Participatory
Democracy

D1198319

Participatory Democracy

Terrence E. Cook

Patrick M. Morgan

Washington State University

Canfield Press
San Francisco

A Department of Harper & Row, Publishers
New York · Evanston · London

Participatory Democracy

Copyright © by Terrence E. Cook and Patrick M. Morgan
1971

Printed in the United States of America.
All Rights Reserved.
No part of this book may be used or reproduced
in any manner whatsoever without written permission
except in the case of brief quotations embodied
in critical articles and reviews.
For information address
Harper & Row, Publishers, Inc.
49 East 33rd Street, New York, N.Y. 10016

STANDARD BOOK NUMBER: 06–382517–1

LIBRARY OF CONGRESS CATALOG CARD NUMBER: 72–150863

Cover Design by Robert Bausch

Interior Book Design by Gracia A. Alkema

71 72 73 74   9 8 7 6 5 4 3 2 1

Preface

This is a book about participation, and it is also a book about democracy. The question is whether participation should be expanded in order to gain more democracy. Although the answer would seem to be a simple "yes," the readings in this text will help you understand how complex the subject is.

The issues posed by participatory democracy are all about us—in schools and universities, in the courts, in communes, in the streets. The slogan "power to the people" may have radical origins, but such language now echoes within the Establishment. Consider, for example, this passage from the Port Huron Statement of the early SDS:

> . . . we seek the establishment of a democracy of individual participation, governed by two central aims: that the individual share in those social decisions determining the quality and direction of his life; that society be organized to encourage independence in men and provide the media for their common participation.

Now compare it with these passages from President Nixon's 1971 State of the Union Address:

> . . . to all Americans let us say: We hear you and we will give you a chance. We are going to give you a new chance to have more to say about the decisions that affect your future—to participate in government. . . .

> . . . Let us give the people a chance, a bigger voice in deciding for themselves those questions that so greatly affect their lives.

Both here and abroad, a debate is now in progress on the meaning and prospects of participatory democracy. We hope this book will contribute to your understanding and perhaps equip you to join the dialogue.

In preparing this work we have enjoyed the editorial assistance of Joseph Dana and Gracia Alkema at Canfield Press, and, at Washington State University, the typing assistance of Norma Day and Joyce Lynd, research help by Steve Cragg, and criticisms of our essay by Take Tsurutani. We appreciate their important "participation," and we also thank the many authors and publishers whose works are included here.

Terrence E. Cook

Patrick M. Morgan

Chapter One

An Introduction to Participatory Democracy

Power to the people! Community control! Let the people make the decisions that affect their lives! Such slogans reflect the contemporary emergence around the globe of demands for "participatory democracy." In 1963 two prominent political scientists wrote, "If there is a political revolution going on throughout the world, it is what might be called the participation explosion."[1] But the belief that the ordinary man should be politicized—mobilized into continual political concerns and involvement— has assumed a new form in the last half decade. The participatory-democracy movement, seeking to distribute decision-making powers more equitably, has been encouraged by a wide range of theorists, such as Paul Goodman, Tom Hayden, and Frantz Fanon, and it has closely followed the contours of New Left student rebellions. In a recent book on student revolutions in ten countries, Joseph Califano has written, "The demands of Sorbonne or Rome students mirror those of our own: more control over courses; more control over administration; more control over faculty—more control."[2] But students are not unique in demanding a voice in decisions that involve their own interests: especially in the developed or postindustrial countries, a wide spectrum of groups has protested the trend toward swollen and centralized

---

[1] Gabriel Almond and Sidney Verba, *The Civic Culture: Political Attitudes and Democracy in Five Nations* (Boston: Little, Brown, 1965), p. 2.

[2] Califano also shows how the challenges on the campus extend to political systems: "The rebel students consider representative democracy a failure. Radical students in France and elsewhere argue for some kind of Utopia where everybody votes on everything that affects them." *The Student Revolution: A Global Confrontation* (New York: Norton, 1970), pp. 23, 72.

1

authority structures that bring impersonality and hierarchy and that need generous doses of expertise to be controlled.

Although many have advocated participatory democracy as the appropriate response to twentieth-century challenges, theory about the ideal and practice of this method of decision-making has remained quite limited. Sociologist Lewis Feuer, noting that participatory democracy is likely to be widely accepted, has warned us of the need for knowledge.[3] Whether we ultimately choose to reject participatory democracy, as does Feuer, or to support it, we should be prepared to make a choice. In order that this choice may be made intelligently, we have gathered a wide range of carefully selected readings on the theory and practice of participatory democracy in the United States and abroad. Neither these readings nor our comments provide simple answers, but it is hoped that they will raise the correct *questions* for evaluation of the promises and problems of participatory democracy. This introductory essay will first attempt a definition of the concept and then explore the case for its implementation, the possible alternatives, and, finally, the range of problems to be considered in developing a theory of participatory democracy.

Definition of Participatory Democracy

One definition of participatory democracy may be based on the origins of its two constituent terms: the Latin *partis* (part) and *capere* (to take) and the Greek *demos* (people) and *kratein* (to rule) suggest "taking part in rule by the people." But etymologies are always dull and seldom helpful. A more fruitful effort to define participatory democracy consists of examining some key developments of modern "representative democracy," so that participatory democracy can be contrasted with it.

Two major aspects of Western democracies are (1) the growth in functions performed by the modern state and (2) an increasing concentration of decision-making power in some aspects. As a general rule, the more crucial the issue under consideration is, the fewer the people who seem to be directly involved in making the decision (for example, the 1962 Cuban Missile Crisis).

It is vital for understanding the contemporary demand for participatory democracy that we note the political "division of labor" between the average citizen and his elective and appointive public officials that exists in representative democracy. After city-states of Renaissance Italy organized along the lines of ancient direct democracies, territorial expansion and population growth soon forced recourse to the principle of representation,

---

[3] *The Conflict of Generations: The Character and Significance of Student Movements* (New York and London: Basic Books, 1969), p. 408.

popular consent to authoritative decisions through elected proxies. The popular electoral base for the selection of representatives has been progressively expanded, in accord with Alexis de Tocqueville's dictum,[4] in a process that has continuted to the present day. Lowering the voting age is a recent example of this process. Paradoxically, at the very moment when suffrage is most extensive, criticism of representation and electoral politics has become most intense. For some, the ideal of universal suffrage loses its luster when suffrage means no more than the right periodically to cast one vote among thousands or even millions. And it seems that when citizenship is somehow cheapened, it is more readily extended by the privileged. In the early Roman Republic, men fought for the privilege of Roman citizenship, but an edict of the Roman Emperor in about 212 A.D. magnanimously extended citizenship to nearly all free men in the Empire as a matter of administrative convenience.

Another component of the political division of labor, in addition to the selection of representative officials, was recruitment of appointive officials, usually for administrative or judicial functions. Appointment of such officials came to be based on objective achievement criteria, such as test scores and credentials of formal training, and thus a system of "meritocracy" developed. Usually this development came in the wake of the appearance of representative democracy, but occasionally it antedated widespread expansion of suffrage as in Imperial Germany. "Meritocratic" staffing of administrative posts triumphed in the United States with the victory of civil service reforms over the spoils system. Seeing in this step a further erosion of the influence of the ordinary citizen, many proponents of participatory democracy have been tacitly or expressly issuing a qualified challenge to the reign of expertise.

The concept of participatory democracy seems to be in part a critique of the zealous democrat's utopia of only yesterday: universal suffrage for selection and control of elective officials claiming to be representative of the electors and meritocratic selection and control of other officials. Now the advocates of participatory democracy, seeking egalitarianism through a new and broader concept of citizenship as well as democracy, wish to enhance the citizen's role by reversing the trend toward concentration of political authority in the hands of elected representatives and appointed

---

[4] ". . . There is no more invariable rule in the history of society: the further electoral rights are extended, the greater is the need of extending them; for after each concession the strength of the democracy increases, and its demands increase with its strength. The ambition of those who are below the appointed rate is irritated in exact proportion to the great number of those who are above it. The exception at last becomes the rule, concession follows concession, and no stop can be made short of universal suffrage." *Democracy in America*, Vol. I, trans. by Henry Reeves, Francis Bowen, and Phillips Bradley (New York: Vintage, 1945), p. 59.

experts. Interestingly, it seems that the movement for participatory democracy is most intense where citizenship is most extensive and meritocracy is most developed.

Against the background of the development of representative democracy, we can attempt a definition of participatory democracy that best adheres to current usage. It seems that participatory democracy connotes two broad features in patterns of decision-making: (1) *decentralization or dispersion of authoritative decision-making*, whereby the authority to make certain decisions is to be displaced downward from remote points near the top of administrative hierarchies or outward from central geographical locations, thus bringing authority closer to the people affected by it; and (2) *direct involvement of amateurs in the making of decisions*. Some participatory-democracy structures drop the representative principle; those that retain it at all require that representation be kept "close" to the people, with amateur representatives selected from a relatively small-scale or immediate constituency. In any case, some amateurs are to move beyond participation in the form of merely *influencing* officials to actually *being* authoritative decision-makers.[5] When we say that "amateurs" are admitted to authoritative roles, we do not use the term in a disparaging sense. Rather, we mean they need not carry credentials as formally trained experts or professionals serving in career capacities and are not regularly elected officials; they are laymen, not professional participants.

In sum, we shall broadly apply the term "participatory democracy" to those decision-making structures that adhere to basic democratic procedural norms, such as equality and majority rule, yet tend to extend equality by some sort of "grass-roots" decision-making of an authoritative nature. In other words, participatory democracy connotes decentralization of power for direct involvement of amateurs in authoritative decision-making.

To develop a deeper understanding of participatory democracy, we should distinguish the forms that have been realized or proposed. First, we can distinguish between two basic types of participatory-democracy structures: the "co-determination" models and the "self-determination" models. Second, in terms of *functions*, we can distinguish between those participatory-democracy units that have some measure of authority to make rules and those that are limited to the implementation of rules arising from

---

[5] This definition excludes many phenomena otherwise similar to participatory democracy. For example, the public hearing may allow direct participation on a consultative or advisory basis, but it is limited to *influencing* authoritative decision-makers. Again, a wide variety of voluntary associations—beginning with Protestant churches during the seventeenth century—have admitted direct participation in decision-making, but those decisions are not politically "authoritative"—that is, they are not ultimately backed by legitimate coercive sanctions. Exceptions include basic party organizations in authoritarian single-party political systems.

another source. Who makes the decisions depends on the type of participatory-democracy structure; which decisions are made by means of participatory democracy depends on the functions assigned to that structure.

The degree of autonomy that amateurs enjoy in decision-making is
determined by whether the participatory-democracy structure is the co-
determination or the self-determination form. The co-determination form
involves joint decision-making by amateurs and nonamateurs (formally
trained experts or regularly elected officials), and it usually provides for the
election or appointment of amateur representatives by or for some immediate and intimate grass-roots constituency of other amateurs. Ordinarily, new positions for amateurs are created within existing structures in
which they were previously excluded from any direct participation. Whenever amateurs move beyond consultation to voting, they may acquire a
minority, parity, or even majority of amateur and nonamateur seats. We
can often recognize co-determination structures by the identifying flag of a
hyphen, for example, student-faculty committees and the West German co-
determination or labor-management councils. In contrast, the self-determination structure is a participatory-democracy unit with a sphere of power
at least formally reserved to amateurs alone, not to be shared with elective
or appointive officials of other political structures. Examples of self-determination structures include the town governments of New England and
the Midwest, the Swiss cantons that still retain direct democracy, the
Israeli kibbutzim, and some of the community-action programs in the War
on Poverty. The extreme form of the self-determination unit is that of the
sovereign direct-democracy city-states of ancient Greece and Rome, and
the extreme is projected as well in the anarchists' ideal—the fragmentation
of nation-states into myriad community-control units.[6]

Once we have understood whether the participatory-democracy structure is one of co-determination or self-determination, we may distinguish
the unit by the nature of its functions. We are not concerned here with
the *substance* of its functions (economic policy, etc.), but rather with the
phases of authoritative decision or action exercised by the unit. Does this
unit have the authority to initiate, deliberate on, and ratify new rules or
changes in old rules, or is it confined to the implementation of rules, as in
administrative or judicial application? At least some rule-making authority
is enjoyed by such participatory-democracy units as the town government
and many student-faculty committees. Often, as is the case with the volunteer fire department, such units will have the authority to implement as
well as make rules. However, other units are limited to the implementation
of rules that originate elsewhere. The latter type is frequently found in co-

---

[6] Something similar is reflected in the "Port Huron Statement" of the Students for
a Democratic Society. See Kenneth Dolbeare, ed., *Directions in American Political
Thought* (New York: Wiley, 1969), p. 472.

determination arrangements in judicial decision-making, in which amateurs join legal experts. In Anglo-Saxon legal systems the judge and jury perform complementary judicial functions, and the Popular Courts of the Soviet Union place "people's assessors" on the bench with judges. A broad range of lower-level "democracies" has been used in Communist countries, and most of these "democracies" have been confined essentially to implementation of rules given from above. For example, James R. Townsend has written of those in Communist China: ". . . the most significant aspect of basic-level government is its subordination to higher administrative levels and its obligation to assist in the propagation and execution of state policy."[7]

Although our division of participatory-democracy structures into co-determination and self-determination forms should be relatively clear, our distinction between those units with authority to make rules and those limited to implementation of rules will be inadequate in practice. For when functions are viewed as phases of decision or action, all authoritative decision-making structures tend to be omnifunctional. A student-faculty discipline committee will, in effect, make some rules as well as implement them, even if it is formally confined to adjudication of rules respecting student conduct. In any case, we can better understand the essence of participatory democracy as well as the various forms covered in the readings if we keep in mind the four basic models of participatory democracy:

1. a co-determination structure confined to rule-implementation authority;
2. a co-determination structure including rule-making authority;
3. a self-determination structure confined to rule-implementation authority;
4. a self-determination structure including rule-making authority.

In our introductions to the various readings, we will occasionally identify the type of participatory-democracy system involved, but the readings will show that the four categories cannot adequately encompass the wide variety of forms.

The Case for Participatory Democracy

Having attempted a definition of participatory democracy and its basic forms, we will review the arguments used to establish the value of direct involvement of amateurs in authoritative decision-making. The arguments can be divided into two types: first, those that emphasize *the beneficial learning experience of the very process of participation*, or that direct

---

[7] *Political Participation in Communist China* (Berkeley: University of California Press, 1967), p. 106.

participation in some way makes the participants "better" men or citizens; second, those that stress *the beneficial end results of the decisions made through such participation,* or that the decisions shaped by direct participation mean "better" consequences.[8] We will review these two classes of arguments in order.

Participation as a Learning Experience. It can be argued that political participation is an educational process in that it changes the psychology of participants. From Alexis de Tocqueville to Frantz Fanon, many theorists have argued that the experience of direct participation can shape a new man, since it socializes people into new beliefs, attitudes, and values. The idea that political participation can have an intrinsic as well as an instrumental value, that it can be an important factor in human growth and development, has often been ignored by modern "democratic elitists," who applaud the apathy and noninvolvement of ordinary people as essential for political stability.[9] As for the leisure necessary for direct political participation, while ancient theorists of the city-state believed that direct democracy presupposed slavery to provide citizens with the time for intelligent participation, automation could now provide the requisite leisure.[10]

Perhaps the primary change in the participants as a consequence of their direct involvement might be an increase in their sense of what political scientists call "political efficacy," or a person's sense of his capacity to effectively manipulate his environment through political participation. In an age of bigness and bureaucratization, people experience a feeling of helplessness, of being "administered" in the complexity of a Kafkaesque world. Only a change in decision-making patterns can overcome this sense of powerlessness and the resultant apathy; for it is not by occasionally voting for authorities in the isolation of a curtained booth, but by actual engagement in making authoritative decisions in concert with persons like

---

[8] Although it can be argued that participation is "drive-creating" as well as drive-reducing, the distinction between the psychological and environmental benefits of participation roughly parallels Lester Milbrath's distinction regarding the *motives* of political participants: In "expressive" political action, "mere engagement in the behavior is satisfying or drive-reducing," whereas "instrumental" behavior "is primarily oriented toward manipulating and changing things." Alternatively, "expressive acts are immediately drive-reducing to the actor, while instrumental acts lead through a chain of action to a final goal." Lester Milbrath, *Political Participation: How and Why Do People Get Involved in Politics?* (Chicago: Rand McNally, 1965), pp. 12, 87.

[9] For an analysis and rebuttal of the case made by those who fear the political mobilization of the apathetic, see Peter Bachrach, *The Theory of Democratic Elitism: A Critique* (Boston: Little, Brown, 1967), esp. pp. 93–106.

[10] Although only a minority of Athenian citizens owned slaves, Aristotle assumed the need for slaves to free citizens from menial labor. But even he imagined the possibility of inanimate instruments to replace slaves. See Ernest Barker, ed. and trans., *The Politics of Aristotle* (New York: Galaxy, 1962), p. 10.

himself, that will serve to reinforce the average man's appreciation of his own political capacities.[11]

Just as political knowledge may increase political self-confidence, a system that opens channels for direct political participation may encourage acquisition of political information. This was the contention of John Stuart Mill in his argument against the antithesis of most understandings of participatory democracy, absolute despotism:

> A person must have a very unusual taste for intellectual exercise in and for itself who will put himself to the trouble of thought when it is to have no outward effect, or qualify himself for functions which he has no chance of being allowed to exercise. The only sufficient incitement to mental exertion, in any but a few minds in a generation, is the prospect of some practical use to be made of its results.[12]

Thus it seems quite plausible that direct participation will stimulate participants to be more attentive to politically relevant information and to put themselves to the trouble of thought on public problems. The amateur participant will be immediately exposed to political stimuli in meetings— not only the political information conveyed by coparticipants like himself, but also the information conveyed by expert counselors. Strongly emphasizing the educative force of direct participation, Frantz Fanon stresses that expert counselors must speak the language of the amateurs:

> It is true that if care is taken to use only a language that is understood by graduates in law and economics, you can easily prove that the masses have to be managed from above. But if you speak the language of everyday, if you are not obsessed by the perverse desire to spread confusion and to rid yourself of the people, then you will realize that the masses are quick to seize every shade of meaning and to learn all the tricks of the trade. If recourse is had to technical language, this signifies that it has been decided to consider the masses as uninitiated. Such a

---

[11] Research by political scientists attempting to isolate the learning experience of participation has been quite thin, perhaps because of two problems: first, the need for obtaining measurements over time rather than merely examining correlations at one point in time, and, second, the need to control for a vast range of other variables in order to plausibly suggest that any correlations are causal relations. However, Robert Dahl has suggested that the objective behavior of participation and the subjective sense of political efficacy feed each other in a circular process (see Milbrath, note 8, p. 58).

[12] Marshall Cohen, ed., The Philosophy of John Stuart Mill (New York: Modern Library, 1961), p. 403. More generally, Robert Pranger, defining "the politics of power" as the antithesis of participatory democracy, has written: "What is sometimes taken as the cause of the politics of power, the unpolitical nature of ordinary citizens, turns out to be an effect of the politics of power and one which further reinforces this politics." The Eclipse of Citizenship: Power and Participation in Contemporary Politics (New York: Holt, Rinehart and Winston, 1968), p. 52.

language is hard put to it to hide the lecturers' wish to cheat the people and to leave them out of things. . . .[13]

Beyond information provided within meetings, it is also possible that a participant will be stimulated to acquire on his own more information of relevance to the problems he confronts. By extension, this drive to acquire information may rise to broader political horizons, to the major political problems outside the immediate context of his direct participation. In sum, it can be argued that participatory democracy leads participants to acquisition of more abundant, accurate, and coherent information on public affairs; thus these participants become aware of possible alternative solutions to problems and are better equipped to make a rational selection of policy means appropriate to goals. The fact that participation stimulates acquisition of political knowledge suggests that the experience of direct participation in local affairs engenders civic and even leadership competence for political participation at higher levels of government.

Beyond improvement of the participant in the matter of knowledge, direct participation may also effect beneficial changes in attitudes and values. To the extent that it overcomes the syndrome of helplessness and ignorance, it may also overcome the political malaise of modern man: his political cynicism, alienation, and anomie.

Participatory democracy would revive and invigorate small communities while fostering the feelings of community solidarity that strengthen abilities to cope with the psychic tensions of modern life. The exhilaration of a participant in the occupation of the Low Library at Columbia University is illustrative:

> Always meetings and more meetings lasting long into the night. Participatory democracy. There was a real community of spirit; everything belonged to everybody; the building was "liberated." . . . Here was a single commune in which adult hypocrisies did not apply any longer, where people shared and shared alike, where democracy decided everything.[14]

Many students of social transition are aware of the costs paid by individuals and societies because of the modern world's loss of small-scale religious, social, and political communities in which the individual may anchor his identity and through which he can structure many of his relationships with the rest of society.[15] Discussing the New Left, Colin Crouch

---

[13] *The Wretched of the Earth* (New York: Grove Press, 1968), pp. 188–189.

[14] Cited from Stephen Spender, "Crisis at Columbia," *The New York Times Magazine*, Mar. 30, 1969.

[15] Among the many books that discuss man's loss of community and longing to regain it, see Erich Fromm, *Escape from Freedom* (New York and Toronto: Rinehart, 1941); David Riesman, *The Lonely Crowd* (New Haven: Yale University Press, 1950);

sees participatory democracy as its answer to the problem of maintaining individualism while returning to the warmth of belonging to an intimate community:

> . . . the resolution of the demand for individuality with that for community is seen through the creation of a participative society; community is assured through the possibility of direct and immediate participation, through simple and democratic organizational forms, in all decisions which will affect one's life, while individuality is assured through the equality of the participation and the ending of a society which demands conflicts between men.[16]

Thus participatory democracy may gratify man's need for community in an age of massive bureaucratic institutions.

Proponents of participatory democracy may differ as to what changes will take place in the average citizen's political orientation. Some argue that being given "a piece of the action" will engender more positive attitudes toward the wider political community, its basic norms, and the public officials of representative-democracy structures. Just as the drive to acquire information on political issues, once stimulated by the experience of participation, may extend beyond issues confronted in the participatory unit, so identifications with the structures and participants in the parochial unit can extend to similar positive identifications with more inclusive units. That is, some would argue that participation in narrow units engenders a less selfish, more socially-oriented attitude and thus serves, in the words of John Stuart Mill, as a "school of public spirit." The participant, he writes,

> is called upon . . . to weigh interests not his own; to be guided, in case of conflicting claims, by another rule than his private partialities; to apply, at every turn, principles and maxims which have for their reason of existence the general good. . . . He is made to feel himself one of the public, and whatever is their interest to be his interest.[17]

If Mill is correct, it would seem that participatory democracy could enhance the legitimacy of the larger political system by fostering loyalties

---

Robert Nisbet, *The Quest for Community* (New York: Oxford University Press, 1953); and Sebastian de Grazia, *The Political Community: A Study of Anomie* (Chicago: The University of Chicago Press, 1963).

[16] "The Chiliastic Urge," *Survey*, No. 69 (October 1968), p. 57.

[17] Cohen, note 12, pp. 419–420. Earlier, Thomas Jefferson had also stressed that political participation—especially when personal rather than by proxy—would increase feelings of loyalty to the wider political community as well as to its democratic regime. See his letters to Samuel Kercheval and Joseph Cabell (1816), in Edward Dumbauld, ed., *The Political Writings of Thomas Jefferson* (New York: Bobbs-Merrill, 1955), pp. 99, 117.

that expand to wider horizons. If so, participatory democracy could be a partial remedy for the disturbing erosion in the domestic authority of Western governments in recent years. We need not look far to see evidence of that decline: riots, radicalism, and lawbreaking in the United States; French separatism in Canada; riots, unrest, and the unseating of De Gaulle in France; religious and linguistic friction in Belgium; the rise of nationalistic or religious discontent in Scotland, Wales, and Northern Ireland; and general unrest on university campuses around the world. Perhaps participatory democracy is one element in the solution of the modern crisis of legitimacy.[18]

However, there are other proponents of participatory democracy who attack the foundations rather than just the functioning of representative democracies. They may view political participation as a salutary school of subversion rather than as Mill's "school of public spirit." Many radical groups in the United States have sought to organize the poor, minorities, high school students, and others not so they will become better and more effective citizens within the existing order, but so they can be mobilized to change it. Radicals see possibilities of using participatory democracy to undermine representative democracy as well as other features of the status quo. Among others, Staughton Lynd has argued that participatory democracy can mean radicalization.[19]

All the above arguments claim that the process of direct participation effects salutary changes in the psychology of participants, both by gratifying existing psychological needs and by creating new beliefs, attitudes, and values. Such psychological changes will supposedly contribute to the age-old utopian dream of a new and superior man and citizen. However, such arguments when considered alone are weak, for they ignore the possible consequences if new patterns of decision-making produced poor decisions. Such arguments claim direct participation is beneficial regardless of the actual decisions made. However, it is far from obvious that the nature of the decisions reached is less important than whether the manner in which they are reached produces personal satisfaction with oneself and one's society. To have participated in the making of decisions does not necessarily mean greater satisfaction with the results. These considerations lead advocates of participatory democracy to the further contention that the system would be of great value because it would result in "better" decisions.

---

[18] One could argue that participatory democracy socializes participants to an ascending authority pattern that is more in keeping with democratic political institutions than the descending authority patterns of hierarchical institutions. On the importance of authority patterns that are congruent, see Harry Eckstein, "A Theory of Stable Democracy," appendix to his *Division and Cohesion in Democracy: A Study of Norway* (Princeton, N.J.: Princeton University Press, 1966).

[19] See Lynd's "The New Radicals and 'Participatory' Democracy," *Dissent*, XII, No. 3 (Summer 1965), pp. 324–333.

Participation as the Means to Better Decisions. The preceding section strongly suggests that participation is of such value in itself that, even if we believed an elite could make "better" decisions, few would ever want to grant *all* decision-making authority to it. However, many advocates of participatory democracy go further, and claim that direct involvement of the people would result in finer decisions as well. Of course, arguments of this nature use a variety of definitions of what is "better," but in general they mean effective problem-solving (rather than efficient decision-making in terms of speed, human energy involved, and so on).

In defining participatory democracy, we suggested that it is in part a contemporary revolt of "everyman" against the expert. It could be said that the amateur himself is really an "expert" in certain matters—whether because of the learning experience of the participation process or because of knowledge acquired in his normal activity. Amateur experts may be superior to elective or appointive officials because their feelings, reflections, and experiences lead them to better choices of ends and means. To extend a venerable democratic argument, they will know where and why the shoe pinches as well as what ought to be done. There are many obvious examples: it could be argued that students are best situated to evaluate the teaching of faculty members; the poor may have much to contribute to the diagnosis of the causes of their own poverty and that of their neighbors on welfare rolls; and workers may have fresh insights for raising the efficiency of economic enterprises.

From another point of view, it could be said that amateur participants can offset one another's deficiencies to make a decision-making unit competent for the tasks at hand. In his *Politics*, Aristotle commented that popular assemblies could possess by aggregation the qualities essential for good decision-making:

> There is this to be said for the Many. Each of them by himself may not be of a good quality; but when they all come together it is possible that they may surpass—collectively and as a body, although not individually—the quality of the few best. Feasts to which many contribute may excel those provided at one man's expense. In the same way, when there are many, each can bring his share of goodness and moral prudence; and when all meet together the people may thus become something in the nature of a single person, who—as he has many feet, many hands, and many senses—may also have many qualities of character and intelligence. . . .[20]

This Aristotelian idea of collective wisdom may be especially relevant to our era of rapidly expanding higher education in the postindustrial countries. The division of labor in research and teaching has made possible an

---

[20] Barker, note 10, p. 123.

explosion in the quantity and quality of human knowledge, but the more mankind knows *collectively*, the less the proportion of human knowledge that can be mastered by men *individually*. Hence, to rely on expertise rather than collective knowledge is to choose an uncertain foundation for decision-making. The example of Lysenko in the USSR warns us that the certainty of today's experts can often become tomorrow's joke. Furthermore, even if our meritocrats are no longer recruited on the sterile standard of the Mandarin's "eight-legged essay," it is possible that top administrative experts may be the least competent of those who possess the requisite expertise;[21] after all, movement toward the top can often require seniority and an obsequious posture toward those already there, rather than demonstrated excellence. But the decisive danger is that previously intimated: to debar amateur participants is to risk losing that one fresh perspective most relevant to the problem at hand. Many heads mean more vantage points.

Shifting to another matter, it can be argued that participatory democracy can produce better decisions because of the nature of certain modern problems. It seems that the crucial decisions facing modern industrial societies will be on qualitative rather than quantitative matters. Many have contended that much of modern life is ugly, that our life-styles are empty of content, that our societies reflect excessive materialism and commercialism, and that we are destroying our natural environment. Could it possibly be that such problems are by their very nature best left to far smaller, more personal communities for resolution? In fact, are they fit subjects for political institutions of any sort other than those at the lowest level? It can be argued that large, bureaucratized systems are to a considerable extent responsible for the existence of many of these problems. Emphasizing mechanical or engineered solutions to problems, such systems find it difficult to detect problems that cannot be physically measured and attacked. When a concern such as the beautification of a decaying neighborhood arises, the issue is increasingly distorted into cold statistical tables or sterile generalizations as it ascends through layers and layers of bureaucracy. If the personal or social nuances of a problem are thus neglected, the solutions adopted may often make matters worse, especially when decisions are further stultified by routine implementation structures. Because our primary problems are increasingly of a nonquantifiable nature, we may be witnessing the progressive deterioration of the relevance of our present decision-making structures. The political institutions developed to meet the challenges of industrialization may be inadequate for the problems of postindustrialization—problems that we are just beginning to perceive.

Even if a proponent of participatory democracy conceded that elites may have a superior *capacity* for intelligent decision-making, he might

---

[21] This is the half humorous thesis of *The Peter Principle*, by L. Peter and R. Hull (New York: Morrow, 1969).

argue that lack of *will* to make "better" decisions makes the matter of capacity irrelevant. One such argument centers on the status of minorities in modern societies. This case can be stated as follows: Most Western democracies harbor disadvantaged minorities—groups of people receiving more than their share of societal burdens or deprivations and less than their fair share of the benefits or rewards. To a considerable degree, the political structures of these democratic systems are unresponsive to the grievances of such minorities. First, what Robert Michels called "the iron law of oligarchy" ensures that elites will emerge that reflect the will of majorities at best and their own particular interests the rest of the time. In other words, these systems respond well to advantaged minorities, not their poor relations. And when the majority will prevails over that of an elite, the disadvantaged minorities still lose. Robert Dahl has noted that this is especially galling when that majority preference is of low intensity of feeling: "How can we restrain a nearly indifferent majority from imposing its preference on a highly intense minority?"[22] But a majority will that is unjust to minorities often is intense in its preferences: the majority may be committed to limiting the responsiveness of the system to minorities out of emotional antagonism or because the appropriate responses would involve serious costs in terms of the majority's interest. For example, the solution to the deplorable problem of housing in black communities may well require either massive expenditures in the ghettos or the forced integration of urban neighborhoods on a quota system, neither of which is consonant with the basic emotional and economic interests of most white citizens. Thus only participatory democracy can offer an alternative to the violence born of despair by allowing disadvantaged minorities to affect directly decisions that shape their lives. The only way to break either the "iron law of oligarchy" or the "tyranny of the majority" is to shift toward nonelitist decision-making units that permit a minority to avoid being submerged in majority sentiment and preference. Hence workers should participate directly in making and applying rules on working conditions, wages, and similar matters; students should participate in decision-making on teaching, curriculum, and campus life; and racial or ethnic minorities should be maximally involved in decisions regarding their housing, schools, welfare payments, and the like.

Since by some criteria and on some issues we are all minorities, it can also be said that *most* of the people frequently find the routine decision-making processes unresponsive. Political scientists have often demonstrated that well-financed, well-organized interest groups linked to the resources of public relations have an impact on the political process that is

---

[22] Viewing the problem of intensity of preference as "almost a modern psychological version of natural rights," Dahl doubts that this problem can be solved by constitutional or procedural rules. See his *A Preface to Democratic Theory* (Chicago: The University of Chicago Press, 1956), pp. 90–119; citations pp. 90, 103.

disproportionate to the size of their memberships. E. E. Schattschneider has suggested that vast numbers of people are effectively excluded from use of organized interest groups as channels for influencing authoritative decision-making: "The flaw in the pluralist heaven is that the heavenly chorus sings with a strong upper-class accent. Probably about 90 percent of the people cannot get into the pressure system."[23] Hence it is possible that participatory-democracy schemes of some sort could result in better decisions that would benefit majorities as well as disadvantaged minorities, for such majorities could contribute a great deal to both the previously mentioned qualitative problems such as environmental quality and quantitative problems such as tax structures.

The classic argument for participatory democracy—one that greatly influenced such thinkers as Madison and Jefferson—is that of protection from tyranny by dispersion of power. This idea acquires a new urgency today, for continuing progress in the natural and behavioral sciences ultimately translates into better instruments and techniques of political control. This is, after all, the message of Orwell's *1984*. Recent "failures" of control—guerrilla warfare, urban riots, bombings—have led to the explosive expansion of research in electronic surveillance and detection, crowd control (MACE, for example), and antiguerrilla weapons. This technological revolution is largely one-sided; its advantage goes to those who have access to the results of research because of their superior economic and political power. One of the major checks on the growth of governmental ability to repress and coerce could be the dispersion of authority among many units. It could help prevent the horror of technological power in the hands of those with a will to abuse it.

Up to this point we have attempted to show that advocates of participatory democracy might claim it is beneficial as a learning experience or in terms of the results of decisions reached by this method. A final argument relevant to making both better citizens and better decisions involves an insidious consequence of the division of labor. The complexity of modern society's division of labor tends to isolate men from a sense of moral responsibility for the ultimate consequences of their actions. As a cog, the individual may be ignorant of or simply indifferent to the impact of the wheel. An Adolf Eichmann could coordinate a complex project of genocide, and his subordinates could play their fractional parts in the plan with detachment; human beings had become simple digits in the flow of paperwork crossing their desks. Participatory democracy may be able to contribute to meeting the psychological and ethical problem of relating personal conduct to social consequences. It could rescue our individual

---

[23] *The Semisovereign People* (New York: Holt, Rinehart and Winston, 1960), p. 35. Even those with privileged access to interest-group channels may find that such groups are "organized internally as hierarchical structures often more severe than those found in the national government itself" (Pranger, note 12, p. 33).

moral sensibilities from the debilitating effects of serving as depersonalized and detached functionaries.

The Alternatives to Participatory Democracy

In stating the case for participatory democracy, our arguments have been illustrative rather than exhaustive, since the majority of the readings will elaborate further the rationale for it. To this point we have taken an affirmative position; but from here on we will be critical as we review some of the alternatives to participatory democracy and some of the theoretical problems that would arise in attempts to achieve it.

The brief review of the case for participatory democracy considered a number of shortcomings in representative systems that it is hoped would be remedied by permitting citizens to participate personally in authoritative decision-making. However, alternative solutions to these problems have been or could be proposed. Before examining them, we should review briefly arguments that reject the fundamental thesis of advocates of participatory democracy, which is that serious problems beset existing representative systems and that these systems cannot handle them. First, the evidence that modern mass democracies produce alienated, isolated citizens may be skimpy at best. The same could be said of the assertion that there has been a breakdown in the authority and legitimacy of those governments. Very few modern democracies have ever collapsed from internal causes. Indeed, in terms of stability, the mass democracies of the Anglo-Saxon and Scandinavian countries must be considered among the most successful governments in history.

Societies with such governments continue to be the world's leaders both in technological innovation and in the application of technology to social problems. They continue to produce the leading innovations in art and music. They have adapted to shifts in fashions, dietary habits, sexual mores, and definitions of masculinity and femininity. They have been willing to give serious consideration to population and conservation problems and to reform of educational and other institutions. Although it cannot be said that these societies have handled all changes and problems successfully and with a minimum of friction, a strong case can be made that they have substantially adapted to emerging problems and have created governments with considerable capacity for continuing to do so. It would be very difficult to point to other forms of government, of either the past or present, that have a record of equal or greater success in this regard.

Critics of participatory democracy claim that the "real" problems of modern society are beyond the scope not of representative democracy, but of participatory democracy. Here emphasis is put on the mass character of society: problems such as production and distribution of goods, communication, transportation, conservation, and provision for leisure activities all require huge expenditures and coordination of a multiplicity of activities. Thus it is considered utopian at best and probably very dangerous for anyone to expect that extreme decentralization will satisfy our political and social needs. Such critics also emphasize that a sizable number of "quantitative" problems still remain: such problems as poverty, adequate medical care for all citizens, and employment require the rather traditional mobilization of resources through large bureaucratic structures.

Some critics of participatory democracy might concede that existing democratic systems are inadequately representative, but they hold that there are alternatives for reform that do not require the personal presence of amateurs in face-to-face decision-making. There are many reforms appropriate to secure both more responsive and better decisions within representative-democracy structures, and we can only review a sample of them here. These alternatives can be broadly grouped under two headings: those not particularly relevant to the complaints of minorities and those aimed precisely at their criticisms.

Among reforms that have been proposed to make representative democracy more responsive to the *majority* will are those of the American Progressives. Their leader, Robert La Follette (evidently adhering to the maxim that the cure for the evils of democracy is more democracy), advocated a variety of measures to further popular sovereignty. One was the direct primary—an attempt to eliminate the selection of candidates for public office by corrupt bosses or by party professionals and a wealthy elite. Voters would participate directly in nominations rather than be confined to simply choosing at election time between candidates selected by others. La Follette also proposed initiative, referendum, and recall —reforms designed to allow expression of public opinion on actual or potential legislation and to permit removal of a public official prior to the expiration of his term in office.

However, the Progressive reforms have not been fully implemented on a national scale in Western democracies, and the quest for greater political participation by citizens could well lie in this direction. In the Democratic Party, interest in direct primaries has revived because of complaints that the 1968 national convention in Chicago was "rigged" far in advance by practices that minimized—often deliberately—popular participation in the selection of delegates. Implementation of the second group of reforms at the national level has not been widespread, although countries such as Switzerland and France have national referenda on certain matters.

Recourse to representation originally was premised on the obstacles to direct democracy presented by the massive size, in territory and population, of the modern state, but the technological developments of the age of Marshall McLuhan's "global village" have collapsed the barriers of distance and numbers. Computerized data processing and modern survey techniques for opinion sampling can facilitate more extensive use of the referendum by making it possible to hold referenda quickly, easily, and inexpensively. Modern mass media developments could permit an instantaneous plebiscite on a political issue. The idea of modifying television for this purpose has been proposed in an electrical engineering journal[24] and espoused by an executive of RCA. In speculating on the future, Martin Shubik has written:

> With the availability of a computer console as a standard consumer good, as commonly available as a television set, it would be feasible to present the electorate with the opportunity to vote directly and immediately on a variety of issues. Not only could they be asked to vote, but they could be supplied with information by direct library interrogation prior to casting their vote.[25]

The difficulties of using such means for regular consultation of a people are obvious. Among other things, even if the phrasing of questions is not biased, one might ask whether it is desirable to have a political system highly sensitized to a public opinion that is instantaneously formed and fixed. Also, far from being relevant to the complaints of minorities, this approach would vastly increase the power of majorities and of those elites with ready access to the media and the necessary financial resources.[26] In addition, it does not meet the contention, frequently documented by political scientists' research, that the bulk of the population is relatively uninformed, and not interested in becoming well-informed, about most major political issues. Democracy need not mean rule of the ignorant through instant majorities.

Another variety of reforms involves modification of the representative structures of political systems: one example proposes a hierarchy of assemblies. Selection of national legislatures by means of a hierarchy of assemblies, each composed of delegates elected from below, is the theoretical model for democratic practice in Communist parties. In the Communist Party of the Soviet Union, primary party organizations elect delegates to city and district conferences, which in turn elect delegates to higher conferences, and so on up to the national CPSU Congress. Unfortunately, in practice this system has never turned out to be anything that even remotely resembles democracy. But in nations that are "democracies" as we understand them, a hierarchy of assemblies instead of one national legislature would have the merits of permitting amateurs at the basic level to directly

---

[24] Robert H. Cushman, "Real-Time, Two-Way Communications Between Citizens and Leaders," *EDN Magazine* (June 1, 1969), pp. 28, 112–113.

[25] "Information, Rationality, and Free Choice in a Future Democratic Society," *Daedalus* (Summer 1967), p. 777.

[26] For a critical appraisal of the referendum as a "Progressive" device, see Howard Hamilton, "Direct Legislation: Some Implications of Open Housing Referenda," *American Political Science Review*, LXIV, No. 1 (March 1970), pp. 124–137.

participate in deliberating on issues of national importance. Since the ultimate decision would not be made entirely by a potentially selfish local unit, the system would preserve accountability to the whole nation. However, such a hierarchy would seem most appropriate to parliamentary systems in which the executive grows out of and has its roots in the national legislature, thus allowing in theory for considerable mass participation in determining the basic policies and selecting the personnel of both branches of the government.

It is worth repeating that none of the above reform proposals deals directly with political grievances of minorities. Since these alternatives tend to make the political system more responsive to majorities, some of them would only make the plight of minorities worse. We turn now to still other reform proposals expressly constructed with this problem in mind.

In democratic theory the most venerable means of protecting minorities is the practice of strictly limiting the powers of government by custom or constitution. The limits may be of two kinds. First, sizable areas of social activity may be placed outside the scope of *political* decision-making; that is, the authority of government to act in such areas may be strictly limited. The United States Constitution puts religion, among other things, in this category. Second, areas deemed to be open to governmental action may be left explicitly to lower-level institutions in order to prevent national majorities from working their will on local minorities. The principle of "states' rights" in the United States is an excellent example. For years Southerners have been demanding a "strict constructionist" viewpoint from the Supreme Court, believing the Court would then reimpose restrictions on the federal government's power to intervene in civil rights matters, which Southerners insist were intended to be left to state and local governments.

Clearly, reserving some areas of authority to lower levels of government is most beneficial to minorities when they are local *majorities* by being concentrated in one geographical section of the society, since the result of this practice is to retain or expand the sphere of policy-making autonomy of a section or region. In effect, this limitation of the authority of higher levels of government corresponds to "home rule" and other forms of autonomy sought by minorities around the world, such as the Kurds in the Middle East, several important nationalities in India, and French-Canadian separatists. But what about the dispersed minority, whose members find themselves outnumbered in their region or even in their local community? Such is often the case for blacks, chicanos, and off-reservation American Indians. Also, numerous disadvantaged (or at least dissatisfied) minorities, students and intellectuals, for example, have a class or occupational base, not a geographic or ethnic one.

A variety of possible reforms promise greater relevance to the complaints of these groups. Perhaps the most familiar of these is proportional representation. There are a number of different principles that may be applied, but the general object is the same: to enable minorities to secure seats in a legislative body in proportion to their weight in the electorate in the hope that they will thus secure a commensurate amount of influence over policy-making. The legislature would then mirror the spectrum of political interests and ideals of the society.

The obvious defect here is that the majority representatives may dominate policy-making just as effectively anyway, as long as simple majority rule prevails. Communists in France and Italy could undoubtedly expound at length on this matter. Thus rules might well have to be added to limit the power of the majority in the legislature. The classic theory of such limits is Calhoun's "concurrent majorities" doctrine. Historically, the most extreme solution was the requirement of unanimity in the eighteenth-century Polish Parliament (the "free veto"), a solution also attempted in the League of Nations. Rather than this extreme, a two-thirds or a three-fourths majority could be required. A less complicated procedure is to grant specified minorities or individual members a veto over decisions, thus requiring both adherence and a simple majority to make policy. The United Nations Security Council is the best formal example, but there are numerous informal or customary practices of this kind.

There are still other variations of this theme. The early electoral rules of the Soviet state were expressly designed to give the votes of workers far more weight in determining the composition of the soviets than those of any other social group or class. The idea of applying some variant of proportional representation to the executive branch of government has also been tried in such countries as Uruguay and Lebanon. The best recent example was the attempt to give the Turkish minority in Cyprus an allotment of posts in the government, among them the vice-presidency, which included veto power on a wide range of policy matters. International civil service posts, in the United Nations Secretariat for example, have often been filled through the use of a quota system so as to distribute them among member states' nationals.

One final possibility for increasing the influence of minorities is to provide for functional representation, that is representation based on occupational categories or interests rather than residence. The now defunct Parliamentary seats for Oxford and Cambridge illustrate the principle. Although students and similar groups could secure a voice through such a scheme, no society has relied on functional representation as the sole means of representation in modern times; even as an auxiliary device it has not proven to be effective. However, functional representation is rather commonly applied within organizations, institutions, and bureaucracies in the structure of interdepartmental committees, advisory councils, and similar bodies. Within the executive branch of governments, cabinets and bodies such as the National Security Council or the Joint Chiefs of Staff are composed on the principle of granting seats to representatives of major functional units. Obviously the utility and feasibility of this approach decline if the boundaries between different functional groups are not very precise—hence the difficulty of applying functional representation to society at large.[27]

Our review of alternatives suggests a wide range of possibilities for reform without recourse to dispersing authority among face-to-face decision-making units accessible to amateurs. Although there are many ways in which representative-democracy structures can be made more responsive to majorities, it can be said that protection of minorities relies chiefly on various ways of institutionalizing the minority veto. But an ability to block governmental action may no longer satisfy minorities with *positive* expectations of government, except insofar as their vetos can be bargained to secure coalition policies that advance their interests or ideals. Thus we return to participatory democracy, focusing now on its problems rather than its promises.

Problems of Theory

For some radicals, participatory democracy has emerged as a kind of panacea for contemporary political discontent. Unfortunately, a panacea, by its very nature, does not lend itself to rigorous theoretical analysis of the problems it is to solve or the solutions it embodies. For several reasons, the advocates of participatory democracy have developed little in the way of systematic theory. For one thing, many of them are hostile to elaborate theorizing at an abstract level, regarding abstractness as one of the chief defects of today's "irrelevant" academic communities. Others fall in the anarchist tradition of asserting that the proper forms and patterns of human interaction cannot be ascertained but will emerge after the old order has been destroyed.[28] This view corresponds to Napoleon's dictum "First one engages, then one sees"—a maxim appropriate to the battlefield but less suited to political programs. For still others this aversion to theory is merely a convenient rationalization for a shallower conviction that "anything would be better than what we have now." However, lest we

---

[27] For some additional ideas on representation of minorities, see Lewis A. Dexter, "Standards for Representative Selection and Apportionment," and Joseph P. Witherspoon, "The Bureaucracy as Representatives," in *Nomos X: Representation* (New York: Atherton Press, 1968), pp. 155–166 and 229–256.

[28] Tariq Ali, speaking on the BBC, provides an example: "It would be incorrect of us to lay down dogmatic rules or lay down even a dogmatic blueprint of the society which is going to emerge. We feel that such a society will evolve through the process of struggle itself." In Leopold Labadz, "Students and Revolution," *Survey* (July 1968), p. 14. In an essay entitled "Rebels Without a Program," George F. Kennan has said that it is difficult to sympathize with rebels who have no "program of constitutional amendment or political reform." Kennan *et al.*, *Democracy and the Student Left* (Boston and Toronto: Little, Brown, 1968), p. 16. See also p. 55 for a reply to this criticism.

mistakenly minimize the difficulties of theory building, we must note that the most theoretically oriented radicals in history, the Marxists, have avoided all but the vaguest of speculations about the nature of a true communist society.

The following comments focus on the elements that would be critical in the formulation of a sound theory of decentralized and direct political decision-making in the modern world. The discussion is organized in the form of questions that a theory of participatory democracy must confront. The questions cannot be fully explored here, but they do provide a framework for examining the subject in depth, and the reader is urged to pursue further those aspects that intrigue him.

1. The first question that a theory of participatory democracy must consider is: *What would be an appropriate unit or context for this kind of decision-making?* Should changes be effected only in traditional political units, or should participatory democracy also be applied to schools, the armed forces, industrial enterprises, and so forth? Sidney Hook, among others, has contended that at present there is no theoretical justification for extending forms of political democracy to all aspects of social organization. In an article critical of the New Left, Hook has commented:

> . . . Despite all their talk about "participatory democracy" they are actually ignorant of its nature as thinkers from Thomas Jefferson to John Dewey have described it. Because society enjoys a democratic political system, this does not mean that all its institutions must be run on the same principle that guides political decisions. After all, an army cannot function that way, neither can the courts or a symphony orchestra, and certainly not a family of many small children. One man, one vote, from professor to janitor, is more in keeping with an intellectual pogrom than with a dedicated search for truth.[29]

We may begin our discussion here by reviewing the position of classical Marxism. In general, Marx and Engels considered administration to be distinct from politics.[30] When they talked of smashing the old state machinery they did not envision the end of authority, order, and discipline in other areas of society. The "withering away of the state" was meant to apply to the bureaucratic and coercive elements of the political system, not

---

29 "Academic Freedom and Academic Anarchy," *Survey* (October 1968), p. 69.

30 Jeremy Azrael, *Managerial Power and Soviet Politics* (Cambridge, Mass.: Harvard University Press, 1966), pp. 12–19. Engels, for example, envisioned a condition in which the "repressive force"—the state—would no longer be necessary, but in which "the government of persons is replaced by the administration of things. . . ." *Socialism: Utopian and Scientific* in Lewis Feuer, ed., *Marx and Engels: Basic Writings on Politics and Philosophy* (Garden City, N.Y.: Doubleday Anchor, 1959), p. 106.

to the decline of economic and other organizations. Lenin adopted this position as well.[31] However, many of Lenin's supporters were far more interested in direct and decentralized decision-making in all spheres of social activity, and they moved to secure the election of officers in the armed forces, workers' control in the factories, and the like. Many elements of the New Left are clearly in sympathy with this latter position: they want to extend direct decision-making to a wide range of institutions and activities. Jerome Skolnick has written:

> Almost uniformly, the participants in mass protest today see their grievances as rooted in the existing arrangements of power and authority in contemporary society, and they view their own activity as political action—on a direct or symbolic level—aimed at altering those arrangements. A common theme, from the ghetto to the university, is the rejection of dependency and external control, a staking of new boundaries, and a demand for significant control over events within those boundaries.[32]

How, then, do we determine where participatory democracy is relevant? Some of its advocates urge that particular groups they consider disadvantaged (workers, students, blacks, etc.) be granted more involvement in actual decision-making. Quite often all they are really asking is that these people be granted "representation" in existing decision-making structures. The co-management or co-determination schemes for enterprises and universities are intended to meet this objective, as are efforts to place blacks on school or draft boards. Here the disadvantaged secure seats on decision-making councils while the councils themselves—their general responsibilities and procedures—are largely undisturbed.[33]

However, other partisans of participatory democracy demand the complete revitalization of existing decision-making units or the formation of new ones. Very often the political units under fire are territorial in nature. They are deemed inadequate for several reasons. First, such units do not meet minorities' needs because ethnic minorities are often too dispersed to constitute majorities at even the local level. This situation leads to calls for further narrowing of the territorial constituency, as in many community-action programs that have a ghetto or neighborhood as their basis. Second, territorial units are considered unsatisfactory because it is believed that decision-making, if it is to be meaningful, must be decen-

---

[31] For example, see Lenin's *State and Revolution*, Vol. II of *Selected Works* (New York: International Publishers, 1967), pp. 314, 344.

[32] *The Politics of Protest* (New York: Ballantine, 1969), p. 7.

[33] It should be noted that many who advocate putting blacks on school boards, for example, are thinking of the proposed members not as representatives in the traditional sense but as the physical embodiment of the black community. Such a notion allows them to see far more participation on the part of the "people" than would be expected with an ordinary representative.

tralized to institutional units, such as factories and schools, and further dispersed within them. Such decentralization requires the application of nongeographic criteria. The importance of devising such criteria is well illustrated by Sir Ivor Jennings' critique of Woodrow Wilson's principle of national self-determination of geographic frontiers: "On the surface it seemed reasonable: let the people decide. It was in fact ridiculous because the people cannot decide until somebody decides who are the people."[34] This problem of defining the "people" is often largely ignored, as in Norman Mailer's case for making New York City the fifty-first state. Mailer writes:

> Power to the neighborhoods! In the new city-state, every opportunity would be offered to neighborhoods to vote to become townships, villages, hamlets, sub-boroughs, tracts or small cities at which legal point they would be funded directly by the fifty-first state. . . . [T]he real significance of power to the neighborhoods is that people could come together and constitute themselves upon any principle. . . .[35]

Mailer refuses to be more specific about how the size and functions of such units would be decided, emphasizing only that they will not be determined by the mayor.

The fact that no clear guidelines yet exist as to the appropriate context for participatory decision-making is illustrated by the contradictions that beset the views of the proponents. Many who support local control over schools in Northern cities would have no sympathy for application of the same principle in the South. Many Southern Congressmen who have consistently deplored federal intervention in local affairs have been the chief opponents of greater self-government for the citizens of Washington, D.C. Many radical students in favor of some form of participatory democracy, and violently opposed to the entry of police on campus, have rejected discipline boards and other traditional devices that have permitted considerable university autonomy and self-government.

The problem with trying to define theoretical guidelines is that there is little similarity among the kinds of groups participatory democracy is supposed to benefit. Blacks in the United States have constituted a *disenfranchised* minority with a territorial base, in part, in the ghettos. Students, on the other hand, are an *unenfranchised* majority in a much more fluid community. Territorial definitions of local political communities make sense for those of us who live and work in small towns and rural

---

[34] *The Approach to Self-Government* (Cambridge University Press, 1956), p. 56.

[35] See his article, "Why Are We in New York?," *The New York Times Magazine*, May 18, 1969, p. 103.

areas, but for many citizens they are not very meaningful because people cross the boundaries every day for work and recreation. In addition, residential communities have become rather fluid: for example, about 20 percent of the United States population moves every year. Thus it is difficult to envision general principles for establishing participatory democracy that would meet the expectations of all who hope to benefit by it.

The examples in the preceding paragraphs imply two other points that can be made about the difficulty of securing adequate theoretical guidelines. The first is that conservatives (at least in the United States) often wish to remove elements of decision-making from the hands of central authorities in order to lodge it with already established local government institutions, while radicals often want decision-making to be decentralized to new units that bypass state and local governments. Hence it is difficult to arrive at generally acceptable definitions of the appropriate units for participatory democracy.

The other and more important point is that, regardless of the rationale offered, a chief motive of many who advocate participatory democracy is *to secure a more favorable arena for decision-making to advance the ideals or interests of their preferred groups*. Again, on this basis, people will differ as to the proper locus of decision-making. Adding to the complexities is the fact that each group may consider a variety of arenas most favorable to their interests, depending on the matter to be decided.

2. The matter of size of participatory-democracy units, both optimum size in terms of the mechanics of decision-making and size in relation to the functions to be performed, must be considered in a theory of participatory democracy. Therefore, our second question is the following: *What would be the proper size and functions of a participatory-democracy unit?* We will first consider the question of proper size in terms of the mechanics of decision-making: that is, what is the optimum scale of a unit for getting people together to make decisions? Then we will turn to the relationship between the size of a participatory-democracy unit and the kinds of decisions to be made. Some issues may involve far more people than others, in which case participatory-democracy units of varying sizes could be necessary.

The very small scale of the classic Greek city-state made it possible for citizens to participate directly in political decision-making. With the largest unit encompassing no more than a few hundred or a few thousand citizens, direct participation did not have to be supplanted by some sort of representative system. It should be noted that the Greek definition of "citizen" excluded a large portion of the adult population and that a modern city of approximately the same size as a Greek city-state would have a much larger body of citizens under contemporary conceptions of citizenship.

As Robert Dahl has pointed out, the adult male citizenry in Athens was, at a maximum, perhaps 40,000.[36] Is this the optimum size for participatory democracy? Or is it the maximum size? The answer depends on one's conception of adequate participation. If everyone is to have a reasonable opportunity to express his views, then the proper size of a decision-making unit cannot exceed several hundred. If participation means the opportunity to be physically present when discussions of issues take place, and that the ultimate decisions are reached by all who are present, then the acceptable size of the unit might be as high as 500,000, although this number would clearly be awkward in many ways. If participation requires the opportunity for citizens to communicate personally with their leaders, then the optimum size would be far smaller, at least as small as ancient Athens.

Some anthropologists feel that tribes of hunters and gatherers have a tendency to average about 500 in size.

> There seems to be a basic limit to the number of persons who can know one another well enough to maintain a tribal identity at the hunter-gatherer level, who communicate by direct confrontation and who live under a diffuse and informal authority, . . . rather than an active centralized political authority.[37]

A hunter-gatherer society is not a long way, in some respects, from a hippie commune in terms of what the hippies have in mind (although the latter groups are typically much smaller), and a similar upper limit might well apply.

Historically, as Western societies became larger and more complex, they moved away from participatory democracy in two ways. On the one hand, they adopted systems of representation, abandoning all attempts to attain citizen participation. In Dahl's words:

> What happened is simply this: In the course of the nineteenth century, the nation-state displaced the city-state as the appropriate unit for democracy. The change, when it came, came swiftly. We can bracket the transition quite nicely by comparing Montesquieu and Rousseau, who still see the city-state as the only proper and indeed viable unit for a democratic republic, with John Stuart Mill, who in *Representative Government* dismisses as irrelevant in a single sentence at the end of a

---

[36] "The City in the Future of Democracy," *American Political Science Review*, LXI, No. 4 (December 1967), p. 957. In modern Appenzell Outer Rhodes, one of the five Swiss direct-democracy or *Landsgemeinde* cantons, more than 10,000 may attend the assembly, where each citizen wears a symbolic dagger and participates in singing the hymn that opens the meeting. See Hans Huber, *How Switzerland Is Governed* (Zurich: Schweizer Spiegelverlag, 1968), p. 30.

[37] John Pfeiffer, *The Emergence of Man* (New York: Harper and Row, 1969), p. 334.

chapter, almost as an afterthought, the two-thousand-year-old tradition. By Mill's time the nation-state had triumphed, the city-state was for all practical purposes an historical curiosity, and if democratic ideals were to survive they had to survive, it seemed, in the form of representative governments for nation-states and subordinate—but not autonomous—territorial units within nation-states.[38]

At the same time these societies did not try to inject participatory democracy, or even representative democracy, into the various nonpolitical subordinate units—into the factory and the corporation, the family, the school.

The advocates of participatory democracy today would have us reverse both these developments. At a minimum this objective would require either decentralization and fragmentation of the existing nation-state or the use of the plebiscite and electronic referendum to inject a large measure of direct decision-making. And it would mean abandoning the hierarchical, autocratic patterns of organization and decision-making in many of our basic institutions. These changes, in turn, would necessitate thinking anew about the relationship between the size of a decision-making unit and the opportunity for people to participate.

We do not mean to ignore the probability that a participatory-democracy society would have a wide variety of units in terms of size or that an individual would simultaneously be a member of several units that might vary considerably in size. The point is that there is an inverse relationship between the size of a unit and its members' opportunity to participate directly; at the same time there are severe pressures to handle major social and political problems in very large units. Every participatory-democracy unit would face essentially the same question: at what point should it compromise between the size necessary to deal with relevant matters and the size most conducive to member participation?

The problem of proper size is obviously intimately linked with the scale of the matters on which decisions must be made. In decentralizing decision-making, provision must be made for dealing with those problems that concern the society as a whole, that is, national problems, as well as local and regional problems. If we assume that the degree of participatory democracy declines as decision-making units grow larger, then the question is: which problems may be left to participatory-democracy units and which ones must be handled by larger, more inclusive units?

Classical theorists have wrestled with the problem but offer no overly persuasive solutions. Rousseau sought a system that would permit a renaissance of direct participation in national decision-making while allowing participation to flourish in local communities as well.[39] Thomas Jefferson's

---

[38] Dahl, note 36, p. 955.

[39] See his *Considerations on the Government of Poland,* trans. by Frederick Watkins (New York: Nelson, 1953), Chap. VII, pp. 192–244.

solution was to have matters of general concern decided at the national center of the political system and particular matters left to the local units. He wanted a "gradation of authorities" such that, when a substantive function was beyond the competence of an individual, it would be delegated upward to the *lowest level* of government competent to perform the function: wards (townships), counties, states, and, finally, the nation.[40] Jefferson's bias against central decision-making is reflected in the principle of "subsidiarity" long advocated by the Roman Catholic Church. This principle starts with the assumption that problems should be solved where they originate; every effort should be made in political and social organizations to deal with problems at the lowest feasible level. Alexis de Tocqueville attempted to make a similar point by using the terms "centralized government" and "decentralized administration." He believed the latter produced a more successful pursuit of local interests and a more satisfactorily socialized citizen.[41]

More recently, Karl Deutsch has argued that the growth and political prosperity of large communities (and the creation of still larger ones) are directly dependent on the growth of the capabilities of the various subsystems that compose them. Thus there is no necessary contradiction between the growing importance of national governments and the flourishing of local governments.

The problem, of course, is that none of these theories provides guidelines for defining the boundaries between what is "national" and what is "local" in nature and interest. Much of American political history has revolved around clashes on just this point, as the nation has gradually expanded the areas deemed to be of "general" concern and thus subject to federal action. A theory of participatory democracy that did not attempt to provide such guidelines would run the risk of creating decision-making units that are seriously deficient in one of two ways.

First, participatory-democracy units could be overburdened with problems and decisions that they could not handle by themselves or with functions that could be performed far more effectively or efficiently elsewhere. A major criticism of participatory democracy that any systematic theory must confront is that the primary problems of our world and its national communities are not amenable to solution by small-scale direct democracy. Leaving aside international problems, we may note that to meet the challenges posed by transportation needs and environmental quality, for example, many analysts have been urging that we create new regional authorities to coordinate city and county governments. They have proposed moving up the scale of government rather than down it, because

---

[40] See his letter of Feb. 2, 1816, to Joseph Cabell, in Edward Dumbauld, ed., *The Political Writings of Thomas Jefferson* (Indianapolis and New York: Bobbs-Merrill, 1955), pp. 98–99.

[41] *Democracy in America*, Vol I (New York: Vintage, 1945), pp. 89–101.

the nature of the problems requires action beyond the capabilities of existing units.

Second, we could find ourselves in exactly the opposite position. Participatory democracy could proliferate decision-making units with essentially parochial concerns, absorbing all attention in the trivial at the expense of what is significant. We may assume that such a situation would quickly erode the citizen's interest and desire to participate actively in such units. The psychological importance of a political unit for its members rarely exceeds its functional significance in their lives.[42] In surveying modern examples of direct participation in political decisions, we find that they are usually fragments of a total nation, such as the old New England town governments or the Swiss cantons, with rather limited involvement in any of the important decisions being made on behalf of their society or region. As we might expect, they are not outstanding examples of public participation.

This fact suggests a further point, which is that curious paradoxes beset contemporary concern about the viability of our political institutions. One of these is that demands for dispersion of political authority into smaller units have become more intense at a time when many believe the nation-state itself is too narrow for adequate performance of key functions. Can men be united by further fragmentation of their political units? A second paradox is that many who are increasingly apprehensive over the omnipresence of politics want to proliferate the number of political units.[43] What if the nature of our problems is such that we require larger, not smaller, political units and fewer of them?

Guidelines are necessary not only to determine which issues are appropriate to national and which to local levels of decision-making within the political system, but also to indicate what is properly political. Often "power to the people" is meant to suggest less power for the politician at any level. This goal raises some complex questions. To take just one example: is a decision to go to war a matter for political units or for all decision-making units that would be involved? If the answer is the latter, then much of the distinction between political and nonpolitical units disappears. If the distinction is retained and political units have made the decision, could a participatory-democracy unit running a factory decide not

---

[42] Robert Nisbet applies this principle not only to political units but also to other social institutions to explain their inability to attract widespread allegiance and participation (Note 15, p. 54).

[43] We already have a vast patchwork of often overlapping political units in the United States. If we include such units as school, water, and park districts, there are more than 91,000 units of local government. Illinois alone has 6,400 units! See James MacGregor Burns and Jack Peltason, Government by the People: The Dynamics of American National, State and Local Government, 6th ed. (Englewood Cliffs, N.J.: Prentice-Hall, 1966), pp. 779–780.

to produce war materials? This move would be a political decision by what is not, ostensibly, a political unit.

3. The third major question that a theory of participatory democracy must confront is: *How are decisions to be made within such units?* Many critics of participatory democracy argue that its partisans have given little thought to this matter and, in fact, seem to care little about it. Critics also charge that a participatory-democracy unit can be extremely undemocratic, inefficient, or incompetent in making decisions.

For one thing, there is the danger of small-scale tyranny. Advocates of participatory democracy have often discounted the value of formal procedures for decision-making in stark contrast to the elaborate rules of procedure used in other assemblies, such as legislatures. In general, advocates emphasize the spontaneous, unstructured, rather amorphous realization of the will of those assembled, as in many SDS meetings. Explicit written rules on membership, elections, and parliamentary procedure are usually not in evidence. The idea is that unstructured discussions, resolutions, and voting will generate the truest expression of the people's will. As described by one unsympathetic to the procedure:

> Participatory democracy is the contribution of the New Student Left to political theory. It was born of their meetings, small and large, minute and mass, where the speaker, heckler or chairman would feel that he had articulated in words what was trying to emerge from a long, often inchoate discussion. Suddenly the mass seemed inspired; words passed to action; the spontaneity of the mass broke through the formal paraphernalia of formal democracy with its parliamentary rules.[44]

Many have seen this unstructured form of decision-making as a mask for what in the end amounts to elitist manipulation. Feuer argues that this "democratic anarchy" is a myth legitimizing an undemocratic reality. An eyewitness account of Haydenesque participatory democracy during the 1968 crisis at Columbia attempts to make the same point. Dotson Rader writes:

> . . . participatory democracy was much like a town meeting where a highly organized minority, in firm agreement on objectives, is able to cow the unorganized, apolitical majority into acting against its better judgment. . . . Nothing was to be written that did not conform with the immediate demands of the "revolution." Every word had to follow the SDS line. . . . I was told by members of the Steering Committee that I had to clear anything written about the commune with them.[45]

---

[44] Feuer, note 3, p. 408. See also pp. 408–412.
[45] "More About Columbia," *The New Republic* (June 8, 1968), pp. 23–24.

Irving Kristol has argued that in modern industrial society participatory-democracy advocates would eventually end up creating dictatorial institutions alleged to incorporate the will of the people.[46]

One of the objectives of participatory democracy is the emergence of psychological changes that will leave people better equipped to participate. However, until these changes occur the ignorance and apathy of the bulk of a group would only encourage elitist tendencies within it. A few activists could quickly become the "spokesmen" or "coordinators" (really the "deciders") of the community. Thus one critic of school board decentralization and local control of ghetto industrial enterprises has argued that black separatism in such matters is usually prompted not by ordinary residents but by a few who stand to benefit personally from it:

> Those blacks who consider it in their interest to promote separation are, as a rule, not workers but members of the middle class. Where separation has been supported in the past by middle-class blacks, it has enabled them to assume positions of leadership (in churches and universities) that would be denied them in integrated situations, and it has enabled them to monopolize the Negro market. Thus, a new black professional elite is demanding all-black schools so that they can monopolize the jobs in those schools, and black entrepreneurs are calling for a separate black economy which they can dominate.[47]

Daniel Moynihan has made a similar point in discussing government by the "people-in-council" as a demand that grew out of community-action programs.

> The institutions of representative government, imperfect as they may be, have the singular virtue of defining who speaks for the community in certain set circumstances. Thus, the elected (black) representatives of the Harlem community had several times ratified the construction by Columbia University of a gymnasium in Morningside Park. But the black students of the University decided that the assemblymen and senators, councilmen and borough presidents did not speak for the community, and that they did. This quickly enough becomes government, as one observer has noted, by a process of private nullification, which has never been especially good news for democracy.[48]

---

[46] "The Old Politics, the New Politics, the New, New Politics," *The New York Times Magazine*, November 24, 1968, p. 174. See also Tom Kahn, "Direct Action and Democratic Values," *Dissent*, XIII (January–February 1966), pp. 22–30, esp. pp. 29–30.

[47] Carl Gershman, "Black Separatism: Shock of Integration," *Dissent*, XVI (July–August 1969), p. 296.

[48] *Maximum Feasible Misunderstanding* (New York: The Free Press, 1969), pp. 182–183.

All such criticisms suggest that participatory democracy could very easily degenerate into some sort of plebiscitary democracy in which popular participation is only a matter of acclamation politics—the enthusiastic ratification of elite decisions by the popular assembly.

The opposite criticism would be that, instead of tyranny from above, the end result would be tyranny from within. There is always pressure for conformity within a group, and that pressure can be stifling. This is especially true of large, amorphous assemblies in which a premium is placed on unanimity and solidarity as weapons in the struggle with society at large. Also, many studies of the behavior of members of small groups document the impact of a subtle psychological manipulation that arises because most people want the approval of the other members of the group. The pressure is particularly significant when membership in the group is attractive to them and when that group is fairly homogeneous in the first place.[49]

The essence of all of these criticisms, then, is that the fears of elitism or of excessive pressures to conform that were originally directed at mass political systems are equally if not more relevant to small-scale decision-making units. Clearly, there is no simple correlation between abuse of power and the remoteness of power from those finally affected by it. The theorists of participatory democracy must come to grips with dangers to democracy that are essentially the same as those perceived in mass society. This fact suggests that perhaps elitism, indifference, manipulation of others, pressures to conform, and so forth, are fundamental political aspects of the human condition. If so, then the claim that participatory democracy can free us from such problems is open to serious question.

Thus far we have considered elitist manipulation and group pressures as separate problems. But what if these two forms of tyranny were combined? The result would be the use of large—even mass—organizations in which everyone is urged to participate in implementing decisions already reached by higher authorities. Participation would appear to be concerned with decision-making, but actually group pressures to conform would be mobilized in support of and to carry out decision implementation. Is this not precisely what has happened in the Soviet Union and China? Participation is ubiquitous there, but it is deliberately manipulated to enhance obedience to decisions from above. On numerous occasions mass participation has been used for the direct purpose of implementing policies: for

---

[49] Plato, an early critic of direct democracy, stressed that not even a man born for philosophy could resist the molding force of the torrent of public opinion in mass meetings, since the people, "with a great deal of uproar, blame some of the things said or done, and praise others, both in excess, shouting and clapping, . . . the rocks and the very place surrounding them echo and redouble the uproar of blame and praise." *Republic*, trans. by Allan Bloom (New York and London: Basic Books, 1968), p. 172.

example, Stalin's creation of a "revolution" of poor peasants against kulaks to introduce collectivization. More recently the Red Guards have been turned loose to implement Mao's designs.

In the twentieth century it has become clear that organization is a major foundation of power in the corporate state, where power belongs to those who dominate the organization. Furthermore, it is an elementary maxim in political science that possession of formal authority can seldom be equated with effective power. Thus provision for grass-roots decision-making can often mean effective manipulation of participant activity from without. Modern authoritarian regimes of both the Left and Right have often combined two approaches to political control: first, isolation of subjects by undermining traditional voluntary associations and, second, promotion of the togetherness of pseudocommunities—mass organizations ingeniously designed for manipulation of memberships. The participatory-democracy forms designed by Mussolini and Stalin victimized people by granting them the psychologically satisfying experience of ostensibly helping to make the decisions affecting their lives, when, in fact, the content of decisions was programed in advance. In brief, to pursue participant activity in the corporate state is to assist in one's own subjection.

It may be objected that such examples, drawn from bureaucratized political systems, have little to do with participatory democracy, in which the object is government by the people. The answer is that what Stalin called "engineering of the soul" may be inherent in direct democracy, not just the product of a tyrant's design. Irving Kristol writes:

> . . . participatory democracy requires that all people be fit to govern; and this in turn requires that all people be made fit to govern, by rigid and uniform educational training, constant public indoctrination, close supervision of private morals and beliefs, and so forth. No legislator can be as free as a private citizen, and to make all the people legislators is willy-nilly to abolish the category of private citizen altogether.[50]

It would be sadly ironic if those who advocate escaping manipulation via participatory democracy became, in the end, manipulators themselves "for the good of the people."

The question of how decisions are to be made must also take efficiency and competence into account. As for efficiency, participatory democracy would inevitably involve a very large part of the ordinary citizen's time, both for participation and to prepare adequately for it. There is no overwhelming evidence that most people want to devote this much time and effort to politics; for many, nothing would destroy enthusiasm for participatory democracy as much as a little experience with it. Representative

---

[50] "What's Bugging the Students," *The Atlantic* (November 1965), p. 111.

democracy does not require such an elaborate investment of the society's time and energy in its governance.

Another aspect of efficiency is the costs that have to be paid to secure a working consensus on issues. Participatory democracy could impose rather high bargaining costs because of the diffusion of decision-making. After all, representatives are able to bargain and compromise with one another in a way that participating citizens cannot. In a society without ethnic, ideological, and economic homogeneity, the result of participatory democracy could be incessant strife aggravated by the costs of bargaining amid a multiplicity of units.

Once again we should reiterate the danger of having participatory-democracy units make something epic of the trivial, of being preoccupied with matters of lesser consequence at the cost of inadequate attention to important issues. We may assume that a society can devote only so much attention and energy to political matters. Political efficiency, then, consists of seeing to it that the most pressing and significant problems get their fair share of attention. In this sense, too, participatory democracy could produce considerable political inefficiency.[51]

Decision-making may be not only inefficient but also incompetent. Since participatory democracy would place the power to make decisions in the hands of ordinary citizens to a far greater extent, a question inevitably arises as to the likelihood that these citizens will make "good" decisions. If we are trying to estimate the probability that a majority in an assembly will make the correct decision, we may use a formula discovered by Condorcet (as summarized by Brian Barry):

> To illustrate its power, here is an example: if we have a voting body of a thousand, each member of which is right on average fifty-one per cent of the time, what is the probability in any particular instance that a fifty-one per cent majority has the right answer? The answer, rather surprisingly perhaps, is: better than two to one (69%). Moreover, if the required majority is kept at fifty-one per cent and the number of voters raised to ten thousand, or if the number of voters stays at one thousand and the required majority is raised to sixty per cent, the probability that the majority (5,100 to 4,900 in the first case or 600 to 400 in the second) has the right answer rises virtually to unity (99.97%). . . .[52]

---

[51] Something like this concept of political efficiency is implicit in portions of Deutsch's discussions in *The Nerves of Government* (New York: Free Press, 1963). See, for example, his remarks that "curiosity may lead to drifting" in systems (p. 236).

[52] "The Public Interest," in Anthony Quinton, ed., *Political Philosophy* (Oxford University Press, 1967), p. 122. The paper first appeared in *Proceedings of the Aristotelian Society*, Suppl. Vol. XXXVIII, pp. 1–14. © 1964 The Aristotelian Society. Reprinted by permission of the Editor of the Aristotelian Society. The mathematical formula can be found in Barry's *Political Argument* (New York: Humanities Press, 1965), p. 293.

Notice the key assumption—namely, that each participant has a better-than-even chance, however slight, of being right. However, what if we assume that he has a less-than-even chance of being right? Then the odds are very good that the majority will be wrong, and, in fact, the probability that the majority will be right sinks rapidly to zero as we expand the voting membership.

This sobering thought is a useful context in which to consider a major argument on behalf of government by administrative expertise and representatives: that they will have a higher probability of making good decisions. Representatives will normally be of above-average intelligence; they can devote more time to the consideration of issues and to gathering relevant information; and they can become specialists in areas of particular concern. The administrative expert possesses the advantages of time and specialization to an even greater degree. Both representatives and administrators possess uncommon expertise for solving the problems of the common man, who may know his shoe is pinching but needs a cobbler to correct it.

A good many advocates of participatory democracy are opposed to government by "experts." Thus they must demonstrate either that bad decisions result about as frequently now as would result from more reliance on "everyman" or that everyman's abilities in this regard can be improved. Some proponents argue that increased participation would give people the motivation to become better informed about political matters; but many others seem to be content with listing "expert" failures—Vietnam, the cities, pollution, etc.—and implying that we could hardly be worse off if we stopped relying on the so-called experts. Unfortunately, pointing out the defects in a system does not prove that a proposed alternative would be better.

The privileged advocate of "power to the people" sings the praises of the political virtues of the disadvantaged while claiming that deprivations inherent in the status quo have stunted their mental development. In assailing this practice of hailing the victims of poverty as models, Edgar Friedenberg writes:

> . . . if we had sought to eliminate [polio] in the prevailing spirit of our attacks on poverty, we would all, I suspect, be pushing one another around in wheelchairs in order to demonstrate our identification with its victims; while genuine polio victims were sought out and worshipped for their putative political virtues.[53]

4. The final set of theoretical problems for the potential theorist is encompassed by this question: *How will the decision-making of a partici-*

---

[53] "Outcasts," *New York Review of Books*, XIII, No. 11 (December 18, 1969), p. 23.

patory-democracy unit relate to other political decision-making structures in society and to the "interest" of the society at large? First, there is the matter of whether participatory-democracy units would complement or replace other political structures. For Lenin, in his *State and Revolution*, the state as *political* structure would begin to "wither away." Administration would remain, but it would be performed largely by ordinary citizens. Lenin insisted, as did the Anarchists, that revolution would be necessary to begin the transition because the existing system would never permit the development of participatory-democracy units.[54]

Staughton Lynd, by contrast, refers to the development of "parallel structures" within *existing* society:

> The intent of these structures is still unclear, even to those involved in organizing them. At one end of the spectrum is the concept of using parallel institutions to transform their Establishment counterparts. . . . [A]t the spectrum's other end is the conviction that in an America whose Establishment is inherently and inevitably hostile, existing institutions cannot be transformed, participation will always mean cooptation and merely token successes, hence parallel institutions must survive and grow into an anti-Establishment network, a new society.[55]

Lynd suggests that the latter end of the spectrum is least feasible with regard to economic institutions.

Tom Hayden has written in a similar vein about the creation of rival institutions outside the system.

> . . . this means building institutions outside the established order which seek to become the genuine institutions of the total society. Community unions, freedom schools, experimental universities, community-formed police review boards, people's own anti-poverty organizations fighting for federal money, independent union locals—all can be "practical" pressure points from which to launch reform in the conventional institutions while at the same time maintaining a separate base and pointing towards a new system. Ultimately, this movement might lead to a Continental Congress called by all the people who feel excluded from the higher circles of decision-making in this country. This Congress might even become a kind of second government, receiving taxes from its supporters, establishing contact with other nations, holding debates on American foreign and domestic policy, dramatizing the plight of all groups that suffer from the American system.[56]

---

[54] See, for example, Lenin, note 31, pp. 277–282.

[55] Lynd, note 19, p. 328.

[56] "The Politics of 'The Movement,'" *Dissent*, XIII (January–February 1966), pp. 75–87; citation from p. 87.

A good many advocates of more involvement of ordinary citizens in decision-making, however, seem to want any new units to be complementary to existing ones and want conventional institutions to be more loosely structured. In this way they hope to correct the failure of representative assemblies and distant executives to represent and respond to personal views and minority interests.

There are essentially three preeminent questions that a potential theorist must face. The first is: will existing societies allow "parallel institutions" of real import to flourish and permit institutions to be adapted to participatory democracy? Lenin's answer was "no," and he is joined in this opinion by the most radical of today's New Left critics. Perhaps the classic case study would be the dual government in Russia in 1917, consisting of the Provisional Government and the soviets. Lenin's immediate response was to assume that one of the two would soon collapse, and, although it may not have been inevitable, he turned out to be correct. Ultimately, to quarrel with Lenin's conclusion, we must assume that an establishment will disestablish itself—something that to Lenin sounded distinctly implausible.

The second question is: just how effective can the parallel institutions and new groups be? We have noted Staughton Lynd's doubts about the utility of seeking parallel economic institutions. With regard to the creation of new groups to involve citizens, we must take note of Theodore Lowi's bitter critique of community-action programs. He comments:

> Delegation of the program to private groups requires official recognition of groups and representatives. . . . However, once the situation is stabilized by official recognition of groups and representatives, the situation tends to militate against emergence of still newer groups. Official recognition is a very conservative force; at the neighborhood level, Federal recognition becomes a valuable resource with which some groups can demoralize others. . . .
>
> Organizing poverty groups in and for the ghetto, and making money and recognition available as systematic rewards, tends to reinforce the ghetto in a most systematic way. The rewards tend strongly to tip the balance arbitrarily toward those prospective leaders who are most strongly pro-ghetto, economics oriented, and separatist.[57]

Lowi's belief that the increased participation of community action has led to the cooptation of some groups and has had a negative, conservative impact clashes sharply with the idea that existing institutions can decentralize or that decentralization is an effective road to reform.

The third question is: are the benefits of creating parallel structures

---

[57] Theodore Lowi, *The End of Liberalism* (New York: Norton, 1969), pp. 245, 247. For somewhat similar comments see Moynihan, note 48, pp. 185–190.

greater than the costs? New participant groups and institutions would tend to weaken existing representative institutions, particularly legislatures. It is not immediately obvious that the society's welfare would be clearly enhanced, especially if the effectiveness and efficiency of the new organs are open to question.

Next there is the matter of the relationships among participatory-democracy units. Unless their spheres of action are severely restricted, the decision-making of one group will always affect others who are not participants in it. When this happens to me, I may find that participatory-democracy unit just as damaging to my interests and values and just as unresponsive to my views as a representative assembly or central bureaucracy. One can imagine jurisdictional disputes and other quarrels that beset contemporary state and local political institutions cropping up just as frequently among these new units.

We must also assume that participatory democracy does not mean a return to city-states or town meetings as the ultimate in political community. The larger society will remain, which raises the question of the proper ties between the participatory unit and overarching community institutions. Many units may well have to continue to rely on the sanctions of the larger political structure. They may require at least the financial assistance of the old structure, with its instruments for raising revenue in one area and transferring it to another. How can this reliance be combined with local "independent" decision-making? Would participatory democracy make it easier or more difficult to tax wealthier sections of society for the benefit of poorer ones? These and other questions come to mind immediately in considering intergovernmental relations within the new society.

One final point is of relevance for those who advocate participatory democracy as a solution to the problem of minority interests. If we accept the idea that a revision of our decision-making procedures would benefit minorities, what happens to the interests of majorities? If one is not a student, worker, or member of an ethnic minority, what does he stand to gain that is of major consequence? It has been asserted that existing representative, centralized, bureaucratic systems inadequately respond even to majority interests, but this allegation does not in itself demonstrate that small-unit participatory democracy would be any improvement. To prevent the domination of the parochial outlook and the particular interest, it may be necessary to define precisely (and thus limit) the decision-making province of each participatory-democracy unit.

The problem is illustrated by the events leading to the New York City teachers' strike in 1968. Without presuming to assign responsibility for this paralysis of a city's educational system for more than two months, it should be noted that the strike was closely related to a community-control project backed by the Ford Foundation. In this experiment with a self-determination model of participatory democracy in the Ocean Hill–Brownsville school district, we can see how various groups can be more or less equally concerned with a decision "affecting" their lives. Simplifying the various points of view, we move from the least inclusive to the most general "interests" involved:

1. Most of the black-dominated community and school board of the Ocean Hill–Brownsville school district: from their vantage point, their "interest" required exercise of community-control powers to transfer out of the district a number of white teachers potentially obstructive to their programs.

2. Most of the members of the white-dominated United Federation of Teachers of New York City: from their vantage point, their "interest" required protection of professional careers by preserving "meritocratic" or colorblind standards for teacher assignment, uniform for all of New York City's school districts; seeing violation of "due process" in the transfer of some of the white teachers from Ocean Hill, they determined that their interest required a citywide teachers' strike.

3. Most of the adult residents of New York City, especially the parents of school-age children: from their vantage point, their "interest" was simply to get the teachers and children back in the classrooms.

The above example shows that what may be in the interest of a minority is not always in a natural or preordained harmony with the wants of those who are not members of a participatory-democracy unit.[58] Hence if we reject the Jefferson-Mill hypothesis that participant activity socializes participants into an unselfish concern with the public interest of the wider community, it is clear that an adequate theory must carefully weigh questions of appropriate contexts, size and functions, and institutional structures. If one ignores such problems, direct democracy may lead to decision-making that is neither in the interest of the members nor satisfactory to other groups of people who may be affected by the results.

Conclusion

This essay has attempted to define the concept of participatory democracy, discussed the arguments for it, reviewed the alternatives to it, and explored the problems of theory that it raises. Should we endorse or reject it? We have dwelled at length on the problems of participatory democracy, not out of hostility to it but because of our concern for the development of both normative and empirical theory. Evaluation of participatory democ-

---

[58] That "responsiveness" to local concerns may conflict with accountability to others is especially obvious in problems of environmental quality, such as air and water pollution. We could suggest a general principle: the narrower the democratic unit, the less its will—and perhaps capacity—to confront problems that are especially noxious to wider communities and that arise from its decisions.

racy surely requires an estimate of the probable benefits and costs, especially when implementation of direct participation in authoritative decision-making would be resisted by some.

This is an age when not even the most dedicated hermit has the capacity to make *all* the decisions that affect his life, for the decisions of others may corrupt the very air he breathes and put insecticide in his flesh and radioactive material in his bones. And even if we could directly participate in making all the decisions that affect us, most of us would want to economize our energies at some point through a division of political labor.

Yet plausible claims for the benefits of both the activity and results of a new degree of participation suggest the importance of its thorough exploration. This exploration would benefit from experimentation, especially on a small scale, where some of the problems and dangers of abruptly altering large political institutions can be avoided. It would also benefit from analysis in theoretical terms, guidelines for which we have attempted to set forth.

We hope that the essay and the readings that follow convey our sense of the importance of the subject. The call for "power to the people" raises issues of enduring concern to political analysts and political activists, for it is in keeping with an ancient and honorable tradition in Western thought. It is the tradition of seeking to make man the master of his communities, and those who pursue it today must be said to be in high company.

Chapter Two

Participatory Democracy in Theory

The readings in this section deal with broad theoretical aspects of participatory democracy. The first four articles provide an outline of the contemporary debate—two of them propose and two question participatory democracy. The rest provide a more elaborate discussion of the subject.

It may be interesting to point out that the drive for direct democracy and decentralization is one of the things that distinguishes the New Left from much of the Old. The traditional objective of socialist parties has been centralized planning and administration of the economy. We may be witnessing a historic turning point at which the traditional goals of radical political thought and action are being reversed.

It should also be noted that this reversal would be a return to influence by the anarchist strand in Western political thought, and we have accordingly included an essay by Paul Goodman to represent such theorists. Several works on anarchism are listed in the bibliography as well.

The reader will notice that in this section there are no references to classical theorists prior to Rousseau. It will be recalled that there are two sorts of arguments for participatory democracy—that it can produce better citizens and that it results in better decisions. The former is relatively new in Western thought; prior to Tocqueville there appears to be no sustained argument that participation is salutary in and of itself.

As a final point, in political science proponents of participatory democracy are usually found to be attacking the fact that the pluralist model is widely used in the discipline today to describe the American political system. Usually they offer some form of elitist model to explain why existing "democracies" are insufficiently democratic to suit them. They are particularly unhappy with the notion (widely prevalent in the discipline) that greater public participation would be bad for democracy—that is, would be incompatible with stability in democratic systems.

On Trial

Tom Hayden

---

*In this selection Hayden links participatory democracy to the most
active elements of the New Left. He outlines the nature of many efforts
to seek a new form of community and tries to indicate the ways in which
this new form will be a force for change in our society. His program is
somewhat reminiscent of the long tradition of utopian enclaves in the
United States, except that he intends his enclaves to be more subversive
than demonstrative, as he has insisted for nearly a decade that "we
visualize and then build structures to counter those which we oppose."**
We should recall that most experimental "island" communities in the
United States have failed within a few years because of finances and
factionalism and that the enduring exceptions were those knit in religious
zeal.*

If we look at any revolutionary movement, we see that it evolves
through three overlapping stages. The first is *protest*, in which people
petition their rulers for specific policy changes. When the level of protest
becomes massive, the rulers begin to apply pressures to suppress it. This in
turn drives the people towards the second stage, *resistance*, in which they
begin to contest the legitimacy of the rulers. As this conflict sharpens,
resistance leads to a *liberation* phase in which the ruling structure disinte-
grates and "new guards" are established by the people. America in the
Sixties experienced primarily the protest phase, but resistance has already
become commonplace among the blacks and the young. Temporary periods of liberation have even been achieved—as when students occupied
Columbia University for one week and learned they could create new
relationships and govern themselves. Of course, these experiences only
provide a glimpse of liberation as long as the government has sufficient
police power to restore university officials to office.

In the resistance phase it becomes necessary to lay plans for defeating
the police and building a new society. It is a time of showdown in which
the government will either crush the resistance and restore its own power,

---

From Tom Hayden, "On Trial," *Ramparts* (July 1970), pp. 53–58. Copyright
Ramparts Magazine, Inc., 1970. Reprinted by permission of the editors.

* "Letter to the New (Young) Left," in Mitchell Cohen and Dennis Hale, eds.,
The New Student Left: An Anthology (Boston: Beacon Press, 1966), p. 7.

or undergo constant failure, eroding its own base to a very dangerous point. Because it challenges the legitimacy of the way things are ordered, resistance acquires the responsibility of proposing and creating new arrangements.

The general outlines of what we want are by now as clear as possible without developing a rigid blueprint. We have to abolish a private property system which turns over the benefits of our wealth and technology to a few, and which in its drive for new markets collides with the aspirations of people all over the world. We need to turn this situation around so that our technology can be used by the world's people for the development of their economies and cultures. In this socialist transformation, decision-making power must be in the hands of the people most affected.

What is less clear is the kind of structural rearrangement which will be required to achieve these goals. A radical movement always begins to create within itself the structures which will eventually form the basis of the new society. So it is necessary to look at the structure of motion-now-in-progress to understand what must be destroyed and what must be built. We need a new Continental Congress to explore where our institutions have failed and to declare new principles for organizing our society.

The first principle of any new arrangement is *self-determination for our internal colonies*. In the Seventies the Third World revolutions will sharpen not only on other continents but here inside the U.S. The black ghettos are a chain of islands forming a single domestic colony. The same is true of the Puerto Rican people struggling for independence in San Juan, New York and Chicago; the Chicano people of the Southwest; and the Asians and Indians struggling in their small urban and rural communities. The concept of "integration" which so dominated consciousness in the Sixties is now blinding most people to the new reality of self-determination. Underlying the desire for integration is the even deeper belief that America is "one nation, indivisible." It seems unthinkable that this country might literally be broken up into self-determining parts (nations on the same land), yet that is more or less what is evolving. The failure of the U.S. to make progress in the areas of education, jobs, housing and land reform here at home, the constant recourse to repressive violence at a time when the "revolution of rising expectations" is nowhere stronger than in America, can only make Third World people turn towards independence.

The second principle of rearrangement should be the creation of *Free Territories in the Mother Country*. Already we are seen as alien and outside White Civilization by those in power. It is necessary for us to create amidst the falling ruins of this Empire a new, alternative way of life more in harmony with the interests of the world's people.

Abbie is a pioneer in this struggle, but so far "Woodstock Nation" is purely cultural, a state of mind shared by thousands of young people. The next stage is to make this "Woodstock Nation" an organized reality with its own revolutionary institutions and, starting immediately, with roots in its own territory. At the same time, the need to overcome our inbred, egoistic, male, middle-class character, and especially to create solidarity with Third World struggles, has to become a foremost part of our consciousness.

The new people in white America are clustering in ghetto communities of their own: Berkeley, Haight-Ashbury, Isla Vista, Madison, Ann Arbor, the East Village, the Upper West Side. These communities, often created on the edge of universities, are not the bohemian enclaves of ten years ago. Those places, like Greenwich Village and North Beach, developed when the alienated were still a marginal group. Now millions of young people have nowhere else to go. They live cheaply in their own communities; go to school or to various free universities; study crafts and new skills; learn self-defense; read the underground press; go to demonstrations. The hard core of these new territories is the lumpen-bourgeoisie, drop-outs from the American way of life. But in any such community there is a cross-section of people whose needs overlap. In Berkeley, for example, there are students, street people, left-liberals and blacks, together constituting a radical political majority of the city. Communities like this are nearly as alien to police and "solid citizens" as are the black ghettos.

The importance of these communities is that they add a dimension of territory, of real physical space, to the consciousness of those within. The final break with mainstream America comes, after all, when you literally cannot live there, when it becomes imperative to live more closely with "your own kind."

Until recently people dropped out in their minds, or into tiny bohemian enclaves. Now they drop out collectively, into territory. In this situation feelings of individual isolation are replaced by a common consciousness of large numbers sharing the same needs. It is possible to go anywhere in America and find the section of town inhabited by the drop-outs, the freaks and the radicals. It is a nationwide network of people with the same oppression, the same language, the same music, the same styles, the same needs and grievances: the very essence of a new society taking root and growing up in the framework of the old.

The ruling class views this pattern with growing alarm. They analyze places like Berkeley as "red zones" like the ones they attempt to destroy in Vietnam. Universities and urban renewal agencies everywhere are busy moving into and destroying our communities, breaking them up physically, escalating the rents, tearing down cheap housing and replacing it with hotels, convention centers and university buildings. Politicians declare a "crime wave" (dope) and double the police patrols. Tens of thousands of kids are harassed, busted, moved on.

In every great revolution there have been such "liberated zones" where radicalism was most deeply rooted, where people tried to meet their own needs while fighting off the official governing power. If there is revolutionary change inside the Mother Country, it will originate in the Berke-leys and Madisons, where people are similarly rooted and where we are defending ourselves against constantly growing aggression.

The concept of Free Territories does *not* mean local struggles for "community control" in the traditional sense—battles which are usually limited to electoral politics and maneuvering for control of funds from the state or federal government. Our struggles will largely ignore or resist out-side administration and instead build and defend our own institutions.

Nor does the concept mean withdrawal into comfortable radical enclaves remote from the rest of America. The Territories should be centers from which a challenge to the whole Establishment is mounted.

Such Free Territories would have four common points of identity:

First, *they will be utopian centers of new cultural experiment.* "All Power to the Imagination" has real meaning for people experiencing the breakdown of our decadent culture. In the Territories all traditional social relations—starting with the oppression of women—would be overturned, or at least re-examined. The nuclear family would be replaced by a mixture of communes, extended families, children's centers and new schools. Women would have their own communes and organizations. Work would be redefined as a task done for the community, or as play. Drugs would be commonly used as a means of deepening self-awareness. Urban structures would be destroyed, to be replaced with parks, closed streets, expanded backyards inside blocks, and a village atmosphere in general would be encouraged. Education would be reorganized along revolutionary lines, with children really participating. Music and art would be freed from commercial control and widely performed in the community. At all levels the goal would be to eliminate egoism, competition and aggression from our personalities.

Second, *The Territories will be internationalist.* Cultural experiment *without internationalism is privilege; internationalism without cultural revolution is false consciousness.* People in our Territories would act as citizens of an international community, an obstructive force inside im-perialism. Solidarity committees to aid all Third World struggles would be in constant motion. Each Territory would see itself as an "international city." The flags, music and culture of other countries and other liberation movements would permeate the Territory. Travel and "foreign relations" with other nations would be commonplace. All imperialist institutions (universities, draft boards, corporations) in or near the Territory would be under constant siege. An underground railroad would exist to support revolutionary fugitives.

Third, *the Territories will be centers of constant confrontation, battle-fronts inside the Mother Country.* Major institutions such as universities and corporations would be under constant pressure either to shut down or to serve the community. The occupying police would be systematically opposed. Stores would be pressured to transform themselves into community-serving institutions. Tenant unions would seek to break the control of absentee landlords and to transform local housing into communal shelter. There would be continual defiance of tax, draft and drug laws. Protest campaigns of national importance, such as the anti-war movement, would be initiated from within the Territories. The constant process of confrontation would not only weaken the control of the power structure, but would serve also to create a greater sense of our own identity, our own possibilities.

Fourth, *they will be centers of survival and self-defense.* The Territories would include free medical and legal services, child-care centers, drug clinics, crash pads, instant communication networks, job referral and welfare centers—all the basic services to meet people's needs as they struggle and change. Training in physical self-defense and the use of weapons would become commonplace as fascism and vigilantism increase.

Insurgent, even revolutionary, activity will occur outside as well as inside the Territories. Much of it will be within institutions (workplaces, army bases, schools, even "behind enemy lines" in the government). But the Territories will be like models or beacons to those who struggle within these institutions, and the basic tension will tend always to occur between the authorities and the Territories pulling people out of the mainstream.

The Territories will establish once and for all the polarized nature of the Mother Country. No longer will Americans be able to think comfortably of themselves as a homogeneous society with a few extremists at the fringes. No longer will politicians and administrators be able to feel confident in their power to govern the entire U.S. Beneath the surface of official power, the Territories will be giving birth to new centers of power.

In the foreseeable future, Free Territories will have to operate with a strategy of "dual power"—that is, people would stay within the legal structure of the U.S., involuntarily if for no other reason, while building new forms with which to replace that structure. The thrust of these new forms will be resistance against illegitimate outside authority, and constant attempts at self-government.

Mother Country radicalism will have its unique organizational forms. Revolutionary movements have turned towards the concept of a centralized, disciplined, nationally-based "vanguard" party which leads a variety of mass organizations representing specific interests (women, labor, students, etc.). This organizational form is logical where people are already disciplined by their situation (as in a large factory) or where the goal is "state power." But it is not so clear that such an organizational form is necessary—at least now—for Mother Country radicalism. Certainly the excessive individualism and egoism which dominate the culture of young people must be overcome if we are going to survive, much less make a revolution. But the organizational form must be consistent with the kind of revolution we are trying to make. For that reason *the collective* in some form should be the basis of revolutionary organization.

A revolutionary collective would not be like the organizations to which we give part-time attachment today, the kind where we attend meetings, "participate" by speaking and voting, and perhaps learn how to use a mimeograph machine. The collectives would be much more about our *total* lives. Instead of developing our talents within schools and other Establishment institutions, we would develop them primarily within our own collectives. In these groups we would learn politics, self-defense, languages, ecology, medical skills, industrial techniques—everything that helps people grow towards independence. Thus the collectives would not be just organizational weapons to use against the Establishment, but organs fostering the development of revolutionary people.

The emphasis in this kind of organization is on power from below. It begins with a distrust of highly centralized or elite-controlled organizations. But we should also recognize that decentralization can degenerate into anarchy and tribalism. Collectives must stress the need for unity and cooperation, especially on projects which require large numbers or when common interests are threatened. We should seek the advantages of co-ordinated power while avoiding the problem of an established hierarchy. A network of collectives can act as the "revolutionary council" of a given Territory and a network of such councils can unite the Territories across the United States. In addition to such political coordination, the Territories can be united through the underground press and culture, through conferences and constant travel.

People or Personnel

Paul Goodman

Paul Goodman is a self-proclaimed anarchist who has for many years championed the virtues of decentralization. Almost all his works are concerned with this matter. Here Goodman tries to build a case for decentralization by confronting the standard arguments against it.

Throughout society, the centralizing style of organization has been pushed so far as to become ineffectual, economically wasteful, humanly stultifying, and ruinous to democracy. There are overcentralized systems in industry, in government, in culture, and in agriculture. The tight interlocking of these systems has created a situation in which modest, direct, and independent action has become extremely difficult in every field. The only remedy is a strong admixture of decentralism. The problem is where, how much, and how to go about it.

Let me give some rough definitions. In a centralized enterprise, the function to be performed is the goal of the organization rather than of persons (except as they identify with the organization). The persons are personnel. Authority is top-down. Information is gathered from below in the field and is processed to be usable by those above; decisions are made in headquarters; and policy, schedule, and standard procedure are transmitted downward by chain of command. The enterprise as a whole is divided into departments of operation to which are assigned personnel with distinct roles, to give standard performance. This is the system in Mr. Goldwater's department store, in the Federal government and in the State governments, in General Motors and in the UAW, in the New York public schools and in many universities, in most hospitals, in neighborhood renewal, in network broadcasting and the Associated Press, and in the deals that chain-grocers make with farmers. The system was devised to discipline armies; to keep records, collect taxes, and perform bureaucratic functions; and for certain kinds of mass production. It has now become pervasive.

The principle of decentralism is that people are engaged in a function

---

From Chapter One of *People or Personnel* by Paul Goodman (New York: Random House, 1963). Copyright © 1963, 1964, 1965 by Paul Goodman. Reprinted by permission of Random House, Inc.

and the organization is how they cooperate. Authority is delegated away from the top as much as possible and there are many accommodating centers of policy-making and decision. Information is conveyed and discussed in face-to-face contacts between field and headquarters. Each person becomes increasingly aware of the whole operation and works at it in his own way according to his capacities. Groups arrange their own schedules. Historically, this system of voluntary association has yielded most of the values of civilization, but it is thought to be entirely unworkable under modern conditions and the very sound of it is strange. . . .

Decentralization is not lack of order or planning, but a kind of coordination that relies on different motives from top-down direction, standard rules, and extrinsic rewards like salary and status, to provide integration and cohesiveness. It is not "anarchy.". . .

As an example of decentralist coordination, the Anarchist Prince Kropotkin, who was a geographer, used to point spectacularly to the history of Western science from the heroic age of Vesalius, Copernicus, and Galileo to his own time of Pasteur, Kelvin, and J. J. Thomson. The progress of science in all fields was exquisitely coordinated. There were voluntary associations, publications, regional and international conferences. The Ph.D. system was devised to disseminate new research to several hundred university libraries. There was continual private correspondence, even across warring boundaries. Yet in this vast common enterprise, so amazingly productive, there was no central direction whatever. . . .

Over the centuries, not only scientific truth but most other objective values, like beauty or compassion, have thrived by voluntary association and independent solitude. (Theological salvation is perhaps the only spiritual good that has usually been centrally regulated.) Almost by definition, the progress of social justice has been by voluntary association, since the central authority is what is rebelled against. And, of course, to preserve liberty, the American political system was deliberately designed as a polarity of centralist and decentralist elements, with limitations on the power of the Sovereign and in-built checks and balances at every level. We must also remember that in its heyday, celebrated by Adam Smith, the free-enterprise system of partnerships and vigilant joint stockholders was in theory a model of decentralist coordination, as opposed to the centralized system of mercantilism, royal patents, and monopolies that it replaced. . . .

"How can you decentralize air-traffic control?" asks a student.

You can't. There are many functions that are central by their natures, and it is useful to enumerate some of the chief kinds.

Central authority is necessary where there are no district limits and something positive must be done, as in epidemic control or smog control; or when an arbitrary decision is required and there is no time for reflection, as in traffic control; or when we have to set arbitrary standards for a whole field, but the particular standard is indifferent, e.g., weights and measures or money.

Centralization is temporarily necessary when an emergency requires the concentration of all powers in a concerted effort. But history has shown that such emergency centralization can be fateful, for the central organization tends to outlive the emergency, and then its very existence creates a chronic emergency; people soon become helpless unless they are told what to do.

Central authority is convenient to perform routine or "merely" administrative functions, when people have more important things to do. This is the Marxist theory of the withering away of the State to "mere" administration. But this too can be fateful, for administration soon encroaches on every function. It is thus that the executive secretary of an organization ends up running the show.

Central organization is the most rational kind when the logistics of a situation outweigh consideration of the concrete particulars involved. These are all the cases of ticketing and tax collecting, where one person is like another. . . .

My bias is decentralist, yet in some functions I think we need more centralization than we have. For instance, there ought to be uniform modular standards in building materials and fixtures. Building is a typical example of how we do things backwards. Where there ought to be decentralization, for instance in the design which requires artistry and in the decision of each neighborhood on how it wants to live, we get bureaucratic routine design, national policy, the standards of absentee sociologists, and the profits of promoters. But where there could be important savings, in materials and the process of construction, we do not standardize. . . .

A Marxist student objects that blurring the division of labor, local option, face-to-face communication, and other decentralist positions are relics of a present ideology, provincial and illiberal. . . .

Any decentralization that could occur at present would inevitably be post-urban and post-centralist; it could not be provincial. There is no American who has not been formed by national TV, and no region that has not been homogenized by the roads and chain stores. A model of twentieth-century decentralization is the Israeli *kibbutz*. Some would say that these voluntary communities are fanatical, but no one would deny that they are cosmopolitan and rationalistic, post-centralist and post-urban.

Decentralizing has its risks. Suppose that the school system of a Northern city were radically decentralized, given over to the control of the parents and teachers of each school. Without doubt some of the schools would be Birchite and some would be badly neglected. Yet it is hard to imagine that many schools could be worse than the present least-common-denominator. There would certainly be more experimentation. There would be meaningful other choices to move to. And inevitably all the schools would exist in a framework of general standards that they would have to measure up to or suffer the consequences.

Invariably, some student argues that without the intervention of the Federal government, the Negroes in the South will not get their civil rights. This may or may not be so, but certainly most of their progress toward civil rights so far has come from local action that has embarrassed and put pressure on Washington. By the same token the Negro organizations themselves have been decentrally coordinated; as Dr. King has pointed out, the "leadership" is continually following the localities. But the basic error of this student is to think that the "States' Rights" of the segregationists is decentralist. (An authentic regionalism would be decentralist.) If each locality indeed had its option, the counties where Negroes are in the majority would have very different rules! And they would provide a meaningful choice for other Negroes to move to.

The relation of decentralization to physical and social mobility is an important topic; let us stay with it for another page. . . . Decentralist philosophies have prized stability, "rootedness," subtle awareness of the environment, as a means to the integration of the domestic, technical, economic, political, and cultural functions of life, and to provide a physical community in which the young can grow up. . . .

Yet Americans have always been mobile—usually going away, individuals and families leaving communities that did not offer opportunity, in order to try new territory known by hearsay. Historically, the country was open at the margins, because of either the geographical frontier or new jobs that attracted immigrants. . . .

At present, however, the country is closed at the margins, yet the physical (and social) mobility is even greater. Negroes migrate north because the sharecropping has failed and they are barred from the factories; Northern middle-class whites move to the suburbs to escape the Negroes; farm families have dwindled to 8 percent. Unfortunately, none of these groups is moving *to* anything. And much moving is ordered by the central organization itself: national corporations send their employees and families to this or that branch; universities raid one another for staff; promoters and bureaucrats dislocate tenants for urban redevelopment.

Under such conditions people must end up in total anomie, with no meaningful relation to the environment and society. There seem to be two alternative remedies. One was proposed forty years ago by Le Corbusier: to centralize and homogenize completely, so that one dwelling place is exactly like another, with identical furniture, services, and surroundings. When all live in identical hotel rooms, mobility does not involve much dislocation. The other alternative is to build communities where meaningful voluntary association is again possible; that is, to decentralize. This has, of course, been the wistful aim of suburbanism, and it continually appears in the real estate advertisements. But a suburb is not a decentralist community; its purposes, way of life, and decisions are determined by business headquarters, the national standard of living, and the bureau of highways. The hope of community is in people deciding important matters for themselves.

A student raises a related objection: Decentralism is for small towns; it cannot work with big dense populations. But I don't think this objection has any merit. Decentralism is a kind of social organization; it does not involve geographical isolation, but a particular sociological use of geography.

In important respects, a city of five million can be decentrally organized as many scores of unique communities in the framework of a busy metropolis.

Usually in modern urban administration, the various municipal functions—school, job induction, social work, health, police and court for misdemeanors, post office, housing and rent control, election district, etc.—are divided into units only for the administrative convenience of City Hall. The districts do not coincide with one another or with neighborhoods. A citizen with business or complaint must seek out the district office of each department, or perhaps go to City Hall. And correspondingly, there is no possible forum to discuss the coordination of the various functions except at the very top, with the Mayor or before the City Council.

Decentralist organization would rather follow the actuality of living in an urban community, where housing, schooling, shopping, policing, social services, politics are integrally related. Each neighborhood should have a local City Hall. Such *arrondissements* could have considerable autonomy within the municipal administration that controls transit, sanitation, museums, etc., whatever is necessarily or conveniently centralized. Taxes could be collected centrally and much of the take divided among the neighborhoods to be budgeted locally.

For the average citizen, the convergence of all kinds of related business in one local center is not only convenient but must lead to more acquaintance and involvement. Poor people especially do not know their way around, are stymied by forms to fill out, and have no professional help; they are defeated by fighting City Hall and soon give up. Besides, each neighborhood has interlocking problems peculiar to itself. These can be reasonably confronted by citizens and local officials, but they are lost in the inner politics of central bureaucracies that have quite different axes to grind.

. . . The say of a neighborhood in its destiny can be meaningful only if the neighborhood has begun to be conscious of itself as a community. For this, mere "consent" or "participation" is not enough; there must be a measure of real initiating and deciding, grounded in acquaintance and trust.

However, the question is not whether decentralization can work in dense urban populations, but how to make it work, for it is imperative. The increase of urban social disease and urban mental disease is fundamentally due to powerlessness, resignation, and withdrawal, as if people's only way to assert vitality is to develop symptoms. The central authorities try to cope as stern or hygienic caretakers; the citizens respond by becoming "community-dependent"—in jail, in the hospital, on relief; that is, they become chronic patients. With many, this has gone on for two and three generations. . . .

A student hotly objects that decentralism is humanly unrealistic, it "puts too much faith in human nature" by relying on intrinsic motives, like interest in the job and voluntary association. . . .

This objection is remarkably off-base. . . . The moral question is not whether men are "good enough" for a type of social organization, but whether the type of organization is useful to develop the potentialities of intelligence, grace, and freedom in men.

More deeply, the distrust of "human nature," of course, is anxious conformism. One must save face, not make a mistake in any detail; so one clings to an assigned role. But, unfortunately, the bigger the organization, the more face to save. For instance, . . . the government Peace Corps is many times as expensive as similar less official operations largely because an errant twenty-year-old well-digger might become an International Incident, so one cannot be too careful in selecting him. Convenience of supervision overrides performance. And the more "objective" the better. If the punch card approves, no one is guilty. To bureaucrats, a fatal hallmark of decentralist enterprises is their variety in procedure and persons; how can one know, with a percentage validity, that these methods and persons are right?

. . . The centralizing style makes for both petty conforming and admiration for bigness. The more routine and powerless people are, the more they are mesmerized by extrinsic proofs of production and power. An enterprise that is designed on a small scale for a particular need of particular people comes to be regarded as though it were nothing at all. To win attention and support, it must call itself a Pilot Project, promising mighty applications.

Nevertheless, still deeper than these neurotic confusions, there is, in my opinion, an authentic confusion in the face of unprecedented conditions of modern times, that makes for rigidity and fear of social experiment. . . . The leap in technology, the galloping urbanization, nuclear weapons, the breakdown of the colonial system—all involve threats and dilemmas. The inevitable response of people is to rally to the style of strict control by experts. In emergencies, centralized organization seems to make sense and often does make sense. It is also comfortingly dictatorial.

Finally, the moral objection is stated also the opposite way: decentralizing is impossible, not because people are incapable but because the powers-that-be won't allow it. (This student is an Angry Young Man.) Granting that in some areas decentralization is workable, how could it possibly be brought about? We cannot expect central powers to delegate autonomy any more than we can expect the nation-states to give up any of their sovereignty and grandeur. Indeed, the tendency is entirely in the other direction, toward bigger corporations, combinations, and tie-ins, toward tighter scheduling and grading in education, toward increased standardization and the application of automatic and computer technology in every field, and of course toward the increase of power in Washington to become the greatest landlord, the greatest sponsor of research, and the greatest policeman. . . .

In principle, there are two ways in which an overcentralized system can become more mixed. Voluntary associations form spontaneously because of pressing needs to which the central system is irrelevant or antipathetic. Or the central authority itself chooses, or is forced, to build in decentral parts because its method is simply not working.

There is a marked trend toward spontaneous associations that indicates first a despair of, and then an indifference to, the regular methods. One must "do it oneself." We have already noticed the spontaneity, localism, and decentralist federation of the Negro civil rights movement, as different from the more conventional maneuvering of the Urban League and the older NAACP. But this is part of a general spread of para-legal demonstrating, boycotting, and show of power that express dissent with formal procedures that are not effective. . . .

Do-It-Yourself can be para-institutional if not overtly para-legal. Beat youth withdraws from the economy and tries to contrive a community culture of its own. Off-Broadway first withdraws from Broadway, dissident artists first withdraw from the big commercial galleries and set up their own galleries, etc.; but then there spreads a distaste for formal showings altogether. Students quit famous universities because they decide they are not being educated; then they form, for instance, the Northern Student Movement in order to tutor backward urban children; but then the Northern Student Movement decides that the public school curriculum is inadequate, and the tutors will teach according to their own lights. Freedom Now sets up what amounts to a para-party in Mississippi.

And there is a similar tone even within the political framework. Contrasted with older "reform" movements which were devoted to purging the bosses and grafters, the new urban reform movements rapidly constitute themselves ad hoc for a concrete purpose other than getting hold of the party machinery, usually to block outrageous encroachments of government or big institutions. . . .

I do not notice any significant disposition of central powers to decentralize themselves. Rather, when the organization begins to creak, their disposition is to enlarge it further by adding new bureaus and overseers, to stall by appointing committees without power, to disregard difficulties and hope they will go away, or to call hard cases "deviant" and put them out of circulation.

Nevertheless, there are examples to show how decentralization can be built in.

[Quite] interesting for our purposes is the multifarious application of industrial psychology. For the most part, the psychologists are decentralist by disposition and have taught a wisdom opposite to the time-motion studies of "scientific business management." Rather than subdividing the workman further and departmentalizing further, they have urged that it is efficient to allow more choice and leeway, to ask for suggestions from below to increase "belonging." To give a typical example: In one plant it has been found more productive in the long run for half a dozen workmen to assemble a big lathe from beginning to end and have the satisfaction of seeing it carried away, than to subdivide the operation on a line.

Needless to say, our industrial psychologists cannot pursue their instincts to the logical conclusion, workers' management. Yet questions of degree are not trivial. Consider the following example: In an area of England, it is traditional to work by a gang or collective contract. (This "Coventry system" has been studied by Professor Melman of Columbia.) A group of workmen agree to complete in a period a certain quantity of piecework, for which they are paid a sum of money divided equally. The capitalist provides the machinery and materials, but everything else—work rules, schedule, hiring—is left to group decision. The group may be half a dozen or a couple of thousand. Humanly, such an arrangement has extraordinary advantages. Men exchange jobs and acquire new skills; they adjust the schedule to their convenience or pleasures; they bring in and train apprentices; they invent labor-saving devices, which are to their own advantage; they cover for one another when sick or for special vacations.

Obviously such a system, so amazingly at variance with our minute top-down regulation, time-clock discipline, labor-union details, and competitive spirit, is hard to build into most of American industry. Yet where it would suit, it would make a profound difference. . . .

It seems to me as follows. We are in a period of excessive centralization. . . . Therefore we might adopt a political *maxim*: to decentralize where, how, and how much is expedient. But where, how, and how much are *empirical* questions. They require research and experiment.

In existing overcentralized climate of opinion, it is just this research and experiment that we are not getting. Among all the departments, agencies, and commissions in Washington, I have not heard of one that deals with the organizational *style* of municipalities, social work, manufacturing, merchandising, or education in terms of technical and economic efficiency and effect on persons. Therefore, I urge students who are going on to graduate work to choose their theses in this field.

Participatory Democracy: Lenin Updated

Lewis S. Feuer

Lewis Feuer here attempts to briefly summarize the view of participatory democracy held by the New Left and then strongly attacks it as a
formula for antidemocratic elitism. Most important is the argument that
the advocates are ready to usurp the privilege of representing "the
people" with little justification beyond the "rightness" of their views.

"Participatory democracy" is the contribution of the New Student
Left to political theory. It was born of their meetings, small and large,
minute and mass, where the speaker, heckler or chairman, would feel that
he had articulated in words what was trying to emerge from a long, often
inchoate discussion. Suddenly the mass seemed inspired; words passed to
action; the spontaneity of the mass broke through the formal paraphernalia
of formal democracy with its parliamentary rules. "Participatory democracy" was "democratic anarchy" fulfilled. The phrase appeared in the Port
Huron statement of the founding convention of Students for a Democratic
Society in 1962: "In a participatory democracy, the political life would be
based . . . (on the principle that) decision-making of basic social consequence be carried on by public groupings." An issue of the pacifist Bulletin
of the Committee for Nonviolent Action undertook to explain how it had
operated in the Assembly of Unrepresented People (AOUP), a group of
two thousand, mostly composed of students, drawn from all segments of
the "New Left," which convened for four days in Washington in August
1965 to press for peace in Vietnam, and which led to the arrest of more
than 350 demonstrators:

> AOUP had no organizational structure nor established discipline
> because its decision-making process was by "participatory democracy."
> This meant that not a single policy was predetermined and imposed; all
> policies could be established or modified by the participants in the
> Assembly. Because participatory democracy is likely to be around the
> radical movements for some time and may eventually be accepted almost

From pp. 407–412 of The Conflict of Generations by Lewis S. Feuer. © 1969 by
Lewis S. Feuer, Basic Books, Inc., Publishers, New York.

universally, it is important that this mode of organization be studied and understood.

Participatory democracy has no initial organization or policies for a demonstration. . . . Decision is by neither voting nor consensus. In fact, decisions in the usual sense don't occur. Policies are set and action determined by those who in the maelstrom of discussion and debate, exert the most influence through courage, articulateness, reasonableness and sensitivity to the feelings of the group. Influence is enhanced by image characteristics such as reputation, looks and style of living that appeal to young people. . . .

Participatory democracy is unsuited for steady activities in which careful reason dominates, clear policy statements are important, and dissonant minorities would become conspicuous. The method is best suited to an action movement, mobilizing and focusing the moral energies of young people in brief, one-event actions. In such a milieu a leader's declaration of intent is a policy, his actions a decision; all currents move toward a crescendo, overwhelming discordant notes.[1]

The advocates of the new "participatory democracy" explained that what they were advocating was a democracy of direct action in which the concerned activists could intervene directly in political processes, and affect their outcome without the intervention of an electorate and the machinery of representative democracy. The direct actions of a "participatory democracy" would be set up parallel to the institutions of representative democracy which they would then supersede. Staughton Lynd, an active civil rights worker and an assistant professor at Yale, saw "participatory democracy" as an American version of the Russian Soviet, with admixtures of Gandhi's pro-village ideology and of the back-to-the-people spirit of the Russian student movement of the nineteenth century. Staughton Lynd wrote:

In form, parallelism suggests a kinship between participatory democracy and Trotsky's conception of the Soviets as a "dual power," or Gandhi's concern to preserve the Indian village analogy. . . . Let the teacher leave the university and teach in Freedom Schools; let the reporter quit his job on a metropolitan daily and start a community newspaper; generally, let the intellectual make insurgency a full-time rather than a part-time occupation. As the Russian radical movement grew from Tolstoyism and the Narodniks' concern to dress simply, speak truth, and "go to the people," so participatory democracy at this point speaks most clearly to the middle-class man, daring him to forsake powerlessness and act.[2]

The participatory democrat saw the people bestirring themselves spontaneously from the fetters of the System, throwing off its rigidities, its formalistic elections and bureaucracies, and acting directly, humanly. A spontaneous protest might suddenly grow into a direct action against the government itself. Lynd wrote, with apocalyptic emotion, of a demonstration in Washington against the war in Vietnam:

> Still more poignant was the perception—and I checked my reaction with many others who felt as I did—that as the crowd moved down the Mall toward the seat of government . . . so that there was nowhere to go but forward toward the waiting policemen, it seemed that the great mass of people would simply flow on through and over the marble building, that our forward movement was irresistibly strong, that had some been shot or arrested nothing could have stopped that crowd from taking possession of its Government. Perhaps next time we should keep going. . . .[3]

The kinship between "participatory democracy" and "Soviet democracy," which Lynd acknowledges, takes us to the heart of the political theory of the New Left. In essence, it is Lenin's theory of revolutionary action by a small, dictatorial elite translated into the language of the "nonviolent" movement. Where Lenin wrote that the people would dispense with parliamentary procedure and substitute for it the direct action of "the simple organisation of the armed masses (such as the Soviets of Workers' and Soldiers' Deputies . . .),"[4] Staughton Lynd has the nonviolent student mass surging forward to take possession of the government. The Senate and House of Representatives would be closed permanently, as the Constituent Assembly was in St. Petersburg in 1918. The "complex machinery" (as Lenin called it) of people's formal elections in representative democracy would be replaced by "participatory democracy." Just as Lenin promised that in the soviets within twenty-four hours of the revolution, there would be a "universal participation of the people" to replace all the machinery of the bourgeois state and economic administration, so the New Leftist envisages the direct action-participation of the moving mass as supplanting the Establishment, the organs of the System. As Lynd writes:

> One can now begin to envision a series of nonviolent protests which would from the beginning question the legitimacy of the Administration's authority where it has gone beyond constitutional and moral limits, and might, if its insane foreign policy continues, culminate in the decision of hundreds of thousands of people to recognize the authority of alternative institutions of their own making.[5]

The crux of a revolution, says Lynd, learning from Trotsky, occurs when the troops desert to the side of the rioters. This he envisages as a "scenario" for America. "A constitutional crisis" exists in America, he declares, "we have moved into a twilight zone between democratically elected authority and something accurately called 'fascism.' " He envisages the denouement of the next major demonstration: "Perhaps next time we should keep going, occupying for a time the rooms from which orders issue . . . until those who make policy . . . consent to enter into dialogue with us and with mankind."

Behind all the phraseology of dialogue there is the simple fact that the ideology of the New Left is one of imposing the will of a small elite, a band of activists, on national policy. The students are summoned to be the shock troops of the elite: "If students chained themselves to the Capitol this summer in wave after wave of massive civil disobedience, even the Johnson Administration would be constrained in its choice of means." What begins as talk of a higher form of democracy, of people directly participating in decisions, turns out to be the defensive formula for action by a student elite which would contravene the will of the majority as expressed in the institutions of representative democracy. "The Movement," like "the Party," seizes power; the one invokes the myth of "participatory democracy," the other invoked the myth of the soviets.

As the civil rights leader, Bayard Rustin, trenchantly declared, "Under whose mandate are the 20,000 Washington marchers entitled to occupy 'their government' for even ten minutes? Does Lynd believe that they represent the views of anything approaching the majority of the people on the question of Vietnam? . . . What gives the disaffected sons and daughters of the middle class the right even symbolically to become the government?"[6]

The tactical means of "participatory democracy" was identical (though translated into ostensibly "nonviolent" terms) with the principle of political tactics which Lenin enunciated in justifying the seizure of power, and in defending his dissolution of the democratically elected Constituent Assembly: "Have an overwhelming superiority of forces at the decisive moment at the decisive point—this 'law' of military success is also the law of political success, especially in that fierce, seething class war which is called revolution."[7] It was simply not possible, said Lenin, for the working class to acquire a sufficient firmness of character, perception, and wide political outlook to enable them to vote intelligently;[8] therefore, he argued, a minority must seize the state power; then, holding power, it would in "a long and fierce struggle" "'convince'" the majority of the workers to accept its policies. The "participatory democrat" likewise has no use for elections, votes, parliamentary procedures; his basic argument is that since the masses are nonparticipant, the elite activists must act on their behalf. The votes of the electorate and of Congress are simply dismissed; somehow the "power structure" has purloined or befuddled the masses and their political expression. The "participatory democrats" will surge forward, take hold of the state, and establish new organs of rule, of their own hegemony. Thus, the line of reasoning which began with the intellectual elitism of C. Wright Mills, with his ridicule of the "labor metaphysics," culminated in Staughton Lynd's conception of the dictatorship of a student elite in the guise of "participatory democracy."

The notion of "participatory democracy" involved a basic alteration in the concept of civil disobedience. Originally, as conceived by such persons as Martin Luther King, it was basically an appeal to the conscience of the community; the civilly disobedient undertook to violate some unjust or unconstitutional ordinance in order to draw the attention of the electorate and the government to ignored wrongs. The civil disobedient still retained a faith in the workings of representative democracy. The student movement, on the other hand, rapidly losing faith in representative democracy, began to conceive of civil disobedience as a first step in a "confrontation" with the "power structure" which would lead in some vague, undefined way to a seizure of power by the student movement. The two conceptions of civil disobedience clashed basically in Selma, Alabama, in the spring of 1965. As Staughton Lynd writes:

> The old politics and the new confronted each other once again in Selma. SNCC was the first civil rights group on the ground there. . . . Then, by agreement with SNCC but nonetheless traumatically for the SNCC workers in Selma, Dr. King's Southern Christian Leadership Conference moved in. SCLC's focus was the passage of national legislation, not the political maturing of persons in the Alabama Black Belt. . . . SNCC could only experience Selma with mixed feelings and considerable frustration. The "march" of March 9, when Dr. King led people to a confrontation he knew would not occur and then accused the police of bad faith for exposing his hypocrisy, must have seemed to those in SNCC a symbolic summation of much that had gone before.[9]

"SNCC," wrote James W. Silver, "is seldom amenable to compromise. . . . These activists were unimpressed with legalism and constitutionalism; they were the 'new abolitionists.' "[10]

What SNCC had wanted was the kind of movement Staughton Lynd had dreamed of, the confrontation, the unpredictable occurrence, the elite and their allies surging forward, the seizure of power, the creation of the New Society, the release of the creative energies of all activists in the student movement and their allies, and finally, though it was only slowly avowed, violence.[11]

The fate of the notion of "participatory democracy" is instructive. It began as the apparent expression of a strong populist identification, with the "unstated assumption," in Lynd's words, "that the poor, when they find voice, will produce a truer, sounder radicalism than any which alienated intellectuals might prescribe."[12] As the doctrine evolved, however, it became the ideological bearer of elitism. It began ostensibly by seeking a political participation by the American citizen which would be more than "the annual act of pulling a lever in a little curtained room."[13] But as the citizenry proved quiescent, or failed to follow the students' lead, the doctrine, with its "insistence that decisions should come about through a process of personal confrontation and encounter," metamorphosed into an apologetic for the "putschist" action of a small student elite, abetted by the violence of the alienated "guerrillas," to impose its will on the recalcitrant majority of the people. Thus, "participatory democracy" was recapitulating in large measure the career of "proletarian democracy." Between the intellectual elitism of C. Wright Mills and the "participatory democracy" of Tom Hayden and Staughton Lynd there was a clear line of continuity; the last fulfilled the first. All were intellectual authoritarians, the only difference being that Hayden and Lynd used an existentialist vocabulary whereas Mills spoke in neo-Marxist terms.

Notes

[1] Bradford Lytle, "After Washington?—Three Views," *Committee for Nonviolent Action Bulletin*, V, No. 5 (Aug. 27, 1965), 1–2.

[2] Staughton Lynd, "The New Radicals and 'Participatory Democracy,'" *Dissent*, XII (1965), 328–329.

[3] Staughton Lynd, "Coalition Politics or Nonviolent Revolution?" *Liberation*, X, No. 4 (June–July 1965), 21.

[4] V. I. Lenin, *The State and Revolution* (New York, 1932), p. 75.

[5] Lynd, "Coalition Politics or Nonviolent Revolution?" pp. 19–21.

[6] Bayard Rustin, "The New Radicalism: Round III," *Partisan Review*, XXXII, No. 4 (1965), 537.

[7] V. I. Lenin, *The Constituent Assembly Elections and the Dictatorship of the Proletariat* (Moscow, 1954), p. 14.

[8] *Ibid.*, pp. 27, 31.

[9] Lynd, "The New Radicals and 'Participatory Democracy,'" pp. 326–327.

[10] James W. Silver, *Mississippi: The Closed Society* (New York, 1966), pp. 342–343.

[11] In 1967, the Student Nonviolent Coordinating Committee dropped its tactical fiction of "nonviolence" and advocated violence, especially "guerrilla warfare." Curiously, in its espousal of "guerrilla warfare," it was following in Lenin's footsteps. William English Walling, activist at the turn of the century, reported from Russia how Lenin favored "guerrilla warfare," and how the lesson of the Revolution of 1905 was "the possible success of guerrilla tactics in a modern city"; guns could be passed, house owners could be terrorized, and the chance of detection was small. See William English Walling, *Russia's Message* (New York, 1909), pp. 358, 370.

[12] Lynd, "The New Radicals and 'Participatory Democracy,'" p. 328.

[13] Lynd, "Socialism, the Forbidden Word," *Studies on the Left*, III, No. 3 (1963), 19.

The Fallacy of Decentralization

Amitai Etzioni

In this selection Etzioni, a noted sociologist, suggests that some crucial problems cannot be handled in a decentralized fashion. He also questions the impact of "micro-participation" on the individual, thereby attacking a key justification for participatory democracy presented in the introductory essay. Finally he challenges the notion that the present system (in the United States) really suffers from overcentralization

---

In 1947, I was delivering hay from Tel Yoseph, an Israeli kibbutz, to Ein Harod, another kibbutz less than a mile away. The farm manager of Ein Harod signed the delivery papers for twenty-eight bales, and I filed the papers with the office of Tel Yoseph. "How much will Ein Harod be charged?" I asked the clerk. He was astonished by my question. "By Afula prices, of course." Afula is a town not far from both kibbutzim. While the kibbutzim neither use money nor set prices in their internal transactions, they charge each other the prices which prevail in the "free" (i.e., capitalistic) market of Afula. The national kibbutz associations help fledgling kibbutzim, but in general the mechanisms for transfer payments are very weak. No wonder that rather well-off kibbutzim are to be found next to extremely poor ones. And over the years, the rich kibbutzim get richer while the poor ones remain poor.

The kibbutz movement is of considerable interest to those who favor decentralization as a way of providing a genuinely participatory system. But it also illustrates the fact that decentralization often serves ineffectively those values which require a national mechanism that is sufficiently powerful to reallocate resources among local units (a prerequisite for social justice) and the handling of many other "inter-unit," nation-wide issues and values (e.g., the financing of institutions of higher education which would advance the movement).

I am far from being an expert on Yugoslavia, but I understand from those who are that the relatively considerable decision-making power given to small residential and work units generates some similar, symptomatic

---

From Amitai Etzioni, "The Fallacy of Decentralization," *The Nation* (August 25, 1969), pp. 145–147. Reprinted by permission of *The Nation*.

problems. Thus, for instance, I am told that there is little "income transfer" from the more affluent parts of Yugoslavia to such poverty-stricken, underdeveloped regions as Macedonia, Yugoslavia's equivalent of our South. Efforts to establish inter-local bus lines, especially, those which require inter-regional coordination, are said to face difficulties similar to those encountered in attempts to establish rapid transit systems in our cities, when the consent and financial support of a large number of independent local governments are needed.

To generalize, a truly decentralized participatory system will tend to be highly responsive to the needs of the members in each participatory locality, but will tend to neglect inter-local, inter-regional and national needs, both of the allocative (e.g., social justice) type and those which are best served collectively (e.g., a priming of the economy).

Decentralization offers a significant basis for participation. It fosters a citizenry that is informed and in control, tending to make society and its governance more humane. Hence, it is not surprising that many attempts are made to explain, or to explain away, the drawbacks of decentralization. Some anarchists suggest that the values fostered by decentralization are of such high priority that its disadvantages are more than acceptable. Laissez-faire liberals say, as Kenneth Boulding has argued, that once we have a large number of small, competitive political units, the laws of free competition will operate so as to promote various "inter-unit" values without the need for an institutionalized "super-unit" (or national) mechanism.

Another "automatic" solution comes from the New Left; Berndt Rabehl has written, "How will the structure of the city look? It can be divided up into many, individual collectivities of three, four or five thousand men, who center themselves around a factory. Thereby the factory becomes not merely a work center, but a place offering all possibilities for the unfolding of life. Computers will be used to figure what has to be built, how the plans must look, what dangers may appear." This approach ignores moral and political questions, making all of the issues seem to be merely factual. In short, it may be said that what we seek for America is a system that is less centralized than the existing one, but not a system which is completely or even highly decentralized.

This brings up the question of the nature of our national system and what its decentralization would entail. As I see it, the formulation of military, foreign and space policy is centralized, especially those decisions which may involve life or death for millions in nuclear war. If there were a realistic way by which these decisions could be decentralized, the welfare of all of us would probably be enhanced. (Even here, however, there would be a hidden assumption: that people are good, at least peace-loving, while governments, ours at any rate, are evil and war-oriented. Possibly the increased participation of citizens in foreign-policy decisions would have the desired effect only when the citizens themselves were liberated from the effects of the centralized society. How we might survive the transition period is a problem almost as intractable as the original one of a decentralized power to declare war.)

For domestic policy, quite a different system seems to prevail in the contemporary United States; hence an approach quite different from decentralization may be required to make the governance of society in this area more participatory and humane. While the foreign-policy state is run chiefly from Washington by generals and bureaucrats in coalition with national power groups, the domestic state is largely fragmented and controlled locally from city halls, state capitals and "private governments" (such as universities and hospitals) in coalition with local power groups and with only spot interference from Washington. Thus, for example, it is empirically incorrect to assume that anyone in Washington has effective control over the educational system; decisions are made by fifty state Departments of Education, thousands of local school boards, and the trustees of 2,000 colleges and universities, with surprisingly little coordination. The same holds for police departments, health and welfare services, etc. Even the funds which come from Washington are spent largely according to local decisions. When national standards exist at all, they are frequently not effectively enforced; the HEW guidelines for desegregation are a case in point.

Domestic policy cannot be much more decentralized than it is now. And in considering whether or not to decentralize further, one must take into account that, by and large, the domestic services provided by the federal government—while highly bureaucratic, too-late too-little, slow to reflect innovations, and more slanted toward the middle class than the underclass—are more responsive to human needs, minority groups, etc., than those provided by most local authorities. Some, actually surprisingly few communities, are progressive but the administration of most cities and states (and, I suspect, of the remaining villages) is significantly inferior to that provided by federal agencies on all conceivable criteria. On the local level, power elites can gain their way more readily, nepotism and unvarnished corruption are more rampant, civil service standards are lower, the cost per unit of achievement is higher, and disregard for minorities is greater. It is the pull of national forces—both the organization of people on relief, and HEW—which increases the level of welfare payments, while most states seek to keep it down; the desegregation that has occurred is due largely to nation-wide efforts by such forces as the civil rights movement and the Department of Justice, and so forth. It is quite unclear, at least to me, why the sum of the parts of this country is less reactionary (when one reviews domestic programs) than most of the parts taken singly, but I am quite sure that it is so.

Those who favor decentralization, at least if they come from the Left, will say that they have in mind units smaller than states or cities. But even these units—South Boston or East Palo Alto—tend to be monopolized and corrupt in their governance. The reformers may say that they seek still smaller units, like the student communes, but these are at best a way of life for a very tiny minority. Moreover, they are too small to attend to most human needs, and the coordination of scores of such units to provide the needed services collectively is nearly impossible.

It is further said that local units can more easily be made participatory. This may be true for a few communities, mainly campus towns and select suburbs, but is not the case for most localities. On the contrary, it seems to me comparatively easier (though still far from easy) to gain participation in decisions made on the national level and to achieve the measure of transformation (e.g., untightening) of which this society is capable by joining into national social movements such as peace, civil rights, and now that of the students. By coordinated effort, scores of Congressmen can be influenced, the outcomes of elections affected, Washington (or the Pentagon) confronted, etc. All this does not yield an open, participatory society, but it does fuel more reforms and radicalization than most strictly local efforts (as distinct from local projects which are part of a national movement).

Furthermore, I hold, though this cannot be elaborated here, that from a psychological viewpoint, participation will have a restless, Sisyphean quality unless it is tied to causes beyond personal gratification. Without helping to liberate others, without helping to create the societal conditions for personal liberation—without macro-participation—there cannot be authentic micro-participation.

The main opportunities to broaden the participation of all citizens in domestic policies—and, to the degree that the national Establishment does not respond to this pressure, the radicalization of those not yet radicalized—lie in national social movements, usually combining a broad critical perspective with mobilization around a specific issue. To anchor this point further, I must digress briefly to indicate my views of the national power structure and of how it may be transformed. The American reality seems to me to stand somewhere between the vulgar conception of the power elite, which sees the control of society as monopolized by one well-coordinated group, and the conception of democratic pluralism, which sees the country taking its direction as the result of interaction among a large variety of autonomous "interest groups." There is, I think, a plurality of national actors, but they are far from being equal in power. In other words, there is a highly slanted pluralism, with the country's course being determined to a large extent, but not exclusively, by a not well coordinated group of powerful actors (e.g., the National Association of Manufacturers, the Armed Services), with a significant role being played—especially on the domestic front—by secondary groups (e.g., AFL–CIO) and, occasionally, by the least powerful groups, such as the farm workers.

To view the same structure dynamically, there is an option other than the four now most frequently discussed: disintegration or anarchy, revolutionary change, token ameliorations ("reforms"), or open authoritarianism following a right-wing backlash. The fifth alternative consists of significant and accumulative changes that result in a gradual although not necessarily slow transformation to a fundamentally different society.

The extent to which this option is realizable depends directly on whether or not change in the *national* power balance is possible. The more the least powerful groups become politically aware and mobilized for political action on the national level (as is gradually happening with the blacks), and the more they find partners in "secondary" groups which have some power but also have, or can find, an interest in societal transformation (e.g., students, middle-class ethnic minorities), the greater the chance that a fundamental transformation will take place. In short, national movements are an essential propellant for social change. And only after such transformation is accomplished can I foresee the conditions under which decentralization would lead not to greater oligarchization but rather to the local transformation of ecological units in the direction of broadened participation.

I deliberately focus here on power, mobilization for political action and national coordination—issues which to some members of the New Left seem rather old-fashioned as compared to "deeper" existential matters. The mere fact that these issues have been raised before does not automatically make them obsolete. And while I can see the appeal of the short cuts offered by the Theatre of the Absurd, the student communes, and even the social islands of the hippies, the integrated and spontaneous way of life cannot, as I see it, be sustained unless the *national* structures are first transformed. Moreover, whatever progress can be made locally, unless it is very microscopic (limited to a few pads or barns), depends on the moral and intellectual sustenance as well as the political protection of a national movement.

There seems to be one exception to this sociological iron law: participation in "private governments" of corporate units as distinct from ecological-residential ones. Universities, churches, hospitals and some places of work can be made more participatory without first transforming the national structures. Again, I am much more confident about the sociological observation than about the reasons. Perhaps this capacity to evolve autonomously in smaller units without first unlocking larger structures is due to the fact that forces of control and sanctioning, that is, the police, are more closely tied to ecological units and elites than to private governments. These governments seems reluctant to resort to such forces because a measure of corporate autonomy serves their interests, and they are afraid— as university faculties so obviously are—that once the government is regularly invited to deal with their rebels, it will stay to deal with them. The result is well illustrated by the relative reluctance of churches, universities and other private governments to call in the police, as compared with the cities of Boston, Detroit, Los Angeles, Oakland and Newark, and by the difficult time Congress has in finding ways to legislate about conduct in the action-space of these private units.

In short, on the domestic front (as distinct from military and foreign policy), little will be achieved by most forms of decentralization, because the system is already rather decentralized, and the local-ecological units are chiefly controlled by oligarchies which are tighter than the national domestic system. The greatest, although far from great, opportunities for mobilizing power toward transformation are on the national level, including unlocking the system for broader local participation. Participation in "private governments" is an exception so far, but it is not clear how long it will remain so; they, too, may become tied into municipal and state sanctioning systems to be controlled like local-ecological units.

The Pitfalls of National Consciousness

Frantz Fanon

Frantz Fanon, a black psychiatrist who became a major theorist on revolution in the Third World before his death, writes of the need to decentralize the dominant political party in any developing country. This article is a direct attack on the Nkrumah-style political system, based on Communist models, in which a centralized, highly organized political party becomes the key political institution in the society. Although inspired by the Marxist tradition, Fanon rejects the idea that such an apparatus is necessary or desirable for rapid economic and social development. He believes that the government should be made physically accessible by moving it out into rural areas. Finally, Fanon insists that the language of expertise be avoided in order not to cut the people off from public affairs.

Contrast this belief in political participation in developing nations with Ithiel de Sola Pool's rejection of it:

> *In the Congo, in Vietnam, in the Dominican Republic, it is clear that order depends on somehow compelling newly mobilized strata to return to a measure of passivity and defeatism from which they have recently been aroused by the process of modernization. At least temporarily, the maintenance of order requires a lowering of newly acquired aspirations and levels of political activity.**

It is conclusions such as these that cause people of Fanon's persuasion to reject much of contemporary American political science.

The bourgeois caste in newly independent countries have not yet the cynicism nor the unruffled calm which are founded on the strength of long-established bourgeoisies. From this springs the fact that they show a certain anxiety to hide their real convictions, to side-track, and in short to set themselves up as a popular force. But the inclusion of the masses in politics does not consist in mobilizing three or four times a year ten thousand or a

From Frantz Fanon, *The Wretched of the Earth* (New York: Grove Press, 1965), pp. 181–205. Copyright © 1963 by *Presence Africaine*. Reprinted by permission of Grove Press, Inc.

* Ithiel de Sola Pool, *Centemporary Political Science* (New York: McGraw-Hill, 1967), p. 26.

hundred thousand men and women. These mass meetings and spectacular gatherings are akin to the old tactics that date from before independence whereby you exhibited your forces in order to prove to yourself and to others that you had the people behind you. The political education of the masses proposes not to treat the masses as children but to make adults of them.

This brings us to consider the role of the political party in an under-developed country. . . . [V]ery often simple souls, who moreover belong to the newly-born bourgeoisie, never stop repeating that in an under-developed country the direction of affairs by a strong authority, in other words a dictatorship, is a necessity. With this in view the party is given the task of supervising the masses. The party plays understudy to the adminis-tration and the police, and controls the masses, not in order to make sure that they really participate in the business of governing the nation, but in order to remind them constantly that the government expects from them obedience and discipline. That famous dictatorship, whose supporters believe that it is called for by the historical process and consider it an indispensable prelude to the dawn of independence, in fact symbolizes the decision of the bourgeois caste to govern the under-developed country first with the help of the people, but soon against them. The progressive trans-formation of the party into an information service is the indication that the government holds itself more and more on the defensive. The inco-herent mass of the people is seen as a blind force that must be continually held in check either by mystification or by the fear inspired by the police force. The party acts as a barometer and as an information service. The militant is turned into an informer. He is entrusted with punitive expedi-tions against the villages. The embryo opposition parties are liquidated by beatings and stonings. The opposition candidates see their houses set on fire. The police increase their provocations. In these conditions, you may be sure, the party is unchallenged and 99.99% of the votes are cast for the governmental candidate. We should add that in Africa a certain number of governments actually behave in this way. All the opposition parties, which moreover are usually progressive and would therefore tend to work for the greater influence of the masses in the conduct of public matters, and who desire that the proud, money-making bourgeoisie should be brought to heel, have been by dint of baton charges and prisons condemned first to silence and then to a clandestine existence.

The political party in many parts of Africa which are today indepen-dent is puffed up in a most dangerous way. In the presence of a member of the party, the people are silent, behave like a flock of sheep and publish panegyrics in praise of the government or the leader. But in the street when evening comes, away from the village, in the cafés or by the river, the bitter disappointment of the people, their despair but also their unceasing anger makes itself heard. The party, instead of welcoming the expression of popular discontentment, instead of taking for its fundamental purpose the free flow of ideas from the people up to the government, forms a screen, and forbids such ideas. The party leaders behave like common sergeant-majors, frequently reminding the people of the need for "silence in the ranks." This party which used to call itself the servant of the people, which used to claim that it worked for the full expression of the people's will, as soon as the colonial power puts the country into its control hastens to send the people back to their caves. As far as national unity is concerned the party will also make many mistakes, as for example when the so-called national party behaves as a party based on ethnical differences. It becomes, in fact, the tribe which makes itself into a party. This party which of its own will proclaims that it is a national party, and which claims to speak in the name of the totality of the people, secretly, sometimes even openly organizes an authentic ethnical dictatorship. We no longer see the rise of a bourgeois dictatorship, but a tribal dictatorship. The ministers, the members of the cabinet, the ambassadors and local commissioners are chosen from the same ethnological group as the leader, sometimes directly from his own family. Such regimes of the family sort seem to go back to the old laws of inbreeding, and not anger but shame is felt when we are faced with such stupidity, such an imposture, such intellectual and spiritual poverty. These heads of the government are the true traitors in Africa, for they sell their country to the most terrifying of all its enemies: stupidity. This tribalizing of the central authority, it is certain, encourages regionalist ideas and separatism. All the decentralizing tendencies spring up again and triumph, and the nation falls to pieces, broken in bits. The leader, who once used to call for "African unity" and who thought of his own little family wakes up one day to find himself saddled with five tribes, who also want to have their own ambassadors and ministers; and irresponsible as ever, still unaware and still despicable, he denounces their "treason."

We have more than once drawn attention to the baleful influence frequently wielded by the leader. This is due to the fact that the party in certain districts is organized like a gang, with the toughest person in it as its head. The ascendency of such a leader and his power over others is often mentioned, and people have no hesitation in declaring, in a tone of slightly admiring complicity, that he strikes terror into his nearest collaborators. In order to avoid these many pitfalls an unceasing battle must be waged, a battle to prevent the party ever becoming a willing tool in the hands of a leader. "Leader": the word comes from the English verb "to lead," but a frequent French translation is "to drive." The driver, the shepherd of the people no longer exists today. The people are no longer a herd; they do not need to be driven. If the leader drives me on, I want him to realize that at the same time I show him the way; the nation ought not to be something bossed by a Grand Panjandrum. We may understand the panic caused in governmental circles each time one of these leaders falls ill; they are obsessed by the question of who is to succeed him. What will happen to the country if the leader disappears? The ruling classes who have abdicated in favor of the leader, irresponsible, oblivious of everything and essentially preoccupied with the pleasures of their everyday life, their cocktail parties, their journeys paid for by government money, the profits they can make out of various schemes—from time to time these people discover the spiritual waste land at the heart of the nation.

A country that really wishes to answer the questions that history puts to it, that wants to develop not only its towns but also the brains of its inhabitants, such a country must possess a trustworthy political party. The party is not a tool in the hands of the government. Quite on the contrary, the party is a tool in the hands of the people; it is they who decide on the policy that the government carries out. The party is not, and ought never to be, the only political bureau where all the members of the government and the chief dignitaries of the regime may meet freely together. Only too frequently the political bureau, unfortunately, consists of all the party and its members who reside permanently in the capital. In an under-developed country, the leading members of the party ought to avoid the capital as if it had the plague. They ought, with some few exceptions, to live in the country districts. The centralization of all activity in the city ought to be avoided. No excuse of administrative discipline should be taken as legitimizing that excrescence of a capital which is already over-populated and over-developed with regard to nine-tenths of the country. The party should be de-centralized in the extreme. It is the only way to bring life to regions which are dead, those regions which are not yet awakened to life.

In practice, there will be at least one member of the political bureau in each area and he will deliberately not be appointed as head of that area. He will have no administrative powers. The regional member of the political bureau is not expected to hold the highest rank in the regional administrative organization. He ought not automatically to belong to the regional administrative body. For the people, the party is not an authority, but an organism through which they as the people exercise their authority and express their will. The less there is of confusion and duality of powers, the more the party will play its part of guide and the more surely it will constitute for the people a decisive guarantee. If the party is mingled with the government, the fact of being a party militant means that you take the short cut to gain private ends, to hold a post in the government, step up the ladder, get promotion and make a career for yourself.

In an under-developed country, the setting up of dynamic district officials stops the process whereby the towns become top-heavy, and the incoherent rush towards the cities of the mass of country people. The setting up early in the days of independence of regional organizations and officials who have full authority to do everything in their power to awaken such a region, to bring life to it and to hasten the growth of consciousness in it is a necessity from which there is no escape for a country that wishes to progress. Otherwise, the government big-wigs and the party officials group themselves around the leader. The government services swell to huge proportions, not because they are developing and specializing, but because new-found cousins and fresh militants are looking for jobs and hope to edge themselves into the government machine. And the dream of every citizen is to get up to the capital, and to have his share of the cake. The local districts are deserted; the mass of the country people with no one to lead them, uneducated and unsupported, turn their backs on their poorly-labored fields and flock towards the outer ring of suburbs, thus swelling out of all proportion the ranks of the lumpen-proletariat.

The moment for a fresh national crisis is not far off. To avoid it, we think that a quite different policy should be followed: that the interior, the back-country ought to be the most privileged part of the country. More-over, in the last resort, there is nothing inconvenient in the government choosing its seat elsewhere than in the capital. The capital must be de-consecrated; the outcast masses must be shown that we have decided to work for them. It is with this idea in mind that the government of Brazil tried to found Brazilia. The dead city of Rio de Janeiro was an insult to the Brazilian people. But, unfortunately, Brazilia is just another new capi-tal, as monstrous as the first. The only advantage of this achievement is that, today, there exists a road through the bush to it.

No, there is no serious reason which can be opposed to the choice of another capital, or to the moving of the government as a whole towards one of the most under-populated regions. The capital of under-developed countries is a commercial notion inherited from the colonial period. But we who are citizens of the under-developed countries, we ought to seek every occasion for contacts with the rural masses. We must create a na-tional policy, in other words a policy for the masses. We ought never to lose contact with the people which has battled for its independence and for the concrete betterment of its existence.

The native civil servants and technicians ought not to bury themselves in diagrams and statistics, but rather in the heart of the people. They ought not to bristle up every time there is question of a move to be made to the "interior." We should no longer see the young women of the country threaten their husbands with divorce if they do not manage to avoid being appointed to a rural post. For these reasons, the political bureau of the party ought to treat these forgotten districts in a very privi-leged manner; and the life of the capital, an altogether artificial life which is stuck onto the real, national life like a foreign body ought to take up the least space possible in the life of the nation, which is sacred and funda-mental.

In an under-developed country, the party ought to be organized in such fashion that it is not simply content with having contacts with the masses. The party should be the direct expression of the masses. The party is not an administration responsible for transmitting government orders; it is the energetic spokesman and the incorruptible defender of the masses. In order to arrive at this conception of the party, we must above all rid ourselves of the very Western, very bourgeois and therefore contemptuous attitude that the masses are incapable of governing themselves. In fact, experience proves that the masses understand perfectly the most complicated problems. One of the greatest services that the Algerian revolution will have rendered to the intellectuals of Algeria will be to have placed them in contact with the people, to have allowed them to see the extreme, ineffable poverty of the people, at the same time allowing them to watch the awakening of the people's intelligence and the onward progress of their consciousness. The Algerian people, that mass of starving illiterates, those men and women plunged for centuries in the most appalling obscurity have held out against tanks and airplanes, against napalm and "psychological services," but above all against corruption and brain-washing, against traitors and against the "national" armies of general Bellounis. This people has held out in spite of hesitant or feeble individuals, and in spite of would-be dictators. This people has held out because for seven years its struggle has opened up for it vistas that it never dreamed existed. Today, arms factories are working in the midst of the mountains several yards underground; today, the people's tribunals are functioning at every level, and local planning commissions are organizing the division of large-scale holdings, and working out the Algeria of tomorrow. An isolated individual may obstinately refuse to understand a problem, but the group or the village understands with disconcerting rapidity. It is true that if care is taken to use only a language that is understood by graduates in law and economics, you can easily prove that the masses have to be managed from above. But if you speak the language of every day; if you are not obsessed by the perverse desire to spread confusion and to rid yourself of the people, then you will realize that the masses are quick to seize every shade of meaning and to learn all the tricks of the trade. If recourse is had to technical language, this signifies that it has been decided to consider the masses as uninitiated. Such a language is hard put to it to hide the lecturers' wish to cheat the people and to leave them out of things. The business of obscuring language is a mask behind which stands out the much greater business of plunder. The people's property and the people's sovereignty are to be stripped from them at one and the same time. Everything can be explained to the people, on the single condition that you really want them to understand. And if you think that you don't need them, and that on the contrary they may hinder the smooth running of the many limited liability companies whose aim it is to make the people even poorer, then the problem is quite clear.

For if you think that you can manage a country without letting the people interfere, if you think that the people upset the game by their mere presence, whether they slow it down or whether by their natural ignorance they sabotage it, then you must have no hesitation: you must keep the people out. Now, it so happens that when the people are invited to partake in the management of the country, they do not slow the movement down but on the contrary they speed it up. We Algerians have had occasion and the good fortune during the course of this war to handle a fair number of questions. In certain country districts, the politico-military leaders of the revolution found themselves in fact confronted with situations which called for radical solutions. We shall look at some of these situations.

During the years 1956–7, French colonialism had marked off certain zones as forbidden, and within these zones people's movements were strictly controlled. Thus the peasants could no longer go freely to the towns and buy provisions. During this period, the grocers made huge profits. The prices of tea, coffee, sugar, tobacco and salt soared. The black market flourished blatantly. The peasants who could not pay in money mortgaged their crops, in other words their land, or else lopped off field after field of their fathers' farms and during the second phase worked them for the grocer. As soon as the political commissioners realized the danger of the situation they reacted immediately. Thus a rational system of provisioning was instituted: the grocer who went to the town was obliged to buy from nationalist wholesalers who handed him an invoice which clearly showed the prices of the goods. When the retailer got back to the village, before doing anything else he had to go to the political commissioner who checked the invoice, decided on the margin of profit and fixed the price at which the various goods should be sold. However, the retailer soon discovered a new trick, and after three or four days declared that his stocks had run out. In fact, he went on with his business of selling on the black market on the sly. The reaction of the politico-military authorities was thorough-going. Heavy penalizations were decided on, and the fines collected were put into the village funds and used for social purposes or to pay for public works in the general interest. Sometimes it was decided to shut down the shop for a while. Then if there was a repetition of black marketeering, the business was at once confiscated and a managing committee elected to carry it on, which paid a monthly allowance to the former owner.

Taking these experiences as a starting-point, the functioning of the main laws of economics were explained to the people, with concrete examples. The accumulation of capital ceased to be a theory and became a very real and immediate mode of behavior. The people understood how that once a man was in trade, he could become rich and increase his turnover. Then and then only did the peasants tell the tale of how the grocer gave them loans at exorbitant interest, and others recalled how he evicted them from their land and how from owners they became laborers. The more the people understand, the more watchful they become, and the more they come to realize that finally everything depends on them and their salvation lies in their own cohesion, in the true understanding of their interests and in knowing who are their enemies. The people come to understand that wealth is not the fruit of labor but the result of organized, protected robbery. Rich people are no longer respectable people; they are nothing more than flesh-eating animals, jackals and vultures which wallow in the people's blood. With another end in view the political commissioners have had to decide that nobody will work for anyone else any longer. The land belongs to those that till it. This is a principle which has through explanation become a fundamental law of the Algerian revolution. The peasants who used to employ agricultural laborers have been obliged to give a share of the land to their former employees.

So it may be seen that production per acre trebled, in spite of the many raids by the French, in spite of bombardments from the air, and the difficulty of getting manures. The *fellahs* who at harvest-time were able to judge and weigh the crops thus obtained wanted to know whence came such a phenomenon; and they were quick to understand that the idea of work is not as simple as all that, that slavery is opposed to work, and that work presupposes liberty, responsibility and consciousness.

In those districts where we have been able to carry out successfully these interesting experiments, where we have watched man being created by revolutionary beginnings, the peasants have very clearly caught hold of the idea that the more intelligence you bring to your work, the more pleasure you will have in it. We have been able to make the masses understand that work is not simply the output of energy, nor the functioning of certain muscles, but that people work more by using their brains and their hearts than with only their muscles and their sweat. In the same way in these liberated districts which are at the same time excluded from the old trade routes we have had to modify production, which formerly looked only towards the towns and towards export. We have organized production to meet consumers' needs for the people and for the units of the national army of liberation. We have quadrupled the production of lentils and organized the manufacture of charcoal. Green vegetables and charcoal have been sent through the mountains from the north to the south, whereas the southern districts send meat to the north. This co-ordination was decided upon by the F.L.N. and they it was who set up the system of communications. We did not have any technicians or planners coming from big Western universities; but in these liberated regions, the daily ration went up to the hitherto unheard-of figure of 3,200 calories. The people were not content with coming triumphant out of this test. They started asking themselves theoretical questions: for example, why did certain districts never see an orange before the war of liberation, while thousands of tons are exported every year abroad? Why were grapes unknown to a great many Algerians whereas the European peoples enjoyed them by the million? Today, the people have a very clear notion of what belongs to them. The Algerian people today know that they are the sole owners of the soil and mineral wealth of their country. And if some individuals do not understand the unrelenting refusal of the F.L.N. to tolerate any encroachment on this right of ownership, and its fierce refusal to allow any compromise on principles, they must one and all remember that the Algerian people is today an adult people, responsible and fully conscious of its responsibilities. In short, the Algerians are men of property.

If we have taken the example of Algeria to illustrate our subject, it is not at all with the intention of glorifying our own people, but simply to show the important part played by the war in leading them towards consciousness of themselves. It is clear that other peoples have come to the same conclusion in different ways. We know for sure today that in Algeria the test of force was inevitable; but other countries through political action and through the work of clarification undertaken by a party have led their people to the same results. In Algeria, we have realized that the masses are equal to the problems which confront them. In an under-developed country, experience proves that the important thing is not that three hundred people form a plan and decide upon carrying it out, but that the whole people plan and decide even if it takes them twice or three times as long. The fact is that the time taken up by explaining, the time "lost" in treating the worker as a human being, will be caught up in the execution of the plan. People must know where they are going, and why. The politician should not ignore the fact that the future remains a closed book so long as the consciousness of the people remains imperfect, elementary and cloudy. We African politicians must have very clear ideas on the situation of our people. But this clarity of ideas must be profoundly dialectical. The awakening of the whole people will not come about all at once; the people's work in the building of the nation will not immediately take on its full dimensions: first because the means of communication and transmission are only beginning to be developed; secondly because the yardstick of time must no longer be that of the moment or up till the next harvest, but must become that of the rest of the world, and lastly because the spirit of discouragement which has been deeply rooted in people's minds by colonial domination is still very near the surface. But we must not overlook the fact that victory over those weaknesses which are the heritage of the material and spiritual domination of the country by another is a necessity from which no government will be able to escape. Let us take the example of work under the colonial regime. The settler never stopped complaining that the native is slow. Today, in certain countries which have become independent, we hear the ruling classes taking up the same cry. The fact is that the settler wanted the native to be enthusiastic. By a sort of process of mystification which constitutes the most sublime type of separation from reality, he wanted to persuade the slave that the land that he worked belonged to him, that the mines where he lost his health were owned by him. The settler was singularly forgetful of the fact that he was growing rich through the death-throes of the slave. In fact what the settler was saying to the native was "Kill yourself that I may become rich." Today, we must behave in a different fashion. We ought not to say to the people: "Kill yourselves that the country may become rich." If we want to increase the national revenue, and decrease the importing of certain products which are useless, or even harmful, if we want to increase agricultural production and overcome illiteracy, we must explain what we are about. The people must understand what is at stake. Public business ought to be the business of the public. So the necessity of creating a large number of well-informed nuclei at the bottom crops up again. Too often, in fact, we are content to establish national organizations at the top and always in the capital: the Women's Union, the Young People's Federation, Trade Unions, etc. But if one takes the trouble to investigate what is behind the office in the capital, if you go into the inner room where the reports ought to be, you will be shocked by the emptiness, the blank spaces, and the bluff. There must be a basis; there must be cells that supply content and life. The masses should be able to meet together, discuss, propose and receive directions. The citizens should be able to speak, to express themselves and to put forward new ideas. The branch meeting and the committee meeting are liturgical acts. They are privileged occasions given to a human being to listen and to speak. At each meeting, the brain increases its means of participation and the eye discovers a landscape more and more in keeping with human dignity.

The large proportion of young people in the under-developed countries raises specific problems for the government, which must be tackled with lucidity. The young people of the towns, idle and often illiterate, are a prey to all sorts of disintegrating influences. It is to the youth of an under-developed country that the industrialized countries most often offer their pastimes. Normally, there is a certain homogeneity between the mental and material level of the members of any given society and the pleasures which that society creates for itself. But in under-developed countries, young people have at their disposition leisure occupations designed for the youth of capitalist countries: detective novels, penny-in-the-slot machines, sexy photographs, pornographic literature, films banned to those under sixteen, and above all alcohol. In the West, the family circle, the effects of education and the relatively high standard of living of the working classes provide a more or less efficient protection against the harmful action of these pastimes. But in an African country, where mental development is uneven, where the violent collision of two worlds has considerably shaken old traditions and thrown the universe of the perceptions out of focus, the impressionability and sensibility of the young African are at the mercy of the various assaults made upon them by the very nature of Western culture. His family very often proves itself incapable of showing stability and homogeneity when faced with such attacks.

In this domain, the government's duty is to act as a filter and a stabilizer. But the youth Commissioners in under-developed countries often make the mistake of imagining their role to be that of Youth Commissioners in fully developed countries. They speak of strengthening the soul, of developing the body, and of facilitating the growth of sportsmanlike qualities. It is our opinion that they should beware of these conceptions. The young people of an under-developed country are above all idle: occupations must be found for them. For this reason the Youth Commissioners ought for practical purposes to be attached to the Ministry for Labor. The Ministry for Labor, which is a prime necessity in an under-developed country, functions in collaboration with the Ministry for Planning, which is another necessary institution in under-developed countries. The youth of Africa ought not to be sent to sports stadiums but into the fields and into the schools. The stadium ought not to be a show place erected in the towns, but a bit of open ground in the midst of the fields that the young people must reclaim, cultivate and give to the nation. The capitalist conception of sport is fundamentally different from that which should exist in an under-developed country. The African politician should not be preoccupied with turning out sportsmen, but with turning out fully conscious men, who play games as well. If games are not integrated into the national life, that is to say in the building of the nation, and if you turn out national sportsmen and not fully conscious men, you will very quickly see sport rotted by professionalism and commercialism. Sport should not be a pastime or a distraction for the bourgeoisie of the towns. The greatest task before us is to understand at each moment what is happening in our country. We ought not to cultivate the exceptional or to seek for a hero, who is another form of leader. We ought to uplift the people; we must develop their brains, fill them with ideas, change them and make them into human beings.

We once more come up against that obsession of ours—which we would like to see shared by all African politicians—about the need for effort to be well-informed, for work which is enlightened and freed from its historic intellectual darkness. To hold a responsible position in an under-developed country is to know that in the end everything depends on the education of the masses, on the raising of the level of thought, and on what we are too quick to call "political teaching."

In fact, we often believe with criminal superficiality that to educate the masses politically is to deliver a long political harangue from time to time. We think that it is enough that the leader or one of his lieutenants should speak in a pompous tone about the principle events of the day for them to have fulfilled this bounden duty to educate the masses politically. Now, political education means opening their minds, awakening them, and allowing the birth of their intelligence; as Césaire said, it is "to invent souls." To educate the masses politically does not mean, cannot mean making a political speech. What it means is to try, relentlessly and passionately, to teach the masses that everything depends on them; that if we stagnate it is their responsibility, and that if we go forward it is due to them too, that there is no such thing as a demiurge, that there is no famous man who will take the responsibility for everything, but that the demiurge is the people themselves and the magic hands are finally only the hands of the people. In order to put all this into practice, in order really to incarnate the people, we repeat that there must be decentralization in the extreme. The movement from the top to the bottom and from the bottom to the top should be a fixed principle, not through concern for formalism but because simply to respect this principle is the guarantee of salvation. It is from the base that forces mount up which supply the summit with its dynamic, and make it possible dialectically for it to leap ahead. Once again we Algerians have been quick to understand these facts, for no member of the government at the head of any recognized state has had the chance of availing himself of such a mission of salvation. For it is the rank-and-file who are fighting in Algeria, and the rank-and-file know well that without their daily struggle, hard and heroic as it is, the summit would collapse; and in the same way those at the bottom know that without a head and without leadership the base would split apart in incoherence and anarchy. The summit only draws its worth and its strength from the existence of the people at war. Literally, it is the people who freely create a summit for themselves, and not the summit that tolerates the people.

The masses should know that the government and the party are at their service. A deserving people, in other words a people conscious of its dignity, is a people that never forgets these facts. During the colonial occupation the people were told that they must give their lives so that dignity might triumph. But the African peoples quickly came to understand that it was not only the occupying power that threatened their dignity. The African peoples were quick to realize that dignity and sovereignty were exact equivalents, and in fact, a free people living in dignity is a sovereign people. It is no use demonstrating that the African peoples are childish or weak. A government or a party gets the people it deserves and sooner or later a people gets the government it deserves.

Practical experience in certain regions confirms this point of view. It sometimes happens at meetings that militants use sweeping, dogmatic formulae. The preference for this shortcut, in which spontaneity and over-simple sinking of differences dangerously combine to defeat intellectual elaboration, frequently triumphs. When we meet this shirking of responsibility in a militant it is not enough to tell him he is wrong. We must make him ready for responsibility, encourage him to follow up his chain of reasoning and make him realize the true nature, often shocking, inhuman and in the long run sterile, of such over-simplification.

Nobody, neither leader or rank-and-filer, can hold back the truth. The search for truth in local attitudes is a collective affair. Some are richer in experience, and elaborate their thought more rapidly, and in the past have been able to establish a greater number of mental links. But they ought to avoid riding roughshod over the people, for the success of the decision which is adopted depends upon the co-ordinated, conscious effort of the whole of the people. No one can get out of the situation scot free. Everyone will be butchered or tortured; and in the framework of the independent nation everyone will go hungry and everyone will suffer in the slump.

The collective struggle presupposes collective responsibility at the base and collegiate responsibility at the top. Yes; everybody will have to be compromised in the fight for the common good. No one has clean hands; there are no innocents and no onlookers. We all have dirty hands; we are all soiling them in the swamps of our country and in the terrifying emptiness of our brains. Every onlooker is either a coward or a traitor.

The duty of those at the head of the movement is to have the masses behind them. Allegiance presupposes awareness and understanding of the mission which has to be fulfilled; in short, an intellectual position, however embryonic. We must not voodoo the people, nor dissolve them in emotion and confusion. Only those under-developed countries led by revolutionary élites who have come up from the people can today allow the entry of the masses upon the scene of history. But, we must repeat, it is absolutely necessary to oppose vigorously and definitively the birth of a national bourgeoisie and a privileged caste. To educate the masses politically is to make the totality of the nation a reality to each citizen. It is to make the history of the nation part of the personal experience of each of its citizens. As president Sékou Touré aptly remarked in his message to the second congress of African writers: "In the realm of thought, man may claim to be the brain of the world; but in real life where every action affects spiritual and physical existence, the world is always the brain of mankind; for it is at this level that you will find the sum total of the powers and units of thought, and the dynamic forces of development and improvement; and it is there that energies are merged and the sum of man's intellectual values is finally added together."

Individual experience, because it is national and because it is a link in the chain of national existence, ceases to be individual, limited and shrunken and is enabled to open out into the truth of the nation and of the world. In the same way that during the period of armed struggle each fighter held the fortune of the nation in his hand, so during the period of national construction each citizen ought to continue in his real, everyday activity to associate himself with the whole of the nation, to incarnate the continuous dialectical truth of the nation and to will the triumph of man in his completeness here and now. If the building of a bridge does not enrich the awareness of those who work on it, then that bridge ought not to be built and the citizens can go on swimming across the river or going by boat. The bridge should not be "parachuted down" from above; it should not be imposed by a deus ex machina upon the social scene; on the contrary it should come from the muscles and the brains of the citizens. Certainly, there may well be need of engineers and architects, sometimes completely foreign engineers and architects; but the local party leaders should be always present, so that the new techniques can make their way into the cerebral desert of the citizen, so that the bridge in whole and in part can be taken up and conceived, and the responsibility for it assumed by the citizen. In this way, and in this way only, everything is possible.

A government which calls itself a national government ought to take responsibility for the totality of the nation; and in an under-developed country the young people represent one of the most important sectors. The level of consciousness of young people must be raised; they need enlightenment. If the work of explanation had been carried on among the youth of the nation, and if the Young People's National Union had carried out its task of integrating them into the nation, those mistakes would have been avoided which have threatened or already undermined the future of the Latin American Republics. The army is not always a school of war; more often, it is a school of civic and political education. The soldier of an adult nation is not a simple mercenary but a citizen who by means of arms defends the nation. That is why it is of fundamental importance that the soldier should know that he is in the service of his country and not in the service of his commanding officer, however great that officer's prestige may be. We must take advantage of the national military and civil service in order to raise the level of the national consciousness, and to de-tribalize and unite the nation. In an under-developed country every effort is made to mobilize men and women as quickly as possible; it must guard against the danger of perpetuating the feudal tradition which holds sacred the superiority of the masculine element over the feminine. Women will have exactly the same place as men, not in the clauses of the constitution but in the life of every day: in the factory, at school and in the parliament. If in the western countries men are shut up in barracks, that is not to say that this is always the best procedure. Recruits need not necessarily be militarized. The national service may be civil or military, and in any case it is advisable that every able-bodied citizen can at any moment take his place in a fighting unit for the defense of national and social liberties.

It should be possible to carry out large-scale undertakings in the public interest by using recruited labor. This is a marvelous way of stirring up inert districts and of making known to a greater number of citizens the needs of their country. Care must be taken to avoid turning the army into an autonomous body which sooner or later, finding itself idle and without any definite mission, will "go into politics" and threaten the government. Drawing-room generals, by dint of haunting the corridors of government departments, come to dream of manifestos. The only way to avoid this menace is to educate the army politically, in other words to nationalize it. In the same way another urgent task is to increase the militia. In case of war, it is the whole nation which fights and works. It should not include any professional soldiers, and the number of permanent officers should be reduced to a minimum. This is in the first place because officers are very often chosen from the university class, who would be much more useful elsewhere; an engineer is a thousand times more indispensable to his country than an officer; and secondly, because the crystallization of the caste spirit must be avoided. . . . nationalism, that magnificent song that made the people rise against their oppressors, stops short, falters and dies away on the day that independence is proclaimed. Nationalism is not a political doctrine, nor a program. If you really wish your country to avoid regression, or at best halts and uncertainties, a rapid step must be taken from national consciousness to political and social consciousness. The nation does not exist except in a program which has been worked out by revolutionary leaders and taken up with full understanding and enthusiasm by the masses. The nation's effort must constantly be adjusted into the general background of under-developed countries. The battle-line against hunger, against ignorance, against poverty and against unawareness ought to be ever present in the muscles and the intelligences of men and women. The work of the masses and their will to overcome the evils which have for centuries excluded them from the mental achievements of the past ought to be grafted onto the work and will of all under-developed peoples. On the level of under-developed humanity there is a kind of collective effort, a sort of common destiny. The news which interests the Third World does not deal with king Baudouin's marriage nor the scandals of the Italian ruling class. What we want to hear about are the experiments carried out by the Argentinians or the Burmese in their efforts to overcome illiteracy or the dictatorial tendencies of their leaders. It is these things which strengthen us, teach us and increase our efficiency ten times over. As we see it, a program is necessary for a government which really wants to free the people politically and socially. There must be an economic program; there must also be a doctrine concerning the division of wealth and social relations. In fact, there must be an idea of man and of the future of humanity; that is to say that no demagogic formula and no collusion with the former occupying power can take the place of a program. The new peoples, un-awakened at first but soon becoming more and more clear-minded, will make strong demands for this program. The African people and indeed all under-developed peoples, contrary to common belief, very quickly build up a social and political consciousness. What can be dangerous is when they reach the stage of social consciousness before the stage of nationalism. If this happens, we find in under-developed countries fierce demands for social justice which paradoxically are allied with often primitive tribalism. The under-developed peoples behave like starving creatures; this means that the end is very near for those who are having a good time in Africa. Their government will not be able to prolong its own existence indefi-nitely. A bourgeoisie that provides nationalism, alone as food for the masses fails in its mission and gets caught up in a whole series of mishaps. But if nationalism is not made explicit, if it is not enriched and deepened by a very rapid transformation into a consciousness of social and political needs, in other words into humanism, it leads up a blind alley. The bourgeois leaders of under-developed countries imprison national consciousness in sterile formalism. It is only when men and women are included on a vast scale in enlightened and fruitful work that form and body are given to that consciousness. Then the flag and the palace where sits the government cease to be the symbols of the nation. The nation deserts these brightly-lit, empty shells and takes shelter in the country, where it is given life and dynamic power. The living expression of the nation is the moving consciousness of the whole of the people; it is the coherent, enlightened action of men and women. The collective building up of a destiny is the assumption of responsibility on the historical scale. Otherwise there is anarchy, repression and the resurgence of tribal parties and federalism. The national government, if it wants to be national, ought to govern by the people and for the people, for the outcasts and by the outcasts. No leader however valuable he may be can substitute himself for the popular will; and the national government, before concerning itself about international prestige, ought first to give back their dignity to all citizens, fill their minds and feast their eyes with human things, and create a prospect that is human because conscious and sovereign men dwell therein.

The City in the Future of Democracy

Robert A. Dahl

The previous selection stressed the countryside in developing nations; this selection examines the city in already developed societies. Robert Dahl reviews the major problems that beset meaningful citizen participation in mass society and settles on the modest-sized city as the community most suitable to participation. Of particular interest is his discussion of the size of various urban communities from the Greek city-state to today's New York and how increased size erodes the meaning of democratic citizenship. Notice that in the end his solution trades a good deal of public participation to obtain other important values; for Professor Dahl, participation is not an absolute value to which all else must necessarily be sacrificed.

The reader may ponder the possible effects of population growth on the relationship between representative and constituency. In 1790 there was a member of the House of Representatives for every 30,000 "free Persons" plus three-fifths of the slaves. Today the ratio is 1 to about 450,000 (the ratio of Representative to voters has become even more extreme because of relaxed suffrage restrictions). Many have argued that this ratio strains the relationship between Representative and represented to the breaking point.* On the other hand, James Madison claimed (in Federalist 10) that the larger the constituency, the higher the quality of its representatives.

I need hardly remind this audience that one of the characteristics of our field is the large number of old and quite elemental questions—elemental but by no means elementary—for which we have no compelling answers. I don't mean that we have no answers to these questions. On the contrary, we often have a rich variety of conflicting answers. But no answer compels acceptance in the same way as a proof of a theorem in mathematics, or a very nice fit between a hypothesis and a satisfactory set of data.

From Robert A. Dahl, "The City in the Future of Democracy," *American Political Science Review*, LXI, No. 4 (December 1967), pp. 953–969. Reprinted by permission of the American Political Science Association and the author.

* See, for example, Giovanni Sartori, "Representation: Representational Systems," in the new edition of the *International Encyclopedia of Social Sciences*, Vol. 13, 470.

Whether the obstacles that prevent us from achieving tight closure on solutions lie in ourselves—our approaches, methods, and theories—or are inherent in the problems is, paradoxically, one of these persistent and elemental questions for which we have a number of conflicting answers. For whatever it may be worth, my private hunch is that the main obstacles to closure are in the problems themselves—in their extraordinary complexity, the number and variety of variables, dimensions, qualities, and relationships, and in the impediments to observation and data-gathering.

However that may be, a question of this sort often lies dormant for decades or even centuries, not because it has been solved but because it seems irrelevant. For even when no satisfactory theoretical answer exists to a very fundamental question, historical circumstances may allow it to be ignored for long periods of time. Even specialists may refuse to take a question seriously that history seems to have shoved into the attic. What seem like fundamental controversies in one age are very likely to be boring historical curiosities in the next. And conversely it is my impression that a great many of the elemental political questions regarded as settled in one age have a way of surfacing later on.

I

One question of this kind is the problem of the appropriate unit for a democratic political system. Some aspects of this problem are, at least to me, quite puzzling. For example, suppose we accept the guiding principle that the people should rule. We are immediately confronted by the question: what people? I don't mean which particular individuals among a collection of people, but rather: what constitutes an appropriate collection of people for purposes of self-rule? Among the vast number of theoretically possible ways of dividing up the inhabitants of this globe into more or less separate political systems, or, if you will, into "peoples," are there any principles that instruct us as to how one ought to bound some particular collection of people, in order that they may rule themselves? Why *this* collection? Why *these* boundaries?

Of course there are answers, like Schumpeter's statement that "a people" must define itself. But answers like these do not take us very far, or else they take us too far toward the simple doctrine that past might makes present right, and hence present might will make future right. A century ago in the United States a Civil War was fought to compel the Southern States by force of arms and military conquest to remain in the Union, a war, it is now painful to recall, that did not have as its official, ostensible, or ideological purpose the noble end of liberating Negroes and incorporating them into American life but, simply, the maintenance of the Federal Union, if necessary at the cost of the Negro. We can understand this easily enough as pure nationalism. But it is more difficult to see that the proclaimed goals of the North were much more than a particular and somewhat arbitrary definition of American nationhood. Do we then conclude that even if the development of a strong and uniform nationhood might be a condition for large-scale representative democracy, the manner and process by which a "people" defines itself—how it becomes a nation—cannot be judged or determined by any criteria derived from democratic theories or principles?

Just in case you may be about to dismiss all the questions I have just raised as irrelevant or uninteresting, let me be deliberately provocative by asking whether it could be wrong for the American South to have seceded in 1861 but right for South Vietnam to do so today. Alternatively, if military conquest of the Southern Confederacy by the North was justified, is military conquest of the South also justified by North Vietnam? If autonomous self-rule was right for Belgium in 1830 is it wrong for the Flemings today? If the independence of Canada from the United States is right, is the independence of Quebec from Canada also right? And if autonomy is right for France is it also right for the Celtic fringe in Brittany? Or in Britain?

I hope I have asked enough questions to persuade you that the problem of what particular and peculiar collections of people can be said to form a proper unit for self-government is relevant. And not only relevant: It is also perhaps just a bit disturbing, quite possibly even a frightening problem. Yet I do not think we are going to be permitted to ignore it in the near future.

Now that the problem of the appropriate unit for a democratic political system has been opened up, I want to skirt around the questions I have just raised in order to focus in the brief time available to me this evening on certain other aspects of the problem. I propose to ask what *kind* of unit is most appropriate for democratic government. Is there a unit within which the policies steadfastly supported by a majority of citizens should prevail against minorities within that unit and against all persons outside that unit? In fact, can we say that any specific unit is more appropriate for popular rule than any other?

Before I proceed, let me clarify what I mean by the kind of unit. Should democracy be based on a territorial unit, like a town, state, or country, or a non-territorial unit, like a labor union, business firm, or industry? How big should the unit be? Small, like a committee or neighborhood, large like a country or world region, or something in between like a state, province, or region? Or should it be any and all of these things?

Like the question of what constitutes a people, the question of what constitutes an appropriate unit is very widely regarded as settled. Yet a little reflection shows that it is actually a wide-open question. The approved school-solution is, of course, the nation-state. Yet the bare possibility that the question has not been so much answered by this solution as ignored is hinted at by the troubling recollection of a simple historical fact:

accepting the nation-state as the appropriate unit for democracy required the flat negation of an older conventional view that prevailed for some two thousand years.

II

The prior view, as I surely need not remind this audience, held that the appropriate unit for democracy is the city-state. The vision of democracy in the city-state that prevailed, by and large, from the Greeks to Rousseau is surely one of the most seductive ever generated in the Western world. Its millennial appeal draws its force, I think, from the vision of man living in a genuine human community of man-sized proportions. In this vision, the city-state must be small in area and in population. Its dimensions are to be human, not colossal, the dimensions not of an empire but of a town, so that when the youth becomes the man he knows his town, its inhabitants, its countryside about as well as any of us knows his own college or university. Given these human dimensions, at its best citizenship would be close to friendship, close even to a kind of extended family, where human relations are intense rather than bland, and where the eternal human quest for community and solidarity can be wholly satisfied within the visible and comprehensible limits of the *polis*. If the city-state is democratic—and it is this particular vision I have in mind—it would be small enough to insure extensive opportunities for direct participation by all free (male) citizens in the management of the community; and in the best of circumstances policies and decisions would reflect wide discussion and a pervasive consensus. Above all, the city-state would be autonomous, in the sense that no one who is not a citizen of that community would possess any legitimate right or power to interfere in the management of the affairs of the city.

I cannot think of any better description of this vision than Kitto's lovely account of an imaginary conversation between an Ancient Greek and a present-day member of the Athenaeum Club in London:

> The member regrets the lack of political sense shown by the Greeks. The Greek replies, "How many clubs are there in London?" The member, at a guess, says about five hundred. The Greek then says, "Now if all these combined, what splendid premises they would build. They could have a clubhouse as big as Hyde Park." "But," says the member, "that would no longer be a club." "Precisely," says the Greek, "and a polis as big as yours is no longer a polis."[1]

One cannot help wondering how much the geography of Greece helped to stimulate this vision, for that land of mountains, valleys, islands and the sea provided magnificent natural boundaries for each community and such a limited supply of arable land for each valley and island that it is only the barest poetic license to say that nature herself suggested the small, autonomous city-state—and with this hint from nature a people to whom Prometheus himself had given the first elements of civilization were bound to elaborate among themselves the ideal form of the harsher and very often uglier reality they knew so intimately.

If the deficiencies of the vision seem obvious to the modern man who prefers the grandeur of the great nations and the glories of great metropolises like New York, London, Tokyo, and Calcutta, it is worth recalling that the Greeks, too, understood that a price had to be paid for the small, autonomous city-state. If the city were to maintain its autonomy, and particularly if it were to be truly self-sufficient the price included a frugal and austere standard of daily life, pervasive violence and anarchy in inter-city relationships, and the need to defend one's city against all comers, including the giants. The Athenians, as we know, proved unwilling to accept the first and developed an empire; they suffered horribly from the second; and in the end they could not pay the last.

Nonetheless, for two thousand years thereafter the vision of democracy in the city-state dominated thought about democratic-republics. Today, that vision may be seen by a few people as a beguiling form of political life; but as a reality and as an ideal it is in no sense fundamental to modern political culture, it is known mainly to specialists, and almost no one seriously proposes that the modern democratic nations be carved up into genuinely autonomous city-states.

What happened is simply this: In the course of the nineteenth century, the nation-state displaced the city-state as the appropriate unit for democracy. The change, when it came, can swiftly. We can bracket the transition quite nicely by comparing Montesquieu and Rousseau, who still see the city-state as the only proper and indeed viable unit for a democratic republic, with John Stuart Mill, who in *Representative Government* dismisses as irrelevant in a single sentence at the end of a chapter, almost as an afterthought, the two-thousand-year-old tradition. By Mill's time the nation-state had triumphed, the city-state was for all practical purposes an historical curiosity, and if democratic ideals were to survive they had to survive, it seemed, in the form of representative governments for nation-states and subordinate—but not autonomous—territorial units within nation-states.

In retrospect, the change seems simpler and more complete than it was. Nonetheless, it is almost as if Americans were to go away for a long week-end and come back on Monday morning believing that the Soviet Union represented free enterprise and bourgeois democracy.

We could zero-in even more precisely on this historic cross-roads by looking at the debate in our own Constitutional Convention of 1787, which was to create a constitution for the first of the giant representative democracies. By 1787, the population of the United States was already greater than that of all of Ancient Greece; in area it was immense, and everyone knew that its territory would go on growing. Yet the traditional view that a republic could flourish only in relatively small communities still persisted even among leading members of the Convention. In his famous argument in *Federalist No. 10*, which he originally advanced in the Convention itself, Madison met this prejudice head-on and in a brilliant exercise turned it upside down by arguing that faction, the inevitable and fatal disease of small republics, could be mitigated only in a republic of large size. Extend the bounds of a republic, the old tradition argued, and you destroy it. Narrow the bounds of a republic, Madison argued in rebuttal, and you make it vulnerable to the dread disease of all small republics—factionalism. Extend the bounds of a republic and you help to generate immunity to that disease.

As we all know, the institutional innovation that made it possible to extend the bounds of a republic was representation: an innovation that democrats like Madison, Jefferson, their French contemporary whose work Jefferson so much admired, Destutt de Tracy, and James Mill all regarded as one of the most profound political inventions of all time.

When the years of the American republic grew into decades, its mere existence stood as living proof that a democratic republic need not be as small as the city; thanks to representation it might indeed be gigantic. In the contest for supremacy in Europe the nation-state had long since come to prevail over the city-state; and as democratic ideas spread, they were focussed not on the obsolete and by now largely forgotten city-state but, naturally, on the nation-state. By the middle—and certainly by the end—of the nineteenth century the idea of democracy in the city-state had been entirely displaced by the idea of representative democracy in the nation-state. The triumph was complete.

Although it is often thought that the older view was refuted, it seems to me that it was not so much refuted as rejected. It is not clear, at least to me, that the kind of political life the Greeks thought possible in the small, autonomous, democratic city-state—even if these possibilities were not often fulfilled—is even theoretically possible with representative government in the large nation-state. Perhaps we create needless trouble for ourselves by claiming that the ideals and potentialities of democracy in the city-state are realized, or theoretically capable of being realized, through the institutions of representative government in the nation-state. One may question the value of the city-state ideal, and suspect the extent to which it was ever realized, for practice fell far short of the ideal even in Athens, and the seamy side of the city-state was, if one looks as it unromantically, pretty appalling. Yet, however one may feel about these matters, the essential point is that representative government in the nation-state is in many respects so radically—and inescapably—different from democracy in the city-state that it is rather an intellectual handicap to apply the same term, democracy, to both systems, or to believe that in essence they are really the same.

III

In any case it would surely be a sign of *hubris* to assert that the ideals and institutions of democracy have reached or will reach their final destination, and their fulfillment, in the nation-state. For one thing, with each passing day it grows more reasonable to see the nation-state as a transitory historic form, to foresee that the nation-state will some day cease to exist as an autonomous unit, just as the city-state did. I do not mean to rush things. The nation-state is a tough organism, with great capacities for survival; it is still far and away the strongest and most durable political unit we know. In much of the world political leaders are even now struggling desperately to create their own nation-state out of the fragments of traditional societies; or, having achieved a momentary success, they go to bed each night half sick with worry lest they awake next morning and find their fragile nation has fallen into fragments during the night. In many parts of the world, it will be generations before peoples have defined themselves and have arrived at that state of confident nationhood where it finally becomes possible to imagine, without panic, the decline and supercession of the nation.

Those Western nation-states in which democracy has flourished for some generations are not only tough, but on the whole, I believe, extraordinarily benign units of government. Historically and comparatively, all the alternatives to representative government in the nation-state seem to me, and I imagine to most of us here, markedly inferior by comparison and often malignant, vicious, and anti-human. Nonetheless, straining to peer into the thick murk of the future, it is difficult, at least for me, to see mankind still existing on this globe without larger political orders than the nation-state, without greater displacement of international anarchy by constitutionalism and the rule of law. In the West, the nation-state has already lost some of its autonomy; it will lose more. Unless we political scientists are to be overswept by events, as we usually are; if we try, as Bertrand de Jouvenel keeps urging us, to conjecture about the future, in order to help shape it; if we use the past to help foresee the longer stretch ahead and not merely to dissect yesterday in order to understand a moment in the past and a moment today—then it is not too soon for us to anticipate a future for democracy when the major unit that has prevailed during the past two centuries, the nation-state, has become an integral and subordinate unit in some larger legal and constitutional order.

There is a second and more immediate reason why the nation-state is not an altogether satisfactory fulfillment of the ancient and continuing aspiration for democratic self-government: its immensity—immensity not so much of territory, which becomes less and less important, as immensity of numbers, of population, of citizens.

Unless wholly new evidence turns up, we shall never have anything more than the shakiest estimates of the population of Athens, but there are some reasonable if very rough guesses as to the approximate number of adult male citizens at about the time of Pericles—the demos, then, in the Athenian democracy. A quorum in the Assembly was fixed for some purposes at 6,000. There were about 18,000 seats in the Pnyx, where the Assembly met. An estimate of 40,000 adult male citizens may be high; it is surely not too low.[2] And Athens, remember, was the largest of the ancient Greek city-states.

Consider, now, some present-day nation-states. The smallest democratic nation-state, Iceland, has more than twice as many adult citizens as Athens had by our outside estimate. What we ordinarily call small democracies are, in fact, gigantic. The number of adult citizens in New Zealand is around 30 times that of Athens, while the Netherlands has more than 100 times as many adult citizens as Athens had. France has more than 500 times as many, the United States about 2500, and India, the largest representative democracy in the world, five to six thousand times as many. In fact the number of new voters coming of age each year in India would supply a citizen body for more than a hundred city-states the size of Athens.

Fortunately for these giant systems, there are some important ways of participating in the political life of a democracy that are not significantly limited by the size of the citizen body or its territory. One of these, happily, is voting. Because different individuals can vote more or less simultaneously, and in different places, time and space do not limit the size of an electorate. Nor do time and space limit the number of citizens who can engage in various forms of consummatory and symbolic participation, such as reading about politics in the press, listening to the radio, or watching TV.

Some kinds of participation, on the other hand, cannot be performed simultaneously. Instead they have to be carried on sequentially. In these cases, time does impose restraints on size, and particularly on the number of individuals who can participate. For example, time's harsh and inescapable constraints impose severe limits on the size of a group that is intended for full and free discussion—a group, that is, in which every member has an opportunity to present his views to all the other members. I shall come back to these constraints in a moment.

Returning to our question of the appropriate unit for democracy, and keeping in mind time's inexorable constraint, we discover that this simple and elemental limit on human behavior cuts both ways: Whenever the number of citizens grows large, to maximize their equal opportunities to control their government people must resort to representation. They have no alternative. Yet if time's constraint demands this shift from direct democracy to representative government, it also reduces and ultimately eliminates the possibility that every citizen can engage in a discussion that includes the officials who are charged with the authority to decide.

The greater the number of citizens, then, the longer and more indirect must be the channel of communication from the citizen to his top political leaders. But the communication between a citizen and his leaders is not a symmetrical relationship. Even in the Assembly at Athens, Pericles could speak directly and at great length to many more Athenians than could ever hope to speak directly to Pericles. But where the size of Pericles' audience was limited by the range of the unamplified human voice, radio and television have eliminated all constraints on the size of a speaker's audience. As a result, the larger a system grows, the more and more one-sided becomes communication between citizens and top leaders: the President of the United States can, in principle, speak directly to a hundred million potential voters, of whom only an infinitesimally small fraction can ever speak directly to him. If you doubt that the fraction is infinitesimally small, I urge you to try a few simple arithmetical exercises using the most generous calculations as to the President's time and the most severe restrictions on the length of the conversation between citizen and President.

There are, of course, ways of coping with this asymmetry in communications, but it would take me too far afield to explore them here. The essential point is that nothing can overcome the dismal fact that as the number of citizens increases the proportion who can participate *directly* in discussions with their top leaders must necessarily grow smaller and smaller. The inherent constraint is neither evil men nor evil institutions, nor any other eradicable aspect of human life, but rather a dimension of all existence that is morally neutral, because it is implacable, unswerving, and inescapable—time.

IV

I have a fantasy in which a modern Constitutional Convention assembles a group of 55 men or thereabouts whose commitment to democracy and whose wisdom are neither of them in doubt. Their task is to design democratic institutions suitable for this small planet in the year 2000. And so they come to the problem of the unit.

Being learned, as well as wise, naturally they recall the city-state. Well, says one, since full civic participation is possible only if the number of citizens is small, let us arrange for a world of small democratic city-states. Let the unit of democracy, then, be the small city.

Ah, says another, you forget that the world of the twenty-first century is not ancient Greece. You even forget that ancient Greece was the setting for a highly defective international system. The trouble with the small city in the modern world is that there are too many problems it cannot cope with, because they go beyond its boundaries. Think of some of the problems of American cities: revenues, transportation, air and water pollution, racial segregation, inequality, public health. . . . I would make the list longer, but it is already long enough to show that the small city is obviously an inappropriate unit and that we have to locate democracy in a larger unit. I urge that we consider the metropolis.

But, says a third, even the boundaries of the metropolis are smaller than the kinds of problems you mention. The legal boundaries of the metropolis are an obsolete legacy of the past. What we need is metropolitan governments with legal boundaries extending to the limits of the metropolitan area itself, boundaries set not by obsolete patterns of settlement but by present densities.

Your argument is persuasive, says a fourth, but you do not carry it far enough. Demographers and planners now tell us that in the United States, to take one example, there is an uninterrupted urban area on the East Coast extending from Virginia to Maine. Even your metropolitan governments will be too small there. And in the future much of the world will surely be as densely settled as our Eastern seaboard. Consequently, I believe that we must design regional democracies, controlled by democratic governments responsive to the electorate of a whole region.

Well, says a fifth, I notice you have already bypassed such things as states and provinces, which is all to the good, since they are as anachronistic as the small city. But you will have to agree that even if you carve up the world into regional governments big enough, for instance, to cover the Eastern seaboard, you cannot expect these units to be adequate for very long. With the population of the world reaching six billion, or ten billion, most of the United States will soon be a vast, undifferentiated, urban mass. Other countries are headed in the same direction. There is, then, a good deal to be said for the only traditional unit that enjoys consensus and allegiance on a scale commensurate with the problems. I mean, of course, the nation-state. If we were to think of the United States as one city, as we shall have to do in the future, it is obvious that the proper unit to bound our sovereign electorate cannot be smaller than the United States. With minor changes here and there, the nation-state is probably good for another century or so. So let us proceed to make use of it by eliminating the powers of all the intermediate units, which are, after all, only obstacles that permit local groups to frustrate national majorities.

But, objects a sixth, you are still too much the victim of the past to think clearly about the future. Obviously our very existence depends on our capacity to create a government that will subordinate the nation-state to a larger legal order. Just as your villages, towns, cities, metropolises, and regions are too small to cope single-handedly with their problems, so too is your nation-state, even one as big as the United States, the USSR, or China. The fatal flaw of the nation-state is its inability to eliminate interstate violence; and because of our genius for violence we can now destroy the species. Even prosaic problems are now beyond the control of the nation-state: the efficiencies that come from world markets, monetary problems, the balance of trade, the movement of labor and skills, air and water pollution, the regulation of fishing, the dissemination of nuclear weapons. . . . I know it is bold, but we must plan for a world govern-ment, and to us that surely means a democratic world government. The appropriate electorate for the twenty-first century is nothing smaller than the human race. The only legitimate majority is the majority of mankind.

At this point there is a tumult of objections and applause. Finally the first speaker gains the floor. Each speaker, he says, has been more persua-sive than the last. But, he adds, I simply cannot understand how my learned friend, the last speaker, proposes to govern the world, if he has in mind, as I thought, a single world-wide electorate, a single parliament, a single executive, all attempting to represent that non-existent monstrosity, a single world-wide majority. I say that even if it would miraculously hold together, which I doubt, a democracy with six billion citizens is no de-mocracy at all. I, for one, do not wish to be only one six-billionth part of any government. One may as well accept a despot and have done with the Big Lie that what we have is a democracy.

Ah, the advocate of a democratic world government now replies, of course I meant that there would be subordinate governments, which would be democracies.

I thank my learned colleague for this important clarification, says the advocate of the small city-state. I now propose that these subordinate gov-ernments consist of units about the size of small cities.

Again there is tumult. The speaker who now gains the floor is the one who had earlier spoken in behalf of the metropolis. Hold on, he objects, if we are to have a subordinate unit, surely it must be one large enough to deal with the problems of an urban society. Obviously this unit should be the metropolis. . . .

Suddenly it becomes as clear to everyone at the Constitutional Con-vention as it has become to you that the argument over the unit has gone completely around in a circle, that it has now started all over again, that is has no logical terminus, that it could go on forever. Perhaps that is why we still talk about the city-state.

For the logic seems unassailable. Any unit you choose smaller than the globe itself—and that exception may be temporary—can be shown to be smaller than the boundaries of an urgent problem generated by activities of some people who are outside the particular unit and hence beyond its authority. Rational control over such problems dictates ever larger units, and democratic control implies a larger electorate, a larger majority. Yet the larger the unit, the greater the costs of uniform rules, the larger the minorities who cannot prevail, and the more watered down is the control of the individual citizen. Hence the argument for larger units does not destroy the case for small units. What it does is to make a seemingly small but radical shift in the nature of the arguments.

For we drop completely the notion so dear to the Greeks and early Romans that to be legitimate a unit of government must be wholly autonomous. With autonomy we also drop the belief that there is a single sovereign unit for democracy, a unit in which majorities are autonomous with respect to all persons outside the unit and authoritative with respect to all persons inside the unit. Instead we begin to think about appropriate units of democracy as an ascending series, a set of Chinese boxes, each larger and more inclusive than the other, each in some sense democratic, though not always in quite the same sense, and each not inherently less nor inherently more legitimate than the other.

Although this may be a discomforting and alien conception in some democratic countries where political tradition has focussed on the overriding legitimacy, autonomy, and sovereignty of the nation-state and of national majorities, even in these countries the evolution of pluralistic institutions has vastly modified the applicability of monistic conceptions of democracy. And of course in democracies with federal systems, like Switzerland, Canada, and the United States, or in non-federal countries like the Netherlands that inherit a political tradition powerfully shaped by federalism and the legitimacy of pluralist institutions, to see the units of democracy as a set of Chinese boxes is very much easier—though even in these countries it will take some re-thinking and a vast amount of institution-building before any of us can think easily about the nation-state as a Chinese box nested in yet larger ones of equal legitimacy.

Our imaginary Constitutional Convention, and our Chinese boxes do not, of course, bring us much closer to a solution to our original problem of the appropriate unit for democracy. But they do suggest that there is not necessarily a single kind of unit, whether it be city-state or nation-state, in which majorities have some specially sacred quality not granted to majorities in other units, whether smaller or larger, more or less inclusive.

A Frenchman, perhaps even an Englishman, or any strong believer in majority rule will tell me that surely in one of these boxes there must be a majority that is sovereign, or else conflicts between different majorities, one of which may in a larger perspective be only a minority, can never be resolved. I ask, very well, a majority of what unit? And my critic will say, the majority, naturally, of the nation. To which I reply, why is this more sacred than the others? Because it is larger? But I can point to still larger majorities in the making in this world. Will you remain faithful to your answer when your nation is a unit in a world polity? Or will you not, instead, revert to federalist conceptions? Anyway, I might add, in a number of federal countries, including some rather old and respectable representative democracies, citizens have grown moderately accustomed to the idea that national majorities—or rather their spokesmen—are not necessarily more sacred than majorities or minorities in certain kinds of less inclusive units. This is logically untidy, and it requires endless readjustments as perspectives and levels of interdependence change. But it makes for a better fit with the inevitable pluralistic and decentralizing forces of political life in nation-states with representative governments.

The hitherto unreported debate at our imaginary Convention also suggests that in a world of high population densities, ease of communication, and great interdependence, where autonomy is in fact impossible short of the earth itself, we confront a kind of dilemma that the Greeks could hardly have perceived. Let me suggest it by advancing a series of propositions:

> The larger and more inclusive a unit, the more its government can regulate aspects of the environment that its citizens want to regulate, from air and water pollution and racial justice to the dissemination of nuclear weapons.
>
> Yet, the larger and more inclusive a unit with a representative government, and the more complex its tasks, the more participation must be reduced for most people to the single act of voting in an election.
>
> Conversely, the smaller the unit, the greater the opportunity for citizens to participate in the decisions of their government, yet the less of the environment they can control.
>
> Thus for most citizens, participation in very large units becomes minimal and in very small units it becomes trivial. At the extremes, citizens may participate in a vast range of complex and crucial decisions by the single act of casting a ballot; or else they have almost unlimited opportunities to participate in decisions over matters of no importance. At the one extreme, then, the people vote but they do not rule; at the other, they rule—but they have nothing to rule over.

These are extreme cases, and if they were all there were, it would be a discouraging prospect. But may there not be others in between?

Before we turn to this question, I want you to notice that our hypothetical Constitutional Convention and the Chinese boxes also hint at the possibility that we may need different models of democracy for different kinds of units. By models I mean here both empirical models that would help us to understand the world as it *is* and normative models that would guide us in shaping the world we believe *ought* to be. We need models that approximate reality in the world of history and experience, and models that indicate standards of performance by which we can appraise the achievements of a particular democracy. I see no reason to think that all kinds of units with democratic institutions and practices do, can, or should behave in the same way—no reason, then, why we should not expect democracy in a committee, in a city, and in a nation to be markedly different both in fact and in ideal. If we expect that representative government in the nation-state is roughly equivalent to democratic participation in a committee then we are bound to be misled in our understanding of political life, in our hopes, and in our strategies for changing the world from what it is to what it ought to be.

V

Let me rephrase my question. If the nation-state is too immense, and if interdependence and population densities render the autonomous self-governing city-state too costly, are there units powerful enough, autonomous enough, and small enough to permit, and in the right circumstances to encourage, a body of citizens to participate actively and rationally in shaping and forming vital aspects of their lives in common? Is there, in this sense, an optimal unit?

There are a number of candidates for this position. Occasionally, for example, one still runs across a nostalgia for the village—a nostalgia strongest, I suspect, among people who have never lived in small towns. There are also suggestions going back nearly a century that we shift our search for the democratic unit away from the government of the state to the government of non-state institutions, such as the workplace, business firm, corporation, or industry. And lately there has been a resurgence of interest, especially among young political activists, in the old and recurring idea of reconstructing democracy around small units that would offer unlimited opportunities for participation.

Although I cannot possibly do justice to these various alternatives in the brief time available to me here, I would like to venture a few comments on each.

The fragmented and even shattered community in which modern man seems condemned to live tempts one to suppose that the appropriate unit for democratic life might be the village or small town. Only there, it might be thought, could one ever hope to find a center of life small enough so that it permits wide participation, and small enough besides to foster the sense of unity, wholeness, belonging, of membership in an inclusive and solidary community which we sometimes seem to want with such a desperate yearning. Speaking for myself, I doubt whether man can ever recapture his full sense of tribal solidarity. Like childhood itself, there is no returning to the childhood of man. What is more, the attempt to satisfy this craving, if carried far on a densely packed globe, leads not to community but to those hideously destructive forms of tribalism that this century has already seen too much of.

Anyway, I suspect that the village probably never was all that it is cracked up to be. The village, including the pre-industrial village, is less likely to be filled with harmony and solidarity than with the oppressive weight of repressed deviation and dissent which, when they appear, erupt explosively and leave a lasting burden of antagonism and hatred. I have not been able to discover much evidence of the consensual *gemeinschaft* in descriptions of the small town of Springdale in upstate New York, or St. Denis in Quebec, or Peyrane, the village in the Vaucluse, or the small English town of Glossop near Manchester, or the peasant village of Montegrano in South Italy, or the Tanjore village in South India that André Betéille recently described.[3]

Here, for example, is how Horace Miner saw political life in the French Canadian parish of St. Denis thirty years ago:

> Politics is a topic of continual interest and one which reaches fever heat during election time . . . The whole parish is always divided between the "blues" or Conservatives, and the "reds." Party affiliations follow family lines and family cliques and antagonisms. The long winter *veillées* are attended almost invariably by family groups of similar political belief. Constituents of each party have a genuine dislike for those of the other . . . Election time is one of great tension, of taunts and shouting as parishioners get their evening mail . . . Insults are common, and many speaking acquaintances are dropped. During the last election the minority candidate had to have one meeting in the parish in secret, another open but under provincial police protection . . . Campaigns reach their climax with the *assemblée contradictoire*, at which both candidates speak. Characteristically at these meetings there are organized strong-arm tactics, drinking, and attempts to make each candidate's speech inaudible . . .
> The chicanery of politicians is a byword in the parish. Factional strife threatens the life of every organized association . . . On the whole the associational life of the community is weak. The people are not joiners.[4]

Thus the village democracy before the demos was ruined by industrialization and urbanization!

If the democratic village seems hardly worth seeking in this industrial and post-industrial epoch, the prospect is all the more appealing that democracy might be extended to the place where most adult citizens spend most of their time—their place of work. Professional people with a great deal of autonomy, academics like ourselves who enjoy an extraordinary amount of autonomy and a fair measure of self government in our universities, executives and administrators who see authority relationships from above rather than from below, all are likely to underestimate the consequences for the average citizen in a modern industrial society flowing from the fact that at his place of work he is a rather low-level subordinate in a system of hierarchical relationships. Although the term democracy has been prostituted in the service of employee relationships, the fact is that practically everywhere in the world, the industrial workplace—the factory, industry, or corporation, whether owned privately or publicly—is no democracy in any sense consistent with our usage in the realm of the state.

"The idea of a factory, nationalized or privately-owned," it has been said, "is the idea of command."[5] The factory, the enterprise, the industry, the corporation is a hierarchy; it may be an aristocracy, an oligarchy, a monarchy, a despotism, but it is not a democracy. This is as true in socialist economies as in capitalist and mixed economies. A century ago Engels asserted that hierarchy would be necessary in the factory even under socialism, that even in a socialist enterprise the worker would lose his autonomy. Over the entrance to the factory, he said, recalling *The Inferno*, the words should be written:

Lasciate ogni autonomia, voi che entrate![6]

Whether the workplace should be democratized, and if so how and how much, are questions that need to be distinguished from the problem of regulating the enterprise, industry, or corporation to insure that it accomplishes the social and public functions that are the only reason the rest of us are willing to grant its vast legal rights, privileges and immunities, and extraordinary power. If democratic states have become immense, so have corporations. There are privately owned corporations that have gross annual revenues greater than the GNP of most countries of the world, that spend annually sums greater than the entire budgets of the governments of most of the nation-states in the world. To insure that these immense resources and powers are used for public purposes is a staggering problem. But internal democracy in the factory, firm, industry, or corporation is not necessarily a more effective means of public control than regulating a hierarchically administered firm by competition and the price system, by a regulatory agency, by government ownership, or by various combinations of these and other possibilities. Indeed, even if the modern corporation were internally democratic, no matter whether it were public or private and no matter whether it were to operate in an economy predominantly privately owned or predominantly publicly owned, I do not think we any more than the Soviets or Yugoslavs would want to dispense entirely with such external controls as competition and the price system. In short, no system of *internal* control negates the need for a system of *external* controls that compel or induce those who exercise authority within the enterprise, whether these managers are chosen by and are accountable to stockholders, workers, or the state, to employ their power and resources for jointly beneficial purposes rather than for exploiting consumers.

But even if we can distinguish the problem of internal democracy from that of external control, the problem does not vanish. And even if this problem is extraordinarily difficult—as I think it is—it seems to me too important to be neglected, particularly by political scientists. It is true that in many developed countries with representative governments, trade union power has substituted bargaining for undiluted hierarchy in the control of wages and working conditions. But even where they are most powerful, labor unions have by no means created a democratic factory or industry; moreover, as a result more of apathy than of repression, few unions anywhere have developed a really high degree of internal democracy. Aside from a few scattered instances elsewhere,[7] the most massive, ambitious, and far-reaching experiment in democratizing the workplace has been taking place in Yugoslavia since 1950. Sober studies[8] suggest that while the system of workers' control has problems—some of them, like apathy and Michel's iron law of oligarchy, familiar to every student of democratic organizations—it might well prove to be a viable system of internal control. If it does, it will surely stand as an alternative with a very great appeal—at least in the long run—to workers in other industrial nations. If workers can participate in the government of their factories in Yugoslavia, and if these factories prove to be relatively efficient, surely the whole question of internal democracy will come alive in other countries.

Yet even if it should prove to be possible, efficient, and desirable, I do not believe that democracy in the workplace is a substitute for democracy in the state. For one thing, I doubt whether democracy in the work-place can be preserved indefinitely unless there is democracy in the state. Moreover, where an opposition party is illegal in the state, opposition in the factory has distinct limits.[9] Finally—and this is the most important point—the work-place is not as important as the state and with increasing leisure it may grow less so. To accept as a focus for self-government a type of unit that is and must be concerned with only a small part of the range of collective concerns would be to trivialize the democratic idea. I find it hard to believe that man's aspiration toward rational control over his environment by joint action with his fellow men will ever be satisfied by democratizing the production of aspirin, cars, and television sets.

As I have already suggested, any form of political participation that cannot be performed more or less simultaneously but must be carried on sequentially runs into the implacable barrier of time. Time's relentless arrow flies directly to the Achilles' heel of all schemes for participatory democracy on a grand scale. It is easy to show that any unit small enough for all the members to participate fully (where each member has the opportunity to present his views and have them discussed) cannot be larger than a working committee. If you doubt this, I ask you to sit down with pencil and paper and do a few exercises with various assumptions as to the time available for decisions and the time required for each participant to make his point or at least present his point of view.[10] You will quickly see how cruel is time's neutral guillotine. Or let me simply evoke your own experience with committees to remind you how quickly a committee grows too large for every member to participate fully. Or consider the experience of legislative committees, cabinets, regulatory commissions, judicial bodies.

Would we not all agree that an effective working committee can have no more than—let us err on the side of generosity—30 to 40 members?

Drawing on your own experience, most of you, I imagine, would cut these figures by a half or two-thirds.

Now if the great advantage of a unit the size of a working committee is that it allows full participation by its members, its great drawback, from a democratic point of view, is that unless it is a representative body or an agent of a representative body it ought not be given much public authority. Either the unit, though small, is granted authority because it represents a much larger number of citizens; or else, not being a representative body, it has little authority other than to recommend and advise; or else, if it has much power and is not a representative body, its power is illegitimate. In an interdependent society, any significant power wielded by a body the size of a working committee is bound to have important effects on citizens not sitting on that committee. Consequently either the committee is representative or its power is illegitimate. We can hardly espouse the small, self-governing, fully participatory unit as a normative goal if it is illegitimate. If it is representative, then it is no longer a body in which all citizens can participate fully. We have run into a cul de sac, as you see, and so we must get back to the starting point.

Some of you may regard this as a pessimistic analysis. It is, I admit, a very large fly in the ointment. Like death, it may be a brutal and perhaps even a tragic limit on man's possibilities, but I do not see why this conclusion must lead to pessimism. The idea of democracy would never have gotten off the ground if enthusiastic democrats had not been willing to settle for something a good deal less than complete and equal participation by all citizens in all decisions. It is worth recalling that in Athens, where the opportunities for free male citizens to participate in running the city seem to have been about as great as they have ever been anywhere, citizens were chosen for what was probably the most coveted participation in the life of the polis—a seat on the Council of Five Hundred, the inner council, or the various administrative boards—by lot or, in the case of the Board of Generals, by election, and to that extent these bodies were instances of representative government and not direct democracy. Participation in the Assembly, which met about once a month, was scarcely the fullest flowering of participatory democracy. I have been to enough town meetings myself to know something of their limitations. If you think of a town meeting in which a quorum sometimes required the presence of 6,000 people, where maybe as many as 30–40,000 were eligible to attend, and where perhaps 4–5,000 were frequently present, it is obvious that most Athenian citizens must have lived their lives without once speaking to their fellow citizens in the Assembly. That, one judges from the reports in Thucydides, was a forum that gave preference to orators.

Nonetheless, I doubt—although we shall never know—whether many Athenians felt frustrated because their opportunities to participate were not as unlimited as their skies. Between the working committee and the nation-state there is, I think, a critical threshold of size, below which the opportunities for participation can be so great and so fairly meted out that no one feels left out and everyone feels that his viewpoint has been pretty fairly attended to. Athens was far too large for the democracy of the working committee; de facto it had to employ a certain amount of representation. Yet I suspect that it was below the critical threshold. And even if we now reject as unattainable the ideal of full, equal, and direct participation by all citizens in all collective decisions—the ideal of committee democracy—we can still search for a unit that remains within this critical threshold for widespread participation.

VI

We have travelled a long trail and turned into a number of branching paths in our quest but we have not found a unit that seems optimal for rational self-government. The journey would have been much longer had we taken the time to explore the by-ways as carefully as they deserve. Yet if we keep going, I think that we shall finally end up about at the place where the Greeks left off: somewhere within view of the democratic city.

Yet what we come to is not the Greek city, nor can it be; not the *polis*, then, but a democratic city that would be consistent with the presence of the nation-state, the institutions of representative government, a level of technology beyond anything the Greeks dreamed of, and huge populations densely spread over the face of our shrunken earth.

If ancient Greeks were the first truly modern people, choice shaped by geography and historical accident made them also city people. So, too, choice shaped by demography and technology makes us a city people. But even if the Greeks were a city people and though they were modern in almost every important sense, our cities must differ in fact and in ideal from their actual and ideal cities. For one thing, the proportion of the residents of a modern democratic city eligible to participate in political life will be very much larger—something like half of the population, so that even a city of 100,000 will have around 50,000 adult citizens. Much more quickly than the Greeks, we reach the limits of direct democracy. Moreover, the citizens of a modern city will also be highly mobile. A resident of Athens was a citizen only if his ancestors were Athenians; in any modern city, many citizens are recent arrivals, or are about to move to another city. In 1960 more than one resident out of every six in American cities had moved there within the last five years.[11] As a result of our mobility, socialization into the political life of the modern democratic city is enormously more difficult for us than for the Greeks. Then, too, the Greek city was completely autonomous in ideal and pretty much so in fact. Our cities are not autonomous in fact nor would many of us offer total autonomy as an ideal. Finally, the citizen of a Greek city ordinarily had one inclusive loyalty to the city of his ancestors and to its gods. He invested in his city a kind of engagement in comparison with which patriotism in the nation-state must seem either shallow or strident. But the citizens of our modern cities will have no single loyalty and no single community; they will have multiple loyalties to many associations; and nowhere will they find the all-inclusive community.

If for these reasons a modern city cannot be a *polis*, we can nonetheless reasonably hope one day to achieve great democratic cities. As the optimum unit for democracy in the twenty-first century, the city has a greater claim, I think, than any other alternative.

To begin with, from now on into the next century man seems clearly destined to live in cities. If to live in cities is our fate, to live in great cities is our opportunity. Is it not of some significance that of the four great waves of experimentation in the West with popular government, during three of these—the Greek, the Roman, and the medieval communes of North Italy—popular governments managed to construct cities of exceptional and enduring beauty?

Yet during the fourth wave, that of representative democracy in the nation-state, we have so far failed most profoundly in our cities. Is it too much to hope that we might be on the verge of a fifth wave, the age of the democratic city within the democratic nation-state? By we, I mean of course, the whole of the Western democratic world and its off-shoots. But most of all, I mean we here in the United States.

City-building is one of the most obvious incapacities of Americans. We Americans have become an urban people without having developed an urban civilization. Though we live in cities, we do not know how to build cities. Perhaps because we have emerged so swiftly out of an agrarian society, perhaps because so many of us are only a generation or two removed from farm and field, small town and peasant village, we seem to lack the innate grasp of the essential elements of the good city that was all but instinct among Greeks, Romans, and the Italians of the free communes. Our cities are not merely non-cities, they are anti-cities—mean, ugly, gross, banal, inconvenient, hazardous, formless, incoherent, unfit for human living, deserts from which a family flees to the greener hinterlands as soon as job and income permit, yet deserts growing so rapidly outward that the open green space to which the family escapes soon shrinks to an oasis and then it too turns to a desert.

One advantage of the city as a unit for democratic government is, then, that it confronts us with a task worthy of our best efforts because of its urgency, its importance, its challenge, the extent of our failure up to now, and its promise for the good life lived jointly with fellow citizens.

These considerations point to another asset of the city as a democratic unit. While the city is not and cannot be autonomous, the policies of city hall and the totality of city agencies and activities are so important to our lives that to participate in the decisions of the city means, or anyway can mean, participating in shaping not merely the trivial but some of the most vital aspects of our environment. I say shaping and not totally controlling because the city is only one of our Chinese boxes. But it is in the city and with the powers and resources made available to cities that we shall deal with such crucial problems as the education of our children, our housing, the way we travel to and from our place of work, preventive health measures, crime, public order, the cycle of poverty, racial justice and equality—not to mention all those subtle and little understood elements that contribute so heavily to the satisfaction of our desires for friendship, neighborhood, community, and beauty.

Yet if the city and its government are important to us, can the good city today be small enough to remain below that critical threshold for wide participation that I mentioned a moment ago? I do not know any question more important to us as political scientists, nor any that we have so completely ignored. From evidence and analysis that are both all too incomplete, I should like to hazard an answer.

The existence of a few giant metropolises here and there may mislead us as to fact and possibility. Only a modest percentage of the world's population lives even today in the giant metropolis. Indeed, in 1960 only one-fifth of the people of the world lived in cities over 100,000. It is true that in the most urbanized region of the world, North America, in 1960 six out of every ten people lived in cities over 100,000. Yet even in the United States, less than one out of every ten lived in cities over a million.

It will take some doing, but we do not have to end up all jammed together in the asphalt desert of the large metropolis—unless that is really what we want. And Americans pretty clearly do not want to live in the large metropolis but rather in cities of modest dimensions. For example, in a survey by Gallup last year nearly half the respondents living in cities of 500,000 and over said they would like to live somewhere else—suburb, small town, farm; by contrast, few of the people living in suburb or town wanted to move to the big cities. About three out of four respondents are distressed by the prospect that their own community will double in population.[12] Census figures for the past several decades tell us that Americans have been acting out these preferences.

What, then, is the optimum size for a city? Curiously, this question, which so far as I know was first asked by political philosophers in Athens over 2,000 years ago, is no longer a subject of discussion among political scientists. I do not know why this should be so, but I wonder if it is because we have come to take a purely passive and defeatist view: the size of a city, we say, is beyond control, so the best we can do is to adapt political institutions to the facts. I am reminded of Rousseau's comment on Grotius, that his invariable mode of reasoning was always to establish right from fact. One might employ a more logical method, Rousseau remarked, but not one more favorable to tyrants.

If to our own loss we have ignored the question of the optimum size of cities, fortunately it has been examined by scholars in a variety of fields other than our own. It is impossible to do justice to this discussion here but the analysis and the evidence are too important for us to ignore.[13] It is only fair to warn you that this is a controversial area, yet the evidence seems to me to support the conclusion that the all-round optimum size for a contemporary American city is probably somewhere between 50,000 and 200,000, which, even taking the larger figure, may be within the threshold for wide civic participation.

There is, for example, no worthwhile evidence that there are any significant economies of scale in city governments for cities over about 50,000. The few items on which increasing size does lead to decreasing unit costs, such as water and sewerage, are too small a proportion of total city outlays to lead to significant economies; and even these reductions are probably offset by rising costs for other services, such as police protection.[14]

Per capita city expenditures increase with the size of city, at least in the United States. In 1960 the mean expenditure for U.S. cities over 150,000 was $123 per capita compared with $70 per capita for cities in the 25–50 thousand range. Yet there is no evidence that these higher costs per capita provide residents of large cities with a better life, taking it in the round, than the life enjoyed by residents of smaller cities. If it costs more in a city of a million than in a city of 25,000 to build, maintain, and police a park within walking distance of every citizen, then higher per capita expenditures for parks in big cities hardly signify that their residents have better public services than residents of smaller cities. What is more, the outlays in larger cities are actually less for some key functions than in smaller cities. For example, even though larger cities employ more persons per capita in public administration than smaller cities, per capita employment in education is on the average lower in larger cities than in small cities.[15]

Roads and highways nullify the older economic advantage of the metropolis as a market and a source of specialized labor. A student of urban economics argues, for example, that

> A half-dozen towns of, say, 25,000 population with two or three main industries each plus a dozen small one- or two-industry towns of half that size add up to a 300,000 population, extended local labor market, built on the moderately broad base of a couple of dozen separate industries.[16]

The oft-cited cultural advantages of a metropolis are also largely illusory. On the basis of his research on American cities, Duncan estimates that the requisite population base for a library of "desirable minimum professional standards" 50,000–75,000, for an art museum, 100,000, "with a somewhat higher figure for science and historical museums." Yet, even though larger cities have larger libraries, the circulation of library books per capita markedly decreases with size of city. There is also a negative correlation between city size and per capita museum attendance.[17] Moreover, just as smaller cities can retain their collective identities and yet form a larger economic unit, thanks to ease of transportation and communication, so we have barely begun to explore the ways in which small cities by federating together for specific purposes might enjoy all of the cultural advantages of the large city and yet retain their individual identities, the pleasures of living in communities of lower densities and more open spaces,[18] and relatively greater opportunities for political participation.

When we think about the size of a city in which a high culture may flourish, it is instructive to recall that Rome in the Augustan age probably had a population of about 350,000. During the Renaissance the city that produced Machiavelli and, I think it fair to say, an outpouring of great paintings, sculpture, and architecture beyond anything we Americans have yet created, had a population of around a hundred thousand. This was probably about the population of the city of Venice during the Renaissance, and of Rome when Michaelangelo chiselled out his Moses and painted his frescoes in the Sistine Chapel.

Now what is strangely missing from the discussion of the optimum size of cities is the voice of the political scientist. The question is, of course, broader than the problem of what size of city may be optimal for a democratic political life. But political life is not trivial. Surely political criteria have a place among the criteria for the optimum size of cities; and among these political criteria surely one of the most important is whether a city is beyond the threshold for widespread participation. The whole question needs more study than it has had. But it looks to me as if the all-round optimum size for a city—the range, say, from 50 thousand to about 200 thousand—is below this threshold. If this is so, then there is no other unit in the nest of Chinese boxes that is at once so important and so accessible; a unit that can and must be clothed with great powers, if it is to manage its problems, and yet can be small enough so that citizens can participate extensively in determining the ways in which this great power will be used. Only the city, it seems to me, can avoid the extremes we began to confront some time back. For the city need not be so huge that, like the nation-state, it reduces participation to voting, nor so small that its activities are trivial.

The city has at least one more advantage: it has great potentialities as a unit for educating citizens in civic virtue or—if I must use a term that comes more readily to the lips of a contemporary political scientist—for political socialization.

We may be approaching a crisis in the socialization of citizens into the political life of the democratic nation-state, a crisis that the challenges of nation-building, democratization, and overcoming the most blatant evils of industrialism have delayed or obscured. There are signs of malaise among young people, among the very citizens who shortly before the dawn of the twenty-first century will have become—to use the word that has now become a mindless cliché—the establishment. If the malaise were only

American, one could put it down to television, over-permissive child-rearing, the persistence of an unpopular and ugly war, or other causes more or less specific to the United States; but there are signs of this malaise among youth in almost all the democratic countries.

I am not going to try to explain here a phenomenon too complex for brief analysis. But a part of the phenomenon—I don't know how much it is symptom and how much underlying cause—is a belief that the government of the nation-state is remote, inaccessible, and unresponsive, a government of professionals in which only a few can ever hope to participate actively and a still smaller number can ever gain great influence after years of dedication to political life.

What we need, what they need, and what some of them are trying to create (often with incredible ignorance of elementary political wisdom) is a political unit of more truly human proportions in which a citizen can acquire confidence and mastery of the arts of politics—that is, of the arts required for shaping a good life in common with fellow citizens. What Pericles said of Athens, that the city is in general a school of the Grecians, may be said of every city of moderate size: it is a marvelous school. I have no doubt that a modern city even of moderate size is a good deal more complicated than Athens was. It has a much greater need for highly trained professionals, permanent administrative agencies, full-time leaders. Yet in the main, its problems are, I believe, within reach of the average citizen. And I believe it may be easier for citizens to reason about the good life and the ways to reach it by thinking in the more immediate and palpable context of the city than in the context of the nation-state or international politics. Even if solving the problems of the city is not quite enough for the good life, it is a great, indispensable, and comprehensible prerequisite.

VII

What I have presented is not a program but a perspective, not a prophecy but a prospect. It is not a solution to the problems of the city or of democracy, but a viewpoint from which to look at the problems of democracy and the city. If it does not lead directly to the answers, it might nonetheless help one to see the questions.

I have already suggested one implication of this way of looking at things—if popular governments in the modern world are a series of Chinese boxes, then we obviously need different models, theories, and criteria of excellence for each. I may seem to be repeating only what was commonly said nearly two centuries ago as ideas about representative government began to develop, that we cannot judge representative government in the nation-state as if it were or could be democracy in a committee, or, for that matter, a town meeting. Yet it is interesting to me that we have made so little of these palpable and evidently inherent differences in the performance of different kinds of units, all of which we are prone to call democratic.

Yet if the democratic city lies somewhere between democracy in the committee or in the town meeting and representative government in the nation-state, then it would be important to know what the similarities and differences are, and what standards of excellence we can apply to one but not the other. Even the democratic city, I fear, cannot satisfy anyone who has a vision of leaderless and partyless democracy, for at its best the politics of the democratic city will be more like a competitive polyarchy than a committee; organized parties and interest groups are more likely to exist than the free and spontaneous formation and dissolution of groups for every issue; a full-time leader or activist will exert more influence than any of his followers; institutionalized conflict is more likely than uncoerced consensus. Yet these are hunches that do no more than point to new worlds that need exploring.

The perspective I have been describing also bears on the way we think about units of government intermediate between nation-state and city. An American obviously must take the 50 states into account. These are too solidly built to be done away with and I don't propose to break any lances tilting against them. Yet in the perspective I am suggesting the states do not stand out as important institutions of democratic self-government. They are too big to allow for much in the way of civic participation—think of California and New York, each about as large in population as Canada or Yugoslavia and each larger than 80% of the countries of the world. Yet an American state is infinitely less important to citizens of that state than any democratic nation-state is to its citizens. Consequently the average American is bound to be much less concerned about the affairs of his state than of his city or country. Too remote to stimulate much participation by their citizens, and too big to make extensive participation possible anyway, these units intermediate between city and nation are probably destined for a kind of limbo of quasi-democracy. They will be pretty much controlled by the full-time professionals, whether elected or appointed. Moreover, many of the problems that states have to deal with will not fit within state boundaries. It cannot even be said that the states, on the whole, can tap any strong sentiments of loyalty or like-mindedness among their citizens. Doubtless we shall continue to use the states as important intermediate instruments of coordination and control—if for no other reason than the fact that they are going institutions. But whenever we are compelled to choose between city and state, we should always keep in mind, I think, that the city, not the state, is the better instrument of popular government.

This argument also applies to megalopolis, to the city that is not a city, to the local government that is not a local government. The city of New York, for example, has about the same population as Sweden or Chile. It is twice as large as Norway, three times the size of New Zealand.

To regard the government of New York as a local government is to make nonsense of the term. If the Swedes were to rule their whole country from Stockholm with no local governments, I am quite sure that we would begin to question whether the people of Sweden could rightly be called self-governing. Where, we might ask the Swedes, are your local governments? But should we not ask the same thing of New Yorkers: Where are your local governments? For purely historical and what to me seem rather irrational reasons, we continue to regard the government of the giant metropolis as if it were a local government, when we might more properly consider it as the equivalent of a state or a provincial government—and hence badly in need of being broken up into smaller units for purposes of local government. If it turns out that the government of a metropolis cannot be decentralized to smaller territorial units, then should we not quite openly declare that the metropolis cannot ever be made into a democratic city? This may be an inconvenient truth, but if it is true, it may be—like much truth—liberating in the end.

Yet I must admit that problems like these involving the metropolis demand more than we now know. The metropolis is a world to be explored, so let us explore it, hoping that we may discover how even it might be turned into a democratic city.

VIII

There are many questions that I shall have to leave unanswered. I could plead lack of time, but the fact is I don't know the answers, nor perhaps does anyone else quite yet.

There is above all the question that now overshadows all else in American life of how we shall solve the problems presented by race, poverty, inequality, discrimination, and centuries of humiliation. No failure in American society has been as enduring, as profound, as visible, as corrosive, as dangerous, and as tragic as our refusal to enable black Americans to share in equal measure with white Americans the realities of the American dream. Now this problem has become central to the whole future of our cities and indeed to the future of the country. I scarcely need to say that unless and until it is solved neither we nor our children nor our grandchildren nor any future generation can have anything like a decent urban life.

There is also the question of how the city can acquire adequate resources, particularly funds, without becoming excessively subordinated to higher levels of government. The bloc grant is a very promising solution, but only if grants are made directly to the cities and not, as is often proposed, exclusively to the states. In the perspective that I have been suggesting, to think of the states as the natural and exclusive recipients of bloc grants is anachronistic; for if the autonomy that is promised by the bloc grant is desirable for states—those barely democratic units in the limbo—autonomy is all the more desirable, and indeed necessary, if citizens are to enjoy the power to shape their cities.

A third question is how to control the size of cities. If there is an optimum size in the broad range from about 50,000 to about 200,000, as I have suggested further inquiry might show, then how can cities be maintained within this range—to say nothing of breaking up the giant metropolis? Typically, the people who influence decisions about the future of cities have acted on the simple-minded axiom: the bigger the better. This is most notably true here in America where the rational prospect of great gain encourages an almost pathological obsession with the virtues of sheer bigness, as if the very bigness of the city, the height of its buildings, and the crowds on its streets must somehow outweigh all squalor and ugliness. There seems to be a fear, too, that the moment we stop growing we start to die, a half truth that overlooks the fact that in nature the mouse and the sparrow have outlasted the brontosaurus and the sabre-toothed tiger. There are, I suspect, all sorts of devices we could use to control the growth of a city when it reaches the optimum range. These need to be explored, but they will be of little use until we decide that this is what we really want to do.

A closely related though much more formidable question is how we can make the legal boundaries of a city coincide more closely with what might be called its sociological boundaries. As I suggested earlier, our view up to now has been passive or defeatist: we say that we must constantly change legal boundaries to fit social boundaries. But as I tried to suggest with my fantasy of a Constitutional Convention, this way lies madness; for the legal boundaries must be extended until they cover the whole globe, which, whatever else it may be, cannot be a complete substitute for smaller territorial units. In general, the political autonomy allowed a territorial unit is likely to be less, the higher the amount of interaction with others outside the legal boundaries. In building nations or international systems, the greater the interaction; and consequently the less "real" the significance of local boundaries, the easier the task. Yet if we are to build democratic cities with enough autonomy to permit their citizens to participate extensively in significant decisions about their environment, we must somehow reverse the tendency for the legal boundaries of the city to lose all social and economic significance. Nor can we simply go on creating separate authorities for each problem. Obviously different problems call for different boundaries, and we may have to live in a network of authorities. Yet the indefinite multiplication of units of government is bound to fragment the control of the ordinary citizen over a broad range of policies.

The problem of fragmented authority touches closely upon another, the problem of decentralization of authority and power within the city. Even in a city in the range from 50,000–200,000 political participation is reduced for most people to nothing more than voting in elections—as it is in the representative government of the nation-state—unless there are smaller units within which citizens can from time to time formulate and express their desires, consult with officials, and in some cases participate even more fully in decisions. Unfortunately, I can only indicate the problem; I have no answers to it. There are a number of proposals floating around for creating smaller participatory units in the city, the oldest and most popular candidate being the neighborhood; and there are even some interesting experiments of this kind going on. So far as I know none of the proposals or experiments triumph over the universal tendency for a few activists to engage in most of the overt activities while the rest participate only sporadically, symbolically, or not at all. Although this limitation seems to me to deflate rather cruelly the most grandiose and utopian claims for citizen participation, and in addition raises serious problems, I do not think it is a reason for rejecting these efforts and experiments out of hand, if we are aiming not for committee democracy but, as I suggested a moment ago, a degree of participation so great and so fairly spread about that no one feels neglected and everyone feels, with justice, that his viewpoint has been pretty fairly attended to. To aim for the point at which practically everyone in the city believes with good reason that his claims ordinarily receive a fair hearing, and decisions, even when adverse to his claims, have been arrived at with understanding and sympathy, is already so distant and so splendid a goal that I am quite content to leave the exploration of what lies beyond it to someone in the twenty-first century.

If there were time, I know that one could turn up more questions, more problems, more obstacles. We might even conclude that the fifth high tide of democracy, the age of the democratic city in the democratic republic, is not after all in our destiny.

Or it may be within the possibilities of other countries, but not our own, to achieve in the rest of this century what the Greeks did 2,500 years ago, to develop an urban civilization founded on the democratic city, only consistent this time with the imperatives of modern technology, the existence of representative governments ruling over huge populations and territories, and the extension of constitutionalism and the rule of law to vast areas of the earth—ultimately, perhaps, to the globe itself.

Yet even if no one can say whether this will ever come about, or where, for everyone stirred by the prospect of shaping politics now toward the good life in the twenty-first century—or at least toward a better life—the opportunities lie all around.

Notes

1 H. D. F. Kitto, *The Greeks* (Baltimore: Penguin Books, 1951, 1957), p. 79.

2 Various classical scholars have made valiant attempts to guess the population of Athens and its composition—citizens, adult males, metics, slaves—from the most frag-

mentary bits of evidence. I have not been able to locate any estimate that does not seem to leave great room for error. Kitto suggests "30,000 as a reasonable estimate of the normal number of citizens" in the Fifth Century: op. cit., p. 131.

[3] Arthur J. Vidich and Joseph Bensman, Small Town in Mass Society (Garden City, N.Y.: Anchor Books, 1960); Horace Miner, St. Denis, A French Canadian Parish (Chicago: University of Chicago Phoenix Books, 1939, 1963); Laurence Wylie, Village in the Vaucluse (New York: Harper Colophon, 1957, 1964); A. H. Birch, Small-Town Politics, A Study of Political Life in Glossop (Oxford: Oxford University Press, 1959); Edward C. Banfield, The Moral Basis of a Backward Society (New York: The Free Press, 1958); André Betéille, Caste, Class and Power (Berkeley: University of California Press, 1966).

[4] Miner, op. cit., 58–61.

[5] Graham Wooton, Workers, Unions and the State (London: Routledge and Kegan Paul, 1966), 36.

[6] Ibid., 36. The quotation is from Engels' essay "On Authority" in Lewis S. Feuer (ed.), Marx and Engels: Basic Writings (New York: Doubleday Anchor, 1959), 481–484.

[7] Wooton, op. cit., 113–124.

[8] Cf. Albert Meister, Socialisme et Autogestion, L'Expérience Yougoslave (Paris: Éditions du Seuil, 1964); and Jiri Kolaja, Workers Councils: The Jugoslav Experience (New York and Washington: Frederick A. Praeger, 1966).

[9] See the comments of Kolaja, op. cit., 7 and 66 ff.; and Meister, op. cit., 240–245, 263–278, 373.

[10] Cf. Bertrand de Jouvenel, "The Chairman's Problem," American Political Science Review, 55 (June, 1961), 368–372.

[11] In 1960 the percentage of migrants from another country since 1955 for all U.S. cities 25,000 and over was 18.4%. The percentages ran slightly higher (19.7%) in small cities of 25–50,000 than in cities over 150,000 (15.6%). See Jeffrey K. Hadden and Edgar F. Borgatta, American Cities, Their Social Characteristics (Chicago: Rand McNally, 1965), Appendix, Table 1, variable #19, p. 108.

[12] American Institute of Public Opinion release, April 24, 1966.

[13] The most extensive survey and analysis of the evidence seems to be the work of Otis Dudley Duncan. The findings of his Ph.D. dissertation, An Examination of the Problem of Optimum City-Size (University of Chicago, 1949) have been summarized in Otis Dudley Duncan, "Optimum Size of Cities" in Paul Hatt and Albert Reiss (eds.), Reader in Urban Sociology (Glencoe, Ill.: Free Press, 1951), 632–645; and James Dahir, "What is the Best Size for a City?," American City (August, 1951), 104–105. Robert A. Lillibridge, "Urban Size: An Assessment," Land Economics, 38 (Nov., 1952), 341–352, summarizes Duncan and others. In addition, see William Fielding Ogburn and Otis Dudley Duncan, "City Size as a Sociological Variable," in Ernest W. Burgess and Donald J. Bogue, eds., Urban Sociology (Chicago: The University of Chicago, Phoenix Books), 58–76; Otis Dudley Duncan, "Optimum Size of Cities" in Joseph J. Spengler and Otis Dudley Duncan (eds.), Demographic Analysis (Glencoe, Ill.: The Free Press, 1956), 372–385.

[14] I am indebted to Mr. Garry D. Brewer for undertaking an extensive survey of the writings and findings dealing with economies of scale in American cities. The relevant literature is extensive, but the most relevant studies appear to be Amos H. Hawley's seminal article, "Metropolitan Population and Municipal Government Expenditures in Central Cities," Journal of Social Issues, 7, nos. 1 and 2 (1951), 100–108; Werner Z. Hirsch, "Expenditures Implications of Metropolitan Growth and Consolidation," Review of Economics and Statistics, 41 (August, 1959), 232–241; Harvey E. Brazer, City Expenditures in the United States, National Bureau of Economic Research Occasional Paper no. 66 (New York, 1959). See also the analysis of the evidence of

these studies in Wilbur R. Thompson, A *Preface to Urban Economics* (Baltimore: Johns Hopkins Press, 1965), Ch. 7, "The Urban Public Economy," 255–292.

[15] Data in the paragraph above are from Hadden and Borgatta, *op. cit.*, Appendix, Table 1, p. 110, variables 57, 58, and 65.

[16] Thompson, *op. cit.*, 34.

[17] Duncan, "Optimum Size of Cities," *op. cit.*, 381.

[18] ". . . museums, professional athletic teams, complete medical facilities, and other accoutrements of modern urban life could be supported collectively. As the federated places grew and prospered the interstices would, of course, begin to fill in, moving the area closer to the large metropolitan area form. But alert action in land planning and zoning could preserve open spaces in a pattern superior to those found in most large urban areas." Thompson, *op. cit.*, 36.

Social Contract (*III, XV*) and *Poland* (*VII*)

Jean-Jacques Rousseau

This selection, the first of three that introduce the ideas of classical theorists, is from the most prominent advocate of direct democracy in modern political thought. Less than a century after Locke's Second Treatise endorsed representative democracy, Rousseau called for a return to the classical tradition of participatory democracy, charging that the arbitrary will of a legislative elite would corrupt and cheat the people. The first selection from his Social Contract denies that any man can make laws on behalf of others. Although the governmental function of enforcement of law should be entrusted to representatives, only the people themselves could perform the sovereign function of enactment of law.

Rousseau later suggested that the people should enact their laws by assembling in smaller territorial units containing roughly equal populations. In the excerpt from his Considerations on the Government of Poland, Rousseau is trying to show how direct participation in basic level democracies could control national legislation, with strictly bound deputies conveying will from below. Ultimately all Polish men would directly vote their wills on national legislation through a three-tiered system of linked assemblies: the mass participation assemblies of the rural and urban communes, the thirty-three provincial or palatine assemblies (dietines), and the national assembly (diet). In theory, Rousseau's combination of the principles of instructed deputies and federated assemblies would permit small-scale participatory units to vote on legislative matters of national importance.*

Deputies or Representatives

As soon as public service ceases to be the main business of citizens, and they prefer to serve with their purses rather than with their persons,

---

From *Rousseau: Political Writings*, trans. and ed. by F. M. Watkins (London: Thomas Nelson and Sons, 1953), pp. 102–106, 192–195. Reprinted by permission of Thomas Nelson and Sons, Ltd.

* The very opposite of Edmund Burke's ideal of the autonomous representative (see his "Speech to the Electors of Bristol"), the use of strictly bound delegates to form legislative assemblies was the practice of many American colonial governments prior to the American Revolution.

115

the state is already on the brink of ruin. Is it necessary to go forth to war? They hire troops and remain at home. Is it necessary to take counsel? They appoint deputies and remain at home. By dint of laziness and money, they end by having mercenaries to enslave their country, and representatives to sell it.

Preoccupation with commerce and the arts, greedy interest in profits, effeminacy and love of comfort, these are the motives that convert personal services into money payments. People give up a part of their profits in order that they may have leisure to increase them. Give money, and you will soon have chains. *Public finance* is a slavish word unknown to republics. In a truly free country, the citizens do everything with their own hands, nothing with money; far from paying to be exempted from their duties, they would pay for the privilege of performing them in person. I am far from taking the common view; I consider corvées to be less inconsistent with liberty than taxes.

The better the state is constituted, the more does public rather than private business preoccupy the minds of citizens. The amount of private business will even be greatly reduced, for the aggregate of common happiness will constitute a larger fraction of the happiness of each individual, and he will therefore have less happiness to seek on his own account. In a well conducted republic, everyone rushes to the assemblies; under a bad government no one likes to move a step in that direction, because no one has any interest in what is done there, because it is foreseen that their proceedings will not be dominated by the general will, and finally because domestic interests are all-absorbing. Good laws cause better laws to be made, while bad ones lead to worse. As soon as any man says of the affairs of the state, "What do I care?," the state should be accounted lost.

The cooling off of love of country, the activity of private interest, the immensity of states, conquests, and the abuse of government have suggested the device of sending deputies or representatives of the people to the assemblies of the nation. This is what, in some countries, has presumptuously been called the Third Estate, which means that the particular interest of two classes is placed in the first and second place, the public interest in the third only.

Sovereignty cannot be represented, for the same reason that it cannot be alienated. It consists essentially in the general will, and will cannot be represented; will either is, or is not, your own; there is no intermediate possibility. Thus deputies of the people are not, and cannot be, its representatives; they are merely its agents, and can make no final decisions. Any law which the people has not ratified in person is null and void; it is not a law. The English people thinks it is free; it is very much mistaken. It is free only when it is electing members of parliament; as soon as they are elected, it is enslaved and reduced to nothing. The use it makes of its liberty, during these brief moments, shows that it well deserves to lose it.

The idea of representatives is modern; it comes to us from the feudal system, that absurd and iniquitous government which degrades the human species, and dishonors the name of man. In the republics and even in the monarchies of antiquity, the people never had representatives; the very word was unknown. In Rome, where the tribunes were so sacrosanct, it is remarkable that no one ever so much as dreamed that they could usurp the functions of the people; and that in the midst of so great a multitude they never tried to pass a single plebiscite on their own authority. And yet the difficulties occasionally caused by such a crowd may be judged by what happened in the time of the Gracchi, when a part of the citizens cast their votes from the rooftops.

Where rights and liberties are everything, no difficulties are too great. Among this wise people, everything was given its proper value; it allowed its lictors to do what its tribunes would never have dared to do, for it had no fear that its lictors would try to represent it.

To explain, however, the way in which the tribunes sometimes did represent it, we need only think of the way in which the government represents the sovereign. Since law is only a declaration of the general will, it is clear that the people cannot be represented in the legislative power; but it can and must be represented in the executive power, which is merely the enforcement of law. This shows that, if the matter were properly examined, we should find that very few nations have laws. Be that as it may, it is certain that the tribunes, since they had no share in the executive power, were never able to represent the Roman people by virtue of their own office, but only by usurping the functions of the senate.

Among the Greeks, the people did for itself everything it had to do; it remained constantly assembled in the market-place. It lived in a mild climate; it was not greedy; slaves did its work; its primary business was its liberty. Lacking the same advantages, how can you preserve the same rights? Your harsher climates add to your needs;[1] for six months of the year the public square is uninhabitable; your muffled tongues cannot be heard in the open air; you are more interested in profit than in liberty; and you are much less afraid of slavery than of poverty.

What is this? Can liberty be maintained only on the basis of slavery? Perhaps. The two extremes meet. All artificial things have disadvantages, civil society most of all. There are some unfortunate situations where you can only preserve your own liberty at the expense of the liberty of others, and the citizen can only be perfectly free if the slave is extremely enslaved. Such was the case in Sparta. As for you, modern peoples, you have no slaves, but you are slaves yourselves; you have bought their freedom at the price of your own. It is in vain that you boast of this choice; I find in it more cowardice than humanity.

By all this I do not mean that it is necessary to have slaves, nor that the right of slavery is legitimate, since I have proved the contrary. I am simply showing why modern peoples, which consider themselves free, have representatives; and why the peoples of antiquity did not. Be that as it may, as soon as a people gives itself representatives, it is no longer free, and no longer exists.

All things considered, I do not see how any future sovereign can preserve its rights among us unless the republic is very small. But if it is very small, will it be subjugated? No. I shall show hereafter how it is possible to combine the external power of a large people with the simple administration and good order of a small state. . . .

One of the greatest disadvantages of large states, the one which above all makes liberty most difficult to preserve in them is that the legislative power cannot manifest itself directly, and can act only by delegation. That has its good and its evil side; but the evil outweighs the good. A legislature made up of the whole citizen body is impossible to corrupt, but easy to deceive. Representatives of the people are hard to deceive, but easy to corrupt; and it rarely happens that they are not so corrupted. You have before you the example of the English Parliament and, through the *liberum veto*, that of your own nation. Now, it is possible to enlighten someone who is mistaken; but how can you restrain someone who is for sale? Without being well versed in Polish affairs, I would wager anything in the world that there is more talent in the diet, and more virtue in the dietines.

I see two means of preventing this terrible evil of corruption, which turns the organ of freedom into the instrument of slavery.

The first, as I have already said, is to have the diets elected frequently, for if the representatives are often changed it is more costly and difficult to seduce them. On this point your constitution is better than that of Great Britain; and when you have abolished or modified the *liberum veto*, I can see no other changes to be made in it, unless it would be to add certain obstacles to the sending of the same deputies to two successive diets, and to prevent them from being elected a great many times. I shall return to this point later on.

The second means is to bind the representatives to follow their instructions exactly, and to make them render their constituents a strict account of their conduct in the diet. In this respect I can only marvel at the negligence, the carelessness and, I would even venture to say, the stupidity of the English nation, which, after having armed its deputies with supreme power, has added no brake to regulate the use they may make of that power throughout the seven years of their mandate.

I observe that the Poles are not sufficiently aware of the importance of their dietines, of all they owe to them, nor of all they might get from them by extending their authority and by regularizing their form. I myself am convinced that, if the confederations have saved the fatherland, it is the dietines that have preserved it, and that they are the true palladium of liberty.

The instructions of the deputies should be drawn up with great care, not only on the subjects listed in the royal agenda, but also on the other current needs of the state or province; and this should be done by a committee presided over, if you will, by the marshal of the dietine, but otherwise composed of members chosen by majority vote; and the nobility should not disperse until these instructions have been read, debated and approved in plenary session. In addition to the original text of these instructions, handed to the deputies together with their patents of election, a copy signed by them should remain in the archives of the dietine. It is on the basis of these instructions that they ought, on their return, to report on their actions at a session of the dietine convened expressly for that purpose, a custom which must absolutely be revived; and it is on the basis of this report that they should either be excluded from all subsequent candidacy for the deputyship, or else declared eligible, if they have followed their instructions to the satisfaction of their constituents. This examination is of the utmost importance; it would be impossible to pay too much attention to it, or to observe its results too carefully. With each word the deputy speaks in the diet, and with every move he makes, he must already see himself under the eyes of his constituents, and feel the future influence of their judgment both on his hopes of advancement, and on that good opinion of his compatriots which is indispensable to the realization of those hopes; for, after all, it is not to express their own private sentiments, but to declare the will of the nation, that the nation sends deputies to the diet. This brake is absolutely necessary to hold them to their duty, and to prevent any sort of corruption from any source. Whatever may be said, I cannot see any disadvantage in this limitation, for the chamber of deputies, which does not, or should not, participate in the details of administration, can never have to deal with any unexpected matter; but if such a matter did arise, and a deputy did nothing contrary to the express will of his constituents, they would not blame him for having expressed his opinion, like a good citizen, on a matter they had not foreseen, and on which they had reached no decision. I will add, in conclusion, that if there were actually some disadvantage in holding the deputies thus bound by their instructions, it could not outweigh the immense advantage of preventing the law from ever being anything but the real expression of the will of the nation.

Once these precautions have been taken, furthermore, there should never be a conflict of jurisdiction between the diet and the dietines; and when a law has been passed in the plenary diet, I would not even grant the dietines the right to protest. Let them punish their deputies; let them even, if necessary, cut off their heads, if they have prevaricated; but let them obey fully, continuously, without exception and without protest; let them bear the just penalty of their bad choice; except that, at the next diet, they may, if they think proper, make as vigorous representations as they like.

Note

[1] To adopt in a cold climate the luxury and effeminacy of orientals is to desire to assume their chains; it makes submission even more inevitable for us than it is for them.

On Revolution

Hannah Arendt

If a revolution is worthwhile because it means men are acting freely to shape their lives, what happens when the revolution triumphs? How does the next generation get to enjoy a similar freedom? Hannah Arendt reviews for us Thomas Jefferson's struggle with this dilemma, which leads into problems of direct democracy, representation, rotation in office, and other devices for maintaining the revolutionary spirit and culminates in Jefferson's advocacy of "small republics" within the nation. Miss Arendt is a renowned advocate of the virtues of public life as it existed in the Greek city-state and of participatory assemblies such as the soviets, which spring up spontaneously in periods of revolutionary turmoil only to be carefully shelved or crushed by the new government. The leaders of the new revolutionary organs at the center strive to destroy these restrictions on their centralized and hierarchical authority and, in so doing, says Arendt, effectively destroy much of the public spirit and revolutionary energy of their societies.

The failure of post-revolutionary thought to remember the revolutionary spirit and to understand it conceptually was preceded by the failure of the revolution to provide it with a lasting institution. The revolution, unless it ended in the disaster of terror, had come to an end with the establishment of a republic which, according to the men of the revolutions, was "the only form of government which is not eternally at open or secret war with the rights of mankind."[1] But in this republic, as it presently turned out, there was no space reserved, no room left for the exercise of precisely those qualities which had been instrumental in building it. And this was clearly no mere oversight, as though those who knew so well how to provide for power of the commonwealth and the liberties of its citizens, for judgment and opinion, for interests and rights, had simply forgotten what actually they cherished above everything else, the potentialities of action and the proud privilege of being beginners of something altogether new. Certainly, they did not want to deny this privilege to their successors,

From On Revolution by Hannah Arendt (New York: Viking Press, 1963), pp. 234–242, 252–259. Copyright © 1963 by Hannah Arendt. All Rights Reserved. Reprinted by permission of the Viking Press, Inc.

but they also could not very well wish to deny their own work, although Jefferson, more concerned with this perplexity than anybody else, almost went to this extremity. The perplexity was very simple and, stated in logical terms, it seemed unsolvable: if foundation was the aim and the end of revolution, then the revolutionary spirit was not merely the spirit of beginning something new but of starting something permanent and enduring; a lasting institution, embodying this spirit and encouraging it to new achievements, would be self-defeating. From which it unfortunately seems to follow that nothing threatens the very achievements of revolution more dangerously and more acutely than the spirit which has brought them about. Should freedom, in its most exalted sense as freedom to act, be the price to be paid for foundation? This perplexity, namely, that the principle of public freedom and public happiness without which no revolution would ever have come to pass should remain the privilege of the generation of the founders, has not only produced Robespierre's bewildered and desperate theories about the distinction between revolutionary and constitutional government, . . . but has haunted all revolutionary thinking ever since.

On the American scene, no one has perceived this seemingly inevitable flaw in the structure of the republic with greater clarity and more passionate preoccupation than Jefferson. His occasional, and sometimes violent, antagonism against the Constitution and particularly against those who "look at constitutions with sanctimonious reverence, and deem them like the ark of the covenant, too sacred to be touched,"[2] was motivated by a feeling of outrage about the injustice that only his generation should have it in their power "to begin the world over again"; for him, as for Paine, it was plain "vanity and presumption [to govern] beyond the grave," it was, moreover, the "most ridiculous and insolent of all tyrannies."[3] When he said, "We have not yet so far perfected our constitutions as to venture to make them unchangeable," he added at once, clearly in fear of such possible perfection, "Can they be made unchangeable? I think not"; for, in conclusion: "Nothing is unchangeable but the inherent and unalienable rights of man," among which he counted the rights to rebellion and revolution.[4] When the news of Shay's rebellion in Massachusetts reached him while he was in Paris, he was not in the least alarmed, although he conceded that its motives were "founded in ignorance," but greeted it with enthusiasm: "God forbid we should ever be twenty years without such a rebellion." The very fact that the people had taken it upon themselves to rise and act was enough for him, regardless of the rights or wrongs of their case. For "the tree of liberty must be refreshed, from time to time, with the blood of patriots and tyrants. It is its natural manure."[5]

These last sentences, written two years before the outbreak of the French Revolution and in this form without parallel in Jefferson's later writings,[6] may give us a clue to the fallacy which was bound to becloud the whole issue of action in the thinking of the men of the revolutions. It was

in the nature of their experiences to see the phenomenon of action exclusively in the image of tearing down and building up. Although they had
known public freedom and public happiness, in dream or in reality, prior
to the revolution, the impact of revolutionary experience had overruled all
notions of a freedom which was not preceded by liberation, which did not
derive its pathos from the act of liberation. By the same token, to the
extent that they had a positive notion of freedom which would transcend
the idea of a successful liberation from tyrants and from necessity, this
notion was identified with the act of foundation, that is, the framing of a
constitution. Jefferson, therefore, when he had learned his lesson from the
catastrophes of the French Revolution, where the violence of liberation
had frustrated all attempts at founding a secure space for freedom, shifted
from his earlier identification of action with rebellion and tearing down to
an identification with founding anew and building up. He thus proposed
to provide in the Constitution itself "for its revision at stated periods"
which would roughly correspond to the periods of the coming and going of
generations. His justification, that each new generation has "a right to
choose for itself the form of government it believes most promotive of its
own happiness," sounds too fantastic (especially if one considers the then
prevailing tables of mortality; according to which there was "a new majority" every nineteen years) to be taken seriously; it is, moreover, rather
unlikely that Jefferson, of all people, should have granted the coming
generations the right to establish non-republican forms of government.
What was uppermost in his mind was no real change of form of government, not even a constitutional provision to hand on the Constitution
"with periodical repairs, from generation to generation, to the end of
time"; it was rather the somewhat awkward attempt at securing for each
generation the "right to depute representatives to a convention," to find
ways and means for the opinions of the whole people to be "fairly, fully,
and peaceably expressed, discussed, and decided by the common reason of
the society."[7] In other words, what he wished to provide for was an exact
repetition of the whole process of action which had accompanied the
course of the Revolution, and while in his earlier writings he saw this
action primarily in terms of liberation, in terms of the violence that had
preceded and followed the Declaration of Independence, he later was
much more concerned with the constitution-making and the establishment
of a new government, that is, with those activities which by themselves
constituted the space of freedom.

No doubt only great perplexity and real calamity can explain that
Jefferson—so conscious of his common sense and so famous for his practical turn of mind—should have proposed these schemes of recurring
revolutions. Even in their least extreme form, recommended as the remedy
against "the endless circle of oppression, rebellion, reformation," they
would either have thrown the whole body politic out of gear periodically
or, more likely, have debased the act of foundation to a mere routine

performance, in which case even the memory of what he most ardently wished to save—"to the end of time, if anything human can so long endure"—would have been lost. But the reason Jefferson, throughout his long life, was carried away by such impracticabilities was that he knew, however dimly, that the Revolution, while it had given freedom to the people, had failed to provide a space where this freedom could be exercised. Only the representatives of the people, not the people themselves, had an opportunity to engage in those activities of "expressing, discussing and deciding" which in a positive sense are the activities of freedom. And since the state and federal governments, the proudest results of revolution, through sheer weight of their proper business were bound to overshadow in political importance the townships and their meeting halls—until what Emerson still considered to be "the unit of the Republic" and "the school of the people" in political matters had withered away[8]—one might even come to the conclusion that there was less opportunity for the exercise of public freedom and the enjoyment of public happiness in the republic of the United States than there had existed in the colonies of British America. Lewis Mumford recently pointed out how the political importance of the township was never grasped by the founders, and that the failure to incorporate it into either the federal or the state constitutions was "one of the tragic oversights of post-revolutionary political development." Only Jefferson among the founders had a clear premonition of this tragedy, for his greatest fear was indeed lest "the abstract political system of democracy lacked concrete organs."[9]

The failure of the founders to incorporate the township and the town-hall meeting into the Constitution, or rather their failure to find ways and means to transform them under radically changed circumstances, was understandable enough. Their chief attention was directed toward the most troublesome of all their immediate problems, the question of representation, and this to such an extent that they came to define republics, as distinguished from democracies, in terms of representative government. Obviously direct democracy would not do, if only because "the room will not hold all" (as John Selden, more than a hundred years earlier, had described the chief cause for the birth of Parliament). These were indeed the terms in which the principle of representation was still discussed at Philadelphia; representation was meant to be a mere substitute for direct political action through the people themselves, and the representatives they elected were supposed to act according to instructions received by their electors, and not to transact business in accordance with their own opinions as they might be formed in the process.[10] However, the founders, as distinguished from the elected representatives in colonial times, must have been the first to know how far removed this theory was from reality. "With regard to the sentiments of the people," James Wilson, at the time of the convention, "conceived it difficult to know precisely what they are," and Madison knew very well that "no member of the convention could say what the opinions of his constituents were at this time; much less could he say what they would think if possessed of the information and lights possessed by the members here."[11] Hence, they could hear with approval, though perhaps not entirely without misgivings, when Benjamin Rush proposed the new and dangerous doctrine that although "all power is derived from the people, they possess it only on the days of their elections. After this it is the property of their rulers."[12]

These few quotations may show as in a nutshell that the whole question of representation, one of the crucial and most troublesome issues of modern politics ever since the revolutions, actually implies no less than a decision on the very dignity of the political realm itself. The traditional alternative between representation as a mere substitute for direct action of the people and representation as a popularly controlled rule of the people's representatives over the people constitutes one of those dilemmas which permit of no solution. If the elected representatives are so bound by instructions that they gather together only to discharge the will of their masters, they may still have a choice of regarding themselves as either glorified messenger boys or hired experts who, like lawyers, are specialists in representing the interests of their clients. But in both instances the assumption is, of course, that the electorate's business is more urgent and more important than theirs; they are the paid agents of people who, for whatever reasons, are not able, or do not wish, to attend to public business. If, on the contrary, the representatives are understood to become for a limited time the appointed rulers of those who elected them—without rotation in office, there is of course no representative government strictly speaking—representation means that the voters surrender their own power, albeit voluntarily, and that the old adage, "All power resides in the people," is true only for the day of election. In the first instance, government has degenerated into mere administration, the public realm has vanished; there is no space either for seeing and being seen in action, John Adams' *spectemur agendo*, or for discussion and decision, Jefferson's pride of being "a participator in government"; political matters are those that are dictated by necessity to be decided by experts, but not open to opinions and genuine choice; hence, there is no need for Madison's "medium of a chosen body of citizens" through which opinions must pass and be purified into public views. In the second instance, somewhat closer to realities, the age-old distinction between ruler and ruled which the Revolution had set out to abolish through the establishment of a republic has asserted itself again; once more, the people are not admitted to the public realm, once more the business of government has become the privilege of the few, who alone may "exercise [their] virtuous dispositions" (as Jefferson still called men's political talents). The result is that the people must either sink into "lethargy, the forerunner of death to the public liberty" or "preserve the spirit of resistance" to whatever government they have elected, since the only power they retain is "the reserve power of revolution."[13]

For these evils there was no remedy, since rotation in office, so highly valued by the founders and so carefully elaborated by them, could hardly do more than prevent the governing few from constituting themselves as a separate group with vested interests of their own. Rotation could never provide everybody, or even a sizable portion of the population, with the chance to become temporarily "a participator in government." Had this evil been restricted to the people at large, it would have been bad enough in view of the fact that the whole issue of republican versus kingly or aristocratic government turned about rights of equal admission to the public, political realm; and yet, one suspects, the founders should have found it easy enough to console themselves with the thought that the Revolution had opened the political realm at least to those whose inclination for "virtuous disposition" was strong, whose passion for distinction was ardent enough to embark upon the extraordinary hazards of a political career. Jefferson, however, refused to be consoled. He feared an "elective despotism" as bad as, or worse than, the tyranny they had risen against: "If once [our people] become inattentive to the public affairs, you and I, and Congress and Assemblies, Judges and Governors, shall all become wolves."[14] And while it is true that historical developments in the United States have hardly borne out this fear, it is also true that this is almost exclusively due to the founders' "political science" in establishing a government in which the divisions of powers have constituted through checks and balances their own control. What eventually saved the United States from the dangers which Jefferson feared was the machinery of government; but this machinery could not save the people from lethargy and inattention to public business, since the Constitution itself provided a public space only for the representatives of the people, and not for the people themselves.

It may seem strange that only Jefferson among the men of the American Revolution ever asked himself the obvious question of how to preserve the revolutionary spirit once the revolution had come to an end, but the explanation for this lack of awareness does not lie in that they themselves were no revolutionaries. On the contrary, the trouble was that they took this spirit for granted, because it was a spirit which had been formed and nourished throughout the colonial period. Since, moreover, the people remained in undisturbed possession of those institutions which had been the breeding grounds of the revolution, they could hardly become aware of the fateful failure of the Constitution to incorporate and duly constitute, found anew, the original sources of their power and public happiness. It was precisely because of the enormous weight of the Constitution and of the experiences in founding a new body politic, that the failure to incorporate the townships and the town-hall meetings, the original springs of all political activity in the country, amounted to a death sentence for them. Paradoxical as it may sound, it was in fact under the impact of the Revolution that the revolutionary spirit in this country began to wither away, and it was the Constitution itself, this greatest achievement of the American people, which eventually cheated them of their proudest possession.

I

"As Cato concluded every speech with the words, *Carthago delenda est,* so do I every opinion, with the injunction, 'divide the counties into wards.' "[15] Thus Jefferson once summed up an exposition of his most cherished political idea, which, alas, turned out to be as incomprehensible to posterity as it had been to his contemporaries. The reference to Cato was no idle slip of a tongue used to Latin quotations; it was meant to emphasize that Jefferson thought the absence of such a subdivision of the country constituted a vital threat to the very existence of the republic. Just as Rome, according to Cato, could not be safe so long as Carthage existed, so the republic, according to Jefferson, would not be secure in its very foundations without the ward system. "Could I once see this I should consider it as the dawn of the salvation of the republic, and say with old Simeon, 'Nunc dimittis Domine.' "[16]

Had Jefferson's plan of "elementary republics" been carried out, it would have exceeded by far the feeble germs of a new form of government which we are able to detect in the sections of the Parisian Commune and the popular societies during the French Revolution. However, if Jefferson's political imagination surpassed them in insight and in scope, his thoughts were still traveling in the same direction. Both Jefferson's plan and the French *sociétés révolutionnaires* anticipated with an almost weird precision those councils, *soviets* and *Räte,* which were to make their appearance in every genuine revolution throughout the nineteenth and twentieth centuries. Each time they appeared, they sprang up as the spontaneous organs of the people, not only outside of all revolutionary parties but entirely unexpected by them and their leaders. Like Jefferson's proposals, they were utterly neglected by statesmen, historians, political theorists, and, most importantly, by the revolutionary tradition itself. Even those historians whose sympathies were clearly on the side of revolution and who could not help writing the emergence of popular councils into the record of their story regarded them as nothing more than essentially temporary organs in the revolutionary struggle for liberation; that is to say, they failed to understand to what an extent the council system confronted them with an entirely new form of government, with a new public space for freedom which was constituted and organized during the course of the revolution itself.

This statement must be qualified. There are two relevant exceptions to it, namely a few remarks by Marx at the occasion of the revival of the Parisian Commune during the short-lived revolution of 1871, and some reflections by Lenin based not on the text by Marx, but on the actual course of the Revolution of 1905 in Russia. But before we turn our attention to these matters, we had better try to understand what Jefferson had in mind when he said with utmost self-assurance, "The wit of man cannot devise a more solid basis for a free, durable, and well-administered republic."[17]

It is perhaps noteworthy that we find no mention of the ward system in any of Jefferson's formal works, and it may be even more important that the few letters in which he wrote of it with such emphatic insistence all date from the last period of his life. It is true, at one time he hoped that Virginia, because it was "the first of the nations of the earth which assembled its wise men peaceably together to form a fundamental constitution," would also be the first "to adopt the subdivision of our counties into wards,"[18] but the point of the matter is that the whole idea seems to have occurred to him only at a time when he himself was retired from public life and when he had withdrawn from the affairs of state. He who had been so explicit in his criticism of the Constitution because it had not incorporated a Bill of Rights, never touched on its failure to incorporate the townships which so obviously were the original models of his "elementary republics" where "the voice of the whole people would be fairly, fully, and peaceably expressed, discussed, and decided by the common reason" of all citizens.[19] In terms of his own role in the affairs of his country and the outcome of the Revolution, the idea of the ward system clearly was an afterthought; and, in terms of his own biographical development, the repeated insistence on the "peaceable" character of these wards demonstrates that this system was to him the only possible non-violent alternative to his earlier notions about the desirability of recurring revolutions. At any event, we find the only detailed descriptions of what he had in mind in letters written in the year 1816, and these letters repeat rather than supplement one another.

Jefferson himself knew well enough that what he proposed as the "salvation of the republic" actually was the salvation of the revolutionary spirit through the republic. His expositions of the ward system always began with a reminder of how "the vigor given to our revolution in its commencement" was due to the "little republics," how they had "thrown the whole nation into energetic action," and how, at a later occasion, he had felt "the foundations of the government shaken under [his] feet by the New England townships," "the energy of this organization" being so great that "there was not an individual in their States whose body was not thrown with all its momentum into action." Hence, he expected the wards to permit the citizens to continue to do what they had been able to do during the years of revolution, namely, to act on their own and thus to participate in public business as it was being transacted from day to day. By virtue of the Constitution, the public business of the nation as a whole had been transferred to Washington and was being transacted by the federal government, of which Jefferson still thought as "the foreign branch" of the republic, whose domestic affairs were taken care of by the state governments.[20] But state government and even the administrative machinery of the country were by far too large and unwieldy to permit immediate participation; in all these institutions, it was the delegates of the people rather than the people themselves who constituted the public realm, whereas those who delegated them and who, theoretically, were the source and the seat of power remained forever outside its doors. This order of things should have sufficed if Jefferson had actually believed (as he sometimes professed) that the happiness of the people lay exclusively in their private welfare; for because of the way the government of the union was constituted—with its division and separation of powers, with controls, checks and balances, built into its very center—it was highly unlikely, though of course not impossible, that a tyranny could arise out of it. What could happen, and what indeed has happened over and over again since, was that "the representative organs should become corrupt and perverted,"[21] but such corruption was not likely to be due (and hardly ever has been due) to a conspiracy of the representative organs against the people whom they represented. Corruption in this kind of government is much more likely to spring from the midst of society, that is, from the people themselves.

Corruption and perversion are more pernicious, and at the same time more likely to occur, in an egalitarian republic than in any other form of government. Schematically speaking, they come to pass when private interests invade the public domain, that is, they spring from below and not from above. It is precisely because the republic excluded on principle the old dichotomy of ruler and ruled that corruption of the body politic did not leave the people untouched, as in other forms of government, where only the rulers or the ruling classes needed to be affected, and where therefore an "innocent" people might indeed first suffer and then, one day, effect a dreadful but necessary insurrection. Corruption of the people themselves—as distinguished from corruption of their representatives or a ruling class—is possible only under a government that has granted them a share in public power and has taught them how to manipulate it. Where the rift between ruler and ruled has been closed, it is always possible that the dividing line between public and private may become blurred and, eventually, obliterated. Prior to the modern age and the rise of society, this danger, inherent in republican government, used to arise from the public realm, from the tendency of public power to expand and to trespass upon private interests. The age-old remedy against this danger was respect for private property, that is, the framing of a system of laws through which the rights of privacy were publicly guaranteed and the dividing line between public and private legally protected. The Bill of Rights in the American Constitution forms the last, and the most exhaustive, legal bulwark for the private realm against public power, and Jefferson's preoccupation with the dangers of public power and this remedy against them is sufficiently well known. However, under conditions, not of prosperity as such, but of a rapid and constant economic growth, that is, of a constantly increasing expansion of the private realm—and these were of course the conditions of the modern age—the dangers of corruption and perversion were much more likely to arise from private interests than from public power. And it speaks for the high caliber of Jefferson's statesmanship that he was able to perceive this danger despite his preoccupation with the older and better-known threats of corruption in bodies politic.

The only remedies against the misuse of public power by private individuals lie in the public realm itself, in the light which exhibits each deed enacted within its boundaries, in the very visibility to which it exposes all those who enter it. Jefferson, though the secret vote was still unknown at the time, had at least a foreboding of how dangerous it might be to allow the people a share in public power without providing them at the same time with more public space than the ballot box and with more opportunity to make their voices heard in public than election day. What he perceived to be the mortal danger to the republic was that the Constitution had given all power to the citizens, without giving them the opportunity of *being* republicans and of *acting* as citizens. In other words, the danger was that all power had been given to the people in their private capacity, and that there was no space established for them in their capacity of being citizens. When, at the end of his life, he summed up what to him clearly was the gist of private and public morality, "Love your neighbor as yourself, and your country more than yourself,"[22] he knew that this maxim remained an empty exhortation unless the "country" could be made as present to the "love" of its citizens as the "neighbor" was to the love of his fellow men. For just as there could not be much substance to neighborly love if one's neighbor should make a brief apparition once every two years, so there could not be much substance to the admonition to love one's country more than oneself unless the country was a living presence in the midst of its citizens.

Hence, according to Jefferson, it was the very principle of republican government to demand "the subdivision of the counties into wards," namely, the creation of "small republics" through which "every man in the State" could become "an acting member of the Common government, transacting in person a great portion of its rights and duties, subordinate indeed, yet important, and entirely within his competence."[23] It was "these little republics [that] would be the main strength of the great one";[24] for inasmuch as the republican government of the Union was based on the assumption that the seat of power was in the people, the very condition for its proper functioning lay in a scheme "to divide [government] among the many, distributing to every one exactly the functions he [was] competent to." Without this the very principle of republican government could never be actualized, and the government of the United States would be republican in name only.

Thinking in terms of the safety of the republic, the question was how to prevent "the degeneracy of our government," and Jefferson called every government degenerate in which all powers were concentrated "in the hands of the one, the few, the well-born or the many." Hence, the ward system was not meant to strengthen the power of the many but the power of "every one" within the limits of his competence; and only by breaking up "the many" into assemblies where every one could count and be counted upon "shall we be as republican as a large society can be." In terms of the safety of the citizens of the republic, the question was how to make everybody feel "that he is a participator in the government of affairs, not merely at an election one day in the year, but every day; when there shall not be a man in the State who will not be a member of some one of its councils, great or small, he will let the heart be torn out of his body sooner than his power wrested from him by a Caesar or a Bonaparte." Finally, as to the question of how to integrate these smallest organs, designed for everyone, into the governmental structure of the Union, designed for all, his answer was: "The elementary republics of the wards, the county republics, the State republics, and the republic of the Union would form a gradation of authorities, standing each on the basis of law, holding every one its delegated share of powers, and constituting truly a system of fundamental balances and checks for the government." On one point, however, Jefferson remained curiously silent, and that is the question of what the specific functions of the elementary republics should be. He mentioned occasionally as "one of the advantages of the ward divisions I have proposed" that they would offer a better way to collect the voice of the people than the mechanics of representative government; but in the main, he was convinced that if one would "begin them only for a single purpose" they would "soon show for what others they [were] the best instruments."[25]

This vagueness of purpose, far from being due to a lack of clarity, indicates perhaps more tellingly than any other single aspect of Jefferson's proposal that the afterthought in which he clarified and gave substance to his most cherished recollections from the Revolution in fact concerned a new form of government rather than a mere reform of it or a mere supplement to the existing institutions. If the ultimate end of revolution was freedom and the constitution of a public space where freedom could appear, the *constitutio libertatis*, then the elementary republics of the wards, the only tangible place where everyone could be free, actually were the end of the great republic whose chief purpose in domestic affairs should have been to provide the people with such places of freedom and to protect them. The basic assumption of the ward system, whether Jefferson knew it or not was that no one could be called happy without his share in public happiness, that no one could be called free without his experience in public freedom, and that no one could be called either happy or free without participating, and having a share, in public power.

Notes

1 Thus Jefferson in a letter to William Hunter, March 11, 1790.

2 In a letter to Samuel Kercheval, July 12, 1816.

3 The two quotations from Paine are from *Common Sense* and the *Rights of Man*, respectively.

4 In the famous letter to Major John Cartwright, June 5, 1824.

5 The much-quoted words occur in a letter from Paris to Colonel William Stephens Smith, November 13, 1787.

6 In later years, especially after he had adopted the ward system as "the article nearest to my heart," Jefferson was much more likely to speak of "the dreadful necessity" of insurrection. (See especially his letter to Samuel Kercheval, September 5, 1816). To blame this shift of emphasis—for it is not much more—on the changed mood of a much older man seems unjustified in view of the fact that Jefferson thought of his ward system as the only possible alternative to what otherwise would be a necessity, however dreadful.

7 In this and the following paragraph, I am again quoting from Jefferson's letter to Samuel Kercheval, July 12, 1816.

8 See Emerson's *Journal*, 1853.

9 See Lewis Mumford's *The City in History*, New York, 1961, pp. 328 ff.

10 William S. Carpenter, *The Development of American Political Thought*, Princeton, 1930, pp. 43–47, notes the divergence between the English and colonial theories of the time with respect to representation. In England, with Algernon Sidney and Burke, "the idea was growing that after the representatives have been returned and had taken their seats in the House of Commons they ought not any longer to have a dependence upon those they represented." In America, on the contrary, "the right of the people to instruct their representatives [was] a distinguishing characteristic of the colonial theory of representation." In support, Carpenter quotes from a contemporary Pennsylvanian source: "The right of instruction lies with the constituents and them only, that the representatives are bound to regard them as the dictates of their masters and are not left at liberty to comply with them or reject them as they may think proper."

11 Quoted from Carpenter, op. cit., pp. 93–94. Present-day representatives, of course, have not found it any easier to read the minds and sentiments of those whom they represent. "The politician himself never knows what his constituents want him to do. He cannot take the continuous polls necessary to discover what they want government to do." He even has great doubts that such wants exist at all. For "in effect, he expects electoral success from promising to satisfy desires which he himself created." See C. W. Cassinelli, *The Politics of Freedom: An Analysis of the Modern Democratic State*, Seattle, 1961, pp. 41 and 45–46.

12 Carpenter, op. cit., p. 103.

13 This, of course, is Jefferson's opinion of the matter which he expounded chiefly in letters. See especially the previously mentioned letter to W. S. Smith, November 13, 1787. About the "exercise of virtuous dispositions" and of "moral feelings," he writes very interestingly in an early letter to Robert Skipwith on August 3, 1771. It is for him primarily an exercise in imagination, hence the great taskmasters of such exercises are the poets rather than the historians, since "the fictitious murder of Duncan by Macbeth in Shakespeare" excites in us "as great a horror of villainy, as the real one of Henry IV." It is through the poets that "the field of imagination is laid open to our use," a field that, if confined to real life, would contain too few memorable events and

acts—history's "lessons would be too infrequent"; at any event, "a lively and lasting sense of filial duty is more effectually impressed on the mind of a son or daughter by reading *King Lear*, than by all the dry volumes of ethics and divinity that ever were written."

14 In a letter to Colonel Edward Carrington, January 16, 1787.

15 In the letter to John Cartwright, June 5, 1824.

16 This quotation is from a slightly earlier period when Jefferson proposed to divide the counties "into hundreds." (See letter to John Tyler, May 26, 1810.) Clearly, the wards he had in mind were to consist of about a hundred men.

17 Letter to Cartwright, quoted previously.

18 Ibid.

19 Letter to Samuel Kercheval, July 12, 1816.

20 The citations are drawn from the letters just quoted.

21 Letter to Samuel Kercheval, September 5, 1816.

22 Letter to Thomas Jefferson Smith, February 21, 1825.

23 Letter to Cartwright, quoted previously.

24 Letter to John Tyler, quoted previously.

25 The citations are drawn from the letter to Joseph C. Cabell of February 2, 1816, and from the two letters to Samuel Kercheval already quoted.

Bicameralism From Below

Staughton Lynd

This essay, part of a draft of a larger work, expresses Staughton
Lynd's contention that communal self-government is deeply rooted in
America's social and intellectual traditions. Someone was bound to discover that today's radicals are really traditionalists. Notice that Tom
Paine's example of effective organization without central government is
similar in nature to the one put forward by Prince Kropotkin as recounted
in Paul Goodman's essay in this section. Lynd, deeply involved in the
affairs of the New Left, has written perceptive articles on its development
and its goal of communities with more effective citizen participation.

I have been developing the thesis that there found its way into the
Declaration of Independence—along with a wholly bourgeois picture of
society, descending from Harrington and Locke—an essentially religious
vision of a covenanted community under the law of God. Originating in
the Radical Reformation of the sixteenth century, this vision was translated
into eighteenth-century terms by non-Anglican Protestants such as Price,
Paine and Woolman. Later, when radical abolitionists appealed to the
authority of the Declaration, it was to this vision as interpreted by these
men that they appealed.

I have argued previously that the American revolutionary tradition
had close ties to the revolutionary experience of continental Europe. It
began with a concept of freedom which it shared with Rousseau, and
culminated in a critique of capitalist acquisition and the nation-state
shared with Marx. All variants of this transnational body of belief agreed
that human powers had been "alienated" by society, and that nature intended men to reclaim them.

I

What kind of society did the exponents of the revolutionary tradition
want? In general, they rejected "government" in the name of "society."

From Staughton Lynd, "Bicameralism From Below," *Liberation* (July 1967), pp.
15–19. Reprinted by permission of *Liberation* and the author.

But unlike laissez-faire liberalism which it superficially resembled, the revolutionary tradition did not see freedom and fraternity as contradictory goals. The "government" rejected was national. Self-government in the sense of communal decision-making at a local level was considered, even by Godwin and Thoreau, as the condition for other freedoms. The revolutionary tradition, moreover, took as its point of departure not property but conscience, and imagined that free men might manage their economic affairs in the manner of a family rather than on the model of a market.

LOCAL INSTITUTIONS

In the American tradition, too, rebellion against inherited authorities was not mere "anti-institutionalism." Implicit, sometimes explicit, in the American revolutionary tradition was a dream of the good society as a voluntary federation of local communal institutions, perpetually recreated from below by what Paul Goodman calls "a continuous series of existential constitutional acts."

The models for radical American imaginings of a good society were English and American local institutions that combined sacred and secular functions: the parish, the congregation, the town meeting. Anglo-American utopianism from the seventeenth to the nineteenth centuries consistently gravitated to these homely exemplars. Gerard Winstanley, with his belief that "there cannot be a universal libertie, til . . . universal communitie be established," desired "that the People in a Parish may generally meet together to see one another's faces, and beget or preserve fellowship in friendly love." Winstanley's Buckinghamshire followers accordingly demanded

the government to be by Judges, called Elders, men fearing God and hating covetousness; Those to be chosen by the people, and to end all controversies in every Town and Hamlet, without any other or further trouble or charge.

The Levellers, similarly, proposed "to erect a court of justice in every hundred in the nation, for the ending of differences arising in that hundred, by twelve men of the same hundred annually chosen by freemen of that hundred," and the popular election of "mayors, sheriffs, justices of the peace, deputy lieutenants, etc. . . . in case there be any need, after the erection of hundred courts." An attenuated echo of this custom of neighborhood arbitration was heard at the Constitutional Convention of 1787, when Franklin described how members of the Society of Friends settled their differences through committees of their Meetings without going to court.

It was still of parishes that Paine and Godwin spoke when they put forth their plans for a better England in the 1790's. Proposing as one part of his elaborate scenario for welfare spending in "The Rights of Man" that every poor family receive a supplement to assist in the education of its children, Paine suggested that "the ministers of every parish, of every denomination" administer the fund. Sketching the outlines of a still more radical scheme for French land reform in "Agrarian Justice," Paine advised that "each canton shall elect in its primary assemblies, three persons, as commissioners for that canton, who shall take cognizance, and keep a register of all matters happening in that canton," and administer property inheritance.

Godwin, too, proceeded on the assumption that "neighbours are best informed of each other's concerns, and are perfectly equal to their adjustment." It followed that government should be decentralized to the district or parish. The districts should "make laws for themselves, without intervention of the national assembly" so that "political power is brought home to the citizens and simplified into something of the nature of a parish regulation." General laws would be unnecessary for these small-scale governments, since "the inhabitants of a small parish, living with some degree of that simplicity which best corresponds to the real nature and wants of a human being, would soon be led to suspect that general laws were unnecessary."

American radicals more often invoked the town meeting, lineal descendant of the English parish. Jefferson urged his native state to subdivide its counties into townships or "wards" similar to the towns of New England. These new bodies would administer the laying out of highways, public elementary education, poor relief, and other matters "relating to themselves exclusively." Supplanting the oligarchical authority of justices of the peace, the townships would give "every citizen, personally, a part in the administration of public affairs."

Abolitionists, as they built the mighty engine of "self-constituted" abolition societies, expressed similar confidence in the town-meeting prototype. Even Thoreau declared himself ready to pay the local highway tax, "because I am as desirous of being a good neighbor as I am of being a bad subject," and maintained that "when, in some obscure country town, the farmers come together to a special town meeting, to express their opinion on some subject which is vexing the land, that, I think, is the true Congress, and the most respectable one that is ever assembled in the United States." He delivered his celebrated defense of John Brown to just such a special town meeting.

SELF-GOVERNING COMMUNITY AS UTOPIA

One of the most systematic presentations of the town meeting as Utopia came from the New England non-resistant, Adin Ballou. "When we get beyond our common Town and Municipal officials, who for the most part render much useful service for small pecuniary compensation,"

Ballou wrote, government was hardly necessary. It might "triumphantly dispense with its army, navy, militia, capital punishment," and make room for "reconstructed neighborhood society by voluntary association." Echoing Winstanley and Godwin, and anticipating Lenin's *State and Revolution*, Ballou affirmed that if in such a social state an occasional individual "broke over the bounds of decency, the whole force of renovated public sentiment would surround and press in upon him like the waters of the ocean."

The vision of a decentralized network of self-governing communities continued to dominate the speculations of late nineteenth-century American radicals. Lawrence Gronlund, for instance, proposed a "co-operative commonwealth" which rejected "the whole system of representation." Political parties, appointments from above, and checks and balances, would be abolished. State and society would become synonymous. All laws would be passed by referendum, as first proposed by Robespierre. All public functionaries would be elected (letter carriers would elect postmasters) and hold office during good behavior. "Anybody can now construct a Socialist administration in his imagination as well as we can," Gronlund remarked,

> if he will only bear in mind that all appointments are to be made from below; that the directors are to stay in office as long as they give satisfaction and not longer; and that all laws and regulations of a general nature must be ratified by those immediately interested.

Edward Bellamy, his reputation as a planophile notwithstanding, imagined in his book *Equality* a new society which "greatly diminished the amount of governing." The representative government of late nineteenth-century America was a "negative democracy," a "pseudo-republic," a "sham democracy": "the period might be compared to the minority of a king, during which the royal power is abused by wicked stewards." The new society would institutionalize the initiative, referendum and recall. Representative bodies would function like congressional committees, responsible to the people at large. Citizens would vote perhaps a hundred times in a year. Recurring to the famous image in *Looking Backward* of capitalist society as a coach groaning upward in which the rich man sat at ease, Bellamy said that the government of the future would operate in the spirit of a wealthy man who liked to drive the coach himself.

PRE—WORLD WAR I FERMENT

There was a resurgence of such thinking in the generation just before the First World War, when a current of speculation about post-capitalist society swept through America and Western Europe. During those years thinkers as different as Rosa Luxemburg and Robert LaFollette shared a concern to promote what has since been called "participatory democracy." Between those extremes, men and movements such as G. D. H. Cole, the young Harold Laski, the Industrial Workers of the World, French Syndicalism and English Guild Socialism sought to envision a modern industrial society which would simultaneously enable the people to control their economy and decentralize the operations of the bureaucratic state.

That intellectual moment is of particular importance because Marxists and "bourgeois democrats" shared a concern to make politics more democratic, whether through workers' councils—the "soviet," originally, was simply a central trade union of all workingmen in a locality—or through initiative, referendum and recall. Marx's idealization of the union of legislative and executive powers in the Paris Commune inspired one strand of this thought, paralleling the persistent reversion of American radicals to the town meeting as an exemplar.

The American thinkers who sought most creatively to develop the traditions which Marxism and native American radicalism share were, in my opinion, Thorstein Veblen and W. E. B. DuBois. Both these great outsiders—the son of Norwegian immigrants who did not speak English well until he reached college, the Negro who ended his life as a citizen of Ghana—studied philosophy before they became social scientists. Both interested themselves particularly in Kant, the philosopher who had systematized the insights of Price and Rousseau. Veblen's doctoral dissertation on Kant's theory of retribution, DuBois reading *The Critique of Pure Reason* in an attic room of Cambridge with William James, are two more illustrations of the fact that in a surprisingly strict and technical sense the American radical tradition has been based on a philosophy of free will. Consistently, its standpoint has been the self-determining human protagonist rather than the impinging environment. For all his awareness of social conditioning, Veblen followed James and Dewey in insisting that man was an active agent. Similarly, DuBois, although he died a Communist, never abandoned the philosophical idealism of his teachers James and Royce.

Neither man saw community as a threat to freedom. DuBois hoped that Afro-Americans could transfer to this country "the communalism of the African clan." Veblen shared Marx's affection for primitive communism, as in his description of those peaceable "savage" communities characterized by a "certain amiable inefficiency when confronted with force or fraud." Characteristically, he reserved his most passionate advocacy of that way of life for an appendix to a book on another subject. Here he praised the old Scandinavian "small-scale, half-anarchistic, neighborhood plan of society," a "conventionally systematized anarchy regulated by common sense" in which justice meant a readiness to "live and let live" and "no public authority and no legally concerted action ordinarily is called in to redress grievances." These little Utopias had been destroyed by technological advance. But ever since men passed the technological limit of tolerance of that archaic scheme of use and wont they have been restlessly casting back for some workable compromise that would permit their ideal of "local self-government" by neighborly common sense to live somehow in the shadow of the large-scale coercive rule that killed it.

II

A natural question arises as to whether the good society envisioned by Winstanley and Lilburne, Paine and Godwin, Ballou and Thoreau, Gronlund and Veblen—a league of self-governing fraternities, a national association of congregations concerned not only (if at all) with religion but with all the affairs of life—is hopelessly utopian.

The American Revolution provides a working model for an answer. In 1775–1776 Americans dismembered and overthrew their government. Whether the American War for Independence was also an American revolution is debatable if one looks to the war's effect on American economy or society: slavery, for example, was left essentially undisturbed. But if revolution is defined in its simplest sense, as the overthrow of constituted authority, a revolution obviously occurred. Not only was the jurisdiction of the British government rejected, but in each of the thirteen colonies old political institutions lost their authority and new ones—committees of safety and correspondence, provincial conventions—took power.

RULE BY LOCAL COMMITTEES

It was primarily the work of these committees that convinced Tom Paine that most of what central governments did could better be done by autonomous local bodies. "For upward of two years from the commencement of the American War, and for a longer period in several of the American states," Paine wrote, "there were no established forms of government. The old governments had been abolished, and the country was too much occupied in defense, to employ its attention in establishing new governments; yet during this interval, order and harmony were preserved as inviolate as in any country of Europe."

The American Revolution suggests that decentralized, self-governing institutions of the kind idealized by American revolutionaries of the past (and present) tend to emerge spontaneously in revolutionary situations. When masses of people are drawn into resistance to oppressive authorities, institutions more accessible to those masses will arise of their own accord. They will arise not because someone envisions them beforehand or desires their appearance on grounds of abstract principle; but because they are necessary. "Common interest," as Paine said, "produces common security." Characteristically, such institutions will be open to anyone who wants to come, not merely authorized representatives, and will in fact take their tone from the physical presence of "the mob." So it was with the French National Assembly, when the common people of the Paris "sections" invaded the galleries; or with the Petrograd Soviet, where (according to John Reed) workingmen debated until exhausted, slept in the halls, then returned to the continuous process of decision making; or with the Boston Town Meeting, in which, so British officials complained, men voted who had no legal right to.

The democratic movement in the American Revolution has usually been associated with the demand for single-chamber legislatures. What the ad hoc bodies of the Revolution signified, however, was the additional insistence that the best of legislatures be continually checked and guided by "the people out of doors," acting through new institutions of their own devising. This was a demand not simply for an end to conventional bicameralism, but for what might perhaps be termed "bicameralism from below."

This process is not inconsistent with the recognition, emphasized by recent scholarship, that the character of the Revolution was defensive. In fact most revolutions, including the French Revolution of 1789, are at the outset not aggressive attempts to achieve something new but efforts to defend what already exists. But in our revolution as in so many others, the mob called onto the stage as puppets remained as protagonists, the institutions devised to transmit orders from above began to send up orders from below, old families found themselves thrust out of places of leadership in favor of "new men," and the words of the revolution's manifesto began to quiver with new meanings.

BICAMERALISM FROM BELOW

The process of revolution begins when, by demonstrations or strikes or electoral victories in the context of supplementary direct action, the way a society makes its decisions is forced to change. This is something very real even when the beginnings are small. It means, not just that a given decision is different in substance, but that the process of decision making becomes more responsive to the ordinarily inarticulate. New faces appear in the group that makes the decision, alternatives are publicly discussed in advance, more bodies have to be consulted. As the revolutionary situation deepens, the broadening of the decision-making process becomes institutionalized. Alongside the customary structure of authority, parallel bodies —organs of "dual power," as Trotsky called them—arise. All that had been closed and mysterious in the procedure of the parent institution becomes open and visible in the workings of its counterpart. Decision makers, appointed to the former, are elected to the latter. Parallel bodies in different communities begin to communicate, to devise means of coordination: a new structure of representation develops out of direct democracy and controlled by it. Suddenly, in whole parts of the country and in entire areas of daily life, it becomes apparent that people are obeying the new organs of authority rather than the old ones. Finally, an act or a series of acts of legitimation occur: ad hoc committees lay down their powers, submit to reelection, are given new names. The challenge becomes the building into the new society of something of that sense of shared purpose and of tangibly shaping a common destiny which characterized the revolution at its most intense.

Of course, such institutional improvisation is made easier if there are pre-existing organizations of the poor. Thus in England, when Elizabethan Puritans abandoned their first hope of reorganizing the national church immediately, they were nevertheless able to go a "longer way around" to revolution by organizing on the basis of "household discussion and education" and "congregational independency." When the revolution ultimately did come about in the 1640's, the Baptist congregations of London ratified the Leveller manifestoes and the soldiers of the New Model Army drew on their experience of religious organization to throw up a network of "agitators" to enforce their demands. E. P. Thompson writes of the similar apparent quiescence of early eighteenth-century Dissenters: "the resolution of the sects to 'patiently suffer from the world' while abstaining from the hope of attaining to its 'Rule and Government' enabled them to combine political quietism with a kind of slumbering Radicalism—preserved in the imagery of sermons and tracts and in democratic forms of organization— which might, in any more hopeful context, break into fire once more." And in the Industrial Revolution, according to the Hammonds, Methodist congregations served English workingmen as improvised schools where they might learn the skills of chairmanship and public speaking required to build trade unions.

In our own time, Negro Baptist congregations in the American South served in the same way as organizational nuclei for the civil-rights revolt.

III

What, therefore, calls for final emphasis is the fact that "bicameralism from below" is not simply a Utopian vision but a means of struggle toward that vision.

The intellectual origins of the American radical tradition were rooted in men's efforts to make a way of life at once free and communal. What held together these dissenters from the capitalist consensus was more than ideology; it was also the daily practice of libertarian and fraternal attitudes in institutions of their own making. The clubs, the unorthodox congregations, the fledgling trade unions were the tangible means, in theological language the "words," by means of which revolutionaries kept alive their faith that men could live together in a radically different way. In times of crisis resistance turned into revolution; the underground congregation burst forth as a model for the Kingdom of God on earth, and an organ of secular "dual power."

The revolutionary tradition is more than words and more than isolated acts. Men create, maintain and rediscover a tradition of struggle by the crystallization of ideas and actions into organizations which they make for themselves. Parallel to Leviathan, the Kingdom is dreamed; discussed; in miniscule form, established. Within the womb of the old society—it is Marx's metaphor—the new society is born.

Notes on Democracy

H. L. Mencken

Our final selection in this section is by a man who found democracy "charming" and hilarious. "I enjoy democracy immensely. It is incomparably idiotic, and hence incomparably amusing." Such caustic comments could come from none other than H. L. Mencken, who, as the following selection makes clear, saw representative democracy as rather incompetent but thought direct democracy would be no improvement.

I

THE TWO KINDS OF DEMOCRACY

The lowly Christian I have limned is not only the glory of democratic states, but also their boss. Sovereignty is in him, sometimes both actually and legally, but always actually. Whatever he wants badly enough, he can get. If he is misled by mountebanks and swindled by scoundrels it is only because his credulity and imbecility cover a wider area than his simple desires. The precise form of the government he suffers under is of small importance. Whether it be called a constitutional monarchy, as in England, or a representative republic, as in France, or a pure democracy, as in some of the cantons of Switzerland, it is always essentially the same. There is, first, the mob, theoretically and in fact the ultimate judge of all ideas and the source of all power. There is, second, the camorra of self-seeking minorities, each seeking to inflame, delude and victimize it. The political process thus becomes a mere battle of rival rogues. But the mob remains quite free to decide between them. It may even, under the hand of God, decide for a minority that happens, by some miracle, to be relatively honest and enlightened. If, in common practice, it sticks to the thieves, it is only because their words are words it understands and their ideas are ideas it cherishes. It has the power to throw them off at will, and even at whim, and it also has the means.

A great deal of paper and ink has been wasted discussing the differ-

---

From *Notes on Democracy* by H. L. Mencken, pp. 71–78. Copyright 1926 by Alfred A. Knopf, Inc. and renewed 1954 by H. L. Mencken. Reprinted by permission of the publisher.

ence between representative government and direct democracy. The theme is a favorite one with university pundits, and also engages and enchants the stall-fed Rousseaus who arise intermittently in the cow States, and occasionally penetrate to Governors' mansions and the United States Senate. It is generally held that representative government, as practically encountered in the world, is full of defects, some of them amounting to organic disease. Not only does it take the initiative in law-making out of the hands of the plain people, and leave them only the function of referees; it also raises certain obvious obstacles to their free exercise of that function. Scattered as they are, and unorganized save in huge, unworkable groups, they are unable, it is argued, to formulate their virtuous desires quickly and clearly, or to bring to the resolution of vexed questions the full potency of their native sagacity. Worse, they find it difficult to enforce their decisions, even when they have decided. Every Liberal knows this sad story, and has shed tears telling it. The remedy he offers almost always consists of a resort to what he calls a purer democracy. That is to say, he proposes to set up the recall, the initiative and referendum, or something else of the sort, and so convert the representative into a mere clerk or messenger. The final determination of all important public questions, he argues, ought to be in the hands of the voters themselves. They alone can muster enough wisdom for the business, and they alone are without guile. The cure for the evils of democracy is more democracy.

All this, of course, is simply rhetoric. Every time anything of the kind is tried it fails ingloriously. Nor is there any evidence that it has ever succeeded elsewhere, to-day or in the past. Certainly no competent historian believes that the citizens assembled in a New England town-meeting actually formulated *en masse* the transcendental and immortal measures that they adopted, nor even that they contributed anything of value to the discussion thereof. The notion is as absurd as the parallel notion, long held by philologues of defective powers of observation, that the popular ballads surviving from earlier ages were actually composed by the folk. The ballads, in point of fact, were all written by concrete poets, most of them not of the folk; the folk, when they had any hand in the business at all, simply acted as referees, choosing which should survive. In exactly the same way the New England town-meeting was led and dominated by a few men of unusual initiative and determination, some of them genuinely superior, but most of them simply demagogues and fanatics. The citizens in general heard the discussion of rival ideas, and went through the motions of deciding between them, but there is no evidence that they ever had all the relevant facts before them or made any effort to unearth them, or that appeals to their reason always, or even usually, prevailed over appeals to their mere prejudice and superstition. Their appetite for logic, I venture, seldom got the better of their fear of hell, and the Beatitudes moved them far less powerfully than blood. Some of the most idiotic decisions ever come to by mortal man were made by the New England town-meetings, and under the leadership of monomaniacs who are still looked upon as ineffable blossoms of the contemporary *Kultur*.

The truth is that the difference between representative democracy and direct democracy is a great deal less marked than political sentimentalists assume. Under both forms the sovereign mob must employ agents to execute its will, and in either case the agents may have ideas of their own, based upon interests of their own, and the means at hand to do and get what they will. Moreover, their very position gives them a power of influencing the electors that is far above that of any ordinary citizen: they become politicians *ex officio*, and usually end by selling such influence as remains after they have used all they need for their own ends. Worse, both forms of democracy encounter the difficulty that the generality of citizens, no matter how assiduously they may be instructed, remain congenitally unable to comprehend many of the problems before them, or to consider all of those they do comprehend in an unbiased and intelligent manner. Thus it is often impossible to ascertain their views in advance of action, or even, in many cases, to determine their conclusions *post hoc*. The voters gathered in a typical New England town-meeting were all ardent amateurs of theology, and hence quite competent, in theory, to decide the theological questions that principally engaged them; nevertheless, history shows that they were led facilely by professional theologians, most of them quacks with something to sell. In the same way, the great masses of Americans of to-day, though they are theoretically competent to decide all the larger matters of national policy, and have certain immutable principles, of almost religious authority, to guide them, actually look for leading to professional politicians, who are influenced in turn by small but competent and determined minorities, with special knowledge and special interests. It was thus that the plain people were shoved into the late war, and it is thus that they will be shoved into the next one. They were, in overwhelming majority, against going in, and if they had had any sense and resolution they would have stayed out. But these things they lacked.

II

THE POPULAR WILL

Thus there is no need to differentiate too pedantically between the two forms of democratic government, for their unlikeness is far more apparent than real. Nor is there any need to set up any distinction between the sort of democracy that is met with in practice, with its constant conflicts between what is assumed to be the popular will and the self-interest of small but articulate and efficient groups, and that theoretical variety which would liberate and energize the popular will completely. The latter must remain purely theoretical for all time; there are insuperable impediments, solidly grounded in the common mind, to its realization. Moreover, there is no reason for believing that its realization, if it should ever be attained by miracle, would materially change the main outlines of the democratic process. What is genuinely important is not that the will of mankind in the mass should be formulated and made effective at all times and in every case, but simply that means should be provided for ascertaining and executing it in capital cases—that there shall be no immovable impediment to its execution when, by some prodigy of nature, it takes a coherent and apposite form. If, over and beyond that, a sufficient sense of its immanent and imminent potency remains to make politicians walk a bit warily, if the threat always hangs in the air that under x circumstances and on y day it may be heard from suddenly and devastatingly, then democracy is actually in being. This is the case, it seems to me, in the United States.

Chapter Three

Theory Into Practice

This section is a transition between Chapter Two, which concerned direct democracy in general, and later chapters, which examine it in specific contexts. These selections are about the efforts of proponents of direct involvement of the people to implement their ideas. The first selection is a historical case study on the evolution of Lenin's views about letting ordinary citizens run the government; the other articles deal with today's radicals.

In general, this section has a pessimistic air about it, because there are not very many examples of organizations or groups run effectively on participatory democracy principles. However, this situation is offset somewhat by the fact that the other sections present articles that are predominantly by supporters of such principles.

From the Port Huron Statement to the present, a consistent element in the demands of the New Left has been "Power to the People." This principle was reflected in key organizations like SDS and SNCC, which in their early years were rather amorphous, with no elaborate leadership structures, central headquarters, or staff. However, in recent years a bitter debate has broken out over whether to retain such organizational forms. Staughton Lynd, writing in 1968, found sentiment growing that it is too early for real democracy:

> Nonviolence and participatory democracy will exist in the good society created after the revolution, it is increasingly said. But the work of transformation requires tools suited to this age of blood and iron: insurrectionary violence and a Marxist-Leninist party.[1]

---

[1] "The New Left," *The Annals*, Vol. 382 (March 1969), 71.

Some persons are bound to question the feasibility of participatory democracy in theory if those most committed to it find it unsatisfactory in practice.

What Is to Replace the Smashed State Machine?

V. I. Lenin

The first two excerpts from Lenin's writings are from The State and
Revolution *and from his draft of a worker's control decree. These writings
date from the time of the Russian Revolution. The main points may be
briefly summarized as follows: The proletarian revolution makes possible
popular control of and participation in state administration. Capitalism
has reduced the tasks of administration to such an extent that ordinary
people can perform them for ordinary wages. The bureaucracy and the
state as a coercive apparatus will begin to wither away.*

The State and Revolution

WHAT IS TO REPLACE THE SMASHED STATE MACHINE?

In 1847, in the *Communist Manifesto*, Marx's answer to this question
was as yet a purely abstract one; to be exact, it was an answer that indicated
the tasks, but not the ways of accomplishing them. The answer given in
the *Communist Manifesto* was that this machine was to be replaced by
"the proletariat organized as the ruling class," by the "winning of the
battle of democracy."

Marx did not indulge in utopias; he expected the experience of the
mass movement to provide the reply to the question as to the specific
forms this organization of the proletariat as the ruling class would assume
and as to the exact manner in which this organization would be combined
with the most complete, most consistent "winning of the battle of
democracy."

Marx subjected the experience of the Commune, meager as it was, to
the most careful analysis in *The Civil War in France*. Let us quote the
most important passages of this work.

Originating from the Middle Ages, there developed in the nineteenth century "the centralized state power, with its ubiquitous organs of

---

Excerpts from V. I. Lenin, *Selected Works*, Vol. 2 (New York: International
Publishers, 1967), pp. 296–345, 474. Reprinted by permission of International Publishers Co., Inc. Copyright © 1967.

standing army, police, bureaucracy, clergy, and judicature." With the development of class antagonisms between capital and labor, "state power assumed more and more the character of a public force for the suppression of the working class, of a machine of class rule. After every revolution, which marks an advance in the class struggle, the purely coercive character of the state power stands out in bolder and bolder relief." After the revolution of 1848–49, state power became "the national war instrument of capital against labor." The Second Empire consolidated this.

"The direct antithesis to the empire was the Commune." It was the "specific form" of "a republic that was not only to remove the monarchical form of class rule, but class rule itself. . . .

What was this "specific" form of the proletarian, socialist republic? What was the state it began to create?

. . . The first decree of the Commune . . . was the suppression of the standing army, and its replacement by the armed people. . . .

This demand now figures in the program of every party calling itself socialist. The real worth of their programs, however, is best shown by the behavior of our Socialist-Revolutionaries and Mensheviks, who, right after the revolution of February 27, actually refused to carry out this demand!

The Commune was formed of the municipal councillors, chosen by universal suffrage in the various wards of Paris, responsible and revocable at any time. The majority of its members were naturally working men, or acknowledged representatives of the working class. . . . The police, which until then had been the instrument of the Government, was at once stripped of its political attributes, and turned into the responsible and at all times revocable instrument of the Commune. So were the officials of all other branches of the administration. From the members of the Commune downwards, public service had to be done at workmen's wages. The privileges and the representation allowances of the high dignitaries of state disappeared along with the dignitaries themselves. . . . Having once got rid of the standing army and the police, the instruments of the physical force of the old Government, the Commune proceeded at once to break the instrument of spiritual suppression, the power of the priests. . . . The judicial functionaries lost that sham independence . . . they were thenceforward to be elective, responsible, and revocable. . . .

The Commune, therefore, appears to have replaced the smashed state machine "only" by fuller democracy: abolition of the standing army; all officials to be elected and subject to recall. But as a matter of fact this "only" signifies a gigantic replacement of certain institutions by other institutions of a fundamentally different type. This is exactly a case of "quantity being transformed into quality": democracy, introduced as fully and consistently as is at all conceivable, is transformed from bourgeois into proletarian democracy; from the state (a special force for the suppression of a particular class) into something which is no longer the state proper.

It is still necessary to suppress the bourgeoisie and crush their resistance. This was particularly necessary for the Commune; and one of the reasons for its defeat was that it did not do this with sufficient determination. The organ of suppression, however, is here the majority of the population, and not a minority, as was always the case under slavery, serfdom and wage slavery. And since the majority of the people *itself* suppresses its oppressors, a "special force" for suppression *is no longer necessary!* In this sense, the state *begins to wither away.* Instead of the special institutions of a privileged minority (privileged officialdom, the chiefs of the standing army), the majority itself can directly fulfill all these functions, and the more the functions of state power are performed by the people as a whole, the less need there is for the existence of this power.

In this connection, the following measures of the Commune, emphasized by Marx, are particularly noteworthy: the abolition of all representation allowances, and of all monetary privileges to officials, the reduction of the remuneration of *all* servants of the state to the level of "*workmen's wages.*" This shows more clearly than anything else the *turn* from bourgeois to proletarian democracy, from the democracy of the oppressors to that of the oppressed classes, from the state as a "*special force*" for the suppression of a particular class to the suppression of the oppressors by the *general force* of the majority of the people—the workers and the peasants.

The reduction of the remuneration of high state officials seems to be "simply" a demand of naïve, primitive democracy. One of the "founders" of modern opportunism, the ex-Social Democrat Eduard Bernstein, has more than once repeated the vulgar bourgeois jeers at "primitive" democracy. Like all opportunists, and like the present Kautskyites, he did not understand at all that, first of all, the transition from capitalism to socialism is *impossible* without a certain "reversion" to "primitive" democracy (for how else can the majority, and then the whole population without exception, proceed to discharge state functions?); and that, secondly, "primitive democracy" based on capitalism and capitalist culture is not the same as primitive democracy in prehistoric or precapitalist times. Capitalist culture has created large-scale production, factories, railways, the postal service, telephones, etc., and on this basis the great majority of the functions of the old "state power" have become so simplified and can be reduced to such exceedingly simple operations of registration, filing and checking that they can be easily performed by every literate person, can quite easily be performed for ordinary "workmen's wages," and that these functions can (and must) be stripped of every shadow of privilege, of every semblance of "official grandeur."

All officials, without exception, elected and subject to recall *at any time,* their salaries reduced to the level of ordinary "workmen's wages"—

these simple and "self-evident" democratic measures, while completely uniting the interests of the workers and the majority of the peasants, at the same time serve as a bridge leading from capitalism to socialism. These measures concern the reorganization of the state, the purely political re-organization of society; but, of course, they acquire their full meaning and significance only in connection with the "expropriation of the expropri-ators" either being accomplished or in preparation, i.e., with the trans-formation of capitalist private ownership of the means of production into social ownership.

> "The Commune," Marx wrote, "made that catchword of all bour-geois revolutions, cheap government, a reality, by abolishing the two greatest sources of expenditure—the army and the officialdom."

From the peasants, as from other sections of the petty bourgeoisie, only an insignificant few "rise to the top," "get on in the world" in the bourgeois sense, i.e., become either well-to-do, bourgeois, or officials in secure and privileged positions. In every capitalist country where there are peasants (as there are in most capitalist countries), the vast majority of them are oppressed by the government and long for its overthrow, long for "cheap" government. This can be achieved *only* by the proletariat; and by achieving it, the proletariat at the same time takes a step towards the socialist reorganization of the state.

ABOLITION OF PARLIAMENTARISM

> "The Commune," Marx wrote, "was to be a working, not a parlia-mentary, body, executive and legislative at the same time. . . .
> "Instead of deciding once in three or six years which member of the ruling class was to represent and repress [verund zertreten] the people in parliament, universal suffrage was to serve the people constituted in communes, as individual suffrage serves every other employer in the search for workers, foremen and accountants for his business."

The way out of parliamentarism is not, of course, the abolition of representative institutions and the elective principle, but the conversion of the representative institutions from talking shops into "working" bodies. "The Commune was to be a working, not a parliamentary, body, executive and legislative at the same time."

"A working, not a parliamentary, body"—this is a blow straight from the shoulder at the present-day parliamentarians and parliamentary "lap dogs" of Social-Democracy! Take any parliamentary country, from America to Switzerland, from France to Britain, Norway and so forth—in these countries the real business of "state" is performed behind the scenes and is carried on by the departments, chancelleries and General Staffs. Parliament is given up to talk for the special purpose of fooling the "common people."

This is so true that even in the Russian republic, a bourgeois-democratic republic, all these sins of parliamentarism came out at once, even before it managed to set up a real parliament.

The Commune substituted for the venal and rotten parliamentarism of bourgeois society institutions in which freedom of opinion and discussion does not degenerate into deception, for the parliamentarians themselves have to work, have to execute their own laws, have themselves to test the results achieved in reality, and to account directly to their constituents. Representative institutions remain, but there is no parliamentarism here as a special system, as the division of labor between the legislative and the executive, as a privileged position for the deputies. We cannot imagine democracy, even proletarian democracy, without representative institutions, but we can and must imagine democracy without parliamentarism, if criticism of bourgeois society is not mere words for us, if the desire to overthrow the rule of the bourgeoisie is our earnest and sincere desire, and not a mere "election" cry for catching workers' votes.

Abolishing the bureaucracy at once, everywhere and completely, is out of the question. It is a utopia. But to smash the old bureaucratic machine at once and to begin immediately to construct a new one that will make possible the gradual abolition of all bureaucracy—this is not a utopia, it is the experience of the Commune, the direct and immediate task of the revolutionary proletariat.

Capitalism simplifies the functions of "state" administration; it makes it possible to cast "bossing" aside and to confine the whole matter to the organization of the proletarians (as the ruling class), which will hire "workers, foremen and accountants" in the name of the whole of society.

We are not utopians, we do not "dream" of dispensing at once with all administration, with all subordination. These anarchist dreams, based upon incomprehension of the tasks of the proletarian dictatorship, are totally alien to Marxism, and, as a matter of fact, serve only to postpone the socialist revolution until people are different. No, we want the socialist revolution with people as they are now, with people who cannot dispense with subordination, control and "foremen and accountants."

The subordination, however, must be to the armed vanguard of all the exploited and working people, i.e., to the proletariat. A beginning can and must be made at once, overnight, to replace the specific "bossing" of state officials by the simple functions of "foremen and accountants," functions which are already fully within the ability of the average town dweller and can well be performed for "workmen's wages."

We, the workers, shall organize large-scale production on the basis of what capitalism has already created, relying on our own experience as workers, establishing strict, iron discipline backed up by the state power of the armed workers. We shall reduce the role of state officials to that of simply carrying out our instructions as responsible, revocable, modestly paid "foremen and accountants" (of course, with the aid of technicians of all sorts, types and degrees). This is our proletarian task, this is what we can and must *start* with in accomplishing the proletarian revolution. Such a beginning, on the basis of large-scale production, will of itself lead to the gradual "withering away" of all bureaucracy, to the gradual creation of an order—an order without inverted commas, an order bearing no similarity to wage slavery—an order under which the functions of control and accounting, becoming more and more simple, will be performed by each in turn, will then become a habit and will finally die out as the *special* functions of a special section of the population.

A witty German Social-Democrat of the seventies of the last century called the *postal service* an example of the socialist economic system. This is very true. At present the postal service is a business organized on the lines of a state-*capitalist* monopoly. Imperialism is gradually transforming all trusts into organizations of a similar type, in which, standing over the "common" people, who are overworked and starved, one has the same bourgeois bureaucracy. But the mechanism of social management is here already to hand. Once we have overthrown the capitalists, crushed the resistance of these exploiters with the iron hand of the armed workers, and smashed the bureaucratic machine of the modern state, we shall have a splendidly-equipped mechanism, freed from the "parasite," a mechanism which can very well be set going by the united workers themselves, who will hire technicians, foremen and accountants, and pay them *all*, as indeed *all* "state" officials in general, workmen's wages. Here is a concrete, practical task which can immediately be fulfilled in relation to all trusts, a task whose fulfillment will rid the working people of exploitation, a task which takes account of what the Commune had already begun to practice (particularly in building up the state).

To organize the *whole* economy on the lines of the postal service so that the technicians, foremen and accountants, as well as *all* officials, shall receive salaries no higher than "a workman's wage," all under the control and leadership of the armed proletariat—this is our immediate aim. This is the state and this is the economic foundation we need. This is what will bring about the abolition of parliamentarism and the preservation of representative institutions. This is what will rid the laboring classes of the bourgeoisie's prostitution of these institutions.

THE TRANSITION FROM CAPITALISM TO COMMUNISM

Marx continued:

Between capitalist and communist society lies the period of the revolutionary transformation of the one into the other. Corresponding to this is also a political transition period in which the state can be nothing but *the revolutionary dictatorship of the proletariat.*

Marx bases this conclusion on an analysis of the role played by the proletariat in modern capitalist society, on the data concerning the development of this society, and on the irreconcilability of the antagonistic interests of the proletariat and the bourgeoisie.

Previously the question was put as follows: to achieve its emancipation, the proletariat must overthrow the bourgeoisie, win political power and establish its revolutionary dictatorship.

Now the question is put somewhat differently: the transition from capitalist society—which is developing towards communism—to communist society is impossible without a "political transition period," and the state in this period can only be the revolutionary dictatorship of the proletariat.

What, then, is the relation of this dictatorship to democracy?

We have seen that the *Communist Manifesto* simply places side by side the two concepts: "to raise the proletariat to the position of the ruling class" and "to win the battle of democracy." On the basis of all that has been said above, it is possible to determine more precisely how democracy changes in the transition from capitalism to communism.

In capitalist society, providing it develops under the most favorable conditions, we have a more or less complete democracy in the democratic republic. But this democracy is always hemmed in by the narrow limits set by capitalist exploitation, and consequently always remains, in effect, a democracy for the minority, only for the propertied classes, only for the rich. Freedom in capitalist society always remains about the same as it was in the ancient Greek republics: freedom for the slave-owners. Owing to the conditions of capitalist exploitation, the modern wage slaves are so crushed by want and poverty that "they cannot be bothered with democracy," "cannot be bothered with politics"; in the ordinary, peaceful course of events, the majority of the population is debarred from participation in public and political life.

The correctness of this statement is perhaps most clearly confirmed by Germany, because constitutional legality steadily endured there for a remarkably long time—nearly half a century (1871–1914)—and during this period the Social-Democrats were able to achieve far more than in other countries in the way of "utilizing legality," and organized a larger proportion of the workers into a political party than anywhere else in the world.

What is this largest proportion of politically conscious and active wage slaves that has so far been recorded in capitalist society? One million members of the Social-Democratic Party—out of fifteen million wage-workers! Three million organized in trade unions—out of fifteen million!

Democracy for an insignificant minority, democracy for the rich—that is the democracy of capitalist society. If we look more closely into the machinery of capitalist democracy, we see everywhere, in the "petty"—supposedly petty—details of the suffrage (residential qualification, exclusion of women, etc.), in the technique of the representative institutions, in the actual obstacles to the right of assembly (public buildings are not for "paupers!"), in the purely capitalist organization of the daily press, etc., etc.—we see restriction after restriction upon democracy. These restrictions, exceptions, exclusions, obstacles for the poor seem slight, especially in the eyes of one who has never known want himself and has never been in close contact with the oppressed classes in their mass life (and nine out of ten, if not ninety-nine out of a hundred, bourgeois publicists and politicians come under this category); but in their sum total these restrictions exclude and squeeze out the poor from politics, from active participation in democracy.

Marx grasped this essence of capitalist democracy splendidly when, in analyzing the experience of the Commune, he said that the oppressed are allowed once every few years to decide which particular representatives of the oppressing class shall represent and repress them in parliament!

But from this capitalist democracy—that is inevitably narrow and stealthily pushes aside the poor, and is therefore hypocritical and false through and through—forward development does not proceed simply, directly and smoothly, towards "greater and greater democracy," as the liberal professors and petty-bourgeois opportunists would have us believe. No, forward development, i.e., development towards communism, proceeds through the dictatorship of the proletariat, and cannot be broken by anyone else or in any other way.

And the dictatorship of the proletariat, i.e., the organization of the vanguard of the oppressed as the ruling class for the purpose of suppressing the oppressors, cannot result merely in an expansion of democracy. Simultaneously with an immense expansion of democracy, which for the first time becomes democracy for the poor, democracy for the people, and not democracy for the money-bags, the dictatorship of the proletariat imposes a series of restrictions on the freedom of the oppressors, the exploiters, the capitalists. We must suppress them in order to free humanity from wage slavery, their resistance must be crushed by force; it is clear that there is no freedom and no democracy where there is suppression and where there is violence.

Engels expressed this splendidly in his letter to Bebel when he said, as the reader will remember, that "the proletariat needs the state, not in the interests of freedom but in order to hold down its adversaries, and as soon as it becomes possible to speak of freedom the state as such ceases to exist."

Democracy for the vast majority of the people, and suppression by force, i.e., exclusion from democracy, of the exploiters and oppressors of the people—this is the change democracy undergoes during the transition from capitalism to communism.

Only in communist society, when the resistance of the capitalists has been completely crushed, when the capitalists have disappeared, when there are no classes (i.e., when there is no distinction between the members of society as regards their relation to the social means of production), only then "the state . . . ceases to exist," and "it becomes possible to speak of freedom." Only then will a truly complete democracy become possible and be realized, a democracy without any exceptions whatever. And only then will democracy begin to wither away, owing to the simple fact that, freed from capitalist slavery, from the untold horrors, savagery, absurdities and infamies of capitalist exploitation, people will gradually become accustomed to observing the elementary rules of social intercourse that have been known for centuries and repeated for thousands of years in all copy-book maxims. They will become accustomed to observing them without force, without coercion, without subordination, without the special apparatus for coercion called the state.

The expression "the state withers away" is very well chosen, for it indicates both the gradual and the spontaneous nature of the process. Only habit can, and undoubtedly will, have such an effect; for we see around us on millions of occasions how readily people become accustomed to observing the necessary rules of social intercourse when there is no exploitation, when there is nothing that arouses indignation, evokes protest and revolts, and creates the need for suppression.

And so in capitalist society we have a democracy that is curtailed, wretched, false, a democracy only for the rich, for the minority. The dictatorship of the proletariat, the period of transition to communism, will for the first time create democracy for the people, for the majority, along with the necessary suppression of the exploiters, of the minority. Communism alone is capable of providing really complete democracy, and the more complete it is, the sooner it will become unnecessary and wither away of its own accord.

In other words, under capitalism we have the state in the proper sense of the word, that is, a special machine for the suppression of one class by another, and, what is more, of the majority by the minority. Naturally, to be successful, such an undertaking as the systematic suppression of the exploited majority by the exploiting minority calls for the utmost ferocity and savagery in the matter of suppressing, it calls for seas of blood, through which mankind is actually wading its way in slavery, serfdom and wage labor.

Furthermore, during the transition from capitalism to communism suppression is still necessary, but it is now the suppression of the exploiting minority by the exploited majority. A special apparatus, a special machine for suppression, the "state," is still necessary, but this is now a transitional state. It is no longer a state in the proper sense of the word; for the suppression of the minority of exploiters by the majority of the wage slaves of yesterday is comparatively so easy, simple and natural a task that it will entail far less bloodshed than the suppression of the risings of slaves, serfs or wage-laborers, and it will cost mankind far less. And it is compatible with the extension of democracy to such an overwhelming majority of the population that the need for a *special machine* of suppression will begin to disappear. Naturally, the exploiters are unable to suppress the people without a highly complex machine for performing this task, but *the people* can suppress the exploiters even with a very simple "machine," almost without a "machine," without a special apparatus, by the simple *organization of the armed people* (such as the Soviets of Workers' and Soldiers' Deputies, we would remark, running ahead).

Lastly, only communism makes the state absolutely unnecessary, for there is *nobody* to be suppressed—"nobody" in the sense of a *class*, of a systematic struggle against a definite section of the population. We are not utopians, and do not in the least deny the possibility and inevitability of excesses on the part of *individual persons*, or the need to stop *such* excesses. In the first place, however, no special machine, no special apparatus of suppression, is needed for this; this will be done by the armed people themselves, as simply and as readily as any crowd of civilized people, even in modern society, interferes to put a stop to a scuffle or to prevent a woman from being assaulted. And, secondly, we know that the fundamental social cause of excesses, which consist in the violation of the rules of social intercourse, is the exploitation of the people, their want and their poverty. With the removal of this chief cause, excesses will inevitably begin to "wither away." We do not know how quickly and in what succession, but we do know they will wither away. With their withering away the state will also *wither away*.

THE HIGHER PHASE OF COMMUNIST SOCIETY

Marx continues:

> In a higher phase of communist society, after the enslaving subordination of the individual to the division of labor and with it also the antithesis between mental and physical labor has vanished, after labor has become not only a livelihood but life's prime want, after the productive forces have increased with the all-round development of the individual, and all the springs of co-operative wealth flow more abundantly—only then can the narrow horizon of bourgeois right be crossed in its entirety and society inscribe on its banners: From each according to his ability, to each according to his needs!

Only now can we fully appreciate the correctness of Engels' remarks mercilessly ridiculing the absurdity of combining the words "freedom" and "state." So long as the state exists there is no freedom. When there is freedom, there will be no state.

The economic basis for the complete withering away of the state is such a high stage of development of communism at which the antithesis between mental and physical labor disappears, at which there consequently disappears one of the principal sources of modern *social* inequality—a source, moreover, which cannot on any account be removed immediately by the mere conversion of the means of production into public property, by the mere expropriation of the capitalists.

This expropriation will make it *possible* for the productive forces to develop to a tremendous extent. And when we see how incredibly capitalism is already *retarding* this development, when we see how much progress could be achieved on the basis of the level of technique already attained, we are entitled to say with the fullest confidence that the expropriation of the capitalists will inevitably result in an enormous development of the productive forces of human society. But how rapidly this development will proceed, how soon it will reach the point of breaking away from the division of labor, of doing away with the antithesis between mental and physical labor, of transforming labor into "life's prime want"—we do not and *cannot* know.

That is why we are entitled to speak only of the inevitable withering away of the state, emphasizing the protracted nature of this process and its dependence upon the rapidity of development of the *higher phase* of communism, and leaving the question of the time required for, or the concrete forms of, the withering away quite open, because there is *no* material for answering these questions.

The state will be able to wither away completely when society adopts the rule: "From each according to his ability, to each according to his needs," i.e., when people have become so accustomed to observing the fundamental rules of social intercourse and when their labor has become so productive that they will voluntarily work *according to their ability*. "The narrow horizon of bourgeois right," which compels one to calculate with the heartlessness of a Shylock whether one has not worked half an hour more than somebody else, whether one is not getting less pay than somebody else—this narrow horizon will then be crossed. There will then be no need for society, in distributing products, to regulate the quantity to be received by each; each will take freely "according to his needs."

In its first phase, of first state, communism *cannot* as yet be fully mature economically and entirely free from traditions or vestiges of capitalism. Hence the interesting phenomenon that communism in its first phase retains "the narrow horizon of *bourgeois* right." Of course, bourgeois right in regard to the distribution of *consumer* goods inevitably presupposes the existence of the *bourgeois state*, for right is nothing without an apparatus capable of *enforcing* the observance of the standards of right.

It follows that under communism there remains for a time not only bourgeois right, but even the bourgeois state, without the bourgeoisie!

This may sound like a paradox or simply a dialectical conundrum of which Marxism is often accused by people who have not taken the slightest trouble to study its extraordinarily profound content.

But in fact, remnants of the old, surviving in the new, confront us in life at every step, both in nature and in society. And Marx did not arbitrarily insert a scrap of "bourgeois" right into communism, but indicated what is economically and politically inevitable in a society emerging out of the womb of capitalism.

Democracy is of enormous importance to the working class in its struggle against the capitalists for its emancipation. But democracy is by no means a boundary not to be overstepped; it is only one of the stages on the road from feudalism to capitalism, and from capitalism to communism.

Democracy means equality. The great significance of the proletariat's struggle for equality and of equality as a slogan will be clear if we correctly interpret it as meaning the abolition of classes. But democracy means only formal equality. And as soon as equality is achieved for all members of society in relation to ownership of the means of production, that is, equality of labor and wages, humanity will inevitably be confronted with the question of advancing farther, from formal equality to actual equality, i.e., to the operation of the rule "from each according to his ability, to each according to his needs." By what stages, by means of what practical measures humanity will proceed to this supreme aim we do not and cannot know. But it is important to realize how infinitely mendacious is the ordinary bourgeois conception of socialism as something lifeless, rigid, fixed once and for all, whereas in reality only socialism will be the beginning of a rapid, genuine, truly mass forward movement, embracing first the majority and then the whole of the population, in all spheres of public and private life.

Democracy is a form of the state, one of its varieties. Consequently, it, like every state, represents, on the one hand, the organized, systematic use of force against persons; but, on the other hand, it signifies the formal recognition of equality of citizens, the equal right of all to determine the structure of, and to administer, the state. This, in turn, results in the fact that, at a certain stage in the development of democracy, it first welds together the class that wages a revolutionary struggle against capitalism— the proletariat, and enables it to crush, smash to atoms, wipe off the face of the earth the bourgeois, even the republican-bourgeois, state machine, the standing army, the police and the bureaucracy and to substitute for them a more democratic state machine, but a state machine nevertheless, in the shape of armed workers who proceed to form a militia involving the entire population.

Here "quantity turns into quality": such a degree of democracy implies overstepping the boundaries of bourgeois society and beginning its socialist reorganization. If really all take part in the administration of the state, capitalism cannot retain its hold. The development of capitalism, in turn, creates the preconditions that enable really "all" to take part in the administration of the state. Some of these preconditions are: universal literacy, which has already been achieved in a number of the most advanced capitalist countries, then the "training and disciplining" of millions of workers by the huge, complex, socialized apparatus of the postal service, railways, big factories, large-scale commerce, banking, etc., etc.

Given these *economic* preconditions, it is quite possible, after the overthrow of the capitalists and the bureaucrats, to proceed immediately, overnight, to replace them in the *control* over production and distribution, in the work of *keeping account* of labor and products, by the armed workers, by the whole of the armed population. (The question of control and accounting should not be confused with the question of the scientifically trained staff of engineers, agronomists and so on. These gentlemen are working today in obedience to the wishes of the capitalists, and will work even better tomorrow in obedience to the wishes of the armed workers.)

Accounting and control—that is *mainly* what is needed for the "smooth working," for the proper functioning, of the *first phase* of communist society. *All* citizens are transformed into hired employees of the state, which consists of the armed workers. *All* citizens become employees and workers of a *single* country-wide state "syndicate." All that is required is that they should work equally, do their proper share of work, and get equal pay. The accounting and control necessary for this have been *simplified* by capitalism to the utmost and reduced to the extraordinarily simple operations—which any literate person can perform—of supervising and recording, knowledge of the four rules of arithmetic, and issuing appropriate receipts.[1]

When the *majority* of the people begin independently and everywhere to keep such accounts and exercise such control over the capitalists (now converted into employees) and over the intellectual gentry who preserve their capitalist habits, this control will really become universal, general and popular; and there will be no getting away from it, there will be "nowhere to go."

The whole of society will have become a single office and a single factory, with equality of labor and pay.

But this "factory" discipline, which the proletariat, after defeating the capitalists, after overthrowing the exploiters, will extend to the whole of society is by no means our ideal, or our ultimate goal. It is only a necessary *step* for thoroughly cleaning society of all the infamies and abominations of capitalist exploitation, *and for further* progress.

From the moment all members of society, or at least the vast majority, have learned to administer the state *themselves*, have taken this work into their own hands, have organized control over the insignificant capitalist minority, over the gentry who wish to preserve their capitalist habits and over the workers who have been thoroughly corrupted by capitalism—from this moment the need for government of any kind begins to disappear altogether. The more complete the democracy, the nearer the moment when it becomes unnecessary. The more democratic the "state" which consists of the armed workers, and which is "no longer a state in the proper sense of the word," the more rapidly *every form* of state begins to wither away.

For when *all* have learned to administer and actually do independently administer social production, independently keep accounts and exercise control over the parasites, the sons of the wealthy, the swindlers and other "guardians of capitalist traditions," the escape from this popular accounting and control will inevitably become so incredibly difficult, such a rare exception, and will probably be accompanied by such swift and severe punishment (for the armed workers are practical men and not sentimental intellectuals, and they will scarcely allow anyone to trifle with them), that the *necessity* of observing the simple, fundamental rules of the community will very soon become a *habit*.

Then the door will be thrown wide open for the transition from the first phase of communist society to its higher phase, and with it to the complete withering away of the state.

Draft Regulations of Workers' Control

1. Workers' *control* over the production, storage, purchase and sale of all products and raw materials shall be introduced in all industrial, commercial, banking, agricultural and other enterprises employing not less than five workers and office employees (together), or with an annual turnover of not less than 10,000 rubles.

2. Workers' control shall be exercised by all the workers and office employees of an enterprise, either directly, if the enterprise is small enough to permit it, or through their elected representatives, who shall be elected *immediately* at general meetings, at which minutes of the elections shall be taken and the names of those elected communicated to the government and to the local Soviets of Workers', Soldiers' and Peasants' Deputies.

3. Unless permission is given by the elected representatives of the workers and office employees, the suspension of work of an enterprise or an industrial establishment of state importance, or any change in its operation is strictly prohibited.

4. The elected representatives shall be given access to *all* books and documents and to *all* warehouses and stocks of materials, instruments and products, without exception.

5. The decisions of the elected representatives of the workers and office employees are binding upon the owners of enterprises and may be annulled only by trade unions and their congresses.

6. In all enterprises of state importance *all* owners and *all* representatives of the workers and office employees elected for the purpose of exercising workers' control shall be answerable to the state for the maintenance of the strictest order and discipline and for the protection of property. Per-

sons guilty of dereliction of duty, concealment of stocks, accounts, etc., shall be punished by imprisonment for a term of up to five years.

Note

[1] When the more important functions of the state are reduced to such accounting and control by the workers themselves, it will cease to be a "political state" and "public functions will lose their political character and become mere administrative functions" (cf. above, Chapter IV, 2, Engels' controversy with the anarchists).

The Immediate Tasks of the Soviet Government

V. I. Lenin

The first of these three selections dates from April 1918, the second from January 1922, and the third from February 1922. Here Lenin has completely reversed his views. It now seems that administration is vital, experts are needed, and ordinary citizens are simply not equipped to run affairs of state. Thus bureaucrats (the experts) should be paid much more than workers, and workers' control in the factories should be ended. In the third selection Lenin insists that even communist party members are inadequate, and he condemns the red tape and bureaucratism that the revolution was to have ended.

A third task is now coming to the fore as the immediate task and one which constitutes the peculiar feature of the present situation, namely, the task of organizing *administration* of Russia. Of course, we advanced and tackled this task on the very day following October 25, 1917. Up to now, however, since the resistance of the exploiters still took the form of open civil war, up to now the task of administration *could not* become the *main*, the *central* task.

Now it has become the main and central task. We, the Bolshevik Party, have *convinced* Russia. We have *won* Russia from the rich for the poor, from the exploiters for the working people. Now we must *administer* Russia. And the whole peculiarity of the present situation, the whole difficulty, lies in understanding *the specific features of the transition* from the principal task of convincing the people and of suppressing the exploiters by armed force to the principal task of *administration*.

For the first time in human history a socialist party has managed to complete in the main the conquest of power and the suppression of the exploiters, and has managed to *approach* directly the task of *administration*. We must prove worthy executors of this most difficult (and most gratifying) task of the socialist revolution. We must *fully realize* that in order to administer successfully, *besides* being able to convince people, besides being able to win a civil war, we must be able to do *practical*

Excerpts from V. I. Lenin, *Selected Works* (New York: International Publishers, 1967), Vol. 2, pp. 649–673, and Vol. 3, pp. 655–699. Reprinted by permission of International Publishers Co., Inc. Copyright © 1967.

organizational work. This is the most difficult task, because it is a matter of organizing in a new way the most deep-rooted, the economic, foundations of life of scores of millions of people. And it is the most gratifying task, because only *after* it has been fulfilled (in the principal and main outlines) will it be possible to say that Russia *has become* not only a Soviet, but also a socialist, republic.

THE GENERAL SLOGAN OF THE MOMENT

Keep regular and honest accounts of money, manage economically, do not be lazy, do not steal, observe the strictest labor discipline—it is these slogans, justly scorned by the revolutionary proletariat when the bourgeoisie used them to conceal its rule as an exploiting class, that are now, since the overthrow of the bourgeoisie, becoming the immediate and the principal slogans of the moment. On the one hand, the practical application of these slogans by *the mass* of working people is the *sole* condition for the salvation of a country which has been tortured almost to death by the imperialist war and by the imperialist robbers (headed by Kerensky); on the other hand, the practical application of these slogans by the Soviet state, by *its* methods, on the basis of *its* laws, is a necessary and *sufficient* condition for the final victory of socialism. This is precisely what those who contemptuously brush aside the idea of putting such "hackneyed" and "trivial" slogans in the forefront fail to understand. In a small-peasant country, which overthrew tsarism only a year ago, and which liberated itself from the Kerenskys less than six months ago, there has naturally remained not a little of spontaneous anarchy, intensified by the brutality and savagery that accompany every protracted and reactionary war, and there has arisen a good deal of despair and aimless bitterness. And if we add to this the provocative policy of the lackeys of the bourgeoisie (the Mensheviks, the Right Socialist-Revolutionaries, etc.) it will become perfectly clear what prolonged and persistent efforts must be exerted by the best and the most class-conscious workers and peasants in order to bring about a complete change in the mood of the people and to bring them on to the proper path of steady and disciplined labor. Only such a transition brought about by the mass of the poor (the proletarians and semi-proletarians) can consummate the victory over the bourgeoisie and particularly over the peasant bourgeoisie, more stubborn and numerous.

THE NEW PHASE OF THE STRUGGLE AGAINST THE BOURGEOISIE

This is a peculiar epoch, or rather stage of development, and in order to defeat capital completely, we must be able to adapt the forms of our struggle to the peculiar conditions of this stage.

Without the guidance of experts in the various fields of knowledge, technology and experience, the transition to socialism will be impossible, because socialism calls for a conscious mass advance to greater productivity of labor compared with capitalism, and on the basis achieved by capitalism. Socialism must achieve this advance *in its own way*, by its own methods— or, to put it more concretely, by *Soviet* methods. And the specialists, because of the whole social environment which made them specialists, are, in the main, inevitably bourgeois. Had our proletariat, after capturing power, quickly solved the problem of accounting, control and organization on a national scale (which was impossible owing to the war and Russia's backwardness), then we, after breaking the sabotage, would also have completely subordinated these bourgeois experts to ourselves by means of universal accounting and control. Owing to the considerable "delay" in introducing accounting and control generally, we, although we have managed to conquer sabotage, have *not yet* created the conditions which would place the bourgeois specialists at our disposal. The mass of saboteurs are "going to work," but the best organizers and the top experts can be utilized by the state either in the old way, in the bourgeois way (i.e., for high salaries), or in the new way, in the proletarian way (i.e., creating the conditions of national accounting and control from below, which would inevitably and of themselves subordinate the experts and enlist them for our work).

Now we have to resort to the old bourgeois method and to agree to pay a very high price for the "services" of the top bourgeois experts. All those who are familiar with the subject appreciate this, but not all ponder over the significance of this measure being adopted by the proletarian state. Clearly, this measure is a compromise, a departure from the principles of the Paris Commune and of every proletarian power, which call for the reduction of all salaries to the level of the wages of the average worker, which urge that careerism be fought not merely in words, but in deeds.

Moreover, it is clear that this measure not only implies the cessation— in a certain field and to a certain degree—of the offensive against capital (for capital is not a sum of money, but a definite social relation); it is also a *step backward* on the part of our socialist Soviet state power, which from the very outset proclaimed and pursued the policy of reducing high salaries to the level of the wages of the average worker.

Of course, the lackeys of the bourgeoisie, particularly the small fry, such as the Mensheviks, the *Novaya Zhizn* people and the Right Socialist-Revolutionaries, will giggle over our confession that we are taking a step backward. But we need not mind their giggling. We must study the specific features of the extremely difficult and new path to socialism without concealing our mistakes and weaknesses, and try to be prompt in doing what has been left undone. To conceal from the people the fact that the enlistment of bourgeois experts by means of extremely high salaries is a retreat from the principles of the Paris Commune would be sinking to the level of bourgeois politicians and deceiving the people. Frankly explaining how and why we took this step backward, and then publicly discussing what means are available for making up for lost time, means educating the people and learning from experience, learning together with the people how to build socialism. There is hardly a single victorious military campaign in history in which the victor did not commit certain mistakes, suffer partial reverses, temporarily yield something and in some places retreat. The "campaign" which we have undertaken against capitalism is a million times more difficult than the most difficult military campaign, and it would be silly and disgraceful to give way to despondency because of a particular and partial retreat.

We shall now discuss the question from the practical point of view. Let us assume that the Russian Soviet Republic requires one thousand first-class scientists and experts in various fields of knowledge, technology and practical experience to direct the labor of the people towards securing the speediest possible economic revival. Let us assume also that we shall have to pay these "stars of the first magnitude"—of course the majority of those who shout loudest about the corruption of the workers are themselves utterly corrupted by bourgeois morals—25,000 rubles per annum each. Let us assume that this sum (25,000,000 rubles) will have to be doubled (assuming that we have to pay bonuses for particularly successful and rapid fulfillment of the most important organizational and technical tasks), or even quadrupled (assuming that we have to enlist several hundred foreign specialists, who are more demanding). The question is, would the annual expenditure of fifty or a hundred million rubles by the Soviet Republic for the purpose of reorganizing the labor of the people on modern scientific and technological lines be excessive or too heavy? Of course not. The overwhelming majority of the class-conscious workers and peasants will approve of this expenditure because they know from practical experience that our backwardness causes us to lose thousands of millions, and that we have not yet reached that degree of organization, accounting and control which would induce all the "stars" of the bourgeois intelligentsia to participate voluntarily in our work.

It goes without saying that this question has another side to it. The corrupting influence of high salaries—both upon the Soviet authorities (especially since the revolution occurred so rapidly that it was impossible to prevent a certain number of adventurers and rogues from getting into positions of authority, and they, together with a number of inept or dishonest commissars, would not be averse to becoming "star" embezzlers of state funds) and upon the mass of the workers—is indisputable. Every thinking and honest worker and poor peasant, however, will agree with us, will admit, that we cannot immediately rid ourselves of the evil legacy of capitalism, and that we can liberate the Soviet Republic from the duty of paying an annual "tribute" of fifty million or one hundred million rubles (a tribute for our own backwardness in organizing country-wide accounting and control from below) only by organizing ourselves, by tightening up discipline in our own ranks, by purging our ranks of all those who are "preserving the legacy of capitalism," who "follow the traditions of capital-ism," i.e., of idlers, parasites and embezzlers of state funds (now all the land, all the factories and all the railways are the "state funds" of the Soviet Republic). If the class-conscious advanced workers and poor peas-ants manage with the aid of the Soviet institutions to organize, become disciplined, pull themselves together, create powerful labor discipline in the course of one year, then in a year's time we shall throw off this "trib-ute," which can be reduced even before that . . . in exact proportion to the successes we achieve in our workers' and peasants' labor discipline and organization. The sooner we ourselves, workers and peasants, learn the best labor discipline and the most modern technique of labor, using the bour-geois experts to teach us, the sooner we shall liberate ourselves from any "tribute" to these specialists.

Our work of organizing country-wide accounting and control of pro-duction and distribution under the supervision of the proletariat has lagged very much behind our work of directly expropriating the expropriators. This proposition is of fundamental importance for understanding the specific features of the present situation and the tasks of the Soviet gov-ernment that follow from it. The center of gravity of our struggle against the bourgeoisie is shifting to the organization of such accounting and control. Only with this as our starting-point will it be possible to determine correctly the immediate tasks of economic and financial policy in the sphere of nationalization of the banks, monopolization of foreign trade, the state control of money circulation, the introduction of a property and income tax satisfactory from the proletarian point of view, and the intro-duction of compulsory labor service.

THE SIGNIFICANCE OF THE STRUGGLE FOR COUNTRY-WIDE ACCOUNTING AND CONTROL

The state, which for centuries has been an organ for oppression and robbery of the people, has left us a legacy of the people's supreme hatred and suspicion of everything that is connected with the state. It is very difficult to overcome this, and only a Soviet government can do it. Even a Soviet government, however, will require plenty of time and enormous perseverance to accomplish it. This "legacy" is especially apparent in the problem of accounting and control—the fundamental problem facing the socialist revolution on the morrow of the overthrow of the bourgeoisie. A certain amount of time will inevitably pass before the people, who feel free for the first time now that the landowners and the bourgeoisie have been overthrown, will understand—not from books, but from their own, *Soviet* experience—will understand and *feel* that without comprehensive state accounting and control of the production and distribution of goods, the power of the working people, the freedom of the working people, *cannot* be maintained, and that a return to the yoke of capitalism is *inevitable*.

All the habits and traditions of the bourgeoisie, and of the petty bourgeoisie in particular, also oppose *state* control, and uphold the inviolability of "sacred private property," of "sacred" private enterprise. It is now particularly clear to us how correct is the Marxist thesis that anarchism and anarcho-syndicalism are *bourgeois* trends, how irreconcilably opposed they are to socialism, proletarian dictatorship and communism. The fight to instill into the people's minds the idea of *Soviet* state control and accounting, and to carry out this idea in practice; the fight to break with the rotten past, which taught the people to regard the procurement of bread and clothes as a "private" affair, and buying and selling as a transaction "which concerns only myself"—is a great fight of world-historic significance, a fight between socialist consciousness and bourgeois-anarchist spontaneity.

We have introduced workers' control as a law, but this law is only just beginning to operate and is only just beginning to penetrate the minds of broad sections of the proletariat. In our agitation we do not sufficiently explain that lack of accounting and control in the production and distribution of goods means the death of the rudiments of socialism, means the embezzlement of state funds (for all property belongs to the state and the state is the Soviet state in which power belongs to the majority of the working people). We do not sufficiently explain that carelessness in accounting and control is downright aiding and abetting the German and the Russian Kornilovs, who can overthrow the power of the working people *only* if we fail to cope with the task of accounting and control, and who, with the aid of the whole of the rural bourgeoisie, with the aid of the Constitutional-Democrats, the Mensheviks and the Right Socialist-Revolutionaries, are "watching" us and waiting for an opportune moment to attack us. And the advanced workers and peasants do not think and speak about this sufficiently. Until workers' control has become a fact, until the advanced workers have organized and carried out a victorious and ruthless crusade against the violators of this control, or against those who are careless in matters of control, it will be impossible to pass from the first step (from workers' control) to the second step towards socialism, i.e., to pass on to workers' regulation of production.

The socialist state can arise only as a network of producers' and consumers' communes, which conscientiously keep account of their production and consumption, economize on labor, and steadily raise the productivity of labor, thus making it possible to reduce the working day to seven, six and even fewer hours. Nothing will be achieved unless the strictest, country-wide, comprehensive accounting and control of *grain* and the *production of grain* (and later of all other essential goods) are set going.

In regard to the significance of individual dictatorial powers from the point of view of the specific tasks of the present moment, it must be said that large-scale machine industry—which is precisely the material source, the productive source, the foundation of socialism—calls for absolute and strict unity of will, which directs the joint labors of hundreds, thousands and tens of thousands of people. The technical, economic and historical necessity of this is obvious, and all those who have thought about socialism have always regarded it as one of the conditions of socialism. But how can strict unity of will be ensured? By thousands subordinating their will to the will of one.

Given ideal class-consciousness and discipline on the part of those participating in the common work, this subordination would be something like the mild leadership of a conductor of an orchestra. It may assume the sharp forms of a dictatorship if ideal discipline and class-consciousness are lacking. But be that as it may, unquestioning subordination to a single will is absolutely necessary for the success of processes organized on the pattern of large-scale machine industry. On the railways it is twice and three times as necessary. In this transition from one political task to another, which on the surface is totally dissimilar to the first, lies the whole originality of the present situation. The revolution has only just smashed the oldest, strongest and heaviest of fetters, to which the people submitted under duress. That was yesterday. Today, however, the same revolution de-mands—precisely in the interests of its development and consolidation, precisely in the interests of socialism—that the people unquestioningly obey the single will of the leaders of labor. Of course, such a transition cannot be made at one step. Clearly, it can be achieved only as a result of tremendous jolts, shocks, reversions to old ways, the enormous exertion of effort on the part of the proletarian vanguard, which is leading the people to the new ways.

The Role and Functions of the Trade Unions

THE TRADE UNIONS AND THE MANAGEMENT OF INDUSTRY

Following its seizure of political power, the principal and fundamental interest of the proletariat lies in securing an enormous increase in the productive forces of society and in the output of manufactured goods. This task, which is clearly formulated in the Program of the Russian Commu-nist Party, is particularly urgent in our country today owing to post-war ruin, famine and dislocation. Hence, the speediest and most enduring success in restoring large-scale industry is a condition without which no success can be achieved in the general cause of emancipating labor from the yoke of capital and securing the victory of socialism. To achieve this success in Russia, in her present state, it is absolutely essential that all authority in the factories should be concentrated in the hands of the management. The factory management, usually built up on the principle of one-man responsibility, must have authority independently to fix and pay out wages, and also distribute rations, working clothes, and all other supplies on the basis and within the limits of collective agreements concluded with the trade unions; it must enjoy the utmost freedom to maneuver, exercise strict control of the actual successes achieved in increasing production, in making the factory pay its way and in increasing profits, and carefully select the most talented and capable administrative personnel, etc.

Eleventh Congress of the R.C.P.(B.)

And here we must squarely put the question: Wherein lies our strength and what do we lack? We have quite enough political power. I hardly think there is anyone here who will assert that on such-and-such a practical question, in such-and-such a business institution, the Communists, the Communist Party, lack sufficient power. There are people who think only of this, but these people are hopelessly looking backward and cannot understand that one must look ahead. The main economic power is in our hands. All the vital large enterprises, the railways, etc., are in our hands. The number of leased enterprises, although considerable in places, is on the whole insignificant; altogether it is infinitesimal compared with the rest. The economic power in the hands of the proletarian state of Russia is quite adequate to ensure the transition to communism. What then is lacking? Obviously, what is lacking is culture among the stratum of the Communists who perform administrative functions. If we take Moscow with its 4,700 Communists in responsible positions, and if we take that huge bureaucratic machine, that gigantic heap, we must ask: who is directing whom? I doubt very much whether it can truthfully be said that the Communists are directing that heap. To tell the truth, they are not directing, they are being directed. Something analogous happened here to what we were told in our history lessons when we were children: sometimes one nation conquers another, the nation that conquers is the conqueror and the nation that is vanquished is the conquered nation. This is simple and intelligible to all. But what happens to the culture of these nations? Here things are not so simple. If the conquering nation is more cultured than the vanquished nation, the former imposes its culture upon the latter; but if the opposite is the case, the vanquished nation imposes its culture upon the conqueror. Has not something like this happened in the capital of the R.S.F.S.R.? Have the 4,700 Communists (nearly a whole army division, and all of them the very best) come under the influence of an alien culture? True, there may be the impression that the vanquished have a high level of culture. But that is not the case at all. Their culture is miserable, insignificant, but it is still at a higher level than ours. Miserable and low as it is, it is higher than that of our responsible Communist administrators, for the latter lack administrative ability. Communists who are put at the head of departments—and sometimes artful saboteurs deliberately put them in these positions in order to use them as a shield— are often fooled. This is a very unpleasant admission to make, or, at any rate, not a very pleasant one; but I think we must admit it, for at present this is the salient problem. I think that this is the political lesson of the past year; and it is around this that the struggle will rage in 1922.

Will the responsible Communists of the R.S.F.S.R. and of the Russian Communist Party realize that they cannot administer; that they only imagine they are directing, but are, actually, being directed? If they realize this they will learn, of course; for this business can be learned. But one must study hard to learn it, and our people are not doing this. They scatter orders and decrees right and left, but the result is quite different from what they want.

The competition and rivalry that we have placed on the order of the day by proclaiming NEP is a serious business. It appears to be going on in all government offices; but as a matter of fact it is one more form of the struggle between two irreconcilably hostile classes. It is another form of the struggle between the bourgeoisie and the proletariat. It is a struggle that has not yet been brought to a head, and culturally it has not yet been resolved even in the central government departments in Moscow. Very often the bourgeois officials know the business better than our best Communists, who are invested with authority and have every opportunity, but who cannot make the slightest use of their rights and authority.

When we rap the exploiters' knuckles, render them innocuous, over-power them, it is only half the job. In Moscow, however, ninety out of a hundred responsible officials imagine that all we have to do is to over-power, render innocuous and rap knuckles. We must make these hands work for us, and not have responsible Communists at the head of depart-ments, enjoying rank and title, but actually swimming with the stream together with the bourgeoisie. That is the whole point.

The idea of building communist society exclusively with the hands of the Communists is childish, absolutely childish. We Communists are but a drop in the ocean, a drop in the ocean of the people. We shall be able to lead the people along the road we have chosen only if we correctly deter-mine it not only from the standpoint of its direction in world history. From that point of view we have determined the road quite correctly, and this is corroborated by the situation in every country. We must also deter-mine it correctly for our own native land, for our country. But the direc-tion in world history is not the only factor. Other factors are whether there will be intervention or not, and whether we shall be able to supply the peasants with goods in exchange for their grain. The peasants will say: "You are splendid fellows; you defended our country. That is why we obeyed you. But if you cannot run the show, get out!" Yes, that is what the peasants will say.

We Communists shall be able to direct our economy if we succeed in utilizing the hands of the bourgeoisie in building up this economy of ours and in the meantime learn from these bourgeoisie and guide them along the road we want them to travel. But when a Communist imagines that he knows everything, when he says: "I am a responsible Communist, I have beaten enemies far more formidable than any salesman. We have fought at the front and have beaten far more formidable enemies"—it is this prevailing mood that is doing us great harm.

We must see to it that the numerous elements with whom we are co-operating, and who far exceed us in number, work in such a way as to enable us to supervise them; we must learn to understand this work, and direct their hands so that they do something useful for communism. This is the key point of the present situation; for although individual Communists have understood and realized that it is necessary to enlist the non-Party people for this work, the rank-and-file of our Party have not. Many circulars have been written, much has been said about this, but has anything been accomplished during the past year? Nothing. Not five Party committees out of a hundred can show practical results. This shows how much we lag behind the requirements of the present time; how much we are still living in the traditions of 1918 and 1919. Those were great years; a great historical task was then accomplished. But if we only look back on those years and do not see the task that now confronts us, we shall be doomed, certainly and absolutely. And the whole point is that we refuse to admit it.

I should now like to give [an example] . . . to illustrate how we administer. [This] . . . is the accusation of bureaucracy leveled at the People's Commissariat of Foreign Trade by the Moscow Consumers' Co-operative Society. . . .

As you know from the newspapers, I have been unable to deal with affairs directly during these past few months. I have not been attending the Council of People's Commissars, or the Central Committee. During the short and rare visits I made to Moscow I was struck by the desperate and terrible complaints leveled at the People's Commissariat of Foreign Trade. I have never doubted for a moment that the People's Commissariat of Foreign Trade functions badly and that it is tied up with red tape. But when the complaints became particularly bitter I tried to investigate the matter, to take a concrete example and for once get to the bottom of it; to ascertain the cause, to ascertain why the machine was not working properly.

The M.C.C.S. wanted to purchase a quantity of canned goods. A French citizen appeared and offered some. I do not know whether he did it in the interests of the international policy and with the knowledge of the leadership of the Entente countries, or with the approval of Poincaré and the other enemies of the Soviet government (I think our historians will investigate and make this clear after the Genoa Conference), but the fact is that the French bourgeoisie took not only a theoretical, but also a practical interest in this business, as a French bourgeois turned up in Moscow with an offer of canned goods. Moscow is starving; in the summer the situation will be worse; no meat has been delivered, and knowing the merits of our People's Commissariat of Railways, probably none will be delivered.

An offer is made to sell canned meat for Soviet currency (whether the meat is entirely bad or not will be established by a future investigation). What could be simpler? But if the matter is approached in the Soviet way, it turns out to be not so simple after all. I was unable to go into the matter personally, but I ordered an investigation and I have before me the report which shows how this celebrated case developed. It started with the decision adopted on February 11 by the Political Bureau of the Central Committee of the Russian Communist Party on the report of Comrade Kamenev concerning the desirability of purshasing food abroad. Of course, how could a Russian citizen decide such a question without the consent of the Political Bureau of the Central Committee of the Russian Communist Party! Think of it! How could 4,700 responsible officials (and this is only according to the census) decide a matter like purchasing food abroad without the consent of the Political Bureau of the Central Committee? This would be something supernatural, of course. Evidently, Comrade Kamenev understands our policy and the realities of our position perfectly well, and therefore, he did not place too much reliance on the numerous responsible officials. He started by taking the bull by the horns—if not the bull, at all events the Political Bureau—and without any difficulty (I did not hear that there was any discussion over the matter) obtained a resolution stating: "To call the attention of the People's Commissariat of Foreign Trade to the desirability of importing food from abroad; the import duties . . . ," etc. The attention of the People's Commissariat of Foreign Trade was drawn to this. Things started moving. This was on February 11. I remember that I had occasion to be in Moscow at the very end of February, or about that time, and what did I find? The complaints, the despairing complaints of the Moscow comrades. "What's the matter?" I ask. "There is no way we can buy these provisions." "Why?" "Because of the red tape of the People's Commissariat of Foreign Trade." I had not been taking part in affairs for a long time and I did not know that the Political Bureau had adopted a decision on the matter. I merely ordered the Executive Secretary of our Council to investigate, procure the relevant documents and show them to me. The matter was settled when Krasin arrived. Kamanev discussed the matter with him; the transaction was arranged, and the canned meat was purchased. All's well that ends well.

I have not the least doubt that Kamenev and Krasin can come to an understanding and correctly determine the political line desired by the Political Bureau of the Central Committee of the Russian Communist Party. If the political line on commercial matters were decided by Kamenev and Krasin, ours would be the best Soviet Republic in the world. But

Kamenev, a member of the Political Bureau, and Krasin—the latter is busy with diplomatic affairs connected with Genoa, affairs which have entailed an enormous, an excessive amount of labor—cannot be dragged into every transaction, dragged into the business of buying canned goods from a French citizen. That is not the way to work. This is not new, not economic, and not a policy, but sheer mockery. Now I have the report of the investigation into this matter. In fact, I have two reports: one, the report of the investigation made by Gorbunov, the Executive Secretary of the Council of People's Commissars, and his assistant, Miroshnikov; and the other, the report of the investigation made by the State Political Administration. I do not know why the latter interested itself in the matter, and I am not quite sure whether it was proper for it to do so; but I will not go into that now, because I am afraid this might entail another investigation. The important thing is that material on the matter has been collected and I now have it before me.

On arriving in Moscow at the end of February I hear bitter complaints, "We cannot buy the canned goods," although in Libau there was a ship with a cargo of canned goods, and the owners were prepared to take Soviet currency for real canned goods! (*Laughter.*) If these canned goods are not entirely bad (and I now emphasize the "if," because I am not sure that I shall not call for another investigation, the results of which, however, we shall have to report at the next Congress), if, I say, these goods are not entirely bad and they have been purchased, I ask: why could not this matter have been settled without Kamenev and Krasin? From the report I have before me I gather that one responsible Communist sent another responsible Communist to the devil. I also gather from this report that one responsible Communist said to another responsible Communist: "From now on I shall not talk to you except in the presence of a lawyer."

But why was it necessary, three years after the revolution, in the capital of the Soviet Republic, to have two investigations, the intervention of Kamenev and Krasin and the instructions of the Political Bureau to purchase canned goods? What was lacking? Political power? No. The money was forthcoming, so they had economic as well as political power. All the necessary institutions were available. What was lacking, then? Culture. Ninety-nine out of every hundred officials of the M.C.C.S.— against whom I have no complaint to make whatever, and whom I regard as excellent Communists—and of the Commissariat of Foreign Trade lack culture. They were unable to approach the matter in a cultured manner.

When I first heard of the matter I sent the following written proposal to the Central Committee: "All the officials concerned of the Moscow government departments—except the members of the All-Russia Central Executive Committee, who, as you know, enjoy immunity—should be put in the worst prison in Moscow for six hours, and those of the People's Commissariat of Foreign Trade for thirty-six hours." And then it turned out that no one could say who the culprits were (*laughter*), and from what

I have told you it is evident that the culprits will never be discovered. It is simply the usual inability of the Russian intellectuals to get things done—inefficiency and slovenliness. First they rush at a job, do a little bit, and then think about it, and when nothing comes of it, they run to complain to Kamenev and want the matter to be brought before the Political Bureau.

Notes

V. I. Lenin

These final items are from the last days of 1922 and January 1923. They are among his last writings and were dictated to secretaries because of his illness. They reveal his deep despair over bureaucracy in both the party and the state. He now sees it as simply left over from the tsars and only "slightly anointed with Soviet oil." However, the solutions he proposes go in two directions at once—more ordinary workers in some official bodies, more "expert" training for officials in others. Thus he reflects both phases of his earlier thinking and seems to draw no lessons from the experiences of the revolution.

Letter to the Congress

DECEMBER 23, 1922

I would urge strongly that at this Congress a number of changes be made in our political structure.

I want to tell you of the considerations to which I attach most importance.

At the head of the list I set an increase in the number of Central Committee members to a few dozen or even a hundred. It is my opinion that without this reform our Central Committee would be in great danger if the course of events were not quite favorable for us (and that is something we cannot count on).

Then, I intend to propose that the Congress should on certain conditions invest the decisions of the State Planning commission with legislative force, meeting, in this respect, the wishes of Comrade Trotsky—to a certain extent and on certain conditions.

As for the first point, i.e., increasing the number of C.C. members, I think it must be done in order to raise the prestige of the Central Committee, to do a thorough job of improving our administrative machinery and to prevent conflicts between small sections of the C.C. from acquiring excessive importance for the future of the Party.

Excerpts from V. I. Lenin, *Selected Works*, Vol. 3 (New York: International Publishers, 1967), pp. 737–779. Reprinted by permission of International Publishers Co., Inc. Copyright © 1967.

It seems to me that our Party has every right to demand from the working class 50 to 100 C.C. members, and that it could get them from it without unduly taxing the resources of that class.

Such a reform would considerably increase the stability of our Party and ease its struggle in the encirclement of hostile states, which, in my opinion, is likely to, and must, become much more acute in the next few years. I think that the stability of our Party would gain a thousandfold by such a measure.

DECEMBER 26, 1922

The increase in the number of C.C. members to 50 or even 100 must, in my opinion, serve a double or even a treble purpose: the more members there are in the C.C., the more men will be trained in C.C. work and the less danger there will be of a split due to some indiscretion. The enlistment of many workers to the C.C. will help the workers to improve our administrative machinery, which is pretty bad. We inherited it, in effect, from the old regime, for it was absolutely impossible to reorganize it in such a short time, especially in conditions of war, famine, etc. That is why those "critics" who point to the defects of our administrative machinery out of mockery or malice may be calmly answered that they do not in the least understand the conditions of the revolution today. It is altogether impossible in five years to reorganize the machinery adequately, especially in the conditions in which our revolution took place. It is enough that in five years we have created a new type of state in which the workers are leading the peasants against the bourgeoisie: and in a hostile international environment this in itself is a gigantic achievement. But knowledge of this must on no account blind us to the fact that, in effect, we took over the old machinery of state from the tsar and the bourgeoisie and that now, with the onset of peace and the satisfaction of the minimum requirements against famine, all our work must be directed towards improving the administrative machinery.

I think that a few dozen workers, being members of the C.C., can deal better than anybody else with checking, improving and remodeling our state apparatus. The Workers' and Peasants' Inspection on whom this function devolved at the beginning proved unable to cope with it and can be used only as an "appendage" or, on certain conditions, as an assistant to these members of the C.C. In my opinion, the workers admitted to the Central Committee should come preferably not from among those who have had long service in Soviet bodies (in this part of my letter the term workers everywhere includes peasants), because those workers have already acquired the very traditions and the very prejudices which it is desirable to combat.

The working-class members of the C.C. must be mainly workers of a lower stratum than those promoted in the last five years to work in Soviet bodies; they must be people closer to being rank-and-file workers and peasants, who, however, do not fall into the category of direct or indirect exploiters. I think that by attending all sittings of the C.C. and all sittings of the Political Bureau, and by reading all the documents of the C.C., such workers can form a staff of devoted supporters of the Soviet system, able, first, to give stability to the C.C. itself, and second, to work effectively on the renewal and improvement of the state apparatus.

The Question of Nationalities or "Autonomization"

I suppose I have been very remiss with respect to the workers of Russia for not having intervened energetically and decisively enough in the notorious question of autonomization, which, it appears, is officially called the question of the union of Soviet socialist republics.

When this question arose last summer, I was ill; and then in autumn I relied too much on my recovery and on the October and December plenary meetings giving me an opportunity of intervening in this question. However, I did not manage to attend the October Plenary Meeting (when this question came up), or the one in December, and so the question passed me by almost completely.

I have only had time for a talk with Comrade Dzerzhinsky, who came from the Caucasus and told me how this matter stood in Georgia. I have also managed to exchange a few words with Comrade Zinoviev and express my apprehensions on this matter. From what I was told by Comrade Dzerzhinsky, who was at the head of the commission sent by the C.C. to "investigate" the Georgian incident, I could only draw the greatest apprehensions. If matters had come to such a pass that Orjonikidze could go to the extreme of applying physical violence, as Comrade Dzerzhinsky informed me, we can imagine what a mess we have got ourselves into. Obviously the whole business of "autonomization" was radically wrong and badly timed.

It is said that a united apparatus was needed. Where did that assurance come from? Did it not come from that same Russian apparatus which, as I pointed out in one of the preceding sections of my diary, we took over from tsarism and slightly anointed with Soviet oil?

There is no doubt that that measure should have been delayed somewhat until we could say that we vouched for our apparatus as our own. But now, we must, in all conscience, admit the contrary; the apparatus we call ours is, in fact, still quite alien to us; it is a bourgeois and tsarist hotchpotch and there has been no possibility of getting rid of it in the course of the past five years without the help of other countries and because we have been "busy" most of the time with military engagements and the fight against famine.

It is quite natural that in such circumstances the "freedom to secede from the union" by which we justify ourselves will be a mere scrap of paper, unable to defend the non-Russians from the onslaught of that really Russian man, the Great-Russian chauvinist, in substance a rascal and a tyrant, such as the typical Russian bureaucrat is. There is no doubt that the infinitesimal percentage of Soviet and sovietized workers will drown in that tide of chauvinistic Great-Russian riffraff like a fly in milk.

It is said in defense of this measure that the People's Commissariats directly concerned with national psychology and national education were set up as separate bodies. But there the question arises: can these People's Commissariats be made quite independent? and secondly: were we careful enough to take measures to provide the non-Russians with a real safeguard against the truly Russian bully? I do not think we took such measures although we could and should have done so.

I think that Stalin's haste and his infatuation with pure administration, together with his spite against the notorious "nationalist-socialism," played a fatal role here. In politics spite generally plays the basest of roles.

How We Should Reorganize the Workers' and Peasants' Inspection

(RECOMMENDATION TO THE TWELFTH PARTY CONGRESS)

It is beyond question that the Workers' and Peasants' Inspection is an enormous difficulty for us, and that so far this difficulty has not been overcome. I think that the comrades who try to overcome the difficulty by denying that the Workers' and Peasants' Inspection is useful and necessary are wrong. But I do not deny that the problem presented by our state apparatus and the task of improving it is very difficult, that it is far from being solved, and is an extremely urgent one.

With the exception of the People's Commissariat of Foreign Affairs, our state apparatus is to a considerable extent a survival of the past and has undergone hardly any serious change. It has only been slightly touched up on the surface, but in all other respects it is a most typical relic of our old state machine. And so, to find a method of really renovating it, I think we ought to turn for experience to our Civil War.

How did we act in the more critical moments of the Civil War?

We concentrated our best Party forces in the Red Army; we mobilized the best of our workers; we looked for new forces at the deepest roots of our dictatorship.

I am convinced that we must go to the same source to find the means of reorganizing the Workers' and Peasants' Inspection. I recommend that our Twelfth Party Congress adopt the following plan of reorganization, based on some enlargement of our Central Control Commission.

The Plenary Meetings of the Central Committee of our Party are already revealing a tendency to develop into a kind of supreme Party conference. They take place, on the average, not more than once in two months, while the routine work is conducted, as we know, on behalf of the Central Committee by our Political Bureau, our Organizing Bureau, our Secretariat, and so forth. I think we ought to follow the road we have thus taken to the end and definitely transform the Plenary Meetings of the Central Committee into supreme Party conferences convened once in two months jointly with the Central Control Commission. The Central Control Commission should be amalgamated with the main body of the reorganized Workers' and Peasants' Inspection on the following lines.

I propose that the Congress should elect 75 to 100 new members to the Central Control Commission. They should be workers and peasants, and should go through the same Party screening as ordinary members of the Central Committee, because they are to enjoy the same rights as the members of the Central Committee.

On the other hand, the staff of the Workers' and Peasants' Inspection should be reduced to three or four hundred persons, specially screened for conscientiousness and knowledge of our state apparatus. They must also undergo a special test as regards their knowledge of the principles of scientific organization of labor in general, and of administrative work, office work, and so forth, in particular.

Better Fewer, But Better

Our state apparatus is so deplorable, not to say wretched, that we must first think very carefully how to combat its defects, bearing in mind that these defects are rooted in the past, which, although it has been overthrown, has not yet been overcome, has not yet reached the stage of a culture that has receded into the distant past. I say culture deliberately, because in these matters we can only regard as achieved what has become part and parcel of our culture, of our social life, our habits. We might say that the good in our social system has not been properly studied, understood, and taken to heart; it has been hastily grasped at; it has not been verified or tested, corroborated by experience, and not made durable; etc. Of course, it could not be otherwise in a revolutionary epoch, when development proceeded at such breakneck speed that in a matter of five years we passed from tsarism to the Soviet system.

It is time we did something about it. We must show sound skepticism for too rapid progress, for boastfulness, etc. We must give thought to testing the steps forward we proclaim every hour, take every minute and then prove every second that they are flimsy, superficial and misunderstood. The most harmful thing here would be haste. The most harmful thing would be to rely on the assumption that we know at least something, or that we have any considerable number of elements necessary for the building of a really new state apparatus, one really worthy to be called socialist, Soviet, etc.

No, we are ridiculously deficient of such an apparatus, and even of the elements of it, and we must remember that we should not stint time on building it, and that it will take many, many years.

What elements have we for building this apparatus? Only two. First, the workers who are absorbed in the struggle for socialism. These elements are not sufficiently educated. They would like to build a better apparatus for us, but they do not know how. They cannot build one. They have not yet developed the culture required for this; and it is culture that is required. Nothing will be achieved in this by doing things in a rush, by assault, by vim or vigor, or in general, by any of the best human qualities. Secondly, we have elements of knowledge, education and training, but they are ridiculously inadequate compared with all other countries.

Here we must not forget that we are too prone to compensate (or imagine that we can compensate) our lack of knowledge by zeal, haste, etc.

In order to renovate our state apparatus we must at all costs set out, first, to learn, secondly, to learn, and thirdly, to learn, and then see to it that learning shall not remain a dead letter, or a fashionable catch-phrase (and we should admit in all frankness that this happens very often with us), that learning shall really become part of our very being, that it shall actually and fully become a constituent element of our social life. In short, we must not make the demands that are made by bourgeois Western Europe, but demands that are fit and proper for a country which has set out to develop into a socialist country.

The conclusions to be drawn from the above are the following: we must make the Workers' and Peasants' Inspection a really exemplary institution, an instrument to improve our state apparatus.

Let us say frankly that the People's Commissariat of the Workers' and Peasants' Inspection does not at present enjoy the slightest authority. Everybody knows that no other institutions are worse organized than those of our Workers' and Peasants' Inspection, and that under present conditions nothing can be expected from this People's Commissariat. We must have this firmly fixed in our minds if we really want to create within a few years an institution that will, first, be an exemplary institution, secondly, win everybody's absolute confidence, and, thirdly, prove to all and sundry that we have really justified the work of such a highly placed institution as the Central Control Commission. In my opinion, we must immediately and irrevocably reject all general figures for the size of office staffs. We must select employees for the Workers' and Peasants' Inspection with particular care and only on the basis of the strictest test. Indeed, what is the use of establishing a People's Commissariat which carries on anyhow, which does not enjoy the slightest confidence, and whose word carries scarcely any weight? I think that our main object in launching the work of reconstruction that we now have in mind is to avoid all this.

The workers whom we are enlisting as members of the Central Control Commission must be irreproachable Communists, and I think that a great deal has yet to be done to teach them the methods and objects of their work. Furthermore, there must be a definite number of secretaries to assist in this work, who must be put to a triple test before they are appointed to their posts. Lastly, the officials whom in exceptional cases we shall accept directly as employees of the Workers' and Peasants' Inspection must conform to the following requirements:

First, they must be recommended by several Communists.

Second, they must pass a test for knowledge of our state apparatus.

Third, they must pass a test in the fundamentals of the theory of our state apparatus, in the fundamentals of management, office routine, etc.

Fourth, they must work in such close harmony with the members of the Central Control Commission and with their own secretariat that we could vouch for the work of the whole apparatus.

In substance, the matter is as follows:

Either we prove now that we have really learned something about state organization (we ought to have learned something in five years), or we prove that we are not sufficiently mature for it. If the latter is the case, we had better not tackle the task.

I think that with the available human material it will not be immodest to assume that we have learned enough to be able systematically to rebuild at least one People's Commissariat. True, this one People's Commissariat will have to be the model for our entire state apparatus.

We ought at once to announce a contest in the compilation of two or more textbooks on the organization of labor in general, and on management in particular.

We ought to send several qualified and conscientious people to Germany, or to Britain, to collect literature and to study this question. I mention Britain in case it is found impossible to send people to the U.S.A. or Canada.

We ought to appoint a commission to draw up the preliminary program of examinations for prospective employees of the Workers' and Peasants' Inspection; ditto for candidates to the Central Control Commission.

Young Radicals and the Fear of Power

Kenneth Keniston

Our introductory essay suggested that there is a danger that an articulate and knowledgeable few can manipulate the many in participatory-democracy units. This interesting piece by Kenneth Keniston describes the discomfort many young radicals feel in positions of power because they realize that the possibilities for manipulation exist. He reviews their hostility to formal roles and office routine. Such inner feelings can have significant consequences in terms of the kinds of organizations that are created.

In the middle of Vietnam Summer, there occurred a "revolt of the secretaries" which can stand as introduction to the vexed and unresolved problems of authority, leadership, power and control which continue to plague the participants in organizations of young radicals.

As Vietnam Summer was originally organized, the national office was divided into two groups: "political" staff concerned with questions of national organizing, coordination, publicity, the funding of local projects, and so on; and "office" staff, who addressed envelopes, typed, ran the mimeograph, and answered the telephone. This second group was largely recruited from among college girls and recent college graduates in the Boston area. It was a group of attractive and unusually intelligent young women. As the summer progressed, and as members of the political staff and the office staff came to know one another, a blurring and overlapping of functions began to occur. Most of the members of the political staff seemed embarrassed that, often for the first time in their Movement experience, they had others to do their routine work for them. Furthermore, it became obvious to all that the office staff was not only talented but that they had volunteered to work for subsistence wages because of their strong commitment to the goals of Vietnam Summer.

In the middle of the summer, then, the secretaries were "organized" by the political staff. "It was a classic organizing situation," said one of the political staff who engineered the revolution. "They were underemployed,

---

From Kenneth Keniston, "Young Radicals and the Fear of Power," *The Nation* (March 18, 1968), pp. 370–373. Reprinted by permission of the author.

dissatisfied with the work they were doing, and had a lot of good ideas about what they should do instead. It was simply a matter of organizing them, encouraging them to speak out." The organized confrontation occurred, the political staff (who constituted both the exploiters and the organizers of the exploited) capitulated immediately, and the distinction between political and office work was abolished. The ex-secretaries were more or less integrated into the political staff and given "political" responsibilities, especially for the organization of publicity and public functions. Girls who had been typing letters one week found themselves negotiating with Sol Hurok the next. To be sure, the completeness of the "revolt of the secretaries" should not be exaggerated. In the end, the superior training and skills of the political staff meant that they continued to make most of the "major decisions"; but the participation of the ex-office workers increased as their experience and competence grew.

This paradoxical revolt, organized by the "bosses" against whom it was directed, illustrates some of the strengths and problems of work in the New Left Movement. The incident points to the extreme discomfort felt by most young radicals when they are in a position of power and control over another person, especially if that person is then expected to do routine, boring or unenjoyable work. At another level, it points to the great value the New Left places on participation, and to its continual effort to devise new institutional forms that will give concrete meaning to the vague phrase, "participatory democracy." The goal behind this slogan is to create an informed group, rather than a single informed person with power over others; to elaborate new techniques for collective decision making; to eliminate traditional bureaucratic organizational structures and hierarchies of power; to develop new social groups that enhance the self-esteem of those who form them and permit the "creative" participation of those involved in decisions that affect them.

All of these issues were raised with singular intensity because of the condensed history of Vietnam Summer. Less than two months elapsed between the conception and the start of the project. Unlike most Movement organizations, Vietnam Summer was at the beginning a "top-down" project with no basis in local communities, with no "constituency." Indeed, one of the prime objectives of the project was to create such constituencies in local communities, with the explicit hope and plan that as the summer progressed they would increasingly take over the organization from the bottom up.

As a result, Vietnam Summer leaders and organizers at all levels found themselves in a conflict-filled situation: by joining together to create an initially "top-down" organization, they violated the Movement's objectives of participatory democracy and grass-roots organizing. But simultaneously, the national office and its field workers had to deal continually with local anxieties that the Movement was excessively dominated from what was sometimes called the "walled city of Cambridge," while other local workers questioned the source of Vietnam Summer funds (did they perhaps come from Bobby Kennedy's political machine?). Members of local projects, especially those in large cities, sometimes expressed concern that the entire summer "achievement" would simply be "turned over" to some existing political machine for use in the conventional party politics shunned by the New Left.

The leaders of the project, then, whether located in Cambridge or moving across the country, had to try to reassure others about aspects of Vietnam Summer which in fact worried them as well. The extent of their discomfort was reflected in the heated arguments, especially in the early summer, between national office staff members and "older members" of the National Steering Committee, a group that included a number of "old New Leftists" plus representatives of a traditional peace organization. In all such arguments, the national office staff made it extremely clear that they were not interested in joining into conventional political alignments, that their emphasis was on community organizing, and that they considered civil disobedience (for example, organized draft resistance) a valid tactic. The national office staff was in the position of defending its own "radical" position from the somewhat more "liberal" position of some of the National Steering Committee, while at the same time allaying the worries of those in the field that it was not radical enough. Further, and even more important, their leading role in a national organization not only provided these young radicals with opportunities but also created considerable personal anxiety because it conflicted with their own values of participatory democracy.

The acceptance of leadership roles, particularly when they entailed the possibility of exercising authority and power, also seemed difficult for many of those I interviewed. In their manner and style, these young radicals are extremely "personalistic," focused on face-to-face, direct and open relationships with other people; hostile to formally structured roles and traditional bureaucratic patterns of power and authority. Although most possessed a great capacity for personal organization, psychological structuring and individual orderliness, they were almost uniformly opposed to bureaucratic organization, tight institutional structure or organizational orderliness. For example, when one of those interviewed was "officially" given increased responsibilities in the national office, and a title to go with them, he was the object of merciless teasing from his friends. This teasing expressed not only the affection others felt for him but their (and his) embarrassment that he should have a position with "bureaucratic" implications. Throughout the summer, a deliberate and consistent effort was made to play down formal leadership and organizational structures within Vietnam Summer. Although "leaders" often had clearly defined regional or task responsibilities, project decisions were generally made on a group basis of those involved, with very little "pulling of rank." At times this suppression of leadership and the power that accompanies it was extreme: individuals not adequately informed of the issues or facts were included in policy-making discussions; while those "natural" leaders who had the most experience and the best grasp of the issues sometimes seemed deliberately to refrain from voicing their opinion lest they appear to "dominate" others. Indeed, I sometimes felt that too little distinction was made between the rational use of authority based on competence and the irrational and authoritarian exploitation of leadership roles. Similarly, power based on capacity and role sometimes seemed confused with domination and sadistic control.

A closely related issue is that of manipulation as contrasted with "sincerity." In keeping with their open and personalistic style, most young radicals seek in relationships with others a direct, unmanipulative and honest encounter. For example, what little organizational in-fighting occurred during Vietnam Summer seemed extremely overt, with disagreements directly stated. And in their interviews with me, these young radicals expressed considerable affection for their co-workers, and often, after stating a controversial view, would add, "But you should talk with X—he will give you a very different picture." Yet this eagerness to maintain open, direct and unmanipulative personal relationships, to avoid controlling others, seemed at times to obstruct other organizational needs. Thus, if everyone is to be honest, open and direct with everyone else and to allow all others a full say, decision making is often slow, especially in times of crisis. Furthermore, decisions which might best be made by a small group of the most experienced and best informed tend to be turned over to larger groups and to become rather blurred. The extent to which it is possible to retain an open, personalistic, unmanipulative and extremely trusting style, and yet mount an effective program on a national scale, is one of the key unresolved questions of the New Left.

The fear of manipulation, for example, seemed to impede organizational effectiveness on a broad scale. Like those involved in more conventional politics, Movement workers sometimes face the problem of how to make people want what they do not at present want. In recent years, conventional American politics has raised to high art public relations techniques like "managing the image" of political candidates, suppressing, selectively presenting, or neglecting crucial facts, deliberately appealing to the irrational anxieties of the electorate, and creating "pseudo-candidates" by publicity. All these tactics are closed to the New Left by their own principles. Indeed, so strong is the fear of manipulation that at times Movement workers found it difficult to appeal to the "rational" anxieties of their constituencies, even by suggesting appropriate efforts to remove the cause of these anxieties. For example, behind the many discussions during the summer over the usefulness of publicity there often seemed to run a conviction that "flashiness" and "publicity seeking" were somehow in themselves illegitimate forms of manipulation, regardless of whether the cause for which publicity was sought was legitimate or the facts to be presented were true. Thus, while intensive, long-range and largely unpublicized community organizing has many other arguments to recommend it, the appeal of this method is increased in the New Left by the fact that community organizing under the banner of "let the people decide" seems perhaps the least "manipulative" political tactic available.

The attitude of Vietnam Summer workers toward the National Conference for a New Politics, which was to be held in Chicago at the end of the summer, illustrates another dilemma of the contemporary New Left. What was to happen at the Chicago meeting, intended as a meeting of all "radical" political and social groups in the country to formulate plans for national action, was of considerable importance, both personal and organizational, to many of those I interviewed. A few had been involved in developing and planning NCNP, and others, when discussing their futures, imagined that they might later become associated with this effort to form a radical coalition in America. Furthermore, as fall approached, discussions of "what would become of" Vietnam Summer were frequently connected with what might emerge from the Chicago conference.

But despite the importance of the NCNP to those interviewed, the national office staff of Vietnam Summer made no prior effort, formal or informal, to "organize" so as to influence, much less control, the proceedings at Chicago. There were many rumors that the conference might be dominated by highly disciplined groups representing older leftist factions, or else by a coalition of black power and insurrectionist militants. The loosely defined voting rules at NCNP were intended to give maximum voice to organizations with a strong community base; the existence of active local projects was therefore crucial in determining voting power. But even though Vietnam Summer had created a large number of such local projects, and was in a position to wield considerable voting power, a number of those interviewed three days before the opening of the Chicago conference had not even secured individual voting rights for themselves. Under the same circumstances, other, old Left groups would have made consistent and perhaps successful efforts to "control" NCNP by exploiting the organizations they had helped create.

What actually happened at the large, tumultuous and confused Chicago conference has been discussed at length elsewhere. Some days after the development of a "black caucus" which demanded and obtained equal representation for the minority of Negroes present, a "white caucus" was slowly organized, largely around a nucleus of Vietnam Summer staff workers. But this "organization" grew up after the beginning of NCNP, as an ad hoc response to the cross currents within that meeting. Whether the chaos and the ultimate results of NCNP could have (or should have) been avoided is an open question. What is clear is that as individuals and in groups, young radicals like those interviewed are surprisingly nonfactional, nonparanoid, trusting, guileless and anti-organization. And what remains to be seen is whether this style, and the rudimentary organizational forms to which it has so far led, is capable of operating effectively in the same socio-political arena as highly organized, bureaucratized, manipulative and centrally controlled groups.

Throughout Vietnam Summer, then, issues of power, leadership, manipulation and control were continually visible. Although the importance of "power" is increasingly stressed in the rhetoric of the New Left, the actual exercise of power produces considerable discomfort in individual New Leftists. Indeed, it seems conceivable that the tough talk of "power" is a compensation for a group that is essentially so unmanipulative and unsuspicious.

The fear of the abuse of power, of irrational authority, and of dominating leadership is in many respects a legitimate reaction to a world in which power, authority and leadership are used cruelly rather than benignly. The various positions, styles and forms that cluster around the concept of participatory democracy are an important attempt, no matter how incomplete and experimental, to devise new forms of organization and action that will humanize the organized and vitalize the actors. The strength of this position is seen in the revolt of the secretaries; its potential weakness in the dilemma inherent in trying to devise large, effective national programs that maintain their participatory basis. In small, face-to-face groups, participatory democracy works relatively well; it has yet to devise suitable forms and strategies for large-scale organization.

But although participatory democracy is more than just a matter of individual psychology, it has deep psychological roots for the New Left. In many of the young radicals interviewed, discomfort at manipulating, controlling, or wielding power over others was related to their previous experiences within the Movement and to their own individual development. If one concentrates within small, tight groups a considerable number of individuals who have been accustomed from childhood to positions of leadership, participatory democracy can be seen as a "compromise" which permits a certain degree of group harmony, although possibly at the expense of speedy decision making and organizational effectiveness. According to this compromise, everyone agrees to give up his own leadership potential in return for the assurance that no one else will try to lead him. The ability to maintain this compromise requires highly developed self-control, especially among those who enjoy dominating or being dominated.

At a more individual level, discomfort with power is related to personal concerns over dominance, control, superiority and ultimately aggression. For example, several of those interviewed commented on how difficult it had been to learn in Movement work not to be excessively impatient when others did a less adequate job than they themselves might have done. Similar themes appeared in other interviews: difficulties in delegating responsibilities to others, in learning to work cooperatively with other people, in overcoming their own tendency to "take over" groups by using their articulateness to dominate group discussions. Moreover, the fusion of will and conscience which one finds in many young radicals requires special restraint if it is not to become smugness and self-righteousness. Those I interviewed had this restraint, often holding themselves back in dealing with others whom they considered less competent, less experienced, or simply wrong. On one or two occasions, for example, these young radicals' enthusiastic praise for the superlative human qualities and talents of those with whom they had worked in previous projects had a faintly hollow ring, as if the interviewee were protesting too much. In most cases, then, these young radicals were still quite consciously attempting to overcome in themselves any propensity to dominate, control, feel superior or be impatiently angry with others.

It is axiomatic that the issues which produce in us the greatest distaste are the same issues with which we have struggled most intensely in ourselves. And in the early lives of a number of these young radicals, the issue of struggle, and even of violence, looms large. Their early experiences had accustomed them to conflict and yet inoculated them against it, teaching them how to cope with anger in themselves and in others, how to respond "rationally" to provocation, how to avoid violence. Yet the special sensitivity to dominating control, to exploitative power and sadistic anger remains, and may help explain why in this group the avoidance of anything that approximates such abuses of power is so intense. The avoidance is almost completely successful; whatever sadism, rage and violence lie within is now expressed only directly in a quickly rejected feeling of one's own superiority, a fleeting fantasy that one could have more power, or the determination not to manipulate others.

Yet the fear of power and control in oneself and others—the avoidance of violence, inner or outer—cannot be fully explained by such psychological issues as these. It is a fear with historical as well as psychological roots and it constitutes, understandably, a central theme in this group of young radicals who came together for a summer to attempt to persuade their fellow Americans to make peace.

Radical Student Organizations

E. Joseph Shoben, Jr., Philip Werdell, and Durward Long

The last selection described some of the feelings characteristic of many of today's radicals. This item describes the kind of organization that is the result of such feelings, since it outlines the nature of the early SDS as well as SNCC. These two groups are significant examples of what a participatory-democracy organization that is nationwide could look like.

SDS

Beginning its active career, as has been the case with most relatively militant student organizations, during the civil rights drives of 1960–61, Students for a Democratic Society emerged from the youthful arm of the League for Industrial Democracy. Essentially an organizational vehicle for a wide variety of welfare-oriented liberals like Harold Taylor, Bayard Rustin, Michael Harrington, and Norman Thomas, the LID paid little attention to the Student League for Industrial Democracy until the youngsters broke away from it. The break apparently was animated largely by the model presented by the Student Nonviolent Coordinating Committee and its vigorous activity in the South.

In June, 1962, some 150 students, the great majority of them undergraduates, gathered in Port Huron, Michigan. The major enterprise of the meeting was the discussion and revision of a long and analytical paper, the first draft of which was prepared by Tom Hayden, recently graduated from the editorship of the *Michigan Daily* at the University of Michigan. By the time the group adjourned on June 15, *The Port Huron Statement* had acquired substantially both the form and the content in which it was published shortly afterward. The first major pronouncement of the New Left, the *Statement* was the founding document on which Students for a Democratic Society was based. With Hayden elected as its first president, SDS announced its basic goals in this fashion:

From "Radical Student Organizations" by E. Joseph Shoben, Jr., Philip Werdell, and Durward Long, in PROTEST! *Student Activism in America*, ed. by Julian Foster and Durward Long (New York: Morrow, 1970), pp. 206–209, 212–214. Reprinted by permission of William Morrow and Company, Inc. Copyright © 1970 by Julian Foster and Durward Long.

We seek the establishment of a democracy of individual participation with two central aims: that the individual share in those social decisions determining the quality and direction of his life, and that society be organized to encourage independence in men and to provide the media for their common participation.

By the opening of the academic year of 1962–63, the new organization had established 11 chapters on various campuses and had enrolled about 300 members. Although friendly relations with the League for Industrial Democracy for the most part were preserved, all formal connections with the parent body very quickly were broken; and, in the early part of 1963, SDS had set up an independent national headquarters in Chicago from which it conducts its national business.

Structurally, SDS is an individual membership organization, but both its requirements and its bookkeeping are essentially casual. To belong, one need only pay annual dues of $2.00 and offer a "reaffirmation of one's belief in democracy." From the beginning, however, there consistently have been at least as many students who associate themselves with SDS activities and ideas without formally becoming affiliated as there have been dues-paying members. In a roughly similar fashion, there always have been regional and national offices in the organization, but the local chapters, granted an extremely high degree of autonomy, regularly have been perceived as the central source of strength. When national policies are formulated, they virtually always are phrased as "recommendations" to the membership, and they typically contain explicit statements like "local chapters must decide for themselves what is appropriate and effective action."

Even under these conditions, however, the regional and national patterns of leadership are kept under constant and stringent review in an attempt to make them "more democratic." Voting at quarterly regional meetings and at the annual national convention follows the one-member, one-vote principle, with an emphasis on direct participation in the meetings rather than on representation by chapter, by region, by college or university, or by some other basis. After some years of continuing debate, the offices of president and executive secretary were abolished in 1966 on the ground that such offices, willy-nilly, had an excess of authority and that it was impossible for two people to serve as spokesmen for so diverse a constituency. Three national secretaries and a National Interim Council were established to serve in lieu of officers of a more conventional kind. In 1967, the council was enlarged to 11, including the secretaries, to involve more people, to permit the interplay of more points of view, and to divide the responsibility for keeping in relatively close touch with local chapters. Members of the council are required to work actively with campus-based groups in order to maintain a loose, but personalized, liaison between the national office and the rank-and-file membership. The rapidity of structural and procedural changes within SDS makes its leadership rather amorphous to an outsider, but reflects its apparently deliberate struggles to avoid bureaucratization and to operate internally in as democratic a manner as it demands in its literature that the larger society observe.

Since its founding, SDS has gained annually in both chapters and individual members. Founded by fewer than 60 students from 11 institutions, by 1964 it had about 2,000 members on some 75 campuses. In 1966, the numbers had grown to almost 20,000 in nearly 200 institutions. Currently, chapters in 275–300 colleges and universities enroll nearly 30,000 individuals. These figures apply only to formal members; many more students can be rallied to participate in the discussions, programs, and demonstrations which SDS often catalyzes.

The dynamic quality of this sort of growth seems to stem from two principal factors in the group's appeal and its mode of operation. First, its ideological umbrella is a very wide one. Sharply critical of contemporary American society, SDS accommodates people whose views range from straightforward anarchy to ideas deriving from what is called the "Old Left." The great majority of members seem to fall between these two extremes, finding the organization a comfortable base from which to develop their own political style and stance. It is from this large middle range that the national leadership has been elected quite consistently. Second, the local leaders, schooled by those who participated in the civil rights movement, have been unusually successful in developing the strategy and (especially) the tactics by which students can take direct and immediate action with respect to issues on which their feelings run high. At the local level—which is the level that is looked upon as counting—the development of SDS can be understood as a function of the almost yearly generation of new programs and emphases, coupled with tactical innovations that have given them a considerable proportion of successes. . . .

SDS continues to be a highly diversified and heterogeneous organization in both its membership and its activities. Community organizing programs, cut very much from the original ERAP cloth, continue to grow. "Radical education," taking its cue from REP, but not bound by its recommendations, is the central concern of a number of local chapters. In a variety of colleges and universities, the main investment of energy is in challenges to the in loco parentis doctrine and to parietal rules; on such issues, SDS rapidly forms alliances with representatives from the National Student Association, with the official personnel of formal student governments, and even with members of the highly conservative Young Americans for Freedom. Older SDS members, often calling themselves "alumni" of the organization, are busy in several institutions with efforts to build radical professional and professorial associations. In short, the evidence suggests that SDS has combined with reasonable effectiveness the business of generating new programs almost every year with the ability to retain old enterprises that appear particularly relevant and rewarding in special communities or on special campuses.

Financially, SDS clearly functions mainly because of a willingness among its leadership to participate in the affairs of the organization with little or no compensation. The annual budget nationally has never been more than $100,000; currently it is reported as between $80,000 and $90,000. Something over half, but under two-thirds, of this amount comes from dues and subscriptions; the balance comes from contributions, nearly all of which are reported as small, mostly under $10.00 in size, and virtually all of them under $25.00. "Alumni" are apparently the most reliable donors. For local programs or projects, money often is raised locally, typically from wealthier but sympathetic students. Such local fund drives seem to be too sporadic, unsystematic, and diffused for their results to be estimated with any accuracy.

About half of the expenditures at the national level are for staff salaries, which seem to average a little less than $20.00 per week, for the travel expenses of secretaries and members of the National Interim Council, and for similar costs. The balance of the budget is for the production and distribution of New Left Notes and other publications, the rent of the national office in Chicago, stationery and postage, telephone, and equipment items like duplicators and a mimeograph machine. Small amounts of money sometimes are contributed to local chapters to meet special needs. Legal costs are negligible; by means of closely maintained relationships with the American Civil Liberties Union, both through the ACLU's national headquarters in New York and its offices in a number of cities, the services of lawyers can be obtained for virtually nothing if, as is usually the case, an issue of civil liberties either is inherent in the situations that demand legal aid or can be injected into them.

Both by principle and as a result of its experience, SDS works with virtually any individual or group with whom sympathies are shared in relation to any given issue. This point holds for both local and national activities. Indeed, there are many ways in which the potency of the organization lies in its capacity to develop constituencies outside of its own membership around the problems to which it chooses to address itself. One of its reasonably clear goals is that of "radicalizing" these constituencies, inducing a widening circle of young people to join it in its ambitions, as well as in its programs, through the personal relationships, the sense of belonging, and the experience of participation that collaboration with SDS tends to provide. Without contradiction, the organization also is quite willing to play a kind of bridging or linking role, holding more militant and more moderate factions in a particular situation in a working relationship. As more "alumni" become available to it, this kind of function becomes somewhat more apparent on campuses where student and faculty elements not infrequently are joined through the efforts of SDS into functional coalitions.

SNCC

The origins of the Student Nonviolent Coordinating Committee, like the origins of many such groups, are lost in the complexities of recent history. Perhaps the most obvious beginning can be attached to February, 1960, when four Negro students from the A. & T. College, Greensboro, North Carolina, after long and serious discussion among themselves, decided that direct action was required of *individuals* to achieve equal rights for black people. On February 1, they sat down at a lunch counter, requesting service which always had been reserved for whites. Within a week, learning of the action in the newspapers and by word of mouth, students on several other campuses in the South were organizing sit-ins of their own. With white and black students over the country joining the movement, over 100 sit-ins took place in the next two months. For the first time in America, young people—almost all of them college undergraduates—had seized political initiative with respect to a vital social issue.

By April 15, there already were over 60 centers of sit-in activity. With a major role played by Ella Baker (formerly with the NAACP and the Urban League, and associated with the late Martin Luther King's Southern Christian Leadership Conference since 1957), a conference was called in 1961 at Shaw University, Raleigh, North Carolina, including 126 students and 58 adult delegates from different southern communities. Most of the participants already were experienced in direct-action techniques, and their meeting concentrated on questions of strategy and tactics and on how they might support one another most effectively as they continued to press for change through variations of the sit-in. The conference has been described as an *ad hoc* committee with mutual assistance and reinforcement as its major goal. To the dismay of some adults present, the students clearly voiced their disinterest in joining or becoming affiliated formally with established civil rights organizations. Although the students then developed no formal organization of their own, the conference foreshadowed the mood and behavior which would dominate SNCC meetings from its inception until 1966.

A month later, at Atlanta University, the Temporary Student Nonviolent Coordinating Committee was formed. Marion Barry, then a student at Fisk University, was elected chairman. The abolition of racial segregation was the central and explicit goal, and the sit-in mode of direct, nonviolent civil disobedience was identified as the most legitimate form of action. Despite the considerable diversity of the participants, agreement on a basic statement was not very difficult. Its essence was contained in the opening sentences:

> We affirm the philosophical or religious ideal of nonviolence as the foundation of our purpose, the presupposition of our faith, and the manner of our action. Nonviolence as it grows from the Judaic-Christian tradition seeks a social order permeated by love. Integration represents the first step toward such a society. . . .

During the summer, SNCC set up temporary headquarters in a corner of the SCLC offices in Atlanta. Jane Stembridge dropped out of Union Theological Seminary to become the first office secretary. Julian Bond, then in student status, and Robert Moses, a Harvard graduate teaching high school in New York City, came to Atlanta for the summer. Together with SNCC officers and a growing number of part-time volunteers, they began to raise money, to plan nonviolent institutes for the summer, to print a newsletter called the *Student Voice*, and to attempt to coordinate student activities throughout the South. "Coordination" meant keeping abreast of plans for local action and, when possible, putting people in touch who might be able to help each other—e.g., protest leaders and sympathetic lawyers. This pattern set the norm and, with a few important exceptions, the limits of national organization throughout SNCC's history. By October, 1960, the number of sit-ins was increasing and winning attention in the national press; the Freedom Rides and other new thrusts were being planned; and the increased communication and travel of student activists nationally were making the vision of a "movement" seem, in student activists' minds, more and more capable of realization. Several hundred delegates met in Atlanta a little over a year later and put SNCC on a permanent basis.

SNCC was not at its beginnings and never has been a membership organization. "Members" are simply those people who share its sympathies and objectives, who by their own individual work and action define its activities, and who attend its meetings. Consequently, there is no structure of local chapters; and, until 1967, participation in SNCC's annual summer conference was entirely self-selective. (Even then, it possibly could be argued, whites did not attend out of respect for the blacks' decision to take responsibility for what they saw as a black problem, not out of explicit policies of exclusion.) Everyone attending these conferences was eligible to vote for national officers, for a 21-man executive committee, and on any statements presented for consideration.

Many student activists in other groups now point to SNCC as having pioneered a politically viable "staff organization," a critical concept in understanding contemporary student politics. Young people who take individual responsibility for direct action and community organizing are the self-selected staff, identifying themselves in terms of their commitments to issues or to the community in which they are organizing, rather than to a formal organization per se. To put this vital notion another way, responsibility is defined as much in terms of the responsiveness of SNCC "members" to the needs of the poor and the disenfranchised as in terms of the responsiveness of national officers to the mandates of members. A feeling of political, though emphatically non-ideological, fraternity and the mutual reinforcement of individual actions replace traditional organizational machinery in holding together these different levels of responsibility. SNCC always has been better understood as a movement than as an organization.

Without a central office, and with Stokely Carmichael under surveillance and Rap Brown under sentence, SNCC has been described recently as "merely a group of 150 wandering, homeless, hard-core militants." There is much that seems accurate in this characterization. But for all its shapelessness, this organization appears to enjoy a discipline, a flexibility, and a degree of sympathy and loyalty—among some white young people as well as Negroes—that make it a strong, serious force despite (or even because of) its lack of firm outlines. Some of those "wandering militants" show up on campuses that are ripe for trouble or after protest activities have broken out, and it is reported by student and faculty sources from some colleges that both the intensity and the discipline of black students can be accounted for significantly by this kind of outside leadership.

The funding of SNCC never has been easy to understand. Its decentralized and fragmentary organization is complicated by the fact that financial records, apparently seldom adequate at any point in SNCC's history, have been lost or destroyed. Three points seem relatively sure. One is that SNCC began with no money at all in any central organizational till, and that the local projects which it has emphasized consistently more often than not have returned to a state of no money at all. In these local enterprises, office space was borrowed, donations or loans of second-hand equipment were solicited, and field workers lived with families in the region in which they happened to be working. In many ways, it is the SNCC field workers' strong and articulate tradition of living on "subsistence or less" that has made both them as individuals and the organization itself beyond fiscal comprehension in the usual sense and beyond financial constraints when outside funds have not been available. Second, the peak annual budget was reached, it would seem, in 1963–64, when about $250,000 was raised by direct-mail appeals, benefit performances by Negro entertainers and artists, and occasional foundation grants. In this period, it must be remembered, SNCC was concerned much more with desegregation than with Black Power, and was inclined less toward the militancy that has marked its activities in more recent years. Estimates indicate that about a fourth of that top budget was spent for field staff salaries that averaged $10–$15 per week. Another quarter, roughly, went for supplies, printing, and postage—mainly in the service of publishing pamphlets, posters, newsletters, press releases, etc. The balance, possibly running as high as $150,000, went into local projects in Mississippi, Alabama, and Georgia. Third, since 1965, money for this kind of loosely conducted, informal, and overwhelmingly and almost exclusively Negro civil rights work has become increasingly hard to come by; and since 1966, when SNCC vociferously espoused the Black Power doctrine and stance, both Negro and white sources of funds virtually have dried up. Some field workers have taken jobs in order to support their community efforts; some have taken to panhandling as a way of acquiring the small amounts of money necessary to their continuing to function in some minimal fashion. Most of Carmichael's money—and it has obviously been a good deal—has come from speaking engagements, and a fair proportion of it is understood as having been reinvested in the purposes SNCC has represented, if not directly in SNCC itself. The same seems to be generally true of Rap Brown. Although there is some talk about money for SNCC through "sources at the United Nations" and through Communist sources, there seems to be no way to verify these notions, and there seems to be little evidence of money being spent that could not be explained as earned by SNCC people or as donated in small amounts. The amounts are far from large, and, insofar as one can determine from a confused and cloudy picture, finances are not central to SNCC's influence.

With respect to its relationships with other groups, SNCC has maintained an insistent independence. When they have joined coalitions or organizations, SNCC has been clear about its own stand on the particular issue, and regularly has tended to pull the other associations into more radical positions. As the integrationist phase of the civil rights movement has faded, however, it has withdrawn from national programs and shown much less interest in united fronts. Its stress has been on local communities, including some college campuses, where SNCC representatives have shown a good deal of talent in building alliances among highly diverse people, including some whites as well as blacks. As in the early sit-ins, the criterion of these alliances has been a matter of commitment to issues felt as important by local people, and this sensitivity to grass-roots frustration and discontent gives it a potency that seems to exceed by far its organizational resources, its financial capability, or its numbers of active workers. If SNCC has become more a psychological force than a national association, it is not without a shadowy but considerable power.

"New" vs. "Left" in the SDS

Tom Milstein

The preceding selection described the SDS as it originally existed. Its participatory-democracy spirit was reflected in its conventions, which shunned elaborate credentials for delegates, complex parliamentary rules, and the like. But here is an account of the convention in 1968. Participatory democracy was no longer in evidence, and virulent factionalism emerged—an illustration of what participatory democracy can lead to, or at least fail to prevent.

We might contrast this situation with an account of direct democracy out in the woods among the ancient Germans. According to Tacitus:

> They assemble, except in the case of a sudden emergency, on certain fixed days, either at new or at full moon. . . . When the multitude think proper, they sit down armed. Silence is proclaimed by the priests, who have on these occasions the right of keeping order. Then the king or the chief . . . is heard, more because he has influence to persuade than because he has power to command. If his sentiments displease them, they reject them with murmurs; if they are satisfied, they brandish their spears.*

Let us hope that the key to making participatory democracy work does not lie in having priests and carrying spears.

The Students for a Democratic Society held its annual convention June 9–15 at Michigan State University, and delegates witnessed some dramatic new developments without precedent in the history of the organization. "Old-timers" who held out so much hope for the SDS in the early sixties will soon discover, if they have not already done so, that very little is left of that unique spirit of innocent idealism which then characterized the group. SDS has come the full circle from other-worldliness to under-worldliness.

From Tom Milstein, " 'New' vs. 'Left' in the SDS," Dissent (September–October 1968), pp. 447–450. Reprinted by permission of Dissent Publishing Corporation and the author.
* Tacitus, Germany, in Moses Hadas, ed., The Complete Works of Tacitus, Modern Library Edition (New York: Random House, 1942), p. 714.

The convention proper was preceded by three days of workshops on such staples of "the movement" as "GI Organizing," "Marcuse and (Norman O.) Brown," "White Racism," "Movement Media, including Underground Papers, Radio Free People, etc.," and so on. Interspersed among these relatively noncontroversial (in the New Left) topics were a few—"Progressive Labor party and the SDS"—that foretold of the important issues to be debated at the convention, but the substantive issues everybody knew to be at stake were at most only obliquely reflected in the workshops. This generated an atmosphere of frustration and irritability that dominated the rest of the proceedings.

By the time things actually got underway, tensions were acute. Wednesday evening was taken up by a plenary session devoted to a panel and discussion on the "black liberation struggle." Four persons (SDS requested that no one be quoted by name in the press) delivered talks on the subject. The first was a rather mundane exhortation to the delegates to support the Peace and Freedom party on the basis of that party's work with the Black Panther Party for Self-Defense. The second was an entertaining account of a young radical's life with proletarians in a farm-implement factory. The speaker gave a lively description of the difficulties involved in raising the workers from economic consciousness to class consciousness, and he dwelt at length on the phenomenon of racist, white, skilled workers and their vested interest in holding down black unskilled labor, even within the same union. The third speaker was a Progressive Labor party SDS'er; he took up this implied challenge to PL's working-class orientation by noting that "fascism" was not restricted to the working class—there is such a thing as middle-class student fascism, as exemplified by certain features of the recent San Francisco State College fracas. This speaker was (to me) the surprise of the evening. He went on to describe the counterproductive consequences of the San Francisco State incident, and sounded quite chastised by the whole affair. Imagine that—a chastised Maoist! He had just finished criticizing the Kerner report for its wholesale indictment of "white society and white racism" as being responsible for Negro oppression—when this potentially fruitful controversy was interrupted by a floor demonstration.

The "anarchist" contingent at the convention, consisting primarily of members of the "Up Against the Wall, Motherfucker" chapter of SDS, of the Lower East Side, New York, continually disrupted the convention proceedings with planned "spontaneous" demonstrations, perhaps a case of chickens coming home to roost. These young people are a demoralized collection of acid-heads and sociopaths with a flair for surpassing in their personal and "political" conduct every gutter-level smear hurled at the Left by reactionaries. When they broke into the developing controversy on race and radicalism, by means of Algerian war-cries and unbelievable profanity, they effectively terminated intelligent discussion and nearly provoked a physical struggle. Passions grew quite heated as the delegates polarized between the ideologues of all persuasions who wanted to carry on the discussion, and the nihilists of no persuasions who feel automatically excluded whenever rational debate threatens to break out. Convention observers began edging toward the exits, but the conflict was resolved short of violence—after all, these are college students—by allowing a Motherfucker to present his views on the subject of racism after the panel had concluded.

But the atmosphere of the convention was no longer conducive to a joining of the issues. The rest of the evening was taken up with speeches. One speaker dealt with "racism in the Left" and cited Harold Cruse, the Negro intellectual who believes that Jewish Communists are responsible for the emasculation of black manhood in America. He concluded by saying that the principal contradiction in American society is not class, but race. This pessimistic conclusion was joyously affirmed by the Motherfuckers' speaker, who carried the logic one step further. It was absurd, he said, for white radicals to discuss ways of "supporting the Black Liberation struggle." Such "support" is itself racist. When the war begins, "the color of your skin will be your uniform, and if you're carrying food to the guerrillas, well, I hope they get it when you drop it." A PL spokesman rose to comment that it was such views which were themselves "racist." Only one thing seemed clear to both sides: SDS is full of "objective" racists.

The formal session began with outgoing national officers' reports. The immediate past was characterized as one in which SDS had evolved an "anticapitalist" perspective. The rottenness in America was gradually revealing itself to be the rottenness of America—not atypical, but essential. The enemy was not "corporate liberalism," which is a euphemism, but "fascism." The blatant rightist repression, which everyone in SDS regards as coming, should be welcomed, even stimulated: the true beastiality that is America will, when no longer obscured, provoke a universal confrontation.

Following that, the "Program Proposals" document was taken up by the convention. This document was explained to me as proposing the reorganizing of SDS along centralist lines, and the transformation of the membership into a vanguardist, disciplined cadre. It was written in a clotted organizational mandarin, and I could not clearly discern these features. Also, during the first two hours the debate on the proposition was conducted in SDS-speak, which is difficult to describe to anyone who has never heard it. It consists of the ritualistic repetition of certain catchphrases like "organize people to take control of the conditions that determine their lives," "structure radical life-styles outside the system," "constituency-based organization leading to regional program exposing the corporate interrelationships among the processing apparatus of the establishment," etc. These phrases are woven together and declaimed in the most passionate style. The audience divides into two factions upon receipt of the message: those who lack self-confidence because of newness to SDS and who hide their failure to comprehend what is being said by mimicking the responses of those around them, occasionally even taking the floor to try stringing together a few phrases on their own—and those who do not hide their inability to comprehend, but who restrict themselves to muttering "bullshit." These latter are the ideologues; they refrain from popping the bubble because to do so usually provokes an enraged counterattack by the non-ideologues on "Old Leftism" in the SDS.

The debate on the "Program Proposals" document went on and produced its corresponding behavioral reaction: a rise in the anxiety level of the convention. The pretense that important things are being hashed out becomes more difficult to maintain after the discussion has droned on for several hours without any apparent resolution. It is at this point that the SDS elite, capitalizing on the exhaustion of the delegates, tries to pass whatever is the object of the discussion.

This discussion was different, however. A Progressive Labor speaker rose to denounce a section of the document which reflected the influence of Herbert Marcuse's ideas on the revolutionary bankruptcy of the proletariat in modern capitalist society. This shrewd move took the supporters of the document by surprise. At last the convention had something real to discuss.

The "Program Proposals" document was a product of the "National Office" grouping within SDS. This faction is a conglomeration that claims to represent the true spirit of New Leftism against the depredations of PL and other "external cadre." The fact is that the original spirit of "participatory democracy" has all but disappeared from the organization, and the National Office grouping, as will be made clear, waged its fight against PL in an obscurantist and manipulative fashion. Their aim in centralizing SDS by means of the "Program Proposals" was, pure and simple, to purge PL and consolidate their power as the only organized faction in SDS. Nothing was said of this in the document, however. There, the sole motivation for centralization was that the "revolutionary situation in America" demanded a "revolutionary vanguard" organization.

In order to portray themselves as authentic heirs to the SDS tradition, the National Office faction must mount an effective critique of PL's Marxism-Leninism-Stalinism, and forward an alternative radical ideology. By their own admission, they are capable of doing neither "at this time." So when PL attacked the document, not for its ostensible purpose, centralization, nor for its real purpose, to purge SDS, but for its Marcuse-ish contempt of the working class, the National Office faction was caught flat-footed.

The debate that followed, on the role of the working class in contemporary capitalist society, enabled PL and its supporters to claim the events in France as its model. Correspondingly, the recent events at Columbia University, for which the National Office faction takes credit, declined in importance. "The seizure of power in one of the most important links in the structure of establishment power" (Columbia University) didn't look so impressive when contrasted to the proletarian seizure of the means of production in France.

Thus trapped into defending an anti-working-class perspective in the midst of the French events, the National Office faction was smashed in debate. Progressive Labor conducted itself with great polemical skill and actually won a clear majority of the convention—both in opposition to the Program Proposals document and to a big piece of its ideology. The longer the debate continued, the more PL's prestige grew. Large numbers of delegates who had come to the convention uncommitted rose to announce that they "couldn't buy this Marcuse crap about the workers."

Hoping to rescue something of its position, the National Office faction made a hasty decision to bring its politics out into the open. A spokesman for the "Program Proposals" document stated that he was sorry that the debate had confused people about the meaning of his document, but that since Progressive Labor had seen fit to utilize its elite cadre to distort and smear, there was nothing honest participatory democrats could do to stop them.

This news produced an audible gasp among the delegates. Except for a few snide remarks about "external cadre" operating in SDS, no one had dared to bring this matter out in open debate in the history of SDS. This spokesman was followed by speaker after speaker from the National Office faction, each denouncing Progressive Labor more vituperatively than the last. All thought of "non-exclusion," once a cardinal principle of SDS doctrine, was forgotten. As the National Office speakers worked on the convention, seeking to build up resentment against PL to a fever pitch, PL, anticipating a siege, sat tight and confined themselves to hisses and an occasional charge of "red-baiting." They knew the politics of desperation when they saw it.

In the meantime, what can only be described as a lynch spirit was building up among the delegates who supported the National Office faction. As the scene approached its climax, they were literally snarling. I have never witnessed comparable behavior in some years of activity in youth politics. The final speaker concluded with the scream "PL must go!" and this signalled his supporters to begin a floor demonstration. About two-fifths of the delegates rose and began chanting "PL must go," stamping their feet and clapping their hands, and the din grew deafening. The chant lasted five minutes, but it seemed endless. PL sat tight.

The National Office faction was gambling that it could stampede the convention. With only about two-fifths of the delegates, they needed support from the SDS center. But their effort to lynch PL, coming on the heels of a weak performance in the debate on the role of the working class, was such a radical departure from SDS tradition (which, while not demo-cratic, was at least not totalitarian) that it backfired and produced only stunned disbelief among the swing delegates. But you can't intimidate a disciplined cadre like PL with a chant, no matter how intimidating it sounds, and when it became apparent that the convention wasn't going to stampede, the demonstration petered out. What would have happened if the National Office faction had managed to isolate PL, I shudder to imagine.

After this remarkable event, all was anti-climactic. Progressive Labor rode out the storm in a manner that did credit to their discipline and strategic abilities. They succeeded, not because they are totalitarians (although they are), but because their opposition was even more totalitarian. As a result, Progressive Labor was the clear victor at the 1968 SDS convention.

Because PL placed none of its cadre in the SDS national office, the National Office faction and its supporters in the radical and liberal press have claimed the victory. The fact is, however, that PL only ran one candidate for national office, and he lost not so much because he lacked support as because of a poorly organized voting system. Progressive Labor is not interested in SDS except as an arena of potential recruits. Least of all is it interested in taking responsibility for such SDS activities as the San Francisco State and Columbia University putsches.

Some myths have arisen among well-wishers of SDS in the adult liberal community, and they ought to be dispelled. One is that SDS's recent conduct is due to the machinations of Progressive Labor, which is viewed as a tiny but incredibly effective band of ultra-leftist Maoist maniacs. Nothing could be farther from the truth. PL has tried to exert a restraining influence on SDS, and was generally regarded as the "Right Wing" of the SDS at the convention. The National Office faction, which claims to represent the authentic SDS and New Left spirit, at all times attacked PL *from the Left*. PL's "labor line" was constantly cited as a major *conservative* influence in the organization. And in fact, it is. Because PL stresses the interests of the working class, it regards university seizures and Black nationalism, which are dear to the hearts of the National Office faction, as irresponsible and (in private) semifascist adventures that can only provoke a rightist reaction and alienate the working class from radicalism. PL seems gradually to be moving toward the Right, away from its earlier Third Period Communism. Its commitment to the working class, even though for the most part cerebral, forces a minimal concept of responsibility for the consequences of action to take hold. The National Office faction, on the other hand, with its half-baked melange of Marcuse, Sorel, Bakunin, Calvin, and Guevara, pridefully sees itself as the revolutionary vehicle, and consequently feels a responsibility for the consequences of its actions to no one and nothing but History.

Progressive Labor's achievements at the SDS Convention should be taken as a measure of the current state of the SDS, rather than as an indication of political superiority. The level of political sophistication within SDS has been severely debased by romanticism and anti-anti-

Communism, and virtually any well-organized and ideologically coherent political tendency could have triumphed. PL, burdened with its surreal commitment to "the red, red sun of the East," its glorification of Stalin, and its willingness to fight the war in Vietnam to the last Vietnamese, could only flourish in the hermetic environment such as the New Left provides.

Where SDS will go in the future is difficult to predict, because its conventions are not very representative of the SDS membership. Although split wide open, it is quite conceivable that it will continue to grow, since no other organization exists to absorb New Left youth. Something very profound and basic is occurring within the upper-middle-class strata from which SDS recruits, and it must be said that the National Office faction's brand of radicalism more accurately reflects this mood than does PL. If SDS does disintegrate or become moribund, we still may expect further outbursts of middle-class radicalism, expressed through different channels.

On the other hand, events can kill movements. Nothing has done more damage to SDS than the McCarthy campaign and the opening of peace negotiations. These events have hit SDS where it lives—on the campuses. The outcome of the French "revolution"—Gaullist victory on an unprecedented scale—will hit SDS also. The important question is whether the current wave of middle-class radicalism can survive the cumulative effect of these events, or whether it will dissolve back into the suburbias which hatched it.

The Flowering of the Hippie Movement

John R. Howard

In a sense this excerpt does for the hippie movement what the previous one did for the SDS: it attempts to explore some of the consequences, or at least occurrences, of rather unstructured communal living.*

The Life and Death of Haight-Ashbury

Before the rise of Haight-Ashbury, the aspiring writer or artist from the Midwest fled to Greenwich Village. By the summer of 1967, Haight-Ashbury had replaced the Village as the place to go, and, indeed, people were leaving the Village to move to San Francisco. The words of Horace Greeley, "Go west, young man," had rarely been so diligently heeded.

The Haight-Ashbury area was for many years an upper-middle-class neighborhood. Haight Street was named for Henry Haight, a conservative former governor of California, who would be appalled could he have foreseen that his name was to be associated with the "love generation."

As the city grew and the residents of the area prospered, they moved out and rented their property. Eventually, the expanding black population began to move in and, in the late 1950's and early 1960's, were joined by beatnik refugees from the North Beach area of the city. Eventually, in this relatively tolerant community, a small homosexual colony formed. Even before the hippies appeared, then, Haight-Ashbury had become a kind of quiet Bohemia.

"Hippie" is a generic term. It refers to a general orientation of which there are a number of somewhat different manifestations. . . .

THE VISIONARIES

The visionaries gave birth to the movement. It lived and died with them in Haight-Ashbury. Let us attempt here to understand what happened.

From John R. Howard, "The Flowering of the Hippie Movement," *The Annals*, Vol. 382 (March 1969), pp. 45–48. Reprinted by permission of the author and the American Academy of Political and Social Science.

* For a similar account of a new commune beset by some traditional problems, see Jack Swanson, "A New Way of Life—Or Is It?" *National Observer*, March 23, 1970, p. 22.

The hippies offered, in 1966 and 1967, a serious, though not well-articulated, alternative to the conventional social system. To the extent that there was a theory of change implicit in their actions, it might be summed up by the phrase "transformation by example."[1] Unlike political revolutionaries, they attempted no seizure of power. Rather, they asked for the freedom to "do their thing," that is, to create their own social system. They assumed, implicitly, that what they created would be so joyous, so dazzling, so "groovy" that the "straight"[2] would abandon his own "up-tight" life and come over to their side. A kind of anti-intellectualism pervades hippie thinking; thus, their theory of change was never made explicit.

The essential elements in the hippie ethic are based on some very old notions—the mind-body dichotomy, condemnation of the worship of "things," the estrangement of people from each other, and so on. Drastically collapsed, the hippie critique of society runs roughly as follows: Success in this society is defined largely in terms of having money and a certain standard of living. The work roles which yield the income and the standard of living are, for the most part, either meaningless or intrinsically demeaning. Paul Goodman, a favored writer among the young estranged, has caught the essence of this indictment.

> Consider the men and women in TV advertisements demonstrating the product and singing the jingle. They are clowns and mannequins, in grimace, speech, and action. . . . What I want to call to attention in this advertising is not the economic problem of synthetic demand . . . but the human problem that these are human beings working as clowns; and the writers and designers of it are human beings thinking like idiots. . . .
> "Juicily glubbily
> Blubber is dubbily
> delicious and nutritious
> —eat it, kitty, it's good"[3]

Further, the rewards of the system, the accouterments of the standard of living, are not intrinsically satisfying. Once one has the split-level ranch-type house, the swimming pool, the barbecue, and the color-television set—then what? Does one, then, measure his progress in life by moving from a twenty-one-inch set to a twenty-four-inch set? The American tragedy, according to the hippies, is that the "normal" American evaluates himself and others in terms of these dehumanizing standards.

The hippies, in a sense, invert traditional values. Rather than making "good" use of their time, they "waste" it; rather than striving for upward mobility, they live in voluntary poverty.

The dimensions of the experiment first came to public attention in terms of a number of hippie actions which ran directly counter to some of the most cherished values of the society. A group called the Diggers came into existence and began to feed people free in Golden Gate Park in San Francisco and in Constitution Park in Berkeley. They themselves begged for the food that they prepared. They repudiated the notion that the right of people to satisfy their basic needs must be mediated by money. If they had food, one could share it with them, no questions asked. Unlike the Salvation Army, they did not require prayers as a condition of being fed; unlike the Welfare Department, they did not demand proof of being without means. If a person needed lodgings, they attempted to make space available. They repudiated the cash nexus and sought to relate to people in terms of their needs.

Free stores were opened in Berkeley and San Francisco, stores where a person could come and take what he needed. Rock groups such as Country Joe and the Fish gave free concerts in the park.

On the personal level, a rejection of the conventional social system involved dropping out. Given the logic of the hippie ethic, dropping out made sense. The school system prepares a person for an occupational role. The occupational role yields money and allows the person to buy the things which society says are necessary for the "good life." If society's definition of the good life is rejected, then dropping out becomes a sensible action, in that one does not want the money with which to purchase such a life. By dropping out, a person can "do his own thing." And that might entail making beads or sandals, or exploring various levels of consciousness, or working in the soil to raise the food that he eats.

They had a vision of people grooving together, and they attempted to remove those things which posed barriers—property, prejudice, and preconceptions about what is moral and immoral.

By the summer of 1968, it was generally felt by those who remained that Haight-Ashbury was no longer a good place. "It's pretty heavy out there on the street," a former methedrine addict remarked to me as we talked of changes in the community, and his sentiments were echoed in one of the underground newspapers, The San Francisco Express Times: "For at least a year now . . . the community as a common commitment of its parts, has deteriorated steadily. Most of the old crowd is gone. Some say they haven't actually left but are staying away from the street because of bad vibrations."

In those streets, in the summer of 1968, one sensed despair. Significantly, the agencies and facilities dealing with problems and disasters were still very much in evidence, while those which had expressed the élan and hope of the community either no longer existed, or were difficult to find. The Free Clinic was still there, as was the shelter for runaways, and the refuge for persons on bad trips; but free food was no longer served in the parks, and I looked for several days before finding the Diggers.

Both external pressures (coercion from the police and various agencies of city government) and internal contradictions brought about the disintegration of the experiment. . . . At this point, I am analyzing only the internal contradictions of the hippie ethic.

Stated simply, the argument is as follows. The hippies assumed that voluntarism (every man doing his thing) was compatible with satisfying essential group and individual needs and with the maintenance of a social system in which there was an absence of power differentials and invidious distinctions based on, for example, wealth, sex, or race. That assumption is open to question. Voluntarism can work only where the participants in a social system have a sufficient understanding of the needs of the system to be willing to do things which they do not want to do in order for the system to persist. Put somewhat differently, every system has its own needs, and where voluntarism prevails, one must assume that the participants will both understand what needs to be done and be willing to do it.

Let me clarify by way of illustration. I asked one of the Diggers why they were no longer distributing food in the park.

> Well, man, it took a lot of organization to get that done. We had to scuffle to get the food. Then the chicks or somebody had to prepare it. Then we got to serve it. A lot of people got to do a lot of things at the right time or it doesn't come off. Well, it got so that people weren't doing it. I mean a cat wouldn't let us have his truck when we needed it or some chick is grooving somewhere and can't help out. Now you hate to get into a power bag and start telling people what to do but without that, man, well.

By refusing to introduce explicit rules designed to prevent invidious power distinctions from arising, such distinctions inevitably began to appear. Don S., a former student of mine who had moved to Haight-Ashbury, commented on the decline of the communal house in which he had lived.

> We had all kinds of people there at first and anybody could stay if there was room. Anybody could crash out there. Some of the motorcycle types began to congregate in the kitchen. That became *their* room, and if you wanted to get something to eat or a beer you had to step over them. Pretty soon, in a way, people were cut off from the food. I don't mean that they wouldn't give it to you, but you had to go on their "turf" to get it. It was like they had begun, in some very quiet and subtle way, to run things.

In the absence of external pressures, the internal contradictions of the hippie ethic would probably have led to a splintering of the experiment. Significantly, many of the visionaries are trying it again outside the city. There are rural communes throughout California. In at least some of them, allocation of task and responsibility is fairly specific. There is the attempt within the framework of their core values—freedom from hang-ups about property, status, sex, race, and the other furies which pursue the normal American—to establish the degree of order necessary to ensure the persistence of the system within which these values are expressed.

Notes

1 Interestingly, Martin Buber, in *Paths in Utopia*, suggested that the example of the *kibbutz* might transform the rest of society. The values of the *kibbutzim* and those of the hippie movement are not dissimilar.

2 We shall have occasion to speak frequently of "straights." The derivation of the word is even more obscure than that of "hippie." At one time, it had positive connotations, meaning a person who was honest or forthright. "He's straight, man" meant that the referent was a person to be trusted. As used in the hippie world, "straight" has a variety of mildly to strongly negative connotations. In its mildest form, it simply means an individual who does not partake of the behavior of a given subculture (such as that of homosexuals or marijuana users). In its strongest form, it refers to the individual who does not participate and who is also very hostile to the subculture.

3 Paul Goodman, *Growing Up Absurd* (New York: Vintage Books, 1960), pp. 25–26.

Chapter Four

Neighborhoods

The concept of neighborhood is not very precise. People use it in many different ways, and here it is used broadly enough to encompass the small town and the ghetto as well as other smaller urban units.

This chapter consists of three parts. The first concerns the neighborhood as a geographical conception—that is, a residential or other kind of community with physical boundaries. The second section deals with black perspectives on community control, where the definition of the community may be more ethnic than geographic. The third section concerns neighborhood control of schools. This is often the most immediate focus of demands for decentralization to the neighborhood level, probably because it is one of the few vital organized social functions still carried on within neighborhoods and because the problems are of immediate and personal interest to the residents. We use the Ocean Hill-Brownsville dispute in New York City as an example of school decentralization. The last part is a good capsule summary of the problems and prospects of neighborhood government in general.

Unhappiness with existing patterns of representation is the basis of proposals for decentralization to the neighborhood level. Thus it is easy to demonstrate that blacks and other minorities are objectively underrepresented in the political system. The crucial point is that representation is also a psychological matter. In the present context of radical thought this means that constituents will seek delegates who are representative *of* them not just *for* them. *If we try to distill a general principle, it would be that like should represent like.* Thus in part of this section we will be dealing with the implicit argument that we should have neighborhood government and local control of the schools so that those who run things are

211

more like their constituents. In another part we are concerned with the argument that blacks must be represented by blacks, a contention widespread among activist blacks that has helped undermine white participation in black political movements.

Of course, if the general principle were pushed to its logical conclusion, no one could ever represent anyone but himself, and this would be the ultimate argument for direct democracy. However, when not extended this far, the principle is actually quite widely used. For example, at election time Congressmen must be like their constituents in terms of residence, and someone from New York would not feel represented by a California Congressman.

What we are presently facing in our racial unrest is a demand by some blacks and other groups that the criteria of likeness be extended to include color as a necessary but not sufficient condition for representativeness. To black radicals no white can speak for them; neither can Roy Wilkins, even though he is not white. For representativeness, ideological agreement is insufficient (in white supporters) and color is insufficient (in Wilkins); the black radical demands both.[1] Exactly the same principle is embodied in the youthful watchword: "Don't trust anyone over 30."

---

[1] In regard to jury selection for the trial of a black man by his "peers," the Black Panthers insist: "A peer is a person from a similar economic, social, religious, geographical, environmental, historical and racial background. To do this the court will be forced to select a jury from the black community from which the black defendant came. . . ." But would the Panthers apply the same criteria in selecting jurors to try their enemies—for example a policeman accused of brutality toward blacks? For the citation see the October 1966 Party Platform in any issue of *The Black Panther*.

Why Are We in New York?

Norman Mailer

The following article by Norman Mailer was written during his campaign for Mayor of New York City, when he and Jimmy Breslin ran on the slogan "Vote the Rascals In." In this article he proposed that New York City become a separate state and that, within the new state, power be decentralized to its neighborhoods. If we recall Dahl's remark that a city like New York has a larger population than a good many countries, we can better appreciate Mailer's program. But note that there are no guidelines for defining neighborhoods; in fact, he clearly expects neighborhoods to define themselves.

. . . We could direct our effort first against the present thickets of the City Charter. The Charter is a formidable document. There are some who would say it is a hideous document. Taken in combination with the laws of New York State, it is a legal mat guaranteed to deaden the nerve of every living inquiry. The Charter in combination with the institutional and municipal baggage surrounding it is guaranteed to inhibit any honest man from erecting a building, beginning an enterprise, organizing a new union, searching for a sensible variety of living zone, or speaking up for local control in education. It would strangle any honest Mayor who approached the suffocations of air pollution or traffic, tried to build workable on-the-job training, faced the most immediate problems of law and order, attacked our shortage of housing or in general even tried to conceive of a new breath of civic effort. There is no way at present to circumvent the thicket without looking to power-brokers in the trade unions, the Mafia and real estate.

Only if the people of New York City were to deliver an overwhelming mandate for a city-state could anything be done about the thicket. Then the legal charter of the new state could rewrite the means by which men and women could work to make changes in the intimate details of their neighborhoods and their lives.

From Norman Mailer, "Why Are We in New York?" *The New York Times Magazine* (May 18, 1969), pp. 101–109. © 1969 by The New York Times Company. Reprinted by permission. Also by permission of the author and the author's agent, Scott Meredith Literary Agency, Inc., 580 Fifth Avenue, New York, N.Y. 10036.

Such a new document would most happily be built upon one concept so fundamental that all others would depend upon it. This concept might state that power would return to the neighborhoods.

Power to the neighborhoods! In the new city-state, every opportunity would be offered to neighborhoods to vote to become townships, villages, hamlets, sub-boroughs, tracts or small cities, at which legal point they would be funded directly by the fifty-first state. Many of these neighborhoods would manage their own municipal services, their police, sanitation, fire protection, education, parks, or, like very small towns, they could, if they wished, combine services with other neighborhoods. Each neighborhood would thus begin to outline the style of its local government by the choice of its services.

It may be recognized that we are at this point not yet vastly different from a patch of suburbs and townships in Westchester or Jersey. The real significance of power to the neighborhoods is that people could come together and constitute themselves upon any principle. Neighborhoods which once existed as separate towns or districts, like Jamaica or New Utrecht or Gravesend, might wish to become towns again upon just such a historic base. Other neighborhoods with a sense of unity provided by their geography like Bay Ridge, Park Slope, Washington Heights, Yorkville, Fordham Road, Riverdale, Jackson Heights, Canarsie or Corona might be able without undue discussion to draw their natural lines.

Poorer neighborhoods would obviously look to establish themselves upon their immediate problems, rather than upon historical or geographical tradition. So Harlem, Bedford-Stuyvesant and the Barrio in East Harlem might be the first to vote for power to their own neighborhoods so that they might be in position to administer their own poverty program, own welfare, their own education systems, and their own—if they so voted—police and sanitation and fire protection for which they would proceed to pay out of their funds. They would then be able to hire their own people for their own neighborhood jobs and services. Their own teachers and communities would, if they desired, control their own schools. Their own union could rebuild their own slums. Black Power would be a political reality for Harlem and Bedford-Stuyvesant. Black people and, to the extent they desired, Puerto Rican people, could make separate but thoroughgoing attacks upon their economic problems, since direct neighborhood funding would be available to begin every variety of economic enterprise. Black militants interested in such communal forms of economic activity as running their own factories could begin to build economies, new unions and new trades in their neighborhoods.

Power to the neighborhoods would mean that any neighborhood could constitute itself on any principle, whether spiritual, emotional, economical, ideological or idealistic. Even prejudicial principles could serve as the base—if one were willing to pay. It could, for example, be established in the charter of the city-state that no principle of exclusion by race or religion would be tolerated in the neighborhoods unless each such neighborhood was willing to offer a stiff and proper premium for this desire in their taxes.

In reaction to this, each and every liberal, Negro and white, who would detest the relinquishment of the principle that no prejudice was allowed by law, might also consider the loss of the dream of integration as the greatest loss in the work of their lives. They would now be free to create neighborhoods which would incorporate on the very base of integration itself—Integration City might be the name of the first neighborhood to stand on the recapture of the old dream. Perhaps it might even exist where now is Stuyvesant Town.

On the other hand, people who wished anonymity or isolation from their neighbors could always choose large anonymous areas, neighborhoods only in name, or indeed could live in those undifferentiated parts of the city which chose no neighborhood for themselves at all. The critical point to conceive is that no neighborhood would come into existence because the mayoralty so dictated. To the extent that they had been conditioned for years by the notion that the government was the only agency large enough and therefore effective enough to solve their problems, so to that extent would many people be reluctant to move to solutions which came from themselves.

To the degree, however, that we have lost faith in the power of the government to conduct our lives, so would the principle of power to the neighborhoods begin to thrive, so too would the first spiritual problem of the 20th century—alienation from the self—be given a tool by which to rediscover oneself.

In New York, which is to say, in the 20th century, one can never know whether the world is vastly more or less violent than it seems. Nor can we discover which actions in our lives are authentic or which belong to the art of the put-on. Conceive that society has come to the point where tolerance of others' ideas has no meaning unless there is benumbed acceptance of the fact that we must accept their lives. If there are young people who believe that human liberty is blockaded until they have the right to take off their clothes in the street—and more! and more!—make love on the hood of an automobile—there are others who think it is a sin against the eyes of the Lord to even contemplate the act in one's mind. Both could now begin to build communities on their separate faith—a spectrum which might run from Compulsory Free Love to Mandatory Attendance in Church on Sunday! Grant us to recognize that wherever there is a common desire among people vital enough to keep a community alive, then there must be also the presence of a clue that some kind of real life resides in the desire. Others may eventually discern how.

Contained beneath the surface of the notion is a recognition that the 20th century has lost its way—the religious do not know if they believe in God, or even if God is not dead; the materialist works through the gloomy evidence of socialism and bureaucracy; the traditionalist is hardly aware any longer of a battlefield where the past may be defended; the technician—if sensitive—must wonder if the world he fashions is evil, insane, or rational; the student rebellion stares into the philosophical gulf of such questions as the nature of culture and the students' responsibility to it; the blacks cannot be certain if they are fundamentally deprived, or a people of genius, or both. The answers are unknown because the questions all collide in the vast empty arena of the mass media where no price has ever to be paid for your opinion. So nobody can be certain of his value—one cannot even explore the validity of one's smallest belief. To wake up in New York with a new idea is to be plunged into impotence by noon, plunged into that baleful sense of boredom which hints of dread and future violence.

So the cry of Power to the Neighborhoods may yet be heard. For even as marriage reveals the balance between one's dream of pleasure and one's small real purchase upon it, even as marriage is the mirror of one's habits, and the immersion of the ego into the acid of the critic, so life in the kind of neighborhood which contains one's belief of a possible society is a form of marriage between one's social philosophy and one's private contract with the world. The need is deeper than we could expect, for we are modern, which is to say we can never locate our roots without a voyage of discovery.

Perhaps then it can be recognized that power to the neighborhoods is a most peculiar relocation of the old political directions. It speaks from the left across the divide to conservatism. Speaking from the left, it says that a city cannot survive unless the poor are recognized, until their problems are underlined as not directly of their own making; so their recovery must be based upon more than their own private efforts, must be based in fact upon their being capitalized by the city-state in order that the initial construction of their community economics, whether socialist or capitalist or both, can begin.

Yet with power in the neighborhoods, so also could there be on-the-job training in carpentry, stone-masonry, plumbing, plastering, electrical work and painting. With a pool of such newly skilled workers, paid by the neighborhood, the possibility is present to rebuild a slum area room by room.

Better! The occupant of an apartment who desires better housing could go to work himself on his own apartment, using neighborhood labor and funds, patching, plastering, painting, installing new wiring and plumbing—as the tenant made progress he could be given funds to continue, could own the pride of having improved his housing in part through his own efforts.

So power to these poor neighborhoods still speaks to conservative principles, for it recognizes that a man must have the opportunity to work out his own destiny, or he will never know the dimensions of himself, he will be alienated from any sense of whether he is acting for good or evil. It goes further. Power to all neighborhoods recognizes that we cannot work at our destiny without a context—that most specific neighborhood which welcomes or rejects our effort, and so gives a mirror to the value of our striving, and the distortion of our prejudice. Perhaps it even recognizes the deepest of conservative principles—that a man has a right to live his life in such a way that he may know if he is dying in a state of grace. Our lives, directed by abstract outside forces, have lost that possibility most of all. It is a notion on which to hit the campaign trail.

American Scene: Participatory Democracy

Time

This brief selection, which describes a town meeting in action, seems to fit with the conclusions reached by a study of Massachusetts town governments:

In general, townsmen appear to be convinced they can make decisions themselves as good as, or superior to, decisions that could be made by a body of elected representatives. . . .

In retrospect, the open town meeting has proved to be a lithe and tenacious institution which demonstrates that government by mass meeting of interested citizens is still possible.*

But our own familiarity with town governments in Wisconsin suggests that the inattentiveness of many residents to such "micropolitical" activities often promotes the self-serving conduct of town officers.

At mud time in New England—a kind of fifth season between winter and spring—residents in scores of towns still assemble for one of American democracy's oldest rites: the town meeting. The tradition is as old as the colonies and, some say, retains about as much relevance as a ducking stool. As population increases and modern municipal problems intrude, many Yankee communities find that they need the expertise and steady ministration of professionals. Yet in smaller towns the annual caucus survives as a functional exercise in participatory democracy.

In mud time 1970, 120 of the 596 inhabitants of Mount Vernon, Me., gathered at the elementary school for the 182nd annual meeting since the first one was held in 1788. Also attending was *Time* Correspondent Gregory Wierzynski. His report:

Twenty miles northwest of Augusta in hilly farm country, Mount Vernon is too poor to be a traditionally quaint New England town. At the

---

From "American Scene: Participatory Democracy," *Time* (April 13, 1970), p. 24. Reprinted by permission from *Time*, The Weekly Newsmagazine. Copyright Time Inc., 1970.

* Joseph Zimmerman, *The Massachusetts Town Meeting: A Tenacious Institution* (Albany, N.Y.: Graduate School of Public Affairs, State University of New York at Albany, 1967), pp. 87–88. For a more pessimistic outlook, see "The Fading Town Meeting," *National Civic Review*, LIV, No. 9 (October 1965), 464–465, 522.

start of the century, it had a flourishing sawmill, gristmill, tannery and barrel factory. By 1940, the industries were gone. Now the townsmen cut lumber or work in neighboring communities in shoe factories, mills or government offices. The average family income runs between $3,000 and $4,000 a year. "Downtown" is a cluster of frame buildings, including the abandoned log mill, a general store and a pizza joint. It was in Mount Vernon, where his mother lives, that Erskine Caldwell wrote *Tobacco Road*—and he might have been inspired by the setting, if not the climate.

Mount Vernon's people are nonetheless proud, independent and intent on keeping the town alive. At least part of their pride derives from the fact that they very literally govern themselves. There is also a sense of stability. Apart from minor vandalism there has not been a crime for years. Despite the poverty, a welfare budget of $1,000 suffices; few are willing to apply for public assistance.

In the schoolhouse, which also serves as the town office, friends who had not seen each other since the first snows of winter exchanged exuberant greetings. Then the townspeople settled down to choosing their three-member board of selectmen and debating a $117,280 town budget. They approved $9,000 for a new school bus and $100 for steel roofing to cover the shed that houses salt to spread on winter roads. But no, they would not repair a section of road leading to the house of the community's second-largest taxpayer. An appropriation for other winter road maintenance was passed, however, because a housewife exclaimed: "I got stuck twice and couldn't get the old man to work."

A proposal to allot $600 to help the state root out a blight called pine blister rust went down because, as one man said: "We can do it better, and for nothing." One item on the "warrant," or agenda, suggested replacing Mount Vernon's 22 conventional street lights with 17 mercury-vapor lights to provide better illumination. When the first selectman explained that the change would increase the monthly electric bill by $25.90, a resident shouted: "Forget it!" It was unanimously voted down.

Short Time. There was some excitement over the town's accounts, which have been in disarray since 1967, when the selectmen did not bother to submit a financial report. "I wish to ask the town treasurer," one citizen snapped, "why there are so many discrepancies in her accounting." Mabel Smith, town clerk and treasurer, a sturdy, pugnacious widow who between meetings virtually runs Mount Vernon, crustily invited any doubters to check the receipts at the bank. One of Mrs. Smith's responsibilities is to record the town's deaths, births and marriages. These days, however, she publicly reports only the deaths, because she noticed a lot of her neighbors snickering at the short time elapsed between some marriages and births.

No Lightning. Before recessing for cookies and coffee provided by the Women's Auxiliary, the townspeople discussed their $64,000 school budget. Superintendent Perry Shibles reported that they would have to spend at least $6,000 on new teachers and raise the salaries of those already working in Mount Vernon. The townspeople gasped but went along with the proposal.

Jefferson called the New England town meeting "the best school of political liberty the world ever saw." To a degree, the town meeting represents an older communal spirit not unlike that of hippie settlements. Now the technology that the communards seek to escape is beginning to close in on towns like Mount Vernon. Until a couple of years ago, Mount Vernon was served by crank telephones and calls routed by two elderly operators who knew everyone in town. One townsman recalls: "They knew where everybody was and used to transfer calls if you were visiting somebody. Now we just have this dial stuff that gets only a lot of noise in the receiver."

There was little superfluous static at the town meeting. Moderator Robert Johnson managed the session with quiet efficiency. For one thing, the townspeople have a deep respect for parliamentary procedure and law. For another, the bootlegger who used to supply enlivening white lightning has been dead for several years. Nowadays the nearest liquor store is twelve miles away.

An Enemy of the People: Act IV

Henrik Ibsen

---

*This selection shows how the ignorance and selfishness of the
"people" in a rural village setting (not unlike the New England town in
many respects) can crush the man of unorthodox views. In Henrik
Ibsen's nineteenth-century play the hero, Dr. Stockmann, has discovered
that the health baths on which the town's economic prosperity depends
have become polluted. Most of the characters are close acquaintances,
and the Mayor is his brother; the bitter confrontation recalls to us the
sobering thought that Socrates was put to death as an "enemy of the
people"—in his case by a mass-participation jury. It is not just the issue
of pollution that gives Ibsen's play contemporary value; at the height of
the cold war and the dawning McCarthy era, Arthur Miller found that
the times demanded a modern adaptation.**

Act Four

A large, old-fashioned room in the house of CAPTAIN HORSTER. At the
back of the room, double doors open on to an anteroom. On the wall,
left, are three windows; against the opposite wall is a dais, on which is a
small table, and on it two candles, a water carafe, a glass, and a bell.

The room is additionally lit by wall lamps between the windows.
Downstage left, a table with candles and a chair. Down right is a door,
and beside it a couple of chairs.

There is a big crowd of townspeople of all classes. A few women and
one or two schoolboys can be seen among them. More and more people
keep coming in through the door at the back, filling up the room.

FIRST MAN [bumping into another man]. Hello, Lamstad! You here as
well?

SECOND MAN. I never miss a public meeting.

THIRD MAN. I expect you've brought your whistle?

From *The Oxford Ibsen*, Vol. VI, trans. and ed. by James Walter McFarlane
(London: Oxford University Press, 1960), pp. 87–105. Reprinted by permission.
* *Arthur Miller's Adaptation of An Enemy of the People* by Henrik Ibsen (New
York: Viking Press, 1951). The decisive meeting occurs in Act Two, Scene Two.

SECOND MAN. You bet I have. Haven't you?

THIRD MAN. I'll say I have. Skipper Evensen said he was going to bring his great big cow-horn.

SECOND MAN. Good old Evensen!

[*Laughter in the group.*]

FOURTH MAN [*joining them*]. Here, I say, what's going on here tonight?

SECOND MAN. It's Dr. Stockmann. He's holding a protest meeting against the Mayor.

FOURTH MAN. But the Mayor's his brother!

FIRST MAN. That doesn't matter. Dr. Stockmann's not frightened.

THIRD MAN. But he's got it all wrong. It said so in the *Herald*.

SECOND MAN. Yes, he must be wrong this time, because nobody would let him have a hall for his meeting—Ratepayers Association, Men's Club, nobody!

FIRST MAN. He couldn't even get the Baths Hall.

SECOND MAN. I should think not.

A MAN [*in another group*]. Whose side are we on here, eh?

A SECOND MAN [*in the same group*]. Just you keep an eye on Aslaksen, and do what *he* does.

BILLING [*with a briefcase under his arm, pushing his way through the crowd*]. Excuse me, gentlemen! May I come through, please? I'm reporting for the *Herald*. Thank you . . . thank you!

[*He sits at the table, left.*]

A WORKMAN. Who's he?

SECOND WORKMAN. Don't you know *him*? That's Billing, he's on Aslaksen's paper.

[CAPTAIN HORSTER *conducts* MRS. STOCKMANN *and* PETRA *in through the door, right front.* EJLIF *and* MORTEN *are with them.*]

HORSTER. I thought perhaps the family might like to sit here. You can easily slip out there if anything happens.

MRS. STOCKMANN. Do you really think things might get out of hand?

HORSTER. You never know . . . with all these people here. But you sit here, and don't worry.

MRS. STOCKMANN [*sits down*].   It was very kind of you to offer my husband this room.

HORSTER.   Well, since nobody else would . . .

PETRA [*who has also sat down*].   And it was brave of you too, Captain Horster.

HORSTER.   Oh, I can't see there was anything particularly brave about it.

[HOVSTAD *and* ASLAKSEN *arrive simultaneously but separately, and make their way through the crowd.*]

ASLAKSEN [*walks over to* HORSTER].   Hasn't Dr. Stockmann arrived yet?

HORSTER.   He's waiting in there.

[*Movement in the crowd near the door at the back.*]

HOVSTAD [*to* BILLING].   Look! Here's the Mayor.

BILLING.   Yes, damn me if he hasn't turned up after all!

[*The* MAYOR *eases his way through the crowd, bowing politely, and takes up a position by the wall, left. A moment later,* DR. STOCKMANN *enters by the door, right front. He wears a black frock coat and a white cravat. Some people clap uncertainly, which is met by subdued hissing. Then there is silence.*]

DR. STOCKMANN [*in an undertone*].   How do you feel, Katherine?

MRS. STOCKMANN.   I'm all right, thanks. [*Lowers her voice.*] Try not to lose your temper, Thomas.

DR. STOCKMANN.   Oh, I can control myself. [*Looks at his watch, steps up on the dais, and bows.*] It's now quarter past . . . so I think we can begin. . . .

[*He produces his manuscript.*]

ASLAKSEN.   First I think we ought to elect a chairman.

DR. STOCKMANN.   No. That's not necessary.

SEVERAL VOICES [*shouting*].   Yes, yes it is!

MAYOR.   I should also have thought that we should elect a chairman.

DR. STOCKMANN.   But I've called this meeting to deliver a lecture, Peter.

MAYOR.   Your lecture might just possibly lead to divergent expressions of opinion.

MANY VOICES [*from the crowd*].   A chairman! A chairman!

HOVSTAD. The consensus of opinion seems to be that we should have a chairman.

DR. STOCKMANN [*controlling himself*]. Very well! Let the "consensus of opinion" have its way.

ASLAKSEN. Wouldn't the Mayor accept nomination?

THREE MEN [*applauding*]. Bravo! Bravo!

MAYOR. For a number of obvious reasons, I must decline. But fortunately we have here with us a man whom I think we can all accept. I refer, of course, to the chairman of the Ratepayers Association, Mr. Aslaksen.

MANY VOICES. Yes, yes. Good old Aslaksen! Bravo!

> [DR. STOCKMANN *gathers up his manuscript and steps down from the dais.*]

ASLAKSEN. If it is the wish of my fellow citizens, I can hardly refuse. . . .

> [*Clapping and cheers.* ASLAKSEN *mounts the dais.*]

BILLING [*writing*]. Let's see—'Mr. Aslaksen elected by acclamation . . .'

ASLAKSEN. And now, perhaps I may be allowed, in this present capacity, to take the opportunity of saying a few brief words. I am a quiet and peace-loving man, who believes in discreet moderation and in . . . and in moderate discretion. Everyone who knows me is aware of that.

MANY VOICES. That's right! That's right, Aslaksen!

ASLAKSEN. I have learnt from long experience in the school of life that moderation is the quality that best befits a citizen . . .

MAYOR. Hear, hear!

ASLAKSEN. . . . and that discretion and moderation are the things whereby society is best served. I might perhaps, therefore, suggest to the honorable gentleman who has called this meeting that he endeavor to keep within the bounds of moderation.

A MAN [*near the door*]. Up the Moderates!

A VOICE. Shut up there!

MANY VOICES. Sh! Sh!

ASLAKSEN. No interruptions, gentlemen, please! Has anybody any comment to make?

MAYOR. Mr. Chairman!

ASLAKSEN. Yes, Mr. Mayor.

MAYOR. In view of the close relationship which, as is doubtless well known, exists between me and the present Medical Officer of the Baths, I should have much preferred not to speak this evening. But my connections with the Baths, to say nothing of my concern for the vital interests of the town, compel me to put forward some sort of proposal. I think I may safely assume that not a single one of us present here today wants to see irresponsible and exaggerated accounts put about concerning the sanitary conditions at the Baths and in the town generally.

MANY VOICES. No, no! Certainly not! We protest!

MAYOR. I should like to propose, therefore, that the Medical Officer be not permitted by this meeting to present his account of the matter.

DR. STOCKMANN [*flaring up*]. Not permitted! What is this . . .?

MRS. STOCKMANN [*coughing*]. Hm! hm!

DR. STOCKMANN [*composing himself*]. Ah! Not permitted, eh!

MAYOR. In my communication to the *People's Herald,* I acquainted the public with the relevant facts, and every right-thinking person can quite well form his own opinion. It clearly shows that the Doctor's proposal—apart from being a vote of censure on the leading citizens of the town—simply means saddling the ratepayers with an unnecessary expenditure of at least several hundred thousand crowns.

[*Cries of disapproval, and whistles.*]

ASLAKSEN [*ringing the bell*]. Order please, gentlemen! I should like to support the Mayor's proposal. I too believe there is some ulterior motive behind the Doctor's agitation. He talks about the Baths, but what he's really after is revolution. He wants to see the control of the council pass into other hands. Nobody doubts but what the Doctor is sincere in his intentions—nobody can be in two minds about that, surely. I too am in favor of self-government by the people, as long as it doesn't fall too heavily on the ratepayers. But that's just what *would* happen here. And that's why I'm damned . . . excuse me, gentlemen . . . why I just can't bring myself to agree with Dr. Stockmann this time. You can pay too dearly even for the best of things sometimes. That's my opinion.

[*Animated applause on all sides.*]

HOVSTAD. I feel I ought to make my position clear, too. Dr. Stockmann's agitation seemed in the early stages to be attracting a certain measure of approval and I supported it as impartially as I was able. But then we got wind of the fact that we had allowed ourselves to be misled by an incorrect account. . . .

DR. STOCKMANN. Incorrect . . . !

HOVSTAD. A not wholly reliable account, then. The Mayor's statement has proved that. I trust nobody here doubts my liberal convictions. The policy of the *People's Herald* on the more important political questions must surely be known to everybody. But I have profited from the advice of experienced and thoughtful men that, when it comes to local affairs, a paper should proceed with a certain caution.

ASLAKSEN. I entirely agree with the speaker.

HOVSTAD. And in the matter under discussion it is now undeniably true that Dr. Stockmann has public opinion against him. But what is the first and foremost duty of an editor, gentlemen? Is it not to work in harmony with his readers? Has he not been given, as it were, a tacit mandate to work loyally and unremittingly for the welfare of his fellows? Or am I perhaps mistaken?

MANY VOICES. No, no! Hovstad's right!

HOVSTAD. It has been a sad thing for me to break with a man in whose house I have of late been a frequent guest—a man who until today has enjoyed the undivided goodwill of his fellow citizens—a man whose only . . . or should we say, whose most characteristic failing is to be guided more by his heart than by his head.

A FEW SCATTERED VOICES. That's true! Good old Dr. Stockmann!

HOVSTAD. But my duty to the community compelled me to break with him. There is also one further consideration that impels me to oppose him and, if possible, to prevent him from going any further along this fateful course he has taken. And that is consideration for his family . . .

DR. STOCKMANN. You stick to the water-supply and the sewers!

HOVSTAD. . . . Consideration for his wife and his helpless children.

MORTEN. Is that us he means, Mother?

MRS. STOCKMANN. Hush!

ASLAKSEN. I shall now put the Mayor's proposal to the vote.

DR. STOCKMANN. You needn't bother! I don't intend speaking about all the dirty business at the Baths tonight. No! You are going to hear about something quite different.

MAYOR [*in an undertone*]. Now what's he up to?

A DRUNKEN MAN [*beside the entrance door*]. If I'm entitled to pay rates, I'm also entitled to my own opinion. And it's my entire . . . firm . . . incomprehensible opinion that . . .

SEVERAL VOICES.   Be quiet over there!

OTHERS.   He's drunk. Chuck him out.

[*The drunken man is put out.*]

DR. STOCKMANN.   May I speak?

ASLAKSEN [*rings the bell*].   Dr. Stockmann has the floor!

DR. STOCKMANN.   If anybody, even a few days ago, had tried gagging me as
they've tried tonight . . . they'd have seen me leaping like a lion to
the defense of my sacred rights as an individual. But that hardly matters
to me now. Now I have more important things to speak about.

[*The crowd presses closer round him.* MORTEN KIIL *can be seen in the
crowd.*]

DR. STOCKMANN [*continues*].   I've been doing a lot of thinking in the last
few days . . . turning so many things over in my mind that in the
end my head was buzzing . . .

MAYOR [*coughs*].   Hm!

DR. STOCKMANN.   . . . but I sorted things out in the finish. Then I saw the
whole situation very clearly. That's why I am here this evening. I am
going to make a great exposure, gentlemen! And the revelation I am
going to make to you is incomparably bigger than this petty business
about the water-supply being polluted and the Baths standing over a
cesspool.

SEVERAL VOICES [*shouting*].   Don't talk about the Baths! We don't want
to hear it! None of that!

DR. STOCKMANN.   I have said I am going to speak about the tremendous
discovery I have made in the last few days . . . the discovery that all
our *spiritual* sources are polluted and that our whole civic community
is built over a cesspool of lies.

DISCONCERTED VOICES [*subdued*].   What's he saying?

MAYOR.   Making insinuations . . . !

ASLAKSEN [*his hand on the bell*].   I call upon the speaker to moderate his
language.

DR. STOCKMANN.   I love my native town as much as ever a man can. I
wasn't very old when I left here; and distance and longing and
memory lent a kind of enchantment to both the place and the people.
[*Some clapping and cheers.*] Then for many a long year I sat up there
in the far North, in a miserable hole of a place. Coming across some

of the people living here and there in that rocky wilderness, I often used to think they would have been better served, poor half-starved creatures that they were, if they had sent for a vet instead of somebody like me.

[*There is a murmuring in the room.*]

BILLING [*putting his pen down*]. Damn me if I've ever heard . . . !

HOVSTAD. That's a slander on a respectable people!

DR. STOCKMANN. Just be patient a little!—I don't think anybody would want to accuse me of having forgotten my home town up there. I sat brooding—rather like an eider duck—and the thing I hatched out . . . was the plan for the Baths. [*Applause and protests.*] And when fate at long last smiled on me, and it turned out I could come home again—yes, my friends, there didn't seem to be very much more I wanted from life. Just one thing I wanted: to be able to work— eagerly, tirelessly, ardently—for the common good and for the good of the town.

MAYOR [*looking away*]. You choose rather a peculiar way of . . . hm!

DR. STOCKMANN. So there I was—deliriously, blindly happy. Then, yesterday morning—no, actually, it was the evening before—my eyes were opened wide, and the first thing I saw was the colossal stupidity of the authorities. . . .

[*Noises, shouts and laughter.* MRS. STOCKMANN *coughs earnestly.*]

MAYOR. Mr. Chairman!

ASLAKSEN [*rings the bell*]. By virtue of my position . . . !

DR. STOCKMANN. Let's not be too fussy about a word here and there, Mr. Aslaksen! All I mean is I got wind of the colossal botch-up our so-called leaders had managed to make of things down at the Baths. If there's anything I just can't stand at any price—it's leaders! I've just about had enough of them. They are just like a lot of goats in a young forest—there's damage everywhere they go. Any decent man and they just get in his way, they're under his feet wherever he turns. If I had my way I'd like to see them exterminated like any other pest. . . .

[*Uproar in the room.*]

MAYOR. Mr. Chairman, is it in order to make remarks like this?

ASLAKSEN [*his hand on the bell*]. Dr. Stockmann . . . !

DR. STOCKMANN. I can't understand why it has taken me till now to wake up to what these gentlemen really are, when practically every day I've had a perfect specimen of them right in front of my very eyes—my brother Peter—slow on the uptake and set in his ideas. . . .

[*Laughter, noise and whistles.* MRS. STOCKMAN *sits coughing.* ASLAKSEN *rings his bell violently.*]

THE DRUNKEN MAN [*who has come in again*]. Are you referring to me? Because they do call me Petersen . . . but I'll be damned if . . .

ANGRY VOICES. Throw that drunk out! Get rid of him!

[*The man is again thrown out.*]

MAYOR. Who was that person?

A BYSTANDER. Don't know him, sir.

A SECOND MAN. He doesn't belong here.

A THIRD MAN. It must be that timber merchant over from . . . [*The rest is inaudible.*]

ASLAKSEN. The man had obviously had too much to drink. Proceed, Doctor, but do please remember—with moderation.

DR. STOCKMANN. Very well, gentlemen, I shall say no more about our leaders. If anyone imagines from what I've just said that I'm out after these gentlemen's blood this evening, then he's wrong—quite definitely wrong! Because I am happily convinced that all these old dodderers, these relics of a dying age, are managing very nicely to see themselves off—they don't need to call in a doctor to hasten the end. And besides they are not the people who constitute the greatest danger to society. They are not the ones who do most to pollute our spiritual life, or to infect the ground beneath us. They are not the ones who are the worst enemies of truth and freedom in our society.

SHOUTS FROM ALL SIDES. Who then? Who is, then? Name them!

DR. STOCKMANN. Yes, I'll name them, don't you fret! Because that's precisely the great discovery I made yesterday. [*Raises his voice.*] The worst enemy of truth and freedom in our society is the compact majority. Yes, the damned, compact, liberal majority. That's what! Now you know.

[*Tremendous commotion in the room. Most of the crowd are shouting, stamping and whistling. Some of the more elderly men exchange glances, and seem to be enjoying things.* MRS. STOCKMAN *anxiously gets to her feet.* EJLIF *and* MORTEN *advance threateningly on some schoolboys who are misbehaving.* ASLAKSEN *rings his bell and shouts for order.* HOVSTAD *and* BILLING *are both trying to speak, but cannot be heard above the noise. At last quiet is restored.*]

ASLAKSEN.   As Chairman, I must request the speaker to withdraw his wild remarks.

DR. STOCKMANN.   Not on your life, Mr. Aslaksen. It is that majority here which is robbing me of my freedom and is trying to prevent me from speaking the truth.

HOVSTAD.   The majority is always right!

BILLING.   And it damn' well always stands for the truth too!

DR. STOCKMANN.   The majority is never right. Never, I tell you! That's one of these lies in society that no free and intelligent man can help rebelling against. Who are the people that make up the biggest proportion of the population—the intelligent ones or the fools? I think we can agree it's the fools, no matter where you go in this world, it's the fools that form the overwhelming majority. But I'll be damned if that means it's right that the fools should dominate the intelligent. [*Uproar and shouting.*] Yes, yes, shout me down if you like, but you can't deny it! The majority has the *might*—more's the pity—but it hasn't *right*. *I* am right—I and one or two other individuals like me. The minority is always right.

[*Renewed uproar.*]

HOVSTAD.   Ha! ha! In the last day or two Dr. Stockmann has turned aristocrat!

DR. STOCKMANN.   I've already said I'm not going to waste any words on that bunch of narrow-chested, short-winded old has-beens. They've no longer anything to give to the red-blooded life of today. I'm thinking of the few, the genuine individuals in our midst, with their new and vigorous ideas. These men stand in the very forefront of our advance, so far ahead that the compact majority hasn't even begun to approach them—and it's *there* they fight for truths too newly-born to have won any support from the majority.

HOVSTAD.   Aha! So now he's a revolutionary.

DR. STOCKMANN.   Yes, by God, I am, Mr. Hovstad! I'm plotting revolution against this lie that the majority has a monopoly of the truth. What are these truths that always bring the majority rallying round? Truths so elderly they are practically senile. And when a truth is as old as that, gentlemen, you can hardly tell it from a lie. [*Laughter and jeers.*] All right, believe it or not! But truths are not by any means the tough old Methuselahs people imagine. The life of a normally constituted truth is generally, say, about seventeen or eighteen years, at most twenty; rarely longer. But truths as elderly as that have always worn terribly thin. But it's only *then* that the majority will have anything to do with them; then it will recommend them as wholesome food for thought. But there's no great food-value in that sort of diet, I can tell you—as a doctor, I know what I'm talking about. All these majority truths are just like salt meat that's been kept too long and gone bad and moldy. That's at the root of all this moral scurvy that's going about.

ASLAKSEN. It appears to me that the honorable gentleman is straying rather a long way from his subject.

MAYOR. I concur very much with what the Chairman says.

DR. STOCKMANN. You must be mad, Peter. I'm sticking as close to my subject as I can. For that's just what I'm trying to say: that the masses, this damned compact majority—*this* is the thing that's polluting the sources of our spiritual life and infecting the very ground we stand on.

HOVSTAD. And this is what happens, you say, just because the great majority of thinking people are sensible enough to keep their approval for recognized and well-founded truths?

DR. STOCKMANN. My dear Mr. Hovstad, don't talk to me about well-founded truths. The truths the masses recognize today are the same truths as were held by advanced thinkers in our grandfathers' day. We who man the advanced outposts today, we don't recognize them any more. In my opinion, only one thing is certain: and that is that no society can live a healthy life on the old dry bones of that kind of truth.

HOVSTAD. But instead of you standing there and giving us all this airy talk, it would be interesting to hear a bit more about these old, dry bones of truth we are supposed to be living on.

[*Approval from several quarters.*]

DR. STOCKMANN. Oh, I could draw up a whole list of these horrors. But for the moment I'll restrict myself to one recognized truth, which is actually a rotten lie but which nevertheless Mr. Hovstad and the *People's Herald* and all the *Herald's* supporters live by.

HOVSTAD. And that is?

DR. STOCKMANN. A doctrine inherited from your forefathers which you fatuously go on spreading far and wide—the doctrine that the general public, the common herd, the masses are the very essence of the people—that they *are* the people—that the common man, and all the ignorant and immature elements in society have the same right to criticize and to approve, to govern and to counsel as the few intellectually distinguished people.

BILLING. Well I'll be damned. . . .

HOVSTAD [*shouting at the same time*]. Citizens, take note of this!

ANGRY VOICES. So we are not the people, eh? Only the top people are to have any say, eh?

A WORKMAN. Chuck him out, saying things like that!

OTHERS. Out with him!

A MAN [*shouting*]. Let's have a blast of it now, Evensen!

[*Great blasts on a horn, along with whistles and tremendous uproar.*]

DR. STOCKMANN [*after the noise has died down somewhat*]. Be reasonable! Can't you bear to hear the voice of truth just for once? I don't expect you all to agree with me straight off. But I must say I expected Mr. Hovstad to admit I was right when he'd got over his first shock. Mr. Hovstad claims to be a free-thinker. . . .

VOICES [*in astonished undertones*]. Free-thinker, did he say? What? Mr. Hovstad a free-thinker?

HOVSTAD [*shouting*]. Prove it, Dr. Stockmann! Have I ever said so in black and white?

DR. STOCKMANN [*reflectively*]. No, damn it, you are right. You've never had the guts. Well, I don't want to embarrass you, Mr. Hovstad. Let's say it's me who's the free-thinker, then. What I'm going to do is prove to you, scientifically, that when the *People's Herald* tells you that you—the general public, the masses—are the real essence of the people, it's just a lot of bunkum. Don't you see it's just a journalistic lie? The public is only the raw material from which a people is made. [*Murmurs, laughter and general disturbance in the room.*] Well, isn't that the way it is with life generally. Look at the difference between pedigree and cross-bred animals. Look at an ordinary barn-yard hen, for instance—fat lot of meat you get off a scraggy old thing like that! And what about the eggs it lays? Any decent, self-respecting crow could do as well. But take a pure-bred Spanish or Japanese hen, or take a pheasant or a turkey—ah! what a difference! Or I might mention dogs, which are so like humans in many ways. Think first of an ordinary mongrel—I mean one of those filthy, shaggy rough dogs that do nothing but run about the streets and cock their legs against all the walls. Compare a mongrel like that with a poodle whose pedigree goes back many generations, who has been properly fed and has grown up among quiet voices and soft music. Don't you think the poodle's brain will have developed quite differently from the mongrel's? You bet it will! That kind of pedigree dog can be trained to do the most fantastic tricks—things an ordinary mongrel could never learn even if it stood on its head.

[*Uproar and laughter.*]

A MAN [*shouts*].   Are you trying to make out we are dogs now?

ANOTHER MAN.   We're not animals, Doctor!

DR. STOCKMANN.   Ah, but that's just exactly what we are, my friend! We are as good animals as any man could wish for. But you don't find all that many really outstanding ones. Oh, there's a tremendous difference between the poodles and the mongrels amongst us men. And the funny thing is that Mr. Hovstad fully agrees with me as long as we are talking about four-footed animals. . . .

HOVSTAD.   Yes, it's all right for *them*.

DR. STOCKMANN.   All right. But as soon as I apply the principle to two-legged creatures, that's the end of it for Mr. Hovstad. He hasn't the courage of his convictions, he doesn't take things to their logical conclusion. So he turns the whole theory upside down and proclaims in the *Herald* that the barn-yard hen and the street-corner mongrel—that these are the finest exhibits in the menagerie. But that's always the way, and always will be as long as a man still remains infected by the mass mind, and hasn't worked his way free to some kind of intellectual distinction.

HOVSTAD.   I make no claim to any kind of distinction. I came from simple peasant stock, and I am proud that my roots go deep into that common people he is insulting.

SOME WORKMEN.   Good old Hovstad! Hurrah! Hurrah!

DR. STOCKMANN.   The sort of common people I'm talking about are not found simply among the lower classes; they are crawling and swarming all round us—right up to the highest social level. You've only got to look at that nice, pretty Mayor of yours. My brother Peter is as mass-minded a person as anything you'll find on two legs. . . .

[*Laughter and hisses.*]

MAYOR.   I must protest against these personal remarks.

DR. STOCKMANN. [*imperturbably*].   . . . and that's not because he's descended, like me, from some awful old Pomeranian pirate or something—because that's what we are . . .

MAYOR.   An absurd story. I deny it!

DR. STOCKMANN.   . . . but because he thinks what his superiors think, and believes what his superiors believe. And anybody who does that is just one of the masses in spirit. You see, that's why my magnificent brother Peter is so terribly lacking in natural distinction—and consequently has so little independence of mind.

MAYOR. Mr. Chairman . . . !

HOVSTAD. So in this country it seems it's the distinguished people who are the liberals! That's a new one!

[*Laughter.*]

DR. STOCKMANN. Yes, that's another part of my discovery. And along with that goes the fact that free-thinking is almost exactly the same as morality. That's why I call it downright irresponsible of the *Herald* to keep putting out this distorted idea, day in day out, that it's the masses, the compact majority that has the monopoly of morality and liberal principles—and that vice and corruption and every kind of depraved idea are an overflow from culture, just as all the filth in our Baths is an overflow from the tannery up at Mölledal! [*Uproar and interruptions.* DR. STOCKMANN, *unperturbed, smiles in his eagerness.*] And yet this same *Herald* can preach about raising the standards of the masses! Good Lord, if what the *Herald* says is right, raising the level of the masses would amount precisely to toppling them straight over the edge to perdition. But fortunately it's just one of those old lies we've had handed down—this idea that culture is demoralizing. No, stupidity and poverty and ugliness are the things that do the devil's work! A house that isn't aired and swept every day—and my wife Katherine says it ought to be scrubbed as well, but that's a debatable point—anybody living for more than two or three years in *that* kind of house will end up by having no moral sense left whatsoever. No oxygen, no conscience! And there must be an awful lot of houses in this town short of oxygen, it seems, if the entire compact majority is so irresponsible as to want to build the prosperity of the town on a quagmire of lies and deceit.

ASLAKSEN. I cannot allow such abusive remarks to be directed at the entire community.

A MAN. I move that the Chairman rule the speaker out of order!

ANGRY VOICES. Yes, yes! That's right. Out of order!

DR. STOCKMANN [*flaring up*]. Then I'll shout the truth on every street corner! I'll write to all the other newspapers! I'll see that the whole country gets to know what's going on here!

HOVSTAD. It might almost seem that Dr. Stockmann is set on ruining the town.

DR. STOCKMANN. I love this town so much that I'd rather destroy it than see it prosper on a lie.

ASLAKSEN. That's putting it pretty strongly.

[*Uproar and whistles.* MRS. STOCKMANN *coughs in vain; the* DOCTOR *no longer hears her.*]

HOVSTAD [*shouting above the din*]. Any man who wants to destroy a whole community must be a public enemy.

DR. STOCKMANN [*with rising temper*]. When a place has become riddled with lies, who cares if it's destroyed? I say it should simply be razed to the ground! And all the people living by these lies should be wiped out, like vermin! You'll have the whole country infested in the end, so that eventually the whole country deserves to be destroyed. And if it ever comes to that, then I'd say with all my heart: let it all be destroyed, let all its people be wiped out!

A MAN [*in the crowd*]. That's the talk of an enemy of the people!

BILLING. That, God damn me, was the voice of the people!

THE WHOLE CROWD [*shouting*]. Yes! Yes! He's an enemy of the people. He hates his country. He hates his people.

ASLAKSEN. As a citizen of this country, and as an individual, I am profoundly shocked by what I have just had to listen to. Dr. Stockmann has betrayed himself in a way I should never have dreamt possible. I must therefore, with great regret, associate myself with the opinion that has just been expressed by my honorable fellow citizens, and I propose we embody that opinion in the form of a resolution. I suggest something like this: "This meeting declares that it considers Dr. Thomas Stockmann, Medical Officer to the Baths, to be an enemy of the people."

[*A storm of applause and cheers. A number of people crowd round* DR. STOCKMANN, *cat-calling.* MRS. STOCKMANN *and* PETRA *have risen.* MORTEN *and* EJLIF *fight with the other schoolboys who have also been booing. Some of the grown-ups separate them.*]

DR. STOCKMANN [*to those whistling*]. You fools! I tell you that . . .

ASLAKSEN [*ringing his bell*]. Dr. Stockmann is out of order. A formal vote must be taken; but so as not to hurt anybody's feelings, we will do it by secret ballot. Have you any paper, Mr. Billing?

BILLING. There's both blue and white. . . .

ASLAKSEN [*stepping down*]. That's fine. We can do it quicker that way. Cut it into strips . . . there we are, now. [*To the meeting.*] Blue means no, white means yes. I'll come round myself to collect the votes.

[*The* MAYOR *leaves the room.* ASLAKSEN *and one or two others carry round the slips of paper in their hats.*]

ONE MAN [*to* HOVSTAD]. What's come over the Doctor? What are you to make of it?

HOVSTAD. Well, you know how impetuous he is.

SECOND MAN [*to* BILLING]. Tell me—you've been in their house quite a bit. Does the man drink, have you noticed?

BILLING. I'm damned if I know really what to say. They always bring the toddy out when anybody calls.

THIRD MAN. No, I think it's more likely he's a bit crazy.

FIRST MAN. Ah, I wonder if there's any insanity in the family.

BILLING. Could very well be.

FOURTH MAN. No, it's just spite, that's what it is. Wants to get his own back about something.

BILLING. He did say something secretly about wanting a rise; but he didn't get it.

ALL THE MEN TOGETHER. Well, there you are then!

THE DRUNKEN MAN [*in the crowd*]. I want a blue one. And I want a white one an' all.

VOICES. Is that that drunk again? Chuck him out!

MORTEN KIIL [*approaches the* DOCTOR]. Well, Stockmann, now you see where these monkey tricks of yours have landed you!

DR. STOCKMANN. I have simply done my duty.

KIIL. What was that you said about the tanneries at Mölledal?

DR. STOCKMANN. You heard. I said that was where all the muck came from.

KIIL. From *my* tannery as well?

DR. STOCKMANN. I'm afraid so. Yours is the worst.

KIIL. Are you going to print *that* in the papers?

DR. STOCKMANN.   I'm not hiding anything.

KIIL.   You might find that costly, Stockmann.

[*He leaves.*]

A FAT MAN [*goes up to* HORSTER, *ignoring the ladies*].   So, Captain Horster, so you lend your house to enemies of the people, eh?

HORSTER.   I think I can do what I like with my own property, Mr. Vik.

THE FAT MAN.   So you won't mind if I do the same with mine.

HORSTER.   What do you mean?

THE FAT MAN.   You'll hear from me in the morning.

[*He turns and goes.*]

PETRA.   Isn't he the owner of your ship, Captain Horster?

HORSTER.   Yes, that's Mr. Vik.

ASLAKSEN [*mounts the platform with the ballot papers; he rings the bell*].   Gentlemen, let me announce the result. With only one vote to the contrary . . .

A YOUNG MAN.   That's the drunk!

ASLAKSEN.   With only one drunken man's vote to the contrary, the resolution of this meeting was carried unanimously: that Dr. Thomas Stockmann is an enemy of the people. [*Shouting and applause.*] Three cheers for our ancient and honorable community! [*More cheers.*] Three cheers for our able and efficient Mayor, for putting duty before family! [*Cheers.*] The meeting is adjourned.

[*He steps down.*]

BILLING.   Three cheers for the chairman!

THE WHOLE CROWD.   Good old Aslaksen!

DR. STOCKMANN.   My hat and coat, Petra! Captain, have you any room aboard for passengers for the New World?

HORSTER.   For you and your family we'll make room, Doctor.

DR. STOCKMANN [*as* PETRA *helps him on with his coat*].   Good! Come on, Katherine! Come along, lads!

[*He takes his wife by the arm.*]

MRS. STOCKMANN [*in low voice*].   Thomas dear, let's go out by the back way.

DR. STOCKMANN. No back way for me, Katherine. [*Raises his voice.*] You'll hear again from this enemy of the people before he shakes the dust off his feet. I'm not as sweet-tempered as a certain person I could mention. I'm not saying: "I forgive you, for you know not what you do."

ASLAKSEN [*shouts*]. That comparison is blasphemous, Dr. Stockmann!

BILLING. Well I'll be . . . ! What dreadful things to say in the presence of decent people.

A COURSE VOICE. And what about those threats he made!

ANGRY SHOUTS. Let's go and break his windows! Duck him in the fjord!

A MAN [*in the crowd*]. Give us another blast, Evensen! Blow! Blow!

> [*The sound of a horn and whistles and wild shouts. The* DOCTOR *and his family make for the exit, and* HORSTER *clears a way for them.*]

THE WHOLE CROWD [*howling after them*]. Enemy of the people! Enemy of the people! Enemy of the people!

BILLING [*tidying his papers*]. Well I'm damned if I would want to drink toddy at the Stockmanns' tonight!

> [*The crowd makes for the exit; the noise is continued outside; shouts from the streets of "Enemy of the people! Enemy of the people!"*]

Neighborhood Government

Milton Kotler

Milton Kotler advocates formally organizing the neighborhood as a corporation in order to create meaningful community control. In this selection from his book Neighborhood Government, Kotler uses the example of the East Central Citizens Organization in Columbus, Ohio, after having reviewed some alternatives.*

The Neighborhood Corporation

Our review of different theories of community organization pointed to certain strengths and defects in their principles of achieving local power for self-rule. But by combining their appropriate elements and rejecting their defects, we can arrive at a practical method of local organization. That method must be directed to a purpose that is natural to men, like liberty; the physical area must be suitable for organizing self-rule; its means must accord with the actual capacities of local power; and its organizational form must serve the purpose of local liberty. We must examine each of these standards for practical organization.

Because the neighborhood originates as a political unit and declines as its local liberties are destroyed, the object of local power can be nothing less than re-creating neighborhood government which has political autonomy and representation in larger units. Some . . . theorists . . . would disagree with this purpose. They see the city as the smallest unit of government and are content to organize neighborhood power to provide continuous pressure for benefits from city government. At the other extreme, some argue for separatism, and this assumes that the neighborhood is capable of total sovereignty. But the middle course of antonomy and representation along with other neighborhoods in a common city body is most practical.

From *Neighborhood Government: The Local Foundations of Political Life*, pp. 39–49, 82–85. Copyright © 1969 by Milton Kotler. Reprinted by permission of the publishers, The Bobbs-Merrill Company, Inc.

* Legislation proposed in Congress to encourage creation of community development corporations is discussed in Gar Alperovitz, "Cooperatives Against Poverty," *Current*, May 1969, pp. 27–31.

We have discussed the historical basis for this middle course, and it remains to comment on its intrinsic characteristics.

Men do not have the patience for the constant militancy which pressure upon the city would require. Nor are they inclined to the terrorism which separatism demands. They prefer the liberties of a recognized civil government, which can be achieved politically, to the constant mobilization of power in an area that is not a political unit.

There is also disagreement on the physical area to be organized for local power. Some theories favor large areas for organization—for instance, the Bedford-Stuyvesant Community Corporation area has a population of 300,000. Others think in terms of a black nation and seek a whole state for their race. Some theories favor a small, specific object in the neighborhood as the unit for organizing control—for instance, a school or a welfare office. Nevertheless, the best practical unit for organization lies in the middle, between large areas and single properties. It is the total territory of the neighborhood. This is because the object of local self-rule can be more nearly achieved in the neighborhood territory than in large urban areas or single institutions within a neighborhood. How can the independent civil government of a school be established, under the final control of its board, self-chosen or elected, unless a neighborhood government binds the school to the local residents? If it were not under the authority of the neighborhood government, such a single popularly controlled school would still be, in effect, a private school, and the children would tend to go to another public school in the neighborhood. Further, where would such a private school get its resources, if not from the neighborhood or city, neither of which has sufficient resources for its own school jurisdiction?

At the other extreme, one cannot organize a territory containing one-half million people like Harlem for civil government without first organizing the neighborhoods within it. This is because people already associate in neighborhoods, and before they join large area governments, they are more inclined to win independence for their own existing local associations. One cannot ask them to abandon the realization of their neighborhood associations in self-government for the sake of authority in a large area with which they feel as little in common as with the entire city. Hence the most practical unit for the struggle for local self-rule is the neighborhood community.

If the purposes of neighborhood organization are government and representation, and the physical area for its organization is the historic neighborhood, the efficient means for gaining local authority for the neighborhood will be by gaining political transfer from existing units of government. This approach lies between the extremes of militant seizures of institutions on the one hand and nonviolent boycotts and abandonment of present public institutions and authorities on the other. Both of these are impractical. Still other approaches fail as efficient means of achieving neighborhood government—for instance, claiming business control by destroying stores instead of claiming government powers for transfer to the neighborhood.

Attempted seizure causes the city government to send the police against the community. This tactic of seizure may be revolutionary in its aim of arousing people to agitate against the current city or national government, but there is no assurance that after a revolution there will be local control. Since local liberty is our object—whether before or after a revolution—it is of greatest importance that the neighborhood gain practical control of the school so that it can defend that control under any change of government.

At the other extreme, nonviolent boycott of schools and abandonment of public institutions in favor of parallel self-help endeavors do not build neighborhood self-rule. The municipal or state government is pleased at boycotts, for they give them time and opportunity to change personnel and methods under emergency conditions for more effective territorial control, and this under the name of improved service.

The efficient means of building neighborhood public authority and civil government lies in following the middle course, in a political strategy of transferring existing public authority and institutions to the control of the neighborhood. This involves organizing to press claims for transfer and local authority and holding flexible the range of tactics for negotiating political transfer.

The best practical organization for the political strategy of securing the transfer of public authority to the neighborhood is the legal incorporation of the local territory and the writing of a formal constitution of internal rule. SDS favors narrow, disciplined party initiative in local organizing, rather than neighborhood membership and decision. It prefers tough and hardened party leadership for maximum flexibility in behalf of revolutionary organization. The difficulty with this extreme is that there is no total legal territorial organization to receive and govern any transferred authority. Thus, for example, it is hard to imagine a city transferring school authority to a political organization like SNCC or SDS. Even if the city should do so, the neighborhood residents would object, and the city would easily be able to regain the authority. Further, the neighborhood unit is too small and familiarly associated to be governed by a party cadre. Such a cadre would force indigenous leadership to take a stance of opposition.

At the other extreme, there is support for informal mass organizing and decision, which is promoted as "participatory" democracy. It opposes any formal organization of the neighborhood into a corporate body with liabilities and internal regulations of rule. It is complained that such formality stifles expression and is intimidating to the people. Mass meetings without control over objectives and strategies are preferred to the binding decision of constituted neighborhood authority.

This argument has romantic appeal, but its strategic difficulty is that it does not provide a legally constituted entity to receive transferred public powers and institutions and to govern to the satisfaction of the residents. Finally, it is an error to suppose informal political organizing is an improvement upon the existing informality of neighborhood association. The neighborhoods are already informally associated for social purposes, and quite ready to be formally constituted for political purposes. Organizers will find that whereas informal mass organizing for political purposes threatens existing neighborhood leadership, formal organization for the political objectives of neighborhood government does not. It attracts local leadership forces, because the political objective of neighborhood government does not threaten existing social leadership.

The best form of neighborhood organization is the corporate organization of a neighborhood territory, chartered by the state and legally constituted for governing public authorities in the neighborhood. We call this form of organization the neighborhood corporation.

One existing neighborhood reflects this method of corporation: the East Central Citizens Organization (ECCO) in Columbus, Ohio. Four years old, ECCO is the oldest of some seventy neighborhood corporations around the country.

The neighborhood of ECCO covers approximately one square mile, with 6,500 residents. It is an area close to the central business district of the city.

Except for a small number of white residents from Appalachia, the people of ECCO are predominantly black. It is a poor community, with an unemployment rate of approximately 25 per cent before ECCO began, compared with a city-wide unemployment level of 2 per cent. Even presently it is estimated that 25 per cent of the residents are on welfare. By all statistical criteria, it is what we now call a poverty area.

ECCO originated early in 1965, when a neighborhood church—the First English Lutheran Church—whose congregation of neighborhood residents had, for the most part, moved to the suburbs, agreed to transfer its settlement house to neighborhood control. This involved a six-year-old agency, which offered a great number of social, educational, and personal services, from a nursery school for retarded children to day care, tutoring, dances, psychological guidance, clubs for young and old, emergency welfare services, and other programs heavily used in the community. Its last annual budget under church sponsorship was $25,000.

Many neighborhood people who had been involved in the settlement on a voluntary and paid basis agreed to organize the neighborhood into a legal corporation of its residents to receive the transferred agency, gain funding for its operation, and independently administer its services through the governing constitution of the corporation.

While the local leadership continued to bring people into the organizing effort and to develop the charter and bylaws of the ECCO corporation, application was made to the federal Office of Economic Opportunity to fund the administrative structure of ECCO for a period of two years.

During that time it was to develop a variety of programs for funding from other government agencies and private sources.

A grant of $180,000 was made to ECCO, and the church agency was transferred to the tax-exempt corporation in January 1966. For the next three months, organizing continued under the authority of an interim council, composed of neighborhood people and former members of the old church board, until March, when the neighborhood met in a general assembly and then elected the first official Executive Council of twenty-one. Thereafter, an executive staff was hired by the Council and its committees. At the election assembly, the authority of the settlement was completely separated from that of the church and vested in ECCO. In its first year, ECCO continued to house its administration in the parish hall. Today, while it rents the parish center from the church, it has its own offices in its own neighborhood building.

The formal legal organization of ECCO is set forth in a democratic constitution. Under the bylaws, as recently amended, any resident at least sixteen years old who lives within the boundaries of the corporate territory can sign the roster and become a member. The fundamental authority of the corporation is derived from its membership, which meets in assembly to elect the council members and chairman, and to transact legislative business over the laws, programs, and budget of ECCO. Its assemblies require a quorum of 10 per cent of the members; they have been legally convened nine times in the past three years. The Executive Council now has thirty members, elected both from the four neighborhood clubs (which existed before ECCO, and were re-formed to comprise four ECCO districts) and at large in an annual assembly. Voting membership on executive committees is open to any member of ECCO, appointed by the chairman. The council has executive authority, and legislative power is vested in the assembly.

The current annual budget of ECCO is approximately $202,947, consisting mainly of a grant from the U.S. Office of Economic Opportunity. A major program is the Youth Civic Center of ECCO, offering many youth activities in delinquency prevention, education, recreation, and job placement, and training in typing, shorthand, and crafts such as upholstering. The youth programs are governed by a youth committee of ECCO which has independence in the programming, management, and budgeting of their center. Although the council has executive authority, it has avoided interference with the youth committee. This Youth Center continues, even though its supporting grant from the now defunct U.S. Office of Juvenile Delinquency has been terminated. Many other programs are now offered in ECCO, and the organization has a full- and part-time staff. The programs of ECCO include educational projects, such as tutoring, nurseries for retarded children, day care, adult education, and community drives for greater local control of administration and management of the local public school in the ECCO territory. In the area of housing, ECCO has a co-operative code-enforcement program with the city government, and is purchasing houses for rehabilitation and leasing to the Metropolitan Housing Agency. In employment, it successfully demonstrated a new plan for operating the state employment service office locally. It is also employing residents in a new sewing center, which is already marketing products. In the field of health, it operates a program with the Public Health Service, and has developed a plan for its own twenty-four-hour Health Clinic, emphasizing night service to meet the needs of residents who work during the day. ECCO also operates a veterinary clinic. In the field of economic development, the organization has a credit union and has scheduled the opening of a supermarket. It also works closely with the federal Small Business Administration to finance local enterprise. It has an emergency welfare service and many other social service programs. Many recreational activities are offered.

This range of programs has been legislated by ECCO. Some are funded and in operation; others have been decided on but await the appropriation of funds. But this list by no means exhausts the subjects of legislative decision in ECCO, or in any neighborhood corporation.

ECCO's existence has been marked by struggle and by political development in both extra-community relations and internal government. The organization is often strongly opposed by both the Columbus Community Action Agency and the Model Cities Agency, which want to control federal antipoverty programs in the ECCO neighborhood. ECCO engages daily in political action against obstructive tactics of the city administration, and it has experienced clear-cut victories and defeats. A history of ECCO is being written, and it will illuminate the trials of the relationship with the city which challenge the object of local self-rule. But it is enough to say here that ECCO grows stronger and continues to thrive.

Within the ECCO area, the politics of democratic constitution over the past few years has enabled the residents to function as deliberative citizens. For the first time, the residents legally decide certain matters of community life. They are steadily practicing the art of political decision-making and living with and learning from the consequences of their decisions. There are factions and rhetoric in ECCO, as in any democratic polity, and new leadership is always generated by the political expression of new problems.

The continuing strategy of ECCO is to develop new, independent programs and to reach agreement with the city for territorial jurisdiction over these public activities. Thus, it succeeded in becoming the exclusive antipoverty authority in its territory. Furthermore, it has de facto territorial jurisdiction for youth programs. ECCO has also jurisdiction over the neighborhood public library, appointing the librarian and selecting books, while the city carries its cost. Gradually new jurisdictions are developing, and ECCO looks toward the time when it will consolidate enough power to achieve public political corporation. Then the neighborhood government will become a political entity of the municipal government.

As far as the present political character of the community is concerned, one might say that having deliberative authority has liberated the political spirit of the residents for internal government and external struggle against the city on such issues as police conduct, administration of public schools, jobs, welfare, and many other issues of public interest. ECCO residents are now orators and officials, and practical political wisdom is developing in a community where earlier the only expressions were frustration and escape. The men, women, and youth of ECCO are prepared to gain political control of their neighborhood.

LEGISLATIVE POWER

Several institutions in which people already assemble exist in any neighborhood. Even before they form neighborhood corporations, people go to church, have mass meetings, and belong to neighborhood clubs. On the basis of these experiences, people are prepared to assemble to make laws. Columbus' ECCO illustrates one way deliberative citizenship can operate.

The corporation meets annually by law to elect the executive council and to conduct legislative business, and for these meetings 10 per cent of the membership constitutes a quorum. It can also meet on the call of fifty members or by decision of any of its four neighborhood districts. Only the assembly has the authority to elect officers, to remove them for cause, to approve or terminate any corporate programs, to amend the by-laws of the corporation, to investigate neighborhood problems, and to initiate programs to meet the community's needs.

An issue always raised by advocates of representative government is the level of attendance at assembly meetings. In ECCO, attendance generally runs between 10 and 25 per cent of the membership. Critics claim 10 per cent is not sufficiently representative of the people for legislative purposes. They argue that representative democracy is more broadly based. But this is a specious argument, amounting to little more than a numbers game. We frequently find, particularly in off-election years, that representatives are elected by only as many—if not fewer—voters as convene in assembly for direct decision. In many election districts, fewer than 25 per cent of eligible voters go to the polls. If it is argued that it is at least possible for a representative to win 70 per cent of the votes in his district, it can be said that it is equally possible for the same percentage of citizens to attend the democratic assembly. When there are political crises, assembly attendance rises.

A more fundamental argument is that a small quorum of members is quite sufficient to bring all political positions of concern and interest to the forum for deliberation. Even a 10 per cent quorum usually encompasses the widest existing range on political opinion and emotion. (Representative government, after all, permits a spectrum of only two candidates, running on two or three issues at best, and on mere personality at worst, every few years.)

Popular deliberation in the ECCO area also takes place through the four districts into which the community is divided. Although these districts are independent organizations, they function as political clubs of the neighborhood corporation. Each club elects four members of the executive council annually; the general assembly elects the remaining fourteen at large. These clubs represent distinct local interests and political attitudes, and through them the deliberation of the membership takes place on a continuing basis. Program development is often initiated by the clubs, for it is within their small districts that dramatic events often occur.

Clubs also represent the sectional interests of the localities within the neighborhood. Because the clubs existed before incorporation, they became factions in the assembly, but they are not political parties.

Finally, a vital function performed by the neighborhood clubs is the development of political leadership. Their independent meetings offer opportunities for formation of new popular leaders, who move into the assembly with district support and eventually achieve official positions on the council or executive staff. It is within the clubs that new leaders get political training and ideas. Since their statements in the assembly are sustained by club support, their rhetoric becomes more confident. An assembly without internal political groups and strategies would have no motion or direction.

Another dimension of deliberation, although relatively minor initially, is the committee structure of the council. Only at a later stage of ECCO's development, when legislation becomes more complex, is it likely that committees will assume major importance. The committees are chaired by council members, but their meetings are open to any member of the corporation. Through an open committee structure, therefore, community participation in the government is further reinforced.

The democracy of the assembly, clubs, and open committees is of crucial importance because it brings the most complete collective agreement to combat political opposition from central power. If a man shares in the deliberative authority of public life, he will commit his own power to defend the corporate body, even though he may be in the minority on many decisions. He will defend the corporation for the sake of his own deliberative right, but he is not apt to defend it if all decision is left to one executive or to an elected council.

Another reason for legislation by assembly is that it will serve the common interest, not special interests. Law-making by an assembly of citizens will favor the many rather than the few, simply because wealth and special interest have a smaller voice in the public assembly than in elected councils.

Mobilization for Youth Lost

Daniel Moynihan

The final item of this first part is by Daniel Moynihan. In his book
Maximum Feasible Misunderstanding, *Moynihan attempts to trace the
genesis and consequences of the provision in War on Poverty legislation
for "maximum feasible participation" of the poor in running antipoverty
programs. This leads him into a discussion of Mobilization For Youth, a
privately organized (government and foundation funded) program aimed
at curbing juvenile delinquency in a ghetto area by giving the adults of
the neighborhood participation in decision-making that affected them.
These excerpts review the reasons for MFY's failure, and the reader will
want to reflect on the problems of "powerlessness" and "ethnic antagonism" that are relevant to subsequent articles on black perspectives. Later
in his book, Moynihan shows himself to be ambivalent on participatory
democracy, viewing it as an unfinished experiment. Commenting on the
participation of the poor, he writes: "It remains to be seen whether it can
do what is promised for it, just as we may discover to our sorrow that
'participatory democracy' can mean the end of both participation and
democracy. But the spirit of the times will not be stayed: these are the
issues of the moment" [p. 164].*

As in the Federal antipoverty program, much the greatest portion of
the MFY budget was devoted to programs in the World of Work, the
World of Education, and its other services of individuals and groups. In its
second year of operation, the Community Program received only $272,000.
On the other hand, from the outset this program received almost all the
publicity, and just as importantly it seems to have been the activity that
most exhilarated the middle-class professionals working at MFY. (One
MFY official told a reporter that the 300-man staff spent 80 to 90 per cent
of its energies "organizing the unaffiliated—the lower fifth of the economic
ladder . . . who will overturn the status quo" in the neighborhood.[1]

This activity, formally titled "Organizing the Unaffiliated" was very
much the prototype of the community action programs of the OEO. As

---

Reprinted by permission of The Macmillan Company from *Maximum Feasible
Misunderstanding* by Daniel Moynihan, pp. 106–118. Copyright © 1969 by The Free
Press, a Division of The Macmillan Company.

with all of MFY's programs it was derived, step by step, from general to specific hypotheses, each step accompanied by citations from the work of major sociologists: Eleanor Maccoby on "Community Integration and the Social Control of Delinquency,"[2] Morris Axelrod on "Urban Structure and Social Participation,"[3] W. G. Mather on "Income and Social Participation,"[4] Peter Rossi on *Why Families Move*.[5] The general hypothesis was direct enough:[6]

> Participation by adults in decision-making about matters that affect their interests increases their sense of identification with the community and the larger social order. People who identify with their neighborhood and share common values are more likely to try to control juvenile misbehavior. A well-integrated community can provide learning experiences for adults which enable them to serve as more adequate models and interpreters of community life for the young. In short, there is an inverse relation between community integration and the rates of juvenile misbehavior.

Four barriers to such integration were identified: lower-class families moved a great deal; community activities were typically staffed by middle-class personnel; the self-defeating attitudes of the lower class made them feel nothing could be accomplished; and, finally, "intergroup tensions" kept the community fragmented. Little could be done about the first difficulty, but tactics were quickly devised for the remaining three: the "indigenous disadvantaged" would be employed by MFY to help organize and stimulate the community; "issues" would be chosen that were at once highly visible and gave promise of immediate payoff; and finally, the groups would be organized along racial and ethnic lines. MFY decided to concentrate almost its entire attention on the Negroes and Puerto Ricans of the neighborhood.

Out of this orderly, and conservative formulation—this was, after all, nothing more than an effort to give grown-ups in the neighborhood roles that would encourage them to teach their kids to behave—came a series of events that many in the larger world, especially the political world, were to view as dangerous and disorderly conduct. The MFY Prospectus had stated, accurately enough, that "The task of developing a theory of action which is consistent with the theory of causation is, of course, immense."[7] As it turned out, however, an even greater if unexpected difficulty was that of retaining over time the same concept of causation and the same object of action. MFY began with the understanding that the problem of the poor was anomie; in short order anomie was replaced by "powerlessness" as the fundamental disorder. It started out to create cooperative arrangements that would open the neighborhood opportunity structure to deviant or potentially deviant youths; in short order the opportunity structure was being defined as a power structure, and itself accused of deviance in the largest social sense of good and bad behavior. Rhetorically at all events, reform inched towards revolution. Right or wrong, MFY did not very long remain the carefully calibrated social experiment it had set out to be.

The shift from anomie to powerlessness would seem in part related to the problem of size. In a city of eight million, Mobilization for Youth represented an area of 100,000 persons and was actively concerned with only a third of these. Almost all of the principal "institutions" that affected the residents of the Lower East Side—the school system, the labor market, the housing, the police force—were at least citywide in their organization and scope, and most had state and national ties. A neighborhood group would sense little leverage in such situations.

The "problem" of powerlessness must surely also have been compounded by the erosion of community-based political power, a change especially to be noted in Manhattan where for so long local political organizations, coalescing in Tammany Hall, had wielded highly visible, even notorious power. Fifty years of municipal reform had just about put an end to that in New York. Not the least ironic of MFY's experience is that much of the impulse to do something about the feeling of powerlessness among the lower-class ethnic minorities of the city came from much the same group that in previous decades had systematically stripped minorities of the very considerable power they had had, and did so in the name of their own good. What more conclusive evidence of evil could be adduced against a local political leader during the 1950's, the more so if he were Italian, say, and had taken to wearing expensive clothes, than to charge that he was a "Boss,"—that is, that he had power! Nothing if ·not self-aware, the MFY Prospectus provided a theory of the urban political machine as well, suggesting in effect that the Italians and Irish had taken Tammany with them, into the lower middle class and would no longer allow it to perform its traditional functions. There was something in this, but the larger fact is that those functions had for the most part been taken out of the political sector and consigned to bureaucracies—the very bureaucracies whose middle-class rigidity and putative disdain for the poor had been responsible for so much of the thinking behind community action! Further, uniformity and consistency, the treatment of like cases alike, is the essence of the bureaucratic method and a central demand of the good government reformers in the campaign against the "favoritism" so characteristic of the working-class style in politics. With the best will in the world, the City departments could not set up special rules for a few square blocks on the Lower East Side. And those few square blocks hardly had the power to force the rules to be changed for the entire city, where in any event their views were not necessarily shared.

During this period, Kenneth B. Clark was preparing the large study from which the community action agency of Harlem, HARYOU-ACT, was shaped. Where MFY had been theory-oriented, Clark's study rested largely on field research: What did the youth of Harlem feel? What did they need? It was in ways even a more impressive piece of work than its downtown counterpart, and came to essentially the same conclusions as did MFY. It was titled: "Youth in the Ghetto: A Study in the Consequences of Powerlessness." Yet by traditional New York standards there was no reason for Harlem to feel powerless. Negroes at this time were in complete control of their local political organizations: Harlem had powerful representatives at the City, State, and National levels of government. Yet somehow the power of such representatives to effect local events had diminished. Thus one of the galling facts of life in Harlem was the treasure that poured out of the community daily in consequence of the gambling and narcotics traffic operated illegally by whites. In an earlier age the police would have regulated this commerce and the political machine would have regulated the police. But, at about this time, when Congressman Adam Clayton Powell, no doubt with other concerns in mind, demanded that a Negro police captain be assigned to Harlem, the Irish Commissioner, not perhaps without a twinge of regret, informed the Congressman that Tammany district leaders (which Powell also was) no longer appointed police captains in New York. Bureaucracy had taken over, the next man on the list would be appointed, etc., etc. As the MFY Prospectus had stated, "the machine humanized and personalized its services. It provided help and favors rather than justice and assistance."[8] Bureaucracies may not do this—must not.

It would appear that these municipal facts of life had important consequences on the tactics of Mobilization's effort to organize the unaffiliated. Inasmuch as so little in the way of institutional change could be accomplished in the neighborhood, it became necessary to escalate the level at which demands were made to that of the City Hall, at very least, where changes in bureaucratic institutions could be affected. This meant expanding the scope of demands from local to citywide propositions. Just possibly the middle-class reformers felt more at home at such levels—their turf—but conditions also encouraged what might have been a predisposition.

The immediate consequence of this was an escalation in rhetoric. More and more George Brager, director of MFY's Action Programs, was talking about the "powerlessness" of the poor *with respect to city government*. A program that had begun as a promising device for helping to resolve the private difficulties of young persons, which in the aggregate were creating a social problem, a device the city government was more than willing to support and encourage, began of a sudden to pose a challenge to that very government. And here the personal qualities of the middle-class professional reformers, elite academics and intellectuals for the most part, contributed not a little to the mounting tension. For if capable of the deepest empathy, the purest Christian compassion for the poor, too frequently they had nothing but contempt for the working-class, lower-middle-class bureaucratic and political cadres that ran the city. The belief that suffering purifies and that security corrupts is deep in Western culture, and nowhere so manifest as among young educated Americans coming of age in the 1950's, having experienced all their lives an absolute minimum of suffering and an absolute maximum of security. One dares to detect a measure of glee, almost, as the MFY theorists turned on City Hall, capitalism, racism, America itself. There is to be seen in their writings, as Leonard Chazen notes, a steady "progression from a politically neutral concern with organizing the slums to a fully engaged animus for the city 'Establishment.' "[9] This is not to be explained in terms of the particular social and political setting in which MFY was trying to function. At this time a radical, middle-class stirring was beginning to be felt throughout the nation. "Expanding Opportunities for Conformity" may have expressed the spirit of the 1950's on the Columbia campus: it was not the "thing" for the 1960's. It is difficult to resist the impression that the MFY principles were as much affected by changing fashions in ideas, as by any pragmatic response to a particular set of circumstances. . . .

The MFY internal notes from the period are filled with the minutiae and the exhilaration of combat. Problem: "No matter how we disguise it, irrespective of letterhead and who signs the letters, telegrams, etc., City agencies quickly begin to realize which letters and which buildings come to them from Mobilization for Youth." Solution: "Transform every housing program currently sponsored by MFY into tenant membership organizations. There need be no exceptions." Future battles were planned. The Housing Committee would become a "rent strike coordinating committee." "We are drawing together and staffing a committee which will coordinate all direct action campaigns in a militant manner. . . . This is an organization of organizations, and contains the kind of fighting, sophisticated politicized organizations who are just itching to play out the 'Jesse Gray' role and 'bring to the Lower East Side what Harlem has begun.' . . . Only massive rent strikes are effective in obtaining publicity, embarrassing the establishment, etc."[10]

It must be kept in mind that Mobilization for Youth was in every sense a creature of that very establishment: Columbia University, the Ford Foundation, the Mayor of New York, the President of the United States. Now it was setting out to embarrass it. That had not been the plan, but that was how it was working out. In Robert F. Wagner they found an especially vulnerable target, an immensely decent man, increasingly worn down by the demands of what was now his third term as Mayor, yet incapable of truly vengeful retaliation, trying only to keep the city running. The trade unions had long ago learned to strike friends first, and MFY understood this about Wagner. But he was human. Herbert Krosney writes:[11]

Mobilization gave counsel to and worked with downtown CORE. This group later dumped dead rats on Mayor Wagner's doorstep, a gesture which, however vivid, was not calculated to gain the Mayor's sympathy.

A second general difficulty which MFY soon encountered, and which would seem to be an endemic risk of community action, involved the issue of ethnic antagonism. In seeking to enlarge the community, to bring in outsiders, they soon found themselves fractionating it. When class conflict is induced in an American urban community, it would seem to have a natural tendency to assert itself in terms of ethnic conflict as well. At the outset MFY made the decision to organize specifically Puerto Rican and Negro groups and to bring them into battle with the establishment. Plans specified the ethnicity of employees: "Henry Street Tenants' Council; Area—Madison to East Broadway, Montgomery to Pike; Staff—Negro community worker to be hired, plus Pedro—." (Such practices were of course to be forbidden by the Civil Rights Act of 1964!)

In one of its first tests, this technique backfired. An organization of Puerto Rican mothers, with the acronym MOM, was put together for the purpose of a "conflict confrontation" with the principal of the local P.S. 140, Irving Rosenbloom. The principal was accused of bigotry and it was demanded that he be fired. The confrontation was noisy, disorderly, and something ominously close to antisemitism made its appearance. Twenty-six public school principals in the area responded with a telegram to Mayor Wagner demanding instead that Brager, head of the MFY action program, be fired. His community workers, the telegram stated,[12]

> [were] becoming full-time paid agitators and organizers for extremist groups. This constitutes an abuse of the noble purpose for which great sums of federal and municipal money were originally appropriated. This movement has been subverted from its original plan to war against delinquency into a war against individual schools and their leaders, to what purpose we cannot at the present time divine.

Now the issue arose as to just how representative the mothers' group was. James McNamara, a member of the local school board and the local leader of the Liberal Party, defended Rosenbloom as a good man, and attacked MOM as a "phantom organization led by MFY staff members." The letter to the superintendent of schools demanding Rosenbloom's resignation contained only twenty valid signatures of 200—"the rest were forgeries." The problem, said McNamara, "stems from the theory that you must get the lower fifth excited and that they must fight the power structure." If that was the problem, it was also the avowed intention of MFY at this point. Shortly after the incident at P.S. 140, the first civil rights boycott of the New York schools occurred. Whether or not there was a valid connection, there were those willing to perceive one.

The Negro Action Group (NAG) took on an even more ominous turn. Although this was a time when relations between Negro militants and white liberals were at their most cordial and effective state, the deliberate effort to bring about conflict between a Negro lower-class group and the city establishment displayed a potential for divisiveness that was to become reality all too soon. NAG was intended to be an outrageous organization, and from all reports it was. Although MFY was to deny the charge when it was made by the *News*, Jesse Gray, the rent strike organizer who had acquired a reputation during the 1963 Harlem riot, was indeed involved with MFY's efforts to start rent strikes on the Lower East Side. He provided an important model for action, and perhaps also a vocabulary that could only inflame relations with whites.[13] An activist in downtown CORE insisted to the journalist Jack Newfield that NAG was "nationalistic and anti-Semitic" and refused to cooperate with CORE, which was vigorously interracial at that time. "This is an inevitable consequence," he continued, "of a strategy that intentionally pits Negroes and Puerto Ricans against a predominantly Jewish establishment."[14] This development was to become even more pronounced later on. Thus in the dispute at I.S. 201 in East Harlem in the winter of 1966–67 in which local residents, much supported by the local community action agency (MEND) demanded the ouster of principal Stanley R. Lisser, the *New York Times* reported that "the street agitation . . . was flagrantly anti-white and anti-Semitic." In 1968 when the issue of community control of the Ocean Hill–Brownsville school district—another Ford Foundation experimental project—was raging, one leaflet took the matter to considerable lengths, declaring:

> If African-American History and Culture is to be taught to our Black Children it Must be Done by African-Americans Who Identify With and Who Understand the Problem. It is Impossible For the Middle East Murderers of Colored People to Possibly Bring To This Important Task The Insight, The Concern, The Exposing of the Truth that is a Must If The Years of Brainwashing And Self-Hatred That Has Been Taught To Our Black Children By These Blood-sucking Exploiters and Murderers Is To Be Overcome. The Idea Behind This Program Is Beautiful, But When The Money Changers Heard About It They Took Over, As Is Their Custom In the Black Community. If African-American History and Culture Is important To Our Children [to] Raise Their Esteem Of Themselves, They Are [sic] The Only Persons Who Can Do The Job Are African-American Brothers and Sisters, And Not the So-Called Liberal Jewish Friend. We know From His Tricksy, Deceitful Maneuvers That He is Really Our Enemy and He is Responsible For the Serious Educational Retardation of Our Black Children.

Pretty sentiments, to which there were Jews capable of responding in kind. Charles E. Silberman, the distinguished author of *Crisis in Black and White*, spotted the trend and in May 1968 demanded of a meeting sponsored by the American Jewish Committee that it "face up to the raw, rank, anti-Negro prejudice that is within our own midst. We talk—endlessly—

about Negro Anti-Semitism; we rarely talk about—let alone try to deal with—the Jewish Anti-Negroism that is in our midst and that is growing very rapidly."[15] Demanding power for a black community rather quickly became a demand for black power. This may have been therapeutic for those involved, but the reaction elsewhere, as Vice President Humphrey later declared in an interview arranged by the American Jewish Community, was "consternation and confusion."[16]

MFY was not responsible for the rise of Negro extremism or black nationalism. It was simply there when the storm broke, and it was useful as a vehicle in its part of the City. It is to the credit of those who conceived and began the program that while the nation generally was either unaware of the mounting fury within the Negro community, or at best indifferent to it, MFY leaders had already set out to do something about it. It is part of the irony that suffuses the MFY experience that the institutions they helped establish were put to uses (miniscule and of no substantive consequence on the Lower East Side, but important in terms of the idea) that were just the opposite of what they had envisaged. Their fondest hope was to enable the slum youth they served to enter the larger society, to conform to its standards, and to succeed by them. Alas, by the time the program was underway the issue had already been raised by Negro writers such as James Baldwin as to whether the standards of the white community were worth conforming to. "Subsequent classes of black students," a Negro youth at Columbia was to declare some years later, "will not only reject the white man's hang-ups, but will also reject the mediocre goals this institution says they ought to aspire to: they will absolutely refuse the white man's benevolent offer of a '32nd vice niggership' at General Motors."[17] Seen from the perspective of other groups, this was rather a conventional statement for a certain type of New York student, but no law provides that Negroes shall follow in the footsteps of those who preceded them in the great city, and certainly there were many who at this point intended nothing of the sort. The extreme left was reasserting its influence, its aim, as Max Lerner writes, "to radicalize the Negro and convert him into the cutting edge that will divide America and throw it into the kind of chaos out of which revolutionary situations are made."[18] This was hardly the intent of MFY, but a whiff of this notion drifted uptown from East Second Street. Rent strikes? School boycotts? Voter registration drives? Mass demonstrations? "What this has to do with curbing juvenile delinquency," declared the New York Herald Tribune "or why public funds should be used, is a cause for bafflement."[19]

Notes

[1] Jack Newfield, New York Post, August 30, 1964, quoting Charles Grosser.

[2] Eleanor Maccoby et al., "Community Integration and the Social Control of Delinquency," Journal of Social Issues, 14 (1958), 38–51.

[3] Morris Axelrod, "Urban Structure and Social Participation," *American Sociological Review*, 21 (February 1956), 13–18.

[4] W. G. Mather, "Income and Social Participation," *American Sociological Review*, 6 (June 1947), 380–381.

[5] Peter Rossi, *Why Families Move* (New York: The Free Press, 1955), p. 58.

[6] MFY Prospectus, p. 126.

[7] *Ibid.*, p. ix.

[8] *Ibid.*, p. 198.

[9] Leonard Chazen, "Participation of the Poor: Section 202 (a) (3) Organizations Under the Economic Opportunity Act of 1964," *Yale Law Journal*, 75 (March 1966), 608.

[10] MFY, The Community Organization Housing Program, Report to the Ad-Hoc Committee on Community Organization, January 7, 1964, mimeographed.

[11] Herbert Krosney, *Beyond Welfare, Poverty in the Supercity* (New York: Holt, Rinehart and Winston, 1966), p. 25.

[12] Quoted in *Ibid.*, p. 23.

[13] See *Herald Tribune* clip in MFY folder.

[14] Jack Newfield, *New York Post*, August 30, 1964.

[15] Charles E. Silberman, "Pieties and Realities: Some Constructive Approaches to Negro-Jewish Relations." Address to the 62nd Annual Meeting of The American Jewish Committee, May 24, 1968.

[16] Hubert H. Humphrey, "Race in a Changing World," American Jewish Committee, 1966, p. 11.

[17] *New York Times*, May 1, 1967.

[18] Max Lerner, *The Washington Evening Star*, April 19, 1967.

[19] *New York Herald Tribune*, August 19, 1964.

Community Control and Black Political Participation

William F. Mullen

With this selection we begin our second part, which is devoted to black perspectives on community control. The opening article, by William Mullen, a specialist on black politics at Washington State University, introduces the major background considerations for the discussions that follow in succeeding articles. The petition for community control of the police mentioned in the article is reproduced in the section on Government Administration and the Legal System.

The pervasive reality for black political participation in traditional modes and within existing structures of the political system is that as a minority of approximately 11 percent of the population, it is almost everywhere impossible for blacks to make the important political decisions that affect their lives. It is true that the passage of the Voting Rights Act of 1965 is responsible for the addition of more than one million blacks to the voter rolls in the South. The 1970 extension of that act should further enhance voting strength by lowering the voting age* and by abolishing literacy tests everywhere. It is also true that in recent years blacks have been elected as mayor in Cleveland, Ohio; Gary, Indiana; and Newark, New Jersey; and have come close in other cities (notably Los Angeles).

At the same time, this litany of "black political progress" should not obscure the under-representation of black people at every level of the political system. Currently, there is one black United States Senator and twelve black members of the House of Representatives; if they were to be represented proportionate to their numbers, we would have 11 black

---

Reprinted by permission of William F. Mullen.

* Since blacks tend to have larger families than whites, a greater percentage of them are under 21. According to recent census figures, the median age for whites is 29; for blacks, 21. This is illustrated by the fact that school enrollment in many core cities is already more than 50 percent black while a majority of the total population of the core is still white. For example, St. Louis' primary school enrollment in 1965 was 63 percent black although the total population was 64 percent white. *Report of the National Advisory Commission on Civil Disorders*, Washington, D.C., March 1968, p. 216.

Senators and 48 black Congressmen.* No black serves in the President's Cabinet. None of the President's closest advisers is black. In not one of our 50 states do we have a black governor, and no state has more than 14 black state legislators.** Chuck Stone estimates that blacks represent less than 1 percent of all elected officials, from school boards through the Presidency.[1]

In the South, where they still constitute their highest percentages of state populations, Afro-Americans continue to meet resistance from many recalcitrant registrars and have yet to elect their first state-wide official. In North Carolina six blacks ran for sheriff this year, and all were defeated. In Alabama, only one black won nomination for the state legislature while George Wallace was defeating a racial "moderate" for the governorship, primarily by appealing to white fears of black political domination. According to the 1960 census, Mississippi's population was 42 percent black, and it therefore ought to offer the greatest opportunity for black representation; however, there are no black sheriffs, one black mayor out of 270, and only one black legislator out of a total of 174.

Recent political campaigns in the North and South have illustrated one of the major liabilities which blacks face in seeking to control political decisions affecting their lives, and that is the manifestation of white racism in the polling booths. Evidence indicates that virtually nowhere is a majority of whites willing to vote for a black candidate.*** Both Gary and Newark have black majorities, and Cleveland is close to one. In none of these cities did the black candidate secure more than a small percentage of white votes in his victory. White racism is revealed in the fact that it is not considered by most to be anything but normal for whites to continue to dominate a city's politics until blacks have a city-wide majority, even though they may represent the largest single group in the city. The traditional American pattern of ethnic groups dominating political machines, electing one of their own as mayor of a city in which they constitute a plurality, is considered exceptional when blacks are that plurality. Witness the national press attention focused on cities where blacks are entered as candidates when compared to the attention given Irish or Italian candidates in other cities. The results of recent elections, then, indicate that there is still a long way to go before black people are represented in anywhere near their proportionate numbers in the political system.****

---

* It should be recalled that one of the major grievances leading to the American Revolution was just such "taxation without representation."

** Georgia and Illinois each have 14.

*** Edward Brooke, elected as Senator from Massachusetts, is, of course, a major exception although he is dismissed by many black militants as a Negro representative of the white power structure.

**** Where blacks have reached majority status in registered voters in a district, some Southern states have devised techniques for limiting their political effectiveness, including: switching from elective to appointive members of boards, changing to "at-large"

The unhappy fact is that unless there is a revolution in white attitudes, the situation is unlikely to be substantially altered. Even if we could assume such an attitudinal change on the part of whites, the basic reality of minority status in most states, Congressional districts, counties, and cities would mean that whites would continue to dominate the political lives of most black people. If geographical dispersion were not a fact, and if true proportionality were to be achieved, blacks would remain subject to the whims of an often hostile, dominant majority, and as Alan Altshuler has pointed out, "Where race is concerned, majority tyranny is much like any other."[2]

If political participation through the ballot is insufficient for a minority in altering either the decisional structures or the policies emanating from those structures, what modes remain? How have blacks attempted to achieve goals toward which whites are either apathetic or overtly hostile? "By whatever means necessary" indicates that all kinds of participation in the political realm are considered legitimate in obtaining from a racist society what is perceived as being withheld illegitimately. This participation has taken the form of marches, demonstrations, strikes, passive non-violent resistance, violence, and rebellions.

> When economic and social institutions fail to provide the life-chances that a substantial part of a population wants, and when political institutions fail to provide a remedy, the aspirations of the people begin to spill over into forms of activity that the dominant society regards either as unacceptable or illegitimate—crime, vandalism, noncooperation, and various forms of political protest.[3]

In other words, participation with the body. Probably the most irksome manifestation of this kind of political activity, at least for the dominant society, is violence. But as H. Rap Brown has said, "Violence is as American as cherry pie." A more scholarly development of this theme is contained in the report to the President's Commission on the Causes and Prevention of Violence:

> Whether in Congress or in the streets, reactions to modern outbreaks of political violence have demonstrated a widely held belief that such outbreaks were "un-American"; that they had occurred infrequently in the past; and that they bore little relationship to the way past domestic groups had succeeded in gaining political power, property, and prestige.

---

elections from district representation, gerrymandering, raising the number of signatures required on filing petitions for office, and increasing filing fees for elective positions. After the recent Newark mayoralty election, a white city councilman said in a television interview that he would immediately begin a drive to change the city's charter to a commission form of government, with five commissioners acting at the apex of the administrative structure.

(Those most vociferous in denouncing the violent were often those who believed, rightly or wrongly, that *their* ethnic, economic, or occupational groups had "made it" in American society without resorting to violent conduct.) Historical study, on the other hand, reveals that under certain circumstances the United States has regularly experienced episodes of mass violence directly related to the achievement of social, political, and economic objectives.[4]

Extra-legal or even illegal participation, then, is part of the American tradition for groups who find office holders or the official governmental structures unresponsive to their demands on the political system. These groups have attempted to change specific individuals populating governmental roles, specific decisions (or the lack of favorable decisions) or even the decisional process itself. Pressure is brought to bear until at least some of the goals are satisfied or the group is crushed. American history is replete with examples: vigilantes, American Indians, the IWW, the Molly Maguires, the KKK, AFL–CIO struggles, the Whiskey Rebellion, the American colonists themselves, the Anti-Saloon League, and White Southerners and the Civil War.

Superficial analyses of the "riots" beginning in Harlem in 1964 and continuing through Watts, Newark, and Detroit make little effort to understand the essentially political nature of these phenomena and concentrate instead on "the criminal behavior," the looting, the breakdown in law and order, the "carnival atmosphere" of the events, or on measures best suited to halting rioting once it has begun. There is evidence, however, that many participants and observers of these uprisings have interpreted them as political events, as alternative ways of making demands upon the political system.* Not only is violence perceived as a political act, but as a helpful one in the cause of black liberation. In a nation-wide survey of black America, Newsweek quotes a Pittsburg housewife, "We got to get to all white people, and some of them, honey, only listen to violence."[5] In fact, the responses reveal that blacks believe by 40 to 29 percent that riots have helped more than they have hurt.[6] From a 1964 survey conducted by the NORC, Gary T. Marx found 55 percent of the blacks in Chicago, 63 percent in Atlanta, and 52 percent in Birmingham felt that riots do some good.[7] Analyzing the U.C.L.A. Watts riot study data, Tomlinson states: "Of the 56 percent who claimed the riot had a purpose, each cited one or another of the following goals of the riot: (a) to call attention to Negro problems, (b) to express Negro hostility to whites, or

---

* In Almond and Coleman's terms, political functions may be performed in the course of this kind of event. Political socialization, interest articulation, recruitment, rule-making, rule application, rule adjudication, interest aggregation, and communication—all may be performed by anomic interest groups in the course of riots and demonstrations. *The Politics of the Developing Areas* (Princeton University Press, 1960), pp. 27–28, 34.

(c) to serve an instrumental purpose of improving conditions, ending discrimination, or communicating with the 'power structure.' "[8]

The rebellions in our cities, then, are perceived as a way to participate directly in making decisions about one's life. Nathan Hare, a former San Francisco State instructor, sees violence as being in some ways superior to more peaceful methods:

> The numbers terrorists advise the black man to seek salvation through voting. Voting is institutionalized and sacred, and it is virtually impossible to vote in a revolution; most certainly it is inconceivable, given the present methods of choosing candidates. Besides, I may be able, through superior fighting skills and stealth, to kill a number of men: slitting the throat of one, choking another, dropping a hand grenade among the rest. But I can vote only once. If my numbers are too few to fight back in self-defense, they are too few to vote out white supremacy.[9]

The Black Panthers have especially been identified with violence (whether directed against them by the state or in terms of their advocacy of armed self-defense). A quotation from Huey Newton, one of their principal leaders, illustrates what the party's position is on the subject:

> In the political arena, a thing is not political unless the people can inflict a political consequence if they don't get what they want. And black people in the past haven't been able to inflict this consequence. . . . We say now that we can develop political power by being a potentially destructive force. That if black people arm themselves in a political fashion, and the aggression is continued against us, we'll be able to offer a political consequence very similar to Detroit.[10]

The citations from militant leaders should not blind us to the facts, cited above, that large numbers of average blacks also share the belief that violence may be a necessary political act to "get the white man off our backs." The Kerner Report, the Commission on the Causes and Prevention of Violence, plus many individual studies such as the ones by Gary T. Marx, Jay Schulman, T. M. Tomlinson, William McCord, and John Howard, etc., have all found the rioters not to be an isolated, malcontented, lunatic fringe of the population.

With the failure of the "melting pot" society to fully integrate blacks into the larger society apparent (especially the masses of people living in ghettos), and the persistence of racism and discrimination, many young black leaders are coming to seek improvement in the conditions of their lives and the lives of other black people by altering some of the political structures which are at least partially responsible for that condition. The major program to achieve amelioration in the perceived situation is community control. The first point in the program of the Black Panther Party, for instance, is: "We want freedom. We want power to determine the destiny of our Black Community."[11]

Jerome Skolnick points out that this is by no means a new type of demand on the political system, that deprived groups in the United States have historically demanded the satisfaction of their group interests in controlling their own social systems.[12]

This demand by blacks is essentially that they be permitted on the community level to control the political and economic institutions that seriously affect their everyday existence—the schools, the police, garbage collection, welfare, government programs in the neighborhood, etc. As Huey Newton has said in explaining "Black Power":

> Black Power is really people's power. The Black Panther program, Panther Power as we call it, will implement this people's power. We have respect for all of humanity and we realize that the people should rule and determine their destiny. Wipe out the controller. To have Black Power doesn't humble or subjugate anyone to slavery or oppression. Black Power is giving power to people who have not had power to determine their destiny. We advocate and will aid any people who are struggling to determine their destiny. . . . We in the black colony in America want to be able to have power over our own destiny and that's Black Power.[13]

An illustration of the movement toward neighborhood power is the Oakland petition for community control of the police. Sponsored by the National Committees to Combat Fascism and by the Black Panthers, this amendment to the Oakland city charter would set up separate and autonomous police departments for the white and black communities. In commenting on the purpose of community control of the police, the Panther paper explains:

> By moving on POLICE CONTROL, we are moving on the most fundamental level possible to obstruct the implementation of that fascist state and thereby give us more time to work with the people in building a revolutionary consciousness among them. It is not mere rhetoric to say that the Community Control of Police petition is a program that will take the power to control the police department out of the hands of the private property and corporate interests and put it directly into the hands of the people of the community. This is the essence of the program; it sets the people diametrically opposed to the interests of the ruling class of the country.[14]

It is obvious from the Kerner report, as well as other studies, that many people living in ghettos view the police as enemies. Robert Fogelson and Robert Hill in Supplemental Studies (for the Kerner Commission) have reported that 50 to 90 percent of the black males studied had arrest records. "Clearly, when the majority of men in a given population are defined as criminal—at least by the police—something more than 'deviant' behavior is involved."[15] At the same time most blacks, like many of the young today, are becoming more unwilling to accept decisions and practices perceived as running counter to their interests—even though these decisions and policies may be supported by a majority of the larger society.

> Almost uniformly, the participants in mass protest today see their grievances as rooted in the existing arrangements of power and authority in contemporary society, and they view their own activity as political action—on a direct or symbolic level—aimed at altering those arrangements. A common theme, from ghetto to the university, is the rejection of dependency and external control, a staking of new boundaries, and a demand for significant control over events within those boundaries.*[16]

It is clear that one way to alter unfavorable outputs of the polity, at least for blacks, is through a change in the decision-making structures themselves—a change in the direction of a devolution of authority to the community level.

Critics of decentralization argue that local control for blacks is essentially a separatist movement aimed at giving black militants power to control in their areas what should be city-wide governmental services. The dispute over decentralization of the schools in the Ocean Hill–Brownsville section of Brooklyn, for instance, was viewed by the teachers' union (the United Federation of Teachers) as primarily involving the protection of job security, tenure, and due process for teachers.[17] Blacks, on the other hand, view these arguments as essentially white rationalizations for the perpetuation of external domination.

Other critics of the black demand for local control deplore the fragmentation of the society with its potential divisiveness if blacks and then other dissatisfied groups were allowed to substantially withdraw into some sort of self-determination units. But as Altshuler has pointed out:

> To endorse this demand is not to say that every group which comes forward with a similar demand in the future should be accorded the same privilege. The fact is that race is the most critical variable in American politics. To be a Negro is to have the fact of race pervade all of one's other roles. It is also to face exclusion and hostility. As the saying goes: we are faced with a condition, not a theory. The Constitution may be color blind, but Americans are not. To be a Negro in white America is to be always in the minority. It is rather difficult to have much sense of self-determination in such a situation. This is especially so if one is poor, and cannot even exercise much choice in the marketplace. It is not significantly less so because the system is democratic.[18]

---

* Emphasis in the original.

As noted above, blacks, like other dispossessed groups in the past, are no longer demanding that single members be integrated or coopted into the dominant society, but that the group *as a whole* be given power to control their lives. Blacks maintain that "tokenism" is merely a "trick" to divide the group by offering the illusion of individual progress. The result of such tactics is to keep the masses of the poor ghettoized and subservient, while at the same time denying to the "integrated" few full acceptance and equality.* As Stokely Carmichael, the originator of the "black power" slogan, has explained:

> In Lowndes County, for example, black power will mean that if a Negro is elected sheriff, he can end police brutality. If a black man is elected tax assessor, he can collect and channel funds for the building of better roads and schools serving black people—thus advancing the move from political power into the economic arena. In such areas as Lowndes, where black men have a majority, they will attempt to use it to exercise control. This is what they seek: control. Where Negroes lack a majority, black power means proper representation and sharing of control. It means the creation of power bases from which black people can work to change statewide or nationwide patterns of oppression through pressure from strength—instead of weakness. Politically, black power means what it has always meant to SNCC: the coming together of black people to elect representatives and *to force those representatives to speak to their needs.* It does not mean merely putting black faces in office. A man or woman who is black and from the slums cannot be automatically expected to speak to the needs of black people. Most of the black politicians we see around the country today are not what SNCC means by black power. The power must be that of a community, and emanate from there.[19]

The working together as a group to achieve shared goals is, of course, not a new phenomenon in American politics. The so-called "bloc-vote" has traditionally been employed to exert pressure to achieve desired results. Blacks are simply carrying the process one step further as an expedient forced upon them by a racist society. Blacks reason that local autonomy would allow the establishment of group economic institutions as well as enhance their national political power through more direct contacts with the federal government. It may also imply a new interdependence "based no longer on favors asked and received but on the respect which power

---

* Malcolm X's famous retort to a black associate professor who had accused him of being a "divisive demagogue" ("Do you know what white racists call black Ph.D.s? Nigger.") illustrates the failure of society to live up to its rhetoric about everyone being able to fully assimilate if only they will adopt the dominant society's styles, mores, speech, etc. *The Autobiography of Malcolm X* (New York: Grove Press, 1964), p. 284.

owes to power."[20] That this kind of power for the group is the goal of militant leaders should no longer be in doubt.*

It is beyond the scope of this paper to analyze the probability that community control for blacks is a possibility in the near future. We may note, however, that for many whites it may be preferable to true integration in schools (through busing, matched schools, etc.) and in residential patterns. It is paradoxical that in the near future it may be whites who are demanding community control and local autonomy in those core cities where blacks are becoming majorities.**

Currently the drive for full integration into American life is no longer perceived by many black people as being a possibility in the immediate future. Thus, the drive has come for community control of those areas where blacks reside. It is a movement to allow black people to experience majority status and to make significant decisions affecting their lives which heretofore have been made by a majority apathetic or hostile to their aspirations. Community control would build black power by providing a locus for organization and through the concentration of resources; but most important, perhaps "It would give blacks a tangible stake in the American political system. By giving them systems they considered their own, it would—hopefully—enhance the legitimacy of the whole system in their eyes."[21]

Notes

[1] Chuck Stone, Black Political Power in America (New York: Dell Publishing Co., 1970), p. 249.

[2] Alan Altshuler, Community Control (New York: Pegasus, 1970), p. 204.

[3] David Boesel, Richard Berk, W. Eugene Groves, Betty Eidson, and Peter Rossi, "White Institutions and Black Rage," Transaction, IV, No. 5 (March 1969), 29.

---

* "The black is moving from dependence and powerlessness to an aggressive pride in collective power." Tom Hayden, "The Trial," Ramparts, IX, No. 1 (July 1970), 48. "Thus we determined to win political power, with the idea of moving on from these into activity that would have economic effect. With power, the masses could make or participate in making the decisions which govern their destinies and thus create basic change in their day-to-day lives." Stokely Carmichael, "Power and Racism," New York Review of Books, September 22, 1966. Reprinted in Floyd B. Barbour, ed., The Black Power Revolt (Toronto: The Macmillan Co., 1968). See also weekly editions of The Black Panther.

** In addition to Gary, Newark, and Washington, D.C., ten other major cities will have black majorities by 1984 if present trends continue. They are, along with their estimated dates of such majority: New Orleans, 1971; Richmond, 1971; Baltimore, 1972; Jacksonville, 1972; Cleveland, 1975; St. Louis, 1978; Detroit, 1979; Philadelphia, 1981; Oakland, 1984; and Chicago, 1984. In addition, other cities in the near future are likely to have black majorities in the schools, including Pittsburgh, Dallas, Cincinnati, Kansas City, and New Haven. Report of the National Advisory Commission on Civil Disorders, March 1968, p. 216.

4 Jerome Skolnick, *The Politics of Protest,* The Report to the National Commission on the Causes and Prevention of Violence (New York: Ballantine, 1969), p. 10. Also see *Violence in America: Historical and Comparative Perspectives,* The Report to the National Commission on the Causes and Prevention of Violence, June 1969.

5 *Newsweek,* LXXIII, No. 26 (June 30, 1969), 23.

6 *Ibid.*

7 Gary T. Marx, *Protest and Prejudice* (New York: Harper and Row, 1967), pp. 32–33.

8 T. M. Tomlinson, "Riot Ideology Among Urban Negroes," in Louis Masotti and Don Bowen, *Riots and Rebellion* (Beverly Hills: Sage Publications, 1968), p. 419.

9 Nathan Hare, "How White Power Whitewashes Black Power," in Floyd B. Barbour, ed., *The Black Power Revolt* (Toronto: The Macmillan Co., 1968), p. 221.

10 "An Interview with Huey P. Newton," *The Black Panther,* March 16, 1968, pp. 4, 16–18; reprinted in John Bracey, Jr., August Meier, and Elliot Rudwick, *Black Nationalism in America* (New York: Bobbs-Merrill Co., 1970), pp. 542–544.

11 Each issue of *The Black Panther* carries the 10-point program of the party adopted in October 1966. See, for instance, *The Black Panther,* III, No. 27 (October 25, 1969),22.

12 Skolnick, *op. cit.,* p. 20.

13 "Huey Newton Talks to the Movement," in Richard P. Young, *Roots of Rebellion* (New York: Harper and Row, 1970), p. 383.

14 *The Black Panther,* IV, No. 21 (April 25, 1970), 9.

15 Boesel, *op. cit.,* p. 29. See also David Bayley and Harold Mendelsohn, *Minorities and the Police* (New York: The Free Press, 1969).

16 Skolnick, *op. cit.,* p. 7.

17 Sol Stern, "Scab Teachers," *Ramparts,* VII, No. 7 (November 19, 1968), 18. For an analysis of the arguments used against community control, see Altshuler, *op. cit.,* pp. 18–65.

18 Altshuler, *op. cit.,* pp. 203–204.

19 Stokely Carmichael, "Power and Racism," *New York Review of Books,* September 22, 1966. Reprinted in Barbour, *op. cit.,* p. 67. Italics in original.

20 Skolnick, *op. cit.,* p. 20.

21 Altshuler, *op. cit.,* p. 199.

Would Community Control Be a Step Toward Racial Separatism?

Alan Altshuler

The next selection is taken from the major work on black community control to date, Alan Altshuler's Community Control, which is an excellent introduction to all facets of the subject. Here he weighs the charge that black community control will promote continued racial segregation.

Most of those who argue that it would assume that community boundaries would be drawn to maximize racial homogeneity. (I shall contend below that this is improbable.) Others simply note that, given existing residential segregation, neighborhood communities would be far more racially homogeneous than the larger cities of which they were part. And they add that, once the boundaries were defined, there would be a very strong tendency for whites to flee those with Negro majorities. In the predominantly white communities, moreover, neighborhood officials might be far less solicitous of Negro interests than today's citywide officials. This would be particularly likely in working class neighborhoods with substantial Negro minorities, or threatened by ghetto expansion. These might become little Mississippis, touching off black migrations comparable to that from the original.

Other arguments advanced under the "separatist" rubric include the following. First, government bureaucracies, very much including those of the nation's large cities, are today the best integrated institutions of American society. The struggle to make them so has been long and hard—and despite their relative position, still has a long way to go. To break them up (dis-integrate them) now would be a colossal retrograde step.[1]

Second, the historic record suggests that progress toward integration is most likely when decision makers drawn from the educational elite are entrusted with power and well insulated from citizen influence. Thus, the Supreme Court has a far better record on race than Congress, and it has

---

Reprinted by permission of Pegasus, a Division of Western Publishing Co., Inc., from *Community Control: The Black Demand for Participation in Large American Cities* by Alan Altshuler, pp. 19–28. Copyright © 1970 by Western.

proven easier to integrate Catholic than Protestant churches. Similarly, Robert Crain, in a study of disputes over school integration in eight nonsouthern cities, concluded that the disposition to combat segregation tended to be a direct function of the extent to which educational decision making was insulated from citizen control.*

Third, it is pointed out that the history of efforts to combat segregation in America has been one of raising the level at which decisions were made. White segregationists are still demanding a reversal of the trend toward federal infringement upon state's rights. In this context it is sometimes pointed out that not too much faith should be placed in the formal power of state authorities to prevent communities from pursuing racist policies. The record of federal enforcement of the 13th, 14th, and 15th Amendments in the southern states is less than reassuring. And even as enforcement of the requirement of formal nondiscrimination has become more vigorous in recent years, the spirit of southern state government has remained profoundly (and quite effectively) racist.**

To all these arguments a few blacks respond, of course, that separation is indeed their goal, that the long quest for integration was both hopeless and misguided—hopeless because the white majority will never permit integration, misguided because the black subculture is superior to mainstream American culture anyway. Why should blacks, these militants ask, rigidly suppress their own personalities in order to resemble and be "accepted" by whites?

What is more important, however, is that at present most black spokesmen whose long-run objective is integration are *also* supporters of community control. They tend to answer the criticisms outlined above as follows.

First, and most important: to proclaim full integration as one's immediate and only goal is idle rhetoric. Only a tiny minority of white Americans are prepared to have their own neighborhoods and schools integrated, except in token proportions and by black families that have adopted white life styles. There is probably a national majority opposed to integration even on these terms. Thus, when open occupancy proposals

---

* Crain and his colleagues found that such factors as region, size of the Negro population, and socioeconomic status of the white population had little predictive value. The variables that appeared to matter were school board characteristics. In particular, appointed boards were much more receptive to integration than elected, and appointed boards composed of blue ribbon civic leaders were more receptive than those composed of professional politicians. Among *elected* officials, mayors (who could seek white support on other issues if they accommodated black demands for school integration) were more receptive than school board members.[2] Almost identical findings have been made, incidentally, with respect to the politics of fluoridation.[3]

** By racist, I mean anti-integrationist as well as tending to deny nonwhites equal social and economic opportunity, equal justice, and an equal share of government benefits.

have been put to American state and local electorates, they have almost invariably been voted down.* [4] When the Survey Research Center (SRC) of the University of Michigan asked a fifteen-city sample of white respondents in 1968 whether they would favor the imposition of limits on further in-migration if a single Negro family moved into their 100-family neighborhood, a majority of those who had opinions (48–40 per cent) replied that they would.** When a sample of whites living in Buffalo, New York, was asked during the winter of 1966–67 whether they favored busing to bring about school integration, only 23 per cent responded positively (vs. 59 per cent opposed).*** [7]

By contrast, an overwhelming majority of blacks has supported integration in the past and continues to do so. An SRC survey in Detroit several months after the Detroit riot of 1967 found Negroes favoring the goal of integration by a ratio of 87–1.[8] In the Buffalo survey cited above, Negroes favored school busing to achieve integration by 67–17 per cent. In this survey, whereas whites said they favored the general concept of integration by 2–1 (46–23 per cent), Negroes favored it by nearly 15–1 (87–6 per cent).[9] In the fifteen-city survey of 1968, only 8 per cent of Negro respondents said that they would prefer to live in a neighborhood with no whites. Only 6 per cent said that they would prefer their children to attend majority-Negro schools. A nationwide poll conducted in mid-1969 by the Gallup organization for Newsweek found Negroes preferring to live in integrated neighborhoods by a ratio of 4½–1 (74–16 per cent), and preferring integrated schools for their children by almost 9–1 (78–9 per cent).[10]

Those who favor both community control and integration maintain that, if history has ever taught a lesson, it has taught that those few white liberals who genuinely desire full integration cannot deliver it—at least not in the foreseeable future. The urban ghettos are growing, not dispersing. In a study of thirteen cities that had special censuses between 1964 and 1967,

---

   * A U.C.L.A. research team which conducted surveys in Los Angeles following the Watts riot, moreover, found that open occupancy was the racial issue that most inflamed whites.[5]

   ** A majority of those with opinions (51–40 per cent) opposed open occupancy legislation, but a slight plurality said that they personally would not mind at all if a Negro family moved in next door (49–44 per cent). A large majority did favor equal employment legislation (67–23 per cent).[6]

   *** Surprisingly, upper income whites were more hostile to busing than lower income whites. By contrast, it was upper income blacks who most favored busing.

   If anything, the Buffalo sample was more favorable to integration than SRC's fifteen-city sample. For example, whereas the SRC respondents opposed open occupancy legislation by a ratio of 5–4, the Buffalo sample favored it by a ratio of 5–2.

   Comparing survey with referendum results on open housing, one is led to the conclusion that whites talk a more integrationist line than they vote. The reason is quite likely that their fears are easily stirred during referendum campaigns. On the other hand, it may simply be that whites are more prone generally to resist integration in practice than when answering pollsters.

Reynolds Farley and Karl Taueber found that in all but two, segregation by census tracts had increased since 1960.*[11] National census analyses show that whites have been fleeing the central cities at an accelerating rate during the 1960's.** Meanwhile, Negroes, who managed to account for 3.4 per cent of suburban growth during the 1950's, accounted for only 1.1 per cent from 1960 to 1966. Census Bureau surveys indicate that Negroes have accounted for a much larger share of suburban growth more recently—an astonishing 14 per cent from 1966 to 1968—but the Bureau warns that high sampling variability makes this finding very suspect.[14]

Black leaders, the "moderate" proponents of community control point out, have rarely opposed integration in practice, even though some have taken to rejecting it as a goal in their rhetoric. None propose denying individual blacks the right to move to predominantly white neighborhoods today. It is still *whites* who provide the political constituency for segregation. All the blacks have done is to change tactics. They have revived the distinction between integration and equality as objectives, and determined to concentrate for the time being upon the latter.

Essentially this decision has been pragmatic. They have judged that if integration ever came about it would do so only *after* black achievement equalled white. (The traditional view, of course, accepted by the Supreme Court in the *Brown* decision, had been that integration was a prerequisite of equal achievement.) They have judged that the real key to unlocking the black potential is self-respect, and that given white resistance to integration, the most feasible way for blacks to acquire it is to exercise responsibility in their own communities.

---

* In a previous article, Taueber had noted that: "In 1910 some ethnic groups were as segregated from native whites as Negroes were. Since 1910, however, the residential segregation of every group of European descent has been declining, whereas segregation of whites from Negroes has been increasing."

Analyzing 1960 census data from specific cities, he had also reached the following conclusions: (a) that Negroes are far more segregated than Puerto Ricans (New York) and Mexican-Americans (Los Angeles); (b) that since 1940 the segregation of Orientals from whites has markedly decreased, while that of Orientals from Negroes has markedly increased (San Francisco); (c) that less than one-eighth of segregation can be explained on the basis of Negro-white income differentials (Chicago and 15 other cities); (d) that the degree of segregation tends to increase as housing vacancy rates go down, and vice versa; (e) that, consequently, segregation increased during the forties and decreased during the fifties (all cities for which the census published adequate data from 1940 through 1960); but (f) that the overall degree of segregation was slightly greater in 1960 than 1940.[12]

** On a national basis, white central city population increased at an annual rate of 220,000 during the 1950's, decreased at an annual rate of 141,000 from 1960 to 1966, and decreased at an annual rate of 486,000 from 1966 to 1968.[13] These figures understate the pace of change in the cities where Negroes are concentrated, because in many of the newer cities of the South and West the Negro population share is small and the white population has continued to grow rapidly.

Similarly, they have concluded that black business is most likely to develop on the basis of ghetto markets and favorable government actions. They have judged that sympathetic government is most likely to be a product of political mobilization, and that residential segregation (even if an evil in most other respects) is a great mobilization asset.* But most of all, they have judged that white America is much more likely (though still not very) to concede a large measure of ghetto self-determination than to accept large numbers of blacks into its neighborhoods.

All black leaders and would-be leaders, moreover, are today in search of mass followings. (Perhaps more than anything else, this is what differentiates them from most civil rights leaders of the past—Marcus Garvey is a conspicuous exception—who did not consider mass followings obtainable.) None believe that the black masses can be mobilized around the remote goal of integration. Popular followings are secured and maintained by focusing on more immediate desires: jobs, physical security, better schools, better housing, more sympathetic treatment from public servants, and so on. They are also secured by establishing cultural rapport: that is, by manipulating the right symbols in the right style. The right style at the present time is militant revivalist. The right symbols are those which express pride in black, and which attempt to purge traditional black self-hatred by ridiculing the traditional aspiration for acceptance into white America.

The evidence available suggests that the calls for black pride and black power have struck responsive chords among the Negro masses, but without substantially altering the basic thrust toward equality and integration. Thus, the SRC fifteen-city survey conducted in 1968 found that, while blacks massively favored integration, 96 per cent felt that blacks should take more pride in Negro history, 70 per cent felt that Negroes should patronize Negro-owned stores whenever possible, and fully 42 per cent felt that Negro schoolchildren should study an African language.**[16] The 1967 Detroit survey, in which the ratio of black support for integration was 87–1, also found widespread support for the term "black power." Only 9 per cent of the black respondents in this survey (by comparison with 39 per cent of the white) thought that "black power" implied blacks ruling over whites. This 9 per cent, moreover, was composed almost entirely of blacks who disapproved the term. The supporters nearly all spoke of equity rather than superiority, and emphasized that they were for black people,

---

* Social science findings tend to bear this out.[15]

** On this point, the authors note: "We had no other question that so clearly taps positive identification with a black heritage without at the same time implying rejection of whites. But the support of this single proposition, which a few years ago was scarcely discussed by most Negroes and still seems exotic and impractical to most white ears, is so impressive that it suggests a considerable potential for the growth of black cultural identity in America."[17]

not against whites.[18] Gallup's 1969 *Newsweek* poll, which found continued mass support for integration, also found a majority of those with opinions favoring the term "black power" (42–31 per cent). Northern respondents under thirty endorsed the term by more than 4–1 (68–16 per cent). The same poll showed massive support for the idea that "Negroes have a special soul that most whites have not experienced" (54 per cent yes, 22 per cent no).*[19]

What all this suggests is that Negroes and whites have radically different views as to whether black power and black pride need violate the traditionally acceptable limits of American ethnic pluralism. The rhetoric and the demands will probably change as and if white America becomes truly receptive to integration. In the long interim, it ill behooves white liberals to reject black-proposed ghetto improvement schemes out of hand. So, at least, the "moderate" supporters of community control maintain.

The critics respond, however, that the intentions of the black masses are not the issue. What *is* at issue is the prospective consequences of community control. Would it, in fact, lead down the paths forecast above? Those I have labelled the "moderate" advocates of community control tend to answer this question—or, rather, these questions—as follows.

First, as to the charge that whites would flee those neighborhoods with Negro majorities: the fact is that whites have been doing so for decades. And it is just as true that they have been trying to keep blacks out of their neighborhoods. Failing in the cities, the whites have adjourned to the suburbs, where they exercise just the sort of community control that blacks are now demanding. The fact is that more than half the whites who now live in metropolitan America live in suburbs rather than central cities. (The estimated 1968 suburban share for whites was 59 per cent; that for blacks 20 per cent. The differential tended to be greatest in the largest metropolitan areas, and in the Northeast and North Central regions.[21]) Taking all Americans together, moreover, only 22 per cent lived in local jurisdictions that had populations larger than 250,000 in 1960, fewer than half of these in cities larger than a million.

Thus, small-scale government is the American norm, even within metropolitan areas. For central city whites who value it, the option of moving to the suburbs is always open. Only blacks have been confined regardless of taste to the central cities, and told that government at a scale which permitted them majority status would be "separatist." Even if this is literally true, to apply it solely to blacks is inequitable. It is, in fact, typical of the white determination to keep blacks power-poor.**

---

* Of related interest is a recent Harris poll of Negro respondents in Harlem. Fully 75 per cent maintained that they watched the program "Soul" on a local educational television station.[20]

** I prefer this term to "powerless," which implies an absolute lack of influence. Parenthetically, this view of the white attitude toward inequality is quite wide-

Second, in answer to the charge that breaking up the city bureaucracies would be a major step away from integration: blacks are inclined to emphasize (a) the current underrepresentation at all but the menial levels of existing city bureaucracies,* (b) the current high levels of tension between city bureaucracies and ghetto populations, (c) the lack of white concern about segregated suburban bureaucracies, and (d) the contrary evidence suggesting that Negro communities would employ integrated staffs.** Given the shortage of black professionals, it would be surprising if many black communities could—even if they wished—get along with all black personnel. Their recruits, presumably, would have to meet state licensing standards. Segregation would more likely be a problem in white neighborhoods, but if Negroes are willing to take this risk it ill becomes whites to refuse it. The reason many Negroes are willing to take it is that they prefer sympathetic and responsive government at home to a few jobs "abroad."

Third, with reference to the historic record (of elites being more favorable toward integration than the citizenry at large): this is no argument for denying blacks the degree of local self-rule enjoyed by suburban whites. If whites are anxious to further integration, let them do so at the metropolitan scale, for suburban and central city communities alike. In any event, blacks are no longer satisfied with paternalism; they value self-governance even more than integration.*** But it should also be recalled that the historic record is one of white mass resistance to integration, not black. The surveys suggest that among Negroes the white pattern is reversed: that is, the masses are more favorable to integration than the elites.****

---

spread. In the Kerner Commission's fifteen-city survey, almost half of the black respondents who thought that whites cared at all thought that their interest was malevolent (27 per cent, vs. 29 per cent who thought that most whites would like to see Negroes get a better break). Those under forty were much less likely to think whites wished Negroes well than those over forty, and the difference was particularly striking among the educated. For example, 46 per cent of Negroes over forty with at least some college education thought that most whites wished Negroes well; the comparable percentage for those under forty was 18.[22]

In the 1969 Newsweek survey, 51 per cent of northern respondents under thirty said they thought that most white people wanted to keep Negroes down. Another 30 per cent thought that most whites were at best indifferent to inequality.[23]

* The Kerner Commission, for example, in a survey of 28 large city police departments, found that the median percentage of Negro policemen was one-fourth (6 per cent) the median Negro share of total population (24 per cent). For the ranks of lieutenant and above, Negro underrepresentation was four to five times greater.[24]

** For example, in New York's controversial Ocean Hill–Brownsville experimental school district, the teaching staff was 80 per cent white as of June 1969.[25]

*** The evidence suggests that in fact this is a minority position. It commands widespread support among the young and the politically active, however.

**** The validity of this assertion depends heavily on how the elites are defined. Elderly Negro men of wealth would doubtless be very favorable to integration. An

Fourth, in response to the charge that the federal record of constitutional enforcement in the South provides little ground for optimism that state authorities would be able to prevent the teaching and practice of race hatred in local communities: community control supporters maintain simply that the analogy is a false one. The Southerners had a position of power in Congress that Negroes cannot hope to achieve in the state legislatures. The national majority had little interest in stamping out southern racism. By contrast, the state majorities will be waiting to pounce at the first excuse. For generations it was accepted that the federal government had little power to intervene in the affairs of southern states. The right of state governments to intervene at will in local affairs, on the other hand, is undisputed.

Notes

[1] Cf. Irving Kristol, "Decentralization for What?" *The Public Interest*, Spring 1968, pp. 17–25. The reference is to p. 25.

[2] Robert L. Crain, *The Politics of School Desegregation* (Aldine, 1968), chs. 10–13; and Robert L. Crain and James J. Venecko, "Elite Influence in School Desegregation," in James Q. Wilson, ed., *City Politics and Public Policy* (Wiley, 1968); pp. 127–148.

[3] Cf. Donald B. Rosenthal and Robert L. Crain, "Structure and Values in Local Political Systems: The Case of Fluoridation Decisions," in Wilson, *op. cit.*, pp. 217–242; and Harvey M. Sapolsky, "Science, Voters, and the Fluoridation Controversy," *Science*, October 25, 1968, pp. 427–433.

[4] Cf. Raymond E. Wolfinger and Fred I. Greenstein, "The Repeal of Fair Housing in California: An Analysis of Referendum Voting," *American Political Science Review*, September 1968, pp. 753–769.

[5] Harry Scoble, "Effects of Riots on Negro Leadership," in Louis H. Masotti and Don R. Bowen, eds., *Riots and Rebellion: Civil Violence in the Urban Community* (Sage, 1968), pp. 329–346. The point cited appears on p. 331.

[6] Campbell and Schuman, *op. cit.*, p. 33.

[7] Everett F. Cataldo, Richard M. Johnson, and Lyman A. Kellstadt, "Social Strain and Urban Violence," in Masotti and Bowen, *op. cit.*, pp. 285–298. The point cited appears on p. 293.

[8] Joel D. Aberbach and Jack L. Walker, "The Meanings of Black Power: A Comparison of White and Black Interpretations of a Political Slogan," paper delivered at the annual meeting of the American Political Science Association, September 1968, mimeo. The point cited appears at p. 12.

[9] Cataldo, *et al.*, in Masotti and Bowen, *op. cit.*, p. 293.

"elite" group consisting of young professionals, intellectuals, and community organizers would presumably include a much higher proportion of separatists (however defined) than the Negro population at large. By way of illustration, the Survey Research Center asked respondents in its fifteen-city survey whether they thought schools with mostly Negro children should have mostly Negro teachers. Overall, 10 per cent of black respondents thought that they should. Among college graduates over the age of forty, only 3 per cent thought so. Among college graduates under forty, 20 per cent thought so.[26]

[10] *Newsweek*, June 30, 1969, p. 20. It should be emphasized that these findings are not strictly comparable to those of the 1968 SRC survey, so no trends can be inferred.

[11] Reynolds Farley and Karl E. Taeuber, "Population Trends and Residential Segregation Since 1960," *Science*, March 1, 1968, pp. 953–956.

[12] Karl E. Taeuber, "Residential Segregation," *Scientific American*, August 1965, pp. 12–19.

[13] U.S. Bureau of the Census, *Current Population Reports*, Series P-23, No. 24 (USGPO, October 1967), p. 8; and No. 27 (USGPO, February 1969), p. 3.

[14] *Ibid.* The Bureau's surveys are designed to provide reliable information on national population trends. The smaller any population group within the nation is, the less reliable are the data bearing on it. Thus, far more confidence can be placed in the data showing an acceleration of the white exodus from the central cities than in that showing a Negro breakthrough in securing access to suburban housing.

[15] Cf. Seymour Martin Lipset, *Political Man* (Anchor, 1963), pp. 200–202; Lester Milbraith, *Political Participation* (Rand McNally, 1965), p. 119; and Jay Schulman, "Ghetto-Area Residence, Political Alienation, and Riot Orientation," in Masotti and Bowen, *op. cit.*, pp. 262–284, esp. p. 281.

[16] Campbell and Schuman, *op. cit.*, p. 20.

[17] *Ibid.*, p. 19.

[18] Aberbach and Walker, *op. cit.*, pp. 3–9.

[19] *Newsweek*, June 30, 1969, pp. 9, 20, 22.

[20] *New York Times*, July 4, 1969, p. 35.

[21] U.S. Bureau of the Census, *Current Population Reports*, Series P-23, No. 27, pp. 2, 7.

[22] Campbell and Schuman, *op. cit.*, p. 26.

[23] *Newsweek*, June 30, 1969, p. 21.

[24] *Report of the National Advisory Commission on Civil Disorders* (Bantam, 1968), pp. 315–316.

[25] *New York Times*, June 25, 1969, p. 39.

[26] Campbell and Schuman, *op. cit.*, p. 19.

The Search for New Forms

Stokely Carmichael and Charles V. Hamilton

The book Black Power by Stokely Carmichael and Charles V. Hamilton has been widely read and discussed among politically active blacks. These passages from Chapter VIII are introductory remarks on the neighborhood ghetto as a basis for black power.

We are aware that it has become commonplace to pinpoint and describe the ills of our urban ghettos. The social, political and economic problems are so acute that even a casual observer cannot fail to see that something is wrong. While description is plentiful, however, there remains a blatant timidity about what to do to solve the problems.

Neither rain nor endless "definitive," costly reports nor stop-gap measures will even approach a solution to the explosive situation in the nation's ghettos. This country cannot begin to solve the problems of the ghettos as long as it continues to hang on to outmoded structures and institutions. A political party that seeks only to "manage conflict" and hope for the best will not be able to serve a growing body of alienated black people. An educational system which, year after year, continues to cripple hundreds of thousands of black children must be replaced by wholly new mechanisms of control and management. We must begin to think and operate in terms of entirely new and substantially different forms of expression.

It is crystal clear that the initiative for such changes will have to come from the black community. We cannot expect white America to begin to move forcefully on these problems unless and until black America begins to move. This means that black people must organize themselves without regard for what is traditionally acceptable, precisely because the traditional approaches have failed. It means that black people must make demands without regard to their initial "respectability," precisely because "respectable" demands have not been sufficient.

The northern urban ghettos are in many ways different from the black-

---

From *Black Power* by Stokely Carmichael and Charles V. Hamilton (New York: Vintage Books, 1967), pp. 164–167, 171–177. Copyright © 1967 by Stokely Carmichael and Charles V. Hamilton. Reprinted by permission of Random House, Inc.

belt South, but in neither area will substantial change come about until black people organize independently to exert power. As noted in earlier chapters, black people already have the voting potential to control the politics of entire southern counties. Given maximum registration of blacks, there are more than 110 counties where black people could outvote the white racists. These people should concentrate on forming independent political parties and not waste time trying to reform or convert the racist parties. In the North, it is no less important that independent groups be formed. It has been clearly shown that when black people attempt to get within one of the two major parties in the cities, they become co-opted and their interests are shunted to the background. They become expendable.

We must begin to think of the black community as a base of organization to control institutions in that community. Control of the ghetto schools must be taken out of the hands of "professionals," most of whom have long since demonstrated their insensitivity to the needs and problems of the black child. These "experts" bring with them middle-class biases, unsuitable techniques and materials; these are, at best, dysfunctional and at worst destructive. A recent study of New York schools reveals that the New York school system is run by thirty people—school supervisors, deputy and assistant superintendents and examiners. The study concluded: "Public education policy has become the province of the professional bureaucrat, with the tragic result that the status quo, suffering from many difficulties, is the order of the day."[1] Virtually no attention is paid to the wishes and demands of the parents, especially the black parents. This is totally unacceptable.

Black parents should seek as their goal the actual control of the public schools in their community: hiring and firing of teachers, selection of teaching materials, determination of standards, etc. This can be done with a committee of teachers. The traditional, irrelevant "See Dick, See Jane, Run Dick, Run Jane, White House, Nice Farm" nonsense must be ended. The principals and as many teachers as possible of the ghetto schools should be black. The children will be able to see their kind in positions of leadership and authority. It should never occur to anyone that a brand new school can be built in the heart of the black community and then given a white person to head it. The fact is that in this day and time, it is crucial that race be taken into account in determining policy of this sort. Some people will, again, view this as "reverse segregation" or as "racism." It is not. It is emphasizing race in a positive way: not to subordinate or rule over others but to overcome the effects of centuries in which race has been used to the detriment of the black man. . . .

Such community control has long been accepted in smaller communities, particularly white suburban areas. No longer is it "white folks' business" only. Ultimately, community-controlled schools could organize an independent school board (like the "People's Board of Education") for the total black community. Such an innovation would permit the parents and the school to develop a much closer relationship and to begin attacking the problems of the ghetto in a communal, realistic way.

The tenements of the ghetto represent another target of high priority. Tenants in buildings should form cohesive organizations—unions—to act in their common interest vis-à-vis the absentee slumlord. Obviously, rents should be withheld if the owner does not provide adequate services and decent facilities. But more importantly, the black community should set as a prime goal the policy of having the owner's rights forfeited if he does not make repairs: forfeited and turned over to the black organization, which would not only manage the property but own it outright. The absentee slumlord is perpetuating a socially detrimental condition, and he should not be allowed to hide behind the rubric of property rights. The black community must insist that the goal of human rights take precedent over property rights, and back up that insistence in ways which will make it in the self-interest of the white society to act morally. Behavior—in this case, the misuse of property—can be regulated to any extent the power structure wishes. No one should be naïve enough to think that an owner will give up his property easily, but the black community, properly organized and mobilized, could apply pressure that would make him choose between the alternatives of forfeiture or compliance. Thousands of black people refusing to pay rents month after month in the ghettos could have more than a salutary effect on public policy.

Virtually all of the money earned by merchants and exploiters of the black ghetto leaves those communities. Properly organized black groups should seek to establish a community rebate plan. The black people in a given community would organize and refuse to do business with any merchant who did not agree to "reinvest," say, forty to fifty percent of his net profit in the indigenous community. This contribution could take many forms: providing additional jobs for black people, donating scholarship funds for students, supporting certain types of community organization. An agreement would be reached between the merchants and the black consumers. If a merchant wants customers from a black community, he must be made to understand that he has to contribute to that community. If he chooses not to do so, he will not be patronized, and the end result will be no profits from that community. Contractors who seek to do business in the black community would also be made to understand that they face a boycott if they do not donate to the black community.

Such a community rebate plan will require careful organization and tight discipline on the part of the black people. But it is possible, and has in fact already been put into effect by some ethnic communities. White America realizes the market in the black community; black America must begin to realize the potential of that market.

Under the present institutional arrangements, no one should think that the mere election of a few black people to local or national office will solve the problem of political representation. There are now ten black people on the City Council in Chicago, but there are not more than two or three (out of the total of fifty) who will speak out forcefully. The fact is that the present political institutions are not geared to giving the black minority an effective voice. Two needs arise from this.

First, it is important that the black communities in these northern ghettos form independent party groups to elect their own choices to office when and where they can. It should not be assumed that "you cannot beat City Hall." It has been done, as evidenced by the 1967 aldermanic elections in one of the tightest machine cities in the country: Chicago. In the Sixth Ward, an independent black candidate, Sammy Rayner, defeated an incumbent, machine-backed black alderman. Rayner first ran in 1963 and missed a run-off by a mere 177 votes. He then challenged Congressman William L. Dawson in 1964 and lost, but he was building an image in the black community as one who could and would speak out. The black people were getting the message. In 1967, when he ran against the machine incumbent for the City Council, he won handily. . . .

The very least which Sammy Rayner can give the black community is a new political dignity. His victory will begin to establish the *habit* of saying "No" to the downtown bosses. In the same way that the black Southerner had to assert himself and say "No" to those who did not want him to register to vote, now the Northern black voter must begin to defy those who would control his vote. This very act of defiance threatens the status quo, because there is no predicting its ultimate outcome. Those black voters, then *accustomed* to acting independently, could eventually swing their votes one way or the other—but always for *their* benefit. Smith signaled this when he said: "The disbelievers who felt that you could not beat City Hall are now whistling a different tune. The victory of Sammy Rayner in the Sixth Ward should serve as a beacon light for all who believe in independent politics in this city. . . . Rayner is going to be responsible for the aldermanic position taking on a new line of dignity. Black people are going to be able to point with pride to this man, who firmly believes that we need statesmanlike leadership instead of the goatsmanship we have been exposed to."[2]

Let no one protest that this type of politics is naïve or childish or fails to understand the "rules of the game." The price of going along with the "regulars" is too high to pay for the so-called benefits received. The rewards of independence can be considerable. It is too soon to say precisely where this new spirit of independence could take us. New forms may lead to a new political force. Hopefully, this force might move to create new national and local political parties—or, more accurately, the first *legitimate* political parties. Some have spoken of a "third party" or "third political force." But from the viewpoint of community needs and popular participation, no existing force or party in this country has ever been relevant. A force which is relevant would therefore be a first—something truly new.

The second implication of the political dilemma facing black people is that ultimately they may have to spearhead a drive to revamp completely the present institutions of representation. If the Rayners are continually outvoted, if the grievances of the black community continue to be overlooked, then it will become necessary to devise wholly new forms of local political representation. There is nothing sacred about the system of electing candidates to serve as aldermen, councilmen, etc., by wards or districts. Geographical representation is not inherently right. Perhaps political interests have to be represented in some entirely different manner—such as community-parent control of schools, unions of tenants, unions of welfare recipients actually taking an official role in running the welfare departments. If political institutions do not meet the needs of the people, if the people finally believe that those institutions do not express their own values, then those institutions must be discarded. It is wasteful and inefficient, not to mention unjust, to continue imposing old forms and ways of doing things on a people who no longer view those forms and ways as functional.

We see independent politics (after the fashion of a Rayner candidacy) as the first step toward implementing something new. Voting year after year for the traditional party and its silent representatives gets the black community nowhere; voters then get their own candidates, but these may become frustrated by the power and organization of the machines. The next logical step is to demand more meaningful structures, forms and ways of dealing with longstanding problems.

We see this as the potential power of the ghettos. In a real sense, it is similar to what is taking place in the South: the move in the direction of independent politics—and from there, the move toward the development of wholly new political institutions. If these proposals also sound impractical, utopian, then we ask: what other real alternatives exist? There are none; the choice lies between a genuinely new approach and maintaining the brutalizing, destructive, violence-breeding life of the ghettos as they exist today. From the viewpoint of black people, that is no choice.

Notes

[1] Marilyn Gittell, "Participants and Participation: A Study of School Policy in New York City." New York: The Center for Urban Education. As quoted in the New York Times, April 30, 1967, p. E90.

[2] Philip Smith, "Politics as I See It," The Citizen, Chicago (March 22, 1967).

The Failure of Black Separatism

Bayard Rustin

The final selection in this second part is a wide-ranging attack by Bayard Rustin on black separation in all its forms—black capitalism, black community control, black studies programs. Of particular importance is his argument that in a large complex society "there is no such thing as an autonomous community within a large metropolitan area." This statement reflects one of Moynihan's points about Mobilization For Youth and strikes at the heart of the movement for neighborhood government in general.

We are living in an age of revolution—or so they tell us. The children of the affluent classes pay homage to their parents' values by rejecting them; this, they say, is a youth revolution. The discussion and display of sexuality increases—actors disrobe on stage, young women very nearly do on the street—and so we are in the midst of a sexual revolution. Tastes in music and clothing change, and each new fashion too is revolutionary. With every new social phenomenon now being dubbed a "revolution," the term has in fact become nothing more than a slogan which serves to take our minds off an unpleasant reality. For if we were not careful, we might easily forget that there is a conservative in the White House, that our country is racially polarized as never before, and that the forces of liberalism are in disarray. Whatever there is of revolution today, in any meaningful sense of the term, is coming from the Right.

But we are also told—and with far greater urgency and frequency— that there is a black revolution. If by revolution we mean a radical escalation of black aspirations and demands, this is surely the case. There is a new assertion of pride in the Negro race and its cultural heritage, and although the past summer was marked by the lack of any major disruptions, there is among blacks a tendency more pronounced than at any time in Negro history to engage in violence and the rhetoric of violence. Yet if we look closely at the situation of Negroes today, we find that there has been not the least revolutionary reallocation of political or economic

From Bayard Rustin, "The Failure of Black Separatism," Harpers (January 1970), pp. 25–32, 34. Copyright © 1969 by Harper's Magazine, Inc. Reprinted from the January 1970 issue of Harper's Magazine by permission of the author.

power. There is, to be sure, an increase in the number of black elected officials throughout the United States and particularly in the South, but this has largely been the result of the 1965 Voting Rights Act, which was passed before the "revolution" reached its height and the renewal of which the present Administration has not advocated with any noticeable enthusiasm. Some reallocation of political power has indeed taken place since the Presidential election of 1964, but generally its beneficiaries have been the Republicans and the anti-Negro forces. Nor does this particular trend show much sign of abating. Nixon's attempt to reverse the liberal direction of the Supreme Court has just begun. Moreover, in the 1970 Senate elections, 25 of the 34 seats to be contested were originally won by the Democrats in the great liberal surge of 1964, when the political picture was quite different from that of today. And if the Democrats only break even in 1970, the Republicans will control the Senate for the first time since 1954. A major defeat would leave the Democrats weaker than they have been at any time since the conservative days of the 1920s.

There has been, it is true, some moderate improvement in the economic condition of Negroes, but by no stretch of the imagination could it be called revolutionary. According to Andrew Brimmer of the Federal Reserve System, the median family income of Negroes between 1965 and 1967 rose from 54 per cent to 59 per cent of that for white families. Much of that gain reflected a decrease in the rate of Negro unemployment. But between February and June of 1969, Negro unemployment rose again by 1.3 per cent and should continue to rise as Nixon presses his crusade against inflation. The Council of Economic Advisers reports that in the past eight years the federal government has spent $10.3 billion on metropolitan problems while it has spent $39.9 billion on agriculture, not to mention, of course, $507.2 billion for defense. In the area of housing, for instance, New York City needs at the present time as many new subsidized apartments—780,000—as the federal housing program has constructed nationally in its entire thirty-four years. The appropriations for model cities, rent supplements, the Job Corps, the Neighborhood Youth Corps, and other programs have been drastically reduced, and the Office of Economic Opportunity is being transformed into a research agency. Nixon's welfare and revenue-sharing proposals, in addition to being economically stringent, so that they will have little or no effect on the condition of the Northern urban poor, are politically and philosophically conservative.

Any appearance that we are in the grip of a black revolution, then, is deceptive. The problem is not whether black aspirations are outpacing America's ability to respond but whether they have outpaced her willingness to do so. Lately it has been taken almost as axiomatic that with every increase in Negro demands, there must be a corresponding intensification of white resistance. This proposition implies that only black complacency can prevent racial polarization, that any political action by Negroes must of necessity produce a reaction. But such a notion ignores entirely the question of what *kind* of political action, guided by what *kind* of political strategy. One can almost assert as a law of American politics that if Negroes engage in violence as a tactic they will be met with repression, that if they follow a strategy of racial separatism they will be isolated, and that if they engage in anti-democratic activity, out of the deluded wish to skirt the democratic process, they will provoke a reaction. To the misguided, violence, separatism, and minority ultimatums may seem revolutionary, but in reality they issue only from the desperate strivings of the impotent. Certainly such tactics are not designed to enhance the achievement of progressive social change. Recent American political history has proved this point time and again with brutal clarity.

The irony of the revolutionary rhetoric uttered in behalf of Negroes is that it has helped in fact to promote conservatism. On the other hand, of course, the reverse is also true: the failure of America to respond to the demands of Negroes has fostered in the minds of the latter a sense of futility and has thus seemed to legitimize a strategy of withdrawal and violence. Other things have been operating as well. The fifteen years since *Brown vs. Topeka* have been for Negroes a period of enormous dislocation. The modernization of farming in the South forced hundreds of thousands of Negroes to migrate to the North where they were confronted by a second technological affliction, automation. Without jobs, living in cities equipped to serve neither their material nor spiritual needs, these modern-day immigrants responded to their brutal new world with despair and hostility. The civil-rights movement created an even more fundamental social dislocation, for it destroyed not simply the legal structure of segregation but also the psychological assumptions of racism. Young Negroes who matured during this period witnessed a basic challenge to the system of values and social relations which had presumed the inferiority of the Negro. They have totally rejected this system, but in doing so have often substituted for it an exaggerated and distorted perception both of themselves and of the society. As if to obliterate the trace of racial shame that might be lurking in their souls they have embraced racial chauvinism. And as if in reply to past exclusions (and often in response to present insecurities), they have created their own patterns of exclusiveness.

The various frustrations and upheavals experienced recently by the Negro community account in large part for the present political orientation of some of its most vocal members: seeing their immediate self-interest more in the terms of emotional release than in those of economic and political advancement. One is supposed to think black, dress black, eat black, and buy black without reference to the question of what such a program actually contributes to advancing the cause of social justice. Since real victories are thought to be unattainable, issues become important in so far as they can provide symbolic victories. Dramatic confrontations are staged which serve as outlets for radical energy but which in no way further the achievement of radical social goals. So that, for instance, members of the black community are mobilized to pursue the "victory" of halting construction of a state office building in Harlem, even though it is hard to see what actual economic or social benefit will be conferred on the impoverished residents of that community by their success in doing so.

Such actions constitute a politics of escape rooted in hopelessness and further reinforced by government inaction. Deracinated liberals may romanticize this politics, nihilistic New Leftists may imitate it, but it is ordinary Negroes who will be the victims of its powerlessness to work any genuine change in their condition.

The call for Black Power is now over three years old, yet to this day no one knows what Black Power is supposed to mean and therefore how its proponents are to unite and rally behind it. If one is a member of CORE, Black Power posits the need for a separate black economy based upon traditional forms of capitalist relations. For SNCC the term refers to a politically united black community. US would emphasize the unity of black culture, while the Black Panthers wish to impose upon black nationalism the philosophies of Marx, Lenin, Stalin, and Chairman Mao. Nor do these exhaust all the possible shades and gradations of meaning. If there is one common theme uniting the various demands for Black Power, it is simply that blacks must be guided in their actions by a consciousness of themselves as a separate race.

Now, philosophies of racial solidarity have never been unduly concerned with the realities that operate outside the category of race. The adherents of these philosophies are generally romantics, steeped in the traditions of their own particular clans and preoccupied with the simple biological verities of blood and racial survival. Almost invariably their rallying cry is racial self-determination, and they tend to ignore those aspects of the material world which point up divisions within the racially defined group.

But the world of black Americans is full of divisions. Only the most supine of optimists would dream of building a political movement without reference to them. Indeed, nothing better illustrates the existence of such divisions within the black community than the fact that the separatists themselves represent a distinct minority among Negroes. No reliable poll has ever identified more than 15 per cent of Negroes as separatists; usually the percentage is a good deal lower. Nor, as I have already indicated, are the separatists unified among themselves, the differences among them at times being so intense as to lead to violent conflict. The notion of the undifferentiated black community is the intellectual creation of both whites—liberals as well as racists to whom all Negroes are the same—and of certain small groups of blacks who illegitimately claim to speak for the majority.

The fact is that like every other racial or ethnic group in America, Negroes are divided by age, class, and geography. Young Negroes are at least as hostile toward their elders as white New Leftists are toward their liberal parents. They are in addition separated by vast gaps in experience, Northern from Southern, urban from rural. And even more profound are the disparities in wealth among them. In contrast to the white community, where the spread of income has in recent years remained unchanged or has narrowed slightly, economic differentials among blacks have increased. In 1965, for example, the wealthiest 5 per cent of white and non-white families each received 15.5 per cent of the total income in their respective communities. In 1967, however, the percentage of white income received by the top 5 per cent of white families had dropped to 14.9 per cent while among non-whites the share of income of the top 5 per cent of the families had risen to 17.5 per cent. This trend probably reflects the new opportunities which are available to black professionals in industry, government, and academia, but have not touched the condition of lower-class and lower-middle-class Negroes.

To Negroes for whom race is the major criterion, however, divisions by wealth and status are irrelevant. Consider, for instance, the proposals for black economic advancement put forth by the various groups of black nationalists. These proposals are all remarkably similar. For regardless of one's particular persuasion—whether a revolutionary or a cultural nationalist or an unabashed black capitalist—once one confines one's analysis to the ghetto, no proposal can extend beyond a strategy for ghetto development and black enterprise. This explains in part the recent popularity of black capitalism and, to a lesser degree, black cooperatives: once both the economic strategy and goal are defined in terms of black self-determination, there is simply not much else available in the way of ideas.

There are other reasons for the popularity of black capitalism, reasons having to do with material and psychological self-interest. E. Franklin Frazier has written that Negro business is "a social myth" first formulated toward the end of the nineteenth century when the legal structure of segregation was established and Negro hopes for equality destroyed. History has often shown us that oppression can sometimes lead to a rationalization of the unjust conditions on the part of the oppressed and following on this, to an opportunistic competition among them for whatever meager advantages are available. This is, according to Frazier, exactly what happened among American Negroes. The myth of Negro business was created and tied to a belief in the possibility of a separate Negro economy. "Of course," wrote Frazier, "behind the idea of the separate Negro economy is the hope of the black bourgeoisie that they will have the monopoly of the Negro market." He added that they also desire "a privileged status within the isolated Negro community."

Nor are certain Negro businessmen the only ones who stand to gain from a black economy protected by the tariff of separatism. There are also those among the white upper class for whom such an arrangement is at least as beneficial. In the first place, self-help projects for the ghetto, of which black capitalism is but one variety, are inexpensive. They involve no large-scale redistribution of resources, no "inflationary" government expenditures, and above all, no responsibility on the part of whites. These same upper-class whites may have been major exploiters of black workers in the past, they may have been responsible for policies which helped to create ghetto poverty, but now, under the new dispensations of black separatism, they are being asked to do little more by way of reparation than provide a bit of seed money for a few small ghetto enterprises.

Moreover, a separate black economy appears to offer hope for what Roy Innis has called "a new social contract." According to Innis's theory, the black community is essentially a colony ruled by outsiders; there can be no peace between the colony and the "mother country" until the former is ruled by some of its own. When the colony is finally "liberated" in this way, all conflicts can be resolved through negotiation between the black ruling class and the white ruling class. Any difficulties within the black community, that is, would become the responsibility of the black elite. But since self-determination in the ghetto, necessitating as it would the expansion of a propertied black middle class, offers the advantage of social stability, such difficulties would be minimal. How could many whites fail to grasp the obvious benefit to themselves in a program that promises social peace without the social inconvenience of integration and especially without the burden of a huge expenditure of money? Even if one were to accept the colonial analogy—and it is in many ways an uninformed and extremely foolish one—the strategy implied by it is fatuous and unworkable. Most of the experiments in black capitalism thus far have been total failures. As, given the odds, they should continue to be. For one thing, small businesses owned and run by blacks will, exactly like their white counterparts, suffer a high rate of failure. In fact, they will face even greater problems than white small businesses because they will be operating in predominantly low income areas where the clientele will be poor, the crime rate and taxes high, and the cost of land, labor, and insurance expensive. They will have to charge higher prices than the large chains, a circumstance against which "Buy Black" campaigns will in the long or even the short run have little force. On the other hand, to create large-scale black industry in the ghetto is unthinkable. The capital is not available, and even if it were, there is no vacant land. In Los Angeles, for example, the area in which four-fifths of the Negroes and Mexican-Americans live contains only 0.5 per cent of all the vacant land in the city, and the problem is similar elsewhere. Overcrowding is severe enough in the ghetto without building up any industry there.

Another current axiom of black self-determination is the necessity for community control. Questions of ideology aside, black community control is as futile a program as black capitalism. Assuming that there were a cohesive, clearly identifiable black community (which, judging by the factionalism in neighborhoods like Harlem and Ocean Hill–Brownsville, is a far from safe assumption), and assuming that the community were empowered to control the ghetto, it would still find itself without the money needed in order to be socially creative. The ghetto would still be faced with the same poverty, deteriorated housing, unemployment, terrible health services, and inferior schools—and this time perhaps with the exacerbation of their being entailed in local struggles for power. Furthermore, the control would ultimately be illusory and would do no more than provide psychological comfort to those who exercise it. For in a complex technological society there is no such thing as an autonomous community within a large metropolitan area. Neighborhoods, particularly poor neighborhoods, will remain dependent upon outside suppliers for manufactured goods, transportation, utilities, and other services. There is, for instance, unemployment in the ghetto while the vast majority of new jobs are being created in the suburbs. If black people are to have access to those jobs, there must be a metropolitan transportation system that can carry them to the suburbs cheaply and quickly. Control over the ghetto cannot build such a system nor can it provide jobs within the ghetto.

The truth of the matter is that community control as an idea is provincial and as a program is extremely conservative. It appears radical to some people because it has become the demand around which the frustrations of the Negro community have coalesced. In terms of its capacity to deal with the social and economic causes of black unrest, however, its potential is strikingly limited. The call for community control in fact represents an adjustment to inequality rather than a protest against it. Fundamentally, it is a demand for a change in the racial composition of the personnel who administer community institutions: that is, for schools, institutions of public and social service, and political organizations—as all of these are presently constituted—to be put into the keeping of a new class of black officials. Thus in a very real sense, the notion of community control bespeaks a fervent hope that the poverty-stricken ghetto, once thought to be a social problem crying for rectification, might now be deemed a social good worthy of acceptance. Hosea Williams of SCLC, speaking once of community control, unwittingly revealed the way in which passionate self-assertion can be a mask for accommodation: "I'm now at the position Booker T. Washington was about sixty or seventy years ago," Williams said. "I say to my brothers, 'Cast down your buckets where you are'—and that means there in the slums and ghettos."

There is indeed profound truth in the observation that people who seek social change will, in the absence of real substantive victories, often seize upon stylistic substitutes as an outlet for their frustrations.

A case in point is the relation of Negroes to the trade-union movement. In their study *The Black Worker*, published in 1930, Sterling D. Spero and Abram L. Harris describe the resistance to separatism among economically satisfied workers during the heyday of Marcus Garvey:

. . . spokesmen of the Garvey movement went among the faction-torn workers preaching the doctrine of race consciousness. Despite the fact that Garveyism won a following everywhere at this time, the Negro long-shoremen of Philadelphia were deaf to its pleas, for their labor movement had won them industrial equality such as colored workers nowhere else in the industry enjoyed.

The inverse relation of black separatism and anti-unionism to the quality of employment available to Negroes holds true today also. In the May 1969 UAW elections, for example, black candidates won the presidency and vice-presidency of a number of locals. Some of the most interesting election victories were won at the Chrysler Eldon Gear and Axle Local 961 and at Dodge #3 in Hamtramck where the separatist Eldon Revolutionary Union Movement (ELRUM) and Dodge Revolutionary Union Movement (DRUM) have been active. At both locals the DRUM and ELRUM candidates were handily defeated by black trade unionists who campaigned on a program of militant integrationism and economic justice.

This is not to say that there are not problems within the unions which have given impetus to the separatist movements. There are, but in the past decade unions have taken significant steps toward eliminating discrimination against Negroes. As Peter Henle, the chief economist of the Bureau of Labor Statistics, has observed:

> Action has been taken to eliminate barriers to admission, abolish discrimination in hiring practices, and negotiate changes in seniority arrangements which had been blocking Negro advances to higher-paying jobs. At the same time, unions have given strong support to governmental efforts in this same direction.

Certainly a good deal is left to be done in this regard, but just as certainly the only effective pressure on the unions is that which can be brought by blacks pressing for a greater role *within* the trade-union movement. Not only is separatism not a feasible program, but its major effect will be to injure black workers economically by undermining the strength of their union. It is here that ignorance of the economic dimension of racial injustice is most dangerous, for a Negro, whether he be labeled a moderate or a militant, has but two alternatives open to him. If he defines the problem as primarily one of race, he will inevitably find himself the ally of the white capitalist against the white worker. But if, though always conscious of the play of racial discrimination, he defines the problem as one of poverty, he will be aligned with the white worker against management. If he chooses the former alternative, he will become no more than a pawn in the game of divide-and-conquer played by, and for the benefit of, management—the result of which will hardly be self-determination but rather the depression of wages for all workers. This path was followed by the "moderate" Booker T. Washington who disliked unions because they were "founded on a sort of enmity to the man by whom he [the Negro] is employed" and by the "militant" Marcus Garvey who wrote:

> It seems strange and a paradox, but the only convenient friend the Negro worker or laborer has in America at the present time is the white capitalist. The capitalist being selfish—seeking only the largest profit out of labor—is willing and glad to use Negro labor wherever possible on a scale reasonably below the standard union wage . . . but if the Negro unionizes himself to the level of the white worker, the choice and preference of employment is given to the white worker.

And it is being followed today by CORE, which collaborated with the National Right to Work Committee in setting up the Black Workers Alliance.

If the Negro chooses to follow the path of inter-racial alliances on the basis of class, as almost two million have done today, he can achieve a certain degree of economic dignity, which in turn offers a genuine, if not the only, opportunity for self-determination. It was this course which A. Philip Randolph chose in his long struggle to build a Negro-labor alliance, and it was also chosen by the black sanitation workers of Memphis, Tennessee, and the black hospital workers of Charleston, South Carolina.

Not that I mean here to exonerate the unions of their responsibility for discrimination. Nevertheless, it is essential to deal with the situation of the black worker in terms of American economic reality. And as long as the structure of this reality is determined by the competing institutions of capital and labor (or government and labor, as in the growing public sector of the economy), Negroes must place themselves on one side or the other. The idea of racial self-determination within this context is a delusion.

There are, to be sure, sources beyond that of economic discrimination for black separatism within the unions. DRUM, ELRUM, and similar groups are composed primarily of young Negroes who, like whites their age, are not as loyal to the union as are older members, and who are also affected by the new militancy which is now pervasive among black youth generally. This militancy has today found its most potent form of expression on campus, particularly in the predominantly white universities outside of the South. The confusion which the movement for programs in black studies has created on campus almost defies description. The extremes in absurdity were reached this past academic year at Cornell, where, on the one hand, enraged black students were demanding a program in black studies which included Course 300c, Physical Education: "Theory and practice in the use of small arms and hand combat. Discussion sessions in the proper use of force," and where, on the other hand, a masochistic and pusillanimous university president placed his airplane at the disposal of two black students so that they could go to New York City and purchase, with $2,000 in university funds, some bongo drums for Malcolm X Day. The foolishness of the students was surpassed only by the public-relations manipulativeness of the president.

The real tragedy of the dispute over black studies is that whatever truly creative opportunities such a program could offer have been either ignored or destroyed. There is, first, the opportunity for a vastly expanded scholastic inquiry into the contribution of Negroes to the American experience. The history of the black man in America has been scandalously distorted in the past, and as a field of study it has been relegated to a second-class status, isolated from the main themes of American history and omitted in the historical education of American youth. Yet now black students are preparing to repeat the errors of their white predecessors. They are proposing to study black history in isolation from the mainstream of American history; they are demanding separate black-studies programs that will not be open to whites, who could benefit at least as much as they from a knowledge of Negro history; and they hope to permit only blacks (and perhaps some whites who toe the line) to teach in these programs. Unwittingly they are conceding what racist whites all along have professed to believe, namely, that black history is irrelevant to American history.

In other ways black students have displayed contempt for black studies as an academic discipline. Many of them, in fact, view black studies as not an academic subject at all, but as an ideological and political one. They propose to use black-studies programs to create a mythologized history and a system of assertive ideas that will facilitate the political mobilization of the black community. In addition, they hope to educate a cadre of activists whose present training is conceived of as a preparation for organizational work in the ghetto. The Cornell students made this very clear when they defined the purpose of black-studies programs as enabling "black people to use the knowledge gained in the classroom and the community to formulate new ideologies and philosophies which will contribute to the development of the black nation."

Thus faculty members will be chosen on the basis of race, ideological purity, and political commitment—not academic competence. Under such conditions, few qualified black professors will want to teach in black-studies programs, not simply because their academic freedom will be curtailed by their obligation to adhere to the revolutionary "line" of the moment, but because their professional status will be threatened by their association with programs of such inferior quality.

Black students are also forsaking the opportunity to get an education. They appear to be giving little thought to the problem of teaching or learning those technical skills that all students must acquire if they are to be effective in their careers. We have here simply another example of the pursuit of symbolic victory where a real victory seems too difficult to achieve. It is easier for a student to alter his behavior and appearance than to improve the quality of his mind. If engineering requires too much concentration, then why not a course in soul music? If Plato is both "irrelevant" and difficult, the student can read Malcolm X instead. Class will be a soothing, comfortable experience, somewhat like watching television. Moreover, one's image will be militant and, therefore, acceptable by current college standards. Yet one will have learned nothing, and the fragile sense of security developed in the protective environment of college will be cracked when exposed to the reality of competition in the world.

Nelson Taylor, a young Negro graduate of Morehouse College, recently observed that many black students "feel it is useless to try to compete. In order to avoid this competition, they build themselves a little cave to hide in." This "little cave," he added, is black studies. Furthermore, black students are encouraged in this escapism by guilt-ridden New Leftists and faculty members who despise themselves and their advantaged lives and enjoy seeing young Negroes reject "white middle-class values" and disrupt the university. They are encouraged by university administrators who prefer political accommodation to an effort at serious education. But beyond the momentary titillation some may experience from being the center of attention, it is difficult to see how Negroes can in the end benefit from being patronized and manipulated in this way. Ultimately, their only permanent satisfaction can come from the certainty that they have acquired the technical and intellectual skills that will enable them upon graduation to perform significant jobs competently and with confidence. If they fail to acquire these skills, their frustration will persist and find expression in ever-newer forms of antisocial and self-destructive behavior.

The conflict over black studies, as over other issues, raises the question of the function in general served by black protest today. Some black demands, such as that for a larger university enrollment of minority students, are entirely legitimate; but the major purpose of the protest through which these demands are pressed would seem to be not so much to pursue an end as to establish in the minds of the protesters, as well as in the minds of whites, the reality of their rebellion. Protest, therefore, becomes an end in itself and not a means toward social change. In this sense, the black rebellion is an enormously *expressive* phenomenon which is releasing the pent-up resentments of generations of oppressed Negroes. But expressiveness that is oblivious to political reality and not structured by instrumental goals is mere bombast.

James Forman's *Black Manifesto,* for instance, provides a nearly perfect sample of this kind of bombast combined with positive delusions of grandeur. "We shall liberate all the people in the U.S.," the introduction to the *Manifesto* declares, "and we will be instrumental in the liberation of colored people the world around. . . . We are the most humane people within the U.S. . . . Racism in the U.S. is so pervasive in the mentality of whites that only an armed, well-disciplined, black-controlled government can insure the stamping out of racism in this country. . . . We say think in terms of the total control of the U.S."

One might never imagine from reading the *Manifesto* that Forman's organization, the National Black Economic Development Conference, is politically powerless, or that the institution it has chosen for assault is not the government or the corporations, but the church. Indeed, the exaggeration of language in the *Black Manifesto* is directly proportional to the isolation and impotence of those who drafted it. And their actual achievements provide an accurate measure of their strength. Three billion dollars in reparations was demanded—and $20,000 received. More important, the effect of this demand upon the Protestant churches has been to precipitate among them a conservative reaction against the activities of the liberal national denominations and the National Council of Churches. Forman's failure, of course, was to be expected: the only effect of an attack upon so organizationally diffuse and nonpolitical an institution as the church can be the deflection of pressure away from the society's major political and economic institutions and, consequently, the weakening of the black movement for equality.[1]

The possibility that his *Manifesto* might have exactly the opposite effect from that intended, however, was clearly not a problem to Forman, because the demands he was making upon white people were more moral than political or economic. His concern was to purge white guilt far more than to seek social justice for Negroes. It was in part for this reason that he chose to direct his attack at the church, which, as the institutional embodiment of our society's religious pretensions, is vulnerable to moral condemnation.

Yet there is something corrupting in the wholesale release of aggressive moral energy, particularly when it is in response to the demand for reparations for blacks. The difficulty is not only that as a purely racial demand its effect must be to isolate blacks from the white poor with whom they have common economic interests. The call for three billion dollars in reparations demeans the integrity of blacks and exploits the self-demeaning guilt of whites. It is insulting to Negroes to offer them reparations for past generations of suffering, as if the balance of an irreparable past could be set straight with a handout. In a recent poll, *Newsweek* reported that "today's proud Negroes, by an overwhelming 84 to 10 per cent, reject the idea of preferential treatment in hiring or college admissions in reparation for past injustices." There are few controversial issues that can call forth greater uniformity of opinion than this in the Negro community.

I also question both the efficacy and the social utility of an attack that impels the attacked to applaud and debase themselves. I am not certain whether or not self-flagellation can have a beneficial effect on the sinner (I tend to doubt that it can), but I am absolutely certain it can never produce anything politically creative. It will not improve the lot of the unemployed and the ill-housed. On the other hand, it could well happen that the guilty party, in order to lighten his uncomfortable moral burden, will finally begin to rationalize his sins and affirm them as virtues. And by such a process, today's ally can become tomorrow's enemy. Lasting political alliances are not built on the shifting sands of moral suasion.

On his part, the breast-beating white makes the same error as the Negro who swears that "black is beautiful." Both are seeking refuge in psychological solutions to social questions. And both are reluctant to confront the real cause of racial injustice, which is not bad attitudes but bad social conditions. The Negro creates a new psychology to avoid the reality of social stagnation, and the white—be he ever so liberal—professes his guilt precisely so as to create the illusion of social change, all the while preserving his economic advantages.

The response of guilt and pity to social problems is by no means new. It is, in fact, as old as man's capacity to rationalize or his reluctance to make real sacrifices for his fellow man. Two hundred years ago, Samuel Johnson, in an exchange with Boswell, analyzed the phenomenon of sentimentality:

> Boswell: "I have often blamed myself, Sir, for not feeling for others, as sensibly as many say they do."
> Johnson: "Sir, don't be duped by them any more. You will find these very feeling people are not very ready to do you good. They pay you by feeling."

Today, payments from the rich to the poor take the form of "Giving a Damn" or some other kind of moral philanthropy. At the same time, of course, some of those who so passionately "Give a Damn" are likely to argue that full employment is inflationary.

We are living in a time of great social confusion—not only about the strategies we must adopt but about the very goals these strategies are to bring us to. Only recently whites and Negroes of good will were pretty much in agreement that racial and economic justice required an end to segregation and the expansion of the role of the federal government. Now it is a mark of "advancement," not only among "progressive" whites but among the black militants as well, to believe that integration is passé. Unintentionally (or as the Marxists used to say, objectively), they are lending aid and comfort to traditional segregationists like Senators Eastland and Thurmond. Another "advanced" idea is the notion that government has gotten too big and that what is needed to make the society more humane and livable is an enormous new move toward local participation and decentralization. One cannot question the value or importance of democratic participation in the government, but just as misplaced sympathy for Negroes is being put to use by segregationists, the liberal preoccupation with localism is serving the cause of conservatism. Two years of liberal encomiums to decentralization have intellectually legitimized the concept, if not the name, of states' rights and have set the stage for the widespread acceptance of Nixon's "New Federalism."

The new anti-integrationism and localism may have been motivated by sincere moral conviction, but hardly by intelligent political thinking. It should be obvious that what is needed today more than ever is a political strategy that offers the real possibility of economically uplifting millions of impoverished individuals, black and white. Such a strategy must of necessity give low priority to the various forms of economic and psychological experimentation that I have discussed, which at best deal with issues peripheral to the central problem and at worst embody a frenetic escapism. These experiments are based on the assumption that the black community can be transformed from within when, in fact, any such transformation must depend on structural changes in the entire society. Negro poverty, for example, will not be eliminated in the absence of a total war on poverty. We need, therefore, a new national economic policy. We also need new policies in housing, education, and health care which can deal with these problems as they relate to Negroes within the context of a national solution. A successful strategy, therefore, must rest upon an identification of those central institutions which, if altered sufficiently, would transform the social and economic relations in our society; and it must provide a politically viable means of achieving such an alteration.

Surely the church is not a central institution in this sense. Nor is Roy Innis's notion of dealing with the banking establishment a useful one. For the banks will find no extra profit—quite the contrary—in the kind of fundamental structural change in society that is required.[2]

Moreover, the recent flurry of excitement over the role of private industry in the slums seems to have subsided. A study done for the Urban Coalition has called the National Alliance of Businessmen's claim to have hired more than 100,000 hard-core unemployed a "phony numbers game." Normal hiring as the result of expansion or turnover was in some cases counted as recruitment. Where hard-core workers have been hired and trained, according to the study, "The primary motivation . . . is the need for new sources of workers in a tight labor market. If and when the need for workers slackens, so will industry's performance." This has already occurred. The *Wall Street Journal* reported in July of 1969 that the Ford Motor Company, once praised for its social commitment, was forced to trim back production earlier in the year and in the process "quietly closed its two inner-city hiring centers in Detroit and even laid off some of the former hard-cores it had only recently hired." There have been similar retrenchments by other large companies as the result of a slackening in economic growth, grumblings from stockholders, and the realization by corporate executives that altruism does not make for high profits. Yet even if private industry were fully committed to attack the problem of unemployment, it is not in an ideal position to do so. Private enterprise, for example, accounted for only one out of every ten new jobs created in the economy between 1950 and 1960. Most of the remainder were created as the result of expansion of public employment.

While the church, private enterprise, and other institutions can, if properly motivated, play an important role, finally it is the trade-union movement and the Democratic party which offer the greatest leverage to the black struggle. The serious objective of Negroes must be to strengthen and liberalize these. The trade-union movement is essential to the black struggle because it is the only institution in the society capable of organizing the working poor, so many of whom are Negroes. It is only through an organized movement that these workers, who are now condemned to the margin of the economy, can achieve a measure of dignity and economic security. I must confess I find it difficult to understand the prejudice against the labor movement currently fashionable among so many liberals. These people, somehow for reasons of their own, seem to believe that white workers are affluent members of the Establishment (a rather questionable belief, to put it mildly, especially when held by people earning over $25,000 a year) and are now trying to keep the Negroes down. The only grain of truth here is that there *is* competition between black and white workers which derives from a scarcity of jobs and resources. But rather than propose an expansion of those resources, our stylish liberals underwrite that competition by endorsing the myth that the unions are the worst enemy of the Negro.

In fact it is the problem of the labor movement that represents a genuine means for reducing racial competition and hostility. Not out of a greater tenderness of feeling for black suffering—but that is just the point. Unions organize workers on the basis of common economic interests, not by virtue of racial affinity. Labor's legislative program for full employment, housing, urban reconstruction, tax reform, improved health care, and expanded educational opportunities is designed specifically to aid both whites and blacks in the lower- and lower-middle classes where the potential for racial polarization is most severe. And only a program of this kind can deal simultaneously and creatively with the interrelated problems of black rage and white fear. It does not placate black rage at the expense of whites, thereby increasing white fear and political reaction. Nor does it exploit white fear by repressing blacks. Either of these courses strengthens the demagogues among both races who prey upon frustration and racial antagonism. Both of them help to strengthen conservative forces—the forces that stand to benefit from the fact that hostility between black and white workers keeps them from uniting effectively around issues of common economic interest.

President Nixon is in the White House today largely because of this hostility; and the strategy advocated by many liberals to build a "new coalition" of the affluent, the young, and the dispossessed is designed to keep him there. The difficulty with this proposed new coalition is not only that its constituents comprise a distinct minority of the population, but that its affluent and youthful members—regardless of the momentary direction of their rhetoric—are hardly the undisputed friends of the poor. Recent Harris polls, in fact, have shown that Nixon is most popular among the college educated and the young. Perhaps they were attracted by his style or the minimal concessions he has made on Vietnam, but certainly their approval cannot be based upon his accomplishments in the areas of civil rights and economic justice.

If the Republican ascendancy is to be but a passing phenomenon, it must once more come to be clearly understood among those who favor social progress that the Democratic party is still the only mass-based political organization in the country with the potential to become a majority movement for social change. And anything calling itself by the name of political activity must be concerned with building precisely such a majority movement. In addition, Negroes must abandon once and for all the false assumption that as 10 per cent of the population they can by themselves effect basic changes in the structure of American life. They must, in other words, accept the necessity of coalition politics. As a result of our fascination with novelty and with the "new" revolutionary forces that have emerged in recent years, it seems to some the height of conservatism to propose a strategy that was effective in the past. Yet the political reality is that without a coalition of Negroes and other minorities with the trade-union movement and with liberal groups, the shift of power to the Right will persist and the democratic Left in America will have to content itself with a well-nigh permanent minority status.

The bitterness of many young Negroes today has led them to be unsympathetic to a program based on the principles of trade unionism and electoral politics. Their protest represents a refusal to accept the condition of inequality, and in that sense, it is part of the long, and I think, magnificent black struggle for freedom. But with no comprehensive strategy to replace the one I have suggested, their protest, though militant in rhetoric and intention, may be reactionary in effect.

The strategy I have outlined must stand or fall by its capacity to achieve political and economic results. It is not intended to provide some new wave of intellectual excitement. It is not intended to suggest a new style of life or a means to personal salvation for disaffected members of the middle class. Nor is either of these the proper role of politics. My strategy is not meant to appeal to the fears of threatened whites, though it would calm those fears and increase the likelihood that some day we shall have a truly integrated society. It is not meant to serve as an outlet for the terrible frustrations of Negroes, though it would reduce those frustrations and point a way to dignity for an oppressed people. It is simply a vehicle by which the wealth of this nation can be redistributed and some of its more grievous social problems solved. This in itself would be quite enough to be getting on with. In fact, if I may risk a slight exaggeration, by normal standards of human society I think it would constitute a revolution.

Notes

1 Forman is not the only militant today who fancies that his essentially reformist program is revolutionary. Eldridge Cleaver has written that capitalists regard the Black Panther Breakfast for Children program (which the Panthers claim feeds 10,000 children) "as a threat, as cutting into the goods that are under their control." He also noted that it "liberates" black children from going to school hungry each morning. I wonder if he would also find public-school lunch programs liberating.

2 Innis's demand that the white banks deposit $6 billion in black banks as reparations for past injustices should meet with even less success than Forman's ill-fated enterprise. At least Forman had the benefit of the white churchman's guilt, an emotion not known to be popular among bankers.

The Federal Principle

H. R. Shapiro

This third part, on neighborhood control of schools, begins with an article by H. R. Shapiro in which he presents local control as a step toward granting citizens power over their community institutions in general. The argument that this is in "the best American tradition" reminds us of the Staughton Lynd article in Chapter One. Shapiro is editor and publisher of The Public Life, A Journal of Politics and executive director of Citizens for Local Democracy.

The essence of the United States Constitution was defined by what Madison called the *federal principle*. (Madison, *Federalist Papers*, No. 51):

> While all authority in it [the U.S. Republic] will be derived from and dependent on the society, the society itself will be broken into so many parts, interests and classes of citizens, that the rights of individuals, or of the minority, will be in little danger from interested combinations of the majority. In a free government the security for civil rights must be the same as that for religious rights. It consists in the one case in the multiplicity of interests, and in the other in the multiplicity of sects; and this may be presumed to depend on the extent of the country and number of people comprehended under the same government. . . . In the extended republic of the United States, and among the great variety of interests, parties and sects which it embraces, a coalition of a majority of the whole society could seldom take place on any other principles than those of justice and the general good; whilst there being thus less danger to a minor from the will of a major party, there must be less pretext, also, to provide for the security of the former, by introducing into the government a will not dependent on the latter, or, in other words, a will independent of the society itself [monarchy, etc.]. It is no less certain than it is important, notwithstanding the contrary opinions which have been entertained, that the larger the society, provided it lie within a practical sphere, the more duly capable it will be of self-government. And happily for the *republican* cause, the practicable sphere may be carried to

---

From H. R. Shapiro, "The Federal Principle," *Liberation* (September 1968), pp. 37–39. Reprinted by permission of *Liberation* and the author.

a very great extent, by a judicious modification and mixture of the *federal principle.*

Black people, non-Europeans in general and city-dwellers have remained outside the federal principle in that they have never had control of their own communities and community institutions. This noninvolvement in the federal principle is a major cause both of our present race conflict in America and of the mass society, but, note the key point: it is not the complexity of modern life that has caused this noninvolvement, for as Madison insisted, it is the very complexity of society that makes the federal principle possible.

Ironically, the average American, although not directly oppressed as are most non-Europeans, is coming to be in the same political position as that faced by black people since Emancipation. The average person has no control over his own life, no say in the running of his own community institutions and, in the case of most city-dwellers, no community institutions of his own. That is, the average American is the subject of a mass society.

It is here proposed that instead of trying to bring black people into the mass society, we work our way back to the federal principle by seeing that all communities, black and white (and integrated) have control over their own community institutions and lives. This then would not only be an extension of the federal principle to black people and other non-Europeans, but to city-dwellers and to those whose community institutions are now being centralized and brought under mega-districts or mega-cities.

The only way individuals can regain control over their lives is by effecting the return of communal and citizen powers to the local communities. The mass society and centralization can only be fought at the local level, the level upon which the mass society feeds. Local communities asserting their rights and controlling their own institutions and interests would have the effect of mountains rising up, penetrating, obstructing and then rolling back the mass cloud, the mass machine which is now devouring the rights and powers of each to participate in the control of his own life.

Public schools in America have traditionally been controlled at the local level. At present, however, when people are acutely concerned (perhaps for the first time in our history) to bring education to their children, the private interest, states and the federal government, assisted by the education establishment, are in a full-scale campaign to take control of the schools from the local level and put them under mega-districts or foundations or state bureaucracies. In the name of an efficiency which doesn't exist, the powers-that-be are attempting to usurp local community and citizen rights over education, a right so basic to democracy that we once thought it the very spirit of the Republic.

If a school district in New York City would assert its rights and regain control over its schools, there would be an immediate obstructing of the mass, centralizing machine. This is no utopian goal. It is concrete, feasible and profoundly within the best American tradition, the very basis of our political structure. It is concrete in that it deals with what people actually do and can do and not with an abstract ideology. It is feasible because local control of local institutions is the basic (if never fully realized or democratically implemented) structure of our politics and society. The feverish efforts of the Establishment to usurp local control demonstrates, indeed, how feasible local control is and how profoundly it is embedded (however much obscured) in the fabric of our national life. All each community would have to do is stand fast and assert its full rights for these rights existed long before teachers' colleges, foundations and unions of experts were born.

A community which controlled its schools could say *no* to: the whole education establishment, to textbook companies, educational-materials peddlers, teaching-machine companies, foundation experiments, phony university, state and federal programs, the compensatory-education business, to the whole mass media and the advertising business, to construction companies, unions and to every other sort of matter, live or otherwise, which is put, pushed or manipulated into the schools. If a textbook company wanted to sell its products to the community, the company would have to serve, not create, the community's needs. In having to serve individual community needs, the companies, foundations, etc., would have to *adjust* to thinking in terms of *people's* needs. Therefore, in *adjusting*, the various businesses will themselves put a halt to the mindless textbooks and empty materials which are the result of having to create a product which must serve uniformly throughout the country and which must thus be emptied of content and removed from reality.

Local control of schools by African-Americans, other minority groups and city-dwellers in general, will also force the education establishment to re-tool and re-think its attitude toward children and its "philosophy." . . . The community's demand for a totally different approach to education (which minority communities must have to save their children and which all communities would have if they actually did or had to take part in the running of their own schools) would be a first and forceful step in the interdicting of the whole educational machine. As is the case with other mass approaches to serving individual needs, the education mass machine cannot tolerate this "seeing" on the part of individual communities, nor can it tolerate individual community assertions, demands and decisions and yet remain a mass machine. The machine which pacifies cannot tolerate any other initiative than its own and on its own terms.

Mass Measures against the mass society tend to be self-defeating. They only feed the monster while legitimizing a mass attitude toward one's own life and political structures. Mass Measures also tend to further condition and "unify" those who have already accepted their position within society and lead others into the bag. The mass society can only be interdicted and fought at the local level because noncommunity organizations, organizations with no *land* under them, have little power or effect on community, city, state and federal government. . . .

People in power only respect and move when either those under them or those in power move or make demands, that is, they only respect others with *political* power. . . .

A community without power is not a community, it is merely a collection of individuals.

Unless people control their own institutions at the local level, anything can happen and does as in the case of the New York City schools where the children are, in the eyes of the Board of Education, mere abstractions. Of the one million children now in New York City schools, some 750,000 have already been segregated out of the academic tracks by discredited achievement tests which label those who have been taught to read at home "gifted" and the others, "average" or "slow." Those not labeled "gifted" are then totally neglected. Segregated in the second grade by these reading tests, the children who have not been taught at home are written off by being placed in "failure" classes. That is, the school informs the children that they are stupid (nonlearners) when they are seven or eight years old and by the time these children reach sixth or seventh grade, they have been virtually de-brained. They no longer listen to or hear anything said in school. This is just one result of people not controlling their own community institutions; the children are reduced to abstractions and no plea or cry can move the bureaucracy, for bureaucracies have no ears.

If African-American (and other minority) groups controlled their own communities, it would be a first step toward a solution of the present civil conflict in America. If each minority group controlled its own local institutions, that is, if each minority controlled its own communities, there would be created *spaces of freedom* for all, for all minorities could then find justice in one community or another. Not only this, but brotherhood, love and integration can only come *after* this democracy through community control for minority groups has been established. Appeals to brotherhood are absurd so long as the supplicants are outside of the political structure and so long as black children are being destroyed in white-controlled schools and black communities are being controlled and raped by white political machines and special interest groups.

If the community controlled its own schools and local institutions, the children, public business and the money involved would be visible. The fact that the children are being miseducated would be a daily reality (not a statistical abstraction) and the community could innovate (begin to teach) until such time as there was education in the schools.

With the public business visible, corruption would be minimized. Central corruption would be unlikely for federal and state monies would come directly and visibly to the districts and then visibly to the subsections of the districts. For instance, each subsection of a district or community would get its allocation just as the district does and this subsection would know just how much money was due it. Along with the allocation of certain funds to subdistricts, there would be allocation of powers to the subdistricts so that each cluster of schools, in fact, each school, would have various powers including the power to hire nonteaching personnel and, in accordance with the district, to hire or select principals or teachers, etc. These powers would bring to life each subdistrict, in fact, each school area. Given the direct allocation of money, powers and the visibility of both, local corruption would be brought and kept within the bounds and limits necessary for the health and life of the community. When people can see how they are affected by public community decisions and where *their* money is going, we can count on human nature for each person to demand what is his, so long as he is able *to know* what is rightfully his.

Community development, extending the *federal principle*, participatory democracy, community control of community institutions will not only serve the schools and children, but the Public Interest, the qualitative life of the community and the qualitative life of the nation. To quote Thomas Jefferson:

The way to have good and safe government, is not to trust all to one, but to divide it among the many, distributing to every one exactly the functions he is competent to do. Let the national government be entrusted with the defense of the nation, and its foreign and federal relations; the State governments with the civil rights, laws, police and administration of what concerns the State generally; the counties with the local concerns of the counties, and each ward district the interest within itself. It is by dividing and subdividing these republics from the great national one down through all its subordinations, until it ends in the administration of every man's farm by himself; by placing under every one what his own eye may superintend, that all will be done for the best. What has destroyed liberty and the rights of every man in every government which has ever existed under the sun? The generalizing and concentrating of all cares and powers into one body, no matter whether of the autocrats of Russia or France, or of the aristocrats of a Venetian senate. And I do believe that if the Almighty has not decreed that man shall never be free (and it is a blasphemy to believe it), that the secret shall be found to be in the making himself the depository of the powers respecting himself, so far as he is competent to do them, and delegating only what is beyond his competence by a synthetic process, to higher and higher orders of functionaries, so as to trust fewer and fewer powers in proportion as the trustees become more and more oligarchical. The elementary republics of the Union would form a gradation of authorities, standing each on the basis of law, holding every one its delegated share of powers, and constituting truly a system of fundamental balances and checks for government. Where every man is a sharer in the direction of his ward republic, or of some of the higher ones, and feels that he is a participator in the government of affairs, not merely at election one day in the year, but every day; when there shall not be a man in the state who will not be a member of one of its councils, great or small, he will let the heart be torn out of his body sooner than his power be wrested from him by a Caesar or a Bonaparte. . . . Begin them [community councils] only for a single purpose; they will soon show for what they are the best instruments. . . .

In New York City, there are some thirty school districts. Half are black and Puerto Rican. Both justice and the only possible solution to the present "race" conflict lie in each community's determining its own affairs. We can start with each community controlling its own schools. We must move past the politicians, bureaucrats, New Deal ideologists and special interests who, along with the mass media, keep us in a dulled state of passivity and away from effecting this only possible solution to the present civil conflict in America.

Why should, for instance, a white district in Queens object to controlling its own schools and the state and federal money involved? Certainly the black and Puerto Rican communities in New York City will not object to running their own schools. We have the beginnings of a solution to our political problems in New York City, but in order to effect this solution, citizens and community groups, from all the communities, must rise up and let the politicians and special interests know that they want no megacity control (nor Tammany control) over their lives, nor experts to run their lives, and that they will no longer tolerate this centrally enforced political impotence . . . and that the communities, all communities, will have control of their institutions and lives.

If African-Americans and other minority groups controlled their own communities (as does Scarsdale, etc.), spaces of freedom would exist for some forty million nonwhite and minority group Americans. Others would not lose control of their communities and lives. In fact, whites would gain or regain control of their lives from the mass machine. In doing so, whites would be able to overcome those abstract fears of the political unknown, that is, fears of anarchy, of black people, of hair and other such mass-media conspiracies. We would have the beginnings of a truly pluralistic society. There would be no effective political persecution for all could find justice somewhere, in one community or another. Injustice would be lessened with this framework or meeting of the various public interests. With community control, integration will first become possible, and we will be able to get on a road leading away from "race" war, from the mass society and toward a real democracy. . . .

With community control of schools and other local institutions, poverty can be abolished. The money now due each community or district from state and federal sources would go directly to the community. Each community could set priorities and hire local residents. In a country where there is more than enough to eat for all, only those who have no political power grow hungry. The point here is that to this extent the political can control the economic. And, in the end, the political must control the economic for the economic is blind, merely production and distribution, while the political is the area where men decide as to the quality of their lives and how they are going to live with one another.

With each community determining its own affairs and looking to its own community welfare, mass movements would, in this pluralistic framework, be highly impossible. Each community would be another obstacle for the mass ideology or irrationality to overcome. For the same reasons, the federal government could no longer totally dominate our foreign policy (soldiers come from communities) and it would be extremely difficult to start any but purely defensive wars. . . .

Fortunately, we do have a tradition of local control; when local control is reasserted and extended to all communities, not only will the pacified "middle-class" communities come to see and live a bit of reality, but our nonwhite and minority communities will be enfranchised and empowered. The country will then be fulfilling one tradition, the democratic, at the expense of the "new" tradition, the imperialistic. By fulfilling our democratic tradition, we can defray the expense caused by the failure of the new tradition and save our national soul. . . .

School Decentralization in New York:
A Case Study

Richard Karp

In this selection we turn to the Ocean Hill–Brownsville dispute in New York City to illustrate the problems that arise in attempting to decentralize existing bureaucratic structures—in this case the city school system. Richard Karp's article is particularly illuminating on the clash of interests involved.

Ocean Hill is a tiny piece of urban blight resting on a gently sloping section of glacial moraine in Brooklyn. From one side of this ancient hill spreads the vast wretchedness of Bedford-Stuyvesant, from the other, the equally vast wretchedness of Brownsville. The two great Negro ghettos of Brooklyn merge at Ocean Hill, but Ocean Hill has never quite belonged to either slum. It is a no-man's-land between two no-man's-lands. Its inhabitants are the overflow of hopelessness and poverty from two of the most desolate communities in the land, perhaps the most unlikely of slum-dwellers to band together for community action.

But in September 1966 an issue arose around which they could rally. That month, parents in a Harlem school district demanded from the New York Board of Education the right to veto the selection of a principal for the newly-completed Intermediate School 201. They had, in effect, asked for the first time to have some real say in the administration of a local school. The cry for "community control" that went up in Harlem was heard far out in the forgotten ghetto of Ocean.

The schooling of children in the Ocean Hill community had long been a failure, and all efforts at reform a failure as well. The Board of Education's plan for "quality integrated education," through busing Negro children to white schools, was a farce. Ocean Hill sent 4,000 black children into white communities. They were put onto buses, dropped off at the white schools and welcomed with little more than suspicion and bigotry. Some principals in the white schools herded the Negro children into sepa-

---

From Richard Karp, "School Decentralization in New York: A Case Study," *Interplay* (August–September 1968), pp. 9–14. Reprinted by permission of *Interplay*.

rate classes because their reading level was lower than the white students'. Many Negro children could not keep up with the work and failed. White parents vehemently protested the arrival of black children in their neighborhoods. Segregated by their school administrators and frozen out by the anger and hatred of the white communities, many Negro children begged to be sent back to their local schools, wretched as those schools were.

As if this weren't enough, there was another cause for desperation by the fall of 1966. Until 1965 the Ocean Hill area had been part of the Bedford-Stuyvesant school district, represented by one member on the district school board. In the spring of 1965 the Board of Education created District 17, a long strip of Brooklyn with white middle-class East Flatbush at one end, the black ghetto of Brownsville in the center, and Ocean Hill at the other end. The school board of this "racially balanced" district was weighted heavily in favor of the white areas: Ocean Hill found itself worse off than it had been as part of the Bedford-Stuyvesant district. On the new board it had no representative at all. The people of Ocean Hill saw acted out before their eyes what they had, perhaps, always believed in their hearts: that the whites would cajole and control them, but never integrate with them.

With talk of "community control" spreading in the Negro ghettos of New York in that fall of 1966, the Ocean Hill community took what must have been to them a drastic step. In November, all the groups with which the Board of Education normally deals, including the parents' associations in the schools, cut off all relations with the District 17 school board and the central Board of Education. Local chapters of the United Federation of Teachers, the official union of New York City teachers, joined and supported them, seeing in the movement for community control a chance to form an alliance with parents against their traditional enemies, the members of the Board of Education. As we shall see, their support was short-lived.

At any rate, in November the loose assembly of parents and sympathetic teachers, now joined by an ever-growing number of agitators, got together and issued a plan for unilateral action. They stated three aims: one, to form a small, totally independent school district of Ocean Hill; two, to create an independent governing school board of teachers and parents; and three, to hold public meetings in the community to discuss school problems and future action. Not constituted into any cohesive body, and without any authority whatsoever, this aggregate of community groups met regularly during that fall and winter. They discussed the chronic problems of the ghetto school: lack of discipline, on the one hand, and, on the other, the suspension of students—the latter a sore point to the parents of Ocean Hill, who had seen large numbers of their young ejected into the streets without diplomas.

Fear in the Ranks of Bureaucracy

The Board of Education, a deeply entrenched and virtually autonomous arm of the city bureaucracy for 70 years, remained disdainful of the pretenses of the Ocean Hill groups. As the central command-post of a centralized system, the Board had complete power, and though its attempts at reform were failures, its authority went unchallenged. But this time a spasm of fear ran through it. Something unprecedented was happening. In December, an angry mob of black parents marched on the Board's headquarters on Livingston Street in Brooklyn, and for three days occupied its executive offices under the name of the "People's Board of Education."

For the first time, the Board realized it was up against real pressure. If its members did not yield, they would, at least, have to listen, or pretend to listen. The people of Ocean Hill did not miss their opportunity, and for the rest of the winter pressured the Board for change. They demanded that it dismiss a principal of one of the Ocean Hill elementary schools, who was considered incompetent and was widely disliked by the parents. The Board acquiesced, and the principal was soon out of the school. Emboldened by this novel success, the insurgents were ready to lay claim to a more fundamental power.

Due to be completed the following fall was Intermediate School 55, and its principal had not yet been named. The Ocean Hill militants began agitating for the right, which no local community in New York possesses, to choose a principal for the new school; they continued agitating until April 1967, when a far broader prospect appeared on the horizon. That April, Mario Fantini of the Ford Foundation appeared on the scene. The Ford Foundation had been working with the parents' groups of IS 201 in Harlem since their September confrontation with the Board, with the idea, according to Fantini, of "seeking out alternatives to the way the schools were being run. We were disturbed at the way the Board of Education was running the school system." Community control in some form was the chief alternative the Ford Foundation had in mind. The Foundation, like other critics of the school system, had lost faith in the system's power to reform itself.

What Were the Foundations' Motives?

Why the Ford Foundation entered the fray between Ocean Hill and the Board of Education is a matter of dispute. Fantini asserts that the Board asked the Foundation to fund such educational programs as the Ocean Hill groups might propose. Ocean Hill community leaders, on the contrary, say that the Board had no intention of asking the Ford Foundation or anyone else to help the community. The Ford Foundation, they believe, saw in the events of that winter a chance to experiment with its own educational theories. "Ford went to the Board of Education, and, with its power and prestige, pushed the Board into accepting them as advisers and letting them use Ocean Hill as a laboratory," says Father John Powis, a white Catholic priest who has been active in the Ocean Hill movement from the beginning. "The 'liaison' business is a lot of nonsense."

Whatever its motives, the Ford Foundation, in April, arranged a meeting between the Ocean Hill parents' groups and Dr. Bernard Donovan, the Superintendent of Schools and the chief executor of Board policies. Although the meeting was ostensibly held to discuss the problem of a principal for Intermediate School 55, it brought to light the basic conflict that was to set the pattern for all future dialogue between the Board of Education and the groups seeking reform in New York City schools. The Ocean Hill parents brought up their plan to create a local governing school board. In their proposal, the board would consist of eight parents, one from each school in the district, elected by the parents of children in the schools, and eight teachers, one from each school, elected by the teachers in each school. There would also be five representatives from the community at large, elected by the eight parent representatives from among Ocean residents on whose behalf petitions had been circulated which contained at least 200 signatures. In addition, there would be two supervisors (i.e., principals) on the board, elected by all the supervisors in the district. The board thus constituted would elect one professional educator from a university faculty.

In essence, the proposal meant direct community control of local schools, and the virtual end to the Board of Education's long-held power to control, down to minute details, the 900 schools and one million students comprising New York's stagnating school system. This the Board dreaded and secretly opposed. Under the eyes of the decentralization-minded Ford Foundation, however, and remembering the seizure of their headquarters by angry parents, the Board agreed to the proposal "in principle." "In principle" meant that the Board of Education would now deal with the Ocean Hill groups simply as upstarts rather than as outlaws.

The reckoning came swiftly. By the end of the month the Board of Education issued its "policy on decentralization." The last article of the document was directly related to Ocean Hill: it proposed to set up "demonstration projects" in certain districts "for increasing parental and community involvement" in order to "strengthen our educational program." Ocean Hill would be the site of a "demonstration project"; two others would be in Harlem and in Manhattan's Lower East Side.

A Significant Substitution

The Board statement of "policy" meant little: for community *control* the Board substituted the term *involvement*, which meant that at its own pleasure it would hear complaints from and grant privileges to the districts in the "demonstration." It would not, however, yield a jot of power. By holding out the promise of local involvement rather than control the Board had perpetuated its authority; by putting some unruly communities in the "demonstration" category, it hoped to make them docile "creatures of the Board of Education." This last remark was actually made a year later, by Norman Brumbacker, the Superintendent of Schools' liaison man with the "demonstration projects."

In April 1967, however, the Board of Education's resolve to obstruct decentralization was not as evident as it is now, and the people of Ocean Hill hopefully began planning for the election of a local governing school board according to its original proposal. Thanks to the Board of Education's acquiescence to a "demonstration," moreover, the Ford Foundation felt sanctioned to give direct aid to the "demonstration projects," and in July announced that it would fund the planning and establishment of governing boards in Ocean Hill and the two other districts. Ocean Hill received $44,000 to plan and hold elections that summer.

Trouble began when the community groups began planning to elect their parent representatives. To register the parents eligible to vote they needed the names and addresses of the students—and these were in the Board of Education's files. They appealed to the Board for help. The Board told them the community groups could get the necessary names and addresses only by hiring two Board of Education secretaries to go into the files. When the community leaders agreed to do this they were informed that the two secretaries had gone on vacation and that no one else was available. The Ocean Hill leaders were dismayed, but they got sympathetic teachers to canvass students for their addresses. Then, by going from door to door, they finally got 2,000 parents registered by August.

On August 3, Ocean Hill parents voted for their representatives. For many of them, it was the first experience of voting in any election. At the polls were observers from the United Federation of Teachers and the Niemeyer Commission, the latter a group of professional educators set up by the Board of Education ostensibly to give assistance to the community. Both groups grumbled about the election: the UFT questioned its legality and the Niemeyer group suggested an irregularity because the Fair Balloting Association did not officiate at the polls. Neither group took a very strong stand, however, and it is fair to assume that neither unearthed any significant mischief.

The Board of Education accepted the election of the governing board and agreed to grant it two important powers: first, to elect a district superintendent, to be known as the "unit administrator," and second, to elect principals to the eight schools in the district. At its first meeting, at the end of August, the governing board held an election for unit administrator. There were two candidates: Rhody McCoy, a Negro, who had been in the school system for many years and had been, until that summer, the acting principal of a school in Manhattan; and Jack Bloomfield, the principal of JHS 271 in Ocean Hill, who was essentially the Board of Education's candidate. Rhody McCoy won the election; the Board of Education recognized him as the unit administrator of Ocean Hill and agreed to pay him a salary as such.

But if the Board of Education had sought to obstruct the election of the governing board by denying help to the community in registering voters in July, it was now bent on pushing the locally-administered school district into chaos. To avoid conflict between himself and the new unit administrator, Bloomfield asked the Board to transfer him out of the district. It was obvious to him, as it would have been to any experienced administrator, that the divided authority and conflicting loyalties would sow discord and confusion in one of the key schools of the district. The Board of Education refused the transfer, and pressured Bloomfield to remain in Ocean Hill for another six months. It was an act that would provoke animosity, and it did. When Bloomfield finally left, in January 1968, the enemies of decentralization could truly say that he had been pushed out by "extremist elements."

The Board of Education was not alone in its determination to disrupt and discredit community control. It had powerful allies of the kind that shows how politics makes strange bedfellows. Among them was the giant United Federation of Teachers, the Board's traditional foe, with its loyal legions of white middle-class teachers. The UFT had seen, in the events of the previous year, that the Board of Education was beginning to lose its grip on the school system. It could no longer be depended upon to preserve the status quo. The union itself would have to fill the gap, and become the first line of defense against reform.

The UFT was ready to move, and on September 2, Ocean Hill received its first volley of shot from the teachers' union. On that day the Ocean Hill governing board held its third meeting and elected five principals for the schools. The five vacancies had been created by the voluntary departure of five incumbent principals after the demonstration project had been established. The teacher representatives on the governing board refused to vote, and bolted the meeting. What irked them, and what frightened a large number of union members, was the fact that the principals chosen by the community were not on the approved Civil Service list. No one denied the merit of the elected principals, but the sight of educators chosen with no regard to bureaucratic procedures seemed to strike symbolically at every teacher's job security, their most precious (and, in some cases, virtually their only) professional possession.

The UFT Calls a Strike

This was a preliminary probe; the fury of the full offensive was unleashed the following week. The UFT called a city-wide teachers' strike that effectively closed down the entire school system. According to the teachers, the strike was aimed at getting a pay increase and smaller classes; in fact, it was a massive show of strength designed to show that no one had better dare make trouble for the teachers. In effect, it threw up a mighty roadblock to the movement toward community control.

Nevertheless, the posture that a "liberal" union cared about reform had to be maintained, so the striking teachers went to the Ocean Hill governing board and asked them to support the strike. When the governing board refused, as the teachers knew they would, the teacher representatives resigned and joined in the chorus of those who were busily fanning public fears that "extremism" and "black power" would prevail in the communities. To prove that black racists had taken over at Ocean Hill, they never returned to the board.

The strike not only brought about a catastrophic suspension of public education in New York, it exposed the deep animosity existing between the white middle-class educational establishment and the Negro community. After the strike the teachers who returned to Ocean Hill did so with bitterness, and were met by the community with equal bitterness. Junior High School 271 was figuratively torn apart by antagonism between the white teachers who had struck in September and the black teachers and parents who saw the strike as a betrayal of community control. When Principal Jack Bloomfield left in February 1968 he was followed by all the assistant principals, 30 teachers and five of the six secretaries.

Junior High School 271 is still the scene of antagonism between white and black. In the teachers' cafeteria the black teachers sit on one side of the room, the white teachers on the other. The wall of fear and hatred between the two groups makes for communication that is at best polite, more often curt, and most of the time non-existent. To the black teachers, their white counterparts are part of the conspiracy to obstruct progress toward local control. "The white teachers are working for the UFT and not the children," the black teachers assert. "They are letting the students run wild to discredit the program. The white community says that Negroes have no pride or ambition, and then, when we show some pride and ambition, they do everything they can to suppress us."

Alleged Sabotage by White Teachers

Any one of the Negro teachers could tell of a dozen instances of white teachers "disrupting the program." On Friday, February 23, the day after

Washington's birthday, one Negro teacher asserted, 28 teachers were out "sick" from one school alone. "Absenteeism" on the part of white teachers is one of the more common complaints of the black teachers. One "incident" which became a *cause célèbre* involved a white teacher who was allegedly found pouring paint on a classroom floor to "blame it on a black student as proof of riot and insurrection in the community."

How true these stories are is hard to determine. They might be exaggerations, but if so, they rise out of the frustrations of trying to deal with men who, because they are still using the rhetoric of another age, cannot and will not understand. The white teachers in Ocean Hill, like the white teachers in the rest of the city, believe in two political principles: labor unionism and the idea that society's problems should be solved by centralized boards of experts and professionals. For these two principles they may well do some improbable things.

Confronted with the Negroes' allegations, the white teachers in Ocean Hill sanctimoniously proclaimed that they were not against, but actually in favor of community control; only, they had reservations. "We believe that the people of this community are not educated and socially elevated enough to run the schools. They must become middle-class before they can participate." These timid and totally uninspired jobholders put themselves forward as paragons, unaware of how fatuous they sound, or, for that matter, of the unfairness of their assertions, considering that, thanks to them, community control has never been given a chance to prove itself.

"We believe in community control," the white teachers say, "but we could only accept a governing school board if it were made up of representatives of the church, the business world, and influential organizations like the NAACP or the Urban League." The teachers ignored the fact that nationwide "influence organizations" have little or no relation to the exercise of power on the purely local scene.

Repugnant and Anti-Democratic Words

The sentiments quoted were not only repugnant to a poor community seeking some influence over the education of its own children; they defied America's enduring faith in the common man. The tenacity with which they were maintained by the white educational establishment in New York made inertia and obstructionism more and more blatant in Ocean Hill as the months passed. Since the July agreement to accept the election of a governing board, the Board of Education has not, in fact, made a single gesture toward recognizing the governing board's authority.

The Board of Education allowed the poor people of Ocean Hill to form an administrative unit with the understanding that it would relinquish some of its authority to it. The Board clearly hoped the experiment would fail and fall into chaos. When the Ocean Hill people demonstrated that they could elect competent administrators, that they could develop, at least on paper, programs to improve education, that, in fact, the "worst damn schools in the city," according to Rhody McCoy, could be improved under community control, the Board merely waited for the Ocean Hill governing board to wither away in bitter impotence.

That it hasn't withered away is a miracle. The planning money granted by the Ford Foundation ran out in the fall of 1967, and an additional $15,000 of Ford money ran out soon after that. After promising $250,000 to fund the Ocean Hill board's programs, the Foundation announced that it could make no more grants until the Board of Education or the state legislature recognized the local board as the official governing authority. Fantini declared, understandably, that "we cannot take the place of the Board of Education." This denial of funds meant that the governing board was reduced to a debating society, without the means to implement any programs in its schools.

Ford's decision was a great blow to Ocean Hill; to the people involved, it was betrayal, pure and simple. The Ford Foundation was, they believe, bending to pressure from the Board of Education, from obstructionist groups like the UFT, and from less organized public pressure generated by racism and an uncomprehending press. Mario Fantini said, "we are waiting to see what happens next." So far, nothing has happened.

The latest and perhaps most effective drive to quash the "rebellion" in Ocean Hill was led by the Council of Supervisory Associations, a quasi-labor union of principals and assistant principals. This group took the Board of Education to court, charging that the principals it had hired in the fall on the recommendation of the Ocean Hill governing board were hired illegally, because they were not chosen from the Civil Service list of candidates. In March, the judge ruled in favor of the CSA, and until an appellate court rules to the contrary—if it does—all the principals elected by the Ocean Hill board are holding their positions illegally.

Without funds to carry out educational reform and the power to hire and dismiss personnel, the school board of Ocean Hill is wholly unable to administer its schools. As the people of Ocean Hill have painfully learned, the ideal of local control of New York schools is, within the framework of existing laws, and confronted with a Board of Education that will not relinquish an iota of its authority, an empty dream.

The so-called decentralization proposals issued by the Ford Foundation, Mayor Lindsay and most recently the State Board of Regents represent an effort to present to the state legislature programs that would break up the Board of Education's power to obstruct reform. The leaders of Ocean Hill are not entirely happy with the various proposals, since they do not, it is asserted, grant enough local power. Experience has made these people skeptical and wary. But if the state legislature could shake itself free of inertia and enact laws that would give real power to the communities, it would relieve a very grave situation.

In Ocean Hill, the situation became critical. Shown to be powerless against a deceitful established bureaucracy, the governing board all but lost the respect and allegiance of the community. Angry and frustrated parents' groups demanded action. Because the governing board could not act, it was ready to turn the schools over to the parents. At a public meeting on March 19, the governing board announced to an auditorium full of parents that if the Board of Education did not accept community control within ten days the governing board would "resign"—that is, end all relations with the Board of Education.

Three weeks later, on April 10, parents staged a boycott that closed down all the eight schools in Ocean Hill. The same day, Superintendent of Schools Donovan publicly declared, "It is unfortunate that the children should be denied education over a matter that should be discussed around the table by adults."

What is really unfortunate is that the Board of Education never looked upon the people of Ocean Hill with anything but contempt. The truth is, the Board of Education never treated the governing board of Ocean Hill as adults.

Awareness of the Crisis Grows

Since last April, events in Ocean Hill have finally demonstrated to the public at large the enormous proportions of the crisis in New York City public education. In the wake of the April 10 student boycott in Ocean Hill, the groups supporting decentralization renewed their efforts to persuade the New York State Legislature to pass a strong decentralization bill. The State Board of Regents, which had announced in March a far-reaching plan for decentralizing New York's schools, now decided to intervene directly in the fray. At the end of April, the Regents went to the legislature and asked it to pass their March proposal into law. At the same time, both Mayor Lindsay and Governor Rockefeller announced their support of the Regents' plan, and urged the legislature to take swift action. But the adjournment-minded legislature remained unmoved. It seemed prepared only to enact a weak bill, proposed by a state senator from New York City, John J. Marchi, which would have sent the decentralization issue back to the Board of Education (whose antipathy to decentralization was by now public knowledge). There it would be "discussed" and then reintroduced to the legislature in 1969. In effect, all action on decentralization would be postponed for at least a year.

While the weak Marchi bill was drifting toward enactment in Albany in early May, the governing board in Ocean Hill, probably with the tacit approval of the Mayor and other sympathetic members of the "establishment," took drastic action. On May 10, the governing board formally dismissed 19 teachers and supervisors in Ocean Hill, charging them with having attempted to "sabotage" the demonstration project. The result of this action was complete dislocation. Superintendent of Schools Donovan ordered the 19 teachers to ignore the governing board's dismissal order and return to their schools. The Ocean Hill parents vowed to prevent the 19 ousted teachers from returning, and on Monday, May 13, blockaded the entrance of Junior High School 271 and told the teachers they could not enter the building. Police, surrounding the school that day, threatened to escort the ousted teachers through the parent blockade, but made no actual move to do so.

The parent blockade of JHS 271 lasted until Wednesday, May 15, when policemen appeared in large numbers, surrounded the school and proceeded to admit all "authorized personnel." Since the end of the blockade, chaos has reigned in Ocean Hill. Parent boycotts have been answered by teacher counter-boycotts. Black parents have hurled charges of racism and police brutality at the city, and they, in turn, have been accused by the United Federation of Teachers of "vigilantism" and black racism. UFT President Albert Shanker hinted at a city-wide teachers' strike, and a prominent civil rights leader who closed the schools in 1964 to protest de facto segregation threatened to do the same thing again if Ocean Hill did not get its way.

With the situation in Ocean Hill threatening to explode into racial violence by mid-May, Governor Rockefeller and the Board of Regents began again to pressure the legislature to pass a strong decentralization bill and drop the meaningless substitute proposed by Senator Marchi. On May 14, legislative leaders agreed to work on a strong decentralization bill based on the Regents' plan, and on the following day, a group of pro-decentralization legislators threatened to "sit-in" outside the governor's office if the plan were not adopted swiftly. On May 18, the Board of Regents announced in Governor Rockefeller's office a new, strong decentralization bill that would replace the Board of Education with a three-member commission that would have one year to decentralize New York's school system, and create nearly autonomous local school boards.

The UFT vs. the People

On May 21, Governor Rockefeller predicted that a strong bill would be passed in Albany. The day before, Albert Shanker and 500 New York City school teachers arrived in that city to lobby against the impending legislation. Two days later, on May 22, the accord reached on a strong decentralization bill collapsed in the legislature. Shanker and his supporters had poured into the corridors of the state capitol, passing out leaflets stating that local school districts would operate "on the basis of local prejudices based on color, race, or religion." They flooded New York's newspapers and radio stations with anti-decentralization advertisements, and threatened the state legislators with massive political retaliation. The legislators, a few days later, enacted a slightly amended Marchi bill, to the consternation of the *New York Times*, among many others.

By almost single-handedly preventing radical school decentralization, the teachers' union, by a single stroke, cleared the air surrounding the school reform controversy in New York City. They revealed that the 50,000 teachers were the real power behind the status quo in New York schools. This was a revelation indeed, since the teachers' union had always before depended on the Board of Education to block reforms, while blandly garbing itself in a cloak of liberal idealism. It now stood plainly exposed as an employee's protective association, and little more. The legislative victory was thus a Pyrrhic one; its vast body of automatic liberal support would soon be looking on it with new eyes.

To the people of Ocean Hill, who were never very satisfied with even the strongest decentralization plans, the teachers' unsheathing of their raw power was a welcome change. The struggle for community control, as they see it, can now be waged in the open field, against an uncamouflaged enemy. Unfortunately for New York, the battle may be fought in the streets. As one observer ominously remarked, "When the summer is over, anyone will be willing to sit down with anyone, to negotiate the decentralizing of this school system."

The Battle for Urban Schools

Wallace Roberts

This last article on community control of schools puts the Ocean Hill–Brownsville dispute into a larger perspective. It reminds us that the proposed reforms threaten to undo the work of earlier reformers, provoking rather violent reactions as a result.

"If anyone walking the streets of New York is under the impression that the teachers are on strike over an educational issue, he is grossly misinformed. The issues are politics and labor."

The speaker was Rhody A. McCoy, unit administrator of Brooklyn's embattled Ocean Hill–Brownsville decentralized school district, an organization that has come to symbolize the spreading struggle for community control of the urban schools. That struggle involves not only a demand by ghetto parents for a direct hand in insuring better education for their children, but a complex of social and political issues that includes the drive for black power, the tenure rights of teachers, black and white racism, and, ultimately, the prerogatives of organized labor. In New York's paralyzing battle these issues have come to a boil, and the ensuing strikes by the city's teachers have closed most of the schools for the opening weeks of the term.

It is clear that the Negro's fight for dignity and equality has come down to something very basic: he wants his share of power, not just a seat in the front of the bus. He wants control over some of the institutions that shape his environment, and the one within easiest reach is the public school. But to obtain power over the schools, the Negro must take it away from others who will not yield it easily. And the objective of the black community puts it on a collision course not only with the increasingly powerful United Federation of Teachers (UFT), but also with many of the traditional assumptions about how "good" schools are run. For the ultimate question of control comes down to whether a semi-autonomous school board has the right to hire and fire its teachers at will.

The concept of "decentralization" grew out of a number of proposals

---

From Wallace Roberts, "The Battle for Urban Schools," *Saturday Review* (November 16, 1968), pp. 97–99, 117. Copyright 1968 Saturday Review, Inc. Reprinted by permission of *Saturday Review*.

made within the past few years to set up "model subsystems" within big-city school systems for experimental purposes. Carried to the logical next step, decentralization involves the reorganization of an entire city school system into a number of semi-autonomous districts. Community control takes the final step of placing authority for most or all major decisions in decentralized districts in the hands of a local school board elected by the community. And it was this final step, taken in one of three experimental districts in New York, that precipitated the bitter impasse that closed the city's schools.

Even before the crisis reached major proportions in New York, however, the groundwork was being laid in the ghettos of nearly thirty other major cities across the country to provide for greater participation in the schools by parents and community leaders. Most of these other cities will not have their own Ocean Hill–Brownsville struggle, but it seems clear that a chain of events has been set in motion that is almost certain to change fundamentally the nation's big-city schools.

The problems of urban education are compounded in New York City, of course, by its size: a $1.4-billion school budget, 1,100,000 students, 57,000 teachers, and 3,700 principals and other administrators. More than half of the students are black or Puerto Rican, while more than 90 per cent of the teachers and about 95 per cent of the administrators are white.

The situation that led to this autumn's explosion was complicated by many other factors as well. Long-standing promises of integration and compensatory programs that never materialized, organizational politics within the union and the politics of race in the community played a part, as well as class and racial tensions in the city at large. The rigidity of the city school administration, the many patch work efforts of the past to shore up the schools, and the long history of educational poverty all contributed to a deteriorating school system.

Some observers assert that when the central Board of Education first authorized three decentralized "demonstration districts" (of which Ocean Hill–Brownsville was one) in 1967, a fundamental mistake was made in giving the local governing boards powers that were broad but too vaguely defined, and that this lack of clarity led to the showdown. Others, however, contend that the situation had become increasingly volatile over the past two years and that the explosion would have come no matter how explicitly the central board had defined the powers of the local governing boards.

In any event, the Ocean Hill–Brownsville governing board, backed—or prodded—by militants in the community forced the issue last May by insisting on its right to transfer out of the district nineteen teachers and assistant principals charged with "sabotaging" decentralization or being "unacceptable" to the community. The UFT supported the teachers and called a strike against the district's eight schools, which remained closed for the rest of the school year.

During the summer of 1968, the governing board recruited new teachers—many of them June college graduates—and the district's schools opened on schedule in September. Unable to close down the Ocean Hill–Brownsville schools, the UFT called a strike that shut down most of the schools in the rest of the city. By the end of October, the union had reached a "settlement" with the central Board on two occasions and had sent the teachers back to open the city's schools. Both times, however, the local community refused to accept the settlement, and the teachers in the rest of the city walked out once more.

Since the series of strikes began, secondary issues have emerged to confuse the situation almost beyond comprehension. Demands on both sides have been made and then withdrawn, agreements were reached, and then ignored. The union is striking against the central Board of Education and must negotiate with it. Yet its real dispute is with the local governing board. To admit that, however, is to recognize community control. Meanwhile, the governing board sits in Brooklyn, quietly running its schools. When the UFT teachers show up after a "settlement," it repeats its position that they are unacceptable, or allows community militants to prevent their return to the classroom.

One secondary issue that has taken on major importance is the racism expressed by both blacks and whites. Because two-thirds of the city's teachers are Jewish, however, the black racism has taken on overtones of anti-Semitism. The Ocean Hill–Brownsville governing board has pointed out that over 50 per cent of the new teachers it hired are Jewish and that none of the board members have made anti-Semitic remarks, but it has not rebuked the members of the community who have. On the other hand, the leadership of the union has referred to "vigilantes" and "Nazi types and gangsters" in the Ocean Hill and Brownsville communities.

The current crisis is directly related to a similar one two years ago when the issue of community control was first raised by the people of Harlem. They demanded that if the city's Board of Education did not integrate a new school, Intermediate School 201, or provide it with enough experienced teachers, as it had promised, then the community wanted the right to run the school itself.

That crisis spread the demand for decentralization and community control through the city's ghettos, and it has been gaining momentum ever since. The idea of decentralization took on official respectability, however, only after a city tax commission reported that the city's schools would be entitled to significantly more state aid if the system were broken up into five districts based on the city's five boroughs.

Shortly after the tax commission report, the Board of Education endorsed the principle of decentralization, and in July 1967, the Ford Foundation announced that, with the approval of the Board of Education, it was going to finance the planning for three decentralized "demonstration districts"; IS 201 in Harlem, Ocean Hill–Brownsville in Brooklyn, and the Two Bridges district on the Lower East Side of Manhattan. Each district would contain at least one intermediate school and its feeder elementary schools.

Meanwhile, the state legislature had appropriated an extra $54,000,000 for the New York City schools on the condition that Mayor John V. Lindsay develop a decentralization plan for the entire city school system. The legislature was thinking in terms of a five-borough plan. However, the panel appointed by Mayor Lindsay and headed by McGeorge Bundy, president of the Ford Foundation, proposed a more radical program of organization reform. The report of the committee, "Reconnection for Learning: A Community School System for New York City," was released exactly a year ago, and called for the creation of thirty to sixty semi-autonomous school districts, each with a governing board composed of eleven members, six elected by the community and five appointed by the mayor.

The Bundy report sparked the immediate opposition of many groups, including the UFT. The New York legislature, under heavy pressure from both the teachers' union and the city's Central Labor Council, failed to approve either the Bundy report or any of several modifications. Instead, it approved a bill delaying effective decentralization for a year, and directed the New York State Board of Regents and the city's Board of Education to produce a temporary decentralization plan. Originally the legislature was expected to approve a final plan when it convened in January, but its action now is an open question.

While New York City has been going through its own agony over decentralization and community control in recent years, related efforts have been made in Boston, Washington, D.C., and Syracuse, New York. Most of these efforts, however, were designed as administrative rearrangements to facilitate widescale educational experimentation and had few formal arrangements for involving the community in planning or operation. These other projects were begun independently but now are in the process of being loosely tied together with more than a score of projects in other cities in a growing movement for decentralization and parental involvement which has the support of the U.S. Office of Education.

Early last spring the Office of Education created a new category for aid under the Elementary and Secondary Education Act. Known as the Central Cities Project, the program is designed to have big-city school departments concentrate their efforts at compensatory education in small "subsystems" and to require that parents and other members of the community are fully involved in the planning and operation of the projects. By June, projects costing $12,800,000 and involving 125,000 children were approved for twenty-six cities stretching from Boston to Los Angeles.

Last month, some 200 school officials and community representatives in the Central Cities Projects gathered for a three-day conference in Detroit. Nearly all the participants felt that their projects provided a loose framework for "plugging in" the ghetto communities to the schools, and to most of them, it seemed inevitable that once the community is aroused, once its expectations about itself and the schools are raised, once the people in the ghettos discover that someone is taking them seriously, then the progression begins. In other words, involvement cannot be sustained unless power is shared.

In New York, this progression was begun without planning and went uncontrolled, producing the confrontation. Other cities have already taken steps that they hope will avoid similar situations. For more than a year, Philadelphia has been laying the groundwork for decentralization by holding training sessions for administrators and teachers and has just ordered a study done on community participation and decentralization. Detroit has been able to win relatively strong support from its teachers' union (which is 35 per cent black) for its decentralization programs by drawing teachers in on the planning.

Boston, once torn over its failure to desegregate its schools, still has controversy, but the people of its Roxbury ghetto literally wrote the proposal for funds in the Central Cities Project last spring with the advice of university and school officials, and are heavily involved in the operations and further planning. Chicago has a twenty-one-member governing board for its Central Cities Project, divided equally among representatives from the city's central school board, the University of Chicago, and a strong community group, The Woodlawn Organization.

Yet, after all the talk of politics, labor, race, bureaucracy, and urban problems, there is more to decentralization and community control than riot prevention or the breakup of the old order. How much more is not yet clear, for there is no single panacea, and none of the advocates find any intrinsic value in the concept, except some black militants who regard separatism as an end in itself.

Community control is seen by most of its other proponents as only a useful political tool for bringing about educational changes. It is relatively inexpensive compared to the costs of busing to achieve integration or of compensatory education. But decentralization without integration, compensatory education, and massive funds will not do the job. The severe problems of urban school systems require an entire range of remedies. Nonetheless, bringing the parents into closer association with the schools can be an effective first step. This rationale for decentralization and community control is based on the theory that parental involvement with the schools and concern over the child's achievement rubs off on the child. The middle-class youngster sees his parents attending teacher conferences, a PTA cake sale, or Visit School Night, and he knows his parents are concerned about his school work. Because he is anxious to please, he learns the expected skills.

The child of the ghetto, on the other hand, does not have this pressure, and too often is not learning. Decentralization and community control are based on the idea that there is a connection between the two and that if the distrust of the school on the part of the ghetto parents can be broken down by involving them in the life of the schools, then the effects will be transferred to the child.

This is the heart of the issue. The people of the ghetto know when they are being used. Community control, if it really is to work, means the dispersal of power. It means allowing parents, mothers on welfare, laborers, and a whole range of people with values different from those of middle-class whites, to sit on boards which have the authority to tell a district superintendent or a principal what kind of results they want. It means creating whole new mechanisms for bringing parents and teachers together, for allowing people with little formal education to work in classrooms and offices, and as liaison workers with the community.

Willard Congreve, director of the Woodlawn Experimental Schools Project in Chicago, has worked out a plausible plan for deciding those instances in which the parents shall have ultimate authority, and those in which the professionals must be allowed to exercise their training and experience. Preston Wilcox, a former Columbia University professor who is now the educational consultant for the IS 201 complex in Harlem, has recently published an essay outlining a whole series of ways in which parents can be genuinely involved in the schools as aides, office workers, and consultants (*The Schoolhouse in the City*, edited by Alvin Toffler).

Another way of looking at community control and decentralization is that it is also an attempt not just to bring the school and the community closer together for the benefit of the parents, but also to make the teachers, principals, and other school officials accountable to the people they serve. As most big city schools now operate, the employees are not directly responsible to the people. The customer is never right. There are many layers of authority, but it is impossible to pin down just where responsibility lies. District governing boards and advisory panels for each school are seen as a means by which the parents can demand satisfactory results.

The central boards of education in Detroit, Chicago, Philadelphia, and Washington, D.C., have already made strong statements or taken decisive actions favoring decentralization and community control. Yet, conditions are volatile everywhere because conditions are basically the same. Any commitment to decentralization requires a sustaining effort not just to pour oil on troubled waters but to make it the kind of experiment that leads to the "reconnection for learning."

The opening chapter of the story on community control is now being written and it seems clear its preface is an obituary for the traditional urban school system. The rest of the story is not clear, but there can be no turning back. Urban schools will never be the same.

This observation may seem mild in light of the intensity of the passions on all sides of the struggle in New York. It is hard to remain sanguine walking through a crowd of 40,000 teachers and labor union members and hear them cursing the mayor, the Board of Education, and the Ford Foundation, or while watching thirteen- and fourteen-year-old boys fight police to get into a school. And it is hard to see more than the immediate hatred expressed by a crowd of angry parents behind the gray police barricades screaming at a small group of teachers.

Yet institutions are such vast structures that often it is only the passionate intensity of a crisis that can bring about the necessary changes. The teachers and the community are profoundly divided by a deep animosity but together they are moving a mountain.

One reason for the high intensity of the emotions on the part of the teachers in the New York battle against community control is that, in effect, decentralization denies all the assumptions about education that have been held for more than a generation. Theories of teacher selection, qualification, tenure, methods, and curriculum—indeed the entire professional ideology is being challenged.

This challenge comes just at a time when the long struggle for teacher recognition seemed to be won. Over the last ten years teachers have acquired, through their unions and increasingly militant teacher associations, substantial influence in educational policymaking. Now, suddenly they are faced with a threat of the disintegration of the very system they were coming to control.

They will not yield without a bitter fight, for they were only able to achieve their power by taking education out of municipal politics. They see decentralization as a hammer about to smash the protective glass of professional standards which were originally developed as a means of improving the quality of teachers and to allow the system to take in minorities kept out through political interference. Now it is the same "professionalized" system which appears to be functioning to keep other minorities out.

And the danger is real that decentralization will be perverted. Educationally, community control has only as much value as each community gives it. If the community allows its schools to be used by ambitious men for their own political purposes, if the community allows teachers to be fired because they are white or Jewish or "not black enough," or because they think differently rather than because of the way they act or teach, then it will be no better than the present system.

But an even greater danger, it seems, especially in light of the current polarization over Ocean Hill–Brownsville, is that other alternatives will be overlooked or disregarded. Community control does not have to mean an all-or-nothing struggle that precludes future consideration of other options. If there is one thing that is clear about the failure of big city schools, it is that no one really knows the answers and that many doors need to be opened.

Yet, community control is probably a political necessity for many cities. More importantly it may be a human necessity as a device to allow black communities to develop their own institutions suited to what they see are their own needs. Rhody McCoy has summed it up: "Everyone else has failed. We want the right to fail for ourselves."

Chapter Five

Colleges and Universities —Student Power?

This chapter is not very extensive because there is already a large number of major, as well as minor, works on student unrest. This avalanche of print has been brought down on us by the string of campus disturbances around the world. A common theme in these events has been the demand for student power.

The introductory essay reviewed the conflicting claims of the expert versus the amateur. Student unrest is most interesting because it is in the university that the demand for amateur participation clashes most graphically with the presence of professional expertise. Student criticisms also raise the crucial issue of the degree to which an institution (here an educational one) can be and/or ought to be separated from the larger society. Some insist it is a corrupted microcosm of the society; others insist it must be separate because it is unique. Finally, there is the issue of whether the democracy we seek for society is appropriate to a university.

In terms of structure, there are two variants of campus participatory democracy. First, there is the ad hoc confrontation model in which rather unstructured mass meetings adopt resolutions and make demands on the administration. In such meetings leadership tends to gravitate to those who are articulate, bold, and fond of long meetings. The participants usually insist that they are speaking for all "concerned" students and faculty, but here they are simply engaging in a disguised form of representative democracy, without using any formal procedures for selecting representatives.

The second type is that of greatly enlarged student participation and influence in the formal decision-making machinery. When extended far enough, this technique becomes codetermination, which is common in

Latin American universities. The trend of events seems to be in that direction.

Campus participatory democracy can also be analyzed in terms of its objective. On the one hand, there is the goal of improving the institution. This means potential student involvement in improving the learning experience (faculty evaluation, curriculum) and in trying to manage things properly (admissions, discipline). One problem that would arise is that there are other members of the community who might now insist on being included in the "people" to whom power is being turned over—clerical staff, maintenance personnel, alumni, parents, contributors or taxpayers, etc. After all, decisions would be made that affect their lives.

On the other hand, there are those who wish to use participatory democracy on campus as a means to larger social change, either by employing the university's resources directly or by setting it up as an example. However, Stanley Hoffmann has defined a problem that arises when radical talk leads to radical action:

> No society ever tolerates a university dedicated to its subversion—indeed, to the making of its future elites into grand agitators. No university can be the commune. . . .[1]

What would be the consequences of campus participatory democracy? Some faculty and administrators fear that familiarity will breed contempt, but it is to be hoped that this applies only to the contemptible. Also, modifying Lord Acton, it may be true that *powerlessness* is corrupting at times and that granting new responsibilities to students will make them more "responsible." Nathan Glazer thinks that something of this sort would occur:

> . . . I think student representation on a greater range of university, college and departmental committees may introduce valuable points of view. But it does not transform education—it only demonstrates that the dilemmas of contemporary higher education are not simply the making of conservative professors or administrators. And if students can be taught that by participation in faculty and administrative committees, well and good.[2]

---

[1] "Participation in Perspective?" *Daedalus*, Winter 1970, p. 217.
[2] " 'Student Power' in Berkeley," *The Public Interest*, No. 13, Fall 1968, p. 17.

Student Social Action: From Liberation to Community

Tom Hayden

This first selection is taken from a 1962 presentation, by Tom Hayden, at the University of Michigan and is an early student viewpoint on the need for university reform. Hayden first discussed the authoritarian nature of the university and then the mindless apathy of contemporary students. In the last part, from which this selection is taken, he prescribes elimination of authoritarianism as one way to awaken students to true citizenship.

To indicate just how far we have come in the short time since Hayden's remarks, we can refer to a recent issue of The New Republic, which proposed that the Congress require as a condition for receiving federal funds that colleges and universities demonstrate that they had given students an ample role on all policy-making boards. The magazine argued that people old enough to vote (because of the lowered voting age) ought to have a similar degree of responsibility on the campus.*

We must have a try at bringing society under human control. We must wrest control somehow from the endless machines that grind up men's jobs, the few hundred corporations that exercise greater power over the economy and the country than in feudal societies, the vast military profession that came into existence with universal military training during our brief lifetime, the irresponsible politicians secured by the ideological overlap, the seniority system and the gerrymandered base of our political structure, and the pervasive bureaucracy that perpetuates and multiplies itself everywhere. These are the dominators of human beings, the real, definable phenomena that make human beings fall—victimized by undefinable "circumstance." Sadly, the university in America has become a part of this hierarchy of power, rather than an instrument to make men free.

It must be said, too, that the university situation in America is more a

---

Excerpts from Tom Hayden, "Student Social Action: From Liberation to Community," in Mitchell Cohen and Dennis Hale, eds., The New Student Left: An Anthology (Boston: Beacon Press, 1966), pp. 283–286. Reprinted by permission of Beacon Press and the author.
* "The Lively Ivy," The New Republic, August 15, 1970, pp. 5–6.

symptom than a basic cause of our problems. But a college is one place to embark on a movement of reform, a place with intellectual equipment and a reservoir of unused creativity, a place from which reason might make a last attempt to intervene in human affairs.

A really excellent university, I believe, would not be organized along corporate and authoritarian lines, but in a way that would truly activate the creative potential of students and faculty. These two communities share the real enterprise of learning, and as there can be no final unamendable Truth in a community of free inquiry, there can be no arbitrary authority structure for the relation of teacher and student. A company of scholars is a company of equals in the crucial sense that none has a premium on truth, though some may be wiser, more literate, more numerous, more knowledgeable than others. Because the faculty has more permanence and more educational training, theirs should be the primary responsibility for the direction of the university. Because education is not a one-way process, because faculty tradition must be balanced by the fresh eye of youth, and because democracy requires popular control over important decisions, students should share with professors in the developing university. Separate student government and faculty government should be abolished and replaced by a cooperative decision-making body. The organized university administration, as it now exists, should be eliminated. In the present form, administrations are increasingly staffed by individuals without backgrounds of significant scholarship, and without a primary interest in the education of students. By the very nature of their constant administrative work, these men assume greater and greater—quite oligarchical—power over the everyday and long-range progress of the university. Therefore, to think of them as "equals" with the faculty and students, is not only to say that bureaucrats should have as much say as scholars, but it is to give bureaucracy an unfair advantage which inevitably leads to dominance. Instead of this system, we should acquire a bureaucracy that is really a bureaucracy: a rational apparatus meant to service the work of the intellectual community. A bureaucracy, for instance, might take care of admissions problems, parking policies, health and medical service, staffing, business management of the dormitories, public relations. All of these functions should be subject to the democratic control of the students and faculty, although they should not be so tightly controlled as to create human problems of alienation within the bureaucracy itself. The more important administrative functions—the presidency, the academic deanships, major rules and regulations, relations with the sources of funds, curriculum content, teaching methods, class sizes—should be the direct and never-delegated concern of the students and faculty. As for the regents and trustees, the present criteria for selection, e.g., wealth, political affiliation, prestige, should be subordinated to educational experience and understanding. This accomplished, regents might properly represent public interests, though with only advisory power, in university decision making.

It will be said that this activity would exhaust the scholarly community. To this I say: Better exhaustion than the present system of nearly total administrative control of the universities. It will be further said that I am being utopian and unrealistic. In response I would ask you to consider whether or not you believe that our current realisms about politics and education are solving human problems; I would then quote Norman Brown's *Life Against Death* (a psychoanalytic study of the meaning of history): "Utopian speculations . . . must come back into fashion. They are a way of affirming faith in the present moment insoluble. Today even the survival of humanity is a utopian hope." Third, I would suggest that without at least a vision of the ideal university, reformers will make no qualitative changes and may even adopt standards that their vision would oppose.

The university I envision will tolerate and even promote student exercise of democratic prerogatives. It will entertain all ideas and make them challenging. It will be culturally, racially, religiously, and internationally integrated. It will appreciate the educational benefits of testing ideas through real action.

In this good university of mine, *in loco parentis* will be replaced by the doctrine that man is meant to live, not to prepare for life. Instead of a system that is paternal and relatively closed, there will be an organic system, where ideas are sharply confronted so that man can comprehend, always developing in the tension between threat and renewal. The good university will be concerned with democracy, too: By its practices, it will counter democracy that depends on authority, elites, and specialization with one that depends on consent, individual participation, and the common intelligence that enables men to deal with confusion, anxiety, and the enormity of events.

Academic Government

Christian Bay

We have chosen this piece by Christian Bay to provide a faculty perspective in favor of participatory reforms in universities. In the earlier segment of the article, Bay calls for the university to be restructured so that it can play a key role in developing self-governing citizens for our society, which means freeing the university from established powers. What a democratic university would look like and how to get there are the subjects of this selection.

It is worth speculating a bit on alternative university structures. In view of our earlier remarks about the problem of excessive size in participatory-democracy units, would direct democracy be inconsistent with an open-enrollments policy? Would it be applicable in our universities at their present size? Perhaps the answer would be Rousseau's model, with basic units in residence or departments binding delegates to higher levels. Alternatively, Paul Goodman suggests that we could let the mass university fall apart into its natural communities of scholars (in his The Community of Scholars).

Now I come, finally, to the question of academic government and citizenship as things ought to eventually become. But the following is not intended as a description of a utopia. I shall argue that this is a practical scheme, and rest my case on that empirical proposition. You will force me to retreat if you can show that I am less than realistic. Crackpot idealism has no greater appeal to me than crackpot realism. Furthermore, I shall argue that the recommended next steps, just discussed, if implemented would bring this desired state of academic government much nearer, with or without Berkeley-type confrontations on the way from here to there.

Being way past thirty, I may be forgiven for being a gradualist. I believe in Freedom Now and Power Now for the blacks but not in Power Now for the Students, handed to them with the trustee's best wishes. I think the students' fight to win their freedom and power from their in-

---

From "Academic Government and Academic Citizenship in a Time of Revolt," by Christian Bay, in The New Politics of American Policy: A Reader, ed. by Edgar Litt. Copyright © 1969 by Holt, Rinehart and Winston, Inc. Reprinted by permission of Holt, Rinehart and Winston, Inc.

transigent elders is a vital requirement for developing a moral and political consciousness among many more students. I don't want to see boards of trustees abolished in the next ten years but to see them include and then gradually increase the proportion of professors and students as voting members. In the final analysis, though, I would like to see boards of trustees given purely ceremonial functions, with or without adademic representation.

Ultimately, I would like to see universities governed democratically much as other communities ought to be, but with the great difference that in the academic community democracy just might work—that is, democracy as envisaged by the classic theorists. For in academic communities people are relatively well educated, relatively nondesperate or nonmiserable, and there are optimal opportunities for a constructive dialogue on normative issues and for recourse to research as a way of resolving the more empirical controversial issues, on any questions of fact subject to dispute.

Ideally, the total voting power of faculty and students should be approximately equal, which raises ticklish questions of differential weighting of votes, because of the far greater number of students, especially undergraduates. John Stuart Mill in his day argued eloquently for differential voting in Great Britain, on the theory that some categories of citizens are likely to be wiser or more conscientious than others.[1] I don't buy this argument as applied to Great Britain, then or now; nor would I buy it for university governments. Granted, professors may average more experience but this is offset by the fact that students, when given political responsibility, may well average not only a fresher vision but quite possibly a much broader and deeper vision of the public interest, being less specialized, that is, having fewer trained incapacities. There are some issues so simple, it has been said, that it takes experts *not* to understand them.

My argument for some kind of differential voting so as to achieve rough parity hinges instead on the view that the welfare of the university and the contributions it can make to society depends on the kind of cooperation that can be achieved, only on a basis of equality I believe, between the two main components of the academic community, professors and students. If one side always were in a position to vote the other side down, the dialogue would suffer and the representative institutions would soon cease representing the minority in any real sense, or so the minority would come to feel.

I would not anticipate any oppression comparable to the experience of the blacks in the United States, who have almost always faced the certainty of being voted down. I would rather compare with the French in Canada; intelligent citizens of that country nowadays realize that Canada can never become united until the achievement of a constitution that grants equal powers, in many areas, to the French minority. Some English-Canadians are as lacking in understanding any basis for the French gripes as some professors and deans are failing to see any merit in the demands for student power; but that does not dispose of the problem of self-government and citizenship for students, or for Quebec in Canada.

It might not be a bad idea to begin by giving students, and especially undergraduates, rather less of a voting representation than would seem fair as a permanent arrangement; first, it may take a little time to get used to exercising new powers and responsibilities and, secondly, it would not be a bad idea to hold back on their rights until a real political demand has been developed. Democratic forms without substance are of little use; witness the decline of democratic participation of Sarah Lawrence as described by Harold Taylor; although these hazards of insufficiently challenging issues are, alas, less likely to be encountered in the years to come.[2]

I shall not go into detail about academic constitution-making. The names and routine functions of administrative offices might not change a great deal; the key point is that the governing boards, with powers corresponding to those of present day boards of trustees, would be elected by professors and students and would be composed of professors and students only (and possibly research scholars and librarians). The administration would be responsible to an executive committee of the Academic Senate, perhaps on a year-to-year basis; I should prefer a university president who would not submit to detailed board supervision but who would report regularly and at maybe yearly intervals see if he still had the Board's confidence.

Within this democratic framework there would still be alienated minorities of students to berate "the system." It would be disquieting if this were not to be the case. The point is not that democratic government with student-faculty power would please everyone; but that a rational, politically responsible dialogue would be brought about which would help educate to citizenship many students who are now robbed of an education and merely acquire skills and attitudes; and the university community as a whole would be far better able than now to contribute to political enlightenment and to political action in the local public interest, in the larger society, and in the international world.

There would presumably be political party slates; hopefully they would be joint student-faculty parties rather than tribal student parties separate from faculty parties; hopefully there would even be an occasional engineer among the humanists and social scientists who might dominate the slates on the left. Presumably there would be proportional representation, with members at large to give minority voices a hearing in the assembly. And surely there would be a bill of individual rights so as to place limits on the majority's powers to infringe on essential human rights such as freedom of speech, of association and so on.

Among the benefits of democratic government on the campus two categories stand out, in my judgment: the likely demonstration that democracy can work, and the likelihood that the university can become true to its own essential mission of uiversality in the pursuit and transmission of knowledge, and in the fostering of education as a liberating force from oppression, individual and collective.

If democratic government can work on the campus, surrounding communities will take note; if students can become self-governing citizens, so can perhaps at a later stage alumni; if full freedom of expression is achieved on the campus, then the normal stifling of radical dialogue in Washington and in most mass media and in many communities will not be tolerated much longer. Real democracy on a national scale may still be a quite utopian ideal, but at least we will all learn the difference between pretended democracy and the real thing and we will cease paying respectful attention to those who now control our destinies when they keep on talking as if democracy has already been achieved in this country. The universities, perhaps starting with campuses like Berkeley, Wisconsin, Harvard, Yale, Stanford, Michigan and Chicago, can become the first demonstration projects in urban America that will show what democracy is and how it can work. If this development can be brought about gradually, I rather think these universities will remain in the front rank among our most distinguished centers of higher learning; and the various political and financial establishments will for their own good (short range, at least) have to put up with us.

How can a democratically governed university hope to become more of a universal city of learning than a trustee-governed one, or a professor-governed one on the continental European models (which in practice tend to function as real gerontocracies, with the influence of youngsters under fifty even more limited than here)? I think the last decade has amply demonstrated that a universalistic moral vision, a disinterested concern for justice is encountered far more often among students than among the faculty, to say nothing of the bulk of university administrators, who so often have been trained to become practical, hard-headed servants of their corporations. What the typical North American and the typical European university have in common today is precisely the absence of effective student influence (official student governments have traditionally been little more than a parody on adult pseudopolitical governments; by hook or by crook, most administrators have had "friendly" immature apoliticals to work with, although the days of this convenient kind of arrangement now appear to be numbered). . . .

The forces that work against full intellectual integrity and against achieving the universal city of learning are in part a matter of PR-conscious university governments, sometimes supported by large sections of the senior faculties as well, who prefer to stifle or forestall dissent by hiring or giving tenure or promotions only to meek or conformist professors. In larger part the problem is that the major foundations and the government and the other main sources of funds and of status and creature comforts outside the universities are exhibiting just the same kinds of preferences: political radicalism is not to be encouraged; it makes people excited, especially the brighter but still immature and malleable students; it rocks the boat, and it is bad business for the university.

But radical intellectual and political inquiry, and perhaps radical politics as well (though about the latter I don't wish to be equally emphatic) is more essential than ever in a world that changes so fast. The really impractical utopians among us are those who believe that our social order can continue to exist without basic changes. Only sheltered societies can sometimes persist unchanged, relying on the conventional wisdom of their unchallenged gerontocrats; in our fast-changing world the premium is on maximal rationality, and political inquiry can be fully rational only to the extent that it is radical, taking no empirical assumptions for granted, however comfortable or crucial they may seem from the perspective of the established powers. Paradoxically, the more turmoil brought about by confrontations between old and young, ins and outs, experts and laymen, and so forth, the greater the prospect that significant parts of our heritage can be adapted to new situations and preserved.

Notes

1 See chapter VIII, "Of the Extension of the Suffrage" in his *Representative Government* (1861), reprinted in Mill, *Utilitarianism, Liberty and Representative Government* (New York: Everyman's Library, E. P. Dutton, 1951), pp. 371–393.

2 See Taylor, "Freedom and Authority on the Campus," chapter 23 in Nevitt Sanford (ed.), *The American College* (New York: John Wiley), pp. 774–804.

More About Columbia

Dotson Rader

---

*Having presented two supporters of participatory democracy in the
university, we now turn to two opponents. The first is another student
viewpoint—that of a participant in the unrest at Columbia in May 1968.
The author concludes that participatory democracy under Hayden's
general direction turned out to be rather undemocratic in practice. Notice
in particular the pressures for conformity that Rader felt he detected.*

There have been so many questions about my May 11 report on the
"disturbances" at Columbia University, some amplification is called for.

I entered Mathematics Hall at the university a few hours after the
building had been seized by 30 students, led by Tom Hayden, at one
o'clock Friday morning, April 26. I remained inside the building as part of
the commune of 200 demonstrators until the police bust on the following
Tuesday morning. Except for the pro-SDS Liberation News Service, no
press was allowed inside. While this prohibition was violated at one or
another of the liberated buildings, it was strictly enforced at Mathematics.

There were several reasons for barring the press, some legitimate, some
not. The radicals believed, perhaps with justification, that plainclothes
police would try to infiltrate the commune in the guise of reporters. Since
Math was the most radical of the five communes, everyone inside risked
retaliation from the administration and the police, especially students with
previous disciplinary records. For this reason it was felt that the police and
persons from the Dean's office should be prevented from taking names and
pictures of the students. All of us faced arrest. Some of us, the pre-profes-
sional students, particularly those in pre-law, had placed our careers in
jeopardy. The protesting foreign students could be deported.

Secondly, some members of SDS have a fanatical distrust of the press.
Their suspicion is based in part on the assumption that in America the
press functions as a propaganda organ for the Capitalist Establishment.
They charge that it is corporate imperialist in its bias, suppressive and
distorted in its effect. During the "liberation" *The New York Times'*

From Dotson Rader, "More About Columbia," *The New Republic* (June 8,
1968), pp. 23–25. Reprinted by permission of *The New Republic*. Copyright © 1969
by Harrison-Blaine of New Jersey, Inc.

reporting of the events at Columbia was continually held up to us as evidence of the prejudice of the liberal press. In the case of the *Times*, the inaccuracies seemed more sinister because of the presence of its publisher on the University Board of Trustees.

But the attempt to prevent the circulation of any independent (*i.e.* non-SDS) account of the life in the commune went beyond simply barring the press. The ban applied to the students in the building. Whenever I attempted to write, self-appointed censors grabbed the offending material from my hands, usually with the rhetorical question, "Who do you work for, motherfucker?" At first I found these interruptions only irritating. Later, when the intimidation went beyond verbal admonishments, I saw them as part of a kind of Stalinist approach to the truth that many of the radicals embraced. Nothing was to be written that did not conform with the immediate demands of the "revolution." Every word had to follow the SDS line.

To write the article on the rebellion which appeared in these pages, I liberated a typewriter from one of the offices, climbed into the attic of Math, sat on a gas drum and wrote. This was necessary to escape constant surveillance in the commune.

After the article appeared I was told by members of the Steering Committee that I had to clear anything written about the commune with them. This apparently had been the policy from the beginning. If I were not willing to put myself under revolutionary discipline I could look forward to having my "revisionist (*i.e.* counterrevolutionary) head busted."

SDS is concerned about the kind of reports that come out, because for them the commune is a prototype of the revolutionary social structure they hope to establish. The word commune is used because of its historical antecedent—the Paris Commune of 1848—and because it takes its basic social organization and much of its style from the type of communal living developed by the hippies. More importantly, the commune is significant as propaganda. It seems to offer young people the promise of functioning within an order based upon Tom Hayden's "participatory democracy." And that, when compared to the straight world most young people know— draft boards, academic bosses, the rat race of business—is a happy prospect.

As it worked inside Mathematics, where Hayden was in charge, participatory democracy was much like a town meeting where a highly organized minority, in firm agreement on objectives, is able to cow the unorganized, apolitical majority into acting against its better judgment. Most of the students in Math were politically undereducated; they had never experienced anything comparable; they were confused and easily led. In Math one had a tendency to vote for radical motions, because the only information one received came from the Steering Committee. It was often untrue. If the quality of political life depends on the information the voters receive about the issues, then ours was a poor experiment in democracy.

In addition to receiving precensored information, we were also kept on a radical course by the fear of being labeled fascist. The mildest statement suggesting a moderation in the demands of the rebellion, especially on the question of amnesty for the six SDS leaders where a hard line was insisted upon, brought charges of revisionist tendencies.

Because we were denied access to independent information, and because we were psychologically vulnerable to being led by the most radical among us (we were isolated from the outside world, expecting a police attack at any time, warned continually to guard against being corrupted by the faculty) our participatory democracy was largely nominal.

An example of the tactic used by the radicals to insure unanimity in the commune came on Sunday afternoon. Earlier in the day the Steering Committee announced that it had broken off negotiations with the Ad Hoc Faculty Group. The usual reasons were given: the faculty was selling out, trying to use the students, stalling to give the administration more time. Nevertheless, over the Steering Committee's strong objections, the commune passed a resolution instructing it immediately to reopen talks with the faculty. This was seen as a weakening of resolve in the commune, and the Steering Committee acted to counter it. It made a dramatic statement that the police bust would come before nightfall. That was completely false, but there were no more calls for moderation.

The radicals reacted in much the same fashion to public suggestions that there had been planning of the Columbia rebellion prior to the event. Those of us who attended the SDS regional meeting at Princeton University (NR, Dec. 9, 1967) knew that the tactics to be used to polarize universities were discussed in detail in the workshop on Campus Organization: Techniques and Strategy. At that meeting the subject of confrontation politics, as applied to a university situation, was analyzed. Various tactics, from the seizure of buildings and the taking of hostages to the disruption of classes and student strikes, were debated. The point of confrontation is to place the administration in the position of having to use great force against its students, hopefully with some blood spilled, so as to polarize the liberal academic community over the use of force itself. That is precisely what happened at Columbia. We also knew, through conversations with members of the Steering Committee, of the SDS caucus at the NSA conference in College Park, Maryland. There the question of SDS's worsening position at Columbia—six of its leaders, including Mark Rudd, faced expulsion and its charter was in danger of being revoked—was discussed. At that meeting a decision, later confirmed in a meeting of the Columbia SDS chapter, was made to attempt a confrontation with the administration in April. There, too, the means were determined: the seizure of university buildings.

The original plan was to take Low Library on Tuesday, April 23. But when the students returned to campus, after scuffling with the police in Morningside Park in protest over the gym construction, they discovered that the university had anticipated them and closed Low Library. The students were in a defiant mood. One of their number, Freddy Wilson, a sophomore, had been arrested in the park. It was then that Rudd made a hurried change of plans and shouted: "They've taken one of ours. Let's take one of theirs! Let's take Hamilton Hall!" They did precisely that.

While there was no conspiracy behind the Columbia rebellion, not as the word is commonly used, there was agreement on the ends and tactics to be used and on the approximate time for the confrontation. SDS has tried to deny the fact of planning, because it conflicts with its official version of the rebellion: that it was a spontaneous outpouring of anger on the part of the majority of students—black and white—against racism, bureaucratic arrogance, and war research at Columbia. This is not the whole truth.

One month before the rebellion the Progressive Labor Party, in coordination with SDS, began in earnest to organize tenants in Columbia-owned buildings to the end that a tenants' strike be called in support of the students. As usual with Progressive Labor projects, the strike never quite came off, its only success being a short-lived seizure of one Columbia-owned tenement by the tenants, with student support, on May 18. In addition, SDS sought the support of the National Mobilization Committee to End the War in Vietnam, a Chicago-based organization with which Tom Hayden is intimately involved. The timing of the Columbia rebellion was coordinated with the antiwar protests. On Saturday, April 27, we were told that a large contingent of the peace demonstrators would march from Central Park up Broadway to Columbia and mass at the gates in support of the strike. Rudd notified the commune that they could expect "around 15,000 marchers." They never appeared. What did appear were several hundred blacks who paused at the gates on their way from Harlem to the Central Park rally downtown.

The effort to get the physical cooperation of off-campus organizations, from CORE and the Black Nationalists to the National Mobilization Committee, was made in order to apply the maximum pressure possible on the administration. It was also done to present the rebellion not as simply a student disturbance but as a full-scale revolt with wide nonuniversity, community support. With opposition to the Institute for Defense Analyses as one of the strike's six issues, the students hoped to rally antiwar liberals who would not otherwise support them. With the issue of the gym, the students tried to expose the whole matter of Columbia's incredibly bad relations with West Harlem, and thus get the backing of civil rights liberals and the black community. It is very difficult to oppose students who are protesting in support of such good causes, especially if you are a left-liberal faculty member who does not like the administration to begin with.

The disruptions will continue at Columbia. SDS will try to uncover new issues on which to build a new coalition, since the old one is getting rather tired of SDS's militancy. The administration will continue to act stupidly, arrogantly, belatedly, playing, as usual, into the hands of SDS. Hayden said, "The only thing we can count on absolutely in this situation is the incompetence of Kirk and Truman." He was right. Twenty-five students have received notices to appear before the administration to answer charges resulting from the rebellion. Four have already been suspended without a hearing. There will be more suspensions. Another 177 persons were arrested early on May 22, as police "swept through the university grounds clubbing, kicking and punching student protesters who flung back rocks, taunts and obscenities" (New York Times, May 23).

The students have responded with two more assaults on university buildings, occupying Hamilton Hall again for a time. They have promised more demonstrations and threatened to disrupt the university's commencement on June 4. The commencement, which is traditionally held outdoors on South Field, will take place instead inside a heavily guarded Cathedral of St. John the Divine, without an address by President Grayson Kirk. SDS will demonstrate outside the building, attempt to organize graduating seniors to disrupt the ceremony inside and, if all else fails, call in bomb threats to the police.

The number of students radicalized by the rebellion continues to grow. Their determination is strong, their patience seemingly unlimited. It will not be until the resignation of Grayson Kirk, probably before November, and the installation of a new president, that Columbia will see the beginning of the end of the rebellion. It will not be until the trustees begin the formal restructuring of the university that the future of Columbia will be clear.

Student Power: The Rhetoric and the Possibilities

Charles Frankel

In the following selection, Charles Frankel opposes any extreme form of "student power." He feels that there are limits, set by the requirements of academic freedom among other things, which should not be exceeded. Of particular interest are his contention that students already have considerable influence and his quite unusual portrayal of the inner workings of the university. This view challenges completely the working model of the university developed by student and faculty radicals and partly reflected in the previous articles by Hayden and Bay.

It has finally come to be accepted that American colleges and universities are in trouble. The questions about them mount in number: Who is to blame for the disruptions and ugly incidents that have left American campuses disturbed? Is it the students? The administrations? The police? Why are the young so angry, and what do they want anyway? Why are the old so dim-witted, and why do they resist change and progress? But the answers to these questions will not tell us what is wrong with American higher education, or what principles should be employed in setting about to improve it.

No reforms can be discussed intelligently unless we take the phrases that are now dominating discussion—"student rights," "student power," "participation," "democracy," "a relevant education," and all the rest— and ask seriously what they mean, and what assumptions are behind them. For it is astonishing how little genuine public discussion there has been of such matters and how little of what has been said has gone beneath the surface of slogan and generality. People have used words to show on which side of the barricades their loyalties lie. But little has been said that suggests that possibly the answers do not all fall neatly on one side of the fence or the other. It is remarkable how many learned men there are, men who enjoy the ambiguities of John Donne's poetry or who spend their lives

---

From Charles Frankel, "Student Power: The Rhetoric and the Possibilities," an article originally appearing in *Saturday Review* (November 2, 1968), pp. 23–25, 73; copyright 1968 Saturday Review, Inc. Based on material drawn from *Education and the Barricades* by Charles Frankel, copyright © 1968 by the author and reprinted by permission of W. W. Norton and Company, Inc.

refining the refinements of Wittgenstein's philosophy, who nevertheless sail into the middle of social controversies with all their answers ready and all their powers of qualified judgment put aside.

Designing a university is not, after all, a form of action-painting. Nor is it a matter of setting forth broad general principles and reasoning deductively from them, so that one is invariably in favor of "student power" or opposed to it, on the side of "university democracy" or against it. General principles are relevant to what one thinks about such matters, but specific problems differ, and the application of these general principles, in consequence, cannot always be the same.

The obvious place to begin is with the concept of "student power." What does the phrase mean? Before we talk about the reforms for which the phrase stands, we should recognize that it also gives a good description of a fact that has long existed. This fact is that students are not only the objects of education, but its principal instruments. An institution and its faculty can provide facilities, stimulation, some guidance and orientation, a sense of standards and of models to emulate. But the primary environment for the student is other students. They set the pace for one another; they have more to do than any other group in the university with what the student pays attention to from day to day; they do much of the teaching that counts.

Moreover, students also have great influence on the evolution of educational theory and practice. They have not, in the past, voted on curricula or met with the faculty in formal sessions. Just the same, they have had an effect—like the effect of the climate—on curriculum, the character of the teaching staff, the rules of campus life, and the composition of future student bodies. General education was for a long time, for example, an exciting and viable part of the curricula of many undergraduate institutions. Increasingly, over the past decade or so, there have been countercurrents. And the largest reason has been that students have changed. They come to college differently and better prepared than their predecessors, or with more highly developed interests in specializing, or with greater impatience to get on to vocationally useful subjects. The colleges have responded to these new attitudes because inattention or resistance in the classroom requires a response.

The power that students have should not, of course, be exaggerated. It works slowly. It is small comfort to a young man or woman to know that, four or five years after he or she has left the university, the dear, slow thing will catch on and mend its ways. And not only is the power that students have slow in achieving an effect, but it is limited. Other sources of power and influence work on a university, as they should, and students do not get everything they want, even slowly. Yet the influence of students, limited though it may be, is nevertheless real and significant. If one has a long enough time-span in mind, students exercise an influence as large as any other group's in bringing about alterations in higher education.

Thus, the question raised by present demands for student power is not really whether students should finally be given the right to say something about what happens to them. It is whether it would be educationally desirable to create arrangements permitting students to participate more visibly and formally in the making of educational decisions. Considered as a general proposition, there can be little doubt, I think, that this is the direction in which change should proceed.

The most important reasons are drawn from educational and democratic theory. If people have some power over the way in which they live and work, they have more interest in their experience, and they learn more from it. If they have some power, they tend to become more responsible. They are more likely to make the connections between ideas and action, rhetoric and reality, that are at once the tests and the pleasures of the moral life. These propositions have been tried in other fields and found to have a substantial amount of truth in them. They have not been tried to the extent that they could be in higher education.

But these are generalities. They tell us about a desirable direction of change. They do not tell us how far the change should go, or if there are any areas in which it should not take place at all. When we get down to brass tacks, what can "student power" mean?

Should students, for example, participate in the selection and promotion of members of the faculty? When they think a good teacher has been fired, they certainly have a right to complain. When faculty members treat them as odd and anonymous objects, to be avoided whenever possible, they have a right to demand the services for which they or the community are paying. Students do not have, in most American universities, the ways and means to assert these rights in an effective and orderly fashion. That situation requires repair.

But students nevertheless cannot have a formal role in the selection of faculty. The most important reason is that this would be incompatible with academic freedom. It exposes the teacher to intimidation. Academic freedom is the product of a long and difficult struggle. It has been achieved by excluding all groups but professors from any formal power over what goes on in the classroom. The exclusion applies to administrators, trustees, legislators, parents, alumni, and the public. There are questions that can be asked about academic freedom—about its range and extent, about mis-interpretations of it, about departures from it that have been defended in its name—but there are no reasons for reconsidering the role of students in relation to it. There is nothing about students to justify giving them power no other group has.

Students have no common professional perspective or shared occupational interest in academic freedom. Judging from the record, numbers of them are subject to the same bouts of intolerance in the face of upsetting ideas that affect bankers or legislators. A wise faculty and administration will do well to try to find out what student opinions about teachers are.

But they had better conduct the canvass informally and discreetly. Teaching is a professional relationship, not a popularity contest. To invite students to participate in the selection or promotion of their teachers is to create a relationship in the classroom inappropriate to teaching.

Should students have the right to demand the introduction of certain courses? Again, there are limits. The fact that students want a course is a reason to consider giving it. But it is not, by itself, a sufficient reason. There may be nobody competent to teach the course. It may be a non-course—an excuse for bull sessions on company time, with no literature worth studying and no tradition of discourse and inquiry to hold things in bounds. Besides, since university budgets have been known to be limited, there is always the disagreeable possibility that the introduction of a new course requires the dropping of an old one. A judgment of comparative worth therefore has to be made. Students are not the right jury to make such a judgment.

Yet these arguments merely define the limits of student power. They do not argue against it. Students have things to teach their teachers. And there are invaluable things they can learn about their education, about universities, about themselves, from taking part in the examination, with their teachers, of the design of their education. The entire spirit within an institution of learning is likely to be better if there is a sense within it that its members are constantly cooperating in the appraisal of what it is doing. There ought to be regular, established procedures for consultation between faculties and student bodies. They should provide for the genuine, serious, and continuing examination of curriculum—a process incompatible with mass meetings, demonstrations, and sloganeering. It should not be expected that all student recommendations be accepted, but it should be expected that the consideration of students' points of view will not be merely pro forma.

Such arrangements would have a number of merits, not least among them the possibility that a myth generally accepted by students would finally be exploded. Students might discover that on many issues, particularly those directly related to courses and curriculum, it is not professors but deans and presidents who are their natural allies. By and large, judging from my own experience, it is members of the faculty, and not administrators, who are the opponents of educational reforms. This is not because deans and presidents are naturally more liberal. It is simply because most men's recognition of the need for reform grows in direct proportion to the distance of the proposed reform from their own territory. If students are talking about the reform of the curriculum, they will probably find more sympathy among deans, who don't work in classrooms. If students have complaints about the food served in dining halls, they will probably find the most sympathetic listeners, on the other hand, among members of the faculty. Professors don't have to balance the budget or hire the cooks.

But what about the largest single demand implicit in slogans such as "student power" and "university democracy"? This is the claim that faculty and students ought to share with trustees and administrators, or take over altogether, the powers which these latter groups have hitherto exercised alone. The claim is a political one. Its justification, if it has any, is the general one that democratic principles call for the establishment of student power in higher education. Is this what "democratic principles" do entail? Indeed, do they apply to institutions of learning? Are colleges and universities sufficiently like cities or national governments, or unions or factories, to justify the use of the same political arguments in relation to them?

There is a fundamental respect in which the administrators of a university are in a different position from the managers of a company. The university administrators cannot create a total plan of work, define jobs within it, and then assign individual workers to them. Of course, now that labor unions have the power they have, managers cannot do this as easily as they once could either. But the difference between their position and that of university administrators is still very great. The product of a factory is a corporate product to which individuals contribute. The product of a university is many separate, individual products, for which the corporate arrangements provide protection and support, but for which the individuals have basic responsibility.

Most of the odd, novel, or shocking things that are being said about the condition of students in the United States today, and many of the discussions taking place about the reallocation of powers within universities, come from the application of loose and unexamined analogies, drawn from other types of social organization, to the structure of institutions of learning. A university is at once a highly individualistic and unavoidably hierarchical human organization. It is based on the premise that some people know more than other people, and that it cannot perform its tasks effectively unless these gradations in knowledge are recognized in its form of government.

This is not an abuse of "democracy." The right of a citizen of the larger society to vote just as the next man can, without regard to hierarchy, is based on the premise that, where the major policies of the state are concerned, where the nature of what is good for society is at issue, only extreme inadequacies, like illiteracy or a criminal record, are disqualifying. The basic reason for this view is that there are no reasonably defensible general procedures by which the citizenry can be divided into the class of those who know enough to have an opinion worth counting or an interest worth expressing, and the class of those who don't.

In contrast, while universities are democratic organizations in the sense that individuals have a broad array of personal rights within them, and that there is a play of opinion inside them which has a massive effect on their evolution, they are not democratic organizations in the sense that majority rule applies to them. For within a university there are acceptable procedures by which people can be graded in accordance with their competence, and grading people in this way is essential to the conduct of the university's special business. The egalitarian ideal does not apply across the board in universities any more than it does in any other field where *skill* is the essence of the issue. To suggest that it should apply is to make hash of the idea of learning. If there is a case to be made for student participation in the higher reaches of university government, therefore, it is a case that is not based upon *rights*, but upon considerations of good educational and administrative practice.

Does this imply that the government of colleges and universities by trustees is a good system? No; but it helps to put this system in perspective. The case which is generally presented against trustee control of universities mixes truths with exaggerations. It is true that most trustees tend to be preoccupied with other matters than education, that they are inaccessible to teachers and students, and that a dispiriting number of them have reached an age and station in life calculated to protect them against fresh ideas. It is not surprising, therefore, that professors and students are sparing in the confidence they lavish on trustees. The government of American universities by boards of trustees is not an example of government by the consent of the governed.

However, neither is it an example of tyranny. The powers of trustees are severely limited by custom and law, and by the realities of a university. In any well established university, trustees normally leave educational decisions to the faculty. One of their primary educational functions, indeed, is simply to provide the educational community of the university—its students and faculty—with protective insulation. The trustees throw their mantle of influence and respectability around it, deflecting and absorbing criticisms and denunciations, and thus guarding the community's freedom. Indeed, it is doubtful that faculties and student bodies could by themselves, in many parts of the country, and without the help of trustees, successfully defend their autonomy, even assuming that their economic problems could be solved. It is odd that trustees should be attacked as though their presence was in contravention of academic freedom. Their presence is usually a condition for it.

Still, it can be asked whether this form of government is the best form for a college or university. Trustees (or regents) do make educational decisions, even if most of these are only indirect. They allocate resources, do more for one field of learning than for another, and make arrangements affecting the relation of the university to the larger society which affect the daily lives of teachers and students. Would it not be better if trustees continued to do their work of finding the money, but surrendered the other powers they exercise to the people who really constitute the university—namely, its students and teachers? Obviously, it is doubtful that many trustees would accept this proposal that they should supply the money but keep quiet about the way it is used. Just to see where the argument goes, however, let us imagine that trustees have a capacity for self-immolation not conspicuous in most human beings. Would it be a good thing for them to retire from the scene?

Not entirely. They are the buffers of the university against external pressures. As we have seen, an educational institution requires such protection. Most organizations, furthermore, benefit from having a lay group of critics with deep commitments to them, who are nevertheless not part of their daily operations. In addition, since universities must maintain relations with the surrounding society, they require people on their board of governors who have interests and experience in that society. And it is always well to remember that though education, like the law, is in part a professional business, it is also everybody's business. If students have a stake in what happens to them, by the same token, so do their parents and so do lay members of the community. In courts of law, juries are not composed of professional lawyers. On the university scene, the outsider, though he should not have as decisive a place as a juror has, also deserves to be represented.

Yet these same considerations call for change in the composition of most boards of trustees. They call, equally clearly, for changes in the manner in which they communicate with the communities they govern. Boards of trustees ought to have more younger people on them, and poorer people. They ought to have recent graduates, not only older ones. They ought to have people who have not yet arrived, not only those swollen with success. The surrounding neighborhood should, if possible, be represented. That is not always easy to arrange because there are so often disagreements about who is "representative" of whom. But if it can be done without creating quarrels that did not exist before, then it should be done. And students and faculty members either should be represented on the board or assured of regular consultation with it.

The participation of students in the supreme governing bodies of a university undoubtedly raises equally subtle issues. Students are inexperienced. They are present on a campus for only a short period, and could serve on committees and boards for only a shorter period. It takes time, on most boards and committees, before new members learn enough to become genuinely useful. Furthermore, student generations change in their styles and opinions and sometimes very quickly. Students, therefore, bring an element of discontinuity, a shortened perspective, and sometimes a short fuse, into the consideration of matters of policy. In educational institutions particularly, continuity of perspective and some sense of the time-dimension are essential.

Nevertheless, the idea is worth experimentation, even though the number of students who belong to a board, or who sit with it when certain issues are discussed, should probably be small. There is little question, apart from the formalities of representation on a board of trustees, that machinery for regular face-to-face meetings between students and trustees is desirable. Discontinuity in policy is dangerous, but so is automatic, thoughtless continuity. The long view is estimable, but impatience is useful too. And if inexperience is a handicap, so is experience: it dulls one to novelty. Trustees could learn things from students that they will never learn from administrators or other trustees.

In the end, we are discussing not matters of right and justice, but matters of political wisdom. Trustees will not know what they should know unless they mix with the people who can tell them. The community they govern will not understand why the trustees have made the decisions they have, and will not have confidence in these decisions, unless it has its own trusted emissaries to keep it in touch with the board. Faulty communication is the heart of the political problem in the American universities that are having trouble today. Demands for "student power" and "faculty power," so interpreted, are more than justifiable.

Ships That Pass in the Night

Ronald Hilton

Many Latin American universities have long had a much higher degree of institutionalized student participation than exists anywhere in the United States. Ronald Hilton here reviews this fact and compares trends in the United States and Latin America indicating that the two are headed in opposite directions.

Where are American universities headed? They are being Latin Americanized. Where are Latin American universities headed? They are being Americanized.

After graduating from Oxford University, I undertook as a modern version of the Grand Tour a methodical plan of graduate study in each of the major countries of the Western world, spending in the course of this program two years (1934–36) in Madrid and two years (1937–39) at Berkeley as a Commonwealth Fund Fellow. In recent years I have visited practically every university in Latin America several times; their traditional structure has been modified by the influence of France, Germany and now the United States, but it is still essentially Spanish. Quite unlike that of Spain and Spanish America, the U.S. university system took on its peculiar form because unconsciously, or sometimes consciously, it imitated the structure of our business corporations. I received, therefore, a sharp impression of the dissimilarity between Spanish and U.S. universities.

One of my first experiences at the University of Madrid was the crisis (this was at the beginning of the Civil War) between the university and the government when students used the Faculty of Medicine to shoot it out with the police. A Civil Guard was killed (usually the students were the victims of these affrays), and the monarchist paper A.B.C. put the tear-jerking caption "Civil Guards also have mothers!" under photographs of the dead member of the elite police. Life at the university college known as the Residencia de Estudiantes was frustrating. The students at one faculty or another would declare a strike. We would learn of it when we went down to breakfast, and the students would stay home all day, playing

From Ronald Hilton, "Ships That Pass in the Night," The Nation (August 28, 1967), pp. 145–148. Reprinted by permission of The Nation.

tennis, talking politics, occasionally doing a little work. They knew Spanish politics inside out, and I learned then that books, journals and newspapers are inadequate for the study of politics in Spanish-speaking countries. Only long hours of conversation open the gate to this fascinating field.

A graduate student in law, a Communist who lived across from me in the Residencia, was killed in one of the battles fought in the university city. My best friend was a conservative who took refuge in the Uruguayan Embassy. When Franco entered Madrid in 1939, this man was released after three years of confinement, drafted into the Blue Legion to fight on Hitler's Eastern front, and died in the snows of Russia.

American universities provided a quite different kind of surprise. No American professor or student in the late 1930s would declare himself to be an "intellectual," a word common on the Madrid academic scene. Professors were described as "employees of the university"; I humbly find this normal now after thirty years, but then it seemed an outrageous affront to the "intellectuals." On the day I arrived in New York, a professor jumped from a skyscraper window, following a disagreement with his university administration. I can understand that too now, but at the time I wondered how universities could possibly have administrations so powerful as to drive the faculty to suicide. In fact, the expression, "university administration," meant little to me; in Europe no such thing really existed. An American businessman whom I met had been a university dean; when I asked why he had left academic life, he answered that he couldn't stand the competition. The universities I visited were efficiently run. The administration ran the corporation; the faculty was busy with research which would bring prestige, promotion and salary increases; the students had a good time and studied enough to acquire the diploma that would bring them, if not prestige, at least a job. Long, fascinating conversations about politics would have interfered with the tedious job of equipping oneself for the struggle for existence in a competitive society.

Since World War II a curious mutual shift has been taking place. Dissatisfied with the inhumanity of the American academic structure, the liberals among the faculty and students have pointed to certain distasteful features of our university system and, in trying to remedy them, have been pushing our universities toward precisely the same solution which the Spanish-American universities found under the impact of the liberalizing movement. Meanwhile, upset by the inefficiency of the liberal university system, the conservatives, the military, the Roman Catholic Church and North American business interests have been urging or even forcing Latin American universities to adopt the traditional structure of U.S. universities. To speed the process, they have established new universities which, for want of a better term, we shall call the "Americanized" universities. Latin American intellectuals are viscerally opposed to the Americanization of their universities, but the money and power behind this movement are hard to resist. Moreover, Latin Americans desperately want their countries to be successful, and since a successful country has as an integral part a successful university system, they are willing to try U.S. academic methods. Few Latin Americans, even those who dislike Americanization, stop to analyze the implications of the U.S. system of higher education. Conversely, very few Americans realize that their universities are being Latin Americanized. The two systems are, therefore, like ships passing in the night. Perhaps a little ship-to-ship conversation would be a good thing, since the seas are uncharted. What are the issues involved?

Faculty and students in the United States are no longer willing to be controlled, through the boards of trustees, by the power elite. They want a say in the conduct of the university's affairs on the highest level. Most Latin American universities have achieved this, usually with a tripartite governing body drawn from the faculty, the alumni and the students. This system is blamed, rather unfairly, for the inefficiency of Latin American university administration. The Americanized universities employ U.S.-style boards of trustees on which the faculty and students have little, if any, representation. Usually a sop is offered in the form of a committee made up of administration, faculty and students, which airs its views but has no real power. It is doubtful that this device will much longer appease the demands of the faculty and students, who want to have their hands on the legal controls of the university. There have not yet been demands for the tripartite system used in Latin America, but they may come later.

In Latin America the Córdoba university reforms of 1917 brought back the medieval democratic system by which university authorities, especially the rector (i.e., president) and the deans are elected by the faculty and students. Faculty members present themselves as candidates, make speeches expounding their programs, and the victorious candidate takes office for a stipulated term. Sometimes the elections are as colorful as a U.S. political convention. By contrast, our university presidents have traditionally been appointed for an unlimited term by the boards of trustees, which can dismiss them at will. There are now demands that the faculty be guaranteed at least some say in the selection of a president. Moreover, academic elections in the United States have been pretty much a formality. They are elections for committees, not for executive posts; candidates do not present themselves, and those elected do not have to state their program. It is now proposed that the elections acquire some reality, that there be effective candidates, and that they be required to state their platforms. Meanwhile, the Americanized universities in Latin America are moving toward the traditional U.S. system; the trustees appoint the rector, who in turn appoints the deans. The circus of elections is abolished.

American university campuses have had no special legal status. In Spanish-speaking countries, university buildings have for centuries been as sacrosanct as the churches, where anyone fleeing from the law could seek asylum. In front of some old Spanish university buildings are stone pillars connected by a chain, beyond which the police could not pass. The tradition of barring police from a university has allowed students in Latin America to barricade themselves inside university buildings and allegedly to convert them into revolutionary barracks. The Americanization of Latin American universities has been accompanied by a flouting of this tradition. When Venezuelan President Leoni recently sent troops into the Central University of Caracas, it did not occur to him that he was acting like the military governments of Argentina and Brazil, which democratic Venezuela has formally denounced. In the United States the reverse trend is perceptible. The presence of the state police on the Berkeley campus has become a major issue, and in a TV interview on February 5 former President Clark Kerr of the University of California said that the assignment of outside police to various campuses had aggravated student unrest. There are demands that university police take care of campus problems, the feeling being that once the campuses are under the thumb of the regular police, academic freedom will vanish. It was precisely this fear that made Latin American universities challenge the right of the government police to enter university buildings.

In the past, most of our great universities were supported by tuition. Since World War II there have been, even in New England and in New York State, moves to provide free higher education on a scale hitherto unknown in the world. Generous California is now wondering how it can afford to maintain its costly state university and college systems, but Governor Reagan's proposal to introduce tuition is generally regarded as a step backward. In Latin America, free university education has been the rule, but in fact the governments have usually been unable or unwilling to pay for a modern university system. Salaries have been low, and funds for libraries and equipment insufficient. The Americanized universities charge tuition and in many cases, as at the Universidad de los Andes in Bogota, offer fair salaries and provide relatively good facilities. The move to introduce tuition would undoubtedly spread were university authorities not afraid of rioting students who will seize and burn buses if fares are raised a cent. Caught in a financial vise, public Latin American universities stress "autonomy," i.e., the state should provide the funds but otherwise not intervene in the affairs of the universities. This cherished autonomy, now being eroded in Latin America, is essentially what the Berkeley liberals demand.

Until now, few Latin American professors have been engaged full time. Most were active in public affairs or supplemented their incomes with outside jobs. Such combinations of activities have been unusual in the United States, but are so no longer. In Latin America faculty absenteeism and lack of concentration on academic duties have been sharply criticized, and U.S. foundations are unwilling to support institutions which do not have a solid core of full-time teachers. Many Latin American administrators claim that their aim is to have a completely full-time faculty. The goal is remote, but it is the direction in which Latin American universities are moving.

The American universities traditionally had church affiliations. However, over the past half century universities associated with Protestant churches have been secularized, and just in the last year there has been a surprising movement to secularize Roman Catholic universities. The reason stated is that higher education is incompatible with Church control; it is also probably feared that control of higher education may embarrass the Church, as for example in the case of the faculty strike at St. John's University. Latin America in modern times has feared such control and has kept higher education separate from the Church. The liberal university movement in Spain got its start in the 19th century from the refusal of a group of professors to swear to support Catholic doctrine—a religious version of the loyalty oath. Now the Latin American power elite and U.S. business interests support Americanized universities controlled by the Roman Catholic Church, which is looked upon as a bulwark against communism. The Creole Foundation, belonging to a subsidiary of the Standard Oil Company, refuses to support the Central University in Caracas but is giving massive aid to the Catholic University. In March, 1967, Episcopal Bishop James A. Pike charged in *Playboy* magazine that the Jesuits had heavy investments in Creole Petroleum. The Jesuits have traditionally been regarded as the allies, and indeed the agents, of conservative ruling groups. Hence they are constitutionally banned from Mexico, but nevertheless operate the Universidad Iberoamericana with the support of commercial companies. In Guadalajara the business community, supported by the U.S. State Department and U.S. foundations, has been promoting the Catholic university to offset the state university, looked upon as "Socialist." In brief, while in the United States there has been a broad move toward the secularization of higher education, in Latin America the trend has been toward clericalization. While in the United States a liberal Supreme Court has been pushing the separation of church and state in education, the thrust of U.S. influence in Latin America has been to strengthen the hand of the Roman Catholic Church in university affairs. The fact that Catholic universities employ some Protestants and Jews should not mislead us as to the focus of power. It must be said that some Catholic universities do an excellent job and that they are usually willing to cooperate with secular, Protestant and Jewish organizations in a way that would have been inconceivable two decades ago. Unfortunately, the death of Pope John XXIII has brought a slight setback in this cordiality.

Thus, American universities are moving toward the position formerly held by Latin American universities, while these are being pushed into "Americanization." This march and countermarch reflect cultural changes. Previously, American faculty and students stuck to their academic business; they did not demonstrate or strike for political reasons. Now alienation from the power elite has produced every form of social protest on our campuses except armed rebellion. In a conscienceless social structure, our academicians have come to regard themselves as the conscience of the nation. That has traditionally been the stance of Latin American intellectuals, but in the Americanized universities of Latin America faculty and students are being told, quite forcefully, that they must concentrate on being good professionals and forget the illusion that they are the conscience of society. The difference is that between the conservative and progressive viewpoints. The managerial class wants universities to turn out competent technicians with a veneer of culture, not independent citizens who will seriously question the origin of power and wealth. In our universities the progressives have become more aggressive; in Latin America they are being weakened or entirely ousted, with the active collusion of U.S. agencies. The Americans who are taking part in what might be called "Operation Latin American University" justify their actions by saying that the liberals who held power in the universities were hostile to the United States and to U.S. business, and had allowed the universities to become chaotic and ineffective. What Latin America needs, the Americans argue, is not campus politicians but qualified engineers and business administrators.

The issue thus enters the domain of foreign policy. What might fairly be called the Reagan viewpoint dominates U.S. influence and aid programs in Latin American education. It is evident in such things as the creation of American-style schools of business, which will turn out U.S.-style business executives. Evident in this emphasis is a curious double standard. We are trying to build academic bridges with the USSR, and government agencies have been inviting a stream of Russian specialists to our campuses. But when a Latin American university enters into relations with the USSR, it is likely to be blacklisted by the United States. When one Latin American university invited some Russian scientists to come as visiting professors, tension between the American Embassy and the university became intolerable, and the rector resigned to lead a leftist political party.

We may be playing with fire. By supporting Roman Catholic universities, we may be unwittingly fanning anti-clericalism, and our university policy generally may become as popular as Governor Reagan's in California. We should study the virulent anti-Americanism of Fidel Castro's Foreign Minister Raúl Roa, an academician who had even been the beneficiary of U.S. largess. The University of Havana was a focal point of the hostility to the academic Americanization described in this article. Without skill and luck our generosity may, as the Spanish say, be *contraproducente*—which seems to be the origin of our neologism "counterproductive." As our two academic ships pass in the night, they could ask each other, "Is this trip worth while?" The trouble is that neither the captains nor the crews seem to know where they are going.

Chapter Six

Economic Institutions
—Workers' Control?

Power to the workers! Since the early nineteenth century, many have argued that because our work fills nearly half our waking lives and shapes our material and psychological existence, the workplace is an obvious context for participatory democracy. Since the decline of the Industrial Workers of the World ("Wobblies"), American unionism has differed from that of continental Europe in its suspicion of workers' participation in management and in its preference for confrontation of management from the outside. But the 1962 Port Huron Statement of the SDS proclaimed:

> . . . that the economic experience is so personally decisive that the individual must share in its full determination; . . . that the economy itself is of such social importance that its major resources and means of production should be open to democratic participation and subject to democratic regulation.[1]

Although workers' participation can concern other enterprises, such as the primarily agrarian *kibbutz* in Israel, our comments and selections focus on the modern industrial sector.

The core of the idea of industrial democracy has always been to increase rank-and-file employee influence in company management.[2] The concept can be further clarified by outlining its chief forms:

---

[1] In Kenneth M. Dolbeare, ed., *Directions in American Political Thought* (New York: Wiley, 1969), p. 472.

[2] Eric Rhenman, *Industrial Democracy and Industrial Management: A Critical Essay on the Possible Meanings and Implications of Industrial Democracy* (London: Tavistock Publications, Ltd., 1968), p. 3.

1. *Joint Consultation Councils.* Representatives of labor sit in a purely advisory capacity with management, often merely extending a form of collective bargaining into a hopefully cooperative rather than combative context. In Britain and the United States, such "partnerships" usually arise with government encouragement to foster industrial peace during wartime, but the committees tend to languish or die during peacetime because of worker apathy and union and management distrust.

2. *Co-Determination or Joint Decision-Making Councils.* Representatives of labor sit in an authoritative voting capacity, thus *sharing* in important managerial functions. This idea arose in Weimar Germany, but Hitler substituted his hierarchical leadership principle in industry. In postwar West Germany this system was developed and made legally mandatory for most industries, in part to curb capitalist owners and managers when nationalization was not politically feasible.

3. *Collective Contract Self-Regulation Councils.* This variant *separates* workers and management in the running of an enterprise, with the transfer of some significant and traditionally managerial functions to groups of workers. Broadly, the negotiated contract specifies what task management wants performed and what the total wage fund will be, while the workers themselves decide how the work is to be performed (e.g., work scheduling and norms) and how the collective piecework fund should be divided.

4. *Workers' Control or Self-Management Councils.* This model makes the workers "sovereign" in the enterprise; that is, they manage the whole enterprise or give binding instructions to professional managers. Practiced when revolutionary upheavals create a vacuum in industrial authority, varieties of institutionalized workers' control were advocated as late as 1920 by the anarcho-syndicalists, IWW, and Guild Socialists. Beyond rarely successful producers' cooperatives in the West, the best approximation of the model is the Yugoslav workers' council.

These sketches move from the lowest degree of worker participation in management to the highest. The reader can further explore these forms by consulting the bibliography section.

Consideration of the prospects and problems of industrial democracy should begin with the general goals. First, claims regarding its value as a learning experience suggest that it increases workers' understanding of the enterprise, fosters a sense of community, and overcomes job alienation. Second, it is asserted that the combination of that experience and their job expertise means worker participation would effect better decision-making, higher efficiency and productivity, and industrial peace. Although such claims seem plausible, there is no consensus among those who have studied the record of practice.

A variety of authoritative decisions are made within any enterprise, and all may affect the lives of workers to some degree. In view of the broad goals, what should be the specific functions to be performed by workers alone or shared with management? Next, problems arise in the area of size and composition of a workers' council. There is some tension between maximal diffusion of the learning experience—which could require large councils or rapid rotation of workers' representatives—and the requirements of effectiveness. Also, "workers" can be defined and classified in many ways, so questions arise regarding fair and responsive representation for all concerned, such as the growing ranks of "brain" workers. Also, can unions be related to the workers' council in such a way that union leaders will not view it as a threat to their survival?

Since management will resist encroachments on its "turf," will participating workers be able to overcome management's ploys of back-office bypassing, withholding crucial information, and misleading those untrained in the complexities of managerial matters?

Even if both workers and managers are satisfied with a system of workers' participation, will others be? Since consumers of a product or service have an interest in its timeliness, quality, quantity, and price, should this public be represented also? Will the owners (private shareholders or public) be satisfied? What are the implications of the new "Proxy Power" movement led by such men as Saul Alinsky and Ralph Nader?

Finally, how will the internally democratized enterprise relate to the larger economic and political system, including political parties affiliated with workers' groups? Workers' councils may attempt to federate and "go political" by assuming a territorial basis or seeking functional representation. Would such industrial democracy promote political democracy and make possible a "humanized" socialism without bureaucratic centralization?

Workers' Councils

Adolf Sturmthal

Although the Yugoslavs deny it, it seems that their fascinating socio-political system is inspired by anarchist theory, which sought to coordinate the future society by linking basic democratic units to higher levels: the commune (basic territorial unit like the county) and the syndicate (basic functional or economic unit like the industrial union in control of an enterprise). In the complex Yugoslav system of many levels of authority and many channels of representation, there has been no real democratization at the top, although considerable democratization has begun at the bottom. Most observers find the Yugoslav system attractive and interesting, but some have contended that the workers' councils do not represent real industrial democracy. Milovan Djilas has written:

> Workers' organizations under the Communist system are really "company" or "yellow" organizations of a special kind. The expression "of a special kind" is used here because the employer is at the same time the government and the exponent of the predominant ideology. . . .*

N. D. Popovic echoes Djilas in adding that self-management organs are merely a cynical effort of the privileged elite to dodge the blame for local grievances.** The reader can weigh Adolf Sturmthal's balanced account with the subsequent selections and judge for himself.

The Yugoslav experiment was partly the result of disillusionment with extreme central planning as it developed in the 1945–1950 period. This is understandable, for in one of those years the complete plan itself weighed one and a half tons!***

Reprinted by permission of the publishers from Adolf Sturmthal, Workers' Councils (Cambridge, Mass.: Harvard University Press), pp. 95–100, 108–113, 115–118. Copyright 1964 by the President and Fellows of Harvard College.

* The New Class: An Analysis of the Communist System (New York: Praeger, 1957), p. 110.

** Yugoslavia: The New Class in Crisis (Syracuse, N.Y.: Syracuse University Press, 1968), p. 33n.

*** David Riddell, "Social Self-Government: The Background of Theory and Practice in Yugoslav Socialism," British Journal of Sociology, Vol. 19 (1968), 52. This account provides a good summary of many empirical studies.

The bulk of Yugoslav business is state-owned. Only in small handicraft and some forms of domestic trade does private business survive. The official term for state-owned enterprises is "general social property." Employment in privately owned handicrafts is limited to five persons in addition to the owner's family. In farming, private owners are restricted to land not exceeding ten hectares of cultivated land; for larger families more may be allotted. Management of the state-owned enterprises on behalf of the community is in the hands of the "working collectivity" (the employees of the firm). Managerial activity is carried on by way of a workers' council, a managing board, and a director. Where there are fewer than 30 employees, the entire "working collectivity" performs the functions of the council, and only a managing board is elected.[1]

The council is the highest authority of the firm. It consists of 15 to 120 members according to its size, elected for a one-year term. By decree, the term of office was extended to two years in 1955 and 1958. The reason given is that a one-year term is too short to acquire the necessary experience. The election proceeds by universal equal suffrage and secret ballot, usually in the first four months of the year. Active and passive suffrage is held by all employees of the firm who have the right to vote in the general political elections. Elections are supervised by an electoral commission selected by the workers' council holding office when the elections are prepared. Lists of candidates are proposed by the trade union branch in the plant, or by at least one tenth of the workers and white-collar employees. In larger enterprises with several plants a joint council may be elected, with each plant choosing an election unit which then selects the members of the council. A proper representation of production workers as against the other workers and office employees must be established. The legality of the election procedure is supervised by the municipal people's committee and the district court.

The council—acting as a body, not as individuals—makes the fundamental decisions for the firm. It adopts the regulations and the plan of the enterprise, its wage and salary schedule, the budget, balance sheets, and profit and loss statements. It makes decisions on sale and purchase of assets, on credits for investment or working capital, on the distribution of that part of the earnings which the enterprise may dispose of, on expansion or the establishment of new plants, and so forth. Moreover, the council elects the managing board and supervises its activities.

The managing board consists of three to eleven members, depending upon the size of the firm, including the director who is a member ex officio. The board, too, acts only as a body, while the director has authority as a person. In general, the board translates the council's policy decisions into more concrete actions; it may also take decisions on current matters not within the province of the council. In particular, the board decides on managerial appointments in the firm and on individual complaints in the area of industrial relations against the director.

At least three quarters of the members of the board must be production workers; not more than one third of the board's members may be re-elected from among the members of the outgoing board; no one may be a member for more than two consecutive years. No such restriction on re-election exists for council members; the reason given for this difference is that the danger of bureaucratization is regarded as larger for the members of the managing board. To protect the members of the board against arbitrariness, they may not be given notice terminating their employment or transferred to another job without their consent during their tenure of office.

The director is the actual manager of the firm. He hires and fires, except for executives whose appointment and dismissal are in the hands of the managing board. He secures discipline within limits still to be discussed. He makes job assignments, and the like. In the area of industrial relations, however, his decisions can be appealed to the managing board.

He is at the same time part of the plant self-government and a representative of the community at large. He is, therefore, entitled to veto decisions of the workers' council or of the managing board which, in his view, contradict state regulations. In the case of continued disagreement, the people's committee of the municipality decides.

Ideally, therefore, all fundamental decisions are to be taken by the council and, in more detail, by the managing board. Day-to-day operations are entrusted to the director. Obviously, the borderline separating these classes of decisions is fluid. The precise location of the boundary will often depend on political circumstances external to the firm; in many other cases on the personalities involved, their competence in general, professional skill in particular, and last, but surely not least, their standing in the all-powerful party.

Theoretical Problems of the Council System. The theoretical model of a council-administered economy would provide for the councils to act as entrepreneurs within a framework to be set by central authority. This "model" gives rise to a number of fundamental issues:

(1) How to enforce observance of this framework by the enterprise;

(2) How to provide a yardstick for rational decision-making by the enterprise;

(3) How to provide incentives for the enterprise as a whole to serve economic progress;

(4) How to provide incentives for the employees to act efficiently.

In attempting to solve these problems, the Yugoslav policymakers were of course not free to choose among the technically available solutions. For political objectives, first the need to ensure the maintenance in power of the Communist Party under Tito's leadership imposed severe restrictions. Second, the regime aimed at high growth rates in the economy, especially in industry. Third, the distance in economic development and living standards between the relatively advanced and the backward regions of the country was to be reduced in order to unify the nation. The evolution of the economic policies of the country since 1950—reflected in changes in the status and functions of the councils—is the story of the regime's attempts to find under changing circumstances appropriate solutions for the fundamental issues within the area of politically tolerable choice.

Planning, in the new system, took on an entirely different meaning from the one in the earlier phase. While formerly the plan authority was concentrated in Belgrade, and all other agencies including the individual firms were merely subordinate administrative parts of this supreme decision-making authority, planning now is limited by decentralized decision-making. The new plan is characterized by its lack of detail,[2] while in the past it provided for every item of output in each plant. Relying on the market, the new system tends to avoid as far as possible the use of direct controls. Price controls were abolished for many, though not all, consumer goods, but were retained for capital goods and raw materials. There is also a check on price increases. Physical controls are rare and apply mainly to foreign trade. Arbitrary and particular rules addressed to a specific enterprise which prevailed under the earlier system were frowned upon. General laws were to be the instruments of economic policy. For every plan goal, there were to be "adequate economic instruments"[3] (incentives to attain it). Since rules are mostly general rather than specific or detailed, enterprises were free to act on their own, within the general framework. The plan, under the circumstances, became a statement of objectives regarded likely to be attained by the effects of incentives, operating through the market, rather than a list of specific instructions.

This compromise between direct controls and the operation of a market underwent several changes as the regime was feeling its way toward a new system. Up to the end of 1961, in spite of ups and downs, the trend seemed to be toward increased reliance upon the market. Changes announced in early 1962 indicated a sharp reversal and a return to tighter direct (particularly price) controls.[4] Whether this represents a more lasting departure from the liberalizing trend than previous changes remains to be seen, although a number of signs point in the direction of a general tightening of the regime. One of the most significant symptoms of this trend was the Djilas trial. However, for the time being the essentials seem still unchanged. . . .

Apart from the key investments of the federal government, the actual operations of the economy are determined by the decisions of the individual enterprises. They are free to make their own plans, within the framework set by tax laws, the guaranteed minimum wages, and some rules on the distribution of net earnings (the word profit being strictly banished from the Yugoslav vocabulary). It would be an obvious misrepresentation to claim that Yugoslav enterprises are as free as American businesses. A list of the restrictions on the freedom of the Yugoslav enterprise appears quite formidable. The main restraints are the following:

(a) The state intervenes in the election of the works council and managing board and may, in certain cases, dissolve them.

(b) The director is elected by a state organ and can be removed only by it.

(c) The state may liquidate an enterprise.

(d) The economic plans of the federation of the republic may provide for specific restrictions and establish obligations for all enterprises or those of certain industries.

(e) Some parts of the plan of the enterprise need, to be effective, the approval of the state and may be amended by it.

(f) Special rules govern the disposition of net earnings by the enterprise.

(g) The pay scale of the enterprise must be approved by the trade union and the local community.

(h) Enterprises are restricted in disposing of their basic assets.

(i) Most of their financial transactions must be carried out on a noncurrency basis by way of state banks.

(j) In some industries, state regulations prescribe the details of cost accounting.[5]

Compared with the system of 1945–50, however, the freedom is considerable. It is, of course, hoped that the plans of the various enterprises will conform to the pattern and the objectives of the over-all plan in that their actions will respond to the incentives provided by the "economic instruments." But this is a hope, and its attainment is not to be furthered by administrative action except when the "base proportions" (most fundamental relationships not clearly defined by the Yugoslav literature) are seriously endangered. In that case, legislative action will be justified. . . .

The Councillors

The first general works council elections took place in 1950, following the enactment of the law about the self-government of the enterprises. Official Yugoslav statistics report that 84 per cent of those eligible to vote took part in the election. Together with the councillors elected prior to the enactment of the law (those with consultative status who continued in their functions until elections took place in their plants), there were altogether 155,166 members of works councils. In enterprises with more than 30 employees, 114,313 members were elected.

Detailed statistics are available for later years. An official study for 1956[6] tells us that the great majority of workers' councils was elected in manufacturing, mining and quarrying, trade, and catering and handicrafts, even though some 7 per cent of all councils functioned in agricultural enterprises. One quarter of the council members represented white-collar employees. Of the others, slightly more than half were skilled workers; highly skilled workers formed less than one fifth of the council membership on the workers' side. The typical council member was male (84.8 per cent) between twenty-six and thirty-five years of age (45.3 per cent), while the council presidents were slightly older (46.9 per cent between twenty-six and thirty-five and 30.6 per cent between thirty-six and forty-five with only 4.4 per cent up to twenty-five years of age as compared with 12.9 per cent of the council members). In professional skill, the presidents ranked far higher than the ordinary members; 85.7 per cent belonged to the two highest skill groups as contrasted with 70.5 per cent of the council members. Only about 10 per cent had secondary school or university education. Presidents of managing boards had about the same characteristics as their colleagues presiding over the councils.

Statistical information is also available on the types of questions dealt with in council meetings. About 40 per cent of all the issues before the councils can be described as economic, financial, or technical problems of the enterprise, ranging from its plan and statements of its accounts to production costs, quality, and realizations. Salary, norms, and distribution of profits—subjects that refer directly to the workers' income—represented only one sixth of the items on the agenda, a smaller fraction than labor relations, labor discipline, and "economic crime" taken together.

According to close observers, an interesting evolution has taken place in the nature of the council's work. Early meetings of the councils, it is said, were taken up overwhelmingly by personal issues, many of them the grievances of one or two individuals. During the next stage, the discussions focused primarily upon methods by which the short-run incomes of the workers in the enterprise in general could be increased. Only gradually did interest shift to long-term consideration of the economic, financial, or technical problems, which are the real assignments of the councils. This shift may reflect progressive education of the council members and of the workers in general, or it may correspond to the growth of the councils' responsibilities under the shifting legislative and administrative arrangements. Whatever the cause or mixture of causes, the evolution seems to indicate that workers' participation in management, as far as subject matter is concerned, has moved in the direction desired by the law-makers.

Of the three types of business issues—technical, financial, and economic—the first seems to be handled best by the councils, while financial issues seem least understood. Moreover, there are substantial regional differences in the level of competency with which the councils handle these issues. As can be expected, the councils in the industrially more developed areas (Slovenia and Croatia, for example) are more effective and deal with wider issues than councils in Macedonia or Montenegro where industry is in its earliest infancy. Interviews have confirmed also the obvious expectation that experienced industrial workers make better councillors than workers from rural areas who are just entering their industrial careers.

The educational effects of the system are closely related to the fact that council members are normally elected for no more than one year.[7] More than a third of all workers and white-collar employees have so far served as members of workers' councils. With the passage of time, more and more workers will have the experience of council membership. The shorter the period of office, the greater is the number of employees who, at one time or another, participate in council work. However, the educational value of the experiment is almost precisely the inverse of its merits as an effective device of management.

Members of the councils are subject to recall, but this seems to occur only in highly exceptional cases. Thus, during 1956 only 998 council members were recalled, 0.8 per cent. Among the reasons given for the recall, laxity and "economic crime" are separately stated in the statistics; about one fifth of the recalls were ascribed to each of these two reasons, with the rest grouped together under "other reasons." Economic crime stands for theft, corruption, and the like. There is a general impression that "economic crimes" have become an important factor in the economic life of the nation. Marshal Tito was reported to have complained that "the provisions of the nation's criminal code dealing with such crimes were mild—the maximum penalty being fifteen years imprisonment."[8] He said that some people had embezzled millions of dinars and had paid with only short prison terms, making the crime worthwhile. Recalls were carried out at the instigation of various authorities: organs of self-government (of the local commune) and the "collective" (the workers in the plant) were responsible in 60 per cent of the cases; state authority, the director, and the political organization in the remainder of the cases (less than 10 per cent).

Somewhat more frequent is the recall of members of the managing boards. This occurred in 476 cases and affected 1.2 per cent of 40,232 board members. Organs of self-government were most frequently responsible for the recall; the political organization was responsible in about 8 per cent of the cases. It is of course possible that political motives were operative in the recall of the council or board members by other bodies.

The above figures refer to enterprises with more than 30 employees. Among them are a few large enterprises—say with more than 1000 employees—or fair-sized enterprises with several shops. Some attempts at adapting the council system to these situations have been made, but it would seem that no full solution has yet been found for the problem of how to make self-government effective under such circumstances. Shop councils, the development of smaller election units in the plant, and so forth, have been proposed.[9] A large percentage of Yugoslav enterprises, on the other hand, has fewer than thirty, but more than six, employees. In these firms, all employees are members of the council; the only elected body is the managing board. Even this seems in many cases excessive organization. It has been suggested that either the workers' council represented by the "working collective" or the managing board be suppressed.[10] (Enterprises with six employees or less do not elect either council or managing board. Their functions are performed by all employees.)

Elections are free and secret, according to the law, and all workers are entitled to vote provided they have the right to vote in political elections. Official statistics for 1956 tell us that of 1,363,788 employees, 1,329,890 were entitled to vote, that is, all but 34,000, or almost 98 per cent. We are further informed that 1,169,058 did vote (all but 160,000, or 88 per cent). Of a total of 6854 lists of candidates, 6599 were proposed by the trade union branch. Only 255 were "unofficial" lists. Of 124,204 workers' councillors, 121,648 were elected from trade union lists. In other words, only 2556 councillors proposed on nonunion lists were elected, that is, about 2 per cent.

Such "unofficial" lists can be proposed by one tenth of the employees of the enterprise in question, but the statistics indicate that this method is not frequently used. In some cases mild pressure has been sufficient to persuade opposition groups to abandon attempts at establishing unofficial lists. In other cases the police or the party intervened. The fact that a few such lists succeeded in getting some unofficial candidates elected is of course no evidence for real freedom in the election procedure.[11]

The supervision of the legality of the elections is in the hands of the local commune and of the district court. Complaints can be formulated by all candidates, proponents of lists of candidates, the union branch of the enterprise, the local commune, and the district authority. If irregularities are established which may have influenced the outcome of the elections, new elections are ordered.[12] This kind of supervision of the regularity of the election will not necessarily inspire confidence among potential oppositionists.

The function of the members of the workers' councils and of the managing boards is honorary; they are not paid for their work in the organs of workers' management. They receive only compensation for wages lost while they are taking part in the meetings of these bodies. Throughout their entire stay in office, they continue to work on their jobs in the enterprise.[13] Decisions of the council are valid provided more than half the council members attend the meeting.

The Managing Board

The board consists of three to ten members, including the director of the enterprise who is a member ex officio. In 1956 there were some 40,000 members of managing boards, most serving on boards with three to eight members.

The boards act as the executive organ of the councils. They implement the council's policy decisions by giving instructions to the director, and they submit policy proposals. But they also act on their own: they decide appointments at higher levels, except for the director who is appointed by the local government; theirs is also the decision on grievances against the director on industrial relations issues.

At least three quarters of the board members must be production workers or otherwise engaged in the fundamental economic activity of the enterprise. Not more than one third of the outgoing members can be re-elected, and no one can be a board member for more than two consecutive years. These clauses naturally act unfavorably on the board's effectiveness, given the small number of workers qualified to serve on it; such restrictions tend to emphasize the educational functions of board membership at the expense of their managerial tasks.

Protection for board members is provided by clauses in the law which prohibit their dismissal during terms of office as well as their transfer to other jobs during that time without their agreement.

The Director

The director is the executive organ of both the workers' council and the managing board and thus the principal representative of the enterprise. At the same time, as appointee of the local people's committee administering the commune, he is a representative of the state and sees to it that the activity of the enterprise corresponds to the laws and administrative regulations. He may, therefore, suspend the execution of any instructions of the council or board which in his view violate law or regulations. In the case of a conflict, the organs of the local community decide.

Among the functions of the director are hiring and firing (except for managerial jobs), job assignments, and discipline (except for severe cases which go before a disciplinary court appointed by the workers' council). Grievances against decisions of the director may be formulated by any worker; as was pointed out above, they come before the managing board for decision.

Almost all directors are male; only 49 out of 6030 (less than 1 per cent) are female. Almost half were in the age group of thirty-six to forty-five which makes them older than members or even presidents of workers' councils. Their educational qualifications do not seem high: less than 10 per cent had university education; less than a quarter, secondary school education. Two thirds had only primary or junior high school education (which ends at the age of 14). Their skill qualification, however, is high: almost 90 per cent belong in the two upper reaches of the four existing skill groups. Only in agriculture are there many unskilled directors—one third of the total.

Nine and three tenths per cent of the directors were relieved of their office during 1956—a total of 563; 61 of them were removed at their own request. Laxity and "economic crime" were the reasons in a quarter of the cases. The supervisory authority was responsible for more than half the dismissals—a sign perhaps of insufficient authority exercised by the councils or managing boards or of excessive outside supervision.

The procedure for the appointment of the director as well as for his dismissal provides for the ultimate decision to be taken by the people's committee of the local commune. For the appointment there is a public competition whose outcome is decided upon by a special committee of the people's committee. This is not a competitive examination, but rather an announcement of the opening in the press. Candidates then submit documents about their education and experience and are interviewed by the selection committee. One third of the members of the special committee consists of persons designated by the workers' council of the enterprise concerned. . . .

The System from the Worker's Angle

How does Stepan Babic, the man on the work bench, experience the new system? There is little doubt that there has been a real improvement in his standard of living compared with the situation up to about 1952. Real wages have risen from their intolerably low level, although they are still among the lowest in Europe. It is difficult to find reliable measures of this change, particularly since the figures of the earlier period—based upon the prices of unobtainable rations—are highly fictitious. But no observer of Yugoslav events would question the fact that real wages have risen. The increase of the domestically produced national income is, however, no reliable guide to this change, not only because of the high and fluctuating level of net investment and national defense spending, but also because of the very profound influence that changes in outside economic relations have played and continue to play in the evolution of the Yugoslav economic system.

Equally important is a distinct improvement in the quality of the products offered the consumer. This is a fact which most Yugoslavs point out, but which finds no expression in the statistics, even though it greatly contributes to the improvement of the standard of living and to bringing some joy into the daily life of the worker. To some extent, it is the result of the element of competition introduced into the Yugoslav economy by the system of decentralized decision-making; another, perhaps immediately more significant, cause was a temporary reduction of inflationary pressure by a combination of circumstances; for as long as inflation was rampant, any merchandise, however shoddy, could easily be sold.

There are some indications, too, that the return to material incentives produced a greater pride in workmanship and increasing recognition of the importance of competency. It is assuredly too much to say that competency has become more important than party membership; a dictatorship could hardly afford to abandon reliance on party loyalty as a primary criterion in the selection for appointments and promotion. But the recognition has been growing that party membership alone is not a sufficient qualification for managerial authority. The selection of directors, though still not free from political considerations, takes competency more and more into account.

Stepan is thus better off than before 1952—provided he has employment. One of the first effects of the introduction of economic accountancy into the system was the release of unnecessary workers from many enterprises in order to increase the volume of profits and decrease the number of those who would share in them. Many of those then rendered unemployed have since found their way back into jobs, but concealed unemployment is still one of the dominant issues of the Yugoslav economy. The system of hiring is, under the circumstances, of great importance to the unemployed.

The intention of the government was to have all hiring go through a public employment service. These offices were established by the local authorities and were supposed to cooperate within each republic to refer job-seekers to any appropriate opening within the republic. However, only a part of the actual hiring seems to pass through these offices. In all cases but one, when we raised the question of how additional workers would be obtained, the answer failed to refer to the public employment service. Instead the enterprises seem to rely on recommendations by current employees or on the job-seekers who present themselves at the factory gate. Stepan, if he were to look for a new job, would most probably make the rounds of the enterprises in the area where he lives. If he is a highly skilled worker, he would have few problems; indeed, if he were willing to go into one of the new industrial areas in Macedonia, Montenegro, or Bosnia, he might find himself the object of relatively enticing offers. But a low-skilled or unskilled worker might go without employment or have to accept inferior and occasional jobs for long periods.

What does Stepan do if he is fired? The dismissal is proposed by the director and ratified by the council or a special council committee for dismissals. Notice given up to the fifteenth of each month takes effect as of the fifteenth; notice given after the fifteenth takes effect on the first day of the following month. The law provides for an appeal to the board of management or, in special cases, to the council. A further protest is possible to an arbitration board set up by the local people's committee; it consists of the president of the people's committee as chairman, an arbitrator proposed by the people's committee of the particular industry, and another proposed by the local union. The ruling of this board is final except in cases of breach of law, when an appeal to a court is possible—for instance if a worker is given notice during illness, sick leave, convalescence, annual leave, during pregnancy or while she has a child up to the age of eight months, during military service, while he is a member of the workers' council or of the managing board, as specified in Article 330 of the act respecting employment relationship of December 12, 1957. If Stepan has served in the enterprise for a long time, a longer period of notice is required (for service of five to ten years, two months notice is required). If it is a case of mass dismissal as a result of a reduction in operations, the workers' council must first decide how many workers are to be laid off, with the director selecting those to be discharged.

The union appears only in a highly subsidiary fashion in this entire procedure, and this opens the general question of to whom Stepan will address himself when he feels unfairly treated in the plant.

There is an almost embarrassing wealth of grievance procedures available to him: the workers' council, the managing board, the director, the union, the Communist Party. Which of these, if any, Stepan selects depends on a great many circumstances. If he is a member in good standing in the party, he will most probably turn to it with his complaint. Where the director is a strong personality, he may be the court of appeal against decisions of the foremen and department heads. In the early stages of the council system, the workers' council was often enlisted in support of personal grievances. Sometimes—although the author has no personal knowledge of such a case—the employee may even follow the course suggested by the law and appeal to the managing board against decisions of the director.

One of the frequently used methods of presenting grievances, particularly those of a whole group, is not listed among the publicly acknowledged ways of grievance handling: The workers present themselves en masse at the director's office and demand redress. This is in effect a suspension of work, comparable perhaps to a sit-down strike, the typical weapon of poorly organized workers.

Equally noteworthy is the fact that the union is hardly ever mentioned by anyone in connection with grievance handling. . . .

Notes

[1] There is ample descriptive literature on the Yugoslav council system. A semi-official description is in A. Deleon, 33 Questions—33 Answers on Workers' Self-Government in Yugoslavia (Belgrade, 1956). See also International Labour Organization "Workers' Management and Labour Relations in Yugoslavia," record of an informal discussion held on June 16, 1958 in connection with the 42nd Session of the International Labour Conference. Labour-Management Relations Series, no. 5 (Geneva, 1958). See also ILO, Workers' Management in Yugoslavia (Geneva, 1962). This is based partly on field investigations. William N. Loucks, "Workers' Self-Government in Yugoslav Industry," World Politics, XI.1 (October 1958). John T. Dunlop, Industrial Relations Systems (New York, 1958), chapter 7.

[2] "The earlier plans were heavy tomes weighing more than three pounds, the new ones were small booklets of some 40 pages," Bicanic, "Economic Growth," p. 66.

[3] Bobrowski, La Yugoslavie Socialiste, p. 162.

[4] New York Times, April 20, 25, and May 7, 1962.

[5] Dr. Lado Vavpetic, Professor at the Faculty of Law, Ljubljana: "On some questions of the relations between the organizations of the State Administration and the organs of Workers' self-government," in "The New Yugoslav Law," Bulletin on Law and Legislation in the Federal People's Republic of Yugoslavia, VIII.2–4:85–102 (April–December 1957). The return of extensive price controls in early 1962 has greatly reduced the area within which the Yugoslav firm can operate by its own decisions.

[6] Federal Statistical Office, Workers' Councils and Managing Boards of Economic Enterprises in 1956, Statistical Bulletin No. 77 (English version). Unless otherwise stated, all figures refer to enterprises with 30 employees or more.

[7] From the point of view of effectiveness of the councils this has been criticized, and the proposal has been made to extend the period of service to two years, with half the council members to be elected each year. Marko Krjichnik, "Organisation et méthodes de Travail des organes d'autogestion ouvrière," Questions Actuelles du Socialisme, 43–4:110 (July–October 1957). In fact, as was mentioned before, decrees in 1955 and 1958 have extended the term of office of council and board members to two years.

[8] New York Times, May 7, 1962.

[9] Krjichnik, "Organisation et Méthodes de Travail," pp. 115–16.

[10] Krjichnik, "Organisation et Méthodes de Travail," p. 116, favors abandoning the managing board.

[11] Benjamin Ward, "Workers' Management in Yugoslavia," Journal of Political Economy, LXV.5 (October, 1957). Branko Horvat and Vlado Rašcović, "Workers' Management in Yugoslavia, A Comment," Journal of Political Economy, LXVII.2 (April 1959).

[12] "Évolution du Système d'autogestion ouvrière," Questions Actuelles du Socialisme, pp. 110–1.

[13] "Évolution du Système d'autogestion ouvrière," p. 112. Krjichnik, "Organisation et Méthodes de Travail," p. 115, rejects categorically proposals to pay the council members. Statisticki Bilten Broj 77, tables 2–34, p. 48, and English text, p. 22, give data on the compensation of council members.

Workers' Councils, The Yugoslav Experience

Jiri Kolaja

Just what goes on in a workers' council meeting? Jiri Kolaja here reports on a meeting of the workers' council of a Belgrade factory. Although the workers' council has the formal right to make all the firm's policy decisions, within the limits of Yugoslav law, Kolaja found that in this factory and in a second factory (Factory B), the managers who attended the meetings tended to dominate them. This factory had a total of some 1,600 blue- and white-collar workers, and both the representative members of the council (about 60) and nonmembers in attendance showed a preoccupation with matters more of personal than production interest, such as the apartments built and allocated by the firm.

This meeting was held in a large room in the accounts office, where more than fifty persons could be easily seated. It was attended by thirty-seven members; thirteen were on vacation, two were sick, and one was officially on a trip outside Belgrade. All the members of the managerial collegium were present. The director did not attend.

The chairman, a floor supervisor, opened the meeting by reading the agenda, which was as follows: (i) production plan for 1960; (ii) balance sheet for the first half of 1959; (iii) regulations concerning premium payments; (iv) allocation of apartments; (v) miscellaneous. He presented the five points skillfully, and throughout the meeting kept the agenda moving, like an efficient parliamentarian.[1] He seemed to be popular.[2]

The head of the production-technical department gave a ten-minute speech outlining the production plan for 1960. Though the previous plan appeared to be only 80 per cent completed, the new plan expected the total volume of production to increase by 8 per cent, as compared with the current plan. The head's talk included a lot of figures and percentages, but none of the members took down any notes. I got the impression that people did not digest all the figures that were thrown at them. However, there were several questions when he had finished his presentation of the plan. A woman asked: "If the plan is enlarged, will we be able to get

---

From Jiri Kolaja, *Workers' Councils, The Yugoslav Experience* (New York: Praeger, 1965), pp. 45–50. Reprinted by permission of Frederick A. Praeger, Inc.

enough raw material?" A man asked: "How will the holiday rota be organized?" Another woman asserted that women with children could not work on the night shift which was being planned for the spinning department. These questions were dealt with by other members of the managerial collegium. It was also stated by the managerial group that for the next few years the purchase of new machines could be planned only for the spinning shop.

The third item on the agenda, the introduction of new rules concerning premium payments, elicited a lively reaction. The head of the personnel department opened the discussion by asking members whether or not they had read the outline he had sent them two weeks prior to the meeting. One person complained that he had not had time to look it over. An older man rose to his feet and said that he was against the whole idea of premium payments because the workers did not like them; furthermore, he asked why white-collar employees got more pay than workers. Another man joined him in his criticism of the premium system. The personnel officer did not accept these views: he said that everybody was paid for what he did. The question at issue was not whether to have a bonus system, but whether the proposed new regulations were satisfactory. There were two further comments by workers and two by other management persons. The young and self-assured head of the production-technical department took the floor and brought the discussion to an end by stating that premium systems were found in both capitalist and socialist societies, that they were necessary in order to maintain quality, and that perhaps there should be a group quality bonus because in the preceding year some products had been returned to the factory on account of their poor quality. It was therefore agreed to set up a committee composed of four specialists to work out further details of the premium system.

The next point on the agenda evoked the most dramatic response. During the discussion on the allocation of accommodation in the new factory-built and -owned apartment house, I noticed that some members of the council took down notes for the first time, and that they really argued the proposals that were put forward.[3] The apartments committee itself had assigned thirty-three units, and had left five to be assigned by the workers' council; a further two were reserved for the director's decision.[4]

The first to raise his voice was the lawyer:[5] "Why was my name dropped from the original list that was previously approved by the workers' council?" The controller, in his role of chairman of the apartments committee, answered that the committee had not been clear about the lawyer's general situation. He was scheduled to get an apartment when the next construction project was completed. Immediately, two other men rose and asked why they had not been considered by the committee. Neither of them was a member of the workers' council. They stood behind the members,[6] who were seated. The head of personnel, who was also on the apartments committee, said that preference had been given according to seniority—whereupon another employee blurted out, "But I have been working here for forty years." The controller told him that his position would be considered later; but the worker, a bricklayer employed by the firm, was not satisfied, and kept protesting. At this, a foreman from the weaving shop, who was a council member, said: "If the bricklayer doesn't get an apartment, I am giving up mine. I don't want it."

Another council member joined in, expressing surprise that the lawyer, and a woman with a child who had to pay a high rent, should have been by-passed. How did it come about that another woman (a member of the League of Communists and a former chairman of the workers' council) who was single had got an apartment? The controller: "Well, we have to look at the person as a human being." The member: "This means that the mother with a child is not a human being?" The audience laughed.

The meeting became noisier, and the chairman banged his gavel to keep order as he put the matter to the vote. He reminded the meeting that there were 260 applications for forty apartments; thus of necessity some people would have to wait for the next opportunity. There were thirty-two persons in favor of the proposed allocation, one against, and four abstentions.

The first matter under the "miscellaneous" heading involved the council's approval for five people to go to Germany to purchase new machinery for the spinning shop; the second was a request for an increase in salary by the head of the personnel department. While this latter point was being discussed, the personnel officer left the room. The chairman of the managing board explained that the head of the personnel department had responsibilities which equaled those of the head of the weaving shop, and yet his salary was 5,000 dinars less, or 30,000 dinars at the time. How much more should he get? One voice suggested that he should have 34,000, another proposed 33,000. The workers' council voted a 3,000 rise, and the personnel officer returned to the meeting.

Another four applications were handled rather more quickly by the council. It was also decided that fifty-six litres of milk (12.3 gallons) should be supplied daily for those whose work involved them in unhealthy conditions; and that a worker who did not give truthful information to the disciplinary committee and who appealed to the workers' council should not be punished financially (the managing board and the disciplinary committee had suggested a 10 per cent cut in pay) but only sternly reprimanded. Finally, because of the lack of further, more detailed, information, an application for financial help addressed to the enterprise by the communal anti-tuberculosis service was adjourned to the following meeting.

Oral exchanges at the meeting were spontaneous. However, the most lively participation occurred, as was to be expected, when a highly personal question was being discussed—the allocation of apartments. It was at this point that some of the council members started to make notes, whereas when the production figures were presented (which hardly anyone could expect to remember without notes), no one cared to jot anything down. In general, all the suggestions put forward by the managerial collegium were accepted, despite the fact that the elderly worker from the finishing department voiced workers' objections concerning premium payments. There was strong moral feeling when a single woman with a good political record got an apartment at the expense of a woman with a child. Nevertheless, a large majority voted approval of the apartment allocation policy.

Notes

1 Seymour Melman, in an unpublished paper, reports that when he attended a labor union meeting at a factory during his visit to Yugoslavia in 1959, he had the feeling that possibly the participants had had virtually no experience in operating a decision-making organization. In our case, however, the chairmen of the councils in Factories A and B had been industrial workers before the second world war, and were efficient in conducting meetings.

2 He wore a blue collar and a short coat, as the other workers did. The managerial personnel were dressed differently, in white shirts, with or without ties.

3 The same happened in Factory B. There, even the proposed distribution of apartments was voted down, and a new allocation had to be undertaken (minutes of workers' council meeting 22 and 23 July 1959).

4 As has already been mentioned, the enterprise had to be able to offer accommodation when it was competing for specialist staff in a free labor market.

5 The enterprise had its own lawyer and two physicians. They were not members of the managerial collegium. However, the lawyer was supposed to attend meetings of the workers' council so that legal advice was available if required. I was later informed that he had been expelled from the League of Communists because he belonged to those who supported Stalin rather than Tito. However, he was presumably doing his best to be accepted again. The lawyer often tried to engage me publicly in debate concerning my political views.

6 Meetings of the workers' council are open to all employees.

On the Job

David Tornquist

Further insights into the operations of workers' self-management are provided by the reports of David Tornquist, an American who worked in a Yugoslav publishing firm. In the first report, he shows that workers' participation failed in his own firm because his coworkers lacked a willingness to participate, although they had the requisite competence. In the second report, an account of management board and workers' council meetings in a pharmaceutical firm, he shows how Sasha, a Communist Party member, sought to teach the workers skills to complement their willingness to speak up and control management.

My enterprise was one of many in which the concept of the economic unit was applied halfheartedly. Partly this was a reflection of the director's ambiguous attitudes. Though he was exceptionally willing to let people work without interference from him, he seemed inherently incapable of letting the formal system of workers' management develop. He had built up a clique to support his policies and he used the party and union organizations to get his own way and keep power in his hands. No more than a minimum attempt was made to keep the workers acquainted with the current financial situation of the enterprise. Although the staff numbered only two hundred people, the details of business were put in the opaque language of tax manuals. There was rarely any "meat" in the meetings of the workers' council or in those to which the entire staff was summoned. The people elected to the workers' council and managing board were either members of the director's clique or people who were too pusillanimous to object to his wishes. The function of these elected bodies was to agree with the director, and the function of the rest of the workers was to sit and squirm during the occasional meeting at which they heard long, dull reports on what their bodies of self-management had agreed to.

At one meeting I attended, for the election of the new workers' council, there was some open political struggle, but it indicated nothing so much as the peculiar conception of democracy held by those who were running the enterprise. The morning of the meeting I heard rumors of a move to change the list of candidates which had been drawn up by the

---

Reprinted by permission of The Macmillan Company from *Look East, Look West: The Socialist Adventure in Yugoslavia* by David Tornquist, pp. 140–147, 183–189. Copyright © 1966 by David Tornquist.

union officials and the director, i.e., by the powers-that-be in the enterprise. A young woman who was an editor and translator and a long-time Communist was behind the move. The original list contained thirty names, of which twenty-five persons were to be elected to the council. This meant that in fact that electorate had to choose at least twenty people nominated by the powers-that-be. But the discussion never turned on this point of principle. The point which the young woman raised was that there were people on the list who had been serving term after term—ever since the beginning of workers' management. She pointed them out in the meeting and asked them one by one how long they had served. She insisted that it was time that other, younger people be put on the list and mentioned several names. The head of the union organization, an essayist and philosopher and one of the senior editors, replied that it was a good list, and he saw no reason why it should be changed or in fact why it should contain more names than the places on the council. But the young woman stuck to her point. Then the question arose of whether the collective should add new candidates to the list—as was its legal right—or whether an old-timer should be taken off the list for every new man put on. The director made a soulful speech expressing his sympathy for those who had to be rejected when there were more candidates than seats. He begged the collective to make replacements rather than additions so that the rejections would be kept to a minimum. In line with this, five of the long-term members—some of them with evident reluctance—stood up and withdrew their names. The workers, without discussion and with the hesitation of people unused to democratic procedures, voted to put five new people on the list to replace them. Since these five received more votes than anyone else in the next day's balloting, the end result was that the collective improved its position by rejecting ten of the original list instead of only five. But the essential question of democracy was approached obliquely, to say the least.

Most people in the enterprise blamed the director for the stagnation of workers' management, and certainly he was in part responsible. A man in his early forties, he had been a Communist since the war, which he spent in a Nazi concentration camp in Belgrade. He had important connections, was generally respected outside the publishing house, and was a good businessman. Under his management the enterprise had come out of the red and prospered financially, partly because he was willing to try new things and partly because he knew how to delegate responsibility. But he was not a literary man. Though he made admirable efforts to improve his literary culture and knowledge of foreign languages, he was ill at ease as director of an enterprise in which many of the workers were writers and intellectuals. Fearing their contempt, he gathered around him the worst party hacks in the enterprise and behaved autocratically in the meetings of the workers' council and managing board. Any attempt to oppose his policy decisions he regarded as a personal insult. One day at a meeting of the managing board a member asked whether the European literary journals to which the enterprise subscribed could be made available to other interested people after the director had read them. He denounced the question as an insinuation that he was spending enterprise funds for his own uses, and walked out of the meeting. His cohorts then pushed through a motion to reject this innocuous proposal. When he was not threatened, the director could be very egalitarian. On business trips he rode in front with the chauffeur and they talked as equals. He attended his meetings while the chauffeur attended to the car, but afterward they lunched together, drank together, and stayed in the same hotels. Though it is true that he had demoralized the staff to such a point that the assistant director left the company saying that he could no longer stand the humiliation of dealing with the director's hacks, it is also no doubt true that the director meant what he said when one day he told me, "The director's position is so confused and his job is so thankless that I would never do it except out of party duty. A director is caught in the middle; he is the only man who's never right."

It is a disappointing truth that people like this director, who have an official responsibility to push the democratic revolution forward, are often actually blocking it. But it is also true that democracy can only be fostered to a certain point. A government can set up democratic institutions which make it possible for more people to participate in political life and influence political decisions, but whether or not a democratic spirit springs up in these institutions is in the last analysis the responsibility of the people. Many people in Yugoslavia are less than willing to assume this responsibility. These are the antiheroes of Yugoslav socialism—the "little citizens," as they are called in Serbo-Croatian.

The man who takes no interest in the social world around him and who works away methodically like an ant, arranging the elements of his private life, securing and furnishing his apartment, maneuvering himself into a comfortable job, weaving himself a nest, is a little citizen. But he is no littler a citizen than the man who applauds everything being done in Yugoslavia but has no wish to get involved because he is bent on making his mark in some specialized field. A professor of electrical engineering at the University of Belgrade told me once that many of his students were little citizens. "They think mathematics is the beginning and end of life and care about nothing else," he said. "I have a hard time convincing them that one can be a mathematician without being a man, that although mathematics is a very fine thing, it is still a rather small part of human civilization, human philosophy, and human life."

Those who criticize the way others conduct public business but refuse to take part themselves or even to make their objections openly are also little citizens. The favorite topic of conversation of one of my landladies was the house council in our apartment building. She gave me daily accounts of the inefficiency, stupidity, and dishonesty of those who were serving on the council. One day I asked her why she didn't attend the meetings or become a member herself. "Surely," she replied, "you don't think I'd get involved with those scoundrels!" I asked another woman one day how well the system of workers' management functioned in the factory where she worked. She shrugged her shoulders. "I never stay for the meetings," she said. "Why not?" I asked. "Oh, let the others run it," she replied. "They don't care what I think."

In my enterprise the six senior editors were called little citizens. Five of them were Communists; all of them had some reputation as men of letters; and they included a poet and a novelist among the best in Yugoslavia. They had no reason to fear the director and did not; if anything, he was afraid of them. These were obviously the people to start a move to put teeth into the managing board and the workers' council, for their position was unassailable. But the editors showed complete indifference toward workers' management. The explanation was fairly simple. They were all involved in their own projects, their poems and plays and essays and novels. They came to work for only a couple of hours a day—from noon to two or two-thirty—while most other employees worked a full eight hours. For those two hours they sat in comfortable armchairs in a newly decorated office, drinking coffee and chatting with prospective authors, arranging for the books they would edit. They had little contact with other workers, never leaving their private world except to confer occasionally with the copy editors who saw to the printing of the books they edited or with the ordinary editors, who did the detailed work on the books (the senior editors did not do such trivial things—their job was to decide which books to publish, arrange for authors or translators, and see to the big problems). Though each of them edited only a half dozen or a dozen books a year, they were very well paid. In short, they had a soft spot, and though their literary work might be important to society, they were not accepting their responsibilities as ordinary employees and ordinary men to act in the political situation before them. They were complacent about a situation which was discouragingly far from the ideal set forth in the program of the League of Communists and in their own novels and essays.

The other workers—the ordinary editors and copy editors and secretaries and accountants and proofreaders and chauffeurs and cleaning women, etc.—resented the senior editors' indifference toward them and their cause, and with some justification. Their positions were not so secure. Many of them were not Communists; if they tried to fight the director, they might be accused of not understanding the aims of the society or of acting out of selfishness. Some excuse might be found to fire a man if he tried to fight alone, and if he tried to organize a group to fight with him, he might be accused of forming a clique. The clique which ran things now watched their critics carefully and were always happy to report opposition to the director in order to win more favor themselves. True, the assistant director, a non-Communist, had quit because of this clique and had had no difficulty getting a similar job in a government publishing house, but he was a highly trained financial expert. It was not so easy to get other jobs in Belgrade if you were a secretary or clerk, for the schools were pouring out people with equal qualifications, and many enterprises were laying off people in the push to raise labor productivity.

Nevertheless, the workers in my enterprise had behind them the force of law, the authority of the government leadership, and the public opinion of the country. If more information was necessary for them to understand the business of the enterprise and participate in the discussion, they could have begun their efforts modestly with a demand that they be given mimeographed copies of all materials before the meetings, in time for them to study carefully what could not be grasped from a mere hearing. If they were afraid to fight openly, they could have fought cautiously. They did not have to attack; they could simply pose innocent questions. "Why, comrade director, is this money necessary?" "Why do we need three company cars?" "Why must this trip be made to Bulgaria or Germany?" Instead they sat silent in the meetings. Afterward each criticized the others for being too timid or indifferent to speak out. Everyone found a reason for waiting until someone else began: "I have a wife and family to support; I have to be careful" or "I'll be on a pension soon, no need to cause trouble" or "I couldn't get such a good job anywhere else." And so here in the publishing house, where the high cultural level of the workers would lead one to believe that the system of workers' management would function smoothly, it was at a disappointingly low stage of development, and demoralization lay over the whole collective.

Even so, the process of development had not come to a complete standstill, and, as I saw at the last meeting I attended, a single incident could change the atmosphere greatly.

The reason for the meeting was a report to the entire staff on the work of the managing board for the previous year. The reading of the report took at least an hour, and at the end we were no more enlightened and a good deal less ready to take an active part in any discussion. We were bored and looking at our watches. We had heard a description of the business of the enterprise during the past year without recognizing any connections with what we had actually been doing, but no one had the energy left to try to pry further information out of the managers.

Then a member of the managing board spoke up. "Comrades," he said, "this report was fine for those of us on the managing board who have already heard reports from the heads of the various departments, but I am not sure how much it means to those who have not heard those reports. Therefore I think it would be in order for the department heads to give us those reports again before the whole collective, so that everyone can know what I have learned about our current business."

The director frowned, but there was no refusing. When the workers make a justified demand, the resistance falls away with remarkable ease.

For the principles of the system are in black-and-white in the Party Program and a director cannot afford to be accused of openly violating these principles. So then we heard detailed reports from the heads of the commercial and export departments and even from the director himself. Here was what the workers should have heard in the first place. Our activity was put into terms of real prospects, real negotiations, and real contracts. It suddenly appeared that the publishing house was doing something an ordinary man could understand: exporting books to America, importing foreign language records from Russia, printing translations of Yugoslav scientific books in English, arranging book sales on the installment plan so that the ordinary worker could buy books, printing art books for the Bulgarians, and so on. I felt that the whole system of workers' management in my enterprise took an enormous step forward in that hour and a half in which the professional staff told us not abstractly but exactly what they were doing, in terms that made sense. For once I felt that these men were acting as if they were responsible to the workers, and not the workers to them. It was a good feeling. . . .

Something in the way Sasha described his efforts to get people to participate in workers' management struck me as smacking of manipulation. I suspected he was really making all the decisions himself and merely pretending to give the workers some say in their affairs. And he did not voice the liberal views on the party I was accustomed to hear. He put too much emphasis on the party's role as initiator of all things and too little on the initiative frequently stifled by party domination. It is intriguing to think of the party as "weak" when it is autocratic, and "strong" when it functions only as a leader and persuader. But this view assumes that the party is ideal, in that it builds its authority through leadership and persuasion; my own skeptical view is that the real party is more likely to manifest the weakness of autocracy. What I saw and heard in Yugoslavia confirmed my view, and the 1964 Congress of the League of Communists adopted a new statute for party organization precisely because the party as theretofore organized was contradicting and stifling the democratic developments described in the Party Program.

I understood Sasha's thinking better, however, after I had sat in on my first meeting in his factory—a session of the managing board. It was quite obvious that workers' management at Galenika was functioning at a high level of competence. Clearly the party did encourage workers' management in this factory, and clearly Sasha had done a good job of drawing in competent people. All the people who sat on the board had already served on the councils of their economic units and had attended the factory's seminars on workers' management. As one executive told me, "We're an up-and-coming enterprise with great ambitions, and we can't let these people learn on the job when that job is making the policy of the enterprise. They already know what they're about." When I went to their meeting, they were still new, but the dispatch and clarity with which they handled the business of the day was extraordinary. (Interestingly enough, it was impossible to pick out the Communists in the discussion. This is a common difficulty in Yugoslavia, and I learned early that guesses were as often wrong as right if one assumed that anyone supporting government policies was a party member. It was also unreliable to assume that people opposing government policies were not members.)

In a meeting that lasted nearly three hours, those twelve men and women on the board, only one of whom was a university graduate, decided on the status of the factory restaurant, the sale of a piece of land, the purchase of a new machine, a bank loan to cover payments to a Hungarian firm installing new chemical apparatus in the factory, the sale of wood scraps, the dissolution of a lease on a building in Belgrade, a loan for the development laboratory, decisions from the economic units to open up new jobs, formation of a commission to oversee the stockroom and warehouse, requests for aid to two workers attending school, a report from the housing commission on several cases of alleged hardship, a mistake in a shipment of pills to Tunis, and half a dozen other matters.

The shipment to Tunis was curious because it touched on factory discipline, a delicate problem in Yugoslav enterprises. In this case, a Tunisian firm had ordered 10,000 pills and only 5,000 had been shipped. The managerial staff now proposed to send the other 5,000 free to make up for the mistake; the managing board was agreeable but wanted to know why the mistake occurred and resolved to penalize the person responsible. The threat of firing as the ultimate penalty is avoided as much as possible in Yugoslav enterprises, both because workers do not like to fire their fellows and because this type of penalty is associated with capitalism. At the same time, however, workers must be held responsible for the quality of their work. This is not easy in a country where workers have few traditions of discipline and responsibility. Every enterprise has a disciplinary commission which investigates complaints of insubordination and negligence and imposes penalties which usually consist of a 5 or 10 percent cut in pay for a period commensurate with the violation. This is not always an attractive solution. The disciplinary commission sometimes seems childish and pompous, and it involves complicated procedures with the possibility of misuse. But it is one way the Yugoslavs have found to hold people to greater responsibility without threatening them with dismissal.

The greatest excitement in the meeting came over one of the alleged hardship cases reported by the housing commission. A young man who had just received the key to a room which he was to share with another man wanted to give it up and resume his position at the head of the waiting list for housing. He complained that the room did not have its own toilet, had no separate closet where he could hang his contaminated work clothes, etc. The members of the board rose up in arms. Why was this man wearing his contaminated work clothes outside the factory? This was a menace to public health. And how could he complain when so many others were just as badly off: men with families, men who had fought in the revolution, men who had worked longer in the factory, and men who gave more time to the burdens of unpaid political work?

A man sitting across from me rose to explain what had been in the young man's mind. A false rumor had gone round that one-room apartments would soon be available for unmarried men and women. His idea was to refuse the double room and then be first to get one of the new apartments.

The board took back the key to the room but angrily resolved to put the young man's name at the bottom of the waiting list.

Then an associate director of the enterprise, who was representing the director at the board meeting, rose to give a survey of the housing situation. The prospects, he said, were that the enterprise would house everyone eligible for an apartment within three years. By that time all hardship cases would be eliminated and the factory could think of keeping up with current housing demands. Until then it would be impossible to think of separate apartments for unmarried persons, except for those suffering from tuberculosis. He closed with a rousing condemnation: "For this man to present his case as one of hardship is an act of inexcusable selfishness." Everyone in the room applauded.

From this meeting it was obvious that the managing board at Galenika was deciding primarily on specific matters. From what Sasha had told me about the party, it seemed pretty clear that the Communists on the board must play a leading role; but this was not apparent to an outside observer. When I checked the reports of their decisions over the last year, I found that the board almost always accepted management proposals, except in the matter of opening up new jobs. It looked as if the management was largely having its way. This is not necessarily a bad thing. There is nothing wrong with giving the director and his staff their head so long as an enterprise is doing well. But when it begins to founder or when the managerial staff begin to abuse this liberty, the managing board and workers' council must be ready and able to take things in hand—and the Yugoslav theory is that they will do so, partly because their own pockets are affected and partly because they will feel some social responsibility for ill effects suffered by the community.

In looking over the work of Galenika's managing board, I found just such an occurrence. Every month the management submits its production plan for the following month, to be approved by the managing board. No plan was submitted in July because the factory was going to be shut down in August for vacations and repairs. But some workers had less than a full month's vacation and were to return to work during August. At its last July meeting the board instructed the management to include the production done by these workers in the September plan. This the management neglected to do. The managing board refused their plan and returned it for correction. Sasha was delighted by the action of the board, for he figured the management had probably not been guilty of an oversight but had hoped those extra working hours would be forgotten so the enterprise's production would show a particularly good record in the following month. This would of course have gone to their credit.

The workers' council at Galenika functioned as a broad policy-making body. Their proposals to the management and managing board were general recommendations: the production superintendent should propose ways to increase labor productivity and prevent increases in the labor force; the managing board should draw up a more effective sales program and increase the advertising staff; unnecessary property, equipment, and materials should be liquidated, and so on.

But the workers' council was not as quick or sharp about management as the managing board. This was quite evident at one meeting I attended. The main business was approval of a statute on the parliamentary procedures of the council and the managing board. Everyone in the room had a copy before him and the president began to call out the page numbers. "Page one." "Approved." "Page two." "Approved." From time to time someone would point out a need for correction, and after a short pause the booming voice of the president would resound again and the weaker voice of the assembly would answer "Approved."

It was a hot day, the statute went on for twenty pages, with minor corrections, neither very vital nor exciting, and I was already disappointed at the fact that everything was so routine, when they reached the last matter on the agenda: approval of some appropriations requested by the management. As everyone waited for the silent approval which would liberate us, a member of the council raised his hand and then lowered it, no doubt having reminded himself of the general discomfort. But the president, a forceful man, insisted gruffly that he speak his mind.

"Well," said the man, "I have a question about the appropriation for those new warehouse shelves. As I understand it, they would have to be imported, and that seems a lot of money in foreign currency when we need other things so badly. Besides, we already have the shelves from the old warehouse. Why don't we use those?"

The director spoke out sharply; he did not ask for the floor. "I suggest that the workers' council approve this appropriation exactly as we presented it."

The suggestion fell like a command. But a man sitting next to me spoke up in support of the workers' council.

Then the associate director stood up. "It seems to me," he said, "that both sides are taking an extreme position in this matter. We need not leave it at all or nothing. I've been told that the old shelves will not finish out the new warehouse because they must be altered to fit. But the resolution could be worded so as to require the management to use up the old shelves first."

Sasha sat on the edge of his seat and beamed with delight. The man who had initiated the discussion presented the reworded resolution. Sasha whispered to himself as the man presented it: "And now cut off the money until it is needed." But the resolution was passed without mention of stopping the money. The workers' council had made a mistake and given the staff money it had not wanted to give it.

Sasha was disappointed. The development of independent workers' management might depend in part on people like himself, but there was only so much he could do. It was his job as information director to teach people enough about factory affairs so that they would know when to put a brake on the professional staff. It was not his job to tell them what to do when the staff caught them off guard. He was not a member of the workers' council and he attended their meetings as an observer—as any other worker in the factory. He could sit on the edge of his seat and hope the board made no mistakes, but that was all. I saw him itching to speak, but I never saw him try to horn in on what was not his affair. . . .

Workers' Control for Poland

Jacek Kuron and Karel Modzelewski

East Europeans often look with envy on the Yugoslav model of
workers' control. But these two Poles insist that, although democracy
begins in the factories, it cannot end there; it requires extension of
workers' democracy into a qualitatively new form of political democracy
based on production units.* In Poland the turbulence of 1956 led to the
formation of workers' councils, but Gomulka curbed them in 1958 when
he saw the efforts of the councils to federate on a territorial basis as a
political threat. Of special interest are the comments on how to control
the police and the armed forces in a society truly dedicated to workers'
control.

Thus far we have considered the revolution as the gravedigger for the
old order. It also creates a new society. Is the working class, which must
be the main and leading force of the revolution, capable of developing a
real, viable program?

The class interest of the workers demands the abolition of the
bureaucratic ownership of the means of production and of exploitation.
This does not mean that the worker is to receive, in the form of a working
wage, the full equivalent of the product of his labor. The level of development of the productive forces in a modern society necessitates a division of
labor in which there are unproductive sectors, supported by the material
product created by the worker. Therefore, under conditions of a workers'

From "Poland" by Jacek Kuron and Karel Modzelewski in The New Revolutionaries: A Handbook of the International Radical Left, ed. by Tariq Ali (New York:
Morrow, 1969), pp. 146–153, 155–158. Published in the British Commonwealth by
Peter Owen, Ltd., London. Copyright © 1969 by Peter Owen, Ltd. Reprinted by
permission of William Morrow and Company, Inc., and Peter Owen, Ltd.

* The ultimate relationship between workers' control and political democracy as
perceived by many has been summarized by André Gorz:

"The demand for self-management which arises out of productive praxis cannot
be contained within the factory walls, the laboratories, and research bureaus. Men
who cannot be ordered around in their work cannot indefinitely be ordered around
in their life as citizens, nor can they submit to the rigid decisions of central
administrations."—[Andre Gorz, Strategy for Labor (Boston: Beacon Press, 1967),
in Carl Oglesby, ed., The New Left Reader (New York: Grove Press, 1969), p.
50.]

democracy, it will also be necessary to set aside from the total product a part earmarked for accumulation, for the maintenance and development of health services, education, science, culture, social benefits and those expenditures for administration and for the apparatus of political power which the working class will recognize as indispensable. The essence of exploitation is not that the working wage represents only a part of the value of the newly created product, but that the surplus product is taken away from the worker by force and that the process of capital accumulation is alien to his interests, while the unproductive sectors serve to maintain and strengthen the rule of a bureaucracy (or *bourgeoisie*) over production and over society, and thus in the first place, over the labor and social life of the working class.

To abolish exploitation means, therefore, to create a system in which the organized working class will be master of its own labor and the resulting product; in which it will set the goals of social production, decide on the sharing and use of the national income, hence define the size and purpose of investments, the size and disbursement of expenditures for social benefits, health services, education, science and culture, the amount for the power apparatus and its current tasks. In brief, a system in which the working class will exercise economic, social and political power in the State.

How should the working class and its state be organized in order to rule over its own labor and its product?

(1) If there is no workers' democracy in the factory, there can be none in the State on any long-term basis. For it is only in the factory that the worker is a worker, that he fulfills his fundamental social function. If he were to remain a slave in his place of work, then any freedom outside the place of work would soon become "Sunday freedom," fictitious freedom.

The working class cannot rule over its own labor and its product without controlling the conditions and goals of its toil in the factory. To that end, it must organize itself in the plants into workers' councils, in order to run the factories. The manager must be made into a functionary subordinate to the council, controlled, hired or dismissed by the council.

However, these days, all key decisions relating to the management of an enterprise are made centrally. Under these conditions, the workers' council would, in practice, be deprived of power. The manager is closely bound up with the offices which make the decisions—the central apparatus of economic management. In this situation, the workers' council would inevitably be reduced to an adjunct of the management, as is the case with the present-day Conferences of Workers' Self-Government.

To manage enterprises through its workers' councils, the working class must make the enterprise independent, creating the preliminary conditions for workers' democracy and, at the same time, adapting management relationships to the new class goal of production. (As we have already shown, the system of centralized management is an organizational tool of production for the sake of production, whereas production for the sake of consumption requires a decentralized system.) Thus, while taking the first step towards realizing its program, the working class achieves that which is most far-reaching and progressive in the program of technocracy: the independence of enterprises. However, the working class and the technocracy imbue this concept with fundamentally different social contents. To the technocracy, independence of an enterprise means that management has full powers in the factory. For the working class, it means self-government for the working force. That is why the working class must go beyond plant management via the councils. Workers' self-rule, limited to the level of the enterprise, would inevitably become fictitious and a cover for the power of management in the factory and for the rule of a new technocratic bureaucracy; exploitation would be maintained and the former state of chaos would return in a new form.

Basic decisions relating to the sharing and use of the national income naturally have a general social character; that is, they are made on an economy-wide scale and, therefore, they can only be made centrally. If these central decisions were to remain outside the influence of the working class, it would not rule over the product that it has created and over its own labor.

(2) That is why, in addition to factory councils, the working class will have to organize itself into a nationwide system of councils of workers' delegates, headed by a central council of delegates. Through the system of councils, the working class will determine the national economic plant and maintain permanent control over its execution. As a result, the councils at all levels will become organs of economic, political, legislative and executive power. They will be truly elective offices, since the electors, organized according to the natural principle of production, will be able at any time to recall their representatives and appoint new ones in their place. In this way, the representatives of working forces in the factories will become the backbone of proletarian State power.

(3) If, however, the workers' representatives in the central council of delegates were to have only one draft plan for the division of the national income laid before them by the Government or by the leadership of the sole political party, their role would be limited to a mechanical act of voting. As we noted earlier, a monopolistic ruling party cannot be a workers' party; it inevitably becomes the party of the dictatorship over the working class, an organization of a bureaucracy designed to keep the workers and the whole of society disorganized and in line.

For the council system to become the expression of the organized will, organized opinion and organized activity of the masses, the working class must organize itself along multiparty lines. In practice, a workers' multiparty system means the right of every political group that has its base in the working class to publish its own paper, to propagate its own program through mass-media, to organize cadres of activists and agitators—that is, to form a party. A workers' multiparty system requires freedom of speech, press and association, *the abolition of preventive censorship,* full freedom of scholarly research, of literary and artistic creativity. Without the freedom to elaborate, publish, express various ideological trends, without full freedom for the creative intelligentsia, there is no workers' democracy.

In the workers' multiparty system, various parties will propose plans for the division of the national income to the central council of delegates, creating conditions for discerning alternatives and for freedom of choice for the central representatives of the working class and for factory workers electing and recalling their delegates.

We speak of a workers' multiparty system, although it would serve no purpose or even be possible to limit membership in the parties to workers only. The working-class character of the multiparty system would follow from the nature of the State power, organized as a system of councils. This means that parties seeking to influence the center of political power would be obliged to win influence among the workers.

By the same token, we are against the parliamentary system. The experience of both twenty-year periods shows that it carried no guarantee against dictatorship and, even in its most perfect form, it is not a form of people's power. In the parliamentary system, parties compete for votes. Once the votes have been cast, election programs can be tossed into the waste-basket. The deputies in parliament feel close only to the leadership of the party which nominated them. The electorate, artificially arranged in purely formal districts, is atomized and the right to recall a deputy is fictitious. The citizen's participation in political life is reduced to his reading statements by political leaders, listening to them on radio or watching them on television, while once every four or five years he goes to the ballot-box to decide which party's representatives are to rule him. Everything happens with his mandate, but without his participation. In addition, parliament is a purely legislative body, which permits executive power to emerge as the only real authority. Thus, in the parliamentary system, the working class and the whole of society, on the strength of their own vote, are deprived of influence on the center of power.

As against this formal, periodic voting, we propose the regular participation of the working class, through its councils, parties and trade unions, in economic and political decision-making at all levels. In capitalist society, above parliament, stands the *bourgeoisie,* disposing of the surplus product; in the bureaucratic system, above the fiction of parliament, the central political bureaucracy rules invisibly. In a system of workers' democracy, if it takes a parliamentary form, the working class will stand above it, organized into councils and having at its disposal the material basis of society's existence—the product of its labor.

(4) The working class cannot decide directly, but only through its political representation at the central level, how to divide the product it

has created. But as its interests are not entirely uniform, contradictions between the decisions of workers' representatives and the aspirations of particular sections of the working class are unavoidable. The very fact of separating the function of management from the function of production carries with it the possibility of alienation of the elected power, at the level of both the enterprise and the State. If the workers were deprived of the possibility of self-defense in the face of the decisions of the representative system, apart from their right to vote (i.e. apart from that very system), then the system would turn against those whom it is supposed to represent. If the working class was deprived of the possibilities of self-defense in its own state, workers' democracy would be fraudulent. This defense should be assured by *trade unions completely independent of the State and with the right to organize economic and political strikes.* The various parties, competing for influence in the trade unions, would struggle for the preservation of their working-class character.

(5) To prevent the institution of workers' democracy from being reduced to a façade, behind which the old disorder would make a comeback, its democratic forms must be the living expression of the activity of the working masses. Administrators, experts and politicians have the necessary time and knowledge to bother with public affairs, while the worker is obliged to stand next to his machine. To take an active part in public life the worker, too, must be provided with the necessary time and knowledge. This requires a certain number of hours to be set aside weekly from the required paid working time to ensure *the universal education of the workers.* During those hours, workers grouped into production complexes will discuss draft economic plans submitted by different parties for the country, factory or region which are too difficult for popular presentation only if an attempt is made to conceal their class content. The representatives of political parties participating in these hours of workers' education will bring both their programs and the working class closer to each other.

(6) In a workers' democracy it will be impossible to preserve the political police or the regular army in any form. The anti-democratic character of the political police is obvious to everyone; on the other hand, the ruling classes have had more success in spreading myths about the regular army.

The regular army tears hundreds of thousands of young people away from their environment. They are isolated in barracks, brainwashed of independent thinking by brutal methods, and taught, instead, to carry out mechanically every order issued by their professional commanders, who are locked in a rigid hierarchy. This organization of armed force is separated from society in order that it may, more easily, be directed against society. The regular army, like the political police, is by its very nature a tool of anti-democratic dictatorship. As long as it is maintained, a clique of generals may always prove stronger than all the parties and councils.

It is said that the regular army is necessary to defend the State. This is true in the case of an anti-democratic dictatorship, where, other than by terror, it is impossible to force the large mass of people to defend a state that does not belong to them. On the other hand, if the masses were allowed to carry arms outside the military organization, they would constitute a dangerous threat to the system. Consequently, for such a system, a regular army is the only possible form of defense force. . . .

To make democracy indestructible, the working class should be armed. This applies, first of all, to the workers in larger industries who should be organized into a workers' militia under the aegis of the workers' councils. The military experts who will train the workers' militia will be employed by the workers' councils and remain subordinated to them. In this, the basic military repressive force in the State will be directly tied to the working class, which will always be ready to defend its own state and its own revolution.

For technical reasons, it is unavoidable to maintain permanent military units within specialized divisions such as the navy, air force, rocketry, etc. The soldiers for those divisions should be recruited among the workers of heavy industry, and during their military service they should remain in touch with their factory teams and retain all their workers' rights.

(7) Agricultural production plays an essential part in the economy, and the peasantry has too important a role in society for the workers' program to by-pass the affairs of the countryside. . . .

Inasmuch as industry plays the decisive role in the economy, the direction of industrial production will determine the general direction of the national economy. And the working class, which will have control of its own product, will thereby create a general framework for the functions of the other sectors, including agriculture. But within these most general limits, determined by the level, structure and development of industrial production, the peasants must also control the product of their labor. The plans for development, for investments, for economic aid, should not be imposed by the State on the peasant population. Otherwise, a specific apparatus of control would come into being and would, finally, also obtain control over the working class. *That is why political self-government by the peasants* is a must for the good of workers' democracy. It is made possible because the interests of the workers and peasants converge.

Economic organizations of peasant producers are not enough to give peasants control over that part of their product taken over by the State and which is to be restored to the countryside in the form of direct State investments and State aid to peasant holdings. This can be assured only by the *political representation of peasant producers on a national scale,* elected on the basis of economic organizations and peasant political parties. . . .

The working class must carry out all these changes in the area of political, social and economic relations in order to realize its own class interest, which is the command over its own labor and its product. Is this program realistic?

Following the initial step towards its realization—making the enterprise independent—the working class would create the conditions for adapting production to needs, eliminating all waste of the economic surplus and ensuring proper use of the intensive factors of economic growth. The same would be carried out by the technocracy, the difference being that the production goal of the working class is consumption by many, not the luxury consumption of privileged strata. That is why workers' control of production would assure the most radical resolution of the contradiction between an expanded productive potential and the low level of social consumption which impedes economic growth today.

The workers' separate class interest coincides with the economic interests of the mass of low-paid white-collar employees and of the small and medium holders in the countryside. Their numbers combined, they comprise the overwhelming majority of the rural and urban population. Since the slavery of the working class is the essential source of the slavery of other classes and strata, by emancipating itself, the working class also liberates the whole of society.

To liberate itself, it must abolish the political police; by doing so, it will free the whole of society from fear and dictatorship. It must abolish the regular army and liberate the soldier in the barracks from nightmarish oppression. It must introduce a multiparty system, providing political freedom to the whole of society. It must abolish preventive censorship, introduce full freedom of the press, of scholarly and cultural creativity, allow social thinking to progress unimpeded. It will thereby liberate the writer, artist, scholar and journalist; it will create, on the widest possible scale, conditions for the free fulfillment by the intelligentsia of its proper social function.

It must subject the administrative apparatus to the permanent control and supervision of democratic organizations, changing existing relationships within that apparatus. Today's common civil servant will become a man free of humiliating dependence on a bureaucratic hierarchy. It must assure the peasant control over his product, as well as economic, social and political self-government. It will thereby change the peasant from the eternal, helpless object of all power into an active citizen sharing in making decisions which shape his life and work.

Because the worker occupies the lowest position in the productive process, the working class, more than any other social group, needs democracy; every incursion on democracy is first a blow against the worker. That is why workers' democracy will have the widest social base and will create the fullest conditions for the free development of the whole of society.

Because the workers' class interest most closely corresponds to the requirements for economic development and to the interests of society, the working-class program is a realistic one.

Will that program be realized? That depends upon the degree of ideological and organizational preparation of the working class in a revolutionary crisis, and therefore also depends upon the present activities of those who identify with workers' democracy.

Attempts to Institute Workers' Control

Daniel and Gabriel Cohn-Bendit

Daniel Cohn-Bendit, declared by the news media to be the student leader of the May 1968 rebellions in France, is a self-styled anarchist who rejects the leadership image and prefers to see untutored spontaneity in the strikes of students and workers. Writing with his brother, he describes the efforts of radical French workers who seized managerial control of French factories, only to have their demands subverted by forces opposed to workers' control, including even the Communist-dominated labor union (CGT). In the sequel to the events here described, the promises of DeGaulle for more workers' participation in French enterprises have largely run aground on the shoals of worker apathy, employer hostility, and the unenthusiastic posture of President Pompidou.

The Case of the AGF

The AGF (Assurance Générale de France) is the second largest French insurance company, a nationalized industry and one which in four years has twice been amalgamated, first with six other companies into a new combine, and then with three more. This "take-over" went hand in hand with the introduction of a high degree of automation and centralization. The trade unions never even raised the question of workers' participation in this "great" State enterprise, and confined themselves to denouncing the arbitrary way in which the management (whom they accused of being a Gaullist clique) ignored the unions.

On Friday, 17 May, a small group of employees raised the question of management, bluntly and clearly, in a pamphlet distributed by students of the 22 March Movement:

> Following the example of the students, we herewith submit a number of proposals to be debated in the general staff assembly of the AGF.
> (1) The AGF should be run by all those working in it.
> (2) The present management should be relieved of their posts.

From *Obsolete Communism: The Left Wing Alternative* by Daniel and Gabriel Cohn-Bendit. Copyright © 1968. English translation by Andre Deutsch, Ltd. Reprinted by permission of McGraw-Hill Book Co., and Andre Deutsch, Ltd.

Every branch should appoint a delegate, chosen solely for his personal qualities and merits.

(3) Those responsible for a particular branch will have a double function—to coordinate the running of the branch under the control of the employees, and to organize, with the delegates from other branches, a council which, again under the control of the employees, will run the enterprise as a whole.

(4) Those responsible for their branch will at all times be accountable for their actions to the entire staff and can be dismissed at any moment by those who have appointed them.

(5) The internal hierarchy is to be abolished. Every employee, no matter what his job, will receive the same pay, based provisionally on the mean wage bill for May (i.e. the sum of all wages divided by the number of workers).

(6) The personal files of employees will be returned to them so that they can remove any item that is not of purely administrative interest.

(7) All property and stock of the AGF will become the property of all, managed by all, and safeguarded by all at all times.

(8) In the case of any outside threat, a voluntary guard under the control of the council will provide protection for the enterprise day and night.

On Monday, 20 May, a new pamphlet was distributed making the following points:

As the fruits of social progress are in danger of being snatched back, we must:
—Beware of false friends and have confidence only in ourselves.
—Elect strike committees.
—Take over control on the lines of the earlier pamphlet.
The strike has been won. Now we must start things up again by ourselves and for ourselves, without any authority other than the council we have elected. Who will then be the forces of disorder? Only those who seek to defend private property, their privilege and jobs as managers, and who stand for oppression, violence, misery and war . . . Where you work is where the action is. There, with all the workers, you can choose to rebuild a new world, a world that will belong to all.

At the beginning, only a relatively small proportion of the employees (500 out of 3,000) participated in the occupation of the AGT Head Office, mainly because of the transport strike. The stay-in was started by a number of young workers, many of whom were not trade union members. Later, the trade unions took over, or rather tried to slow things down. The staff, however, was fully determined not to lose what had already been won. The list of original demands was impressive, and included four conditions, chief among them full strike pay, the right of the strike committee to introduce structural reforms, and worker participation in the decision-making machinery. When the administrative staff joined the strike on 22 May (130 voting in favor, 120 against, with 250 absent) the nature of the strike changed radically. The young technocrats and administrators and the trade union leaders were now in a dominant position on the strike committee. This "take-over" did not pass unchallenged: among other incidents there was a violent row over the function of trade union officials, which led to the break-up of the so-called structural commission, charged with handling the question of workers' management. Some of the young technocrats on this commission, mostly members of the CGC (Confederation of Administrative Staff) had tried to use their vote to force their own conception of management on the workers, to wit the modernization, and not the destruction, of the existing hierarchical structure. Other members of the commission, by contrast, put forward the principle of workers' direct participation in management, on Yugoslav lines.

The interest of these proposals is that they forced the workers to take a very hard look at the possible forms of direct participation in industry. Quite a few of them realized that the so-called co-management proposal of the technocrats was merely a blind that allowed them to strengthen their grip over the rest. In particular, by retaining the system of "points" and promotion, confidential information, and by making profitability the chief criterion, "co-management" must rapidly degenerate into the old system. By contrast, real workers' participation at the decision-making level is bound to weaken the power of the trade union bureaucrats and the technical experts. No wonder then, that the trade unions were so hostile to the following proposals submitted by the more radical members of the structural commission:

(1) Every decision, without exception, must be taken jointly by a rank and file committee consisting of twelve workers and the departmental chief.

(2) If they agree, the decision will be put into force immediately. If there is disagreement, the matter is brought before a works council, on which workers and management have equal representation. The workers' representatives are not permanent, but are appointed for a particular council meeting, and can be recalled at any time. The works council has no power to make decisions, its job is to re-examine the problem, suggest solutions, and refer them back for decision to the particular rank and file committee in which the conflict originated.

(3) If the conflict continues, the whole matter will be brought before a standing committee dealing with departmental affairs in general. This committee too has equal worker-management representation and is elected for a maximum of one year, while subject to immediate dismissal. It decides the issue by a majority, with the head of the department having the casting vote. The decision is then enforced without right of appeal.

Two things are clear: that the experts are reduced to a technical rather than managerial function and that the trade union delegates have no say in departmental affairs. This explains the position of the management and trade unions quoted in Le Monde on 2/3 June, 1968: "We must know exactly what, in practical terms, this involves for us. We are not yet ready for action, but we are keeping an open mind."

In fact, the trade unions and technical staff made no attempt at all to apply these principles, but simply promised to enter into negotiation with the management once the strike was over. The habit of leaving decisions to the management dies hard! The principle of co-management was not even mentioned directly, only the creation of a commission to inquire into new methods of organization. It is evident that, at best, there would have emerged a consultative body, an unholy alliance between the trade unions, administrators, and bosses, who would share out the jobs between them, and agree to preserve the status quo.

This whole situation utterly disgusted the young workers who had thought all along that the strike was for greater things than that. They now had to listen to interminable discussions, to flatulent and hackneyed phrases instead of concrete proposals. And so the strike degenerated and the strike committee, whose 150 members had planned to work without a permanent secretariat, and to allocate their different tasks to a number of autonomous sub-committees, was suborned by the bureaucrats. The lesson is clear: once the workers stop fighting their own battles, they have lost the war.

The TSF Works at Brest

Another attempt to achieve workers' control was made during the general strike at the TSF (Wireless Telegraphy) works in Brest (Brittany).

Some years ago, the TSF opened a factory there as part of the State plan to develop the depressed areas. Technical and administrative experts were brought in from Paris and eleven hundred workers were recruited on the spot, mostly unskilled. The central board, no doubt in order to receive further State subsidies for the Brest factory, only gave it the most un-profitable contracts. As a result, they were able to oppose all wage claims on the grounds that the factory was running at a loss. This caused a great deal of anxiety, particularly among the technical staff who were afraid that the factory might close down and that they would be thrown out of work.

On 20 May, groups representing various branches of the factory (workshops, offices, laboratories) elected a strike committee and then set up "workers' tribunals" which concluded that the administrative staff was incompetent, and insolent in its dealings with subordinates.

A report to that effect was sent out to the management board, and a pamphlet calling for the democratization of the factory was printed and widely distributed. It called for workers' control over training courses, a guaranteed promotions scheme, definition of jobs and responsibilities, and control over the finances of the factory.

On 18 June, after six days of fruitless discussion on various topics, including the setting up of worker-management councils, the workers decided to down tools by 607 to 357 against. The management continued in its refusal to admit workers' delegates to the board, and even the official CFTC representatives were unable to make them change their minds.

Work was restarted on Friday, 21 June (551 for and 152 against), after discussions between local trade union representatives and the Paris Board had led to the creation of a "works council" consisting of five members appointed by the management and twelve appointed by the staff. This was charged with studying "changes in structure" and improvement of working conditions. The works council had no more than an advisory capacity and was expected to submit its suggestions towards the end of the year.

This progressive nibbling away of the claims was very significant! At the beginning, the call was for direct workers' participation in management, then it was workers' councils and finally these became a mere study commission. Once again a real attempt to achieve a workers' democracy had been smartly outwitted.

The Atomic Energy Center at Saclay

Let us now look at what happened at CEA (Atomic Energy Center).

Of the 6 to 7,000 employees at the CEA (Saclay), some 4,500, including 25 per cent of the engineering staff, were covered by collective agreements. The rest were not members of the industry proper; they included charwomen, secretaries, draftsmen, technicians and maintenance men brought in from outside. There were also a number of French and foreign students studying at the CEA.

During the strike, the CEA works were occupied: 83 per cent of the staff stayed in during the entire strike—and even over the Ascension and Whitsun week-ends at least 500 people remained in the Center. During this time, long discussions were held on the subject of works reorganization and allied topics. The strike itself had been started by a small nucleus of research workers (practical and theoretical physicists) most of whom were extremely well paid. Not directly concerned with production, young, and in touch with the universities, these men acted in disregard, and often against the wishes, of the trade unions. The strike lasted for no more than fifteen days, and stopped when the administration promised to introduce a number of structural reforms and to make good all wages and salaries lost during the strike.

As a result of these reforms, a veritable pyramid of works councils was set up, with a consultative council, presided over by a chairman, right on top. In the constitution of the works councils, the trade union machinery was completely by-passed, groups of the workers electing one delegate each. All the delegates were subject to immediate dismissal and, at first, there was a demand that the chairman himself should be answerable to the whole staff. Needless to say, this demand was never met.

It is therefore true to say that, as far as giving the workers a say in management, the famous "pyramid of committees" was completely irrelevant; its only usefulness was to keep the staff informed of what was happening at the top, but even here its work was severely restricted. The old strike committee, which had been formed spontaneously, was re-elected almost to a man, but it was now reduced to a kind of inferior intelligence service; and, moreover, was impeded at every point by the various committee chairmen.

The Rhône-Poulenc Works

It might also be interesting to examine the case of the Workers' Committees in the Rhône-Poulenc works in Vitry.

For years before the strike, the workers here had taken little interest in politics or in trade union activities. But once the student movement started, the young workers in particular suddenly turned militant, so much so that some of them even helped to man the barricades.

The big twenty-four hour strike of 13 May, with its "parliamentary" aims, was joined by about 50 per cent of the workers. The staff grades did not take part and the foremen did so reluctantly. From 13 to 20 May, the factory kept running, but there was a growing sense of unrest among the workers.

On Friday, 17 May, the management decided to stop all assembly lines, probably with the intention of staging a lock-out. On that evening, the trade union liaison committee called a general meeting (from 50 to 60 per cent attended). The majority of those present (60 per cent) voted for an immediate stay-in, but since the trade unions insisted on a clear two-thirds majority, the factory was not occupied that week-end.

On Saturday, the 18th, the trade union liaison committee decided to stage a stay-in strike on Monday, 20th. The CGT then proposed the formation of Shop Floor Committees, and this was accepted for various reasons by the CFDT and the FO.

This extraordinary proposal was probably a maneuver by the CGT to outwit the other two trade unions.

The stay-in strike began and, from the start, about 2,000 workers occupied the factory. At the end of the week, some fifteen staff-grades also decided to join the strike, after many votes and despite the opposition of their own trade union (the CTC).

The Shop Floor Committees

The Shop Floor Committees, as we saw, were formed at the suggestion of the trade unions, but were quickly swamped by non-union members.

There were thirty-nine Shop Floor Committees in all. They elected four delegates each to a central committee whose 156 members were subject to immediate recall. Meetings of the central committee were public and could be reported. Shop Floor Committees were organized in each building, so that while some combined various categories of workers—from unskilled to staff grades, others, for instance in the research buildings, were made up entirely of technicians.

On Sunday, 19 May, the CGT proposed the creation of an executive committee at a general meeting of all trade unionists, in which it held a majority. No member of this executive committee was allowed to serve on the central committee.

There were two ostensible reasons for forming a separate executive committee:

(1) The management was only prepared to discuss matters with trade union members;

(2) Trade union members were the only ones who were legally entitled to go on strike.

After a week of argument, the Shop Floor Committees finally succeeded in getting a non-trade union member into the executive committee.

During the fortnight preceding the Whitsun week-end, the Shop Floor Committees reached the highest peak of their activities. At the time, the workers all thought this was the obvious way to organize: all propositions were listened to and discussed while the better ones were put to the vote, for instance the entry of non-trade union members into the executive committee. During this entire period, the trade union members collaborated with the Shop Floor Committees without any trouble—all of them were simply comrades on strike. The executive committee limited itself to carrying out the decisions of the central committee.

The subject uppermost in all these discussions was direct control of the factory. At the same time, smaller committees of a dozen or so workers discussed such political subjects as the present strategy of the Communist Party, workers' rights, and the role of the trade unions.

By the beginning of the month, all the subjects had been talked out and a certain lassitude set in, although de Gaulle's speech on 30th gave the discussions a shot in the arm. Even so, on 1 June, there was a noisy meeting of the central committee devoted exclusively to the subject of allocating petrol for the Whitsun week-end!

When the factory was re-occupied after Whitsun, the spirit was no longer the same. Serious discussions gave way to card-playing, bowling and volley-ball. The trade unions began to peddle their wares again, sapping the strength of the movement.

It was during this second period that the trade unions started negotiations with the management, and needless to say, their first claims concerned the status of the trade unions in the works.

After the Grenelle agreement, the CGT did not lose any time calling on everybody to go back to work ("the elections . . .," "we can obtain no more . . ."), and despite very strong resistance from those occupying the factory, pulled out its own militants on Monday, 10th.

After this, a number of CGT membership cards were torn up, which did not stop the CFDT from associating itself with the CGT call for a general return to work on 12 May, nor did the fact that the vote for a continued stay-in was 580 against 470.

The Shop Floor Committees at Rhône-Poulenc-Vitry were set up, as we have seen, on a rather unusual work-unit basis, which, in some cases, tended to separate technicians and workers into separate committees. One fact sticks out: although there was some cooperation between the workers and technicians, there was no real fusion between the different committees. Clearly, the division of labor introduced by the capitalists is hard to kill.

Contact with outside strikers was maintained by a small group of radicals, whose example helped to start Workers' Committees in other factories, such as Hispano-Suiza, Thomson-Bagneux, etc. Most workers, however, tried to run their own private little semi-detached strike, just as they tried to lead their own private little semi-detached lives.

What happened at Rhône-Poulenc-Vitry shows clearly why workers as a whole are so apathetic and apolitical: when they took responsibility, they came alive and took an active part in making important decisions, when matters were taken out of their hands and delegated to the unions, they lost interest and went back to playing solo.

Chapter Seven

Government Administration and the Legal System

We have placed a variety of readings under this heading, which covers decentralization of government administration and police and popularization of justice. They are grouped together for two reasons: First, because they concern *implementation* of policy rather than its determination, and, second, because it is most difficult to imagine administration, the police, or the courts becoming fully participatory. Each sphere emphasizes "professionalism"—in part because at various times in the past there were reactions against spoils systems, political machines built on patronage, amateur lawyers, and police corruption—all of which were deemed to be the product of unprofessional practices.

In a brilliant review, Herbert Kaufman perceives that, with the questioning by many of traditional forms of representation, "the quest for representativeness in this generation centers primarily on administrative agencies"—civilian police review boards, decentralized school systems, participation of the poor in poverty programs. But, says Kaufman, we are simply in one phase of a recurring cycle. Decentralization will soon produce disparities and competition among the units, a revival of spoils systems, and other related difficulties:

> So the wave of reform after the one now in progress will rally under a banner of earlier days: Take administration out of politics and politics out of administration.[1]

---

[1] "Administrative Decentralization and Political Power," *Public Administration Review*, Vol. XXIX, No. 1 (January–February 1969), pp. 3–15; citation from p. 12.

This kind of analysis, relying on a cyclical conception of the nature of drives for reform, has been pushed to an even higher level of generality by Robert Michels:

> When democracies have gained a certain stage of development, they undergo a gradual transformation, adopting the aristocratic spirit, and in many cases also the aristocratic forms, against which at the outset they struggled so fiercely. Now new accusers arise to denounce the traitors; after an era of glorious combats and of inglorious power, they end by fusing with the old dominant class; whereupon once more they are in their turn attacked by fresh opponents who appeal to the name of democracy. It is probable that this cruel game will continue without end.[2]

Our selections do not discuss one possible way to escape Michels' pessimistic outlook: the rotation of personnel, perhaps extending to reversals of roles. This technique would break up administrative logjams, preventing officials from building up elaborate nests and then assiduously feathering them. Such rotations have been practiced in Yugoslavia, and something of the sort was tried in the Soviet Union under Khrushchev. In the latter case, the Party Rules of 1961 required that up to as many as half the members of party bodies at various levels not be reelected at the next election and that key officials be limited to two or three successive terms in office.[3] However, it was not very successful, and these provisions were dropped after Khrushchev's departure.

---

[2] *Political Parties* (New York: Crowell-Collier, 1962), p. 371.

[3] Jan Triska, ed., *Soviet Communism Programs and Rules* (San Francisco: Chandler, 1962), p. 170.

Political Effects of Decentralized Administration in the United States

Alexis de Tocqueville

In this first selection Alexis de Tocqueville, an early nineteenth-century French observer of American ways, is using a broad definition of "administration." Tocqueville wanted local affairs handled locally, and to justify this he assembles criticisms of centralized administration that echo through many of the other readings in this section. Notice especially that Tocqueville's assessment of the "political" advantages corresponds to what we would refer to today as benefits in "political socialization" from participation in government.

"Centralization" is a word in general and daily use, without any precise meaning being attached to it. Nevertheless, there exist two distinct kinds of centralization, which it is necessary to discriminate with accuracy.

Certain interests are common to all parts of a nation, such as the enactment of its general laws and the maintenace of its foreign relations. Other interests are peculiar to certain parts of the nation, such, for instance, as the business of the several townships. When the power that directs the former or general interests is concentrated in one place or in the same persons, it constitutes a centralized government. To concentrate in like manner in one place the direction of the latter or local interests, constitutes what may be termed a centralized administration.

Upon some points these two kinds of centralization coincide, but by classifying the objects which fall more particularly within the province of each, they may easily be distinguished.

It is evident that a centralized government acquires immense power when united to centralized administration. Thus combined, it accustoms men to set their own will habitually and completely aside; to submit, not only for once, or upon one point, but in every respect, and at all times. Not only, therefore, does this union of power subdue them compulsorily, but it

From *Democracy in America* by Alexis de Tocqueville, trans. by Phillips Bradley, Vol. I, Vintage Edition, pp. 89–90, 93–101. Copyright 1945 by Alfred A. Knopf, Inc. Reprinted by permission of the publisher.

affects their ordinary habits; it isolates them and then influences each separately.

These two kinds of centralization assist and attract each other, but they must not be supposed to be inseparable. It is impossible to imagine a more completely centralized government than that which existed in France under Louis XIV; when the same individual was the author and the interpreter of the laws, and the representative of France at home and abroad, he was justified in asserting that he constituted the state. Nevertheless, the administration was much less centralized under Louis XIV than it is at the present day.

In England the centralization of the government is carried to great perfection; the state has the compact vigor of one man, and its will puts immense masses in motion and turns its whole power where it pleases. But England, which has done such great things for the last fifty years, has never centralized its administration. Indeed, I cannot conceive that a nation can live and prosper without a powerful centralization of government. But I am of the opinion that a centralized administration is fit only to enervate the nations in which it exists, by incessantly diminishing their local spirit. Although such an administration can bring together at a given moment, on a given point, all the disposable resources of a people, it injures the renewal of those resources. It may ensure a victory in the hour of strife, but it gradually relaxes the sinews of strength. It may help admirably the transient greatness of a man, but not the durable prosperity of a nation.

The partisans of centralization in Europe are wont to maintain that the government can administer the affairs of each locality better than the citizens can do it for themselves. This may be true when the central power is enlightened and the local authorities are ignorant; when it is alert and they are slow; when it is accustomed to act and they to obey. Indeed, it is evident that this double tendency must augment with the increase of centralization, and that the readiness of the one and the incapacity of the others must become more and more prominent. But I deny that it is so when the people are as enlightened, as awake to their interests, and as accustomed to reflect on them as the Americans are. I am persuaded, on the contrary, that in this case the collective strength of the citizens will always conduce more efficaciously to the public welfare than the authority of the government. I know it is difficult to point out with certainty the means of arousing a sleeping population and of giving it passions and knowledge which it does not possess; it is, I am well aware, an arduous task to persuade men to busy themselves about their own affairs. It would frequently be easier to interest them in the punctilios of court etiquette than in the repairs of their common dwelling. But whenever a central administration affects completely to supersede the persons most interested, I believe that it is either misled or desirous to mislead. However enlightened and skillful a central power may be, it cannot of itself embrace all the details of the life of a great nation. Such vigilance exceeds the powers of man. And when it attempts unaided to create and set in motion so many complicated springs, it must submit to a very imperfect result or exhaust itself in bootless efforts.

Centralization easily succeeds, indeed, in subjecting the external actions of men to a certain uniformity, which we come at last to love for its own sake, independently of the objects to which it is applied, like those devotees who worship the statue and forget the deity it represents. Centralization imparts without difficulty an admirable regularity to the routine of business; provides skillfully for the details of the social police; represses small disorders and petty misdemeanors; maintains society in a *status quo* alike secure from improvement and decline; and perpetuates a drowsy regularity in the conduct of affairs which the heads of the administration are wont to call good order and public tranquillity;[1] in short, it excels in prevention, but not in action. Its force deserts it when society is to be profoundly moved, or accelerated in its course; and if once the co-operation of private citizens is necessary to the furtherance of its measures, the secret of its impotence is disclosed. Even while the centralized power, in its despair, invokes the assistance of the citizens, it says to them: "You shall act just as I please, as much as I please, and in the direction which I please. You are to take charge of the details without aspiring to guide the system; you are to work in darkness; and afterwards you may judge my work by its results." These are not the conditions on which the alliance of the human will is to be obtained; it must be free in its gait and responsible for its acts, or (such is the constitution of man) the citizen had rather remain a passive spectator than a dependent actor in schemes with which he is unacquainted.

It is undeniable that the want of those uniform regulations which control the conduct of every inhabitant of France is not infrequently felt in the United States. Gross instances of social indifference and neglect are to be met with; and from time to time disgraceful blemishes are seen, in complete contrast with the surrounding civilization. Useful undertakings which cannot succeed without perpetual attention and rigorous exactitude are frequently abandoned; for in America, as well as in other countries, the people proceed by sudden impulses and momentary exertions. The European, accustomed to find a functionary always at hand to interfere with all he undertakes, reconciles himself with difficulty to the complex mechanism of the administration of the townships. In general it may be affirmed that the lesser details of the police, which render life easy and comfortable, are neglected in America, but that the essential guarantees of man in society are as strong there as elsewhere. In America the power that conducts the administration is far less regular, less enlightened, and less skillful, but a hundredfold greater than in Europe. In no country in the world do the citizens make such exertions for the common weal. I know of no people who have established schools so numerous and efficacious, places of public worship better suited to the wants of the inhabitants, or roads kept in better repair. Uniformity or permanence of design, the minute arrangement of details,[2] and the perfection of administrative system must not be sought for in the United States; what we find there is the presence of a power which, if it is somewhat wild, is at least robust, and an existence checkered with accidents, indeed, but full of animation and effort.

Granting, for an instant, that the villages and counties of the United States would be more usefully governed by a central authority which they had never seen than by functionaries taken from among them; admitting, for the sake of argument, that there would be more security in America, and the resources of society would be better employed there, if the whole administration centered in a single arm—still the *political* advantages which the Americans derive from their decentralized system would induce me to prefer it to the contrary plan. It profits me but little, after all, that a vigilant authority always protects the tranquillity of my pleasures and constantly averts all dangers from my path, without my care or concern, if this same authority is the absolute master of my liberty and my life, and if it so monopolizes movement and life that when it languishes everything languishes around it, that when it sleeps everything must sleep, and that when it dies the state itself must perish.

There are countries in Europe where the native considers himself as a kind of settler, indifferent to the fate of the spot which he inhabits. The greatest changes are effected there without his concurrence, and (unless chance may have apprised him of the event) without his knowledge; nay, more, the condition of his village, the police of his street, the repairs of the church or the parsonage, do not concern him; for he looks upon all these things as unconnected with himself and as the property of a powerful stranger whom he calls the government. He has only a life interest in these possessions, without the spirit of ownership or any ideas of improvement. This want of interest in his own affairs goes so far that if his own safety or that of his children is at last endangered, instead of trying to avert the peril, he will fold his arms and wait till the whole nation comes to his aid. This man who has so completely sacrificed his own free will does not, more than any other person, love obedience; he cowers, it is true, before the pettiest officer, but he braves the law with the spirit of a conquered foe as soon as its superior force is withdrawn; he perpetually oscillates between servitude and license.

When a nation has arrived at this state, it must either change its customs and its laws, or perish; for the source of public virtues is dried up; and though it may contain subjects, it has no citizens. Such communities are a natural prey to foreign conquests; and if they do not wholly disappear from the scene, it is only because they are surrounded by other nations similar or inferior to themselves; it is because they still have an indefinable instinct of patriotism; and an involuntary pride in the name of their country, or a vague reminiscence of its bygone fame, suffices to give them an impulse of self-preservation.

It is not the *administrative*, but the *political* effects of decentralization that I most admire in America. In the United States the interests of the country are everywhere kept in view; they are an object of solicitude to the people of the whole Union, and every citizen is as warmly attached to them as if they were his own. He takes pride in the glory of his nation; he boasts of its success, to which he conceives himself to have contributed; and he rejoices in the general prosperity by which he profits. The feeling he entertains towards the state is analogous to that which unites him to his family, and it is by a kind of selfishness that he interests himself in the welfare of his country.

To the European, a public officer represents a superior force; to an American, he represents a right. In America, then, it may be said that no one renders obedience to man, but to justice and to law. If the opinion that the citizen entertains of himself is exaggerated, it is at least salutary; he unhesitatingly confides in his own powers, which appear to him to be all-sufficient. When a private individual meditates an undertaking, however directly connected it may be with the welfare of society, he never thinks of soliciting the co-operation of the government; but he publishes his plan, offers to execute it, courts the assistance of other individuals, and struggles manfully against all obstacles. Undoubtedly he is often less successful than the state might have been in his position; but in the end the sum of these private undertakings far exceeds all that the government could have done.

As the administrative authority is within the reach of the citizens, whom in some degree it represents, it excites neither their jealousy nor hatred; as its resources are limited, everyone feels that he must not rely solely on its aid. Thus when the administration thinks fit to act within its own limits, it is not abandoned to itself, as in Europe; the duties of private citizens are not supposed to have lapsed because the state has come into action, but everyone is ready, on the contrary, to guide and support it. This action of individuals, joined to that of the public authorities, frequently accomplishes what the most energetic centralized administration would be unable to do.

It would be easy to adduce several facts in proof of what I advance, but I had rather give only one, with which I am best acquainted. In America the means that the authorities have at their disposal for the discovery of crimes and the arrest of criminals are few. A state police does not exist, and passports are unknown. The criminal police of the United States cannot be compared with that of France; the magistrates and public agents are not numerous; they do not always initiate the measures for arresting the guilty; and the examinations of prisoners are rapid and oral. Yet I believe that in no country does crime more rarely elude punishment. The reason is that everyone conceives himself to be interested in furnishing evidence of the crime and in seizing the delinquent. During my stay in the United States I witnessed the spontaneous formation of committees in a county for the pursuit and prosecution of a man who had committed a great crime. In Europe a criminal is an unhappy man who is struggling for his life against the agents of power, while the people are merely a spectator of the conflict; in America he is looked upon as an enemy of the human race, and the whole of mankind is against him.

I believe that provincial institutions are useful to all nations, but nowhere do they appear to me to be more necessary than among a democratic people. In an aristocracy order can always be maintained in the midst of liberty; and as the rulers have a great deal to lose, order is to them a matter of great interest. In like manner an aristocracy protects the people from the excesses of despotism, because it always possesses an organized power ready to resist a despot. But a democracy without provincial institutions has no security against these evils. How can a populace unaccustomed to freedom in small concerns learn to use it temperately in great affairs? What resistance can be offered to tyranny in a country where each individual is weak and where the citizens are not united by any common interest? Those who dread the license of the mob and those who fear absolute power ought alike to desire the gradual development of provincial liberties.

I have visited the two nations in which the system of provincial liberty has been most perfectly established, and I have listened to the opinions of different parties in those countries. In America I met with men who secretly aspired to destroy the democratic institutions of the Union; in England I found others who openly attacked the aristocracy; but I found no one who did not regard provincial independence as a great good. In both countries I heard a thousand different causes assigned for the evils of the state, but the local system was never mentioned among them. I heard citizens attribute the power and prosperity of their country to a multitude of reasons, but they all placed the advantages of local institutions in the foremost rank.

Am I to suppose that when men who are naturally so divided on religious opinions and on political theories agree on one point (and that one which they can best judge, as it is one of which they have daily experience) they are all in error? The only nations which deny the utility of provincial liberties are those which have fewest of them; in other words, only those censure the institution who do not know it.

Notes

[1] China appears to me to present the most perfect instance of that species of well-being which a highly centralized administration may furnish to its subjects. Travelers assure us that the Chinese have tranquillity without happiness, industry without improvement, stability without strength, and public order without public morality. The condition of society there is always tolerable, never excellent. I imagine that when China is opened to European observation, it will be found to contain the most perfect model of a centralized administration that exists in the universe.

2 A writer of talent who, in a comparison of the finances of France with those of the United States, has proved that ingenuity cannot always supply the place of the knowledge of facts, justly reproaches the Americans for the sort of confusion that exists in the accounts of the expenditure in the townships; and after giving the model of a departmental budget in France, he adds: "We are indebted to centralization, that admirable invention of a great man, for the order and method which prevail alike in all the municipal budgets, from the largest city to the humblest commune." Whatever may be my admiration of this result, when I see the communes of France, with their excellent system of accounts, plunged into the grossest ignorance of their true interests, and abandoned to so incorrigible an apathy that they seem to vegetate rather than to live; when, on the other hand, I observe the activity, the information, and the spirit of enterprise in those American townships whose budgets are neither methodical nor uniform, I see that society there is always at work. I am struck by the spectacle; for, to my mind, the end of a good government is to ensure the welfare of a people, and not merely to establish order in the midst of its misery. I am therefore led to suppose that the prosperity of the American townships and the apparent confusion of their finances, the distress of the French communes and the perfection of their budget, may be attributable to the same cause. At any rate, I am suspicious of a good that is united with so many evils, and I am not averse to an evil that is compensated by so many benefits.

Decentralization: Antidote for Remote Control

David E. Lilienthal

Citing a passage from the previous Tocqueville article, David E. Lilienthal proposes "decentralized administration of centralized authority" as the way to obtain the benefits of big government and single-agency coordination of comprehensive planning without abandoning citizen participation. This idea contrasts with Jean-Jacques Rousseau's opposition to involving masses of citizens in the administration of the broad policies they have set down in law. Drawing on his experience as head of the TVA, Lilienthal feels that, in an age when the nature of the problems requires national decision-making, this decentralized administration is vital if we are to retain a healthy democracy. Robert Nisbet has proposed a broad extension of Lilienthal's principle into private organizations and groups as well as public ones, arguing that it is equally valid for business, labor, charitable organizations, etc.* On the other hand, we should keep in mind Montesquieu's contention that democracy can be corrupted by excessive equality in the administration of public affairs; for then the people "want to manage everything themselves, to debate for the senate, to execute for the magistrate and to decide for the judges," despite their obvious inability to do so.**

What I have been describing is the way by which the people of one region have been working out a decentralized administration of the functions of the central government.

The chief purpose of such methods of decentralization is to provide greater opportunity for a richer, more interesting, and more responsible life for the individual, and to increase his genuine freedom, his sense of his

"Decentralization: Antidote for Remote Control" from TVA: Democracy on the March by David E. Lilienthal, Twentieth Anniversary Edition (New York: Harper, 1953), pp. 138–149. Copyright 1944, 1953 by David E. Lilienthal. Reprinted by permission of Harper and Row, Publishers.

* The Quest for Community: Studies in the Ethics of Order and Freedom (New York: Oxford University Press, 1953), see Chapter 11 and Conclusion. Both Lilienthal and Nisbet warn that we cannot decentralize if we make a fetish of uniformity and standardization.

** The Spirit of the Laws, I, viii, 2; trans. by Thomas Nugent (New York: Hafner, 1949), p. 109.

own importance. Centralization in administration tends to promote remote and absentee control, and thereby increasingly denies to the individual the opportunity to make decisions and to carry those responsibilities by which human personality is nourished and developed.

I find it impossible to comprehend how democracy can be a living reality if people are remote from their government and in their daily lives are not made a part of it, or if the control and direction of making a living—industry, farming, the distribution of goods—is too far removed from the stream of life and from the local community.

"Centralization" is no mere technical matter of "management," of "bigness versus smallness." We are dealing here with those deep urgencies of the human spirit which are embodied in the faith we call "democracy." It is precisely here that modern life puts America to one of its most severe tests; it is here that the experience in this valley laboratory in democratic methods takes on unusual meaning.

Congress established the TVA as a national agency, but one confined to a particular region. This provided an opportunity for decentralization. A limited region, its outlines drawn by its natural resources and the cohesion of its human interests, was the unit of federal activity rather than the whole nation.

To the degree that the experiment as administered helps to solve some of the problems raised by the flight of power to the center and the isolation of the citizen from his government, history may mark that down as TVA's most substantial contribution to national well-being and the strengthening of democracy.

TVA's methods are, of course, not the only ones that must be tried. There will be different types and other methods of administration suitable to other problems and different areas. Diversity will always be the mark of decentralized administration, just as surely as uniformity (often for its own sake) is the mark of central and remote control.

Decentralization in action is anything but an easy task. Its course will never be a smooth one, without setbacks and disappointments. Everywhere, nevertheless, the problem must be faced if we are to conserve and develop the energies and zeal of our citizens, to keep open the channels through which our democracy is constantly invigorated.

Overcentralization is, of course, no unique characteristic of our own national government. It is the tendency all over the world, in business as well as government. Centralization of power at our national capital is largely the result of efforts to protect citizens from the evils of overcentralization in the industrial and commercial life of the country, a tendency that has been going on for generations. Chain stores have supplanted the corner grocery and the village drug store. In banks and theaters, hotels, and systems of power supply—in every activity of business—local controls have almost disappeared. Business centralization has brought advantages in lower unit costs and improved services, and in new products of centralized research. Except by the village dressmaker, or the owner of the country store or hotel, the advantages of centralization, at the beginning, at least, were gratefully received. People seemed to like a kind of sense of security that came with uniformity.

The paying of the price came later when towns and villages began to take stock. The profits of local commerce had been siphoned off, local enterprise was stifled, and moribund communities awoke to some of the ultimate penalties of remote control. When a major depression struck in 1929, business overcentralization may well have made us more vulnerable than ever before to the disruption that ensued. Power had gone to the center; decisions had to be made far from the people whose lives would be affected. Cities and states seemed powerless. The federal government had to act. The tendency to centralization in government was quickened.

It was ironic that at this juncture, twenty years ago, centralized businesses should become, as they did, eloquent advocates of the merits of decentralization in government. From their central headquarters they began to issue statements and brochures. And a wondrous state of confusion arose in the minds of men: they ate food bought at a store that had its replica in almost every town from coast to coast; they took their ease in standard chairs; they wore suits of identical weave and pattern and shoes identical with those worn all over the country. In the midst of this uniformity they all listened on the radio to the same program at the same time, a program that bewailed the evils of "regimentation," or they read an indignant editorial in their local evening papers (identical with an editorial that same day in a dozen other newspapers of the same chain) urging them to vote for a candidate who said he would bring an end to centralization in government.

I am not one who is attracted by that appealing combination of big business and little government. I believe that the federal government must have large grants of power progressively to deal with problems that are national in their consequences and remedy, problems too broad to be handled by local political units. I am convinced, as surely most realistic men must be, that from time to time in the future further responsibilities may have to be assumed by the central government to deal on a national basis with issues which our complex economic system calls into being.

The people have a right to demand that their federal government keep clear the channels by which they can enjoy the benefits of advances in science and research, the right to demand protection from economic abuses beyond the power of their local political units to control. But they have the further right to insist that the methods of administration used to carry out the very laws enacted for their individual welfare will not atrophy the human resources of their democracy.

It is folly to forget that the same dangers and the same temptations exist whether the centralization is in government or in mammoth business enterprises. In both cases the problem is to capture the advantages that come with such centralized authority as we find we must have, and at the same time to avoid the hazards of overcentralized *administration* of those central powers.

It can be done. It can be done and is more latterly being done in many business operations, as well as in government activities. I have described the way in which the operations of the Tennessee Valley's power system have been brought close to the people of this valley. Certainly that makes clear that no blind fear of bigness underlies my conviction of the necessity for decentralized administration. Here we have centralized only the activities in connection with electric supply which are common to a large integrated area and can best be carried on by a single agency, that is, producing the power and then transmitting it from the dams and steam-electric plants to the gates of communities. But, as I have pointed out, in the Tennessee Valley system the ownership and management of the distribution systems are decentralized. Here, I believe, is one example, among many, of an effective combination of the advantages of the *decentralized administration of centralized authority*.

The distinction between authority and its administration is a vital one. For a long time all of us—administrators, citizens, and politicians—have been confused on this point. We have acted on the assumption that because there was an increasing need for centralized authority, the centralized execution of that authority was likewise inevitable. We have assumed that, as new powers were granted to the government with its seat at Washington, these powers therefore must also be administered from Washington. Out of lethargy and confusion we have taken it for granted that the price of federal action was a top-heavy, cumbersome administration. Clearly this is nonsense. *The problem is to divorce the two ideas of authority and administration of authority.*

Our task is to invent devices of management through which many of the powers of the central government will be administered not by remote control from Washington but in the field.

A national capital almost anywhere is bound to suffer from lack of knowledge of local conditions, of parochial customs. And in a country as vast as the United States, in which local and regional differences are so vital and so precious, many citizens and administrators are coming to see more and more that powers centrally administered from Washington cannot and do not take into account the physical and economic variations within our boundaries. The national strength and culture that flows from that very diversity cannot be nourished by too greatly centralized administration.

It has become common observation that in Washington it is too easy to forget, let us say, the centuries of tradition that lie behind the customs of the Spanish-American citizens in New Mexico and how different their problems are from those of the men and women whose lives have been spent in the mountains of the South. It is hard, from a distance, with only memoranda before him, for an administrator to be alive to the fact that the ways of suburban New Jersey are alien to the customs of the coast of eastern Maine. And yet the fact that the ancestors of these people brought dissimilar customs from their homelands, that they have earned their living in different manners, that the climates in which they live are not the same—this is all deeply important when a national program is brought to the men and women in cities and villages and farms for application, when their daily lives are visibly affected. When those differences in customs are not comprehended, statutes seem irrelevant or harsh. They destroy confidence, and disturb rather than promote people's welfare.

Centralization at the national capital or within a business undertaking always glorifies the importance of pieces of paper. This dims the sense of reality. As men and organizations acquire a preoccupation with papers they become less understanding, less perceptive of the reality of those matters with which they should be dealing: particular human problems, particular human beings, actual things in a real America—highways, wheat, barges, drought, floods, backyards, blast furnaces. The reason why there is and always has been so much bureaucratic spirit, such organizational intrigue, so much pathologic personal ambition, so many burning jealousies and vendettas in a capital city (any capital city, not only Washington), is no mystery. The facts with which a highly centralized institution deals tend to be the men and women of that institution itself, and their ideas and ambitions. To maintain perspective and human understanding in the atmosphere of centralization is a task that many able and conscientious people have found well-nigh impossible.

Making decisions from papers has a dehumanizing effect. Much of man's inhumanity to man is explained by it. Almost all great observers of mankind have noted it. In *War and Peace* Tolstoy makes it particularly clear. Pierre Bezukhov is standing a captive before one of Napoleon's generals, Marshal Davout.

> At the first glance, when Davout had only raised his head from the *papers where human affairs and lives were indicated by numbers*, Pierre was merely a circumstance, and Davout could have shot him without burdening his conscience with an evil deed, but now he saw in him a human being. . . .

To see each citizen thus as a "human being" is far easier at the grass roots. That is where more of the functions of our federal government should be exercised.

The permanence of democracy indeed demands this. For the cumulative effect of overcentralization of administration in a national capital is greatly to reduce the effectiveness of government. It is serious enough in itself when, because of remoteness and ignorance of local conditions or the slowness of their operation, laws and programs fail of their purposes. We are threatened, however, with an even more disastrous sequence, the loss of the people's confidence, the very foundation of democratic government. Confidence does not flourish in a "government continually at a distance and out of sight," to use the language of Alexander Hamilton, himself a constant advocate of strong central authority. On the other hand, said Hamilton,

> the more the operations of the national authority are intermingled in the ordinary exercise of government, the more the citizens are accustomed to meet with it in the common occurrences of their political life, the more it is familiarized to their sight and to their feelings, the further it enters into those objects which touch the most sensible chords and put into motion the most active springs of the human heart, the greater will be the probability that it will conciliate the respect and attachment of the community.

When "the respect and attachment of the community" give place to uneasiness, fears develop that the granting of further powers may be abused. Ridicule of the capriciousness of some government officials takes the place of pride. Democracy cannot thrive long in an atmosphere of scorn or fear. One of two things ultimately happens: either distrustful citizens, their fears often capitalized upon by selfish men, refuse to yield to the national government the powers which it should have in the common interest; or an arrogant central government imposes its will by force. In either case the substance of democracy has perished.

We face a dilemma; there is no reason to conceal its proportions. I do not minimize the complexities and difficulties it presents. We need a strong central government. This is plain to everyone who sees the changed nature of our modern world. But I have deep apprehension for the future unless we learn how many of those central powers can be decentralized in their administration.

Every important administrative decision need not be made in Washington. We must rid ourselves of the notion that a new staff, with every member paid out of the federal treasury, has to administer every detail of each new federal law or regulation. We who believe devoutly in the democratic process should be the first to urge the use of methods that will keep the administration of national functions from becoming so concentrated at the national capital, so distant from the everyday life of ordinary people, as to wither and deaden the average citizen's sense of participation and partnership in government affairs. *For in this citizen participation lies the vitality of a democracy.*

Federal functions can be decentralized in their administration. But it requires a completely changed point of view on the part of citizens and their representatives. For this business of centralization is not wholly the fault of government administrators. Statutes are rarely designed to provide an opportunity for ingenuity in the development of new techniques in administration. Only infrequently do you find a new law which in its terms recognizes the hazards of overcentralization.

Most public men and editorial writers prefer the privilege of berating administrators as "bureaucrats" to suggesting and supporting ways through which the vices of bureaucracy would have less opportunity to develop. Congress has usually taken the easy course, when new laws are passed, of piling upon the shoulders of an already weary (but rarely unwilling) official the responsibility for supervising a whole new field of federal activity. He has been given a fresh corps of assistants perhaps, but upon his judgment decisions of great detail ultimately rest.

This country is too big for such a wholesale and indiscriminate pyramiding of responsibilities. In the general atmosphere of bigness, men continue to come about the same size. There is a limit to the energy and wisdom of the best; the ancient lust for power for its own sake burns in the worst.

In the case of TVA, Congress did enact a statute which permitted a decentralized administration. Had not Congress created that opportunity, the TVA could not have developed its administration at the grass roots. An area of manageable proportions—the watershed of a river as its base—was the unit of administration. Decisions could be made and responsibility taken at a point that was close to the problems themselves. That is the test of decentralization.

It is not decentralization to open regional offices or branches in each state, if decisions have to be made in Washington and the officers in the field prove to be merely errand boys. It is not decentralization nor genuine regionalism to set up an Inter-Agency Committee, as has been done in the Missouri River Basin, each of the members of the Committee being responsible to a different and separate Washington Department or bureau. The Hoover Commission's Task Force on Natural Resources, criticizing the ineffectiveness of this Inter-Agency device said that such a Committee could not see to it that "the basin is a unit for coordinated management despite the admission of informed public officials that it should be so regarded. The really important plans and decisions are made by separate Federal agencies responsible to a Washington desk or by the Congress or the President. Thus the present [Committee] organization encourages *centralization and the habits of dependence on centralized authority and largesse.*" (My italics.)

This proposition applies equally to the decentralization of huge business undertakings. Genuine decentralization means an entirely different point of view in the selecting and training of personnel. It means an emigration of talent to the grass roots. But if the important tasks, the real responsibilities, are kept at the center, men of stature will not go to the "field."

Neither is it decentralization when bureaus or departments are moved out of crowded Washington. It may be necessary and entirely wise—but it is not decentralization. You do not get decentralization as we know it in the TVA unless you meet two tests:

First, do the men in the field have the power of decision?

Second, are the people, their private and their local public institutions, actively participating in the enterprise?

There is generous lip service to decentralization on every hand. But little will be done about it unless there is real understanding of what it means, and an urgent and never ceasing demand from citizens.

When methods such as those the TVA has used are proposed, the chief objection usually made is that local communities, state agencies, or the field officers of federal agencies cannot be trusted to carry out national policies. Usually the reason is dressed up in more tactful language, but, however disguised, it is the doctrine of the elite nevertheless. The burden of proving that the men who at the time are federal officials in Washington are the only ones competent to administer the laws enacted by Congress certainly lies upon those who advance that reason. Actually such statements often prove the desperate hazards of centralization to the health of a democracy, for they exhibit, in the minds of those who put them forward, a low esteem or affectionate contempt for the abilities of anyone outside the capital city, or else a slavish concern for the existing rituals of bureaucracy.

There are of course many instances where the facts appear to support the claim that good administration of national concerns cannot be obtained through the co-operation of local agencies. Local politics, ineptitude, lack of interest and experience in public matters and in administration, brazen partisanship, even corruption—all these stand in the way. I am sure these hazards exist. I am sure, for most of them were encountered in this valley. But what are the alternatives? Fewer citizens participating in governmental administration. Less and less local community responsibility. More federal employees in the field armed with papers to be filled out and sent to Washington for "processing," because only there is "good administration" possible. The progressive atrophy of citizen interest. An even wider gulf between local communities and national government, between citizens and their vital public concerns. Such are the alternatives.

The often flabby muscles of community and individual responsibility will never be invigorated unless the muscles are given work to do. They grow strong by use; there is no other way. Although it is true that decentralization at times is ineffective because of the quality of local officials or field officers, the virtues, by comparison, of what can be done in central headquarters are somewhat illusory. For, without the co-operation of citizens (an admittedly difficult goal) and of institutions familiar to them, no detailed and far-reaching economic or social policy and no democratic planning can be made effective.

The shortcomings of highly centralized administration of national policies are not due simply to the stupidity or wrong-headedness of particular individuals. Naming a villain whenever a mess is uncovered, a favorite American custom, is of little help; it usually misses the mark. We need perspective about such things, lest we foolishly take out our anger and frustration for ineptitudes upon this man and that, this party or that, instead of turning our attention where it often belongs, viz., upon the limitations and dangers of centralization.

These evils are inherent in the overcentralized administration of huge enterprise, because it ignores the nature of man. There is light on this matter in the words of de Tocqueville, writing a century ago of the relatively simple society of the United States.

> However enlightened and however skillful a central power may be [he wrote in his *Democracy in America*] it cannot of itself embrace all the details of the existence of a great nation. . . . And when it attempts to create and set in motion so many complicated springs, it must submit to a very imperfect result, or consume itself in bootless efforts. Centralization succeeds more easily, indeed, in subjecting the external actions of men to a certain uniformity . . . and perpetuates a drowsy precision in the conduct of affairs, which is hailed by the heads of the administration as a sign of perfect order . . . in short, it excels more in prevention than in action. Its force deserts it when society is to be disturbed or accelerated in its course; and if once the co-operation of private citizens is necessary to the furtherance of its measures, the secret of its impotence is disclosed. Even while it invokes their assistance, it is on the condition that they shall act exactly as much as the government chooses, and exactly in the manner it appoints. . . . These, however, are not conditions on which the alliance of the human will is to be obtained; its carriage must be free, and its actions responsible, or (such is the constitution of man) the citizen had rather remain a passive spectator than a dependent actor in schemes with which he is unacquainted.

Out of my own experience in the Tennessee Valley I became acutely aware of the difficulties of securing the active participation of citizens at the grass roots. I know "what a task" (again using the words of de Tocqueville) it is "to persuade men to busy themselves about their own affairs." But that experience has in it more of encouragement than of despair. For in this valley, in almost every village and town and city, in every rural community, there has proved to be a rich reservoir of citizen talent for public service. The notion that brains, resourcefulness, and capacity for management are a limited commodity in America—and this it is that is behind most of the skepticism about decentralization—is a myth that is disproved in almost every chapter and page of the story of the development of this valley.

The fact that TVA was not remote but close at hand has been the most effective way to dissipate the considerable initial suspicion of this enterprise and secure from citizens of every point of view the continued wide measure of warm co-operation. In the case of the power program of the TVA, for example, if TVA were not in the region and of it, if it could not make decisions until Washington, hundreds of miles away, had "processed" the papers and reached a conclusion, I wonder if more than a handful of these valley communities would have signed a contract with the TVA for power supply. Remote control from Washington might not have seemed greatly to be preferred to remote control from a holding company office in New York. And if TVA had not in turn decentralized its own operations the plan would work badly. TVA's division and area managers and other field officials were not merely office boys with imposing titles but no standing or authority. They were selected, trained, given broad responsibility and discretion.

The decentralized administration of federal functions is no infallible panacea. Of course mistakes are made at the grass roots too. But even the mistakes are useful, for they are close at hand where the reasons behind them can be seen and understood. The wise decisions, the successes (and there are many such), are a source of pride and satisfaction to the whole community. If, as I strongly believe, power of all kinds, economic and political, must be diffused, if it is vital that citizens participate in the programs of their government, if it is important that confidence in our federal government be maintained, then decentralization is essential.

I speak of decentralization as a problem for the United States of America. But the poison of overcentralization is not a threat to us here alone. Decentralized administration is one form of antidote that is effective the world over, for it rests upon human impulses that are universal. Centralization is a threat to the human spirit everywhere, and its control is a concern of all men who love freedom.

Functions of a Bureaucratic Ideology: "Citizen Participation"

Elliot Krause

One wonders if Lilienthal's advocacy of dispersed power at the bottom is an apologetic compensation for his concentrated power at the top. This next selection, by Elliot Krause, is representative of a school of critics aiming directly at the Lilienthal thesis. The main argument is accurately summed up as follows: Citizen participation is an ideal voiced by administrators because it consciously or unconsciously justifies undemocratic administrative behavior in a democratic society; therefore the chief beneficiaries of citizen participation as a bureaucratic ideology are the bureaucrats themselves. On a more elaborate scale, this is the major point of a work by Philip Selznick that takes issue directly with Lilienthal's argument by reference to his own example of the TVA.*

The term "citizen participation" has a long history in political and social philosophy. Fullest participation of the citizen in government is a Jeffersonian ideal, and recent expressions of this philosophy can be seen in the work of Percival and Paul Goodman.[1] Verba has recently discussed the dimensions influencing degree of participation in political activity in America.[2] But besides being a general philosophical idea in American politics, it is, in the present use, a specific set of ideas used by certain types of "action" bureaucracies for a specific set of purposes. This latter use of the term, citizen participation as a bureaucratic ideology, is our topic here.

The two government bureaucracies to be considered in the analysis are: (a) the U.S. Housing and Home Finance Agency, with its local urban renewal agencies, and (b) the Community Action Program of the Office of Economic Opportunity, with its local community action agencies. The activities which are the subject for two closely related statements of the "citizen participation" ideology are, respectively, planning for urban renewal in the community and planning for action programs to improve conditions in poor areas of communities. We can give an example of the

---

From Elliot Krause, "Functions of a Bureaucratic Ideology: 'Citizen Participation,'" *Social Problems*, Vol. 16, No. 2 (Fall 1968), pp. 136–142. Reprinted by permission of the Society for the Study of Social Problems and the author.

* *TVA and the Grass Roots* (Berkeley: University of California Press, 1949).

ideology in each variant, and then discuss the ways in which the text given is ideological in the sense of our own definition of the term.

For urban renewal, the "citizen participation" ideology (in one of its official versions) reads:

> A basic approach to building the kind of citizen participation a Program needs is three-pronged. It must be planned to inform and involve . . .
>
> . . . the community as a whole
>
> . . . special interest groups, enlisting their assistance in solving particular problems
>
> . . . residents of areas to be directly affected by various program activities.
>
> People need to know what is happening to their community; what neighborhoods are going downhill; what is causing blight; what is being done to fight deterioration and what more can be done. They must have every opportunity to take constructive action.[3]

Each local urban renewal agency is allowed to devise its own method for citizen participation, as well as the specific goals and functions of this participation. The only formal requirement of the federal bureaucracy, concerning participation, is that one open hearing be held before final adoption of the urban renewal agency's plan to change the community, at which citizens of the local community may vote yes or no about the plan.[4] This vote carries no legal weight, however, as programs are not disqualified from federal funding because of local opposition.[5] As Dahl points out, this "participation" *in fact* has become an increasingly public ritual.[6]

The Community Action Program of the Office of Economic Opportunity has had a requirement of "maximum feasible participation of the poor" in the planning and carrying out of local community action programs.[7] "Maximum" and "feasible" are nowhere defined in the legislation, although in 1967 an administrative directive was made by OEO that at least ⅓ (a distinct minority) of the local board members be "poor people or representatives of the poor."[8] Again, no definitions are given. A good summation of the main points in the rationale for the Community Action Program—which Riessman calls the ideology of citizen participation—is the statement that:

> Despite the ambiguity in the term "maximum feasible participation," these 30 words open the doors to a new concept of service for the poor. Their implementation will permit the consumer to become a participant with a voice and power in the service system. He can be on the advisory committee of the community action programs; he can become a participating member of the local Neighborhood Service Center; he can become a new kind of client, a citizen-client. He can forge a new unity with professionals; he can bring into the system the best of the methods

and understandings and culture of the poor. The consumer as participant can guarantee that services will be adequate, appropriate, and utilized. The poor can become constituents in the service system. Thus, the anti-poverty legislation provides the opportunity for new forms of representation outside of the traditional one, the ballot box.[9]

In both the cases of urban renewal and community action programs, the *text* of the ideology—the words or phrases or plans being used ideologically—are government rules or "guidelines" on the meaning and importance of participation. In each case, the proponent of the ideology is a governmental or quasi-public bureaucracy on the federal level. The *target* of the ideology and the *client group* differ for the two organizations. Schematically, research evidence on this issue indicates the following approximate set of relationships. When the *proponent* of the "citizen participation" ideology is the *local urban renewal agency*, the *primary clientele group* is the middle and upper class, and the *primary target of the ideology* is the poor neighborhood and its residents. When the *proponent* of the "citizen participation" ideology is the *local community action agency*, the *primary clientele group* is the poor, and the *primary target of the ideology* is also the poor.

Notice that in the case of the urban renewal program, the primary clientele group and the primary target group are different, whereas for the Community Action Program the target group and the clientele group are essentially the same. That is, in our analysis and in that of most researchers who have objective data on urban renewal programs, "citizen participation" is an ideology directed by the urban renewal agency toward the poor residents, in order to energize them to act in favor of the goals set by the urban renewal agency, even if they are against the material interests of these poor residents. For Community Action Programs, the ideology is directed by the formal community action agency professional staff at the poor, to energize them toward the goal of acting "on their own behalf" as members of the advisory board of the local community action agency. In both uses of the ideology, implicit in the text of the message is the positive evaluation of "citizen participation" as a *good and desirable* activity, an activity which is that of participating in the program of the action bureaucracy. To further understand how "citizen participation" functions as an ideology, we must turn to the actual consequences of using it.

The Ideology in Use: Intended and Unintended Consequences

Merton has pointed out an important difference in social processes, between the short-run, intended consequences of given acts and the long-run, unintended, and sometimes even unnoticed consequences of the same acts.[10] The positing and advertising of the ideology of "citizen participation" by the urban renewal and community action bureaucracies, and their direction of this ideology at the poor, is an act which has both intended and unintended consequences for the target group, and for the group which proposes it.

CONSEQUENCES FOR THE TARGET GROUP

First, what were the major consequences for the target groups when they *accepted* the offered ideology and "participated"? In fact, this meant participation in a program which was funded and administered by the bureaucracy. The intended reasons for participating appear to have been those of gaining a "voice," or a share in the decision. For example, in the urban renewal program, what participation there was in the early phases was motivated by poor individuals' interest in improving their living conditions, and in diverting the forces of renewal agencies from destroying the low-rent housing situations, and neighborhood cultures which they found necessary for existence. For participants in local community action agency boards, who were residents of poverty areas, participation was intended to hasten programs which would increase their material and intellectual possessions, or their opportunity for upward social mobility. The poor intended to make their needs felt at the level of "the power structure."[11] In some cases, local community action agency staffs have banded together with the poor to put pressure on local and state politicians, pressure to change conditions, laws, or vocational opportunities for the poor.[12]

There have been unanticipated consequences, however, for those groups within the ghetto who have accepted the ideology of "citizen participation" and have actively participated in the programs of the local urban renewal and community action program bureaucracies. For urban renewal programs, those groups who have cooperated have found that, in ghetto areas, either the entire area has been torn down with them being forcibly relocated, or rehabilitation and clearance together have usually singled out the low-income family's dwellings for clearance and the middle-income ones for rehabilitation.[13] "Participation" in a cooperative sense has thus led in most cases to the acknowledgment and approval of bureaucratic activities which may have benefited the urban renewal program's *clientele* group—central city businessmen—but not the program's *target*—the poor living in the central city.

In community action programs, in precisely those cases where both the action bureaucracy and the poor accepted, believed in, and acted upon their own stated ideology, they have been slapped down by the central OEO bureaucracy in Washington. Because the overall political-attitude climate grew increasingly conservative as more radical activity took place in action programs (in part as a reaction to this activity), local politicians put pressure on state and congressional leaders to pressure the federal OEO, which in turn had to tell its own local action agencies to "go easier" or to "cool it."[14] The leverage used by the middle class and especially conservative groups was, and has continued to be, the yearly congressional appro-priation to the overall agency. At the local level, therefore, if "participa-tion" works in any oppositional, conflict-producing, or boat-rocking sense, the local action bureaucracy has come to expect trouble from their own federal headquarters. The policy in fact used by the bureaucracies has been to avoid conflict at all costs.[15] Recently, successful legislative attempts to change the locale of the community action agency from private, indepen-dently incorporated agencies to supervision by branches of the local government, are simply an inevitable consequence of some groups succeed-ing at their effort of believing in the ideology, and opposing the bureau-cracy in their role as participant.[16] The reason for this consequence—the "City Hall" amendments—would appear to be the group propounding the ideology, and its sponsorship—it is a part of the public, governmental bureaucracy. As Coser noted, "I know of no government in history which has deliberately financed its own opposition."[17]

We have now considered the major consequences for the target group if they were to accept the ideology of "citizen participation" and use it as a guide to cooperative action with the proponent bureaucracies. What would be the consequences for them if they were to reject it? That is, when the agencies urge ghetto residents to participate and they refuse, or participate only in the negative sense of using the opportunity as a forum for actively opposing the aims and plans of the bureaucracy, what would be the result for them?

The rejection of the ideology has usually been made with the clientele group of the bureaucracy in mind. When urban renewal participation has been rejected by the poor, it has usually been with a strong statement that "the one who benefits is not us, it is the downtown businessman." The intent here has been to stop the urban renewal machine in its tracks. It has not worked, in most cases, because both the present laws and time are on the side of the urban renewal agency, in the short run. But the long-term, unanticipated consequence of rejecting the ideology and its bureaucratic proponent has been that other areas of other cities have become more and more alerted to the dangers of urban renewal to them. If they are poor, or even lower middle class, urban renewal itself becomes politically less popular each year. This in turn puts pressure on mayors to slow down the program, on the threat of losing the next election to anti-renewal candi-dates.[18] Thus the rejection of the ideology may be causing greater returns and advantages to the target groups than had they accepted it. For many years, urban design specialists and redevelopment consultants have at-tempted to persuade the poor that renewal is good for them, but much of the evidence thus far indicates rather the opposite.[19]

For the local community action program, the poor could not reject themselves as potential benefiters, but instead chose to focus on the "cooperation" issue and the "feedback cycle" or "cool-it" dilemma. The reason for rejecting the citizen participation ideology is that it is said to be a statement of an agency which is a captive of city hall, or acting out the desires of the middle-class community. From an objective point of view, the rejection of the community action program has in most cases not affected the operation of the local organization. It still gets grants, it still gets someone to act on the community citizen board. But the rejection strongly limits the legitimacy of the program within the ghetto. However, in the long run it also may be the case that those who have rejected the activities and programs of the local community action programs may find that few other legal channels are open to them in expressing grievances. This loss of hope in the efficacy of the community action program and the rejection of the ideology may very well have added to the frustration which explodes in riots.

To sum up, the target group appears to be in a difficult position when the bureaucracy offers them the "citizen participation" ideology. They lose if they participate, and they sometimes lose if they don't participate. This damned-if-you-do and damned-if-you-don't situation is explainable if we ask one final question. Using the ideology as a guide, the question must be asked, "Participation in what?" The answer, participation in the program of the bureaucracy and in the activities desired by the bureaucracy's clientele groups. Either these activities are directly detrimental to the welfare of those asked to participate (urban renewal) or the activities involve the bureaucracy on behalf of a powerless or unliked target group (OEO), which activity is somewhat unacceptable to the wider population. Thus the citizen participation ideology, from the point of view of the target group, is an irrelevant or empty phraseology. From the functional point of view, it appears in most cases to be either detrimental to or ineffective for the target group, if they accept it or act on it, in the present social context.

CONSEQUENCES FOR THE PROPONENTS

Every decision which the poor have made, to accept or reject the offered ideology, has had its consequences for the bureaucracies which proposed it in the first place. Acceptance and participation have allowed the bureaucracy to pursue its aims, but only to a point. When the poor have become extensively involved in active urban planning or in community action work, the administrators have found that things got very complicated, routine decisions were questioned, conflict escalated, and timetables were delayed which in some cases cost money for the urban renewal agency.[20] This is a classic problem in a representative democracy. In Britain, there has been a tradition of electing officials, letting them run the show and then holding them accountable for failure. In America, by contrast, participation at every step of the way is a much stronger tradition.[21] But since it does increase conflict and decrease rationality and predictability in planning, many bureaucratic administrators have been

quiet on pushing the "citizen participation" ideology, fearing over-partici-
pation and its consequences far more than under-participation.[22]

On the other hand, the rejection of the ideology leaves the bureaucracy—and its program—open to the double charge of "undemocratic
procedures" and "arbitrary action." Neither the urban renewal program
nor the community action program agencies have been able to dispense
with the rituals of participation and to ignore completely the demands of
the ghetto. The long-term political consequences of total rejection of
ghetto opinion have been to put pressure on the city administration and
fear into the minds of the residents of lower middle-class areas, that they
might be the next victims of unchecked bureaucratic programs, after the
ghetto has been handled or dispensed with. The unintended long-term
consequence for the action bureaucracies has thus been a state of ambiv-
alence toward their own ideology. In most cases this takes the form of soft-
pedaling it in the community forum, or of carefully selecting cooperative or
passive community members to get the minimum of participation with the
minimum amount of trouble. This results in despair in the poor neighborhoods, the breakdown of communication, and, in some cases, violence as
the last remaining method of reestablishing communication.[23]

The Fate of Ideologies

In most cities studied to date, in both the case of the urban renewal
"citizen participation" ideology and the community action program "citizen participation" ideology, the target groups do not appear to have
benefited extensively when they did participate, and in many cases gained
if they fought the proponent bureaucracy directly and rejected their
ideology, as one power bloc against another. In so doing the ideology has
been denounced by many poor people as a "lie" and a "cheat." Yet,
another bureaucracy—the Model Cities Program of the Department of
Housing and Urban Development—has adopted the term in its community planning approach, and the federal government has just created an
Office of Citizen Participation. It would appear that the use of the ideology has benefited its bureaucratic proponents and their clientele groups,
and its popularity is rising with such groups. But the cynicism of the poor
rises with each increasing use of the ideology which does not produce
positive results for them and their living areas.

Notes

[1] Percival Goodman and Paul Goodman, *Communitas*. New York: Random
House, 1947.

[2] Sidney Verba, "Democratic Participation," *Annals of the American Academy of
Political and Social Science* (September 1967), pp. 53–78.

3 United States Housing and Home Finance Agency, "Workable Program for Community Development." Washington, D.C.: Government Printing Office, 1962, p. 13.

4 Martin Anderson, The Federal Bulldozer. Cambridge: M.I.T., 1964, p. 18.

5 Ibid., pp. 183–193.

6 Robert Dahl, Who Governs? Democracy and Power in an American City. New Haven: Yale, 1961.

7 Office of Economic Opportunity, Community Action Program Guide. Washington, D.C.: Government Printing Office, 1965.

8 Warner Bloomberg, Jr., and Florence W. Rosenstock, "Who Can Activate the Poor: One Assessment of 'Maximum Feasible Participation,'" Society for the Study of Social Problems, Annual Meetings, San Francisco, California, August 29, 1967.

9 Frank Riessman, "The New Anti-poverty Ideology," Poverty and Human Resources Abstracts, 1 (Winter 1966), 5–16.

10 Robert K. Merton, "The Unanticipated Consequences of Purposive Social Action," American Sociological Review, I (December 1936), pp. 894–904.

11 The term "power structure" here refers to the majority of the society and all its institutions, as viewed from the point of view of the poor. Though the "multiple elite" theory is being borne out by some research evidence, it is also true that closing of ranks occurs vis-à-vis the poor on many issues. See William A. Gamson, "Community Power Research and Community Action," paper given at the American Sociological Association, 1967, Annual Meetings, San Francisco, California, August 28, 1967.

12 Such examples as the Syracuse Community Action Program (which was modified, in time) and the Child Development Group of Mississippi are important on this point.

13 Anderson, op. cit., p. 159.

14 Louis A. Zurcher, Jr., "Functional Marginality: The Dynamics of a Poverty Intervention Organization." Paper presented at the Society for the Study of Social Problems, Annual Meeting, Miami Beach, Florida, August 28, 1966.

15 Conflict may have a positive function for the eventual stability of a social system while the avoidance of conflict may not. This is essentially Coser's conclusion. See Lewis Coser, The Functions of Social Conflict. Glencoe: Free Press, 1956, p. 157.

16 The 1967 Amendments to the Economic Opportunity Act of 1964 put greater power and control of local action programs in the office of the city mayor. This is a legislative consequence of the unpopularity of successful local opposition to the community power structure and to the middle-class "business as usual" ethos.

17 Lewis Coser, chairman's remarks at a session of the Society for the Study of Social Problems, August 1966, Miami Beach, Florida.

18 In Boston, the 1967 Mayoral Election was almost won by a candidate whose appeal was based on the twin planks of covert racism and anti-urban renewal sentiment.

19 Anderson, op. cit. See also two compendiums on urban renewal as presently practiced, Jewel Bellush and Murray Hausknecht, Urban Renewal: People, Politics, and Planning. New York: Doubleday, 1967; and James Q. Wilson, Urban Renewal: The Record and the Controversy. Cambridge: M.I.T., 1966.

20 Nathan Leventhal et al., eds., "Citizen Participation in Urban Renewal," Columbia Law Review, 66 (March 1966), pp. 599–600.

21 Edward C. Banfield, "The Political Implications of Metropolitan Growth," Daedalus (Winter 1961), p. 75.

22 Harold W. Demone, Jr., "The Limits of Rationality in Planning," Community Mental Health Journal, I (Winter 1965), pp. 375–381.

23 Lewis A. Coser, "Some Social Functions of Violence," in Continuities in the Study of Social Conflict. New York: Free Press, 1967, pp. 73–92.

Black Panther Petition for Neighborhood Control of the Police

---

The following is the first of two articles on current proposals for decentralization of city police forces. It is a petition circulated by the Black Panthers in Oakland, California, and it indicates how they would like to restructure the police. Of particular interest are the "Neighborhood Divisions," to be headed by councils of representatives elected from precincts, and the residency requirement proposed for police officers.

Petition for Submission to Electors of Proposed Amendment to the City Charter of Oakland

To the City Council of the City of Oakland:

We, the undersigned, registered and qualified electors of the State of California, residents of the City of Oakland, pursuant to Section 8 of Article XI of the Constitution of this State, present to the City Council of the City this petition and request that the following proposed amendment to the charter of the City be submitted to the registered and qualified electors of the City for their adoption or rejection at an election on a date to be determined by the City Council.

The proposed charter amendment reads as follows:

SECTION 1

Repeal Sections - 87, 87-1/2, 88, 88a, 91, 91b, 91c, 91d, 91e, 92, 96-1/2.

SECTION 2

Amend section 30(1) and 30(6) by substituting "Commissioner of Police" for "Chief of Police."

SECTION 3

In article XIV, add new sections

87(s) *Establishment of Separate Police Departments:* For the purpose of providing police services to the people of the City of Oakland,

428

there are established two police departments, one for each of the two Districts into which the City is divided as hereinafter set forth and described.

87(c) *Police Departments:* Each Department of Police shall be administered by a Commission comprised of five members, hereinafter referred to as Commissioners, each of whom is selected by a Division Council as hereinafter provided. The Commissioners shall fix the policies of the police within the Department, shall punish police officers for violations of said policies and for violation of the law, shall determine qualifications of members of the police department and shall fix compensation of all employees of said Department. They may enter into necessary agreements with other police departments and other government agencies and generally conduct the affairs of the police department. Each Commissioner shall bring before the full Commission any matter or proposal which his council instructs him to place before the Commission, and shall vote as his council instructs him. The Police Commission shall hold regular public meetings at a time when the residents of the Department District are most able to attend. The Police Commissioners shall serve on a fulltime basis and shall be compensated therefor. Compensation shall be set by the respective Division Councils. The Departments may enter into agreements with each other for the operation, maintenance and staffing of certain facilities in which there is a common interest, including, but not limited to laboratories, vehicle repair and communications. The Departments may cooperate together in the requisitioning of equipment, including vehicles and weapons. Funds for the Departments shall be appropriated annually for the City of Oakland by the City Council and shall be disbursed to each Department on the basis of the number of people residing in each Department District on the last preceding election.

87(d) *Neighborhood Divisions:* Each Police Department is divided into five neighborhood Divisions described below. . . .

87(f) *Police Council:* Each Neighborhood Division shall be divided into fifteen Police Council Precincts by the City Clerk; the population of each such Precinct is not to exceed any other Precinct by more than 10% of the population of the entire District divided by the number of Precincts therein. The registered voters in each Precinct shall elect a Police Councilman who will serve in that capacity for a term of two years, unless recalled. The Councilmen shall serve on a part-time basis and will be compensated for the time spent in the performance of their duties.

87(g) *Qualifications of Councilmen:* Any person who has resided in the Precinct for six months next preceding the election and is of voting age at the time of elections is qualified to serve as a Councilman. There shall be no other qualifications established for the office.

87(h) *Duties of Council:* The Neighborhood Council shall, within ten days of its own election, select a Commissioner. In addition to selection of Commissioners, the Councils shall review the policies of the Police Department and will recommend changes or modifications of such policies when such policies no longer reflect the needs or will of the populace of the Neighborhood represented by the Council. The Councilmen of each Neighborhood shall have the power, exercised by a vote of the majority of that council, to remove and replace their Commissioner when he is no longer responsive to the Council. Each Council shall establish procedures necessary to hear and process complaints made against individual members of the Police Department by persons residing within the district or concerning police practices within the district, and shall have the power to discipline members of the Department for violations of law or policy occurring within that District.

87(i) *Meetings:* The Neighborhood Council will meet regularly at a time convenient to the Councilmen and at a time when interested persons may attend. Special meetings may be called when requested in writing by 20% of the Councilmen. When requested by a Neighborhood Council, as expressed by a vote of the majority of said Council, the five Councils of the Department shall meet jointly within ten days. At such a joint meeting the councilmen by majority vote may change, institute or modify any Policy of the Department, upon which they fail or refuse to act.

87(j) *Recall of Councilmen:* The people of a precinct may recall their councilman by a petition bearing the signatures of residents equalling 20% of the number of people voting within the precinct in the last preceding general election. Upon certification of the requisite number of signatures an election shall be had not later than 30 days thereafter. Notice of intention to recall a councilman must be given not more than 30 days prior to seeking certification of the requisite number of signatures by the City Clerk.

88 *Recall of Commissioners:* Commissioners may be recalled by a petition bearing the signatures of 20% of the number of people voting in the precincts comprising the neighborhood to which the Commission is responsible.

89 *Annexation:* Whenever 30% of the adult residents of a precinct within one Department District, which is contiguous to another Department District, petition for annexation into said other Department District, an election shall be had within 30 days of certification of the requisite

number of signatures by the City Clerk. Such precinct shall be annexed if the majority of the people voting in such election so indicate, unless a majority of the councilmen of said other Department District reject such annexation within 30 days of said election. A notice of intention shall be given not more than 60 days prior to filing for certification of the petition. Where such annexation has taken place, appropriate adjustments shall be made between the affected Departments in regard to funding, whenever practicable.

90 *Disposition of Current Assets:* All funds, files, records, property, supplies, and other assets currently possessed by the Oakland Police Department shall be divided among the Police Departments herein created in proportion to the population of each Police Department District; provided that police files and other records shall be distributed so that each Department shall obtain all records pertaining to citizens living within its geographic confines, or to organizations operating therein.

91 *Residence:* All Police officers shall reside in the area covered by the department they work for.

92 *Ordinances:* Any ordinance heretofore enacted, prior to the effective date of this within amendment, which is contradictory to any of the provisions hereof, is repealed. . . .

Community Control of the Police

Arthur I. Waskow

Waskow's article is particularly noteworthy for its attack on the idea of police professionalism as, first and foremost, a device for insulating them from public control. The proposed alternative of recruiting temporary policemen from a cross-section of the public rests on the assumption that most of their work is not and should not be considered beyond the capability of amateurs.

In an earlier introductory comment, we noted that there is now considerable pressure for application of the principle that "like should represent like." Applying this principle to Kaufman's remark (cited in the introduction to this chapter) that there is a contemporary quest for representativeness in administration, we must note that this often means discarding professional credentials as criteria for selecting civil servants. Nothing makes a man more unlike his clients, in both his eyes and theirs, than credentials of professional status—indeed, that is their primary purpose.

In almost every American metropolis, the police no longer are under civilian control—that is to say, democratic public control. Whether it be constant harassment of black youth in Los Angeles and white youth in Washington, brutal repression of white dissidents in Chicago and beating of peaceful Black Panthers in New York, refusal to obey the orders of a black mayor in Cleveland and those of a white president of the Board of Education in Philadelphia, or failure to answer routine calls for assistance from black neighborhoods of Detroit and white neighborhoods of Baltimore, it is clear that there are many people in the metropolitan areas who do not believe they can make the police respond to their needs. The problem is clearer and more chronic in black neighborhoods—the consciousness of it is clearer there, so that it is seen not as a "failure" but as the successful accomplishment by the police of their mission as an occupation army. But parts of the white community—the young, dissident middle-class liberal peaceniks, even such Establishments as those that try to set up

---

From Arthur I. Waskow, "Community Control of the Police," TRANS-action (December 1969), pp. 4–7. Copyright © December 1969 by TRANS-action, Inc., New Brunswick, New Jersey.

civilian review boards, even such ethnic working-class communities as those that threw rocks at Martin Luther King's Chicago marches—feel unable to control their police. Increasingly, the police control themselves—almost in the fashion of the Prussian military traditionally so dreaded by democracies. (The fear of police autonomy has probably been because the police were expected to act autonomously in relation to the blacks, the Spanish-speaking and the poor. Only recently have parts of the middle class found themselves powerless vis-à-vis the police.)

There are two ways the police gain their autonomy: First, by constructing a police subculture of lifelong policemen, they insulate themselves against informal social controls—defining their own norms, defending, rewarding and promoting policemen who adhere to these regardless of public pressures or orders from above, insisting that policemen are "professionals" who should be trained by "professionals," so that civilians are increasingly excluded even from police academies. Secondly, they have, on the basis of this subculture, organized quasi-unions with considerable political power, which have been able to "negotiate" practical autonomy on most occasions.

"Professionalized" Cops

During the period from the 1940s to about 1965, when liberal criticism of the police focused on "brutality" toward black people, the liberal solutions were: psychological screening to exclude sadists; human relations training to soften racial "prejudice"; professionalization to reduce "lower-class" or "untrained" reliance on naked violence; and civilian review boards to discipline violators of professional norms. All have failed. Among the most "professional" big city forces has been that of Los Angeles; among those most carefully screened to exclude sadists has been that of Chicago; among those with a "strong" civilian review board has been that of Philadelphia.

There are at least three major possible directions in which to go to achieve the kind of change in police forces that seems necessary to restore democratic, civilian control over the police:

1. Formal restructuring of metropolitan police departments into federations of neighborhood police forces, with control of each neighborhood force in the hands of neighborhood people through election of commissions.

2. Creation of countervailing organizations (in effect, "trade unions" of those policed) responsible to a real political base, able to hear grievances and force change.

3. Transformation of the police "profession" and role so as to end the isolation of policemen from the rest of the community, and thus to establish de facto community control by chiefly informal means.

The neighborhood control approach could be institutionalized by election of neighborhood or precinct police commissions which would (1) appoint high precinct officers (perhaps with approval of metropolitan headquarters, the mayor or a civil service commission); (2) approve the assignment in the precinct of new policemen and be able to require transfers out; (3) discipline officers, perhaps with the concurrence of a city-wide appeal board; and (4) set basic policy on law enforcement priorities in the neighborhood.

Neighborhood Control

Such an arrangement would respond first of all to the possibility that no great metropolis can be democratically governed from City Hall; that departments of education, police, zoning and the like may become far too bureaucratic and too insulated from popular pressures and fresh ideas if they try to govern from a single center a public of more than 100,000 people. It would thus accept the traditions of rural counties and suburban towns that find electing the sheriff or closely supervising the town police workable. Secondly, neighborhood control would respond to the concentration of the black populations in particular neighborhoods, and would thus attempt to deal at least with the "occupation army" aspect of a white-governed police force in black areas. It might also make working-class ethnic neighborhoods and middle- or "new-class" neighborhoods more able to shape their own police forces, and might even provide a framework for dealing with the difficulties that the "youth minority" face with policemen.

As far as the black neighborhoods are concerned, elected precinct commissions with the powers described would make possible great changes in the policemen who walk or ride the beat. Policemen might be chosen from the neighborhood and required to live in it. Black recruits are likely to be far more numerous if the police do not in fact bear the stigma of an occupying army, and they are far more likely to feel and act like members of the black community when they are no longer under pressure from a white-bossed headquarters and overwhelmingly white colleagues. Neighborhoods where back yards and recreation cellars are scarce might decide that enforcement of laws against playing ball in an alley or loitering to talk on the street would not be high-priority matters, and that enforcement of laws for decent housing would. Policemen would be much more likely to take seriously and answer promptly calls for their help. Drunks in the inner city might be taken home to their families like drunks in the suburbs, instead of beaten mercilessly and dumped in jail. The cries of "Nigger!" and "Boy!" would be much less frequent. The black community would almost certainly be living much more comfortably with its police.

The idea of neighborhood control of the police has raised objections on two related "territorial" grounds: that major differences in style of law enforcement would plague any one person as he moved around the metropolis, and that "hot pursuit" questions (and other similar negotiation problems of the neighborhood forces) would be much worse. Both these "difficulties" exist now in rural and suburban jurisdictions, and can only be said to be new in the sense that population density might make a difference. It is true that shifts from one neighborhood to another come more quickly than from town to town and that more people do in fact move from one neighborhood to another during their daily lives. But it should be noted that already, in a city like Washington where U.S. park police, capitol police, White House police and metropolitan police have major geographically distinct jurisdictions within the District of Columbia, solutions for "hot pursuit" and similar problems have been worked out. With reference to the problem of different styles in law enforcement, it seems already true that within a single city there are great differences from neighborhood to neighborhood, especially in the regulation of street conduct—but they are defined by policemen, not the public.

It might also be objected that neighborhood control of the police would destroy some city-wide institutions that ought to be protected. Not necessarily: for example, such divisions as fingerprint files and modus-operandi files, homicide squad and arson squad could still function under metropolitan police headquarters.

Finally, would neighborhood control in itself—regardless of the decisions made by the elected commissions—require changes in the role of the policeman? Perhaps the most politically ticklish question would arise around the function of the policeman as protector of property. In neighborhoods filled with property owners, that role would be supported; but in neighborhoods of the poor, would the residents put great store in the protection of property? It is precisely the fear that they would not that has motivated many property holders to insist that the poor should be policed by outside authority rather than police themselves. But first of all, the poor might turn out to want their few miserable possessions protected as desperately as the rich want their great hoards guarded. The poor might even be prepared to say that all property—that of the wealthy as well as their own—should be protected. The present ideological commitment of the middle class to protect giant property that it does not own suggests that for long-range reasons, intelligently or stupidly conceived, people will protect even interests that in some ways may damage them.

Countervailing Power

The possibility of control of the police through countervailing power is based on two recent models: the emergence of the Community Alert Patrols (CAPs) in Watts and elsewhere as checks on the police, and the Community Review Board created by the Mexican-American community in Denver. Both are vastly different from the conventional neutral civilian review boards, in that they are explicitly based not on a quasi-judicial model but on the necessity of having independent political power to confront that of the police forces. Both assume that the police are themselves either an independent political force or an arm of a powerful establishment, not a neutral peacekeeping body.

Thus both approaches seek some external political support for pressing grievances against the police. In the Denver case, chicano organizations investigate charges of illegitimate or unjust police behavior and, where they regard the charges as well founded, demand punishment of the officers and back up their demands with political pressure (publicity, threatened loss of votes, threatened disorder and others). As for the CAPs, they used the endemic anger of young black men against the behavior of the police in the black community to energize youth patrols that accompany the police on their rounds to take detailed notes and photographs of their behavior. Where the patrols felt the police acted badly, they filed complaints and sometimes tried to turn on some political heat to achieve redress. The Watts CAP tried, notably, to combine the insurgent political energy of the black community with the outside political (i.e., financial) support of the federal government, and thus to box in the police force. But what the Watts CAP hoped to gain from the federal tie in political ability to resist enormous hostility from the police, was lost in the weakening of ties with the black community itself. The CAP's legitimacy within Watts declined; and then, when the Los Angeles police department brought its political power to bear, the federal government backed off.

Nevertheless, the countervailing-power approach may have some advantages over neighborhood control. Perhaps the major one is that it can be undertaken without agreement of those in power, whereas the neighborhood-control model requires governmental acquiescence. It should also be noted that it does not need to be tied to a neighborhood base. Where a given community that feels itself the powerless object of police power, not the defining subject, is scattered across a city, then a countervailing organization along the lines of the Denver Crusade for Justice could be useful. And finally, some activists have argued that at least in the short run it is wiser to organize the powerless to oppose police power than to grasp it—on the grounds that power over one police precinct, or even many, in the absence of drastic social change in other spheres of life, may simply make fuzzy the face of the enemy, require the poor to police themselves in the patterns demanded by the unchanged spheres of social power, and thus stultify movements for more basic change.

As suggested above, the isolation of the police into an angry and frequently frightened subculture with a tight and effective political "face" is at least as important a factor in preventing democratic control as is the formal command hierarchy and its ties to the metropolitan white power structures. So it may be just as important to work for community control by cracking this informal "blue curtain" as it is to change the formal power relations and command hierarchies.

In examining ways to crack the "career" subculture, an important distinction should be kept in mind: the distinction between on-the-street peacekeeping and the more formal and "organized" policing of systematic off-street crime. These are quite different roles of the people we call "policemen."

In the first case, it seems relatively easy to argue that the police should not be "professionals" or career men. The role of peacekeeper on the beat is not a highly technical or specialized one, but depends rather on a fairly widespread and certainly nonprofessional skill in conciliatory human relations. The "false professionalization" of the role is due in part to an effort by policemen to defend their jobs and careers, and in part to the attempt of middle-class liberals to "upgrade" and "retrain" working-class policemen, on the theory that the "uneducated cop" was typically brutal or racist. This process could be reversed; peacekeepers could be recruited for a term of not more than three years from a broad cross-section of the public—especially and deliberately from among women as well as men, and from a wide age range, so as to emphasize the peacekeeping rather than the force-dispensing function. Such peacekeepers would probably not carry firearms, but would probably be trained in such defensive tactics as judo. They should probably wear uniforms quite unmilitary in style, be required to live in the community and keep up strong social contacts in it, and so on. Thus the community should see them as quite unlike traditional "policemen," and this perception should be accurate. Their command line should be totally divorced from that of the regular "police" department, and ideally would run to a neighborhood commission of the kind described above.

If it is true, as has frequently been claimed, that those who volunteer for police duty are especially self-selected for tendencies to sadism, then even a short-term volunteer process might not change the police enough, and one might have to think about selection of police by lottery from the whole population. But most of the evidence suggests that recruitment for the police proceeds on so many different appeals that if sadism is widespread, or becomes widespread on particular occasions, that is because it is learned on the job from other officers and from the nature of the role. If that is so, reducing the "career" line to three years would greatly weaken the informal social pressures from older policemen, and transforming the role would change the direction of the pressures.

The peacekeepers would deal with such traditional worries of the patrolman as family fights, conflicts between a tavern owner and unruly customers or between sleeping old people and singing youngsters. Indeed, some police authorities say patrolmen spend 80 percent of their time on such matters—and resent it terribly. For they are taught that their function is to Enforce the Law, not calm people down. Thus they tend to be bad at what they feel is a waste of their time and training—and of course even worse at it when they are strangers to or contemptuous of the community they are doing it in. Peacekeepers who are recruited for that precise job would do it better.

"Downtown" Policemen

Along with the transformation of the neighborhood street police, there should be a reexamination of the "downtown" policemen. Here there are two issues: Should these men be under neighborhood control? and does their work require professional expertise and training?

On the issue of where to locate authority, the answer seems clear from the kinds of crimes these men must handle: large-scale, quasi-business, "organized" crime; systematic refusal of large-scale land or factory owners to obey laws concerning adequate housing, adequate pollution control, and so forth; embezzlement, tax evasion and other white-collar crimes. It does not seem possible or appropriate to cope with these on a neighborhood basis. Indeed, many such categories of crime are already dealt with on a federal basis, and certainly metropolitan or even regional policing makes sense in these areas. The policemen involved would rarely if ever need to be "on the street" in any particular neighborhood, and their work would affect much wider areas; therefore wider areas should be governed.

"Professional" Danger

But this issue of size leaves open the issue of professionalization. On one hand, there is evidence in this realm of police work—from the growing use of large-scale private detective agencies, the growing importance of electronic detectors and computer analysis of financial accounts—that public police have not kept pace with the degree of technical expertise now required by much of the public. But on the other hand, there is the necessity of making sure that national, regional or metropolitan police forces, as well as neighborhood peacekeepers, are kept under civilian control—a necessity not easily achieved as the history of the FBI makes clear and one that itself will require considerable social innovation. Whether there is any way to meet the requirement for technical skill while still preventing the emergence of a "professional" career subculture in this kind of police work is not clear, and will require further study. If the ultimate goal is not merely representative but participatory democracy, then deprofessionalization of even the technical police must be sought.

Model-building is not enough; we must also examine the politics of change toward one or another of these models of community control of the police.

The only city in which a sustained demand for neighborhood control along the lines of Model I has turned into a serious political issue seems to be Washington, D.C. There the Black United Front has demanded neighborhood election of precinct police commissions—in the context of a series of homicides of civilians (almost all black) by policemen (all white) and the killing of a white policeman by a black civilian. The BUF demand was picked up by a group of black businessmen, some black clergymen and a number of white and racially mixed groups in the city, including the Democratic Central Committee. In the total absence even of a fiction of city-wide democratic control over the police, the claims of neighborhood democracy have been strengthened. The strongest pressure has come from upsurges of rage from the black community after each homicide of a black civilian has been ruled "justifiable." Opposition to neighborhood control has come from the police, the white business community, the two large newspapers and the southern congressmen who control the city's budget. Washington's city government has tried to appease both "law and order" and "community control" pressures by issuing slightly stronger restrictions on police use of guns, by calling for new advisory precinct boards and so forth. Their efforts have had little effect.

Efforts in the direction of Model II have come almost entirely from black or Spanish-speaking communities (perhaps in a few Appalachian white "ghettos" like uptown Chicago), with only momentary outside support from the federal government or foundations.

The radical deprofessionalizing of some police roles, as in Model III, seems not to have become a political issue anywhere; but the splitting of police functions into several distinct roles and the recruitment of more "community" people (but no effort toward democratization of the command line) has been urged by the president's crime commission. A "community participation" (but not control) project in Washington, developed by outside agencies (the National Institute of Mental Heath, especially) to test the crime commission's proposals, has triggered considerable enmity from neighborhood organizers on the ground that it will simply extend and intensify police control over the community (through informers, for example), rather than the reverse.

Obviously, what political strategy is developed in achieving community control over police depends heavily on which model one intends to pursue, and which end result within them one hopes to achieve. Let us assume, however, that a decision is made to pursue a combination of Models I and III—which together seem to offer the fullest control over a police force to those in the neighborhood—by transforming both the formal lines of command and the informal interpersonal processes to converge on the community.

With that goal in view, it would make sense to strive immediately to set up Model II. Such a countervailing "community union to police the police" could then become not simply a grievance-processing organization, but also a continuous pressure group for the adoption of a Model I/III arrangement in the form of a present version of what the future Model I/III control would look like. Imagine an open-ended community group that anyone in a given police precinct could join, the directors of which would be periodically elected, and that would be funded by neighborhood "dues" and, perhaps, matching foundation grants. Such a strong community union to police the police could (1) itself put peacekeepers on the street—unarmed, distinctively uniformed, oriented to conflict resolution rather than enforcing the law, including women, young dropouts and clergymen; (2) itself patrol the police, taking evidence of bad behavior and offering to settle problems instead of the police; (3) hear and investigate and judge complaints; (4) mobilize political pressure for the transfer of bad policemen, bad precinct commanders and others; and (5) keep up constant pressure for the transfer of power over the neighborhood police to the neighborhood itself. It must be clear that such a community union to police the police would be a focus of intense political conflict, including great hostility and possibly physical danger from the police. But if the groundwork in organizing community support for a Model I/III arrangement had been well done, the very intensity of political conflict over a strong Model II might persuade the city to allow Model I/III to be established. In any case, it is hard to see how democratic civilian control over a staff of armed men who are widely believed to hold a monopoly over legitimate violence and who are well organized in a separate subculture and a strong political force can be reestablished without intense political conflict.

Law: The Function of Extra-Judicial Mechanisms in the USSR

Leon Lipson

The last two articles review attempts in the USSR to popularize justice and to increase citizen involvement in the work of the police (the militia). Pressures to do this come from two sources: First, the Soviets believe very strongly in making the collective the key group in character formation, including the rehabilitation of social deviants and criminals. This means giving collectives of citizens some power and responsibility for disciplining wayward citizens. Second, in Marxist thought the state will begin to "wither away" as communism approaches. In practice, the Soviets have taken this to mean that some of the functions of professional, bureaucratic state agencies will gradually be turned over to nonprofessional citizen organizations. Leon Lipson's article reviews all the major forms of popular legal mechanisms.

At the outset we face a problem of scope that cannot be solved except by arbitrary exclusion and inclusion. In contemporary China and the Soviet Union, where society is organized tightly under direction and pressure from state organs and political leadership, many official bodies engage in investigation, fact-finding of a sort, and coercive decision; once the courts are abstracted, we are left with a wide variety of institutions including, in Soviet terms at least, party organs, state organs, and "civic," "public," or "lay" organs (*obshchestvennye*).

Some of the bodies that might fit such a definition have nothing directly to do with adjudication in the usual sense of the term. Take, for instance, the exposé essay or article in the newspaper, written by a special (and specialized) correspondent, reporting abuses of position or authority.[1] Often, according at least to the press reports themselves, a sort of adversary proceeding occurs in which the newspaper correspondent casts himself—or, especially in cases of education, youth or family morality, herself—in the role of judge and hears argument from accusers, the accused official, party committees, local soviets, and witnesses. The follow-up

---

From Leon Lipson, "Law: The Function of Extra-Judicial Mechanisms," in Donald Treadgold, ed., *Soviet and Chinese Communism, Similarities and Differences*, pp. 144–167. Reprinted by permission of the University of Washington Press.

report of "measures taken" continues the informal parallel, for in tone and context it bears some resemblance to a report of compliance with a judicial decree.

In a similar way, it would be possible to include under the head of extrajudicial mechanisms the work of the party-state control committees, which were set up in November 1962 for the primary purpose of helping to increase productivity by exposing slackness in administration of industrial and commercial establishments, by jacking up the procedures of quality control of production, and by uncovering incipient criminality in the management of production and distribution. It is still too early to say what place this new institution is likely to have in the era of Khrushchev's successors or what sanctions committees of party-state control may come to deploy.

A third institution that ought at least to be mentioned before it is banished to a marginal position in this study is that of the "political school" and its associated "circles," which appear to be used primarily for continuing adult indoctrination but also secondarily for verifying the doctrinal orthodoxy of those who perform in the system.[2] Similar tasks are performed for party members and Young Communist League members by special bodies. The institution of criticism and self-criticism, wherever it is practiced, can be thought of as a means toward officially induced correctness of behavior.

At the risk of misusing Western categories, however, it will be convenient here to focus on those bodies that have the most to do with a process most easily recognizable as law enforcement. The description may serve as a basis for discussion of the reason for the inadequacy of those institutions and possibly of the classification itself.[3]

Comrades' Courts

Until their revival in 1959, Soviet comrades' courts were limited chiefly to the hearing of cases of violation of labor discipline, though the decrees under which they were authorized would have enabled them to consider a broader group of cases. In their present form, first sketched in 1959 in obedience to the 21st Congress and adopted after some deliberation in the Russian Republic in July 1961 (in the Ukraine in August 1961), they are "elected organs of society, whose mission it is to assist actively in the inculcation of the spirit of a communist attitude to work and to socialist property, in the inculcation of a spirit of observance of the rules of socialist community life, and in the development among the Soviet people of feelings of collectivism and comradely mutual help." They were to accomplish these ends by deterring violations of the law and acts that caused harm to society, by education through suasion and social influence, by creating a setting in which all anti-social acts would be regarded as intolerable.

Comrades' courts are separate from the regular judicial system, though there is a large jurisdictional overlap. A comrades' court is not a court presided over by a professional judge, it is not a forum in which parties are represented by counsel, it is not governed by the regular judicial codes of procedure, and it is not in general subject to regular review by higher courts.

A Soviet comrades' court is set up either on a territorial or an occupational principle. Thus we cannot arrive at the average size of a comrades' court's constituency by dividing the 220 million inhabitants by the 230,000 courts, for many inhabitants come under the jurisdiction of both a territorial and an occupational comrades' court. If it is set up territorially it takes in an apartment building or a complex of them, or a collective farm, or some other residential unit. If it is set up occupationally, it takes in an industrial or commercial enterprise, or a subdivision of one, or an institution or organization such as an office or a government bureau, or a school. There seems to be no formal maximum number of persons in a collective to support one comrades' court; the minimum number is fifty. ("Comrades' " by the way is not used as a term of art; the court is not limited to party members.) The state does not in terms require such courts to be set up. The decision rests with a general meeting of the respective collective or residential unit; in the residential situation the agreement of the executive committee of the local soviet is required; in the occupational situation the initiative seems to be lodged in the local trade union committee. According to several recent complaints by legal officials and writers, the local trade union committees are frequently slack in forming, supplying, supporting, and superintending the occupational comrades' courts, which seem to work more crudely and irregularly than those at residential collectives.

The comrades' courts, unlike the anti-parasite tribunals, have a group of members, presumably smaller than the number of persons in the appropriate collective, who are elected by the general meeting of the collective and who serve for a term of one year. (The comrades' court thus has a bench; the anti-parasite toilers' collective has only pews; neither has a Bar.) The elected members in turn choose from among their number a chairman, vice-chairmen, and a secretary; if we take the grammar seriously, the number of members of the court must be at least four, unless a secretary doubles with a vice-chairman. A public hearing requires at least three members. The elected members need meet no formal qualifications except that they must qualify as members of the constituency by virtue of their place of residence or their occupational attachment. They need not, of course, have legal training; at each of the six comrades' courts I saw in Moscow in 1963, however, a member or the secretary had had some legal training and experience. It is said by Soviet authors that the great bulk of elected members are old enough to have sufficient "experience of life" and to be capable of deciding cases with patience and attention; but a plea has been made also for drawing into the elected membership some members of a younger generation, "all the more so because not seldom it falls to [the courts] to hear cases on the conduct of young men and young women whose psychology is not always understandable to the older generation."

The range of offenses which the comrades' court has jurisdiction to determine overlaps the offenses that fall within the cognizance of the anti-parasite tribunals (discussed below) or the regular courts when they hear cases of parasitism, and overlaps also the regular criminal code. Comrades' courts (in the RSFSR) hear cases on minor offenses against labor discipline or safety regulations, unworthy public conduct, minor damage to public property, violations of dwelling regulations, some property disputes, and—most important—various minor crimes. Judges of people's courts, prosecutors, and police may transfer cases of certain minor crimes to be heard by comrades' courts. Specific authority was given the comrades' courts in October 1963 to hear cases of petty theft of state or public property, petty hooliganism committed as a first offense, petty speculation, and first-time thefts of consumer goods from citizens belonging to the same collective as the offender.

So much for the targets of the proceedings. The court may (but according to the literature it too seldom does) move *sua sponte* or may be set in motion by a complaint from any citizen, by the transfer of a file by the organs of regular justice, by state agencies, or by various civic (non-state) organizations. The list includes trade union committees; volunteer people's police (public-order squads); street or block committees and other social organizations; gatherings of citizens; executive committees or standing committees of local soviets; state agencies, directors of enterprises, institutions, organizations, administrations of collective farms; a court (the Ukraine adds also "a [single] judge"); the public prosecutor; and the organs of inquiry (i.e., police, investigator) with permission of the public prosecutor.

When a case comes before the comrades' court, or when the comrades' court is convened in order to hear a case, the case may already have been investigated by the members or staff of the court in the fortnight that may intervene between the time the case is brought and the time it is heard. Attempts to compose differences and settle short of hearing have been receiving encouragement in the general press. Legal writers have apparently not resolved the question whether a comrades' court is most successful when it disposes of disputes by quiet mediation and reconciliation or when it stages a public hearing with rhetorical denunciation and the waving of ideological banners. The recent shift of commentators' emphasis toward the frequency with which comrades' courts are used for the prosecution of crimes may be expected to increase the relative weight of the public hearing as against the work behind the scenes.

The court may require witnesses and documentation in its own discretion or on the request of the respondent (*privlekaemyi*, the one brought up). It is not clear whether the court must grant that request; I have seen a case in which it was denied, for what appeared to be good reason. The court does not have the subpoena power, though witnesses are supposed to be obliged to respond to a summons.

The hearing takes place outside the working day (or between shifts), and is public. The respondent may challenge any member of the court for bias; this challenge is weighed, however, by the court itself, including the challenged member. The court hears the witnesses, the complainants, the respondent, and looks over the docmentary material available. The audience may with the court's permission put questions and make comments on the case. Frequently the comments from the audience are dominated by party members, Young Communist League officials, and other activists, whose remarks appear to be preconcerted. The court secretary makes a minute of the session.

If the respondent does not respond—that is, if the person who is summoned fails to appear—the comrades' court must postpone the hearing once, but may later—how much later is not fixed by law—hear the case *ex parte* unless there are good reasons for continued absence; but if the case has come to the comrades' court on transfer from one of the regular organs of justice, the file is returned to the transferor for further action.

The court's decision is taken by a majority of the (elected) members participating, is expressed in signed writing with an account of the gist of the violation and the measure of "influence" or retaliation decided upon, and is announced publicly and further reported.

The measures of "civic influence" at the disposal of a comrades' court are limited. In order of roughly increasing seriousness, they include: letting the respondent off with a sincere repentance and the voluntary[4] compensation of damage he has done; requiring a public apology from the respondent to the injured person or to the collective; issuing a comradely warning; issuing a public reprimand (*poritsanie*); issuing a public censure (*vygovor*), with or without publication in the press; imposing a fine of up to ten rubles except in cases of theft or violation of labor discipline; suggesting to the management of the place of work a transfer to a lower-paid post or a demotion; suggesting the eviction of the respondent from his living quarters when he cannot get along with other tenants or takes a predatory attitude toward housing facilities or maliciously omits to pay his rent; and, along with the other measures, compelling the restitution of harm caused by the illegal actions in an amount up to fifty rubles.

In addition, the comrades' court may decide to transfer the case to a (regular) people's court if the case is too complicated for it, or may bring the case to the attention of the agencies in charge of preparing criminal charges or imposing "administrative" responsibility.

The decisions of a comrades' court may be reviewed, but not ordinarily by a court. Either a trade union committee or the executive committee of the local soviet—probably depending on whether the comrades' court has been set up respectively on an occupational or a residential basis—may, if the decision has been contrary to the evidence or to law, suggest to the comrades' court that it hear the case over again. If the decision has included an order for the payment of money as fine or compensation or some other property transfer, and the respondent refuses to comply with the order, a judge of the *people's* court may be applied to for a writ of execution, and in that event the people's court judge will in effect review the legality of the decision of the *comrades'* court. If his review indicates that the decision of the comrades' court was illegal, the people's court judge refuses to issue the writ and returns the case to the comrades' court and to the trade union committee or executive committee of the local soviet for a decision whether to rehear the case in the comrades' court.

The other sanctions at the disposal of the comrades' court are not apparently reviewable by the people's judge. The warning, censure, and reprimand remain in force for a twelvemonth and then lapse if no new offense has been committed; the court may also lift its sanction before that time, upon its own motion or upon application by the individual concerned or various public organizations vouching for him.

In some cities, including Moscow, the review that is exercisable by the executive committee of the local soviet is in effect done for it at the *raion* or borough by a formally advisory body: the lay council on comrades' courts. This is staffed mainly by pensioners, of whom some have legal training. It has recently been recommended that the lay councils be divided into sections, one of which would work on appeals and be staffed by jurists.

The accounts of cases brought before comrades' courts indicate that the principal object of the proceeding, in the eyes of the Soviet commentators, is not so much the disposition of disputes or the retribution of society upon an offender as it is the conversion of the offender, the setting him on the path of righteousness. The commentators dwell upon the wholesomeness of criticism and self-criticism, of revulsion and self-revulsion, and they stress the deterrent effect on others than the respondent.

Soviet commentaries, though lavish in recounting cases of catharsis and conversion, do mention some abuses. On one side some comrades' courts seem to have been used some of the time to settle private scores, to satisfy the hostility of the community to the non-conformist or its resentment of the "loner," or to prop the self-esteem of elderly busybodies: the pensioners who man the residential comrades' courts give full value to their roles. On the other side, there have been complaints in the lay and legal press of the practice whereby regular courts, public prosecutors, or police allegedly abuse the authority given them by statute to transfer petty crimes under certain conditions to the comrades' courts. There seem to be what one leading article called "profoundly mistaken and harmful views of comrades' courts as if they were organs supposed to 'unburden' the court, the public prosecutors, and the police of 'picayune' matters." Yet that seems to have been one of the motives behind the revival of the comrades' courts. Here, as with the other non-courts, it would be wrong to suppose a simple and consistent unity of motives on the part of the Soviet leadership simply because we have not been able to sort them all and label them with names of persons, parties, or factions.

Similarly, the frequent resort to the levying of fines has been criticized by legal writers as evidence that the comrades' courts have been shirking their social duty of mobilizing community pressure on offenders by the more "moral" sanctions available to them. Yet in January 1965 the Russian Republic increased the maximum fines that might be imposed for thefts coming within the jurisdiction of the comrades' court. Perhaps the conflict over the proper role of fines is symbolic of a difference of opinion over the proper role of the comrades' court itself. Some legal writers, trying to remain faithful to the "withering-away" ideal, look on the courts as a prism through which the moral indignation or exhortation of the local collective is focused upon an offender in the interest of his reform. The authorities are inclined rather to use the comrades' courts, whatever the ideological components in their origin and revival, as a mechanism to handle an administrative problem by processing certain minor offenses and thus relieving the docket of the regular courts. Whether the new emphasis on fines also reflects a theory of deterrence that lays more stress upon economic deprivation than Soviet theory used to is not clear.

The Anti-Parasite Laws

The anti-parasite laws began their modern career before the revival and reformation of the comrades' courts and the volunteer people's guard. Draft statutes appeared in party newspapers through the Union in early 1957. Under those drafts, "able-bodied citizens leading an anti-social, parasitic way of life, deliberately avoiding socially useful labor, and likewise those living on unearned income" could be tried at a public meeting of fellow residents. In cities, the meeting would be convoked by a street committee or apartment-house management's committee for cooperation in maintaining public order; in rural areas, by a village soviet. Sentence could be passed by a majority of those attending, who in turn had only to be a majority of the adult citizens of the given local unit. Although the meeting could confine its action to a warning for a period of probation, the primary sanction was exile at forced labor for two to five years. The sentence would be subject to no judicial review, but would go into effect on being confirmed by the executive committee of the local soviet.

The drafts met opposition, some of which was made public in articles and letters to the newspapers. A number of people asserted that the definition of living on unearned income was vague; that sham workers should be included beside non-workers; that the requirements for a quorum at the public meeting should be tightened. Someone urged that the government prosecutor (prokuror) should be present at the trials to watch over legality; it was suggested that the power of the general meeting should be limited to the uncovering of facts to be brought to the attention of the prokuror for further action in the course of regular criminal prosecution; others urged that the public meeting be vested with a wider range of possible sanctions than the choice between a warning and two-to-five-year exile.

The anti-parasite measures were nonetheless enacted, mostly in a form close to the drafts, in nine "outlying" republics between 1957 and 1960. In the Russian Republic and the Ukraine, no anti-parasite law was enacted until 1961; opposition there may have been even stronger though less visible.

There is reason to think that between 1957 and 1961 the opponents of an anti-parasite law sought to play off one non-court against another. The draft statute for the comrades' courts in the Russian Republic, published in 1959, included a provision that would have let a comrades' court hear parasite cases. As the sanctions available to the comrades' courts did not include anything so drastic as exile to forced labor for two to five years, the suggestion to bestow parasite jurisdiction on comrades' courts may have come from those who thereby desired to forestall the adoption of an anti-parasite law.

In late 1959 and 1960 the drive for more drastic punishment of parasites in the Russian Republic was renewed. A lead seems to have been taken by officials of the Young Communist League (Komsomol), whose institutional connection with the internal security apparatus has long been apparent. First, the Komsomol has administrative responsibility for many of the "welfare" activities aimed at combating the rise of juvenile delinquency. Second, it has special duties in organizing and controlling public demonstrations, both the carefully planned official demonstrations and the more carefully planned "spontaneous" demonstrations. Third, the Komsomol has played an active role in the establishment and staffing of local volunteer people's guards (druzhiny) and the units that the guards superseded. Fourth, the Komsomol, in its public pronouncements, has tended to uphold a stern, xenophobic, and maximalist standard on questions of ideological purity and public morality. Fifth, the leaders of the organization appear to form a pool from which the senior soviet security apparatus draws its staff.

Important, though still general, guidance came in September 1960, through a leading article in the official party theoretical organ Kommunist. The writers of this article acknowledged that "the struggle against parasites is being intensified at the present time"; attributed the persistence of parasitism to private-property psychology, which was nourished by contemporary influences from the bourgeois world; recommended stricter enforcement of existing laws and less emphasis in the press on speculators' ill-gotten gains; and ominously concluded with a word of praise for the anti-parasite law passed shortly before in Georgia and a call for new legislation making it possible to bring "administrative or criminal proceedings" against all parasites.

Jurists moved into the discussion in the latter part of 1960. Two of them agreed that new penalties on parasites had to be set, but they advocated the use of sanctions adjusted to the offense.

Shortly thereafter a people's judge voiced two recommendations which found their way into an RSFSR decree six months later: one, that property acquired by means other than labor be forfeit; the other, that parasites should be not simply banished from the city where they happened to be offending but settled in definite areas and compelled to work there, on pain of criminal punishment.

The year 1961 was marked by the campaign against economic crimes and the expansion of the death penalty; it is not surprising that during that year public opposition to the stiffer form of anti-parasite law came to a halt. On May 4, 1961, the RSFSR at last enacted its decree, to which in the following months the legislation of almost all other union republics was substantially conformed. The opponents of anti-parasite legislation had lost. Comrades' courts, with their lighter sanctions, were not given authority over parasite cases as such; the new legislation retained the sentence of two to five years of exile to specially set-off regions, with compulsory labor at the place of settlement.

Opposition, however, had not proved altogether vain. The 1961 decree did contain one important change from the 1957 drafts, and thus also represented a departure from the legislation of the 1957–60 period. This was a change in the procedure for hearing cases. In the 1961 decree no role was left for the residential public meeting, and the lowest state court of general jurisdiction, the people's court, was assigned important duties. A procedural distinction was drawn between cases of parasites who did not work at all and cases of parasites who had been registered in a job but did not report for work. The parasite who held no job was placed under the exclusive jurisdiction of a people's court, which however was supposed to try the case non-criminally and thus without such safeguards as were contained in the Code of Criminal Procedure. The parasite who was enrolled in a sham job could be tried by a people's court or by a public meeting of workers; discretion to select the forum was not expressly lodged anywhere, but subsequent commentary has made it clear that it is the government prosecutor's office that makes the decisions.

According to the 1961 decree, cases heard by a people's court were not subject to review in ordinary appeal but might be protested by the prosecutor to higher courts. Cases heard by a public meeting were subject to no review in court, but the sentence did not take effect until it had been confirmed by the executive committee of the local soviet, which therefore was in a position to conduct an administrative review of the file; as the convocation of the public meeting might have come at the initiative, or at least with the approval, of the executive committee of the local soviet in the first place, the administrative review probably persuaded the reviewers in most cases that the sentence was right and should be confirmed.

Another change was that under the 1961 decree the warning became not one of the consequences but one of the prerequisites of the trial. An anti-parasite proceeding now was not to be instituted until after the offender had been warned by the authorities to mend his ways and had disregarded the warning. Some convictions have since been set aside, on protest, by appellate courts on the ground that the necessary warning had not been given; more have been set aside on the ground that too little time had been allowed for the warned offender to reform. The warning may be given by "civic organizations or state organs," including the police, the public prosecutor, a trade union, a comrades' court, and perhaps others. In most cases the way for a man to comply with a warning is to get a job, or, if he is already on the rolls, to work regularly at his job; however, sometimes it is hard to tell what the offender could have done after the warning to avert the subsequent proceedings. If the parasite had gone to work by the time his case came to trial or even by the time it came to the attention of a higher court (where that was possible), the exile was considered wrongful and must be set aside even though the offender took the job only after the expiration of a realistic term of warning; but he was to be supervised closely in his work lest the employment prove to have been a maneuver to circumvent the decree.

The role of the public meeting, reduced by the jurisdictional provisions of the 1961 decree, was reduced still further in operation. Most of the prosecutions under the law had to be brought before people's courts because the defendants were unemployed and thus not attached to any occupational collective. It has been said that the sham workers were too often protected by their fellows. Even the few sham workers who were tried were usually brought not to the workers' public meeting but to the people's court. The government prosecutors may have preferred this route because they regard the public meetings as too lenient, too different from ordinary criminal prosecutions, or too unfamiliar.

The compromise of 1961 lasted in its main outlines for four and a half years. In September 1965 a decree issued by the Presidium of the Supreme Soviet altered the procedure, and to some extent the grounds of proceeding, against parasites. The toilers' collective now does not figure at all, unless it counts as a "civic organization" that may issue the preliminary warning. The offender has a month's time, after he is warned by police or civic bodies, to avoid prosecution by getting a job. For offenders who do not heed the warning, further process depends on their place of residence. Those who live in Leningrad, in Moscow, or in Moscow Province around the metropolis may be brought before a (regular) people's court and there sentenced to exile to special locations, as under the 1961–65 version of the law, for two to five years of compulsory labor. Offenders who live elsewhere are liable to be sentenced by the executive committee of a local soviet to socially useful work at enterprises or construction sites located within their own province (*oblast'*), march (*krai*), or autonomous republic.

As before, a convicted parasite who refuses to work under sentence is liable to a term at "corrective labor" with partial docking of his wages, and if he still refuses to work he may be deprived of his liberty in an ordinary penal institution.

So much for a sketch of the way the anti-parasite laws work. Why were they passed?

The official accounts of the enactment of the anti-parasite laws stress the determination of the Soviet people to make every member of "socialist" society willing and eager to do his part, to work to bring a better life to pass in the higher phase of communism. This professed goal appears to have three aspects, which we may conveniently call the productional, the sanitary, and the salvational. Parasites are to be made to work in order that production can be increased, they are to be temporarily isolated from the law-abiding majority in order not to infect their betters with private-property views, and they are to be reformed because civic virtue is good in itself.

May one conclude, from the severity of the sanctions, that the Soviet leaders are alarmed by an increasing incidence of such "parasites"? The inference, though natural, is rejected in Soviet explanations, just as it is in the case of the recent broadening of the application of the death penalty. In both instances we are told that the reduction in crime and the rise in the moral level of the population have produced in the overwhelming law-abiding majority a growing determination to do away with the nuisance created by the ever smaller anti-social minority. Yet in the late 1950's when some criminal penalties were reduced and some criminal procedures were liberalized, one was informed that that change was occasioned by the reduction in crime and the rise in the moral level of the population. An explanation that accounts in the same way for contradictory trends is suspect, and we may be excused for continuing our search.

Until the revision of October 1965, the laws against parasites seemed to look two ways at once. One edge of the sword was turned against the violent drunkard, the wife-beater, the man who had never made it. Thus an American observer described the trial in Moscow of one Zbarski— drunk, loathsome, scandalous, without work—who was exiled under the decree for three years. Sometimes the decree was used to get rid of prostitutes, as appeared to be the case with one Maiseva, sentenced to five years after trial in the city of Chita. The woman who instead of working spent her time slandering her neighbors and complaining to the authorities about imaginary threats was also a fit subject for exile. Many of the offenders were young ne'er-do-wells who were depicted as living off their poor but industrious parents and spending their nights in drinking bouts.

The other edge of the sword was turned against the man who disrupted the economic order by turning an illegal profit, the overprivileged scion who sought shelter behind the broad backs of his rich and powerful relatives, the *stiliaga* in narrow trousers and duck-tail haircut lounging on the sidewalks of Gorky Street, the snob who liked to sport Western clothes and a Western nickname.

At this point the anti-parasite laws meet the problem of juvenile and young-adult delinquency. While the men who make today's Soviet laws are digging themselves out of their history, they are confronted by the perennial and universal revolt of the young, in the special variant of the nuclear era and the even more special subvariant of Soviet conditions. There must not be any admission that there is a conflict between Fathers and Sons. The ideology of Marxism-Leninism, which has paid so much attention to dynamics, which abounds in talk of stages and development and periodization, cannot recognize its own transitory character.

If the revolt of the young were only a political opposition, the regime could apply to it some of the lessons learned in sixty years of battle, before and after the October Revolution. But how shall the aging warriors combat the rebellious apathy of their own progeny? What if posterity simply ignores the victories bought at such a price? The anti-parasite laws show one way of trying to turn this tragedy into melodrama.

Yet it is also possible to speculate that the thrust of the sword is really all one, and that the weapon is being wielded in the interest of the values of a lower middle class rising to power. After all, many of the virtues celebrated in anti-parasite proceedings and in the literature about parasites are just those so often ascribed to a lower middle class: the glory of work in one's appointed calling; modesty in dress, toilet, deportment; adjusting to one's surroundings, making one's peace with the organization. In defense of these values the anti-parasite laws, like the comrades' courts and the volunteer people's guard, were used to repress "excesses" characteristic of either the lower or the upper class. On this view the self-appointed gravediggers of the bourgeoisie would be now busy making the land safe for the *petit bourgeois*.

This explanation of the anti-parasite laws has much in its favor besides irony; yet there are facts in the picture which it fails to fit. First, the men and women in the party establishment do not seem effectively subject to the anti-parasite laws or other non-courts in the public sector, though party discipline may be exerted from time to time for similar reasons on some "upper-class" cases. Second, the Soviet ideologists would deny that a social class structure in this sense exists in Soviet society; anyone in any station can be part of the *narod* (the people) just as anyone in any station can be an *obyvatel'* (Philistine, selfish vulgarian). Third, the procedures used to further these lower-middle-class values are derived from rather unlikely models, such as the village assembly and the pattern of peasant collective censure. Fourth, certain values usually associated with the lower middle class in European and American society are not only absent from Soviet ideology but attacked as unworthy: one thinks in particular of the value of personal thrift (or personal accumulation) and of the value of privacy or discretion in personal relations. The individual pioneer, the self-reliant Titan raising his edifice of thought or invention or production, has not been an approved model in collectivist society.

Volunteer People's Police

The *druzhiny* (Volunteer People's Police, or Guard) grew out of a movement that seems to have started in late 1958 in factory committees in Leningrad, on the outskirts of Sverdlovsk, in Enakievo in the Donets basin, and a few other places. They took some of their tasks and forms from institutions that had operated sporadically before, the most recent having been the *brigadmily* (brigades of cooperation with the police) and the KAO (Young Communist League flying squads). They were set up to help keep public order; in many places the regular police had broken down in its efforts to cope with drunkenness and other breaches of the peace. The organizations were variously named people's police, workers' police, detachments for the preservation of order, etc. They had no common structure; some were set up on a military model, with three hundred to five hundred in a detachment, divided into brigades of fifteen to twenty. The detachment in these cases covered a borough (*raion*) and was headed by a council of five, six, or seven, including workers of the borough party committees, executive committees of the borough soviets, representatives of trade unions, the Young Communist League, and other social organizations. Their initial duties were to patrol the streets. In some places they went out on patrol at first on Saturdays, Sundays, and paydays, which suggests the importance of the drink problem. Later the patrols were made daily; the usual time is in the evening, six to ten or eight to eleven o'clock.

Now there are about 140,000 *druzhiny* in the RSFSR, probably over 200,000 in the whole Soviet Union. Most of the *druzhinniki* are enlisted at their place of work and, mustered in occupational detachments, serve on patrols in rotation. An ordinary *druzhinnik* may find himself on patrol one evening in every fortnight or so.

The offenses against which the *druzhiny* were to act, in aid and in the stead of the militia, were and are various, including besides general rowdyism (hooliganism) and drunkenness the theft of government and private property, violation of regulations of trade, speculation, moonshining, traffic violations, neglect of children, and others. They are also supposed to engage in preventive work, to suggest measures of civic influence to governmental and public organizations, to send materials regarding violations to the comrades' courts or to the administrative agencies, to report offenses where necessary to the procuracy for prosecution, or to the press for exposure, and to conduct public education in the maintenance of public order. The *druzhinniki* are authorized to demand that a citizen stop violating public order and to demand identification where necessary, to draw up statements on certain violations and send them to the *druzhina* commander, to take citizens to the commander (though it is not clear how far he may act to overcome resistance), and to enter public places in order to maintain order.

One of the more picturesque functions of the *druzhiny* is the maintenance of Boards of Shame—the counterpart of the Honor Rolls kept in factories and offices—on which miscreants detected or detained by the *druzhiny* are named, depicted, and lampooned. Some officials, especially in the larger cities, are trying to broaden and refine the activities of the *druzhiny* so as to include social welfare work: children's sport clubs, helping the retired and the aged, marital counseling, coping with alcoholism apart from the direct protection of public order, and organizing adult leisure activities.

Auxiliaries to the Judicial Process

Besides the marginal institutions mentioned briefly at the outset and the three institutions that have been most heavily stressed in the past seven years (comrades' courts, anti-parasite laws, volunteer people's police), the public has been associated in the regular processes of justice by the establishment of certain auxiliary functions.

Under the Criminal Code an offender can be given a suspended sentence (conditional conviction) and placed on probation to a collective that takes responsibility for his good conduct; in some cases, an offender can be released on surety to a collective without conviction. The collective usually is an occupational unit (factory, workers, shop, trade union local, collective farm). Some such device has long been employed in the Soviet Union.

In the last few years the public prosecutor's office (*prokuratura*) in some neighborhoods has had the assistance of groups of lay helpers. So far as appears from the Soviet writing on the lay helpers, they usually have no special training, are not used for legal research or advocacy, but serve under instructions as un-skilled or semi-skilled investigators, checking business documents in economic fraud cases, searching neighborhoods for missing persons, weapons, or goods, and the like.

In the criminal trial, the Soviet judge may entertain argument from a lay defender or accuser, whose authority is decided by delegation from a collective interested in one or more of the parties, usually the accused or the victim. The collective, be it occupational or residential, is supposed to decide who shall represent it in court and whether the representative is to speak as accuser or as defender. Informal comments made by Soviet jurists suggest that lay defenders or accusers appear in as many as 10 to 15 per cent of all criminal cases tried in People's Courts and that defenders are heard more frequently than accusers; it has not been possible to check these statements.[5] The relationship between professional counsel and the lay representatives is unclear. Some writers have recommended that the prosecuting attorney work with the lay accuser, guiding his preparation and perhaps even, where time and the lay accuser's abilities will permit it, assigning certain parts of the case to him, and correspondingly for defense counsel and the lay defender. In practice, it seems, the lay speakers are not trained or qualified for such tasks, and professional counsel on both sides are reluctant to risk the fortunes of their side by relinquishing responsibility even in part. (If the lay accuser or defender were to take over a substantial part of the functions of his professional ally and do unexpectedly well at it, his professional ally might run still a different risk; but it is likely that the pressures of office routine and the traditions of single responsibility are more important than are the apprehensions of eclipse.) The content of the speeches in court is thus usually predictable and canned; the judges seldom interrogate the lay representative, the lay representative seldom interrogates parties or witnesses or offers evidence, the legal or factual merits of the case are seldom mentioned concretely.

If the institution of the civic accuser or defender is to be appraised by its effect upon the establishment of the relevant facts or the decision on relevant legal questions, it has to be written off as negligible. The extent to which the representations of the opinion of the collective affect sentencing is unknown, though judicial decrees will often mention favorable representations as an informal kind of extenuating circumstance and counsel in summing up will use those representations in argument if they are on his side. It would be wrong, however, to suppose that the main purpose of the civic accuser or defender is to contribute to a resolution of the issue before the court. It appears rather to be to help increase the solidarity of the collective by the activity of making the delegation and deciding which way to delegate; to give proof of the watchful concern of the appropriate collective, or its leadership, over the conduct of its members; and to provide yet one more outlet for the expression of certain moral values promulgated in the official culture.

It is worth guessing that the trend toward the transfer of functions from state bodies to nominally unofficial organs is being deflected if not arrested. What is happening is not usually that the lay bodies are being abolished or functions withdrawn from them; indeed, from time to time new groups are added, and new functions are entrusted to the most important of the existing ones. Instead the officials are reinforcing their connection with, and supervision over, the lay bodies. One example is found in the comrades' courts, where the augmented fining power may have the effect of making the people's judge the reviewing authority over a larger fraction of comrades' court decisions. A second concerns the anti-parasite laws; there, even before the amendment of October 1965, the combination of the formal division of jurisdictional authority and practical administration had put more and more of the cases into the line of the regular courts, partly by decision of the public prosecutor. A third is shown by the use made of the lay helpers of the prosecutors and investigators; though the lay helpers are indeed used for some tasks delegated to them by the officials, it now appears that this institution, far from prefiguring a transfer of function, is on the contrary being adapted as a screening and internship stage in the selection of cadres for the official staff.

If we attempt to sort the possible reasons for the prominence being assigned to the non-courts in the period since 1957, we may have provisionally to accept the relevance of a number of factors, among which we cannot be sure of identifying a dominant one.

(1) First we can mention the two explanations offered most often in the Soviet literature.

(a) *Down with Crime.* The argument here is that, thanks to the creation of socialism, the abolition of the exploitation of man by man, and the liquidation of antagonistic classes, all the objective conditions for the persistence of crime have been eliminated. There is no reason for crime to continue, except the survivals of the bourgeois past and infectious influences from the capitalist present.

(b) *"Withering."* As a result of the 21st and 22nd Congresses and the 1961 Party Program the classic Marxist vision of the withering away of the state was revived; its attainment was implicitly regarded as less remote than had once been thought, and the path to it was denominated the transition from socialist statehood to voluntary Communist self-government. One of the operating characteristics of the period upon which party dogma says the Soviet people are now embarked is the progressive transfer of some functions of government from the hands of the state into the hands of non-state, civic, societal organs. (The existence of the state is not immediately threatened by this doctrine; it is now admitted that it will continue, even for the exercise of coercion, well into the stage of communism.)

There is no reason to doubt the genuineness of the desire, on the part of at least some of the persons responsible, to draw in large masses of the people to the work of improving public order, deterring violators, and instilling the moral values of the regime. Sincerity does not guarantee effectiveness or justice. For one thing, the centrality of party control is not to be touched, and the multiplication of instruments is not to be considered an excuse for genuine pluralism of power. The excesses of the past are laid to personal whim, to arbitrary power, to insufficient vigilance, to breach of trust, to anything except systemic features of the Soviet state and party regime. In the field of law, those who have had to pick up the pieces after the breaking of the images are faced with a choice that has troubled them before. One avenue of reform lies through an improvement in procedural regularity and formality; another, through a broadening of the base of justice, bringing the law closer to the people. This conflict, from which no society is altogether free, has been intensified by the characteristics of the Soviet regime. It divides Soviet reformers—one may guess—not so much from one another as within themselves, and tends to make a confused zigzag of the course of reform.

(2) A second explanation would emphasize the economic aims of the regime. Attention has, thus, been drawn by observers abroad—accounting specifically for the 1961 wave of anti-parasite legislation—to the bad harvest of 1960; to the evidence of unexplainable wealth transpiring when old money was exchanged for new in early 1961; to the illegal combinations succeeding the abolished trade cooperatives; to the increasing wealth divertible to commercial use, to the interference with strict organization of distribution wrought by private trading; to the new taste for luxuries unsatisfied through official channels.

(3) A third explanation would account for the non-courts as a response, specifically Soviet to be sure, to problems of industrialization, urbanization, and post-adolescent rebellion that are encountered in not very dissimilar forms in Britain, in the United States, and in many other countries.

(4) To the doctrinal, the economic-determinist, and the sociological explanations we might oppose or add a fourth, which would stress the special need for institutions of control under Soviet conditions. Given the basic premises of the Soviet polity, which I suggest are changing but slowly, and chiefly under the surface, the Soviet state needs machinery of control in a degree not matched by societies that are—to use a reasonably dispassionate word—looser. Not only does it need powerful machinery of control, but it needs large numbers of engines and tends to produce many of them, playing one off against another.

One of the claims made for the non-courts in the Soviet Union is that they bring the processes of justice closer to the people and at the same time induce the people to take part in the processes of justice. In part, the claim is justified. When a lay accuser or defender speaks in a criminal trial, he does represent an organization or collective even though the collective decision authorizing his effort may have been inspired and guided from above. When a court holds sessions in the Little Red Corner of an apartment house or the clubroom of a trade union local, many attend who otherwise probably would not, and the responses of the audience frequently interact (not always in the interest of justice) with the proceedings "on stage." The speeches made by members of the audience toward the end of a trial in a comrades' court, while some of them appear to reflect the instructions of the local *aktiv*, do convey a sense of popular morality—channeled into a state-established, though nominally unofficial, sanction. The authorities go to considerable trouble before and during the trials of accused parasites, both in people's courts and at public meetings of workers, to mobilize the expression if not the reality of public sentiment.

Nonetheless, it is clear that the "popularization" of justice tends to bring an ever larger portion of life under the eye of a watchful regime. The non-courts do not—as is sometimes asserted—merely relieve the official courts from that portion of their case-load that can be handled with less formal procedures and less drastic sanctions. A comparison between all the cases handled by the regular courts in, say, 1956 and those handled by the courts and non-courts today in 1964 would reveal that the range of institutionally supervised conduct has markedly increased. So, probably, have the number of sanctionable offenses, the total number of cases, the amount and perhaps even the median severity of the penalties handed down. The comparison would, very likely, hold good even if the 1956 figures were augmented by the case-load handled by the predecessors of today's comrades' courts and of today's volunteer people's police. The Soviet regime has become less repressive; but it does not show many signs of becoming less comprehensive. The total weight of the blankets is lighter than it was, but there are still many blankets.

Procedures in Soviet non-courts fit into a pattern that has been described more thoroughly in its application to small and limited organizations than in relation to an entire polity. In many countries, certain types of institutions share an approach to the individual, an official ethic, and a mode of operation that have led Erving Goffman to call them "total institutions." Examples may be found in the work of many mental hospitals, insane asylums, prisons, reformatories, army camps, concentration camps, some preparatory schools, and the training programs of certain religious orders. Some of the features of these institutions closely resemble ordinary life in the Soviet Union as a whole, and one of the most striking resemblances is the practice that Goffman has called "looping."

Looping takes place between institution and individual and appears most clearly when the institution is most nearly "total." In those cases, officials of the institution, doing their duty as they see it, have acted upon or against the individual (patient, inmate, prisoner, recruit, novice—or, in the Soviet Union, citizen). The subject responds by defensive reaction. Then—and here is the place where the loop is made—the officials of the institution treat the subject's defensive response as evidence confirming the rightness of their initial judgment or diagnosis or punitive measure, and inflict more of the same. Sometimes the loop is traveled through several circuits.

One instance of looping in Soviet non-courts is the counter-response to the Grin. In anti-parasite cases, as well as in comrades' courts and indeed regular trials, the defendant often reacts to his odd and unpleasant situation (no matter whether he deserves, by his or the regime's criteria, to be put in it) by a tight, fixed grin. Perhaps it is a mask behind which he comes to terms with this newest little defeat. The grin thereupon becomes an added offense; prosecutors, civic accusers, and judges comment on the grin, "which shows that this defendant has no respect for our Soviet laws, has a frivolous attitude toward his social obligations, and mocks the authority of this tribunal." The judgment itself, though it may not mention the grin specifically, will refer to the defendant's contemptuous attitude in court as one of the signs that he is in need of correction. The grin has its counterpart in the smaller "total institutions" when the subject is not permitted the luxury of an autonomous facial reaction (sneer, pout, disgust, frown) and must keep a blank face lest the severity of the sanction be increased.

Another example lies in the blurring of the lines between various parts of a subject's existence. In the mental hospital what the patient does or says in the ward where he sleeps or in the shop where he works is observed, perhaps by different officials, but it is part of the job of the institution to collate the observations, to relate them to a picture of the whole man. The freedom of ordinary civil life, where work, play, family, public service, social life can be kept in separate though not completely sealed compartments, is infringed in the total institution for the subject's own good as the institution views it. Correspondingly, in the Soviet Union it is not only permissible but obligatory for the authorities to collapse the separate structures of a subject's daily life by piecing together, especially in the non-courts, the observations recorded by his family, his colleagues, the housing committee, the union officials, the party representatives.

A third example lies in the use made by the official of information elicited from the subject himself in the interests of the program of the institution (again ostensibly for the good of the individual as well as society). A mild form of this can be seen in the use made of interviews and questionnaires in market research and political polling. A more intensive form is practiced in certain kinds of psychotherapy. In the Soviet Union, the authorities profess to encourage candor but in practice reserve the privilege of using the elicited material to justify further sanctions.

To a lawyer, the closest parallel in a looser society is the process by which a convicted defendant is sentenced. At the point of sentencing, the privacy and autonomy that have been preserved at least in the public forum are discarded; testimony, under safeguards of no great rigor, is taken from the district attorney, police officers, welfare workers, and others; the convict himself is heard, but what he says is likely to be used against or for him. Not only the Soviet non-court but also Soviet life as a whole is governed to some degree by similar rules. It is almost as if a Soviet citizen came into his society already convicted and ripe for the sentencing. The possibility that injustice will be tempered with mercy is real, and politically significant, but Soviet legal institutions are still at least as far as those in other lands from successfully adjusting the competing claims of ideology, public order, criminology, and due process.

Notes

The main stress of this paper is on the Soviet Union. A comparative description of extrajudicial mechanisms in China and the Soviet Union was provided for the Tahoe Conference by Mrs. Virginia Jones of New Haven, Connecticut, to whom the author expresses his thanks for research assistance.

[1] The resemblance to adjudication is enhanced by the arguments used in many exposés. Often the target is an official whose competence and conformity to rule are not only conceded but stressed; and the message in the exposé is that the official violated a policy deeper than that of fidelity to rule by failing to show humane sensitivity. At times the writer of the exposé seems to be appealing from law to equity.

[2] See unpublished Ph.D. dissertation by Ellen Mickiewicz, "Adult Political Education in the U.S.S.R.: The Political Englightenment System of the Communist Party of the Soviet Union," Yale University, Department of Political Science, 1965.

[3] Some of the following text is drawn from my "Soviet Non-Courts," New York County Lawyers Association Bar Bulletin, XXI (1964), 222–29; "Hosts and Pests: The Fight against Parasites," Problems of Communism, Vol. XIV, No. 2 (Mar.–Apr., 1965), pp. 72–82; and "The Future Belongs to . . . Parasites?," Problems of Communism, Vol. XII, No. 3 (May–June, 1963), pp. 1–6.

[4] The term is used in the sense analyzed for the Chinese case by Ezra Vogel.

[5] In Moscow in 1963 I saw no lay defender in about forty trials but three lay accusers: one in a shoplifting case where the accuser was an office-mate of the defendant; one in an anti-parasite trial held before a People's Court in circuit session in an apartment-house clubroom, where the accuser spoke as a neighbor of the defendant; and one in a comrades' court case involving a traffic accident, where the accuser spoke in the name of the defendant's residential collective but was not himself a resident and had performed as lay accuser for several different collectives as part of his extracurricular civic activity. A lay accuser took part in the 1966 trial of the writers Siniavsky and Daniel; his testimony is abridged in the New York Times Magazine, Apr. 17, 1966. There is opinion in the Soviet legal literature that disapproves the use of lay accusers or defenders in comrades' courts; the ground expressed is that lay accusers and defenders are supposed to represent the collective before a court but that a comrades' court, unlike a people's court, is the creature of the collective itself, or else of society directly, and needs no representative of the public to stand between the public and the court.

When Comrades Sit in Judgment

Abraham Brumberg

It is quite common for a newly established revolutionary government to "popularize" justice. Thus the new Castro government conducted mass trials of Batista officials in stadiums. The Communist government in China frequently conducted mass meetings to denounce landlords and other despised persons, who were later dragged through the streets. This kind of justice is also common when law and order have not yet been fully established or have been temporarily undermined—witness the vigilantes of the Old West and the rough trials of "capitalist" or "bureaucratic" elements by the Red Guards in China.* However, the comrades' courts in the Soviet Union were reintroduced when that society had passed far beyond its days of revolutionary turbulence. The following article by Abraham Brumberg is a Western observer's view of such a court in action.

I had long cherished a desire to see a Soviet comrades' court in action, and so it was with considerable excitement that I approached the narrow, dark entrance to the *krasnyi ugolok* (red corner—Soviet equivalent of an American "community center") of a large Moscow apartment project where a session of the local court was about to begin. I had learned about it quite by accident, having stumbled upon a small notice pinned on one of Moscow's ubiquitous bulletin boards the day before, and now, dressed in a blue English raincoat which after weeks in Moscow had come to resemble the local GUM product, I timidly made my way inside. After walking through a dimly lit hallway, I entered a longish, narrow room with a small podium at the far end. The podium was flanked on both sides by portraits of Marx and Lenin (each with an appropriate slogan) and boasted a rectangular table plus a few chairs. In front of the podium were hard

---

From Abraham Brumberg, "When Comrades Sit in Judgment," *Problems of Communism*, Vol. XIV, No. 2 (March–April 1965), pp. 140–144. Reprinted by permission of the author.

* As of 1970 the "juries" in mass public trials in China were running as large as 20,000 persons, and it appears that the larger the juries the more severe the penalties imposed. See Richard Hughes, "Mao Makes the Trials Run on Time," *The New York Times Magazine*, August 23, 1970, pp. 22, 68.

wooden chairs occupied by about two dozen people, almost all of them elderly and—even by Moscow's standards—shabbily dressed.

A few minutes after I seated myself in one of the back rows, the court, in the persons of the chairman—a small, dark-haired man—two other men, and a rather plump, middle-aged woman secretary, entered the room, and the chairman announced that unless anyone in the audience had any objection to the particular *sostav* (composition) of the court (which changes from trial to trial), the session would begin.

The first suit was brought by a tenant whose apartment had been flooded from the apartment on the floor above. The cause was a hot-water faucet, which through oversight had been left open after the entire apartment building had been deprived of hot water for over two weeks. The defendants were a middle-aged mechanic at the Moscow metro (subway), earning a salary of 120 rubles a month, and an infirm pensioner, whose monthly check came to 39 rubles and 25 kopeks. At stake was the sum of 34 rubles, the cost of the damage caused by the men's negligence. The sum was not large, of course; yet, for the pensioner at least, it obviously represented a staggering amount. This much the ensuing debate between the chairman (quiet, paternal), the plaintiff (self-confident, short-tempered), and the two defendants (obeisant and querulous in turn) made clear. Besides, demanded the metro mechanic, why hadn't the ZHEK (apartment administration) fixed the pipes for two weeks? And what about the damage caused to his and his friend's apartment? The exchange became more lively, with the representative of the apartment administration, a rather handsome and well-dressed man, turning to the defendants and warning them that if they didn't pay up, they would be told to hire a carpenter on their own, and he would surely charge more than 50 rubles— and how would they like that? They wouldn't, and so the discussion turned to the question of whether the 34 rubles should be paid in one lump sum or in installments, with the defendants, of course, pleading for the latter. After a few minutes of rather inconsequential wrangling, the chairman announced that the court would adjourn for deliberation, and that another case be heard in the meantime.

Well, I thought to myself, this was rather interesting, but it lacked the dramatic flavor which I had anticipated. The proceedings that started a few minutes later, however—with a new court (and the same secretary) upon the podium—were to bear out my expectations.

A thin, bedraggled man with a dirty patch over his left eye walked up to the front of the room and began reading off a list of names. "Simion Vassilevich Titkin?" Silence. Then a voice from the audience: "He's not here!" The man went on: "Timofiei Alexandrovich Razumnyi?" Again silence, and again a voice from the audience: "Not here!" At this point the chairman man raised his eyes and with a slightly puzzled expression on his face inquired as to Razumnyi's whereabouts. "He couldn't make it," came another voice from the audience. "He's sick." A short woman, bent with age, and with the inevitable kerchief over her head, rose from one of the back rows and approached the podium.

"Comrade Chairman," she began querulously, "what do we need all this fuss and bother for?" Couldn't the whole matter be settled simply, as among friends? Besides, she went on, her son (the reference was to Timofiei Razumnyi) was innocent. He hadn't done a thing.

"But please, citizenness," said the chairman patiently and with good humor, "your son is not accused of anything. He was asked to come here as a witness."

"I don't know—all this business," the woman continued, slowly raising her voice. "He isn't guilty, that's all. He hasn't done a thing!"

"But citizenness," the chairman went on with what I thought was a remarkable display of endurance. "Don't you understand what I am telling you? No one has said that your son has done anything; he's merely to testify here as a witness—understand, witness—W-I-T-N-E-S-S."

But the citizenness would have none of it. In fact, she didn't think that Simion Vassilevich should be brought to trial, either. "He is a good lad—why punish him? He ought to be [this to the audience] supported!"

The audience found this vastly amusing, as did the chairman. "Well, perhaps so," he said at last. "We'll see next time. And perhaps—we shall have to expel him from Moscow . . ."[1]

What with the defendant and one of the witnesses missing, the court adjourned till the following evening, first allowing a member of the previous sostav to announce the finding in the first case: 34 rubles to be divided in half between the two defendants and to be paid in three monthly installments. The two men sighed with relief, the audience was visibly pleased, and everybody made for the exit. I left, too, eagerly awaiting the next chapter of the case of Simion Vassilevich Titkin.

The following evening, the courtroom was filled with people, among them the defendant Titkin, a young man of 26, blond, with an open face and a decidedly uneasy mien. According to the indictment read by the chairman, Titkin had not been working at his factory for almost seven months, coming home every night in a drunken stupor, frequently beating up his wife, and forcing her to hand over her earnings to quench his incessant alcoholic thirst. A general meeting of the workers at his factory had unanimously accused him of parasitic behavior and demanded his exile from Moscow. At home things had come to such a pass that Titkin's wife, fearful of her husband's violent outbursts, had taken to staying away from their apartment, sending their three-year-old child to her mother-in-law for safekeeping.

The chairman asked Titkin to rise. "Well, what about it?"

With a slightly bowed head, and speaking in half-finished sentences, Titkin began to tell his side of the story. Did he occasionally come home drunk? Yes—but only occasionally. (Murmurs in the audience.) But he never used his wife's money for that purpose. ("Then where did you get it?" came a question from the floor. The chairman did not react.) Certainly, he missed work—but after all, he had been sick off and on for more than two months. ("Right!" came another voice.) As for intimidating his wife, why, let the chairman ask her himself—she's sitting right beside him.

The chairman turned to Titkin's wife—a bashful-looking girl carrying a small child in her arms. Before she could say a word, however, another woman rose from her seat and began regaling the court with her observations of the Titkin household. Yes, there have been fights between husband and wife, but then—what's so unusual about that? Everybody gets into an occasional brawl with his or her spouse. (Murmur of approbation in the audience.) The chairman listened to her and then again turned his attention to Titkin's wife. From her recital, I gathered that she bore her husband no ill will. To be sure, there had been fights, he did come home once or twice and beat her up, but. . . .

"Well, then, what do you think we ought to do with your husband?" asked the chairman. And it seemed to me, just then, as if these words suddenly provided the key to the extraordinary nature of the legal proceedings that were going on around me. For what was the specific charge against Titkin? "Parasitism"? "Appearance in an intoxicated state in public places"? "Absence from work without valid reason"? "Unworthy behavior toward women"? "High-handed acts," "abusive language," or perhaps some "other antisocial acts not entailing criminal liability"? (All these and many other transgressions are listed in the USSR "Statute on Comrades Courts.") What is more, it wasn't at all clear who precisely was pressing any of these vague charges. Titkin's fellow-workers? If so, why not either hand over his case to the regular courts, as the statute prescribes, or perhaps try him again before the factory's court? His fellow tenants? From the behavior of those present, I gathered that Titkin's neighbors were not particularly scandalized by his behavior. Well, then, what about his wife? It turned out that she, too, was not eager to press charges. He should be given another chance, she haltingly told the chairman—who knows, perhaps he would stop drinking and become a more responsible husband, father, and citizen. After all, this was his first transgression. At this point Timofiei's warmhearted mother, who the evening before had provided us with such a spirited example of Chekhovian humor, quickly sprang to her feet: "She is right, Comrade Chairman!" she exclaimed. "Cheloveka nado no put povesti (one ought to help straighten a man out) and not punish him." "Right, right!" came a chorus from the audience. "Give him a chance." "He is an orphan!" "Just give him a warning!"

"Well," said the chairman, looking impassively at the audience, "Titkin was accused by his comrades of unsocial behavior. He does not work. He drinks. How, comrades, can we possibly enter communism with such people among us?" (Pause. Silence.) "The court will consider all that has been said here and will announce the verdict later. Now for the next case."

The chairs were reoccupied (for by that time the excitement had caught almost all of Titkin's assembled neighbors), and the next defendant was asked to rise. This time there could be no mistake about the nature of the man. Fifty years old, slightly stooped, with an expression at once cunning and vacuous, he twisted and turned as the indictment was being read. The plaintiff was a middle-aged widow who had wanted to rent a room at the defendant's apartment while he was serving a two-year jail term (only his wife was living there at the time). The room, it seems, was perfectly satisfactory, and she had moved in. One fine day, however (here the story began to be interrupted with sniffles and tears, which slowly infected other women in the audience), there was a knock at the door, and there was the defendant, bowing and scraping and begging to be admitted. Naturally she let him in, but no sooner did he make himself at home than he took out a bottle and started to drink and use foul language. Frightened, she ran into her room and locked the door. (The wife, obviously, was not around—in fact, she didn't seem to be around anywhere. . . .) The defendant began knocking at the woman's door, becoming more abusive and finally committing the ultimate indignity of urinating right outside her room. Having related this incident, the woman, no longer able to contain herself, burst into tears and sat down.

The audience was obviously exercised by the story, and even more so by the behavior of the defendant, who, questioned in turn by the chairman and one of the other members of the sostav, denied the allegations lock, stock and barrel. "Didn't you drink and behave like a hooligan?" "Khospodi pomilui (God forbid)! No, never!" "You're lying," came a voice from the audience. "Well, perhaps I took a drink or two," the defendant admitted indignantly, "but I certainly did not insult anyone." Besides, he informed the chairman, the plaintiff was clearly untrustworthy. "What a reputation she has! Goes around smoking one cigarette after another all day long—word of honor! Ask anyone and you'll hear the same thing—nobody can stand her, nobody wants to live with her." "Lies, all lies," came a chorus. Several people stood up and began to talk in unison, gesticulating, shouting, trying to make themselves heard over the voices of their neighbors. The chairman pounded on the table and asked for quiet. And suddenly at this point my second visit to the comrades' court took an entirely unexpected turn.

As I sat there totally absorbed by what was going on and manfully trying to jot down a few notes, the man with the patch over his eye appeared, glared at me, and demanded to know who I was and what I was doing there. "I am an American," I said, "a journalist, and I am interested in comrades' courts." "Come with me," said the man—and, mindless of my neighbors who had obviously been eyeing my suspicious reportorial activities for quite some time, he led me out of the court room.

I was ushered into a small room where I found the members of the first *sostav* and a man in his late thirties, whose neat, well-groomed appearance clearly distinguished him from the others. A minute later the members of the second court, along with the chairman and the woman secretary (whose name, as I soon found out, was Citizenness Gurvich), entered the room and seated themselves behind a large desk. I was now faced by about ten people, all of them—with the possible exception of Madam Gurvich— staring at me with what I felt was a distinct lack of friendliness, albeit not without curiosity. It was clear that I was in for one of those interrogations to which inquisitive foreign tourists in Russia are so frequently subjected. And it was clear, too, that it was the well-groomed man who was to be in charge of it.

The questions followed one another in rapid succession: Who are you? What is your business here? Who gave you permission to come to our court? I replied that I was an American journalist, that I had long been interested in attending a comrades' court, and that I was not aware of the need to obtain any permission to do so. Then, in turn, I asked my questioner who *he* was. Startled by this unexpected reversal of roles, he replied quickly that he was a member of the comrades' court, and then, realizing perhaps that the reply was less than convincing, he added: "That's none of your business, anyway. So you are an American journalist, eh?" Then, with growing hostility: "Whatever gave you the idea that you can just enter a court without permission? Don't you Americans know anything about etiquette?" I said, again, that I was not aware of any Soviet law that requires a visitor to obtain permission to visit a court (there is none). Of course, I added, if there were such a law, then I was obviously in the wrong and was ready to admit my mistake. At this point the chairman interrupted, saying that the regular "people's courts" were one thing—everyone was welcome there—and "comrades' courts" another. "Perhaps so," I answered, "but all I can say is that I have not been aware of any restrictions."

My replies were obviously not to the liking of the well-dressed "member of the comrades' court," for he resumed questioning me with increasing vehemence. Why hadn't I at least asked the chairman for permission? ("As I said—I didn't know it was necessary.") Didn't I know that the courts were not open to everyone? ("But the chairman just told me differently.") Didn't I realize that what was allowed to Soviet citizens was not necessarily allowed to foreigners? ("No, that's news to me.") Don't Americans have any rules of etiquette at all? What would happen if a Soviet citizen were to enter an American court, just like that, without asking for permission? ("I assure you, no one would dream of bothering him.") Why was I interested in comrades' courts? Why only in the seamy side of Soviet life? ("I am not"—this to the obvious satisfaction of some of the others—"I have seen your university, your Pioneer Palace, the new construction in Volgograd. . . .")

The atmosphere was getting decidedly uncongenial, the questioning more intense. I was told to produce my documents, and when I replied that I had left my passport at the hotel, my interlocutor announced that we would have to go to the nearest militia station. I replied that I would insist on calling my embassy first. My interlocutor relented (it was rather clear that he had no case), but perhaps out of sheer frustration he clenched his fist in front of my face and exclaimed: "You know how we treat people who try to break into our Soviet garden? With our fists—that's how!" I replied that I was unaware of breaking into any gardens whatever. "You have behaved like a scoundrel (po khamski)!" he shouted, livid with rage. I said I was surprised to hear him use such terms—was this in keeping with Soviet etiquette? I took out a cigarette and struck a match. My questioner was beside himself: "Is this how you Americans behave? Don't you first ask the lady whether she minds your smoking?" I turned to Citizenness Gurvich with elaborate courtesy: "May I?"—thus unwittingly succeeding in embarrassing her and her mild-looking chairman, who had been puffing incessantly ever since I had entered the room.

The wrangling went on for another twenty minutes or so, the questions repeating themselves with monotonous regularity (at one point I grew quite exasperated and inquired whether they thought I had come to the courtroom equipped with a capitalist bomb). But it was clear that the charges against me were even more tenuous than those against Simion Vassilevich Titkin, and so, as suddenly as it had begun, the interrogation ceased and I was told that I was free to go. "In that case," I said, "I should like to have permission to go back to the courtroom." My interlocutor was visibly shaken. "No, you can't go back," he said testily. Why not, I demanded—they had heard my story and satisfied themselves as to my intentions, then why was I not permitted to go back? "It is not for me to decide," he said, with cold fury, "it's up to the kollektiv." I turned around to the kollektiv, as I had a few minutes ago to Citizenness Gurvich, and repeated my request. The kollektiv in turn looked at the chairman, who, after a pause, said rather weakly: "There's no point in going back—it's all over; only the verdict is to be announced." "Fine," I said, "I'd like to hear the verdict." "All right," said the chairman resignedly, "go ahead."

I returned to the courtroom, much to the amazement of the assembled audience, again seating myself in one of the back rows. About half an hour later the court reappeared, and the chairman read the verdict. Citizen Titkin was given a warning—if he didn't mend his ways within a month, the comrades' court would refer his case to a people's court with a recommendation that he be exiled from Moscow. (A specialist on Soviet law told me later that my presence in the courtroom may have had something to do with the mildness of the sentence.) The other defendant also got off fairly easily; he was fined ten rubles for vandalism, given a reprimand, and warned sternly by the chairman that if he, too, didn't mend his ways, he would most definitely be exiled from Moscow. "Remember," said the chairman, wagging his finger, "if you should ever find yourself here again, we won't treat you with kid gloves, you understand?" "Yes, Comrade Chairman," exclaimed the man, bowing and clicking his heels grotesquely, "I understand!" "You promise not to drink any more?" continued the chairman. "I promise—not a drop!" "You promise not to create any more scandals?" "Word of honor, Comrade Chairman, may I be struck by lightning if I ever give you trouble again!" It was pure Chekhov once more. "All right, then—you may go," said the chairman. "The court is adjourned."

The tenants slowly filed out of the room. Gathering up my coat and notebook, I followed the others. Before I went out into the courtyard, I stopped to say good-bye to the chairman and Citizenness Gurvich, who were standing nearby and looking at me. "Well, you see," said the chairman pleasantly, "had you come to me and asked for permission, I would have gladly given it to you." I had my doubts, but I didn't voice them. Citizenness Gurvich was the next to speak. "How did you like our court?" she asked with a smile. "Extremely interesting," I replied, in all sincerity, "—extremely." We all shook hands, and I left. The lesson in justice and etiquette was over.

Note

1 This would be strictly illegal, inasmuch as the comrades' court is empowered only to *recommend* exile (or other forms of criminal punishment) to a regular people's court, which may or may not approve it. But the chairman seemed to be oblivious to this legal nicety.

For Further Reading

Those interested in further explorations of participatory democracy can read more of the sources from which our selections were taken, then turn to these additional items.

I. General Theory

Bachrach, Peter. *The Theory of Democratic Elitism: A Critique.* Boston: Little, Brown, 1967. 106 pp.

   Against political scientists who value some political apathy for stability, Bachrach emphasizes the value of participation as a learning experience.

Bay, Christian. *The Structure of Freedom.* Stanford, Calif.: Stanford University Press, 1950. 419 pp.

   This rather difficult and abstract case for expansion of human freedoms can be read as background for a case for participatory democracy.

Dewey, John. *The Public and Its Problems.* Denver: Swallow, 1954. 219 pp.

   Writing in 1927, Dewey stressed the need for the diffusion of scientific knowledge in order to meet public problems, and, although he remains vague on what functions might be performed, he closes the book with an account of the need for participative communities as a learning experience.

Duncan, Graeme, and Steven Lukes. "The New Democracy," *Political Studies,* Vol. XI, No. 2 (June 1963), 156–177.

   Another critique of democratic revisionists—that is, social scientists holding that apathy can be a good thing for political systems.

Flacks, Richard. "On the Uses of Participatory Democracy," *Dissent,* Vol. XIII (November-December 1966), 701–708.

   A short and rather general essay favoring the expansion of participatory democracy beyond mobilization of the disadvantaged to other spheres of life. See also the comments on the article by Tom Kahn and Paul Goodman, with Flacks' reply, Dissent, Vol. XIV (March-April 1967), 247–254.

Frankel, Charles. *The Democratic Prospect.* New York: Harper and Row, 1964.

   Originally written in 1962, the work contains an argument that restoration of participatory democracy is illusory. See especially Ch. IV, pp. 49–71.

Gallup, George, and Saul Forbes Rae. *The Pulse of Democracy: The Public*

Opinion Poll and How It Works. New York: Simon and Schuster, 1940. 290 pp.

Two fundamentalist democrats argue that the supplementary support of polls will lend something of direct democracy to representative democracy. See especially Chs. 1, 21–23.

Girvetz, Harry K. *Democracy and Elitism: Two Essays With Readings*. New York: Scribners', 1967. 349 pp.

Of only indirect relevance, since the focus is on the case for representative democracy against its antidemocratic critics from Plato onward.

Glazer, Nathan. "The New Left and Its Limits," *Commentary*, July 1968, pp. 31–39.

Contains some pointed criticisms of participatory democracy as a political program.

Goodman, Paul. *Growing Up Absurd: Problems of Youth in the Organized System*. New York: Random House, 1960. 296 pp.

Advocating decentralization, he writes of the need for small-scale communities and their "local patriotisms" for good education of youth.

———. "Notes on Decentralization," in Irving Howe, ed., *The Radical Papers*. Garden City, N.Y.: Doubleday, 1966. Pp. 183–201.

———, and Percival Goodman. *Communitas: Means of Livelihood and Ways of Life*. Chicago: The University of Chicago Press, 1947. 141 pp.

Less on participation than on urban planning for the genuine communities that could make it possible.

Goodwin, Richard N. "The Shape of American Politics," in Fred Krinsky, ed., *Democracy and Complexity: Who Governs the Governors?* Beverly Hills, Calif.: Glencoe Press, 1968. Pp. 114–147.

See especially pp. 138–147, where the liberal political speech writer argues for decentralization against the "illusory neatness of central direction and control, under the assumption that it is more effective."

Hayden, Tom. The *"Port Huron Statement"* of Students for a Democratic Society, in Kenneth M. Dolbeare, ed., *Directions in American Political Thought*. New York: Wiley, 1969. Pp. 468–484.

Hayden was the chief author of this 1962 manifesto for participatory democracy.

Joll, James. *The Anarchists*. Boston: Little, Brown, 1964. 280 pp.

Also available in paperback (Grosset and Dunlap), this is a good account of the early communitarian socialists and anarchists—the nineteenth-century advocates of participatory communities.

Kariel, Henry S., ed. *Frontiers of Democratic Theory*. New York: Random House, 1970. 448 pp.

The focus is on the debate between the revisionist (or elitist) theorists of representative democracy and their opponents, but it includes much that is relevant to participatory democracy.

———. *Open Systems: Arenas for Political Action.* Itasca, Ill.: Peacock, 1968. 148 pp.

> Beyond expressing views reminiscent of Herbert Marcuse's *One Dimensional Man,* he argues the need to "open" public and private organizations to more participatory involvement in order to "open" our minds to new possibilities.

Kornhauser, William. *The Politics of Mass Society.* Glencoe, Ill.: Free Press, 1959. 256 pp.

> Warns of the totalitarian dangers of a mass participative society when elite and mass are not insulated from each other by the buffer zone of autonomous intermediate associations.

Kresh, Paul. *The Power of the Unknown Citizen.* Philadelphia: Lippincott, 1969.

> Examples show that ordinary citizens can be politically influential.

Krimmerman, Leonard I., and Lewis Perry, eds. *Patterns of Anarchy.* Garden City, N.Y.: Doubleday Anchor, 1966. 564 pp.

> An excellent anthology of the many varieties of anarchism.

Larson, Calvin J., and Philo C. Wasburn. *Power, Participation and Ideology: Readings in the Sociology of American Political Life.* New York: McKay, 1969. 484 pp.

> Many of these largely sociological writings are relevant to participatory democracy.

Lowi, Theodore. *The End of Liberalism: Ideology, Policy, and the Crisis of Public Authority.* New York: Norton, 1969. 314 pp.

> A general critique of the phenomenon manifest in the community-action programs in the War on Poverty: irresponsible devolution of functions to be performed on behalf of the public by private groups.

Lowry, Ritchie P. "Power to the People—Political Evolution or Revolution?," *The Urban and Social Change Review,* Vol. III, No. 2 (Spring 1970) 2–6.

> Brief and very elementary.

Lynd, Staughton. "The New Left," *The Annals of the American Academy,* Vol. 382 (March 1969), 64–72.

> On antiauthoritarian and proparticipation aspects of New Left ideology.

McClosky, Herbert. "Political Participation," *International Encyclopedia of the Social Sciences,* Vol. 12, pp. 252–265.

> Little on participatory democracy, but good background information on behavioral research findings.

Madison, James, et al. *Federalist Papers,* Nos. 10, 52–58, 62–63.

> There are many editions of this classic, with Madison's No. 10 setting forth a case for large-scale representative democracy instead of small-scale participatory-democracy sovereignties; the other listed papers of Madison set forth his views of representation.

Michels, Robert. *Political Parties: A Sociological Study of Oligarchical Tendencies of Modern Democracy.* New York: Collier, 1962. 371 pp.
    Gloomily dwelling on the dark side of cyclical change, this classical statement is pessimistic on the chances for sustained participatory diffusion of power.

Milbrath, Lester W. *Political Participation: How and Why Do People Get Involved in Politics?* Chicago: Rand McNally, 1965. 159 pp.
    Including a good bibliography, he summarizes empirical research on participation, focusing on representative-democracy electoral politics.

Mill, John Stuart. *Considerations on Representative Government.*
    There are many editions of this classic liberal defense of representative democracy, which betrays Mill's concern to salvage the benefits of participatory democracy in juries and local government offices.

Minar, David, and Scott Greer, eds. *The Concept of Community: Readings with Interpretation.* Chicago: Aldine, 1969. 361 pp.
    Chiefly of interest on the quest for community, but the inclusion of a selection from William Golding's Lord of the Flies reminds us that spontaneity and democratic order may often be in tension.

Nisbet, Robert A. *The Quest for Community: A Study in the Ethics of Order and Freedom.* New York: Oxford University Press, 1953.
    After a long diagnosis of modern man's frustrated search, Nisbet endorses the message in Lilienthal's TVA (our selection) and urges its extension to private associations. See Ch. 11 and Conclusion, pp. 248–284.

Olsen, Marvin E., ed. *Power in Societies.* New York: Macmillan, 1970. 445 pp.
    An anthology of sociological writings on political power in modern societies. Use as background for reflections.

Pennock, J. Roland, and John W. Chapman. *Voluntary Associations: Nomos XI.* New York: Atherton Press, 1969. 291 pp.
    Although the book deals broadly with pluralism, the essays from page 170 ff. offer useful background.

Pitkin, Hanna. *The Concept of Representation.* Berkeley: University of California Press, 1967. 323 pp.
    A rather difficult analysis of conceptual usage in great theorists as well as in ordinary language.

Pool, Ithiel de Sola. "The Public and the Polity," in Pool, ed., *Contemporary Political Science.* New York: McGraw-Hill, 1967. Pp. 22–52.
    After reviewing classical theory on the relationship between mass participation and political stability, turns to findings of modern empirical research.

Pranger, Robert J. *The Eclipse of Citizenship: Power and Participation in Contemporary Politics.* New York: Holt, Rinehart and Winston, 1968. 104 pp.

An abstract case for participatory democracy against oligarchic representative democracy. It fails to show how his large claims for the former could be realized in any specific contexts.

Sartori, Giovanni. *Democratic Theory*. Detroit: Wayne State University Press, 1962.

His Ch. XII (pp. 250–268) contrasts the ancient Greek with modern democracies, stressing the inappropriateness of direct democracy to modern conditions.

Schumpeter, Joseph A. *Capitalism, Socialism and Democracy* (3rd ed.). New York: Harper and Row, 1962. 425 pp.

See especially Part IV (pp. 235–302), where Schumpeter argues that the limits of political rationality suggest that democracy should be defined so that the rule of the people consists in participation—not in deciding of issues, but in competitive election of representatives.

Silvert, Kalman. *Man's Power: A Biased Guide to Political Thought and Action*. New York: Viking, 1970. 163 pp.

Can be read as background for a case for participatory democracy, since his abstract method of analysis and its application seek to maximize "freedom" in defective representative democracies.

Verba, Sidney. "Democratic Participation," *The Annals of the American Academy*, Vol. 373 (September 1967), 53–78.

An excellent short introduction to democratic political participation but touches only briefly on direct democracy.

Walker, Jack L. "A Critique of the Elitist Theory of Democracy," *American Political Science Review*, Vol. LX (June 1966), 285–295.

Essentially the same message as Bachrach (1967).

II. Putting Theory into Practice

Adler, Renata. "Letter from the Palmer House," in William P. Gerberding and Duane E. Smith. *The Radical Left: The Abuse of Discontent*. Boston: Houghton Mifflin, 1970. Pp. 31–49.

A brutally ironic account of the inability of a congeries of leftist groups to practice participatory democracy at the 1967 New Politics Convention in Chicago.

Alinsky, Saul D. *Reveille for Radicals*. New York: Random House, 1969. 235 pp.

Although the bulk of the book dates from 1946, the professional organizer of mass movements has added a fresh introduction and afterword on current developments.

———, with Marion K. Sanders. "The Professional Radical, 1970," *Harpers*, January 1970, pp. 35–42.

An interview colorfully describes his strategy and tactics for organizing those with little participatory power.

Duhl, Leonard J., with Janice Volkman. "Participatory Democracy: Networks as a Strategy of Change," The Urban and Social Change Review, Vol. III, No. 2 (Spring 1970), 11–14.

If participatory democracy is to cease being the prerogative of elites, the new informal style of political organization must build community ties among the disadvantaged.

Hayden, Tom. "The Politics of the Movement," Dissent, Vol. XIII (January-February 1966), 75–87.

After reviewing the failures of the liberals, he shows how the participatory-style movement of the discontented can bring real change.

Kahn, Tom. "Direct Action and Democratic Values," Dissent, Vol. XIII (January-February 1966), 22–30.

Argues that participatory democracy is no substitute for formal rights to vote, to dissent, or to organize opposition.

Kase, Francis J. People's Democracy: A Contribution to the Study of the Communist Theory of State and Revolution. Leyden: A. W. Sijthoff, 1968. 190 pp.

The sequel to Lenin: the theory and practice of popular participation in modern Communist systems. See especially pp. 148–160, the Yugoslav case. Good bibliography included.

Keniston, Kenneth. Young Radicals: Notes on Committed Youth. New York: Harcourt, 1961.

In Ch. 5 the book enlarges on some of the points made in the Keniston selection printed in this reader.

Lynd, Staughton. "Decentralization: A Road to Power?," Liberation, Vol. XII, No. 3 (May-June 1967), 32–34.

Raises questions on Tom Hayden's program.

———, "The New Radicals and 'Participatory Democracy,' " Dissent, Vol. XII, No. 3 (Summer 1965), 324–333.

The focus is on early development of SNCC and SDS.

Mann, Eric. "Electoral Politics and The Movement," Liberation, Vol. II, No. 3 (May-June 1966), 44–49.

Citing the failures of participatory democracy in Newark, N.J., he writes a radical's apologia for electoral activity.

Rubinstein, Richard E. Rebels in Eden: Mass Political Violence in the United States. Boston: Little, Brown, 1970. 192 pp.

Powerlessness (or dependence) has long been the root cause of the violent response of "colonialized" outgroups in America. Endorses self-determination for such groups as ghetto blacks. See especially pp. 116–160.

Swanson, Jack. "A New Way of Life—Or Is It?," National Observer, Mar. 23, 1970, p. 22.

Describes life on the Tolstoy Farm commune in the State of Washington, showing new patterns of communal living beset by some traditional problems.

Thigpen, Robert, and Lyle A. Downing. "Power, Participation and the Politics of Disruption," *The Christian Century*, July 23, 1969, pp. 973–975.

The politics of disruption may be necessary for those who lack and want meaningful participation.

Townsend, James Roger. *Political Participation in Communist China.* Berkeley and Los Angeles: University of California Press, 1967. 233 pp.

Sets forth much information on the theory and practice of Chinese grass-roots participation but sees little of real democracy in it.

III. Neighborhoods

(1) GEOGRAPHICAL CONCEPTIONS AND POVERTY

Alperowitz, Gar. "Cooperatives against Poverty," *Current*, May 1969, pp. 27–31.

Reviews the main provisions of the proposed Community Self-Determination Act aimed at facilitating creation of community corporations for local self-determination.

Bachrach, Peter, and Morton S. Baratz. *Power and Poverty: Theory and Practice.* New York: Oxford University Press, 1970. 240 pp.

After presenting a theoretical framework for the study of community power, they apply it to poverty, race, and political participation in Baltimore, Md.

Bell, Daniel, and Virginia Held. "The Community Revolution," *The Public Interest*, No. 16 (Summer 1969), pp. 142–177.

An excellent essay on demands for participatory democracy in the urban context, focusing on poverty and the model-cities programs.

Citizens For Local Democracy, "How to Make the United States a Democracy: Making Our Cities, Counties and States Democratic."

This ambitious document shows how the United States could be reconstituted on both urban and rural participatory-democracy units. Available from CLD, 111 Mercer Street, New York, N.Y. 10012 ($1.00).

Huber, Hans. *How Switzerland Is Governed.* Zurich: Schweizer Spiegel Verlag, 1968. 63 pp.

Available through the Embassy of Switzerland, contains uncritical accounts of direct participation in the Swiss communes, the Landsgemeinde cantons, the initiative, and referendum.

————, "Swiss Democracy," in Henry W. Ehrmann, ed., *Democracy in a Changing Society.* New York: Praeger, 1964. Pp. 91–116.

The Bernese professor here shows that participatory democracy is threatened by centralizing tendencies even where it has long been at home.

Kramer, Ralph L. *Participation of the Poor: Community Case Studies in the War on Poverty*. Englewood Cliffs, N.J.: Prentice-Hall, 1969. 273 pp.

    Detailed study of community-action programs, examining alternative patterns of participation.

Marris, Peter, and Martin Rein. *Dilemmas of Social Reform: Poverty and Community Action in the United States*. New York: Atherton Press, 1967.

    The most relevant section is entitled "The Voice of the People," pp. 164–190.

National Civic Review, "The Fading Town Meeting," Vol. LIV, No. 9 (October 1965), 464–465, 522.

    Attacks the town meeting as undemocratic because of manipulation by the few and low community participation in general.

Nuquist, Andrew E., and Edith W. Nuquist. *Vermont State Government and Administration: An Historical and Descriptive Study of the Living Past*. Burlington, Vt.: Government Research Center, University of Vermont, 1966.

    See pp. 526–542 for an account of the structure and functioning of the New England town government.

Peterson, Paul E. "Forms of Representation: Participation of the Poor in the Community Action Program," *American Political Science Review*, Vol. LXIV, No. 2 (June 1970), 491–507.

    How forms influenced substance of grass-roots representation on poverty councils of Chicago, New York, and Philadelphia, 1964–1966. Good on conflicts involved.

Riessman, Frank. "Self-Help Among the Poor: New Styles of Social Action —Can Alinsky's Community Projects Become a Nation-wide Model?," *Trans-action*, Vol. 2, No. 6 (September-October 1965), 32–36.

    Argues that Alinsky's approach should become less parochial if it is to really help community organizations conquer poverty.

Shipler, David. "Urban Renewal: Giving the Poor Opportunity to Increase Power," *New York Times*, Nov. 9, 1969, pp. 1, 80.

    Community-based participation of slum residents and its impact on urban renewal decision-making in New York City.

Whitaker, "Participation and Poverty," *Fabian Research Series* No. 272. 20 pp.

    A British view of the American War on Poverty and its community-action programs.

Wickwar, W. Hardy. *The Political Theory of Local Government*. Columbia, South Carolina: University of South Carolina Press, 1970. 96 pp.

    Brief but cogent, this book offers a general overview of theory and practice of local government, although it slights participation.

Wood, Robert C. *Suburbia: Its People and Their Politics*. Boston: Houghton Mifflin, 1958. 340 pp.

Again reminded that the privileged already enjoy much participatory democracy, we here see that suburbanites have a nostalgia for the town meeting that is reflected in their myriads of political decision-making units. Wood is rather critical of the town meeting ideal.

Zimmerman, Joseph E. The Massachusetts Town Meeting: A Tenacious Institution. Albany, N.Y.: State University Graduate School of Public Affairs, 1967. 117 pp.

The history and present status of the town meeting, including an account of the encroachment of the representative principle in lieu of mass meetings.

(2) PERSPECTIVES OF ETHNIC MINORITIES

Aberbach, Joel D., and Jack L. Walker. "The Meaning of Black Power: A Comparison of White and Black Interpretations of a Political Slogan," American Political Science Review, Vol. LXIV, No. 2 (June 1970), 367–388.

Survey results from Detroit, 1967–1968, conjoined with useful interpretations.

Blake, J. Herman. "Black Nationalism," The Annals of the American Academy, Vol. 382 (March 1969), 15–25.

After a broad historical account, turns to contemporary developments and the call for black power.

Browne, Robert S. "The Case for Black Separatism," Ramparts, August 1967, pp. 46–51.

National partition—an alternative to ghetto community control?

Collier, Peter. "The Theft of a Nation: Apologies to the Cherokees," Ramparts, September 1970, pp. 38–45.

Shows the participatory organization called "The Original Cherokee Community Organization" in tension with oligarchic, white-dominated management of tribal affairs in Oklahoma.

Deloria, Vine, Jr. "This Country Was a Lot Better Off When the Indians Were Running It," New York Times Magazine, Mar. 8, 1970, pp. 32ff.

Easily demonstrating the truth of his title, a Sioux offers brief comments on the union of young and old native Americans in the movement to restore the vitality of the open-participation tribal councils in lieu of letting elected representatives run tribal affairs.

Glazer, Nathan. "America's Race Paradox," in William P. Gerberding and Duane E. Smith, The Radical Left: The Abuse of Discontent. Boston: Houghton Mifflin, 1970. Pp. 244–262.

Against the fashionability of Fanon, Glazer argues (pp. 254–262) that the "colonial analogy" used in black demands for separate territory or extraterritoriality is "meaningless."

McEvoy, James, and Abraham Miller, eds. Black Power and Student Rebellion. Belmont, Calif.: Wadsworth, 1969.

See especially Nathan Hare, "The Case for Separatism: 'Black Perspective,'" and Roy Wilkins, "The Case against Separatism: 'Black Jim Crow,'" pp. 233–237.

Moynihan, Daniel P. "The New Racialism," The Atlantic Monthly, Vol. 222, No. 2 (August 1968), 35–40.

Warns liberals to think critically about their turnabout to endorse decentralism and ethnic or racial quotas.

Newton, Huey. "A Prison Interview," in Carl Oglesby, ed., The New Left Reader. New York: Grove Press, 1969. Pp. 223–240.

The theoretician of the Black Panthers defines "Black Power" as "people's power" and explains how to obtain it. Read with Rubinstein (1970) of Section II.

Scott, Robert L., and Wayne Brockriede, eds. The Rhetoric of Black Power. New York: Harper and Row, 1969. 205 pp.

A broad anthology of the various black power positions, with two pages of additional bibliography appended.

Skolnick, Jerome. The Politics of Protest. New York: Ballantine, 1969. The movement for black political autonomy is discussed in Ch. 8.

Steiner, Stan. "Chicano Power," The New Republic, June 20, 1970, pp. 16–18.

Although the parallel is not developed, this new participatory movement bears many similarities to the launching of SNCC.

(3) NEIGHBORHOOD CONTROL OF THE SCHOOLS: PARENT POWER

Berube, Maurice R., and Marilyn Gittell, eds. Confrontation at Ocean Hill-Brownsville: The New York School Strikes of 1968. New York: Praeger, 1969. 340 pp.

Although the editors favor community control of schools, their selections offer thorough coverage of views. A helpful chronological table of events is appended.

Featherstone, Joseph. "Community Control of Our Schools," "Choking Off Community Schools," "Community Control: Down But Not Out," and "The Problem Is More Than Schools," all in The New Republic, Jan. 13, 1968, pp. 16–19; July 19, 1969, pp. 16–18; Aug. 16, 1969, pp. 11–13; and Aug. 30, 1969, pp. 20–23.

Good reporting, focusing on New York City events.

Gittell, Marilyn. Participants and Participation: A Study of School Policy for New York City. New York: Center for Urban Education, 1967. 113 pp.

Since she shows that the "headquarters staff" of the school superintendent's office was the locus of power in the system, this is good background for understanding the Ocean Hill-Brownsville events.

Karp, Richard. "The Siege of Ocean Hill," *Interplay*, January 1969, pp. 21–24.
  Defends community control against its critics.

IV. Colleges and Universities: The Academic Context

Bell, Daniel, and Irving Kristol. *Confrontation: The Student Rebellion and the Universities.* New York and London: Basic Books, 1969. 183 pp.
  The most useful essays are those by Irving Kristol ("A Different Way to Restructure the University") and Talcott Parsons ("The Academic System: A Sociologist's View"), pp. 145–158 and 159–183.

Bourges, Hervé. *The Student Revolt: The Activists Speak.* London: Jonathan Cape, 1968.
  See especially pp. 35–43, where a radical French student leader, Jacques Sauvegot, speaks of the need for an alliance of workers and students to get participatory democracy for both.

Califano, Joseph A. *The Student Revolution: A Global Confrontation.* New York: Norton, 1970. 96 pp.
  See especially pp. 72ff., where this liberal shows how to defuse campus rebellions through provision of a variety of new openings for student participation.

Cockburn, Alexander, and Robin Blackburn. *Student Power: Problems, Diagnosis, Action.* Baltimore: Penguin, 1969. 378 pp.
  This anthology of radical, largely Marxist, essays on student revolts contains scattered passages on campus participatory democracy.

Crouch, Colin. "The Chiliastic Urge," *Survey*, October 1968, pp. 55–61.
  Sees something messianic in the New Left's longing for the participatory community in Great Britain and abroad.

Donahue, Francis. "Students in Latin-American Politics," *Antioch Review*, Vol. XXVI, No. 1 (Spring 1966), 91–106.
  Comments on university autonomy and student-faculty "co-government" in Latin America.

Ehrenreich, Barbara, and John Ehrenreich. *Long March, Short Spring: The Student Uprising at Home and Abroad.* New York and London: Monthly Review Press, 1969. 189 pp.
  An impressionistic but comparative book that frequently comments on student demands for participatory democracy.

Eisen, Jonathan, and David Steinberg. "The Student Revolt against Liberalism," *The Annals of the American Academy*, Vol. 382 (March 1969), 83–94.

Fawthrop, Tom. "Towards an Extra-Parliamentary Opposition," in Tariq Ali, ed., *The New Revolutionaries.* New York: Morrow, 1969. Pp. 54–66.

On student power as well as workers' control. The Ali volume contains other selections relevant to participatory democracy.

Foster, Julian, and Durward Long, eds. *Protest! Student Activism in America.* New York: Morrow, 1970. 596 pp.

See especially the essays by Stanford Cazier, "Student Power and 'In Loco Parentis,' " and G. David Garson, "The Ideology of the New Student Left," pp. 506–527, 184–200.

Goodman, Paul. *The Community of Scholars.* New York: Random House, 1962. 175 pp.

A fascinating application of anarchist philosophy to higher education.

———. Untitled essay, in Samuel Gorowitz, ed., *Freedom and Order in the University.* Cleveland: Western Reserve University Press, 1967. Pp. 31–41.

More on Goodman's answer: let the giant universities fall apart into "natural" and "self-governing" communities of those who want to learn something together.

Hoffman, Stanley. "Participation in Perspective?," *Daedalus,* Winter 1970, pp. 177–220.

An excellent essay arguing that reform needs a prior consensus on the ends of the university; then debate should turn to how various stakeholders can participate. See especially pp. 206ff.

Horowitz, Irving L., and William H. Friedland. "Sit-In at Stanford," in James McEvoy and Abraham Miller, eds., *Black Power and Student Rebellion.* Belmont, Calif.: Wadsworth, 1969. Pp. 122–167.

An account of one form of campus participatory democracy in action.

Larkin, Bruce D. "China," in Donald Emmerson, ed., *Students and Politics in Developing Nations.* New York: Praeger, 1968. Pp. 146–162.

The participatory activity of Chinese students from 1919 to the more recent Red Guards Movement.

Newfield, Jack. *A Prophetic Minority.* New York: New American Library, 1966.

See especially Ch. 6, pp. 115–146, where he discusses the SDS, the "Port Huron Statement," and participatory democracy.

Oppenheimer, Martin. "The Student Movement as a Response to Alienation," *Journal of Human Relations,* Vol. 16, No. 1 (First Quarter, 1968), 1–16.

A sociological explanation of the call for participatory democracy.

Rudd, Mark. "Columbia: Notes on the Spring Rebellion," in Carl Oglesby, ed., *The New Left Reader.* New York: Grove Press, 1969. Pp. 291–312.

The 1968 rebel leader at Columbia University suggests that the call for "student power" or democratic restructuring of the university is a reformist-liberal trap, diverting students from really revolutionary activities to parochial student interests.

Sampson, Edward E. "Student Activism and the Decade of Protest," *The Journal of Social Issues*, Vol. XXIII, No. 3 (July 1967), 1–33.
    See especially pp. 20–25 on participatory democracy as an issue in campus disturbances.
Shover, John L. "Preparation for Dow Day," *The Nation*, Dec. 18, 1967, pp. 648–651.
    On practice: San Francisco State's "War Crisis Convocation."

V. Economic Institutions: Industrial Democracy

Bell, Daniel. *The End of Ideology: On the Exhaustion of Political Ideas in the Fifties*. New York: Free Press, 1962.
    See especially Ch. 2, pp. 227–272, and Ch. 15, pp. 355–392. In the first essay, Bell offers a stimulating analysis of modern work, as well as a critique of "efficiency"; in the second, he examines workers' control against Marxist theory and practice.
Blair, Thomas. *"The Land to Those Who Work It:" Algeria's Experiment in Workers' Management*. Garden City, N.Y.: Doubleday, 1969. 139 pp.
    A favorable account of the seizure of enterprises by workers when European owners and managers fled in 1962. Covers the later institutionalization of workers' control.
Blum, Fred H. *Toward a Democratic Work Process: The Hormel-Packinghouse Workers' Experiment*. New York: Harper and Bros., 1953. 207 pp.
    A study of a Minnesota plant, extending to reflections on how the spirit of Albert Schweitzer could be applied to support participation of those who "invest" their working lives—not just money—in an enterprise.
Blumberg, Paul. *Industrial Democracy: The Sociology of Participation*. London: Constable, 1968. 234 pp.
    A very impressive but occasionally difficult case for workers' participation in management, backed by a comprehensive review of relevant behavioral research.
Blumenthal, W. Michael. *Codetermination in the German Steel Industry*. Princeton, N.J.: Industrial Relations Section of the Dept. of Economics and Sociology, 1956. 114 pp.
    An unenthusiastic account of structure and operation of co-determination, which finds that labor and management tend to define their spheres of influence rather than really sharing management of all matters.
Brooks, John Graham. *American Syndicalism: The I.W.W.* New York: Macmillan, 1913. 264 pp.
    A contemporary account of the rising I.W.W., which is remi-

niscent of our own time. Hopes for some good from the movement but doubts workers are really capable of full workers' control and criticizes I.W.W. "anti-intellectualism," program of sabotage, and tendency toward violence.

Chamberlain, Neil W. *The Union Challenge to Management Control.* New York and London: Harper and Bros., 1948. 338 pp., including long appendices.

Balanced account of American union penetration of traditionally managerial functions through collective bargaining. Reflections on how union and management can be functionally integrated, with some shared responsibilities.

Clegg, Hugh. *A New Approach to Industrial Democracy.* Oxford: Basil Blackwell, 1963. 134 pp.

A broad survey of workers' participation in management, favorable to the collective contract system but suspicious of other forms, since he values independent unions and private enterprise.

Cole, G. D. H. *Guild Socialism.* New York: Frederick A. Stokes Co., 1921. 195 pp.

A theory of industrial democracy permitting representation of "brain" workers as well as "hand" workers, with protection of the consumer interest as well as the producer's interest.

———. *The Case for Industrial Partnership.* New York: St. Martins Press, 1957. 121 pp.

Cole's matured views on industrial democracy.

Dahl, Robert A. "Power to the Workers?" *The New York Review of Books,* November 19, 1970, pp. 20–24.

Offering a preview of part of his forthcoming book, After the Revolution?—Authority in a Good Society, Dahl here tentatively supports Yugoslav workers' self-management.

Das, Nabagopal. *Experiments in Industrial Democracy.* New York: Asia Publishing House, 1964. 158 pp.

Broad survey of forms of workers' participation in management in various countries.

Denitch, Bogdan. "Is There A 'New Working Class,'" *Dissent,* July-August 1970, pp. 351–355.

Argument that mass higher education and professionalization point to a revival of demands for workers' participation.

Engels, Frederick. "On Authority," in Karl Marx and Frederick Engels, *Selected Works,* Vol. 1. Moscow: Foreign Languages Publishing House, 1962. Pp. 636–639.

Warning against anarchism in industrial organization, he argues the need for unambiguous and strict authority within a factory, even if that authority is democratic.

Gomberg, William. "The Trouble with Democratic Management," *Transaction,* July-August 1966, pp. 30–35.

Critique of modern social scientists' arguments for democratization, sensitivity training, and the like.

Greaves, H. R. G. *Democratic Participation and Public Enterprise.* London: University of London, Athlone Press, 1964. 27 pp.

This Hobhouse Memorial Trust Lecture is a British perspective of workers' participation.

Lipset, Seymour Martin, et al. *Union Democracy: The Internal Politics of the International Typographical Union.* Garden City, N.Y.: Doubleday, 1962. 455 pp.

Good on rank-and-file participation within the union.

Mhetras, V. G. *Labour Participation in Management: An Experiment in Industrial Democracy.* Bombay: Manaktalas, 1966. 234 pp.

Good description of joint consultative committees in India but rather barren of significant contributions to theory.

Rhenman, Eric. *Industrial Democracy and Industrial Management: A Critical Essay on the Possible Meanings and Implications of Industrial Democracy.* London: Tavistock Publications, Ltd., 1968. 141 pp.

A Swede advances an analytical framework for study and evaluation of workers' participation. Good on the enterprise "stakeholders."

Rice, A. K. *Productivity and Social Organization: The Ahmedabad Experiment.* London: Tavistock Publications, Ltd., 1958.

The collective contract system in textiles.

Schuchman, Abraham. *Codetermination: Labor's Middle Way in Germany.* Washington, D.C.: Public Affairs Press, 1957. 244 pp.

Useful on the history and rationale of a program aimed toward freedom with order, steering between capitalism and collectivism.

Spiro, Herbert J. *The Politics of German Co-determination.* Cambridge, Mass.: Harvard University Press, 1958. 168 pp.

On the origins, ideology, and operation of the West German system. Argues that economic effects are inconsequential, but more egalitarianism and increased worker status have resulted from a system not really insulated from politics.

VI. Administrative and Legal Contexts

Bennis, Warren G., and Philip E. Slater. *The Temporary Society.* New York: Harper and Row, 1968. 128 pp.

Their essays offer an unconventional argument: The accelerating pace of changing problems requires replacement of rigidly authoritarian and bureaucratic organizations with impermanent and more democratized forms for flexible adaptation.

Drew, Elizabeth. "Reports: Washington," *The Atlantic Monthly,* January 1970, pp. 4 and sequel.

On the emergence of organizations within the federal civil service favoring more political activity for government employees.

Hazard, John N. "Simplicity and Popularity: Early Dreams"; Leon Lipson, "Hosts and Pests: The Fight against Parasites"; and Albert Boiter, "Comradely Justice: How Durable Is It?"; all in *Problems of Communism*, Vol. XIV, No. 2 (March-April 1965), 16–21, 72–82, 82–92.

On popular participation in special courts in the USSR.

Kaufman, Herbert. "Administrative Decentralization and Political Power," *Public Administration Review*, Vol. XXIX, No. 1 (January-February 1969), 3–12.

One of several good articles in this issue of PAR, focused on a symposium regarding "Alienation, Decentralization and Participation."

Miller, S. M., and Martin Rein. "Participation, Poverty and Administration," *Public Administration Review*, Vol. XXIX, No. 1 (January-February 1969), 15–25.

On how popular participation affects administrators.

Plato. Apology. Many editions.

The classic account of Socrates' condemnation by a mass-participation jury in ancient Athens.

Selznick, Philip. *TVA and the Grass Roots: A Study in the Sociology of Formal Organization*. Berkeley: University of California Press, 1949. 274 pp.

Read with the Lilienthal selection printed in this reader.

Wilcox, Herbert G. "Hierarchy, Human Nature, and the Participative Panacea," *Public Administration Review*, Vol. XXIX, No. 1 (January-February 1969), 53–62.

Attacks what he views as an unscientific ideology: the idea that we could better achieve our goals with informal relationships based on sensitivity training, rather than formal and hierarchical coordination. Counters Bennis and Slater (1968).

Wilson, James Q. "The Bureaucracy Problem," *Public Interest*, No. 6 (Winter 1967), pp. 3–9.

Notes that Left has joined Right in seeing this problem and proposes a solution in clarification of objectives and recognition of the inherent limits of using the means of large scale, hierarchical organizations when administrative talent is scarce.

VII. Miscellaneous Contexts

Ashford, Douglas E. *National Development and Local Reform: Political Participation in Morocco, Tunisia, and Pakistan*. Princeton, N.J.: Princeton University Press, 1967. 439 pp.

Good on political mobilization of the peasantry in the Third

World. See especially Ch. 4, pp. 94–97 and 113–134, on Ayub Khan's Basic Democracies" program.

Baker, J. E. "Inmate Self-Government," *Journal of Criminal Law, Criminology and Police Science*, Vol. 55 (March 1964), 39–47.

Favoring inmate councils as a rehabilitation measure, the author reviews the history of prisoners' representation in prisons and reformatories and summarizes responses to his questionnaire mailed to American prisons. See also Section V, Brumberg (1968), pp. 135–138.

Burke, Edmund. *Reflections on the Revolution in France*, II, iv, 3. Indianapolis and New York: Bobbs-Merrill, 1955, pp. 247–260.

The famous conservative opponent of "pure democracy" expresses shock at its march through the French army.

Jain, Sugan Chaud. *Community Development and Panchayati Raj in India*. Calcutta: Allied Publishers, 1967.

Ch. V, pp. 77–162, is a good review of the Indian tradition and theory of village self-government.

Mair, Lucy. *Primitive Government*. Baltimore: Penguin, 1962. 279 pp.

Believing that such forms are now obsolescent, she includes discussions of East African peoples who had no "state," or centralized, hierarchical political system. Among the Nuer, for example, no man was obligated to accept the commands of another!

Middleton, J., and D. Tait, eds. *Tribes without Rulers: Studies in African Segmentary Systems*. London: Routledge and Kegan Paul, 1958. 234 pp.

Difficult because of anthropological jargon, discussions of subSaharan peoples who managed without hierarchical command structures.

Neill, A. S. *Summerhill: A Radical Approach to Child Rearing*. New York: Hart, 1960. 379 pp.

Part of his "radical approach" is participatory-democracy control of the school, where even a child of 5 has a vote equal to that of Neill himself. See esp. pp. 45–55.

Perham, Margery. *Native Administration in Nigeria*. London: Oxford University Press, 1962.

Dating from 1937, contains two chapters (XV–XVI, pp. 221–254) that discuss the participatory structures among the Ibo and Ibibio peoples of Southeast Nigeria.

Rosen, George. *Democracy and Economic Change in India*. Berkeley: University of California Press, 1966.

Briefly reviews and evaluates responsibilities and activities of the Indian village council (panchayat).

Rubinstein, Robert, and Harold D. Lasswell. *The Sharing of Power in a Psychiatric Hospital*. New Haven, Conn.: Yale University Press, 1966.

Perhaps the extreme case of devolving power to those of conventionally questioned competence, this reports on an experiment in rehabilitation of mental patients.

Wilson, James Q. *The Amateur Democrat: Club Politics in Three Cities.* Chicago: The University of Chicago Press, 1962. 370 pp.

How issue-oriented citizens have organized for participatory re-forms of "professional"-dominated parties, focusing on New York, Chicago, and Los Angeles. See especially Ch. 12, pp. 340–370, for Wilson's appraisal of the movement.